About Island Press

Island Press is the only nonprofit organization in the United States whose principal purpose is the publication of books on environmental issues and natural resource management. We provide solutions-oriented information to professionals, public officials, business and community leaders, and concerned citizens who are shaping responses to environmental problems.

In 2000, Island Press celebrates its sixteenth anniversary as the leading provider of timely and practical books that take a multidisciplinary approach to critical environmental concerns. Our growing list of titles reflects our commitment to bringing the best of an expanding body of literature to the environmental community throughout North America and the world.

Support for Island Press is provided by The Jenifer Altman Foundation, The Bullitt Foundation, The Mary Flagler Cary Charitable Trust, The Nathan Cummings Foundation, The Geraldine R. Dodge Foundation, The Charles Engelhard Foundation, The Ford Foundation, The Vira I. Heinz Endowment, The W. Alton Jones Foundation, The John D. and Catherine T. MacArthur Foundation, The Andrew W. Mellon Foundation, The Charles Stewart Mott Foundation, The Curtis and Edith Munson Foundation, The National Fish and Wildlife Foundation, The National Science Foundation, The New-Land Foundation, The David and Lucile Packard Foundation, The Pew Charitable Trusts, The Surdna Foundation, The Winslow Foundation, and individual donors.

GREEN URBANISM

GREEN URBANISM
Learning from European Cities

307.1

Timothy Beatley

ISLAND PRESS

Washington, D.C. • Covelo, California

ISLAND PRESS is a trademark of The Center for Resource Economics.

COVER IMAGES:
Background map: Helsinki master plan, courtesy of City of Helsinki.
Upper photo: Spokes for Folks program, courtesy of City of Boulder, Colorado.
Middle photo: Tram in Freiburg, Germany.
Lower photo: Aerial view of Zwolle, the Netherlands.

Unless otherwise noted, all photos are by the author.

Library of Congress Cataloging-in-Publication Data
Beatley, Timothy, 1957–
    Green urbanism : learning from European cities / Timothy Beatley.
        p.   cm.
    Includes bibliographical references and index.
    ISBN 1–55963–682–3 (acid-free paper)
    1. Urban ecology.   2. City planning—Environmental aspects.   3. Sustainable
    development.   4. Cities and towns—Europe.   I. Title.
HT241.B437   2000
307.1'216'094—dc21   99-052418

Printed on recycled, acid-free paper ✪

Manufactured in the United States of America
10 9 8 7 6 5

Contents

Preface and Acknowledgments   xiii

Part I.   Context and Background   1

Chapter 1.   Introduction: Green Urbanism and the Lessons of
European Cities   3

The Important Role of Cities in Global Sustainability   3

The Vision of Green Urbanism   5

Research Methods and the Cities Examined   9

Issues of Transferability: Why Study European Cities?   13

The Relevance and Role of Urban Sustainability in Europe   15

The Plan of the Book to Follow   24

Part II.   Land Use and Community   27

Chapter 2.   Land Use and Urban Form: Planning Compact
Cities   29

Strategies for Compact Urban Development   32

Compact Growth Districts, with a Green Emphasis   41

Urban Villages and the Importance of City-Centers   43

New Towns and Growth Centers   47

Regional and National Spatial Planning   52

The Value of Rural, Agricultural, and Undeveloped Lands   58

Cultural and Other Influencing Factors   59

Economic Signals and Policy Instruments   60

Sustainable Land Use Trends?   61

Lessons for American Cities: Prospects for More Compact Urban Form   62

Chapter 3.   Creative Housing and Living Environments   76

Planning Livable Environments   76

Urban-Village Living   77

Accessory Units and Mixed Housing Environments   80

Housing over Shops   81

Hofjes, Cohousing, and Ecovillages   83

Preservation and Adaptive Reuse   90

Streets, Urban Design, and the Civic Realm   92

Pedestrianized Centers   93

Lessons for American Cities   101

Part III.   Transportation and Mobility in Green-Urban Cities   107

Chapter 4.   Transit Cities: Public Transport Innovations and Priorities   109

High-Mobility Transit Cities   109

Public Transit Strategies and Solutions   111

Coordinating Transit and Land Use   112

Multimodal, Integrated Systems   113

Systematic Transit Priority   116

The Clear Benefits   118

The Tram City   119

The Special Feel of Trams   122

High-Speed Rail, Green Transit, and Other Creative Mobility Strategies   124

Lessons for American Cities   129

Chapter 5.   Taming the Auto: The Promise of Car-Free Cities   137

The Promise of Car-Free Cities   137

Traffic-Calming and Car-Limiting City Strategies   139

Car-Free Developments and Housing Estates   145

Car-Sharing   150

            Call-a-Car and Demand Management   154

            Road Pricing   156

            Lessons for American Cities   161

Chapter 6.   **Bicycles: Low-Tech Ecological Mobility**   166

            Bicycles as a Legitimate Form of Mobility   166

            Bicycle-Friendly Cities   167

            Public Bikes Programs   177

            Building a Bike-Riding Culture   183

            Lessons for American Cities   184

Part IV.   Green, Organic Cities   195

    Chapter 7.   Urban Ecology and Strategies for Greening the Urban Environment   197

            Cities like Forests   197

            Natural Capital of Cities   198

            Ecological Networks: National and Urban   199

            Reimagining the Built Environment: Organic, Living Buildings and Urban Landscapes   203

            Eco-Bridges   213

            City Farms and Ecology Parks   214

            Green Schools   215

            Desealing and Natural Drainage Strategies   216

            Planning for Local Climate   218

            Ecological Regeneration   219

            Ecological Urban Restructuring   220

            Urban Gardens   221

            Urban Wildlife and Habitat Conservation   222

            Lessons for American Cities   223

    Chapter 8.   Urban Ecocycle Balancing: Toward Closed-Loop Cities   232

            Urban "Ecocycles" and the Metabolism of Cities   232

            Connections between City and Hinterland   238

            Closed-Loop Economies: Industrial Symbiosis in the City   242

            Ecocycle-Balanced Neighborhoods and Urban Development   246

Encouraging Ecocycle Balancing: The Role of Green Taxes   252

Lessons for American Cities   253

Chapter 9. Renewable Energy Cities: Living on Solar Income   258

Low-Energy, Renewable-Energy Cities   258

Municipal Energy Planning and Conservation   258

Decentralized Energy Production   261

Strides in Energy Efficiency   264

Energy Standards for New Development   267

Urban Policies to Promote Renewable Energy   268

Emerging Solar Cities   270

Solar Urban Development   274

Zero-Energy Building and Energy-Balanced Homes   277

Carbon Dioxide Reduction Strategies   282

Lessons for American Cities   284

Chapter 10. Building Ecologically: Designing Buildings and Neighborhoods with Nature in Mind   290

A Revolution in Ecological Building   290

Many Examples of Ecological Building Projects: The Dutch Leading the Way   291

Ecological Urban Renewal   304

Strategies for Promoting Green Building   307

Green Mortgages   309

Green House Numbers   310

Other Important Strategies   312

Lessons for American Cities   313

Part V. Governance and Economy   325

Chapter 11. Ecological Governance in Green-Urban Cities   327

Audits, Indicators, and Targets   328

Sustainability Matrices and Appraisals   331

Environmental Budgets and Charters   333

Procurement and Investment Policies   336

Employee Mobility Strategies   337

Management of Municipal Buildings and Properties   338

Green Energy   342

Environmental Vehicles   343

Ecological Twinnings and Looking Beyond the City's Borders   344

Educating and Engaging the Public: Local Agenda 21 and
  Community-Based Initiatives   345

Public Awareness Campaigns   349

The Role of the Nongovernmental Sector   353

Confronting the Consumer: Eco-Teams and Green Codes   354

Supporting and Encouraging Ecological Communities   358

Lessons for American Cities   360

Chapter 12. Building a Sustainable Economy: Innovations in
             Restorative Commerce   369

Building a Sustainable Local Economy   369

Supporting Sustainable Local Businesses   370

Industrial Symbiosis and Ecoindustrial Parks   374

Envisioning a Sustainable Factory   378

Sustainable Industrial Estates   381

Economic and Ecological Renewal: Economic Development through
  Landscape Recycling   384

Green Offices: More Ecological Ways of Working?   387

Ecobusinesses and Green Consumerism   390

Marketing Sustainable Business and Technologies   400

Lessons for American Cities   401

Part VI.   Learning from Europe   405

Chapter 13. The Promise of Green Urbanism: Lessons from European
             Cities   407

The Challenges of Green Urbanism   407

Creating Green and Sustainable Cities in The United States: Lessons
  from Europe   414

A Final Note: From Aalborg to Austin   427

References   429

Appendix A. Individuals Interviewed   451

Appendix B. Charter of European Cities and Towns: Towards Sustainability   462

Index   471

Preface and Acknowledgments

There are a number of individuals who must be thanked for their kindness and support, without which this book would not have been possible. Much of the initial research and travel occurred while I was on sabbatical in the Netherlands. I was generously hosted during that year by the department of spatial planning and rural development at Wageningen Agricultural University. Particular thanks go to Professor Dr. Hubert van Lier for providing such pleasant facilities and accommodations and for helping me in this work at numerous points along the way. A number of faculty at Wageningen also provided significant help and support. Special thanks are due Adri van den Brink for his kindness and hospitality. And, of course, thanks as well to my friends and colleagues at the University of Virginia School of Architecture for afforcing me the essential time away from normal duties to conduct this research.

Many specific individuals in the cities visited and studied donated tremendous amounts of their time and energy to me. A full list of interviewees and contacts is contained in an appendix, but certain people deserve special recognition for truly going out of their way to help me in this work. Many of these individuals helped set up interviews and site visits and very often spent considerable amounts of time showing me around their respective communities. I owe a special debt to a number of individuals, including the following: Wulf Daseking (Freiburg), Dr. Karl Niederl (Graz), Eric Skoven (Copenhagen DIS), Prof. Dr. Willy Schmid (ETH, Zürich), A.W. Oskam (Amsterdam), Kari Silfversberg (Helsinki), Timo Permanente (Lahti), Micael Hagman (Stockholm), Co Verdaas (Zwolle), Margot Stalk (Utrecht), Jurgen Lottermoser (Saarbrücken), Simonetta Tunesi (Bologna), Poul Lorenzen (Odense), Mayor Finn Aaberg (Albertslund), Annette Vestergaard (Herning), and Peter Newman (Murdock University), among many others.

In writing this book, and in pulling together the stories and cases, I have relied on a number of secondary sources and documents, from technical studies to newspaper clippings. I gratefully acknowledge the research and contributions of the authors of these many sources, and I take responsibility for any misquotes or errors in interpretation or use.

Important early financial support for this project was provided by the Lincoln Institute for Land Policy. Special thanks go to Roz Greenstein and James Brown at the Lincoln Institute for this assistance. Special thanks, as well, go to the German Marshall Fund, which has provided additional funds for production and marketing of the book.

I'd like to thank as well the staff at Island Press, and especially Heather Boyer for her enthusiasm and support for this book and for her invaluable editing suggestions and ideas.

Finally, and most importantly, I wish to thank my wife, Anneke, who endured considerable inconvenience during this period and whose personal support was unlimited. Watching me depart for the airport—and often taking me there—was an all-too-regular event, and she spent much time alone as I wandered around Europe. She has also helped in innumerable other ways, especially by providing hours of help translating Dutch documents and materials into English. Without her love and personal support along the way, this book would not have been completed.

I must also acknowledge the important impact on my thinking of simply living for a year in a country such as the Netherlands. I cannot underestimate the profound life experience this was for me, and in many ways it was as important as, if not more so than, the actual research conducted. I lived in the lovely, old city of Leiden, in the Randstad, or ring city, comprising the western portion of the Netherlands. Leiden, like most Dutch cities, is very compact and contains a rich and vibrant mix of uses and activities. Nothing is very far away. All of my local trips were made by bicycle or on foot (the Netherlands has one of the highest rates of bicycle use—there are more bicycles than people there—and cities are clearly designed for them and for discouraging automobile use). Greenspaces and open lands are accessible by bicycle. Longer trips are made by train (the central station was but 1.5 kilometers from my home), and a high priority is placed at every level on improving and strengthening public transport. The physical environment is an immensely livable one, with canals, plazas, pedestrian-only shopping streets, and some inspirational public buildings and architecture. While the Dutch approach is not perfect (the use of automobiles is on the rise), the national strategy of promoting compact cities—a key feature of its spatial planning system, and a topic I will discuss in considerable detail in the text to follow—generally works well. Understanding this strategy in an intellectual sense is one thing, but experiencing it day to day has clearly had a deeper educational impact on me.

So it was a tremendously enriching year and one in which I learned much from my surroundings. It was a difficult transition, in fact, back to living in the United States in the summer of 1997 (although I would return to the Netherlands several times the following year). The metaphorical transition found me leaving an eminently walkable city, where I could walk or ride my bicycle to the train, take the train to Schiphol, the Amsterdam airport, walk a short distance up the escalator to the airline check-in, all quickly and seamlessly. On the other end of my journey, I arrived at Washington-Dulles airport, with no public transit option to speak of, and quickly found myself in an auto, navigating through traffic, eventually reaching a destination where walking anywhere is difficult. While I was glad to see family and friends, it was certainly a rude awakening. So, I am thankful as well for the chance to experience living in a delightful compact, Dutch city, and trying, for at least that year, a much more sustainable lifestyle. Much of the enthusiasm in the pages to follow is in a small part a result of these firsthand experiences.

Timothy Beatley
Charlottesville, Virginia

Part I

Context and Background

Chapter 1

Introduction: Green Urbanism and the Lessons of European Cities

The Important Role of Cities in Global Sustainability

The world is in the midst of a disturbing period of growing consumption, population, and environmental degradation. From global warming to biodiversity loss to patterns of sprawling land consumption, the environmental trends are increasingly dire. Cities—globally and in the United States—will by necessity play an increasingly important role in addressing these problems, and it is this basic assumption that motivates the work presented here.

Cities must become more central in our global agenda of sustainability for several reasons. The first is the growing acknowledgment—indeed the considerable progress made at documenting and quantifying—that cities have sizeable ecological footprints. The work of William Rees and others has been particularly enlightening in showing the amounts of energy, materials, water, food, and other impacts essential for supporting urban populations. As one recent commentator noted: "The first and most obvious thing about cities is that they are like organisms, sucking in resources and emitting wastes" (Tickell, 1998, p. vi).

American cities, especially, reflect wasteful use of land and resources, with few reflecting any real sense of ecological limits or environmental constraints. In American cities and metropolitan areas, the amount of land consumed by urban growth and development far exceeds the rate of population growth (see Beatley and Manning, 1997). The impacts are clear: loss of sensitive habitat, destruction of productive farmland and forestlands, and high economic and infrastructural costs. The low-density auto-dependent American landscape makes more sustainable living—such as walking, bicycling, or public transport—difficult. American cities consequently have high carbon dioxide emissions, produce large amounts of waste, and draw in large amounts of energy and resources.

The answers to our present environmental circumstances are complex and difficult. They will involve the need for both "cleverer technologies and humbler aspirations," to borrow Bill McKibben's words (1998, p. 75). In both categories, cities—smart cities, innovative cities, green cities—will necessarily play a major role. Green and sustainable cities present fundamental opportunities to both apply new technologies (such as public transit, district heating, and green building and design) and bring about major lifestyle changes (such as walking, bicycling, and reductions in consumption). Indeed, it seems that cities hold the greatest hope for achieving a more sustainable future for our planet. Any effective agenda for confronting global climate change, biodiversity loss, and a host of other environmental challenges must necessarily include cities as a key, indeed *the* key, element.

Agenda 21—the detailed action agenda emerging from the Rio Conference on Environment and Development—reflects an understanding of the key role of local governments. Chapter 28 of this agenda calls specifically for the preparation of local sustainability action plans, recognizing that local governments play a special role. As *Agenda 21* states: " . . . because so many of the problems and solutions . . . have their roots in local activities, the participation and cooperation of local authorities will be a determining factor in fullfilling its [Agenda 21's] objectives. . . . As the level of governance closest to the people, they play a vital role in educating, mobilizing and responding to the public to promote sustainable development" (United Nations, 1992, p. 233). More specific objectives were established in Rio for local involvement, and specifically local authorities were to have undertaken (by 1996) a consultation process and to have achieved consensus around a local sustainability program. As will be discussed in the chapters to follow, many local governments in Europe have made incredible strides in the spirit of *Agenda 21,* and demonstrated in a variety of ways the potential role of cities, towns, and local authorities (see Lafferty and Eckerberg, eds., 1998).

The evidence suggests important differences in the environmental performance of cities—even among the cities in developed countries, there is considerable variation in their ecological footprints. Per capita carbon dioxide emissions, for example, are much higher in American cities; they are almost twice as high as in European cities. What these comparisons suggest is that cities—through their spatial organization, their management practices, and the development of their economic bases—can be the locus for significant reductions in demand and pressure on the planet's resources and ecosystems.

The book that follows is very much founded on the notion that the design, organization, and operation of cities can make a fundamental difference. Comparing the much higher consumption of land and per-capita emissions of carbon dioxide of American cities with European cities, for example, gives some indication of this. A premise of this book is that the most progressive green cities of Europe do provide important guidance and inspiration to American cities in becoming more sustainable, more resource-efficient, and less environmentally extractive and damaging. To be sure, the lessons also flow in the other direction, and most European cities have much work to do to reduce their own impacts. Nevertheless, the programs, policies, and innovative design ideas described here and applied in European cities suggest important new directions for American communities.

The Vision of Green Urbanism

There are, in fact, many different terms used today in discussing efforts to reduce environmental impacts and to live more lightly on the land. *Sustainable development, sustainable communities,* and *sustainable cities* are a few of these terms, and each captures much of the agenda of this book. *Green urbanism* effectively captures both the central urban and environmental dimensions of the agenda I will be discussing. It emphasizes the important role of cities and positive urbanism in shaping more sustainable places, communities, and lifestyles. And, it implicitly emphasizes that our old approaches to urbanism—our old views of cities, towns, and communities—are incomplete and must be substantially expanded to incorporate ecology and more ecologically responsible forms of living and settlement. This need for a revised approach has been an ongoing concern with the so-called *new urbanism,* so enthusiastically endorsed by many American architects and planners. (For a full discussion of the issues and limitations of this movement, see Beatley and Manning, 1997.) What we need today are cities that reflect a *different* new urbanism, a new urbanism that is dramatically more ecological in design and functioning and that has ecological limits at its core.

Precisely what green urbanism implies is evolving and unclear, but in the programs, policies, and creative design ideas found in many European cities, we begin to sharpen our sense of what might be possible. To elaborate on what the vision of green urbanism includes (and incor-

porating and extending the thinking of others), there are several important design qualities or characteristics. Cities that exemplify green
urbanism are:

- *Cities that strive to live within their ecological limits, fundamentally
  reduce their ecological footprints, and acknowledge their connections
  with and impacts on other cities and communities and the larger
  planet.*

  Green urbanism accepts that public (and private) decisions about how
  cities grow, the kinds of transportation systems they employ, and the
  ways they generate and supply energy and food for their populations
  have tremendous environmental impacts. Green urbanism takes as a primary goal the need to greatly reduce the ecological footprints of cities,
  to live within the limit of local and regional ecosystems, and to acknowledge that in a host of ways the decisions in one city affect the quality of
  environment and life in other places, as well as the overall health of the
  planet. Efforts by cities to reduce carbon dioxide emissions and to reduce
  the impact of urban consumption patterns, for example, reflect all of
  these goals.

  As the analysis of Herbert Girardet demonstrates, cities such as London consume large amounts of energy and other inputs and produce
  large amounts of waste. London's population consumes some 55,000
  gallons of fuel and some 6,600 tonnes of food per day, and emits
  160,000 tonnes of carbon dioxide per day (see Girardet, undated). Considerable amounts of this food are (increasingly) transported from far-
  away places: "Early potatoes come from Egypt and Cyprus. Tomatoes,
  cucumbers and asparagus are imported from Spain, Greece and Holland.
  Beans are increasingly flown in from Kenya, 4000 miles away"
  (Girardet, undated, p. 52). Taken together, these inputs and outputs
  require a land base 125 times the size of London to support its population.
- *Cities that are green and that are designed for and function in ways analogous to nature.*

  Green urbanism requires us to overcome our traditional view of the
  polarity of cities and nature. Cities, to many, are indeed the very antithe-
  sis of nature—places of gray, where one finds concrete and asphalt,
  buildings and cars, things that could not be natural. Yet, nature does
  exist in cities, and cities are fundamentally embedded within a larger natural setting.

  Ecological architect William McDonough frequently ponders whether
  towns and cities might function like forests. Indeed, nature is a profoundly helpful paradigm for cities. Cities must strive to be places of

nature; they should be sheltering; cleansing of air, water, and spirit; and restorative and replenishing of the planet, rather than fundamentally extractive and damaging.

Moreover, innumerable ways of restoring, replenishing, and nurturing urban ecology exist, such as daylighting streams, planting green rooftops, bringing forests and greenspaces into the very heart of cities, as well as many other creative planning approaches.

- *Cities that strive to achieve a circular rather than a linear metabolism, which nurtures and develops positive symbiotic relationships with and between its hinterland (whether that be regional, national, or international).*

Nothing in nature is wasted. Wastes become productive inputs for other natural processes. In hundreds of ways, the same principle could apply to the functioning of cities. Wastewater treatment systems can extract biogas to fuel community heating systems; organic household waste can become fertilizer returned to urban populations in the form of food. Industries can feed off each other, with each company's wastes becoming the productive inputs to production processes of the others.

Green urbanism calls for a circular metabolism for cities, rather than the prevailing linear approach. Green urbanism calls for the balancing of the ecocycles of a city, so that its inputs and outputs are harmonized, complementary, and fundamentally in balance.

- *Cities that strive toward local and regional self-sufficiency and take full advantage of and nurture local/regional food production, economy, power production, and many other activities that sustain and support their populations.*

Green urbanism demands cities that assume responsibility for the environmental and other impacts of lifestyle and consumption decisions. Historically, it has been easier to ignore the devastating impacts of conventional energy production and production of food, for example, because these impacts have typically been externalized. They happen far away, in distant places, out of sight and mind. Bringing these many functions closer means greater scrutiny and presents more likelihood that responsible actions and choices will result.

What will also result are more healthful lives, for example by avoiding the consumption of chemicals and level of processing needed to transport food hundreds of miles.

- *Cities that facilitate (and encourage) more sustainable, healthful lifestyles.*

An important measure of a sustainable city, and an important goal of green urbanism, is that such places should make it easier for people to live richer, fuller lives. Most Americans, for instance, have few options besides the automobile. Green urbanism emphasizes giving individuals the ability to walk or ride bicycles if they choose. It gives them the option and the ability to grow food, to live with fewer consumer goods, to live without a car if they choose to, and so on. The benefits again extend beyond the environmental. Such conditions empower individuals and families to change in meaningful ways (if they so desire) the directions of their lives and to emphasize the quality of their relationships, rather than the size of their home or their possessions.

- *Cities that emphasize a high quality of life and the creation of highly livable neighborhoods and communities.*
  Green urbanism gives centrality to creating (and strengthening) neighborhoods and places where people enjoy being, places that are emotionally uplifting and aesthetically inspirational. It is an agenda that emphasizes the provision of adequate housing and services for all members of society and that seeks to be socially and economically inclusive. It is as much about creating highly livable cities as it is about creating ecological cities (indeed, the goals are mutually reinforcing). Nature in cities is important to livability. Green urbanism presumes that connections to nature are important to personal health and well-being.

Are there actually cities in the world that satisfy these ambitious criteria? The insertion of the words strive to is important to note. The many examples of European cities described in the pages that follow, I will argue, often come the closest to meeting the vision. But, in many ways, even the

Many European cities show that human settlements can be green and ecological, at the same time that they are highly desirable places in which to live and work. Shown here is Morra Park, an ecological housing project in Drachten, the Netherlands.

most exemplary individual cities fall short. Nevertheless, the following text contains a menu of creative tools, design concepts, and tangible examples that illustrate how cities—particularly American cities—might move closer to these ideals.

Research Methods and the Cities Examined

The study presented herein had several goals. First, it was an attempt to comprehensively identify and describe the current state of the art in European sustainable cities. What are cities currently doing to advance sustainability and what specific best-practices might be valuable and important for cities elsewhere to learn from and perhaps adopt? It is the author's belief that a large number of creative and unique approaches are being employed, many of which are described in this book, that represent important ideas that American cities will find useful.

A second goal relates to the holistic nature of sustainable cities. Many definitions of sustainability and sustainable development emphasize the need for integrative and holistic approaches. As further discussed below, many of the cities were chosen for the range and number of innovations and sustainable practices undertaken in a number of different sectors. Describing and understanding these more holistic cases is a second, related objective. The process of description helps us to concretely define what a sustainable city might actually consist of and what its qualities and program policies might ideally be. While this research has uncovered no ideal or perfect cities, enough exemplary work is going on in many cities across Europe to be very instructive about what urban sustainability actually implies.

The observations and conclusions presented in this book are primarily the result of visits and extensive interviews in approximately thirty cities in eleven European countries. Table 1.1 presents a full list of these cities. In all, more than 200 interviews were conducted between September 1996 and June 1998, with the bulk of the visits occurring in the spring of 1997. Additional phone interviews were also undertaken. (A partial listing of interviewees is included in the appendix.)

Cities were chosen based on several criteria. With a few notable exceptions, these are cities that are frequently cited in European planning and environmental literature and that have been engaged in a variety of innovative and cutting-edge local sustainability initiatives. Cities were favored that were doing a number of different things and that had adopted and implemented sustainability policies in a wide range of sectoral areas (ideally, these places were not simply doing one thing but were attempting more holistic strategies).

Table 1.1. European Cities in Which
Field Visits and Interviews Were Conducted, 1996–98

Austria	*Ireland*
Graz*	Dublin
Linz	
Vienna	*Italy*
	Bologna
Denmark	
Albertslund*	*Switzerland*
Copenhagen	Zürich
Herning	
Kalundborg	*Sweden*
Kolding	Stockholm*
Odense	
	The Netherlands
Finland	Almere
Helsinki	Amersfoort
Lahti	Amsterdam
	Den Haag*
France	Groningen
Dunkerque*	Leiden
	Utrecht
Germany	Zwolle
Berlin	Others
Freiburg	
Heidelberg*	*United Kingdom*
Münster	Leicester*
Saarbrücken	London (including
	boroughs)

*Indicates recipients of the European Sustain-
able City Award; awarded by the European
Sustainable Cities and Towns Campaign.

Several exceptions should be noted. London and Dublin, while perhaps
not representing cutting-edge sustainable city programs, nevertheless represented important examples of cities with significant social and environmental problems, with each in the early stages of developing a local sustainability agenda. London especially, as Europe's largest city, highlights
both the challenges of local sustainability and the range of problems and
obstacles European cities face in shifting directions. Bologna could be

described in the same way and was included, in large part, to examine sustainability issues and problems in a southern European city.

It should be emphasized, although it is perhaps obvious to the reader, that there is a strong bias in this book toward northern European and western European experiences. The sustainability practices in cities in the Netherlands, Germany, and the Scandinavian countries receive the most attention. In many respects and on many dimensions, these countries have done the most in experimenting with and supporting new sustainable technologies and more sustainable urban development patterns.[1] Given the large amount of time spent by the author in the Netherlands, Dutch projects, programs, and cities are disproportionately represented throughout the book.

In a number of places in this book, I examine innovative local initiatives and projects, many of which may be too new or recent to constitute a trend or to provide a definitive sense of their effectiveness or success. I strongly believe in the value of identifying new planning ideas and concepts, even in the early stages of formation and development. In the chapter on ecocycle balancing, for example, I describe the early efforts of cities such as Stockholm to develop closed-loop relationships within and among their different municipal agencies. This is an emerging and early effort, but it nevertheless puts them ahead of most other cities and is certainly worthy of description and discussion. As another example, in the chapter on greening the urban environment, I describe the proposal to create a Green Radial and eco-station (an ecological community center) in the German city of Leipzig. These are important and powerful planning and design ideas, and although not (yet) put into practice, they need to be discussed. At many points in this book, I have sought to extract from the European green-urban scene those ideas, proposals, and design concepts that hold the most promise, even when applied in only a few places or in an early stage of development.

Several important disclaimers about the text to follow need to be issued. First, as explained above, this book is not intended to serve as a comprehensive study or analysis of European cities. Rather, it constitutes a set of observations and insights derived from examining the initiatives and programs of an explicitly nonrandom set of cities. The cities chosen and discussed here undoubtedly are representative in many ways of European cities more generally, but I make no such claim. For the most part, the cities discussed in this book have been chosen because they have undertaken particularly exemplary or special planning and sustainability programs.

It should also be made clear that I do not pretend to have comprehensively studied or examined even these cities in complete detail. Rather, usually each city is notable for one or more sets of initiatives, and I have often tended to focus in greatest detail on these particular programs. Full-fledged case studies, analyzing such things as demographics, the governmental structure and politics, historic development patterns, and so on, have not been prepared for each city.

Considerable obstacles to fully examining and understanding the experiences of these European cities have arisen along the way, and these obstacles should be stated as further important disclaimers. Language represented a serious obstacle in several respects. Plans, reports, and other documentation associated with the cities was generally (and understandably) written and published in the native language. I made full use of English materials when I found them, but the extent of English language materials was limited. Face-to-face interviews became even more important, then, and I often did not have the ability to cross-check or embellish my notes with written materials. Even face-to-face interviews were limited (by my failure to speak other languages) when key local officials did not speak English. This was almost never a problem, I should note, in the Netherlands, in the Scandinavian cities, and of course in Ireland and the United Kingdom. Occasionally I would also become aware of differing interpretations and meanings given to different terms; there have undoubtedly been many cultural nuances that I was unaware of or failed to pick up on, even when discussions occurred in English. Readers should be forewarned that the accuracy of what follows must certainly be affected by these language limitations.

Field visits ranged from a day or two to more than a week for each city. In some cases, multiple visits (e.g., to Copenhagen) and repeated and frequent visits (e.g., to Amsterdam) were made. Interviews were generally conducted with city staff and other knowledgeable individuals in several key areas, including land use and spatial planning, environmental policy, energy and carbon dioxide reduction, waste management, and transportation. Each city dictated a unique set of interviews, but at a minimum interviews were conducted and information collected on these subjects. Extensive reports, documentation, and other written material were also collected and used extensively in developing conclusions about each city. Personal interviews were also supplemented by follow-up phone interviews (a list of interviewees is included in the appendix). Part of each visit was devoted to visiting local development projects and important sites. An extensive photographic record and personal notes were amassed.

In addition to these case study cities, a number of other specific projects, sites, or housing developments were visited in other cities. These visits were usually made to explore specific examples of innovative practice, and these examples are also discussed throughout the book.

Issues of Transferability: Why Study European Cities?

When I speak or give slide presentations about planning and sustainability strategies in European cities, there is a certain predictability to the response of my American colleagues and students. The reactions, although often mixed with enthusiasm and excitement, are frequently skeptical. There is a feeling that while these things can happen in Europe, the American context is so fundamentally different that these great ideas are not likely to be feasible or applicable to American places. To some degree this is a legitimate reaction, but I disagree with these conclusions for several reasons.

I would not have spent so much time in Europe if I did not believe there is much to be learned from the most exemplary European cities. Yet, having said this, there is no question that there are indeed significant social, cultural, political, and geographical differences between Europe and America. I believe there is considerable long-term transferability, however (ever conscious of the differences in context), and I believe this for several reasons. First, there is already a rich history of powerful environmental, planning, and sustainability ideas firmly established here from Europe. Many examples can be cited. Subscription farming emerged first in Europe, for example, and now there are more than 600 such operations (known as community-supported agriculture) throughout the United States. The concept of the Enterprise Zone, such a cherished element of American urban policy, actually began in the United Kingdom. Cohousing began in Denmark, but it is beginning to catch on in the United States (as will be discussed later) now, with more than 100 cohousing projects under way in various parts of the country (McCamant and Durrett, 1998). The traffic-calming techniques and methods that are becoming increasingly popular throughout the United States were first applied in European cities (e.g., the Dutch *woonerf*, or living street concept). Car-sharing, an increasingly important European practice, is now beginning to find application here. Many other planning ideas and concepts have been successfully drawn from Europe.

Given the great increase in concern about urban sprawl in the United States, European cities—with their historical emphasis on compact urban form (although under assault from growing auto use and decentralization pressures)—are especially promising guideposts of good planning. Many others have made this observation over the years. Alterman, for example, argues that the exemplary urban containment and farmland preservation policies of European countries (in particular the British and Dutch systems) "can serve as models for countries such as the United States . . ." (1997, p. 238). In many respects, European cities arguably represent unusual opportunities for learning by their American counterparts; few other countries or cities outside the United States have as much in common from a historical, cultural, or economic point of view.

Masser (1992) accurately observes that many important social and demographic trends are similarly occuring in Europe and North America. Patterns of urban deconcentration, growing automobile usage, and trends in the direction of emphasis on deregulation and markets-oriented solutions, for example, characterize both the United States and Europe. If anything, European and American cities are becoming more alike than dissimilar. Europe, moreover, is composed essentially of a large number of medium-sized cities (the problems and circumstances of megacities, it can be argued, are quite different), and thus is helpfully analogous to the American context. Cities of this size often have been the most innovative and creative in their local sustainability initiatives and strategies (Mega, 1996; 1997). For these reasons, among others, much can be learned from European cities that can be directly transferred to American communities.

The transfer and application of these lessons are not always a complete success, of course. The experience of creating pedestrian malls in American downtowns that occurred in the 1970s was largely an inspiration from European cities. Many of these spaces (with the exception of places such as Charlottesville, Virginia, and Boulder, Colorado) were not successful and many center-cities have since taken out these pedestrian spaces. But even in cases such as this, much of a positive nature has resulted from a cross-fertilization of European and American ideas.

Probably a more accurate description of the relationship between European and American sustainability policy is one of *coevolution*. In many policy and planning areas, American and European cities are moving in parallel directions. Experiments in road pricing are occurring in both places, for instance, and it is inappropriate to characterize the flow of ideas and experiences as occurring solely in one direction or the other (and indeed, significant lessons are being learned in places such as Curitiba and Singapore). It is also important to understand that while the chapters to follow are aimed at extracting lessons from European initiatives, on many topics and dimensions the Europeans look to the Americans for leadership. American efforts in the areas of transport demand management and auto emissions standards, among many others, are viewed as being ahead of the European efforts.

Another important response is to acknowledge that the United States is a large and diverse country, and thus it is unreasonable to think that any specific idea or program (even those drawn from other American cities) will find successful application or relevance everywhere. Great variations in climate, geography, political culture, and so forth exist, and certain ideas from Europe will find special application in particular cities and in particular regions of the United States. The lessons from those European cities that have aggressively promoted bicycles may be less relevant, for example, in American cities where the topography or climate makes bicycle use difficult. As a further example, clearly places such as the Pacific Northwest (and cities such as Eugene, Portland, Seattle, and Vancouver) will currently be more politically and socially receptive to the lessons of compact cities than other areas of the country. Moreover, there are many American cities that because of their political culture, history, and makeup (examples include Davis, Boulder, and Burlington) will be more inclined to adopt the innovative ideas offered by these European cities. My point is that it is inappropriate to simply dismiss the applicability of many European ideas when there is actually great variation in local and regional circumstances in this country.

Having said this, however, it is important to think carefully about how these European initiatives will or can be invoked with American society in mind. In many instances, because of differing social, legal, and other background conditions, planning and sustainability programs will need to be adapted or modified for American application. In each chapter, I try to explore this possibility and provide suggestions for how this adaptation might occur.

The Relevance and Role of Urban Sustainability in Europe

While the cities visited and studied were not randomly chosen, it is nevertheless impressive how they are embracing and seriously incorporating into their planning and other policies explicit consideration of sustainability. Sustainability is quite important to these cities and is an idea and concept of generally higher priority in Europe than in the United States. This priority has been expressed in many ways and in many forms.

Sustainability has been endorsed through the legislation and directives of the European Union (EU) as a primary Europe-wide objective. The EU's Fifth Environmental Action Program is actually entitled *Towards Sustainability*. And, more recently, the Treaty of Maastricht has been amended to explicitly incorporate sustainable development as an objective of the EU (under the June 1997 Treaty of Amsterdam) (Neild, 1998; O'Riordan and Voisey, eds., 1998). A variety of more specific EU directives mandates strong attention to environmental protection and conservation (e.g., the EU Habitats Directive and Biocide Directive). Most western European nations have prepared national sustainability strategies, as well as a variety of other national-level action plans and standards. The language of sustainability increasingly finds its way into national legislation and programs (O'Riordan and Voisey, eds., 1998).

The topic of sustainable cities has also been given considerable attention within the EU. The *Green Paper on the Urban Environment*, published in

1990, has been seen as a "milestone" document, prompting considerable discussion about the environmental role and context of cities. This document called for more integrated, holistic approaches to planning, and the need to view cities as a necessary part of the solution to global environmental problems (Commission of the European Communities, 1990; European Commission, 1994). An Expert Group on the Urban Environment was formed in 1991, as a follow-up to the *Green Paper*, and with a Sustainable Cities Project as a main area of focus (see Fudge, 1993; Williams, 1996).

The final report of the Expert Group, *European Sustainable Communities*, is impressive in scope and coverage and is another significant milestone. It, like the EU *Green Paper*, advocates more holistic, integrated approaches, but goes further in arguing for an *ecosystems* view of cities. Cities both affect the environments they are situated in (for example, regional hydrologic systems) and are themselves habitats for plants and animals. The city must be viewed as a "complex, interconnected and dynamic system. Cities are both a threat to the natural environment and an important resource in their own right. The challenge of urban sustainability is to solve both the problems experienced within the cities themselves . . . and the problems caused by cities" (European Commission, 1996, pp. 6–7).

The report identifies as an important first step four principles of sustainable development (presented in Box 1.1): the principle of urban management; the principle of policy integration; the principle of ecosystems thinking; and the principle of cooperation and partnerships (European Commission, 1996; see also European Commission, 1994). Much of the report develops a series of detailed recommendations and examples of good practice by which these principles can be implemented. The report has clearly had substantial impact and is the source of "inspirational examples, innovative approaches, and practical tips to demonstrate how much can be done to green cities and regions" (European Environment Agency, 1997, p. 42). A European good practices guide and Internet information service have also been prepared.

One of the key outcomes of the work of the Expert Group was the initiation of the European Sustainable Cities and Towns Campaign, an informal network of European cities begun in 1994. The beginning point of this network was the first significant meeting of the campaign in Aalborg, Denmark. Here, a sustainable cities charter was drafted and signed by participating cities; the charter is now more commonly known as the Aalborg Charter. Participating cities in the network sign the Aalborg Charter as a commitment to work toward local sustainability. To date, nearly 400 local authorities have signed the Aalborg Charter, representing an impressive 100 million Europeans. Among the other activities of this campaign are the

BOX 1.1. Principles of Urban Sustainability

1. *The principle of urban management.*
Management for sustainability is essentially a political process that requires planning and has an impact on urban governance. The process of sustainable urban management requires a range of tools to address environmental, social, and economic concerns in order to provide the necessary basis for integration. By applying these tools, urban policy making for sustainability can become broader, more powerful, and more ambitious than has been generally recognized.

2. *The principle of policy integration.*
Coordination and integration are to be achieved through the combination of the subsidiarity principle with the wider concept of shared responsibility. Integration should be achieved both horizontally, to stimulate synergetic effects of social, environmental, and economic dimensions of sustainability, and vertically, between all levels of the European Union, member states, regional, and local governments, to achieve greater coherence of policy and action and to avoid contradicting policies at different levels.

3. *The principle of ecosystems thinking.*
Ecosystems thinking emphasizes the city as a complex system that is characterized by flows as continuous processes of change and development. It incorporates aspects such as energy, natural resources, and waste production as chains of activities that require maintenance, restoration, stimulation, and closure in order to contribute to sustainable development. The regulation of traffic and transport is another element of ecosystems thinking. The dual network approach, which provides a framework for urban development at the regional or local level, is based on the principles of ecosystems thinking. Ecosystems thinking also includes a social dimension, which considers each city as a social ecosystem.

4. *The principle of cooperation and partnership.*
Sustainability is a shared responsibility. Cooperation and partnership between different levels, organizations, and interests is, therefore, crucial. Sustainable management is a learning process within which "learning by doing"; sharing experiences, professional education, and training; cross-disciplinary working, partnerships, and networks; community consultation and participation; and innovative educational mechanisms and awareness raising are key elements.

Source: EC, European Sustainable Cities, 1996.

publication of a newsletter, networking between cities, and the convening of periodic pan-European conferences. The campaign has also created a European Sustainable City Award, with the first awards issued in 1996 (discussed later in the book). (The full text of the Aalborg Charter is attached as an appendix to this book.)

A second pan-European sustainable cities conference, as a follow-up to Aalborg, was held in Lisbon in 1996, and a third is to be convened in Hannover, Germany, in February 2000. The Lisbon meeting drew one thousand participants and resulted in a more detailed action plan, "From Charter to Action" (Lisbon Action Plan, 1996). A series of regional conferences has also been sponsored, including, for example, the "Towards local sustainability in central and eastern Europe" conference held in the fall of 1998 in Sofia, Bulgaria. (See "Sofia Statement," 1998; other recent regional conferences were held in Turku, Finland, and Sevilla, Spain.) A campaign office in Brussels coordinates the program and serves as a combination network and clearinghouse.

In addition to the Sustainable Cities and Towns Campaign, a number of other groups and organizations in Europe are actively involved in and promoting urban sustainability, and a number of networks of local authorities assist in this work. These important networks include the International Council for Local Environmental Initiatives (ICLEI), the Organization for Economic Cooperation and Development (OECD), Eurocities, the Council of European Municipalities and Regions (CEMR), the United Towns Organization (UTO), and the Commission de Villes.

Much local sustainability innovation has been directly supported by the EU, through a series of funding programs and initiatives. These programs have been important in supporting information dissemination and collaboration between cities and the development of demonstration programs. There are many of these programs, in a number of specific technical areas, and their cumulative effect is difficult to overstate. They include energy pilot programs (e.g., JOULE, SAVE, and THERMIE), urban transportation programs (e.g., JUPITER, DRIVE, and ZEUS), and sustainable economic development and urban regeneration initiatives (e.g., RECITE, PACTE), among others. (See Williams, 1996, for an overview of some of these programs.)

Many EU-funded programs, moreover, have been aimed at both demonstrating new green-urban technologies and helping to build networks and cooperation between European Sustainable Cities. One such initiative is European Green Cities, funded through the EU THERMIE program, and supporting the design and construction of low-energy, ecological housing projects in eleven cities (Green City Denmark, 1997). As these programs are organized often, the cities meet periodically to share information and insights. The resulting housing innovations will in the end represent important demonstrations and "inspirations" for a much wider group of European cities.

A number of efforts have also been directed at understanding and assessing the extent to which European cities are sustainable. The EU has sponsored several sustainability indicator initiatives, some well before much

Freiburg, Germany, has taken many impressive steps to create a pedestrian urban environment, to encourage bicycles and public transit, and to curtail and calm the automobile.

work had occurred in the United States. These initiatives have included the Sustainable Index project, which included twelve European cities in developing a common set of indicators, and the more recent set of indicators prepared for the Dobris Assessment, "Europe's Environment" (International Institute for the Urban Environment, 1994; Stanners and Bordeau, 1995). (See also the updated "Second Assessment of Europe's Environment"; European Environment Agency, 1998.) The latter entailed the development of fifty-five urban indicators, grouped into sixteen attributes and falling under three broad types: indicators of urban patterns, urban flows, and urban environmental quality.

Ecological footprint analysis is also increasingly being applied to European cities, and it is emerging as a powerful technique for understanding extra-local environmental effects and resource demands. Folke et al. (1997), for instance, have calculated the total ecological footprint of the twenty-nine largest cities in the Baltic region (which includes several of this study's cities, including Helsinki, Stockholm, and Copenhagen). They found an immense footprint of 565 to 1,130 times the land area of the cities themselves. Each average citizen requires between 60,000 square meters and 115,000 square meters for food, energy, and waste assimilation needs. Ecological footprint analysis has also been done for other cities, such as London (Sustainable London Trust, 1997).

The EU has also provided substantial support for a number of research organizations and projects focused on urban sustainability. The European Academy of Urban Environment, located in Berlin, has been created with partial funding from the EU and focuses primarily on research, training, and information dissemination on urban sustainability (see Kennedy and Kennedy, eds., 1998). The European Foundation for the Improvement of Living and Working Conditions, based in Dublin, has coordinated several major studies of urban sustainability, especially in medium-sized cities (e.g., see Mega 1977; 1996). There has been a tremendous amount of European literature and writing focused on local sustainability (e.g., Van der Vegt et al., eds., 1994; Municipality of Dordrecht, 1994; see the many ICLEI publications). The literature includes a number of planning guidebooks and manuals, produced by groups such as ICLEI and designed to assist local jurisdictions in embarking on local Agenda 21 and other local sustainability initiatives (e.g., see ICLEI, 1996).

Promoting urban sustainability and green-urban cities has been a high priority for many European countries as well. In Finland, for example, the 1995 Local Government Act calls on municipalities to provide for the "inhabitants' well-being and sustainable development within their boundaries" (Association of Finnish Local Authorities, 1996, p. 10). The Finnish Building Act, moreover, establishes sustainable development as the foundation for land use planning: "Plans shall be drawn up . . . in a manner contributing to sustainable development of natural resources and the environment . . ." (Association of Finnish Local Authorities, 1996, p. 10). In Denmark, a Green Municipalities Project at the national level led to the sponsoring of a number of pilot environmental initiatives (some 500 projects) and the development of a network of communities (Danish Ministry of Environment and Energy, 1995). Similar initiatives have been under way in other European nations.

There is considerable evidence of the greening of city planning and development throughout Europe, but most especially in northern and western European countries. In the last decade, several major green city initiatives have been undertaken through a combination of public and private means. In Germany, for example, the national environmental group Deutsche Umwelthilfe (DU) began ranking cities according to their environmental policies and began designing the first (annual) "federal capital for nature and the environment" (Deutsche Umwelthilfe, undated). Many German cities have adopted an impressive array of local greening and sustainability initiatives, and the winners of the DU designation take great pride in this. A similar municipal ranking system has been established in

Denmark by the environmental group Danmarks Naturfredningsforening, (Danmarks Naturfredningsforening, 1997). In the United Kingdom, Leicester became the first environmental city, a designation co-sponsored by the Royal Society for Nature Conservation, the Wildlife Trust Partnership, and The Leicester Ecology Trust. Leicester has to a large degree defined itself in terms of its environmental aspirations and has actively pursued a range of initiatives in becoming a green city. Three other cities in the United Kingdom, Leeds, Middlesborough, and Peterborough, have also gained the environmental city designation.

The precise form given to urban sustainability varies from city to city in Europe, but overall substantial local activity revolves around the idea. Evidence of the increasing importance of sustainability among European cities abounds. Considerable tangible evidence of sustainable initiatives and efforts can be seen at the local level and many of these detailed efforts are described in the pages that follow. Clearly, in many European cities, and especially in the case study sites examined here, sustainability is increasingly viewed as a primary organizing concept for planning for the future. For example, many of the structure plans, or comprehensive plans, for the cities examined here have taken sustainability as their underlying theme or organizing principle.

The variety and extent of greening initiatives and activities taken at the municipal level in northern and western Europe is impressive, and much of what follows is an accounting of these efforts. The activities range from promotion of compact urban form, to efforts to promote more circular approaches to waste and metabolism, to efforts to fundamentally make cities and the built environment more organic and natural. Substantial progress and innovation can be seen as well in those many sectors where European cities have already tended to excel, for instance in commitment to public transit, pedestrian design, bicycles, and many others areas.

Many cities in Europe have developed sustainability indicators and targets, and many are attempting to creatively implement sustainability concepts and principles. Several U.K. communities have developed sustainability criteria for judging new development proposals (e.g., the London Borough of Ealing). Even among cities such as London, which is not known for its innovative environmental policies, sustainability appears to have great meaning and importance. The London Local Planning Authority's guidance document has a strong sustainability theme, as does the ongoing London study.[2]

Local Agenda 21 (LA21) programs have also been instituted in many European cities, with considerable activity still under way. A response to the 1992 Rio conference, these are local, community-based participation processes, intended to identify citizen ideas and goals about the future and to promote the development of local sustainability action agendas. A high percentage of communities in Europe, especially in northern European nations, is undertaking some form of the LA21 process. As of late 1996, local Agenda 21 initiatives had been started in 1,119 European localities, representing some 62 percent of the global total (European Commission, 1997). Many European cities have gone through, or are currently going through, some form of local Agenda 21 process (including many of the same cities that have signed the Aalborg Charter); this is another important indicator of the relevance of local sustainability. Indeed, in the countries studied, high percentages of municipal governments are participating (e.g., in Sweden 100 percent of all local governments are at some stage in the local Agenda 21 process). Often these programs represent tremendous local efforts to engage the community in a dialogue about sustainability. They typically involve a number of important steps and products, including the creation of a local sustainability forum, sustainability indicators, local state-of-the-environment reports, and the preparation of comprehensive local sustainability action plans.

In many European cities, global environmental issues, such as climate change, have a high degree of currency. Many of the cities have pursued measures to address the issue of climate change. The Climate Alliance of European Cities (Klimabundis), a German-based initiative, boasts participation by more than 400 European cities (Collier and Löfstedt, 1997). To participate, cities set an impressive target of reducing carbon dioxide emissions by 50 percent (by 2010, compared with 1987). ICLEI has sponsored its own Cities for Climate Protection campaign, also with relatively high participation by European cities. Many European cities, such as Graz and Heidelberg, among many others, have prepared ambitious local climate change strategies and have taken substantial actions to reduce greenhouse emissions.

European cities have also been active in the World Health Organization's (WHO's) Healthy Cities program; indeed, the original founding members were European cities (EC Expert Group on the Urban Environment, 1994). There were thirty-nine European cities participating in the WHO network in 1997, coordinated by the Regional Office in Copenhagen.[3] Under this program, cities express commitment to the principles of healthy cities, establish a project office and steering committee, develop and implement a city health plan, and prepare annual city health reports (WHO Regional Office for Europe, 1998). A third phase of the European project has recently been initiated, with the goal of expanding further this network of sustainable european cities.[4]

Many local groups throughout Europe are adopting the language and framework of sustainability. In London, for example, a grassroots group called the Sustainable London Trust has emerged as an advocate for change. Environmental community groups, such as Ecostad Den Haag in the Netherlands, and Environ in Leicester, England, have played major roles in encouraging and facilitating local innovation and progress in urban sustainability. Even more mainstream groups such as London First (an association of businesses) are using notions of sustainability, for example by putting forth proposals for reforming local public transit policy and for promoting the use of bicycles.

Environmental groups have played an active role in Europe in raising awareness about sustainability issues and pushing for action on this agenda. In 1992, Friends of the Earth Netherlands prepared an influential *Action Plan Sustainable Netherlands.* This led to the launching by FOE-Europe of the Sustainable Europe Campaign. An important initial step was the commissioning of a European-wide study entitled *Towards a Sustainable Europe,* prepared by the Wuppertal Institute in Germany. It calculated available *environmental space,* current consumption levels, and reduction targets for the year 2010. *Environmental space* is defined in *Towards a Sustainable Europe* as

> The global total amount of environmental resources: such as absorption capacity, energy, non-renewable resources, agricultural land and forests that humankind can use without impairing the access of future generations to the same amount. Environmental space is limited and (partially) quantifiable. There is, for example, a fixed amount of agricultural land that we can use sustainably; there is a limit (because of the greenhouse effect) to CO_2 emissions and there is a finite amount of non-renewable resources. (Friends of the Earth Europe, 1995, p. 5)

A key element is the equity principle, which states that "(E)ach person in the world has the same right (although no obligation) to use an equal amount of global environmental space." (1995, p. 5) In *Towards Sustainable Europe,* environmental space calculations and target reductions have been prepared for energy, nonrenewable raw materials, land use, wood, and water. These initial results have served as a beginning point and have provided a common methodology for the preparation of national sustainability strategies in thirty European countries. Here extensive discussions and dialogue about sustainability have occurred, with quantitative targets established for resource consumption (European Environment Agency, 1997). A variety of possible strategies are proposed for reaching the targets in *Towards Sustainable Europe,* and much discussion at the national level has centered on these strategies.

In short, sustainable cities, local sustainable development, and thus green urbanism, are very much on the municipal and national agenda in Europe. Sustainability is increasingly seen in Europe as an important and useful framework for envisioning and clarifying a future path. Much of what follows contains detailed descriptions and analyses of the tangible ways in which the most progressive European cities are attempting to move toward greater sustainability.

The Plan of the Book to Follow

The chapters to follow describe and analyze in considerable detail the many green-urban initiatives and strategies pursued by these most impressive cities. Chapters have been organized into several main sections. The chapters in Part II, to follow, describe strategies for promoting compact urban form and a range of creative ideas for housing and living environments in these cities (Chapters 2 and 3).

Part III addresses distinctive mobility strategies in green-urban European cities and, in particular, effective alternatives to the automobile. The chapters describe creative transit programs (Chapter 4), traffic calming, car-free housing, and other strategies for "taming the automobile" (Chapter 5), and an examination of bicycles as a legitimate and important mobility option (Chapter 6). The overall conclusions of this section are that these European cities represent powerful examples of a range of ideas, technologies, and strategies for achieving less environmentally damaging forms of mobility and for loosening the typical heavy reliance on auto-mobility.

The chapters in Part IV take as a common view the city as a living organism, as a place of nature, and as an entity with a metabolism and flows of inputs and outputs. Chapter 7 ponders whether a city can indeed be like a forest, and answers in the affirmative. It reviews the variety of greening initiatives in European cities from greenroofs to natural drainage to urban gardens. It argues that cities are necessarily embedded in a natural context, and that through a host of planning, policy, and interventions, they can be fundamentally greener (more full of nature) than they often are. Chapter 8 extends this reasoning and argues that a more circular, or closed-loop, metabolism for cities is desirable and possible; this can be seen in the emerging ecobalancing initiatives in European cities. Chapter 9 explores the exemplary efforts of many of these cities to achieve tremendous energy efficiency and to power themselves with renewable sources of energy, especially solar energy. Finally, Chapter 10 reviews the extensive experiences of these European cities at building ecologically and also reviews a number of specific ecological building projects throughout Europe.

The chapters in Part V consider the prospects of cities with ecologically restorative economies and economic bases (Chapter 11). Chapter 12 considers the possibility that cities can themselves become more ecological in their decisionmaking, and by so doing can set fundamental, positive examples for businesses and citizens inhabiting these cities.

The final section (Part VI) identifies the broad themes that emerge from the book and extracts some important overarching lessons from these European cases. Extensive references are also contained here, as well as several appendices, including the text of the Aalborg Sustainable Cities Charter.

At the end of each chapter an effort has been made to extract specific lessons for American cities. An attempt has been made here to identify the special or unique opportunities presented in the U.S. context for applying these powerful green-urban ideas.

NOTES

1. Pucher and Lefevre (1996) note the considerable difference in planning approaches and level of planning and development control between northern and southern European nations: "By tradition, the Netherlands, Germany, Switzerland, and the Scandanavian countries have very restrictive laws and regulations on land use. By contrast, Italy, Spain, and Portugal have no significant government control over the use of privately-owned land. France and Britain lie between these two extremes" (p. 28). While the lack of planning in southern European countries is probably overstated here, there are certainly clear and significant differences.

2. The vision presented in the London Planning Advisory Committee (LPAC) guidance emphasizes four key themes for the city: a strong economy, a good quality of life, opportunities for all, and a sustainable future.

3. Among the participating cities are six cities included in the present study: Bologna, London (Camden), Copenhagen, Dublin, Stockholm (Region), and Vienna.

4. The stated goal in phase three is to create "a geographically balanced network of up to 80 cities." (See WHO Regional Office for Europe, 1998.)

Part II

Land Use and Community

Chapter 2

Land Use and Urban Form: Planning Compact Cities

To even the most casual observers visiting Europe from the United States, there are clear and immediate differences between the basic land use patterns and spatial form of American and European cities. Historically, European cities have been fundamentally more compact, with a distinct separation between urban and rural. The cities are walkable, have good public transit, and are generally much less reliant on the automobile. For these reasons these cities are important sources of both practical planning and policy guidance, and sheer inspiration, for American cities and regions struggling to control urban sprawl.

While many European cities themselves, including the cities studied here, have been experiencing decentralization pressures, they remain substantially more compact and dense than American cities. Newman and Kenworthy (1991; Kenworthy, Laube, Newman, and Barter, 1996) have shown this effectively in their comparative global cities work. Table 2.1 presents some of this data, comparing density figures for selected case study cities with American cities. European cities are much more dense and rely significantly less on automobile mobility.

While American cities consume land and growth spatially at a much faster rate than population growth (Leinsberger, 1996), European cities (especially those described here) have generally tended to grow more compactly, at higher densities, and with greater emphasis on the redevelopment and reuse of land within existing urbanized areas. And, even in small countries with relatively large populations such as the Netherlands, the percentage of land devoted to cities and developed areas is a modest 13 percent (Van der Brink, 1997)—this, in a country with one of the highest

Table 2.1. Land Use and Transportation Data for Selected Cities, 1990

	Car use per capita (km)	% of total passenger km on transit	Urban density (persons per ha)
SELECTED EUROPEAN CASE CITIES			
Amsterdam	3,977	17.7	48.8
Zürich	5,197	24.2	47.1
Stockholm	4,638	27.3	53.1
Vienna	3,964	31.6	68.3
Copenhagen	4,558	17.2	28.6
London	3,892	29.9	42.3
SELECTED AMERICAN CITIES			
Phoenix	11,608	0.8	10.5
Boston	10,280	3.5	12.0
Houston	13,016	1.1	9.5
Washington	12,013	4.6	13.7
Los Angeles	11,587	2.1	22.4
New York	8,317	10.8	19.2

Source: Adapted from Kenworthy, Laube, Newman, and Barter, 1996.

population densities in the world. In a less-dense country such as Sweden, only about 2 percent of that nation's land base is reported to be in built-up or urban uses. In Sweden, expansion of urban areas has closely tracked urban population growth. Between 1960 and 1990, for example, population in Swedish cities grew by 31 percent, and the extent of urban or built-up areas grew by a larger but still modest 47 percent (Swedish Ministry of the Environment, 1995). Despite some degree of urban spread, European cities have been largely able to maintain their compactness and density.

Although there is a healthy debate about density and compactness as desirable planning goals (for example, see Jenks et al., 1996), there is considerable consensus among planners and policymakers that this is the appropriate direction for European cities. The *Green Paper on the Urban Environment,* for example, strongly endorses the avoidance of sprawl and instead recommends that new development be guided into existing areas and abandoned lands in need of redevelopment (Commission of the European Communities, 1990).

The cities examined here demonstrate well the many advantages of compact urban form. Ironically, the tight urban structure of these cities, along with the extensive amount of open space and natural lands often owned by cities (e.g., the Vienna woods and the Berlin forest), and good public transit, means that European urban residents have relatively quick access to natural areas. Stockholm and Vienna are two good examples. It is possible to travel by public transit from the center of Stockholm in about thirty minutes to the edge of the archipelago and to resort towns such as Saltsjöbaden. Similarly in Vienna, it is but a brief tram ride from the center of the city to an extensive system of protected forests (more than 7,400 hectares, or about 18 percent of Vienna Province) (City of Vienna, 1992).

European cities also illustrate that density and compactness are not antithetical to economic productivity but, on the contrary, may actually enhance it. Some of the densest, most compact cities are the wealthiest and most economically productive in the world. Kenworthy, Laube, Newman, and Barter (1996) have shown this by calculating per capita regional domestic product for the cities in a worldwide database. The results indicate that per capita Gross Regional Product certainly need not be hindered by density, and may actually be enhanced by it.

The higher densities of European cities and settlement patterns have clear implications for many specific sustainability concerns. Torrie (1993) documents, for example, the substantially lower per capita energy and carbon dioxide emissions for European cities when compared with North American cities.[1]

European cities generally reflect higher average densities than American cities and a more compact urban form, such as in Zwolle, the Netherlands, shown here.

Many factors help to explain these differences, of course, including a historic urban tradition and the fact that many European cities developed their urban core in an era when defensive fortifications were common. The relative scarcity of land in many European countries is also certainly a factor, as is the greater importance placed on protecting rural and resource lands. And certainly, relative scarcity of land and the need to accommodate considerable population growth help explain the cautious use of land in countries such as the Netherlands. Conscious public policy choices and planning traditions are also critical here. While the Netherlands, for example, supports a population of 15 million on a land base of only 400 square kilometers, again it commits only a small portion of its land base to urban development (Van den Brink, 1997). The Netherlands has a long history of supporting compact, contained growth patterns. These European policies and experiences are instructive and need to be carefully considered for the guidance and wisdom they can provide American cities.

Strategies for Compact Urban Development

Although compact urban form has been a priority for centuries, few countries have embraced the virtues of urban compactness in current planning as much as the Dutch. The Netherlands has implemented an explicit national compact cities policy since the mid-1980s. The vast majority of new development in the country occurs in designated development areas (so-called VINEX sites, an abbreviation for Vierde Nota over de Ruimtelijke Ordening Extra, or the Fourth Memorandum on Town Planning Extra), which are generally within or contiguous to existing cities and urban areas. These development areas must meet a minimum overall density target of thirty-three dwelling units per hectare. This system has been reasonably effective at promoting compact development patterns, although problems have been experienced in recent years (e.g., land speculation) and some believe that the density levels must be much higher. Compact growth, especially in the Randstad, is further supported by national transportation and locational policies (which are discussed below).

Alterman (1997, p. 231) eloquently describes the main features of Dutch growth containment:

> The compact city is achieved through careful use of each piece of land. Densities within cities are several times those of United States and Canadian cities. Residential areas are usually planned with multifamily units or mod-

est townhouses. Private conspicuous consumption of space is rare. Despite recent policies to bring more market forces into the Dutch housing system, and also more upscale housing, the national planning authorities are careful to maintain the policies for higher density. Most notably, thanks to a successful battle by Dutch planners, there are few land-gobbling shopping centers or office projects on the suburban fringe, and efficient parking is planned. Visitors today enjoy the picture-book Green Heart area, with its spic-and-span stewardship of every corner, complete with grazing cows, meticulous canals, and dikes. Not the little fingers of the legendary boy, but a concerted planning assault has held back the streams of urban sprawl.

Other European countries have developed similar urban patterns. Indeed, in most of the countries visited and especially in countries such as the Netherlands, Germany, and Denmark, farmland and rural land outside cities receive strong planning protection. More fundamentally, there is a sense that, unlike our American view, these lands are not in a transitional use but should and will remain in an undeveloped state.

In many of the cities studied, the promotion of compact development within each city structure or comprehensive plan is given a clear priority. Stockholm's new structure plan, for example, takes sustainability as a main theme and endorses a compact regional spatial pattern. A number of former industrial sites are identified as the primary areas for future growth in the city (with the Hammarby Sjöstad designated as the first major site to be developed). Generally, this planned development pattern locates new growth in close proximity to existing transportation modes (e.g., the Hammarby project will be served by a new fast tram). These sites are to be developed not as new suburbs, but as mixed urban villages, with shopping, light industry, and residences, all within relatively close proximity to Stockholm's inner city (City of Stockholm, 1996). Similarly, the city of Helsinki has prepared a set of "Sustainable Development Principles for City Planning," and the city's 1992 Master Plan also takes a strong sustainability orientation. Among other things, the plan identifies areas of future development that are "almost without exception, located within the urban structure, supplementing, consolidating, or renovating existing building sites for new uses" (City of Helsinki, 1996, p. 2).

In Odense, Denmark, the vast amount of new growth and development in recent years—owing to Denmark's strong limitation on development outside of urbanized areas—is happening within the city. A number of other smaller towns in the county are entitled to some additional growth, but relatively little development appears to be happening in them. Interestingly, according to planners in Odense, most residents and especially young families would prefer to live in the existing, older parts of the city. The city's structure plan identifies several areas of future growth in the city, all contiguous to and expanding on the existing urbanized area. The city's short-term priority, however, is to promote infill, using available lands within the city before developing new expansion locations. These priority areas are indicated as circles on the city's present plan.

In Groningen, the Netherlands, the city's choices of where to locate new development areas are intended to reinforce the center city and the city's compact urban structure. Major new development areas, such as Beijum, have been located directly adjacent to already developed areas, and bicycle and pedestrian bridges have been built to provide access to the center. The newest residential area, De Helden to the east, will eventually include about 1,500 homes, and is being developed in an area adjacent to existing built-up areas. The city has made a strong attempt to locate major public buildings and attractions close in, within the center or within walking dis-

The city-center of Leiden, the Netherlands, is a mixed-use, highly walkable environment. The city has worked hard to connect its walking streets and urban spaces through, for example, pedestrian and bicycle bridges spanning historic canals, as seen here.

tance of it. Recent examples include the city's new library, the new modern art museum (which serves to link the center with the main train station), a new city hall, a new hospital, and law courts.

Many of the cities studied have followed a strategy of urban form that allows large blocks of open space or green wedges to come very close to urban neighborhoods. In Helsinki, large tentacles of greenspace penetrate into the very center of the city, providing ecological corridors and connections with surrounding countryside (see Figure 2.1). One of the largest of these green tentacles is Keskuspuisto central park—an 11-kilometer-long unbroken green wedge that ends at the periphery of the city in old growth forest (see discussion of Helsinki Urban Biodiversity Strategy, City of Helsinki, 1995). In Copenhagen, high-density development is clustered along transit lines (like "pearls along a neckless"), with large wedges of greenspace between them.

Amsterdam has taken a similar form, beginning with its General Extension Plan approved in 1935. A number of large public parks date to this period, most notably the Amsterdamse Bos, which constitutes one of the most important of the green wedges (see City of Amsterdam, 1994). These green wedges, separating the major new *lobes* of urban development in the city, also connect with and lead into the Randstad's *Green Heart,* a large area of farms and open space in the middle of this urban agglomeration.

Preservation of land in the Green Heart is widely understood and supported by citizens in the Netherlands. Indeed, if surveyed, it is likely that a high percentage of the citizenry would recognize and be able to describe this key planning concept in the Randstad. As Alterman (1997) notes, "commitment to the Green Heart has, since the 1950s, spread beyond professional circles to become part of the national self-image" (p. 230). In the fourth national planning report extra (VINEX), protection of the Green Heart has been reemphasized at the national level, with its physical boundaries now delimited (Van der Valk, 1997). In addition to the Green Heart, major open space buffers and wedges have been set aside to separate major cities in the Randstad. (See also Louisse, 1998.)

The long history of compact spatial form in the Netherlands has undoubtedly made efforts there to protect the Green Heart easier. These efforts at managing and controlling growth date back at least to 1531 when Emperor Charles the Fifth issued an order that precluded many industrial and commercial activities from taking place outside of the walls of existing cities (Geografie, 1996a).

Many German cities have pursued a similar development path. The city of Freiburg, for example, has a development plan that acknowledges and protects five major wedges of open space and natural lands. Development and growth occur outside of these green fingers along the spines of the

Figure 2.1. Helsinki master plan

Helsinki, like many Scandinavian cities, has a compact urban form and large wedges of green penetrating the urban core. Keskuspuisto central park is one of the largest of these wedges, extending a distance of 11 kilometers from old-growth forest to the north of the city-center.

Source: City of Helsinki.

MASTER PLAN SYMBOLS AND REGULATIONS:

City Boundary

HOUSING

Area reserved for housing, including open space and recreational areas, shopping and local services, public utilities and transport infrastructure.

CENTRAL AND LOCAL BUSINESS DISTRICTS

Area reserved for office and commercial use, shopping, housing and open space, including public utilities and transport infrastructure.

INDUSTRY AND WAREHOUSING

Area reserved for general and light industry that does not cause severe nuisance to local neighbourhoods. Warehousing, as well as associated service sectors and office accommodation, will also be permitted, including public utilities, open space and transport infrastructure.

ADMINISTRATIVE AND SERVICE SECTOR

Area reserved for public administration and the service sectors, including housing, open space, public utilities and transport infrastructure.

PUBLIC UTILITIES

Area reserved for public utilities, communication service networks and transport infrastructure.

TRANSPORT

Area reserved for traffic and transport networks, including public utilities.

AREA THAT WILL BE CHANGED TO HOUSING WHERE THE FORMER PRIMARY LAND-USE OF NON-HOUSING ACTIVITIES WILL BE DISPLACED

MAIN MOTORWAYS OR DUAL CARRIAGEWAYS

MAIN ROADS

METRO OR RAILWAY LINES/STATIONS

PROPOSED PUBLIC TRANSPORT CROSS-TOWN CONNECTION BY THE DEVELOPMENT OF A RAPID TRANSIT LIGHT-RAIL/TRAM SYSTEM (JOKER)

Main transport networks underground

PEDESTRIANISED AREA

Area where pedestrians are given preference over other forms of traffic.

RECREATIONAL, SPORT AND OUTDOOR ACTIVITIES

Area reserved for sport and physical recreation activities where it is permitted to build recreational and sport centres and associated facilities, as well as adequate public utilities and local access roads.

OPEN SPACE AND RECREATIONAL AREAS

Area reserved for environmental/open space, parklands, and recreation where it is permitted to build facilities for sport and outdoor activities, including sufficient public utility support systems and local access roads.

Recreational areas where holiday cottages exist

NATURE PROTECTED AREAS

MINISTRY OF DEFENCE AREA

SEA AND WATERWAYS

Area permitted to build facilities associated with water transport and water recreational activities.

CULTURAL AND HISTORICAL AREAS OF SIGNIFICANCE

Area of cultural or historical significance, including buildings of architectural or historic character and special townscape design that may not be materially affected by any proposed development.

WORLD HERITAGE PLACE OF INTEREST

Central Park area covered by an existing Local Plan that has been ratified by the Ministry of the Environment 23.8.1978.

tram lines. All major areas of urban expansion (such as the new Reiselfeld development, the city's primary new development district) are accompanied by expansions of the public transit system. The trams do not come along at some possible future date; they are installed contemporaneously with the construction of housing and development. This is a consistent pattern in most green-urban cities.

The green fingers are an important ingredient in the Freiburg development pattern, and indeed to the local quality of life. Much of these lands are forests, including extensive areas of Black Forest to the east. City officials there strongly declare that the green fingers are considered "off-limits" and vigorously protected by the city. The amount of open and forested land within the city's boundaries (most of it owned, in fact, by the city) is rather high, and urban development within the city boundaries occurs on only about 32 percent of the land.

In Britain, the designation of extensive greenbelts around cities has been a major growth containment strategy and began as early as the late 1930s (under the Greenbelt Corridor and Home Countries Act). London's greenbelt is large in size—some 1.2 million acres—and although urban encroachments and conversions have occurred, it has been mostly successful at preventing sprawl. Extensive greenbelts exist around a number of other British cities (fifteen greenbelts exist, to be precise), and by 1993, the land areas contained within them had grown to 4.5 million acres or about 14 percent of England's land base. Elson (1993) in a comprehensive study of the function of greenbelts found that they are generally effective at restricting sprawl and preventing towns from merging, and they serve to promote urban regeneration. Analyzing alterations to greenbelt boundaries over an eight-year period, he found extremely small levels of change (less than 0.3 percent of greenbelt land affected) (see also Elson, 1986).

In many of these cities, there is simultaneously a strong emphasis on promoting infill development and intensification, and the more efficient use of abandoned or underutilized land within the urban core. Berlin's current land use plan (1994), for example, assumes that 90 percent of the development that will occur to the year 2010 will be accommodated within existing urban areas through strategies that can be broadly termed as *infill*. As Table 2.2 (a rough translation from the German) indicates, the plan assumes that future growth will occur in one of several ways, which interestingly include the conversion of existing rooftops to apartments (some of which can already be seen taking place in the city) and the further subdividing of large single-family lots (especially in the eastern part of the city) (Berlin Senate, 1994).

Examples of resourceful and creative infill projects abound in these European cities, as the goal of compact urban form necessitates looking within the city for development sites wherever possible. The city of Leiden,

Table 2.2. Areas Planned for New Development in Berlin

23%	=	in older industrial areas
24%	=	in vacant sites in eastern part of the city; sites left from World War II destruction
25%	=	division of larger single-family lots (in eastern part of the city)
7%	=	completion of large housing areas
11%	=	roof conversions
10%	=	new development in previously undeveloped (green) areas

Source: Berlin Senate, 1994.

for instance, has been planning the development of one of the last remaining parcels within the city: a 13-hectare former rail yard. What is envisioned is accommodating between 300–400 new dwelling units on this vacant site. The city has been exploring a variety of housing designs and configurations, working with the surrounding neighbors to come up with an acceptable design. Residents were asked to devise their own designs for the site, and thirteen development concepts were offered for what the housing might look like (including an interesting proposal for subterranean homes; see Gemeente Leiden, 1998). The residents prepared their own rough drawings, with city planning staff converting these drawings into a common format and publishing them in a booklet to stimulate further community discussion. The need to directly engage residents in the design of this infill project is a key lesson. The city, at the encouragement of the residents, also commissioned an extensive study of the ecology of site, which resulted in the setting aside of a major portion of the parcel because of its emergence as an important wildlife habitat and movement corridor. The resulting homes will be clustered in a way that will leave a large portion of the parcel untouched. The need to adequately appraise and plan within the urban ecology of a site is another important lesson.

The Dutch government has sought to make it easier for cities like Leiden to develop such sites infill through an innovative pilot program called *Stad en Milieu* (city and environment; See VROM, 1996). Leiden may be given flexibility to exceed noise and other standards (it doesn't know yet if it will need such a waiver) when the result is acceptable to residents and where special compensating features are designed in (for instance, by providing extra amenities in the project, by utilizing special building materials and technologies that minimize the impacts of noise). Leiden and many other cities are working hard to redevelop and reuse important urban sites—locations that provide a high urban quality of life and also conserve the land base.

Stockholm's new structure plan, with sustainability as a central theme, also reflects the importance of reusing lands and not developing any more of the city's greenspaces. A number of former industrial sites are identified as the primary areas for future growth in the city, with the Hammarby Sjöstad (discussed in greater detail in Chapter 8) site the first of these to be developed. Generally, this planned development pattern locates new growth in close proximity to existing transportation nodes, and the Hammarby project will be served by a new fast tram. These sites are to be developed not as new suburbs, but as mixed urban villages, with shopping, light industry, and residences. They will be in close proximity to Stockholm's inner city. The new plan also emphasizes the importance of protecting and strengthening the existing character of the city. To this end, it identifies eleven different types of character by city types. These types include the old stone city, the subway city, and the garden city, and the plan develops a set of design guidelines to govern building and development in each of these different areas. A number of investigations and background studies have gone into the plan, including an inventory of heritage values, the identification of ecologically sensitive lands, the green structure, and issues related to energy, sewerage, and waste (e.g., areas where district heating could be extended are mapped).

The Strøget, Copenhagen's main pedestrian street, is a delightful urban space; a mix of shops, offices, and housing. The city's pedestrian core represents more than thirty years of gradually converting space for the auto to civic and pedestrian spaces.

European cities also generally exhibit a much higher level of mixing and integration of functions. While separate Euclidean-style residential districts do exist, it is much more common to see an interspersing of retail shopping, grocery stores, and even industrial activities in close proximity to where people live. Urban residents are frequently within easy walking distance of a wide variety of services, shops, and community functions. These characteristics, along with the compact nature of the cities, generally means that residents are able to get to many more places and do more things by foot. In the Netherlands, some 35 percent of all trips nationally under 2.5 kilometers are made on foot, with another 40 percent by bicycle. Compact urban form, from the regional level to the design of new districts, makes walkable lifestyles possible.

Compact Growth Districts, with a Green Emphasis

There are many examples of local efforts to design and build new housing areas that continue these patterns. Indeed, the major new growth areas in almost every city studied are situated in locations adjacent to existing developed areas and are generally designed at relatively high densities. Good examples of this can be seen in the new growth areas planned in Utrecht (Leidsche Rijn), Freiburg (Rieselfeld), Amsterdam (IJburg), Copenhagen (Ørestad), Helsinki (Viikki), and Stockholm (Hammarby Sjöstad). IJburg in Amsterdam, for example, is being planned to accommodate a housing density of about 100 dwelling units per hectare.

Many examples of specific development projects and new growth districts that exemplify and strengthen compact urban form can be cited. There are few better examples of Dutch attempts to promote compact development than the new growth district Leidsche Rijn, in Utrecht. An overall master plan and detailed building plans have been prepared for the area, and construction on the first phase of the project has just begun (see Figure 2.2). The plans are ambitious, and this extension of Utrecht will accommodate some 75 percent of the growth in the region for the foreseeable future. In total, the district will accommodate 30,000 houses, as well as 30,000 jobs. The district covers an area of about 2,500 hectares, with an overall development density of about 37 units per hectare.

The most impressive aspect of the new district involves the efforts to connect it to the existing city. The site is immediately to the west of existing Utrecht and takes in the preexisting villages of Vleuten and De Meern. The plan for a compact, contiguous extension of the city has not been easy, and major physical barriers have had to be overcome, most notably the A-2 highway and a large shipping canal (the Amsterdam-Rhine Canal). The plan involves a creative roofing of the highway in several places for a total

Figure 2.2. Leidsche Rijn new town district master plan

Leidsche Rijn is a new compact urban expansion district in Utrecht in the Nether-lands. Typical of new growth districts in Dutch cities, it is adjacent to the existing urban area and offers direct pedestrian and bicycle connections to the city-center.
Source: Gemeente Utrecht.

distance of about 300 meters. An extensive area of greenhouses has had to be relocated as well.

The commitment to connectivity and building on to the existing struc-ture and fabric of the city is truly impressive. In this pursuit, three new bridges are to be constructed, again with the goal of strengthening the con-nections between the old centrum and the new district. One of the bridges (the middle one) will be for bicycles only, while another will be reserved for public transit (buses, at least in the beginning) and bicycles. A third bridge will accommodate these modes, as well as automobiles.

This project also exemplifies an effort to promote a mixture and diversity of people and activities. Approximately 70 percent of the housing will be private sector, and 30 percent public sector; a range of housing types will be provided, including multi-family flats, single-family attached, and single-family detached. While the Utrecht centrum will remain the major shopping area for residents, grocery and other daily shopping will be available close to home. The inclusion of commercial and industrial uses also provides for local employment, and some of the homes will be provided with additional space for in-home offices.

Several innovative environmental features will be included. All homes will be connected to a district heating system (hot water piped to the district from the residual heat of a nearby power plant). Extensive use is to be made of natural stormwater collection, through the use of *wadies*, or green drainage swales to which water is directed. All homes will be provided with two different lines of water—one for clean water (from the city's water treatment facility) for drinking, and a second line supplying less-clean water (from a major water transfer pipe running through the area) to be used for car washing, garden watering, and other nondrinking purposes.

A goal from the beginning is to discourage the use of automobiles. There will be three new stations for the train, as well as new bus service. One transferium (parking deck) will be provided to give automobile drivers the chance to shift to the bus. Higher-density housing and much of the employment will be clustered near the train stations. (It is not clear, however, that the automobile is sufficiently restricted here: the plan still calls for 1.2 spaces per unit.) The area is also designed to facilitate bicycle use (see Figure 2.2). For example, the network includes extensive bike-only routes. The project designers have managed to keep most of the new development within 5 kilometers of the centrum, and they believe this is the distance most people can be expected to ride their bicycles ("autonomic cycle lanes with a mesh-work from 500 meters"). The project also contains extensive green infrastructure. The plan calls for a "central park" of about 300 hectares, in the center of the district, with ecological connections between the district and surrounding areas (the Randstad's Green Heart is immediately to the west). The central park includes, among other things, sporting facilities and allotment gardens for residents.

Urban Villages and the Importance of City-Centers

Although there are certainly examples of communities where the city-center is declining in population and intensity of use, European cities on the whole (and especially the case study communities described here) have been able to maintain and strengthen the vitality of these centers. In no small part, this is a function of density and compactness, but it is also the result of numerous efforts to maintain and enhance the quality and attractiveness of the city-center.

In most of the study cities, the center area has remained a mixed-use zone, with a significant residential population. A common pattern is the location of residential units above retail shops and offices (as in most Dutch cities and towns, for example). Consequently, significant numbers of people still live there. In the city of Münster, some 12,000 residents live in the old center, a fairly sizable portion of the city's population. In Amsterdam, about 80,000 people live in the historic inner city, and the center remains "the economic heart of the entire agglomeration" (Oskam, 1995, p. 32). Sixty-five thousand people live in the historic core of Copenhagen, and some fifty-five thousand residents live in the historic center of Bologna. Odense, Denmark, has a healthy city core, and some 70,000 residents live within its city-center statistical zone. An extensive system of pedestrian streets and the presence of many amenities have made the center an attractive place to live near.

Many European cities are investing major resources in supporting new development in city-center locations. Examples of such projects on quite a massive scale can be seen in Berlin and Den Haag. In Berlin, the largest new development site is the Potsdamer Platz, where 1.1 million square meters of office and residential space are under construction. This new area will be served by major new transit investments—with a planned modal split of 20 percent private car and 80 percent public transit—and will be served with central heating and cooling.

Groningen, in the Netherlands, has undertaken a host of actions to further strengthen its compact urban form and to enhance the attractiveness of its center, especially through its initiative *binnenstad beter* ("a better inner city").

In Den Haag, the Nieuw Centrum is a massive project to create a new office and governmental center in the very heart of the city, and adjacent to the city's central train station. The 4 billion guilders project (about US \$2 million) includes 800,000 square meters of office space to be completed by 2000 (City of the Hague, 1995). Admittedly, both the Potsdamer Platz and the New Centrum have been criticized for not including enough residential units. Nevertheless, residential use is a key component of each project (e.g., in New Centrum, more than 2,150 new residential units will be created, about half above shops).

Other cities have undertaken aggressive programs for improving the look, feel, and functioning of their city-centers. The City of Groningen, for instance, has undertaken a host of actions under its binnenstad beter ("a better inner-city") program. Described as a "cohesive set of measures to improve the center," the measures have included the creation of new pedestrian-only shopping areas (creating a system of two linked circles of pedestrian areas), the installation of yellow brick surfaces in walking areas, the installation of new street furniture, and the adoption of a new public transit concept. The public transit concept includes making the center car free, providing free peripheral parking and direct bus service to the center, replacing street parking with a series of underground car parks on the edge of the center, and increasing the number of cycling paths (Groningen Gemeente, 1993; 1996). Together these measures are designed to improve the access to and attractiveness of the center.

These cities also present excellent, and generally successful, examples of redevelopment and adaptive reuse of older, deteriorated areas within the city-center. Exemplary cases include Amsterdam's eastern port area (8,000 new homes in an abandoned port area) and Bologna's urban plan, which identifies a number of development sites, all within the existing urban area and including the reuse of a former cigarette factory site. In Dublin, the Temple Bar district has emerged as a major new cultural and commercial district in a once-derelict part of the city. Through a combination of tax incentives and creative design ideas (e.g., the creation of a new public square, street resurfacing, and other pedestrian improvements), the district has become a lively and desirable location (see RECITE, undated).

Some cities are attempting to further encourage the injection of residential units in city-center and commercial areas, as a way to both efficiently provide housing and enhance the vitality and livability of these city-center areas. Traditionally, British and Irish center-cities have had fewer residents than continental European cities (Bradshaw, 1996). The cities of Dublin and Leicester have operated (only moderately successful) programs that provide financial incentives to encourage people to relocate to city-centers. One such effort is called the Living Over The Shop program, which seeks to take advantage of the traditional housing opportunities that exist above shops and retail establishments. While this is a common housing option in most Dutch and German cities, much less can be seen in cities such as Dublin. Several major obstacles include the cost of bringing buildings up to the building and fire codes, the fact that shop owners may not be able to effectively use the tax credits provided, and the perception by shop owners of the liabilities of having new residents living above them. Nevertheless, the living-over-the-shops notion is increasingly viewed as a promising strategy for promoting sustainable urban form as well as for providing affordable housing. (This idea is discussed in greater detail in Chapter 3; see also Petherick, 1998, for a discussion of both the promises and obstacles of this program in the United Kingdom.)

Compact urban form and efforts at infill and urban redevelopment go hand in hand in many of these cities. The city of Amsterdam has pursued its own compact cities policy since 1978, a clear reaction to the syphoning off of the city's population by the outlying growth center communities. As a result, the city has vigorously pursued developing and redeveloping close-in areas. One of the centerpieces of this policy has been the redevelopment of the eastern docklands area: formerly vibrant docks during the nineteenth century that were made obsolete by the shifting of activities to the city's western docks (City of Amsterdam, 1994). The city's physical planning department prepared a masterplan for the area that envisions development at about 100 units per hectare, a mixture of uses and activities (including a major new shopping area), and direct (bicycle, pedestrian, auto) connection to the city-center. Eventually, the area will accommodate some 8,500 new dwelling units, about 1,500 of which have already been completed.

Java-eiland—one of the main pieces of the eastern docks redevelopment area in Amsterdam—represents an impressive example of a new compact urban village, one that is in very close proximity to the Amsterdam centrum. It is very much an expression of the city's compact growth strategy. Typical for new Dutch developments, an emphasis has been placed on encouraging a diversity of building styles and architectural designs. An overall masterplan for this island, prepared by urban designer Sjoerd Soeters, sets the stage and the basic physical characteristics of the district; it lays out roads and bikeways, pedestrian and civic spaces, and the block dimensions within which more specific building designs occur. The design creatively incorporates a series of canals crossing the island at several points, reminiscent of old Amsterdam. A bikepath meanders down the center of the quay. Building heights vary from five to ten stories, with the north end of the island accommodating the tallest structures. A wide range of housing types and lifestyle choices are designed from the beginning (types of homes include larger family flats, studio units, senior housing, and work-at-home arrangements), as well as a variation in price levels (the most expensive units are located on the south end of the island).

Scores of architects have been involved in designing the various buildings that make up Java-eiland, which helps explain the unique look and feel of the place. Even the bridges crossing the new canals are each designed by a different architect. The result is a visual and aesthetic diversity, and a successful attempt to overcome the otherwise monotonous feel that often results when new construction occurs mostly at the same time. Fostering design diversity and experimentation is a hallmark (and a key lesson) of the Dutch approach to planning new growth areas.

An important element of the compact development strategy in Zürich Canton, another example, is the reuse of land. A number of former industrial sites in the Zürich area have been or are being planned for redevelopment; most of the development and growth is occurring in these areas. Indeed, the guiding plan of Zürich Canton specifically identifies eleven areas where future redevelopment and growth will be directed. One important example is the Zentrum Nord site, which is located in the Oerlikon area of the city and was at one time a manufacturing site for cannons and other armaments. The city has worked hard to turn the project into a more desirable one from the city's perspective—although the owners originally wanted only office development, 35 percent of the project space will now be devoted to residential development. It will now be a mixed-use neighborhood, with much greater public ownership. The city held a design competition, and the chosen design maintains the existing street grid, with the assumption that not all of the project will be built at once. The design also contains well-defined open spaces (50,000 square meters of park were required by the city), and the project will be in close proximity to the main train station, with the highest residential density closest to the station. A new city bus line will run through the neighborhood, along with a dense network of footpaths and bikepaths.

The cities contain many good examples of locational decisions explicitly intended to support and strengthen city-centers. Cities such as Zürich, Odense, Groningen, and many others are cases in point and provide important models of what can be accomplished when strengthening city-centers is given planning and development priority.

New Towns and Growth Centers

One possible strategy for accommodating population growth in a compact form is the creation of new towns and growth centers. Europe offers many positive examples of successfully designed and implemented new towns, many of which approximate the ideal characteristic of sustainable communities. Sweden and the Netherlands offer the most successful guides.

The Dutch growth centers policy began in the mid-1960s and lasted until the mid-1980s. It was a realistic recognition of the trend of people moving out of city-centers, and it reflected a desire to direct this outward growth to compact nodes. Under a strategy known as *concentrated deconcentration* (or clustered deconcentration); fifteen new growth centers were designated, most in the Randstad, and significant national government subsidies were provided to build them. Each growth center had a target population of between 55,000 and 80,000, and each involved sites ranging from small villages, to medium-sized cities, to entirely new towns. Despite certain perceived negative aspects (e.g., a higher per-unit cost), they have generally been successful and were built as intended. They can be generally characterized as compact and transit-oriented, and of mixed housing types. The most dramatic examples are Almere and Lelystad, which are new towns shaped literally from the sea, built on a reclaimed polder. Their main limitations have been in failing to achieve economic self-sufficiency (there is high out-commuting in Almere, for instance, much of which is by car) and the effect that some of the growth centers have had in siphoning off population from older cities such as Amsterdam.

Nevertheless, Almere is an impressive design creating an urban form that largely approximates our image of an ideal sustainable place. The town's spatial form consists of a polynuclear structure, with three main centers: the first was Almere Haven, then Almere Stad and Almere Buiten. The central train station is at Almere Stad, which represents the main city-center, where most regional entertainment, cultural, and shopping functions are located. A walking boulevard extends immediately from the central train station, with shops and restaurants on the ground level and apartments and multi-family housing above. The city's *stadhuis* (city hall) is located at the other end of the boulevard. Accessibility is a key feature of Almere. Perhaps the most interesting transportation mode is the city's fixed-route bus system. City buses run along bus-only routes and consequently provide very rapid service between different parts of Almere. A separate system of bike lanes, which generally pass under roads and the bus-only routes, makes it easy and comfortable to travel by bicycle. Few living areas are more than a few hundred meters away from a bus stop or a train station, and there are plans to increase the number of train stations from three to seven.

Overall density of the city is about thirty-five dwelling units/hectare, although density is higher in the center of Almere Stad. There are now new plans to intensify activities in the center of Almere Stad, and a new

Stadscentrum 2005 plan was recently proposed by Rem Koolhaas and his Office of Metropolitan Architecture. Even now, Almere's urban form is fairly compact, and each neighborhood has services and small-scale shopping as well as schools, all accessible by a short walk or bicycle ride. One of the most impressive features about Almere is its green network. As a rule, residents are no farther than 500 meters from green areas, and there are extensive forested and nature areas just a few minutes' bike ride away. Other sustainability features include a district heating system fueled by a natural-gas cogeneration plant (district heating is described in more detail later).

Another impressive growth center is Houten, 10 kilometers to the south of Utrecht. Like many of the growth centers, it was a small village before its designation. The initial town plan has brought the population to about 30,000 (a second phase is now under construction), and the design of the town uses a creative "butterfly" structure. A new railway station and town center make up the core of the town. The town center includes grocery and retail shops, a town hall and a library, and denser, multi-family housing. There are sixteen different residential zones, each containing about 600 homes, and no point is further than 1.6 kilometers from the train station and the center of the town (half the homes are within 800 meters).

Perhaps the most creative design feature of this growth center is its approach to mobility. The automobile is explicitly deemphasized in the design. Auto access to residential neighborhoods is by way of an outer ring road that encircles the town, making it difficult to travel from one residential area to another by car. By contrast, the extensive pedestrian and bicycle network is star-shaped (see Figure 2.3), allowing much easier movement by these nonauto modes within the town. A major green corridor runs down the spine of the town. All major destinations in the town, including schools, sport facilities, and the library, are all on the bicycle network, and most residents get around within the town by bicycle.

Houten represents a model of a functional, compact, green new town, where pedestrian and bicycle mobility is encouraged and facilitated and where good public transit is a central element. A relatively high percentage of shopping trips are made within the town (about 50 percent of nonfood shopping), and the vast majority of residents commuting by train get to the station on foot or by bicycle. The town's bicycle network also connects to regional networks, allowing relatively easy bicycle travel to Utrecht, to the north. Kraay (1996) reports that over-the-counter sales are higher in Houten, traffic accidents are substantially lower than the national average (1.1 per 1,000 inhabitants, compared with 3.5 nationally), and automobile use is significantly lower than comparable cities (25 percent lower). These are all good signs. Unfortunately, the number of jobs in Houten is small,

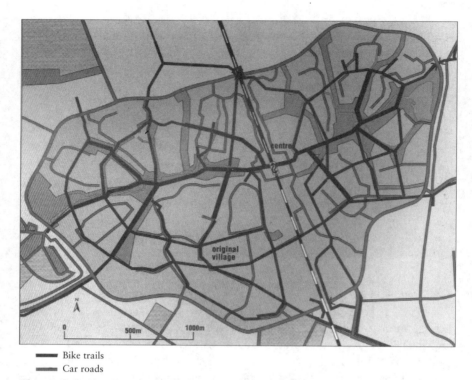

Bike trails
Car roads

Figure 2.3. Houten town plan (butterfly design)

The town of Houten in the Netherlands is designed in a compact butterfly urban form. Two mobility modes are shown here. Traveling by auto requires an outer ring road. More direct travel, however, is accomplished on bike or by foot.

Source: Ministry of Transport, Public Works and Water Management, 1995.

and many residents commute to other areas, typically by auto—a fact that remains an Achilles' heel for Houten planners.

Stockholm provides another impressive example of transit-based, satellite communities. Here, beginning in the 1950s, a series of communities have been built, along the *tunnelbana* regional rail system. Communities such as Kista, Skärpnack, and Vällingby are high-density, high-access communities, designed around subcenters incorporating retail and various community services (e.g., a library, daycare, and movie theaters). Based on Sven Markelius's famous 1945–52 General Plan, these communities are largely walkable, with a discernible town center and higher density housing all within a few meters of the train station. Density is "tapered" around these centers, with lower density housing farther away. The ability to walk to the train station was a key design feature: As Hall notes, these new cities were "developed on the basis that dense flat-block development was within

Houten in the Netherlands has an urban form and spatial plan that make it easier to reach schools, shopping, and greenspace on foot or by bicycle than by automobile. All major community destinations are easily reached through its impressive network of bicycle and pedestrian paths.

500 meters of the subway station; terrace houses, villas and small houses were within 900 meters. The idea was that the multi-story housing should be for a particular clientele of small families and bachelor households, who were less interested in space than in proximity—to transport, shops, restaurants, cinema, theater and collective household sources" (Hall, 1995a, p. 20). While considerable out-commuting and cross-commuting occurs (and indeed these towns were not intended to be self-sufficient), there is a heavy reliance on public transit, and a clear de-emphasis of the automobile. For the most part the communities seem to work well: people appear to enjoy living there, and the communities provide a high degree of access and mobility, along with considerable community amenities.

Vällingby, the first of the satellite towns to be completed (in 1954), remains an impressive example. This town of 25,000 residents is a mix of housing types and uses, with a civic center/shopping complex at the center. An attractive public square makes up the core—for the most part a car-free area—with sitting places, fountains, a theater, stores, a town hall, and an escalator/entrance to the tunnelbana. The town is also surrounded by extensive greenspace. Beyond the main center are neighborhood centers (what Cervero (1995) calls a "hierarchy of centers").

Although as Hall (1995a) and others accurately observe, many of these towns were built before high car-ownership, they are nevertheless impressive, especially for their regional coordination of rail and land use/development decisions. Cervero (1995) and Bernick and Cervero (1997) identify several key ingredients that help to explain Stockholm's success: an effort to keep rail fares relatively low, and costs for owning and operating auto-

Vällingby, one of Stockholm's satellite communities, shows the many benefits of transit villages. A civic plaza, main shopping area, and higher-density housing are clustered around the tunnelbana (train) station. Lower-density housing and green-space are within an easy walk or bicycle ride.

mobiles relatively high (e.g., with high parking fees in the city center and high motor vehicle taxes); a high degree of city ownership of land, and a high degree of public subsidy for housing.

Similarly, the Copenhagen region has developed regionally along its rail lines, with suburban and satellite communities situated like pearls along a necklace. Albertslund is a case in point, with its civic center (city hall) and shopping and office areas adjacent to the main train line, and most residential neighborhoods within a few minutes' walk or bicycle ride to the station. A number of other examples from the case study cities can be mentioned. In Berlin, for example, the regional plan endorses limited "concentrated deconcentration" by designating a series of ten smaller towns, 50 kilometers or more away from the city, each intended to accommodate a population of between 50,000 to 100,000 (including its own economic base).

Regional and National Spatial Planning

These European cities also reflect an ability to influence growth and development patterns through coordination and integration with higher jurisdiction levels of planning and control, including at regional and national

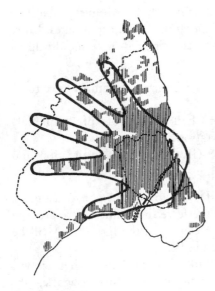

Figure 2.4. Copenhagen regional plan (finger plan)

Much of the urban form of Copenhagen is owed to its famous 1947 regional fingers plan, which required major new growth areas to be sited along the transit lines, with large wedges of greenspace preserved between the growth fingers.

Source: Greater Copenhagen Council.

government levels. Cities such as Copenhagen, for example, have a long tradition of regional planning (dating back to its famous 1947 finger plan; see Figure 2.4). In Denmark, the regional plans are essentially prepared by counties (there are fourteen in Denmark), and municipal plans must be consistent with these regional plans. Municipal plans lay down the broad structure and pattern of development in a city, as well as use, density, height limitations, and other development guidelines for different areas. A specific local plan, usually prepared by the city itself, identifies a more detailed development plan for the site.

In the Netherlands, spatial planning occurs within an integrated national-provincial-municipal framework. Each of the eleven provinces must prepare their own (regional scale) plan. Called a *streekplan* (provincial structure plans), they are not legally binding. However, the municipal plans must take these plans into account in preparing their own plans. This happens because provincial governments must approve every local *bestemmingsplan* (a more detailed development plan) and will not do so if the plans conflict with the direction of the regional plan.

Some cities, such as Berlin, have extremely large city boundaries, encompassing a high percentage of the developable region. Cities such as Stockholm have been able to effectively influence regional development patterns as a result of a high degree of public land ownership and a strong public role in planning and underwriting new development areas.

In the Swiss planning system, cantons (similar to states) must prepare Guiding Plans, and municipal plans must be consistent with these. The

Zürich Canton has adopted an approach explicitly based on the objective of promoting compact growth, oriented along the S-bahn train lines. More specifically, the Guiding Plan identifies three principles that should direct planning at all levels.

1. Future viability of urbanized areas and urbanized structures have to be ascertained and enhanced.
2. Future development of urbanization shall concentrate predominately on areas serviced by public transportation.
3. Existing interrelated natural/rural environments need protection and active management (Zürich Canton).

Zürich Canton planning officials argue for the importance of focusing on only three guidelines. They believe that the fewer guidelines there are, the more emphasis and attention they will receive and the more they will be kept in mind by decisionmakers and the public.

The basic idea behind the Zürich Canton Guiding Plan is that growth will occur in the medium-sized cities and major nodal points along the public transit lines. (Such medium-sized places include, for instance, Winterthur, Aarau, and Baden.) The Guiding Plan specifies where urban development can occur; beyond this zone, development is not allowed. Under the current plan, 25 percent of the canton is in settlement uses (cities and towns), while 30 percent is in forested uses and 45 percent in agricultural uses. More specifically, the Guiding Plan also designates eleven "central areas of Cantonal importance" (Ringli, 1995). These are areas that are at key points along the public transit system where opportunities for urban reintensification and redevelopment exist. It is also expected that these eleven areas will be given priority for canton governmental investments as well (e.g., new government offices).

In a number of these cities, examples of agencies or governmental units effectively operating at regional levels can be cited. In Helsinki, for example, a regional agency, YTV (Metropolitan Area Council) has considerable powers and the primary responsibility for coordinating transportation, waste management, and air quality at a regional level.

Nevertheless, even in many European cities, spatial decentralization has occurred, and the need for more concerted coordination and control at a regional level is increasingly recognized. A new Italian law requires the largest cities in Italy to prepare metropolitan plans, and Bologna has been involved in the preparation of such a plan (which assumes a strong sustainability orientation by setting regional sustainability targets, for example). In Berlin, a regional plan has been prepared jointly by the city and the State of Brandenburg, and special procedures are now in place for coordinating and dealing with land use projects and proposals of a regional nature. London has suffered tremendous problems without the existence of a strategic authority at the metropolitan or regional level (the Greater London Council was abolished in 1986), and most decisions are left to the thirty-three boroughs that make up the city. The Blair government, however, has promised to make the creation of such a metropolitan-wide body a priority.

Although it would be difficult to generalize across Europe, in the countries studied there is a significant degree of control and planning over spatial and settlement policy at the national level. The form this control takes varies. The Netherlands has a long history of national spatial plans, which exert major influence on local development. These plans are administratively binding on lower levels of government, and the national government has the power (infrequently used) to overturn or mandate a specific local decision. In Britain, although no national spatial plan exists, the national government exerts influence through (among other things) a series of planning guidance documents.

The most extensive planning powers in the Swiss system reside at the cantonal level. However, the Swiss central government exercises important influences on cantonal and municipal levels of planning and development as well. The planning function of the national government is largely one of coordination and of laying out broad principles of spatial policy. In May 1996, the Swiss national parliament adopted a new, creative national spatial planning strategy that holds promise for helping to create and reinforce a compact development pattern for other parts of the country similar to what has evolved in Zürich. Called the *polycentric urban network,* the strategy is contained in the national guidelines for Swiss spatial development. The urban network is described in this way by Ringli (1996, p. 203):

> The backbone of the strategy is a polycentric urban network which is based on the existing urban pattern in Switzerland. This urban network forms the functional 'Swiss City' with many but relatively small nodes and with about three million inhabitants and two million work places. The network offers the required critical mass and a large enough market needed for highly specialized services and for skilled top professionals. Therefore it will be able to compete with surrounding metropolitan areas like Munich, Frankfurt, Lyon and so on.

The strategy assumes that future growth should occur in a compact fashion, in the "core city" and near rail stations (Ringli, 1995). Redevelopment and strengthening of existing cities is a key part of the strategy, and sprawl on the fringe is to be avoided. "Generally, the agglomerations are planned to develop in a compact manner, mainly along the axes of the metropolitan railway system, with green wedges between the development axes. This inward urban development shall reduce development pressure on the urban fringes and in the rural areas" (Ringli, 1996, p. 204). Some growth (e.g., new large businesses) would be directed to nearby medium-sized cities, next to train stations (referred to by Ringli as deconcentration centers). An important element of the strategy is the national government's "Rail 2000" program. Actually predating the spatial strategy, this program's invest-ments in rail service are central to bringing about the concept. Basically, the idea is one of connecting and providing regular service to the important nodal points in the polycentric system; emphasis is not on fast trains, but on reliable connections of cities and nodes.

The political and governmental ability of national governments in Europe to take action in support of sustainable land use patterns was demonstrated dramatically in early 1999 in Norway. Here, the govern-ment, by royal decree, banned new shopping malls located outside of city-centers for a period of five years. Seen as a bold and necessary move to prevent further auto traffic and the economic undermining of downtowns, the decree applies to malls of 3,000 square meters or larger (Associated Press, 1999; World Media Foundation, 1999). Similar restrictions have been placed on out-of-town shopping complexes in other European coun-tries.

Even in the United Kingdom, the national government has taken steps to further promote compact growth patterns. Its national strategy of sus-tainable development (U.K. Government, 1994) explicitly calls for efforts to further promote urban compaction. Several important guidance docu-ments have been issued to further encourage compact growth. The U.K. national government has also issued recent policy papers proposing a tar-get that 60 percent of future residential growth occur on reused urban land (Breheny, 1997).[2] National government statistics for 1993 show that 49 percent of residential development occurred on "redeveloped" or brown-field sites, and another 12 percent on vacant urban land. Only 39 percent of residential development (still a large amount by continental European standards) in the United Kingdom occurred on "rural" land (Breheny, 1997, p. 212).[3]

Although a full description of the different planning systems in use in western and northern European nations is not included here, a number of important works can be consulted (e.g., see Newman and Thornley, 1996; Thomas et al., 1983; Hallett, 1989; and Grant, 1992). Even though differ-ences between these systems do exist (e.g., the Netherlands and Britain have, as Alterman (1997) nicely describes, quite different planning sys-tems), they tend to share important characteristics and norms when compared with the United States (see also Pearce, 1992). When it comes to building and development, most European cities exercise a much greater control over, and involvement in, the development process. Typically, cities initiate the development process for major new areas, preparing development plans that specify in great detail the density, form, and other specifics of development. Commonly, European cities acquire the land, and once detailed development plans have been prepared, sell it to private builders and social housing companies with specific conditions attached. Privately initiated development, where a developer buys land, designs and privately finances a project, and then seeks approval from local planning authorities, has been less common. A much higher level of public financial involvement has typically occurred in housing development, with most major projects incorporating significant amounts of social and subsidized housing units.

Moreover, there is a history of extensive public land ownership in many European cities, such as Amsterdam and Stockholm, and this ownership affords a further level of land use control that is uncommon in most American cities. In Amsterdam, the city continues to own a relatively high percentage of the underlying land rights in the city, under a system of long-term land leases. In the Netherlands more generally, municipal governments now have special rights of first refusal, which give them the first option of buying private lands in future development or growth areas.

Planning in German cities, such as Freiburg, occurs on several levels. Two major types of plans are especially key: there is a citywide development plan (the *Flächennutzungsplan*), and then a more detailed development plan for specific districts or development areas within the city. This plan, the *Bebauungsplan,* is binding on private land owners (and must be consistent with the citywide plan) (see Newman and Thornley, 1996). It is through the latter mechanism that the city is able to exercise such a major influence on development, for these district plans are extremely specific. They include not only the types of uses permitted, but they also usually indicate the zones in which the buildings can actually be built and the type of building and number of floors that must be constructed. As the planning director for Freiburg impressed upon me, the district plans can indicate what levels the developer has to build to—rather than simply specifying a limit or maximum, as in typical American zoning.

Urban sprawl is virtually nonexistent in cities such as Freiburg, due in large part to a German planning law, adopted in the early 1960s, that prevents any building outside of established communities. Cities such as Freiburg are also able to exercise great influence by owning the land on which major development is taking place. Freiburg owned the Reiselfeld property, for example, and as a result has been able to place a number of development conditions into the agreement between the city and the developer. These conditions include, for example, important energy efficiency standards (see Chapter 9), which then become contractual obligations.

In the Netherlands, a similar level of detailed planning control occurs through the municipal preparation of a *bestemmingsplan*. This is the only plan at the local level that is legally binding, and it must be prepared by the municipality for any new growth or development area (see Ministry of Housing, Spatial Planning and the Environment, 1996b; and Davies, 1989). It, like the German *Bebauungsplan,* is very detailed in its delineation of roads, public facilities, and the density and types of uses to be permitted. Dutch builders, architects, and housing corporations are thus given a much more detailed development template in which to operate.

The Value of Rural, Agricultural, and Undeveloped Lands

To be sure, one of the reasons compact urban form is considered necessary in many European countries is the value attached to rural and undeveloped lands. In contrast to attitudes (and resulting regulatory systems) about land use in the United States, which historically view farmland and undeveloped land as a temporary use, in Europe rural and agricultural lands are not seen as transient or residual activities but as important primary societal uses. To be sure, generous European Union agricultural subsidies have helped as well.

Rural land, especially agricultural land (such as in Switzerland) is preciously guarded. Generally, only agricultural uses are allowed in these areas. One Swiss planning academician described the importance of Swiss history in understanding protections given to farmland: he explained that it was actually closely tied to national security—a feeling that Switzerland must be prepared to be self-sufficient to the furthest extent possible. Protecting farmland is viewed as one way to do this (Ringli, 1989).

A different social norm also applies concerning the property rights that attach to ownership of private land outside existing urban areas. While in the United States much land use policy and decisionmaking is driven by concern about violating the takings clause of the federal constitution (and similar provisions in most state constitutions), no similar concern exists in the European countries studied. Indeed, the social norms there do not generally support the notion of a right to develop that must be compensated for when taken away or significantly reduced. Local planning authorities in European cities "are not troubled by the shadow of a 'takings clause.' In Britain, development permission is not a right, and its denial does not entail compensation. Thus, greenbelts or agricultural preservation policies are immune from claims for compensation" (Alterman, 1997, p. 228; see also Brussaard, 1991).

When land is acquired, it is usually at its existing use value. This is a result of the limited development potential, the stronger and clearer separation of urban and nonurban uses, and the generally lower inherent expectations that rural land will be permitted to be converted to developed uses. Thus when land is purchased by European municipalities or other governmental authorities, it is typically at its farm or rural land value and not at a higher speculative development value.

Cultural and Other Influencing Factors

To be sure, there are important cultural differences and social norms that also help to explain more compact urban form in European cities. These cultural differences vary to some degree from country to country and certainly merit additional research and study. In the Netherlands, a strong egalitarian ethic works against the desire for large American-style single-family homes on large lots (see Vossestein, 1998). A stronger sense of environmental concern in Scandinavian countries undoubtedly helps explain support for a variety of conservation and sustainable development initiatives there (see Newman and Kenworthy, 1989).[4] European urban traditions and the importance of city living (arguably in contrast to a strong anti-city bias in much American history and thinking, dating back to Jefferson) certainly help make many of the compact urban policies and projects described easier to implement.

There are clear differences, of course, in the ways these European cities have developed compared with the United States, which help to explain why the European land use patterns tend to better exemplify sustainability. Generally, the public sector in the countries studied exerts a much greater degree of control over the development process. Major new development areas are commonly initiated and designed by public sector agencies, with a much higher degree of public financial investment. As noted, in planning systems such as Germany's, no building can take place in the absence of a specific and detailed building plan for an area, usually prepared by government planners, showing great detail down to the placement of trees, the siting of buildings, and the stipulating of a variety of standards including minimum and maximum building heights and densities.

A sustainability agenda that emphasizes encouraging people to return to cities to live in more compact infill environments also requires them to feel safe there. Moreover, feelings of safety have implications for many of the other design and planning ideas discussed in this book, including the potential importance of pedestrianized city-centers and pedestrian and bicycle

networks, among others. Particularly when it comes to fear of gun violence, European cities become more attractive places to live. Homicides
from handguns are dramatically lower in the European countries when
compared to the United States.

Strong controls on gun ownership in Europe, and the inverse of the free
flow of weapons in the United States (where there are some 60 million
handguns), make for the very real personal assessments that the chances of
a fatal robbery attempt while visiting a city-center market in a European
city are much lower. In 1996, for example, there were a reported 9,390
handgun deaths in the United States, compared with only 30 in the United
Kingdom, a country with some of the toughest gun restrictions of any
nation (Overholser, 1999). There is no question that the ubiquity of guns
and the frequency of gun fatalities in the United States affects the locational
and lifestyle choices of Americans. An important lesson from European
countries, then, may be one that is not frequently discussed in planning
texts: serious gun control may be a necessary element in any strategy to
promote sustainable urban form.

Economic Signals and Policy Instruments

More compact European land use patterns are certainly strongly influenced
by a variety of important economic signals that citizens, consumers, and
public officials alike respond to. One significant economic signal is the relatively high price of gasoline in Europe—over $4 per gallon in many places,
a result of a willingness to impose substantially higher taxes on fuel. The
income derived from these gas taxes is substantially higher than the total
direct costs incurred in building and maintaining road systems. The cost of
purchasing a car in most European countries is much higher than in the
United States, again due to tax.[5] Also, most European countries have not
put in place the generous tax subsidies for home ownership found in the
United States. The Europeans have also invested much more heavily in
public transit, as already exhibited in a number of the cities discussed;
sprawl-inducing road and automobile subsidies found in the United States
are very significant factors to the contrary. Higher costs imposed for electricity, and the existence now of a variety of green taxes (including carbon
taxes) also contribute (see Chapter 8), as does the more consumption-
directed nature of European tax systems (e.g., the heavy use of value-added
taxes). In the United States, in the absence of these kinds of consumption
taxes and where sprawl-living is the ultimate form of consumption, Nivola
(1999) does not find the resulting land use patterns at all hard to understand: "The effect of such provisions [a tax system that favors consump-

tion] is to lead most American families into the suburbs, where spacious dwellings are available and absorb much of the nation's personal savings pool" (p. 3).[6]

Sustainable Land Use Trends?

The relatively high density and compact urban structure of European cities are critical features in determining their sustainability on other measures. These features make possible, or at least much easier, many of the other qualities that have been discussed above, including the high use of public transit, high walkability, vital and vibrant civic spaces, the use of extremely efficient district heating systems, and the protection of large systems of extremely accessible greenspaces.

Despite the historic denseness and compactness of European cities, most have experienced considerable deconcentration (beginning as early as the 1950s) of both employment and population. Generally, this has also resulted in significant increases in automobile use and commuting in these cities. But the nature of these deconcentration trends, and the ways in which they have tended to manifest are quite different in European cities compared with the American scene. As Hall (1995) notes, strong systems of public land use planning and development control have been able to guide these forces into more compact urban forms:

> With differences in detail from country to country, the pattern of urban deconcentration has been contained by strong land-use planning systems, either into medium-density contiguous extensions, or into outgrowths of free-standing smaller towns separated from their parent conurbations by greenbelts. In a few countries, planned new towns and satellite towns have played a major role in this pattern. Sometimes (as in the United Kingdom) these were planned as freestanding self-contained communities, though their self-containment seems to have weakened somewhat since 1970. In others (the Paris, Amsterdam and Stockholm areas) they were planned as part-commuter satellites from the start. (1995, p. 68)

Suburbanization has certainly happened in European cities, but generally at much higher densities. (European suburbs are, according to Pucher and Lefevre [1996] four times denser than American suburbs.)

The spreading out of population occurs through different mechanisms in different cities. In Stockholm, an estimated 100,000 small summer cottages are situated along the archipelago, and the trend is that people have gradually moved to these cottages permanently.[7] In the Utrecht area, and in many other Dutch areas, dispersion is occurring through a pattern of growth in smaller outlying villages and towns.

Europe is also consequently experiencing considerable growth in the ownership and use of private automobiles. Auto traffic in western Europe has doubled in the last twenty years, and car ownership and use have risen (Kraay, 1996). Interviewees consistently cited this increase as a major environmental problem. The projections in many western European cities and nations is not encouraging. The Dutch Second Structure Scheme for Traffic and Transport predicts a 70 percent increase in car use in that country by 2010 (from 1986), if current trends continue.

European cities are, of course, experiencing other types of social and environmental problems. Increased traffic levels have resulted in increases in nitrogen oxide and carbon monoxide in all European cities, as well as increases in noise (Stanners and Bourdeau, 1995). Another problem has been the increasing segregation of urban populations by income and race. In cities such as Stockholm and Amsterdam, particular neighborhoods have a very high concentration of immigrants, creating significant spatial differences by income and social group.

Lessons for American Cities: Prospects for More Compact Urban Form

There is little question that future development patterns that are much more compact, contiguous to existing developed areas, and considerably denser than existing development would do much to make American communities more sustainable on a number of ecological and social criteria. But how applicable is the notion of a compact city to American communities, and to what extent are Americans interested or willing to live in more compact communities? Demographic and economic trends toward suburbanization and deconcentration suggest to many that Americans are not yet interested in compact, dense living environments, and attitudinal surveys suggest that most Americans still prefer (at least the image of) the single-family detached home, with house, garden, and garage. What is sometimes described as "the American Dream" seems alive and well, and seemingly contrary to the vision of compact communities that so many of these European cities have been able to achieve.

Nevertheless, there are many important reasons to look to European cities and the planning experiences of European nations. The growing concern in the United States with urban sprawl, as especially evidenced in the large number of sprawl-related ballot measures (and their high rate of passage), suggests the time may be ripe for considering alternative models of growth. The ballot measures passed in Ventura County, north of Los Angeles, were some of the strictest yet, and they speak to the public's growing frustration with the march of urban sprawl. These measures specifically take away from elected officials the power to approve new growth in rural and agricultural areas. Until the year 2020, any growth outside urban growth boundaries must be by a popular vote of the people (Friends of the Earth, 1999). These are some positive signs that Americans (and their political leaders) are increasingly concerned about the patterns of sprawl and their environmental and other costs.

The experiences of the European cities profiled here represent in many important ways more compelling models of future American urban growth: strategies that reinforce and strengthen existing urban patterns and texture, including new developments that are of much higher density but that (while not excluding the automobile) include by design from the beginning public transit, bicycles, and walking, and that perhaps (most importantly) are tightly connected with existing cities. A high premium is clearly placed on connections to, and new growth that links to and is interwoven with, the prevailing urban form.

The European cities profiled here also effectively demonstrate that it is possible to achieve compact urban form at the same time that greenspaces in and around cities are protected. Indeed, in many Scandinavian cities, such as Helsinki, large wedges of greenspace and nature extend into the very center. In many respects, it is the very compactness that allows these networks of greenspace to exist in such proximity to large populations. Good public transit systems that make outlying greenspaces easy to reach, even from the very core of the city, is another important ingredient.

There are many lessons to be learned from these European cities in terms of both design and building of new residential districts and the broader scales of community and regional planning. In the new growth districts examined and described in this chapter (and elsewhere in this book), a strong emphasis is placed on connecting with and building onto the existing city and its fabric, building at densities that make walking and other alternatives to the automobile possible (not to mention the more efficient use of land), and designing new communities with town centers, diverse housing types, and mixtures of uses and activities. Even the best new American communities typically lack these qualities.

In translating the lessons of European cities, several important points should be kept in mind. Preferences and actual decisions about where to live are not made in a vacuum (although surveys and questionnaires often present them as such) but are influenced by price, amenities available in a community, and a package of other important considerations. There is some evidence reported by Pivo (1996), that housing consumers if given the chance would be willing to make trade-offs in their optimal housing choice in exchange for other benefits, such as being closer to their jobs and commuting less:

> Complete communities seem to be attractive to those who are tired of having to commute to work and other destinations. A recent survey of workers in Silicon Valley in California, where there is a shortage of housing relative to jobs, showed that many workers would prefer to live closer to work if they could find an affordable place. They would even be willing to settle for a smaller house and yard if it meant not having to commute as far to work. . . . Other studies have shown that there is an unmet demand for housing close to where people work. The low vacancy rates in rental units around downtown Seattle is further evidence. If better jobs-housing balances can be achieved while not changing the price and type of housing, it would probably be well-received in the marketplace. (Pivo, 1996, p. 351)

As Pivo further notes, there is evidence, not surprising of course, that people are very concerned about keeping taxes low. "This could connect into popular support for compact urban patterns if citizens realize it can lower taxes by reducing spending on public infrastructure" (Pivo, 1996, p. 348). Pivo reports that recent market studies show increasing demand for smaller housing units, and for attached housing. And, there is a significant group of consumers who are only secondarily concerned with housing type and are more interested in other considerations (" . . . such as affordability, security, parking, yards and privacy"). "In other words, they were willing to live in alternatives to detached single family housing if the alternatives could be designed to be affordable and include the features they were looking for" (Pivo, 1996, p. 352).

In thinking about the American translation of compact urban form, it is also important to recognize that substantial additional density is possible and desirable even while maintaining an emphasis on single-family housing units. Single-family detached, or attached, units can be organized in ways that enhance walkability, connectedness, and higher density, while also recognizing the important American home values of privacy and private yard space. Indeed, many of the European development projects profiled here (e.g., many new Dutch projects) also appear to respect these amenity values. It is quite common to include, for example, extensive low-rise, single-family new housing with private backgrounds and gardens. There clearly are ways to build more densely, but with the American sensibilities and vision of what a desirable home includes kept firmly in mind.

One of the clear lessons from research on the visual preferences of Americans (especially the work of Anton Nelessen) is the importance of aesthetics and design in determining acceptability of density. Incorporation of trees, sidewalks, on-street parking, varied rooflines, and so on would substantially improve the attractiveness of higher-density forms of housing (see Beatley and Manning, 1997, for more detail). Objections to density are often founded in a fear about what the visual implications or ramifications will be (and a sort of sterile concrete, higher-bulk image of what multi-family and higher density housing would entail). Careful design and the incorporation of desired amenities would do much to improve acceptability of density in American communities.

The growing interest in and popularity of the New Urbanism in the United States perhaps offers some hope as well. These designs—seen in such places as Kentlands (Maryland) and Laguna West (California)—aspire to many of the features of high-quality compact communities. They are, to be sure, somewhat higher in density, more compact, and more walkable. But in many ways, their reality does not meet their aspirational rhetoric. The densities are often not much higher than conventional suburban development, they are often built on greenfield sites, and they often lack the transit, mixed uses, and other ingredients that could make them fundamentally more sustainable. Moreover, and unfortunately, some believe New Urbanism and sustainable communities to be synonymous, even though such New Urbanism projects rarely reflect a clear or significant concern about reducing ecological impacts or promoting more ecologically sustainable lifestyles (see Beatley and Manning, 1997). Perhaps New Urbanism represents a positive trend upon which to grow a more European-like development style, but it will need to become much greener in the process.

Others have made similar observations and offered similar critiques about the New Urbanism track record to date. Alex Kreiger of Harvard, sympathetic to the goals of New Urbanism, nicely summarizes the extent of what has actually been achieved so far (and what has clearly not). What has been accomplished has been:

> [m]ore subdivisions (albeit innovative ones) than towns;
> an increased reliance on private management of communities, not innovative forms of elected local governance;
> densities too low to support much mixed use, much less to
> support public transportation; relatively homogeneous

demographic enclaves, not rainbow coalitions; a new attractive, and desirable form of planned unit development, not yet substantial infill, or even better, connections between new and existing development; marketing strategies better suited to real estate entrepreneurs than public officials; a new wave of form-follows-function determinism (oddly modern for such ardent critics of modernism), implying that community can be assured through design; a perpetuation of the myth of the creation and sustainment of urban environments amidst pastoral settings; carefully edited, rose-colored evocations of small town urbanism, from which a century ago many Americans fled not to the suburbs but to the city. Such evocations provide a new (if unintended) legitimization of low-density, peripherally-located, home-dominated development. (Kreiger, 1998, p. 74)

Kreiger concludes, as other thoughtful observers of the movement have, that although New Urbanism has helped provoke critical debate and discourse about contemporary development patterns, it has failed to confront the most important challenges we face, which have less to do with "coming up with a better way to subdivide land" than with how "to rescue, reinvigorate, reform, resettle, learn once again to love places already made" (Kreiger, 1998, p. 75). The Europeans have found a way to do this, through a mix of policies, incentives, and supportive norms.

In large part, the different spatial and physical results in European cities are the result of a fundamentally different approach to planning and development, one that American cities should consider adopting in whole or in part. In most American cities, real public planning has arguably been abdicated to developers and the private sector. Planners, and the democratic planning bodies they work for, exercise but a modest control—usually setting broad land use parameters through largely reactive policy instruments, typically zoning and subdivision ordinances. The European model of serious public control and guidance of future growth, the integration of the different spatial levels of planning, and an aggressive and strong public role in shaping the design of new development areas is one that American planning must eventually learn to emulate. Playing a much more active (and forward-looking) role in acquiring land (and both influencing growth patterns and reaping speculative gains) is also needed. At the very least, planning in American cities must do a better job of laying down a sustainable template of connected streets, transportation and other investments, ecological infrastructure, and the spatial outlines of community.

The exemplary growth containment policies of cities such as Portland are much closer to the European model and demonstrate that the more compact model of city growth is indeed possible. In Portland, the planning instruments employed include a regional urban growth boundary, a strong form of regional government, a metropolitan housing rule that stipulates minimum densities in local comprehensive plans, and major investments in the downtown and in public transit (e.g., the MAX light rail system). (See Beatley and Manning, 1997, for more detail on Portland.) The 2040 growth concept that will guide the future of the region calls for more of the same: maintaining a tight urban growth boundary, promoting growth along and around transit lines (a European planning strategy), and creating a series of compact regional centers. A comprehensive regional green-spaces plan and new bond monies for land acquisition emphasize the importance of preserving open space and natural lands outside (and inside) the growth boundary. Portland's growth containment policies are strongly supported by the public, indicating that the more-European notions of urban compactness will be and are already acceptable (and politically feasible) in many parts in the United States. A variety of other cities, from San Jose to Boulder to Sarasota County (Florida) to Lexington (Kentucky), have already adopted similar growth containment programs (Porter, 1996).

The emphasis given to connectedness and weaving into an existing fabric of cities is an important lesson that can find expression in a number of perhaps uniquely American urban and suburban patterns. The most distinctive feature of new growth in the progressive city of Davis (California) is the emphasis on a *connected-cul-de-sac* form of development. While the cul-de-sac is highly criticized by many American planners and new urbanists, it has been used in creative and unusual ways in Davis (Loa and Wolcott, 1994). Cul-de-sac circles have a fairly conventional look, with the important exception that they include direct bicycle and pedestrian connections to the city's extensive greenway network. Instead of isolated residential enclaves, this pattern allows for a tremendous connectedness and mobility for residents (and children especially). As well as a mobility system, the green network includes extensive park and recreational facilities and serves to connect neighborhoods to major public destinations, such as schools and community centers (the city also has a policy of combining schools and major parks at the same location and creating multiple-use activity nodes). In part, this network results from a requirement that each new development set aside at least 10 percent of land for open space (and in exchange, developers are allowed to subdivide into smaller lots). Greater connectedness is possible even in very suburban environments.

Much more emphasis is clearly needed, following the European lead, on reurbanizing already developed areas of our cities and metropolitan regions. That there is space within existing cities to accommodate much of our future growth is without question, although there is certainly a host of obstacles that must be overcome. In one American city, Baltimore, it has been estimated that more than 40,000 vacant lots exist, many already publicly owned, composing an astounding 11 percent of the city's land area (Baltimore Urban Resources Institute, 1997). The vacant lots are often created through demolition or tax foreclosures, and estimates suggest that this number will actually increase over time.

There are some positive signs that compact urban living, as with many of the most exemplary European examples discussed here, is catching on in American cities. In an number of cities, efforts have been under way to enhance and strengthen downtowns and to promote compact, mixed-use urban neighborhoods, often under the banner of creating "urban villages." Seattle is one of the best examples. Its 1994 comprehensive plan (which takes sustainability as its guiding principle) explicitly adopts the concept of urban villages as its centerpiece. Specifically, several types of urban village are designated in the plan, including urban center villages, hub urban villages, and residential urban villages. The key idea here is that much of the new employment and residential growth in the city would be directed into these mixed-use villages. Each would have strong public transit service and would be oriented around a pedestrian core.

Under the Seattle plan, some 72,000 new residents are to be accommodated within the city in the next twenty years, including a doubling of the number of households living downtown. While the comprehensive plan lays out the broad contours of this urban village strategy, much of the more detailed planning is actually being done by the thirty-seven neighborhoods in the city. A neighborhood planning office came into existence in 1995 to help in this effort, and substantial funds have been given to the neighborhoods to help them in preparing their plans. To date, some 20,000 people have been involved in the neighborhood planning process, and most of the plans have been completed or are nearing completion. A key to implementation will be to follow through on the transportation investments, as well as investments in neighborhood parks, infrastructure, and other improvements recommended in neighborhood plans (Byrnes 1997; Stanford and Chirot 1999). While too early to declare a success, already some urban villages have witnessed an influx of population and new development. And certainly a significant part of the reason has been the enactment of new restrictions on growth in rural and exurban locations under the 1990 Growth Management Act (see Pivo, 1998). Successful approaches to compact urban form in the United States must consist of making it more diffi-

Seattle is pursuing an urban villages development policy through its most recent comprehensive plan, Toward a Sustainable Seattle. New development and increased densities have already occurred in some designated villages, such as in the Freemont neighborhood shown here.

cult to build in the wrong places and making it attractive and desirable to grow in the right places.

The American pattern of development offers (in comparison to many European cities) special opportunities to reurbanize and retrofit older inner-ring suburbs. Considerable potential exists to reconfigure early suburban landscapes in ways that accommodate considerable new population growth and help to bring about more European-style compact and walkable urban neighborhoods. A number of recent examples can be cited. (See Beatley and Manning, 1997, for several.) The city of Chattanooga's new smart growth initiative, for example, focuses precisely on these areas. Specifically, a thirty-five-year-old suburban mall is being transformed into a "mixed-use town center with a town square, new office, residential and retail development built in a new street grid carved out of former mall parking" (Chattanooga News Bureau, 1997, p. 2). Many American metropolitan regions have disused or underutilized remnants of earlier suburban development, which were left behind in the march to the urban periphery.

Modifying the existing tax structure could help as well. Compared with many of the European countries discussed here, the United States generally reflects a much less centralized system of raising revenue, as well as much greater dependence on property taxes (see Netzer, 1998). Heavy reliance on property taxes to pay for schools, infrastructure, and other important services has tended to encourage competition among and between American local governments for tax base, and tended to promote land speculation and low-density development. Part of the U.S. strategy for promoting compact urban form, then, must include taxation and public finance reforms. One potential tax solution that could address these different American circumstances would be to seek a shift from traditional taxation of buildings and land improvements, to taxation only (or primarily) of speculative land value. So-called land value taxation (Henry George's original notion of the single tax) has been successfully applied in Pittsburgh and a small number of other American communities and has tremendous potential to help in promoting a more compact urban form. Such a tax reform acknowledges the current local reliance on property taxes, but would modify it in an important way to encourage development of infill and speculative locations within existing urban areas. Other tax reforms, such as regional tax-base sharing, deserve consideration as well if compact American cities are to be achieved.

A number of European countries have also taken important steps to shift tax burdens from payroll and other taxes to green or ecological taxes (i.e., taxes on pollution, energy consumption). Such reforms, which are discussed in greater detail in later chapters, could also help to moderate the sprawl-inducing effects of American property taxes. A recent proposal in Minnesota, for instance, would have imposed a US $50 per ton tax on carbon, resulting in an impressive 25 percent reduction in property taxes.

Arguably the more *laissez-faire* American approach to land use planning will make bringing about more compact urban form more difficult. Although strengthening the American planning and control system is a desirable goal in the long run, in the shorter term utilizing the existing (more limited) array of planning and development tools more creatively may be a valuable approach for many American communities. Austin, Texas, for instance, has embarked on an interesting planning initiative that seeks to apply smart growth ideas at the local level. Austin has a long history of planning, but with little success or genuine implementation. Its official plan—*Austin Tomorrow*—results from an extensive community-based planning process in the late 1970s. Using an extensive overlay system, which identified and mapped environmentally sensitive lands and lands unsuitable for development, a preferred growth corridor was delineated. After an extensive more recent planning initiative called *Austinplan* failed (see Beatley, Brower, and Lucy, 1995), the city has endorsed again the key underlying growth concept of *Austin Tomorrow*.

Austin's *smart growth* system essentially relies on creating a set of sig-

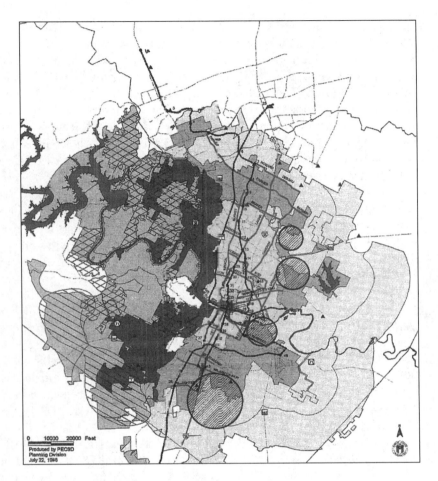

Figure 2.5. Austin smart growth zones

The city of Austin has adopted a smart growth initiative that encourages future development in locations designated as more desirable, namely, away from groundwater recharge zones and other environmentally sensitive lands to the west and into existing urban areas and along planned transit corridors.

Source: City of Austin, Texas, Planning Department.

nificant new incentives for encouraging growth in desired locations and helping to create a more contained, compact urban form. A guiding map has been prepared identifying smart growth zones in which financial and other incentives will be available (see Figure 2.5). Consistent with *Austin Tomorrow,* growth is to be discouraged west and northwest of the city where sensitive lands and habitat are located and where the city's main aquifer (Edwards Aquifer) and groundwater recharge zone lies. Growth is to be encouraged in several desired growth zones, including areas to the east as well as along the main proposed transit corridors in the city.

Several types of incentives are offered to developers: the main financial incentive is a waiver of a portion or all of the development fees that would normally be imposed. The amount of the waiver depends on a point system, which assigns points based on a number of factors, with greatest weight given to new development located downtown and around future light rail stations and that incorporates mixed uses of commercial/office and residential.[7] Expedited permitting in smart growth zones is another incentive (and corresponding greater scrutiny for projects in the western portions of the city, in sensitive environmental zones).

The Austin system is viewed as especially appropriate to that city because it relies more on incentives than on regulations, reflects the important position that Austin is not anti-growth or no-growth, and involves no out-of-pocket funds to implement (rather, foregone revenues). The city of Austin has also adopted a Traditional Neighborhood District (TND) ordinance (that many American communities have adopted to facilitate new urbanist projects), which gives developers greater zoning flexibility, including higher densities, narrower streets, and some combined permit review. Interestingly, in Austin (unlike most places where New Urbanist projects are being promoted) there is also a desire to see ecological or green buildings within these neighborhoods. Under the TND ordinance's requirements (which include a 20 percent green space requirement, among other conditions), all homes must reach at least the One-Star standard under the city's (residential) Green Building Program (City of Austin, 1998a; see Chapter 10).

While encouraging infill and development in the eastern portions of the city, the city has also taken impressive efforts to discourage development in sensitive areas to the west. Considerable land acquisition has occurred under the Balcones Canyonlands Conservation Plan (now called the Balcones Canyonlands Preserve), and a recent bond measure approved new funds to purchase 15,000 acres in the Barton Springs Watershed. The city has also, for a number of years, imposed significant restrictions under its watershed protection ordinance.

There are, then, a host of planning tools (e.g., Austin-style smart growth incentives and land acquisition) available and suited to the American context. In many respects, however, a more cautious and conservative use of land is as much a reflection of a "nation's shared norms for rights and obligations in land development," as are the actual regulatory and other mechanisms used to bring about contained growth and tighter urban form (Alterman, 1997, p. 231). Admittedly, changing prevailing norms about the use of land is a slow process, but perhaps in the long run it is a necessary component of any effort to promote more compact, sustainable land use patterns in the United States. How to accelerate this changing norm or ethic becomes an important question. Alterman (1997) calls for an "Urban Containment Movement," similar to the massive public education and awareness-raising period for environmentalism in the 1970s. "An Urban Containment Movement will focus on improving urban and suburban land utilization through higher densities, infill, use of underground space, and multiple use, and will explain the importance of good land management for future generations" (p. 238).

Setting new and different targets concerning future growth is certainly part of this process of norm-changing. A number of possible targets have been suggested: Beatley and Manning (1997) propose, for example, that urban land conversion should occur at no greater a rate than population growth. Alterman (1997) suggests as a "reasonable target" the "doubling of residential, commercial, and industrial land use densities" (p. 238). The experiences of the exemplary European cities in this study suggest that even higher average densities can be supported at the same time that highly attractive communities and neighborhoods are created.

One significant lesson from Europe is that the tax code can make an important difference in promoting economic and household decisions that support more compact urban form. Indeed, a number of observers over the years have recognized the current system as one that encourages consumptive lifestyles, and the need to move (perhaps modestly at first) in the direction of taxing consumption, as the Europeans have done. Nivola (1999) describes well the decision dynamic that results from the current set of economic incentives:

> Why not pour all of what we do save into as large a dwelling as possible, the mortgage interest of which is deductible? And why should we search anywhere but in suburbia? After all, that's where our mortgage will buy more house, as well as where the latest commercial and recreational conveniences are being built. Life in the suburbs will mean owning several vehicles and driving them more, but this luxury is so lightly taxed it scarcely gives pause. (Nivola, 1999, p. 5)

Nivola points to a number of other potential influences on land use, including the proliferation and impact of unfunded mandates, high expenditure on nonteaching personnel in urban school systems, failed public housing strategies, and disproportionate public investment in roads and highways. He suggests the need for reforms in each of these areas.

The European cities in this study, then, represent positive models of sustainable urban form, with many lessons for their U.S. counterparts. They show convincingly that it is indeed possible to create highly livable and attractive urban spaces—cities with qualities of enduring value—while at the same time conserving land and other resources and allowing for more sustainable lifestyles. A green, compact urban form is possible and cities such as Freiburg, Copenhagen, and Helsinki represent compelling alternative visions to our sprawling land-consumptive, American pattern of growth. Such sustainable land use patterns and urban form in turn set the stage and make possible many of the other urban sustainability strategies discussed in later chapters. As a nation, we seem to be poised at a promising point, where many communities are searching for alternatives to soulless sprawl. While there are no magic bullets, these European cities provide impressive ideas, big and small, for reimagining our urban future.

NOTES

1. For example, per capita carbon dioxide emissions for North American cities participating in the urban CO_2 Reduction Project are reported to be 12.7 tonnes, in 1988, compared with 8.4 tonnes per capita for European cities. Carbon dioxide per capita emissions for study cities such as Copenhagen, Helsinki, and Bologna (7.5, 8.3, and 5.7 tonnes per capita) are dramatically lower than for most American cities (e.g., Minneapolis/St. Paul at 17.5, Dade County/Miami at 11.5, and Denver at 22.3 tonnes per capita) (Torrie, 1993).

2. Breheny (1997) questions the ability to achieve this target, although recent statistics show considerable success in United Kingdom at promoting residential development on reused urban land.

3. Breheny believes future brownfield gains may be more difficult in that the easier sites and more marketable sites have been developed, and he questions whether the political will is there on the part of government to incur the additional needed subsidies and/or legal liability.

4. Newman and Kenworthy (1989) describe some of the reasons why in Sweden, a country with large amounts of space, cities are built in a very compact manner. "The basic reason for this is the long tradition in Sweden to plan urban services in an equitable and efficient manner" (p. 82). They identify the following as elements of what a good city requires in Sweden:
   • a railway station for rapid urban accessibility should be within 500 to 900 meters (i.e., a short walking or cycling distance) of most housing,
   • a train service should not require a timetable, i.e., something less than a 12-minute service should be provided, and
   • people should not be more than 30 minutes from the city center.

5. Pucher (1997) reports the taxes to be double the amount of these direct road expenses, at least in the late 1980s; gas taxes have gone up since then.

6. Nivola (1999) reports that the sales tax on an average new car, for example, is nine times higher in the Netherlands and thirty-eight times higher in Denmark than in the United States.

7. Summer houses in Sweden are reported to have doubled since 1960, now numbering some 650,000 (see Boverket, 1995).
8. *Mixed use* is defined as residential with at least 20 percent of the project in another use. If a project accumulates more than 200 points under the smart growth matrix, 50 percent of the development fees are waived. If more than 270 points are accumulated, 100 percent of the development fees are waived (up to a cap set at five years of property taxes for the project; if more than 350 points are amassed the cap is extended to ten years of property taxes).

Chapter 3
Creative Housing
and Living Environments

Planning Livable Environments

The cities examined in this study present a variety of creative approaches to providing housing and positive living environments. Several themes have emerged. A key message is the viability and high quality of life that can result from relatively high density neighborhoods and development projects. A number of specific housing options are exemplified by these cases, including inner-city or city-center housing, in the form of housing in dense, highly walkable neighborhoods, typically above stores, shops, and offices. In most of the cities examined, a high population of residents lives in these city-center areas. A key theme, then, is the importance of providing a range of housing and living options, many of which are further described later.

Another recurring theme in many of the cities visited was the desirability of "high-density, low-rise" neighborhoods and housing. Compactness and density, as these many European examples show, can be achieved at the same time that very human scale urban environments are created. Manhattan-style development is not required, the Europeans show us. There has, in fact, been a considerable backlash against high-rise dwellings in Europe (especially high-rise block housing estates, discussed later in this book), yet a belief in the need for dense, land-conserving forms of housing. Jan Gehl (1995) describes the dominant type of new construction in Denmark as "dense, low row house-type housing around shared spaces." As Gehl notes, such housing is well-suited to the small (and decreasing) household sizes in Denmark and elsewhere.

Even many of the higher density urban projects being built today in the cities studied (e.g., the new GWL-terrein development in Amsterdam) incorporate a mixture of housing types and styles, including backyard gardens and private spaces—features very important to many prospective residents, who might be looking at more suburban homes. New Dutch housing projects have been particularly impressive in mixing and integrating different forms and types of housing, including single-family/detached and multi-family housing, in the same project. As a result of the high degree of public subsidy and control, most new large housing projects also include a mixture of social (or subsidized housing) and private or market housing. The amount of subsidized housing (social housing) has historically been high in the Netherlands, although these subsidies have been substantially cut back in recent years. New national development sites (so-called VINEX locations) are now to achieve a 70–30 mix of private to social/public housing. Even with the curtailing of social housing, this higher mix of socioeconomic groups is nevertheless unusual by American standards.

Other housing options include the creation of high-density satellite or suburban communities, close to what might be called transit villages (to borrow Bernick and Cervero's term, 1997). As already mentioned, cities such as Stockholm and Copenhagen have developed the very successful model of high-density satellite communities oriented around metro and suburban rail lines. These communities (such as Vällingby and Kista in Stockholm) are mixed-use, with most housing usually within walking distance of a metro or train station, and with shopping, banking, schools, and other public services within close proximity. In the case of Kista, for example, a shopping mall is constructed adjacent to the main metro stop.

Urban-Village Living

Many examples can be cited of fantastically attractive and desirable neighborhoods where the density is quite high. European cities show convincingly that density by itself is not the undesirable quality believed by many in the United States. It is actually now this density is configured and designed, along with the package of urban design, green features, access to transit and other amenities, that will be more important. The notion of urban villages has become a mantra of sorts among American proponents of sustainability, and in these European cities we see both exceptional existing models of urban villages and attempts to design and create new ones.

What these European cities effectively show, then, is that density can be achieved at the same time that attractive and highly desirable living environments can be created. Relatively high density levels by American standards (e.g., 100 or more dwelling units per hectare) can be achieved, without requiring the stark, monolithic high-rise images that the term *high density* tends to evoke. For example, Statenkwartier, a neighborhood in Den Haag, achieves this density level, yet has become a highly desirable place to live, with greenspaces, shops, low-traffic streets, and many of the other qualities planners tend to advocate. Other impressive examples of relatively high density, walkable, transit-friendly neighborhoods include Weststadt in Heidelberg and the Jordaan in Amsterdam. A number of recent positive examples of new urban villages in the study cities can also be cited, including the South Station development in Stockholm, the Nieuw Sloten district in Amsterdam, and the Pikku-Huopalahti district in Helsinki.

Nieuw Sloten, a new district containing about 5,000 dwelling units and built at a density of about 56 units per hectare, illustrates the potential qualities of these new urban villages. One of the most impressive qualities of this new district is the high degree of mobility and accessibility provided to residents (see City of Amsterdam, 1994). The city chose to extend the tram before the housing was even completed. There are stops in Nieuw Sloten and very regular service. It is only about a thirty-minute ride or less to the center of Amsterdam. There is also an extensive system of bike lanes, running alongside the tram corridor and throughout the development. This network provides easy access to the center of Amsterdam (only about a twenty-minute bicycle ride), and the project is actually designed to facilitate bike movement while making it more difficult to traverse the district by car. At the center of the district is a shopping area, a few feet from the main tram stop. Grocery shopping, a community center, and other services and shops are located there on a small pedestrian plaza, with bike-only lanes running down the middle (creating a kind of small main street). Apartments are located above the shops, and there is a mixture of housing types and income levels. The highest density housing is a sixteen-story high-rise building, but most of the units in the district are single-family attached and in low-rise blocks.

Nieuw Sloten has been designed as a kind of garden city. Key elements in the design include a green outline or boundary (the framework) within which the district lies; the district is separated into a series of housing blocks, distinguished by canals and tree-lined streets (see Figure 3.1). Two 45-meter blocks make up each smaller neighborhood, and each block has a different architect and architectural style. Distinctive bridges for bicyclists entering the district further accentuates the feeling of entering Nieuw Sloten. Thus, there is a different feel to each couple of blocks. A central park runs down the center of the district; key objectives of the project were to maintain an open, spacious feeling and to protect vistas. Other interesting features include the designation of housing units in many places for combination housing and working, with a working establishment on ground level and housing above. Neighborhood commercial uses have also been designated at spots throughout the district.

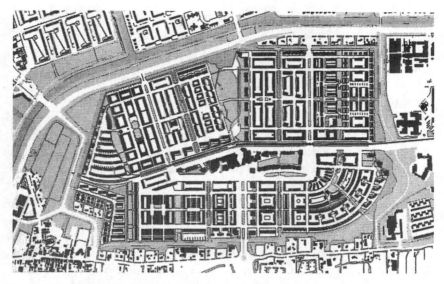

Figure 3.1. Nieuw Sloten plan diagram (Amsterdam)

Nieuw Sloten is a new mixed-use district in Amsterdam that exemplifies the city's strategy of promoting compact urban growth by providing a mix of different types and price levels of housing, as well as shopping and offices. The district contains about 5,000 new dwelling units, which were built at a fairly high density of 56 dwelling units per hectare. In addition to being extremely walkable and bikable, a new tram line serves residents and provides relatively quick and easy access to the city-center. Many of the larger buildings in the community have designs that incorporate extensive solar panels on rooftops and even on building facades.

Source: Plan of Nieuw-Sloten, prepared by the Physical Planning Department, Amsterdam.

While exclusively residential districts exist in many European cities, there has historically been much less emphasis, unlike in American cities, on stridently separating and isolating from one another different types of land uses. Over the course of this study, some dramatic examples of this tendency emerged, including a Freiburg car dealership with housing located above and several auto repair shops in Den Haag with apartments above them.

Moreover, in many new development districts (including many examples already discussed in Chapter 2), an explicit emphasis is given to incorporating retail establishments, grocery stores, shops, and offices, all in close proximity to new housing. A number of new Dutch growth expansion districts illustrate well the priority given to providing a mix of housing types, and access (by walking and bicycling) to community shopping. Nieuwland in Amersfoort, for example, has a basic circular form, with four distinctive residential quarters revolving around a central shopping area. In addition to ready access to the center, the project has included direct bicycle and pedestrian connections to the city-center of Amersfoort. When eventually completed, this new urban district will contain 4,500 homes.

In Leiden, a compact district called Merenwijk assumes a similar circular environment, with a few creative twists. The district contains 5,450 dwelling units, a mix of single-family units and apartments (see Thomas et al., 1983). A circular road distributes auto traffic in the interior, with extensive bicycle and walking paths. This project also includes a neighborhood commercial center as a key design element. An interesting feature of Merenwijk is the city farm in the center. It operates as a kind of petting zoo and green farm-park, easily reached by residents of the neighborhood, and is a great amenity that adds to the appeal of the district. The emphasis in Dutch design given to mixing different types of housing in close proximity is seen clearly in projects like Merenwijk: single-family detached, row houses, and multi-level flats, as well as social (or subsidized) housing mixed with market housing, all together in a compact, walkable district.

Work-at-home arrangements are now frequently planned into many of these new development districts. In the ecological housing district of Morra Park, in Drachten, for example, about one-third of the houses are specifically designed to accommodate in-house businesses. In these homes, 30 percent of the floor area is required to be devoted to the owner's primary economic livelihood. Already, these homes house offices for an architect, a photographer, and an accountant. Similar house designs can be seen in the new growth area of Nieuwland (Amersfoort). Here, a certain number of homes are designed with floor plans and separate entrances to accommodate an in-home office or business. These are common design elements in new Dutch housing estates, and many other examples can be cited.

Accessory Units and Mixed Housing Environments

The cities examined here, and the development projects and initiatives occurring within them, facilitate and encourage a variety of housing types, embedded within a mixed-use environment. This mix takes many forms: rooftop housing conversions, flats above shops, accessory housing units, and live-work designs, among others. American cities can and should strive for such diversity, in particular, by providing a variety of affordable housing and living options that better match our changing demographic trends, especially the projected rise in America's elderly population. Many of the European cities profiled here offer constructive examples of these kinds of creative, diverse housing options. Liebman (1996), in arguing for accessory housing units, notes the European roots:

One advantage of accessory apartments is the way they open good neighborhoods to older relatives of families with young children. The European tradition of *babushka* (grandmother) living in adjoining private quarters could, if imitated, do much to alleviate today's family stresses. Indeed, much of the demand for day care already results from unwise zoning regulations that discourage not only accessory apartments but also home businesses, retailing within walkable distances, and in-home neighborhood child-minding. (p. 98)

Germany provides a sizable tax deduction for the creation of accessory housing units (Liebman, 1996). The need for active support (including financial) for such forms of housing is an important lesson.

Many examples of new Dutch housing projects embody a mixing of housing types, styles, and income levels. GWL-terrein in Amsterdam, illustrates well the belief in mixing people, activities, and housing types. First, the project has an intentional mixing of rental and purchase housing. Special ground-level units have been designed to accommodate handicapped or invalid residents. Retail space is provided on the ground floor of several of the buildings, as well as in the corner units of several of the structures. The master plan for the project creatively preserves and incorporates several of the original buildings associated with this historic water pumping station. An old storage area has been converted into about ten residential flats. The old pumping house itself, right in the center of this new neighborhood, has been converted into offices and a restaurant.

There has also been an effort to blend into the existing street network. The blocks of housing are organized to connect with the sight-lines for the roads and streets of the surrounding neighborhoods. The one exception is the (large) north building, which effectively blocks off visual connection in this direction. This exception was intentional, given the need to shield the neighborhood from the noises of a busy auto road on this edge and from the prevailing winds that come from this direction.

Housing over Shops

As discussed in Chapter 2, European cities, particularly those on the continent, are characterized by a substantial amount of city-center housing and a relatively high population of residents living there. In the central districts of cities such as Amsterdam, Bologna and Copenhagen, relatively large amounts of urban housing can be found. This housing takes many forms, but one style that remains common is flats, or apartments, over shops. In some cities, especially in the United Kingdom and Ireland, many of these spaces above shops are no longer occupied, and a number of programs and policies have been developed to promote reestablishment of these living spaces.

In the United Kingdom, significant efforts have been under way since the late 1980s to promote the notion of converting these above-shop spaces back into housing. A Living Over the Shops (LOTS) campaign, spearheaded by a nonprofit company by the same name, has been instrumental in educating and purchasing for these kinds of conversions. The U.K. government, moreover, has invested £2.5 million in supporting conversions through its earlier social housing over the shops and flats over the shops (no longer operating) programs. So far, it is reported that some 10,000 units have been created above shops under these initiatives, with an estimated potential of half a million units (Petherick, 1998; Forum for the Future, 1997a).

Several LOTS programs in different British cities have been described and profiled in the literature. The LOTS initiative in the northern British city of York has led to the conversion of four buildings to accommodate new housing. In one case, new flats were created above an auto accessories store, and in another above a small grocery. With the University of York serving as an intermediary, these conversions have already provided new housing for seventy-eight students in the historic center (Forum for the Future, 1997a).

Certain difficulties have been encountered in the LOTS scheme, including the considerable cost involved in refurbishing units and bringing them up to current fire and health codes, the hesitancy of business owners to accommodate housing, which they see as a potential economic negative that constrains future options, and the time necessary to convince the business owners otherwise. Shopowners and commercial property owners have certain fears about having flats above their establishments (e.g., it may limit their storage needs or may reduce marketability of the building later). The director of the LOTS project describes the key obstacles from her perspective:

> Owners of commercial property were unwilling to grant residential leases for two reasons: they (rightly) saw residential use as a management problem; and they feared that retrospective legislation following a change of government might re-introduce security of tenure for residents. They were therefore unwilling to become directly involved with creating housing with commercial properties. (Petherick, 1998, p. 35)

To overcome these perceived obstacles, intermediaries, typically housing associations, now act as leasing go-betweens, taking on management responsibilities and shielding the building owners. Studies of LOTS initiatives so far completed suggest that they are generally a cost-effective form of housing, most appropriate for younger single residents without children or families (Goodchild, 1998). Living over shops is clearly not for everyone, and there are distinct advantages and disadvantages. The former include access to urban amenities, shops, and entertainment. The latter include the noise and other inconveniences associated with living close to bars, restaurants, and busy commercial areas. (For a survey of the likes and dislikes of new residents living over shops, see Goodchild, 1998).

Such housing has the potential to further invigorate urban centers and also to provide important crime-prevention benefits. Goodchild (1998), in his study of housing over shops, reaches promising conclusions, although he acknowledges that it is too early to point to quantitative statistics that show a reduction in crime.

- The provision of housing over shops does indeed increase the level of public surveillance in town and city centers and makes access to commercial property more difficult for offenders;
- The reoccupation of empty shops and buildings also reduces the risk of fire and criminal damage, as the remarks of the insurance companies suggest, and squatting, where this is a potential problem;
- As a result, housing over shops schemes are simultaneously welcomed by local police officers and noted as a possible constraint by young offenders (Goodchild, 1998, p. 88).

To be sure, these development ideas are not foreign to the American landscape, as living over the shop was (and still is in many places) a typical main street pattern in many cities and towns. Moreover, in cities from Charleston to Portland, mixed-use urban projects have been successfully undertaken, integrating housing, office, and commercial uses. These American examples demonstrate the clear applicability of European housing and neighborhood design concepts.

Hofjes, Cohousing, and Ecovillages

Other ideas for organizing housing and living, include the extensive cohousing experience in the Scandinavian countries, the unique development of *hofjes* (almshouses) in the Netherlands, and ecovillages in a number of places. Hofjes are a distinctive form of Dutch housing dating back to the fifteenth century. *Hof* means "garden" and hofjes are buildings and housing units clustered around a courtyard or garden. From eight to ten units typically, hofjes can be as large as twenty-five units. Most original

Dutch hofjes, such as this one in Leiden, have been a historically important form of urban courtyard housing. They combine the benefits of urban amenities and living with the privacy of green interior courtyards and gardens sheltered from busy urban streets.

hofjes were intended to provide housing for the poor and were financed by bequests from richer members of the community. Often stipulations about how residents should live were established by benefactors. (One common stipulation was that residents must pray for the souls of their benefactors!) Creating such places to live through a bequeath upon death is an interesting interpretation of one's duties to charity, and perhaps an idea worth resuscitating.

The historic hofjes today are seen as extremely desirable places to live and are frequently owned and managed by a private foundation. Impressively, the interior garden space of each is different from the next. Some are in the form of formal, manicured lawns and gardens, while others are veritable wild oases. Each is entered through a gateway or arch opening on the street sidewalk. One travels down a hallway or corridor, which often dramatically opens up to these delightful green courtyards and the front doors of the typically modest units. The privacy afforded by the courtyard is quite remarkable, and the public and private realms are effectively balanced in this housing design. Interestingly, the hofje design has been used in newer development projects as well. In Den Haag, for instance, a new infill project, Het Haagsche Hof centers the residential units around green court-yards (Den Haag Nieuw Centrum, 1995).

Cohousing has more contemporary origins. The first cohousing projects were established in the early 1970s in Denmark (known as *bofællesskaber* or "living communities"), and now exist in many other European countries (including the Netherlands). Cohousing typically includes attached hous-ing, clustered around a pedestrian-only common street or courtyard. (Cars are usually restricted to an edge parking area.) A common house is a dis-tinguishing feature where residents can eat dinner together (sharing cook-ing responsibilities), and where other collective activities, such as child care, occur (see McCamant and Durrett, 1988). Cohousing has many advantages from a sustainability point of view, including the more efficient use of land, the creation of safer nonauto environments for children, a greater degree of social interaction (and collective watching of children), and the possibility of sharing many things in the community (including automobiles). Residents are also typically very closely involved in the actual design and building of the project and in its operation and gover-nance.

A visit to the Bakken cohousing neighborhood, north of Copenhagen, demonstrates well the social and community-enhancing benefits of the style and design of housing. Here, on a Saturday afternoon, small children were found playing along the pedestrian interior of a neighborhood, some resi-dents were sunning themselves in lounge chairs, and one resident was actively tending her garden. A bit later in the day a group of residents—adults and children alike—seemed to spontaneously assemble and bicycled off for a collective picnic. The common house on that day was being set up for a dinner to celebrate the birthday of one of the residents, which was not an unusual activity. Bakken's compact form clearly allows for both the experience of the public or community realm (those activities taking place in the pedestrian core or center) and the more private realm (including use of private spaces such as the vegetable gardens behind each home). Auto-mobiles, though clearly present in this scheme, are relegated to a side lot. Many residents clearly rely heavily on a bicycle for personal mobility. The many advantages and community-enhancing qualities of this style of hous-ing and spatial organization are immediate to any visitor.

Cohousing projects have been initiated, taking the Danish lead, in a number of places around the United States. Muir Commons, in Davis, Cal-ifornia, was the first to be built new in the United States. Finished in the early 1990s, it contains the main elements of the Danish model: twenty-six two- or three-bedroom units clustered around a common, car-free pedes-trian path. A 3,670-square-foot common house serves as the social center for the neighborhood, providing a collective dining hall for common meals, a craft room, a children's playroom, and other facilities (Norwood and Smith, 1995). Following the Scandinavian model, the design of the community, as well as its ongoing management, was decided on through collective participation and decisionmaking. From the Muir Commons beginnings, many other cohousing examples have emerged around the country, as more and more Americans appear eager for the connection and sense of community they feel are lacking.

Ecovillages are another emerging (similar) housing form, increasingly popular in Scandinavian countries. Typically, ecovillages include sustainable building and energy features (e.g., solar energy) and generally give explicit attention to environmental issues. Many impressive examples of ecovillages have been built in and around the European cities studied.

The Scandinavian cities, for instance, offer substantial examples. In Sweden, some twenty ecovillages have been built in recent years. Like cohousing, they are typically characterized by clustered, attached-housing units, with shared open space, environmental features, and certain collective facilities, such as a meeting house. Often these projects involve efforts to save significant existing forests and natural features, and they incorporate a variety of ecological features and environmental technologies (e.g., rainwater collection systems and composting facilities). Stockholm offers one of the best examples of a recently built ecovillage. Understenshöjden, an ecovillage at Björkhagen, is about 5 kilometers south of the Stockholm city-center. The location is only a ten-minute walk from the Björkhagen metro stop and less than a fifteen-minute metro ride to the city-center. Adjacent to the Nacka nature reserve, the project consists of forty-four attached homes (in fourteen buildings, mostly two-story). The natural qualities of the site are spectacular, and the buildings have been sited in such a way that large amounts of woodland and natural area have been left untouched. An effort was made to minimize impacts on the site. The homes are built on pillars and designed "to look as though they had been lowered 'out of thin air'" (HSB Stockholm, undated). Environmental features include solar orientation and solar panels on each roof (7.5 square meters); central heating through a waste wood pellet system (with auxiliary electric heaters and water-based heating tubes installed in some homes); toilets that separate solid and liquid wastes and an onsite biological treatment system; and composting of organic wastes. There is also a common house, a shared kitchen, and a woodworking shop.

Residents of the project were involved early on in its overall design, as well as in the design of their specific units. (There is considerable variation in the features that can be chosen; the size of the units range from 58 to 144 square meters). The project has reportedly developed into a "strong

Ecovillages, which combine clustered housing, common spaces, and a number of ecological features, are on the rise in Sweden. This one, Understenhöjden, is but a few minutes walk from a tunnelbana station and a brief trip to the center of Stockholm.

social unit." As HSB Stockholm observes: "The residents look after and maintain their area and homes. They collectively purchase organically grown foods, and if a child becomes ill a doctor living in one of the houses stops in for a visit. Everyone helps out where they can" (undated, p. 6).

Many other creative hybrid forms of new housing exist in these study cities as well. In Utrecht, for instance, the housing project Het Groene Dak ("the green roof") includes many of the features of cohousing (e.g., a common house, a collective store for organic foods, and a democratic process for designing the project), but without the common meals. This project involves a number of ecological features (e.g., a green roof on the common house, passive solar, solar hot water heaters, and greywater and rainwater retrieval systems), but perhaps its most distinctive feature is its central courtyard, where a wild natural space has been created.

Het Groene Dak illustrates well the potential for ecological cohousing in the heart of a city. The project was built by a social housing corporation with the active involvement of the future residents in every stage of design and planning. The development consists of sixty-six attached units, of which forty are rentals and twenty-six are privately owned homes. All are publicly subsidized (i.e., social housing). Completed in 1993, the design of the project explicitly and effectively mixes ecological and social dimensions. The first design decision, and probably the most important, was to reconfigure the layout of buildings to maximize the south-facing solar potential, and at the same time to create a marvelous green and wild interior space. (A major north-south street was taken out, in effect allowing for the interior courtyard.) This "communal inner garden" represents important play space for children and access for socializing among residents (Post, undated; for another good discussion of Het Groene Dak, see Roefels, 1996). Many of the units have their own ground-level garden, which transitions into the larger communal space. A common house with a grass roof (from which the development gets its name) lies in the center; community meetings and events are held there, as are a variety of other activities, such as classes and music playing.

The common house, which was actually built by the residents themselves, is also available for rental by the surrounding neighborhoods and is heavily used. While common meals are not served in the community, some of the apartments are configured as group homes, and common meals are eaten there. A store where ecological goods can be purchased is also operated in one of the buildings.

Other ecological features of the project include buildings with 60 percent more insulation than typical, high-efficiency natural gas furnaces, the use of ecological building materials (no tropical hardwoods, insulation from mineral wools), the reuse of concrete in the foundation, and the installation of water-conserving taps, showerheads, and toilets. A rainwater collection system provides water for washing machines and toilet flushing in a number of units. A number of units are supplied with hot water from solar hot-water systems. Ten of the units are independent of the city's municipal sewage treatment system, and instead are connected to a large centralized composting toilet (with organic wastes periodically going to the city's centralized composting plant).

By all accounts, Het Groene Dak is a great success. The reconfiguring of the development's layout has created a strong social connection between residents, as did the consensus-based approach to designing and planning the project. A large number of the original participants in this design process have remained as residents. Most residents know each other, and the collective garden space is heavily used. The ecological features have substantially reduced the ecological footprint of residents: natural gas consumption has been reduced by half, for example, with the passive solar features alone accounting for a 20 percent reduction. The availability of good transit and bikeways (it is a fifteen-minute bike ride to the city-center) and nearby shopping and schools has meant that there are fewer than normal the number of automobiles (about twenty-seven or twenty-eight cars total, in a project of sixty-six units), and that fewer parking spaces are needed (with an accompanying reduction in cost).

The density of this project—sixty-six units per hectare—illustrates effectively that higher density urban living can be achieved at the same time that a strong sense of community and an impressive level of greenness and greenspace is maintained. Ironically, in surrounding neighborhoods there is a common perception that the level of park and open space is higher even though this apparently is not true—it has simply been organized more efficiently. Furthermore, the buildings, although at a considerable density by American standards, are not high-rise, but rather are human scale—most are two stories in height (some are three stories).

In Leiden, an interesting new ecological housing neighborhood—with many of the typical features of ecovillages—is under development. It is located in one of the growth sites for the city, adjacent to and weaving into the existing city. This new neighborhood, called Roomburg, exemplifies, further, the promise of green projects in an urban environment. This new development will consist of approximately 1,000 dwelling units, in a space of 24 hectares. Main ecological features include natural stormwater drainage, through the creation of a closed-loop canal system (with natural reedbed filtration treatment, sufficient to allow residents to swim in the canals), and the extensive use of solar power (both passive through south-orientation and glass rooms, and photovoltaic panels). One of the most interesting energy features under discussion is the incorporation of wind turbines. It is believed that sufficient space will exist on the site to accommodate three turbines, carefully integrated into the project. The internal living streets will be car-limited, with priority given to bicycles, walking, and public transit (see City of Groningen, 1997; Gemeente Leiden, 1998; Sep, 1998).

There are indeed many good examples of ecological buildings and architecture within the urban environment. One example is the so-called Green Building in the Temple Bar district of Dublin. This four-story apartment building, with eight apartments, and offices and shops on the ground floor, generates most of its own power through rooftop solar panels and wind turbines (Temple Bar Properties, undated). The building includes a variety of environmental features, including extensive daylighting and other energy-efficiency features, solar hot water heating, and extensive interior vegetation. Although no parking for cars is provided to residents, special storage areas for bicycles are provided. Especially exciting about this project is the occasional glimpse pedestrians have of the rooftop wind turbines, and the sense of an ecologically restorative housing project in the very heart of a historic city. The building's mixing of uses and its location in a larger mixed-use and highly walkable urban environment also make it a model.

Preservation and Adaptive Reuse

Much of the charm and attractiveness of the European cities studied is the palpable antiquity of the buildings, streets, and neighborhoods. A significant challenge for most of the cities examined is both how to protect and enhance these historic qualities, and how to balance preservation with the needs of a modern and sustainable city.

A number of the case study cities offer compelling examples of preservation planning. For example, Münster, Germany, made a conscious choice to rebuild its heavily bombed center to its pre–World War II historical look and feel; thus, it enforces a fairly stringent monuments law in the historic core (e.g., controlling lighting and exterior and window design). The older city reflects a careful attention to detail, and many small things cumulatively create an extremely pleasant urban feeling. One detail noticed early on is the impressive tile and brick work. The surface of the roads is an interesting mixture of rough cobblestones and finer tiles, the latter often providing design and borders along the sidewalks. In the old city, the stone work in the street is done in such a way that even the streets where bus, taxi, and bike traffic is teeming feel like a part of the public plaza, part of the public space. And the old city, moreover, remains a viable place to live and work. An estimated 11,000 residents live directly in the old center, and there remains a strong tradition of flats and living spaces above the stores and offices.

Much of what Münster has accomplished is the result of a strong preservation or monuments law, which imposes major restrictions on what can be done architecturally in the older sections. The farther away from the central city, the fewer of these building restrictions that are in effect. These standards apply to many of the details of buildings, including the windows and signage (shopkeepers are not permitted to have lighted signs on the outside of arcade facades; shop signs there must be in a consistent gold lettering). There is also a height limitation, which in most places is set at about 20 meters.

Other cities have undertaken similar efforts. Vienna's *gentle urban renewal,* for instance, has emphasized the rejuvenation of historic districts without demolishing buildings and without displacing residents (City of Vienna, 1993). Some impressive urban quarters, including the Spittelberg quarter, are the result. Another city, Bologna, established a program for inventory, classification, and restrictions to alteration of its arcaded-core.

Like Münster, Freiburg (Germany) was heavily bombed by the allies during World War II. There was little remaining after the war but the shells of buildings. Miraculously, Freiburg's most spectacular cathedral (the Münster) survived the bombing (and is perhaps the city's most notable landmark). Rebuilding following the war was skillfully done, and efforts were made to maintain the scale and feel of the older city. Conditions placed on redevelopment, such as height limitations and the use of traditional tiles, have created an urban environment that has the look and feel of the original city. The old city, or Altstadt, has maintained its medieval layout of winding, narrow streets and public squares. Freiburg is blessed with an incredible physical setting. Perched at the foot of mountains, it lies on the western edge of the Black Forest, an ever-present backdrop to the city. The forest has a visual presence from almost any place in the city. From the Altstadt, the Black Forest is literally a few hundred yards away.

Freiburg, especially the Altstadt, is a virtual feast for the eyes. It combines impressive architecture, priority given to pedestrians, abundant shops and restaurants, and an active street life to create an exciting and vibrant city. It is a city of design details, and several stand out. One of the especially interesting (and unique) features is the system of open street drains (drainageways) running through most of the older city. Originally operated by the guilds, their purpose was to bring clean water into the city (by diverting streams). Today, this system has been reconstructed and adds much to the visual charm of the city. The drains are the object of active delight, for example, children enjoy playing in them. In addition to promoting a feeling of uniqueness about the city, they help to make water visible to city residents.[1] (And as one transit planner for the city noted, they also serve as an important barrier between pedestrians and the trams.) This traditional feature of the city is also replicated in many new developments and buildings (e.g., the new Freiburger Verkehrs AG building, headquarters for the city's transport company, has this feature in its front courtyard).

Another feature is the tile detailing around the old city. Elegant lines of stone and tile border streets, and the city has recreated the tradition of store symbols in front of shops (different symbols were originally to indicate the type of product or service being sold in the building). These "pebble mosaics" have done much, as Lennard and Lennard (1995) note, to enhance the distinctive feel and attractiveness of the city:

> Indeed, the floor of the city has been treated as the city's "carpet". It is a work of art, and exhibits fine craftsmanship. Geometric and flower designs, historic, cultural and business symbols, executed by traditional artisans working with the different colored stones, pebbles

and mosaics emphasize the unique character of each street, stimulate a sense of history, and prompt fantasy and imagination.[2] (p. 190)

Reusing buildings where possible, whether historic or not, is an important sustainability strategy (for the purpose of conserving embodied energy as well as preserving urban character and texture). Important examples of adaptive reuse of buildings can be seen in almost every city. In Berlin, interesting examples include a church that has been converted into offices and shops and a former parking garage that has been converted into a primary school.

Blending new buildings and architecture within the context of an existing older center is another challenge, and several of the case study cities have done this especially well. The city of Groningen represents an exemplary case, for example, in its recently built Waagstraat complex. A relatively large multi-level shopping and residential complex, its sensitive design and placement (it wraps around a very historic building) serve to enhance rather than detract from the historic fabric. With retail, offices, and residential units above, it further strengthens the mixed-use character of this city.

Streets, Urban Design, and the Civic Realm

Especially impressive in these European cities is the attention paid to streetscapes and public space. In addition to pedestrian-only streets, there are numerous examples of street enhancement efforts. Many of these cities have taken a host of actions, including extensive tree-planting, increased places to sit, and public sculptures and other forms of art, to make streets and public spaces more desirable places to be.

Understanding one's location and having a clear bearing and orientation when a pedestrian are also important. European cities often have a natural edge here, with their physical layout organized around large and prominent public buildings and civic architecture. In walking around Leiden's center, for instance, the presence of buildings such as the Town Hall, or the St. Peter's Church with its tall steeples and tall looming form, are always felt.

The European cities in this study place a premium on civic spaces—spaces for public meetings and gathering, for strolling and shopping, for outdoor fairs and festivals. Many impressive examples of such civic spaces exist in the cities studied. They include Piazza Maggiore in Bologna, the Nieuwe Markt and Dam Square in Amsterdam, the Domplatz in Münster, Trafalgar Square in London, and the Gammeltorv-Nytorv and Amagertov Squares in Copenhagen, among many others.

Many examples of vibrant well-functioning streets can be cited from this study. These streets include, for example, Mariahilfstrasse in Vienna, Prinzipalmarket in Münster, Las Ramblas in Barcelona, the Hauptstrasse in Heidelberg, the Bahnhofstrasse in Zürich, and the Damrak in Amsterdam. These are exemplars of "great streets" and meet better than most American streets the conditions and qualities frequently admired: definition, human scale, visual complexity, complex and detailed facades, diversity of uses, focal points and significant destinations, and places to sit and stand, among others (see Jacobs, 1994, for a full discussion of these qualities). Leicester's extensive directional signage in its city-center (and similarly used by other communities) is extremely helpful, while minimizing visual intrusion. If visitors to the city-center are comfortable moving in the unfamiliar area, they will want to spend more time there. In Bologna, there are some 40 kilometers of arcaded streets, covering most of the center of the city, which make for an amazingly pleasant environment in which to stroll, shop, or move through on the way to some destination. The arcades, moreover, are of a variety of architectural styles, and include a variety of types and designs of tile, providing a rich architectural and visual experience when walking there. Las Ramblas, in Barcelona, is another amazing street: creatively, car traffic is pulled to each side, with pedestrians, cafes, and street life in the center. (As Jacobs says, the design is "a stroke of genius that establishes the social orientation of the street.") An abundance of places to sit, merchant stalls, and theaters and other destinations make it work, as well as the extensive canopy of trees down the center.

Many of the cities examined illustrate well the visual and experiential benefits of fine-grain street patterns. In Dutch cities such as Groningen, Leiden, or Delft, the dense network of streets provides a great variety of routes, and in turn a diversity of sights and sounds in moving through the city as a pedestrian or bicyclist—what has been called the "permeability" of places (Bentley, 1995). In addition to enhancing enjoyment, people tend to feel safer where many different routes can be chosen.

Pedestrianized Centers

Beginning in the 1960s, and continuing today, many European cities have been gradually pedestrianizing parts of their city-centers—taking space away from cars and parking and returning it to the pedestrian. This has had the effect of not only helping to control the automobile, but also creating city-centers and downtown areas that are much more inviting places to visit and shop.

Copenhagen is perhaps the best example of a successful and continual effort to pedestrianize a city-center. It began the process in 1962, when it pedestrianized its main shopping street, the Strøget. Each year since, the city has maintained a gradual but steady course of expanding its pedestrian areas. By 1996, it had increased by six times the amount of pedestrian space, compared to 1962 (Gehl and Gemzøe, 1996). In total, it has set aside some 96,000 square meters of pedestrian space (including "pedestrian priority" streets, where cars are allowed but only at slow speeds) (see Figure 3.2). Despite the skepticism that residents of a northern European city would not embrace these pedestrian spaces ("We're not Italy" as Gehl and Gemzøe relate), the pedestrian streets and squares have been wildly successful and highly used. The number of people walking along Strøget on a summer day is an amazing 55,000 (about 145 pedestrians per minute), and even during the winter months, the number reaches a high of 25,000. Moreover, a large percentage are getting to the area by public transit (and only about 20 percent by car).

It is hard to underestimate the impact of these pedestrian areas on the public life of the city. Some four times as many people (compared to thirty years ago) are coming to the city-center and spending time there. Surveys of users of the streets and spaces give insights into what attracts them. Factors include the atmosphere, the presence of people and activity, and the presence of many older historic structures. A number of users have observed the important qualities of Strøget: the narrow streets, the verti-

The Strøget is Copenhagen's premiere pedestrian space. It is the result of a long-term policy of converting 2 to 3 percent of the parking in the city-center to civic and pedestrian space each year.

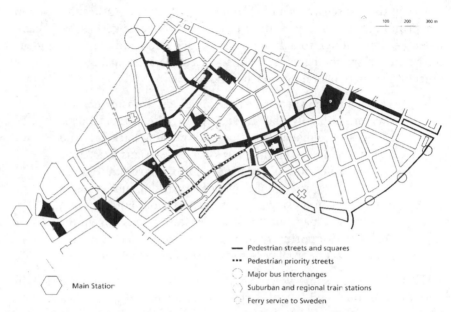

Pedestrian streets and squares
Pedestrian priority streets
Major bus interchanges
Suburban and regional train stations
Ferry service to Sweden

Main Station

Figure 3.2. Map showing extent of Copenhagen pedestrian center

The present extent of the pedestrian network in the city of Copenhagen.
Source: Gehl and Gemzøe, 1996.

cality of buildings, the numerous coors and windows, and the general "richness in visual stimulation."

The Strøget and the other pedestrian areas in Copenhagen are also places to be at night, and they include some interesting differences when compared with most Dutch pedestrian shopping areas. In Copenhagen, shopowners are not permitted to cover or close up their show windows, so there is more reason to visit and stroll in the evening. In most Dutch cities, cold metal security panels are extended at the end of the shopping day, and many of these streets, though inhabited above the shops, become less enticing in the evening.

The activity in Copenhagen's center—shops, cafes (twenty-six outdoor cafes), civic functions, and people—is also obviously crucial. About 7,000 residents live in the historic center of the city, above stores and cafes (Gehl and Gemzøe note the feeling of safety at night that comes from the many lighted windows).

A major lesson from the Copenhagen experience is the importance of gradualism and gradual change. Since the 1960s, the city has followed a policy of converting 2 to 3 percent of its city-center parking (reducing 600 spaces in the last ten years alone) to pedestrian spaces. Rather than sweeping proposals to make the entire center car-free, change has been incremental—slow enough to defuse potential opposition and to allow residents of the city to see the benefits. Gehl and Gemzøe state strongly the importance of the incremental approach taken there:

> The key to the success of these inner city transformations was undoubtedly the gradual way these rather drastic changes were made. The process of pushing back cars and reclaiming streets and squares for pedestrians was done incrementally. In the city proper people have had time to change their patterns of driving and parking into patterns of bicycling and using public transportation. Furthermore, the gradual pace of the transformation has given the Danes the opportunity to figure out what role attractive public spaces can play in today's society. (1996, p. 11)

There has been some worry that visitors to the pedestrian areas will object to the continued loss of parking, but interestingly, surveys show just the opposite. "Cars and traffic" are actually on top of the list of things respondents still do not like about the center. Also important in explaining the success of these changes is the city's transportation strategy. It has been actively promoting bicycle use and public transit, while at the same time raising the cost of parking in the center.

Many other cities in Europe have followed Copenhagen's example, and pedestrianization continues as a trend. Virtually all of the cities studied here have created, and continue to expand, pedestrian-only or pedestrian-priority areas. The most impressive examples include Vienna, Freiburg, Heidelberg, Münster, and Stockholm, and virtually all of the Dutch cities. Although less of a trend in the United Kingdom, even there impressive pedestrian areas have been created. Dublin has its Grafton Street, and Leicester has created an extensive area of pedestrian-only and pedestrian-priority streets. Even in London, groups such as London First have recently been calling for more pedestrian space, and a comprehensive study of opportunities to create more pedestrian areas has been commissioned (it is under preparation by Richard Rogers architects).

In 1973, Freiburg decided to create an entire pedestrian-only precinct in the Altstadt. Although several other German cities had designated one or two streets, Freiburg was the first to designate an entire district. Freiburg has one of the most impressive pedestrian systems of any city in Europe, and it has gradually expanded its coverage over time. The Altstadt has three different pedestrian zones, one that permits no motor traffic at all and two that allow delivery traffic during certain times of the day (in one zone, deliveries are allowed in the morning and evening, in the other deliveries are allowed during the day only). Because of the cobblestones throughout the Altstadt, truck traffic is limited to vehicles that weigh no more than 7.5 tons. Deliveries to merchants do not seem to generally be a problem, although at least one company operates a distribution warehouse from which smaller trucks are dispensed. Also, some special exceptions are made by permit.

The pedestrianization of the central city in Freiburg has had some side effects, which the city has worked hard to address. These include the spillover of cars onto adjoining neighborhood streets. The city has taken a number of measures to mitigate these effects, including the narrowing of some streets, the greening of some streets (e.g. tree-planting), and restrictions on parking.

The Leiden *centrum* is another impressive pedestrian district, especially from the standpoint of permeability. The entire sixteenth-century historic core has been given monument status, and there are an unusual number of historic buildings and streets to experience. Moreover, one can walk or bicycle from one point to any other in the city via a number of routes, each with its own sights and flavor.

The city of Leiden has done much to enhance the pedestrian environment over the years and has officially adopted the goal of making the center "auto-luw," or "auto-calmed." There are two main pedestrian streets—Haarlemmerstraat and Breestraat—both quite long. Haarlemmerstraat is completely pedestrian, with delivery vehicles allowed only between the hours of 9:00 A.M. and 11:00 A.M. Indeed, at 11:00 A.M., the city installs bars that prevent cars from entering the street. Breestraat is not exclusively pedestrian; it allows bicycle and bus traffic, as well as taxis.

Leiden has undertaken a creative approach to providing access to its center through the use of a series of mini-buses and the creation of a low-cost parking lot on the edge of the historic center. Called the "parkeerbus" or "parking bus," the system operates during all shopping days and Saturdays. Eleven buses run along a fixed route, picking people up at the city lot and dropping them at desired points along the route. Parking at the lot costs only 5 guilders per day (about US $2.50).

Leiden has undertaken a series of significant pedestrian enhancements in recent years. A major new pedestrian square (the Beestenmarkt) has been created from an active through street, and the sidewalks along Breestraat have recently been expanded. Pedestrian streets have been created along several other streets, including along the Rijn River, where new bricking has been installed, trees have been planted, and bike racks have been provided. One concern has been to connect these two main pedestrian streets, creating the ability for pedestrians to make walking loops from one to the other. Several pedestrian- and bicycle-only bridges have been built over canals, and to a considerable degree these connections have been enhanced. Leiden's experience at promoting a car-limited center points out some of the inherent difficulties in trying to do so. Expanding pedestrian space along Breestraat, for example, has meant that bicycles and buses must share an even more limited space, and although Leiden planners believe the situation is not unsafe, riding a bicycle here is often an uncomfortable experience. Leiden officials believe that ultimately a new light rail system would represent a major solution. While buses are restricted to 15 kilometers per hour, everyone acknowledges that they often drive much faster than that.

A second difficulty in the Dutch context is the presence of a large number of mopeds. Under Dutch law, mopeds are allowed to go anywhere that bicycles are, and they are often a nuisance and danger along Haarlemmerstraat. Mopeds also create an amazing amount of noise and serve to further diminish the quality of these walking environments.

Leiden's situation also points out the often contradictory impulses concerning control of the automobile. While Leiden has an official policy of promoting an auto-limited core, currently proposals are being promoted by several large businesses in the center to build a new municipal parking garage. The political pressures—particularly by shopowners and businesses—to maintain or expand car access are present even in cities such as Leiden and Groningen, which have accomplished much. Leiden planners see the parking garage as a necessary accommodation, and in this particular case they believe the proposed location (in combination with the fairly circuitous routing that cars in the center must already take) will not be so detrimental.

A variety of strategies for creating and managing these pedestrian areas exists. In Leicester, for example, two pedestrian zones have been created: pedestrian-only areas and *pedestrian-preference zones*. While the former prohibits almost all motorized traffic (except delivery vehicles at certain times), the latter allows bicycles, buses, taxis, and disabled drivers (with an orange badge). In most cases, these pedestrian districts appear to be successful and to generally work well. Delivery vehicles are typically permitted during early morning or late afternoon, and accessibility for merchants and residents appears adequate.

A number of specific calming measures have been used in Leicester's city-center, including road narrowing, placing bends in the road, and elevated brick treatments. Interestingly, road narrowing has lead to the freeing up of some additional sidewalk spaces, which the city has put to creative use. These areas are now used for bike racks, trash receptacles, and the placement of benches and flower pots. In one case, the area has been converted to an elaborate brick design called "the maze," adding an element of civic art. The calming treatments have in some areas substantially added to the width and size of the sidewalk. In walking around Leicester

during the especially active times of day, it is impressive to see how these
calmed streets are treated by pedestrians. It is not uncommon to see people
walking down the streets (in one case, a couple and a baby carriage were
moving right down the center), crossing leisurely, and in general much
more comfortable now that speeding cars are not a threat.

Leicester's downtown is full of good examples of little details that add
to the pleasant walking environment. These features include, most notably,
flower pots (hanging from wrought iron stands) strategically placed
throughout the city-center, and road signs on almost every corner, pointing
the way to various important places in the city (e.g., city hall or De Montfort Castle). As a result of this impressive signage, it is difficult to get lost
or truly disoriented.

Odense has an extremely attractive and well-functioning pedestrian area,
dating back to the mid-1980s. It consists of a series of interconnected walking streets. Vestergaard is the largest of these streets and constitutes the spine,
at about 500 meters long. This area has a number of distinctive features,
including an abundance of sculptures and artwork. The city has a policy of
adding at least one major new sculpture each year. The streets have been
designed creatively to incorporate twists and doglegs to produce a diversity
of sightlines. Trees have been used abundantly, and where tree planting has
not been possible, a number of metal cages accommodate clinging vegetation.
At the intersection of each pedestrian street, elevated stone circles alert the
pedestrian to the upcoming change in streetscape. The city has been sensitive
about expanding the pedestrian zone, believing that it seems about the right
size for the city. It is also worried about too many places where there might
be "holes in the Swiss cheese"—places where foot traffic and people are less
likely to venture. Several off-shooting alleys lead to very interesting restaurants and stores that seem to work, but others do not.

Interestingly, a major east-west bicycle way runs right through the center of the district, and there is a steady stream of bike traffic as a result. Part
of the strategy, as well, is to encourage the parking of cars at the perimeter
of the city-center and to provide ample parking opportunities along the
ring roads that circle the center. For the most part, this has succeeded,
although one parking deck was permitted to be built in the Odense center
(in retrospect believed by some to be a mistake).

Vienna has very successfully revitalized several important streets in the
city. One notable example is Mariahilfstrasse, a bustling market street and
main shopping area that has been partially pedestrianized. The sidewalks
have been made substantially wider, and the auto traffic has been reduced.
For the length of most of the street, there is only one lane of car traffic in
each direction, and on only one side of the street. The intersections have
been narrowed, and in some places elevated, to calm and slow auto traffic.
Cobblestone differentiates the onstreet parking from the main traffic area;

strategically placed flower planters and vertical blue bars provide the pedestrian a sense of protection from the auto traffic. The architecture along the street has much to do with its positive feeling—while not small-scale structures (four to six stories mostly), the buildings have a diversity of color, height, and detail. There is an organic feeling to the street; it clearly was not built at one period or point in time. Colorful banners, usually advertising something, span the street in a number of places, typically at the intersections where the road has been narrowed and where new lightpoles have been installed. Mariahilfstrasse illustrates as well that it is not necessary to completely cut off or eliminate the car. This street is a functional, busy, enjoyable environment, which accommodates cars as well as pedestrians.

Another impressive street in Vienna is Neubaugasse. Here, streetscape improvements and traffic calming have also been implemented successfully. This street intersects with Mariahilfstrasse, and has also narrowed the road, providing just a buses-only lane and a bicycle lane. The sidewalk has been narrowed, and lots of pots with trees have been placed on the street. It is evident that the onstreet parking has been taken away and the area

Vienna's impressive pedestrianized center includes churches, important civic architecture, sculptures and fountains, and other visual delights. Despite merchant fears, a reaction typical in many cities where proposals to create pedestrian commercial areas are made, this pedestrian center has been very economically successful.

absorbed into creating a much wider sidewalk. A street banner indicates that one is entering Neubaugasse (and the tree pots are adorned with "I love Neubaugasse" stickers).

When proposals to pedestrianize city-center districts or specific streets are made, they are invariably met with hostility and opposition from merchants fearing a loss of business. This was (and is) an important issue in many of the communities studied. Generally, the experiences suggest that these fears are unfounded and that business activity and profits are often enhanced when car traffic is restricted. This was the case in Groningen, for example, where business in the area of Fish Market, a street closed to auto traffic, was found to increase. Similar results have been experienced in Vienna and Leicester. In Leicester, a study by the local group Environ found that rents went up 29 percent and the vacancy rate of shops went down along pedestrianized streets. A visual survey of many of these areas confirms a high level of foot traffic. In Stockholm, pedestrian traffic is so great along Drottingatan, the main pedestrian street, that it is actually becoming difficult for visitors to move (suggesting that there may be some practical limits to the commercial benefits of pedestrianization).

When such restrictions are imposed (e.g., streets are closed or parking is taken away), they should be accompanied by simultaneous aggressive programs to improve, upgrade, and enhance the attractiveness of these spaces to the public. Simply banning cars alone is insufficient. The most successful cities appear to understand that they must work to make these spaces where people want to visit, live, and shop. In cities like Vienna, Amsterdam, and Copenhagen, very successful policies for pedestrianization have been implemented; the results have been the creation of some marvelous new public spaces and a gradual increase in the attractiveness of these city-centers.

Lessons for American Cities

European cities represent a source of considerable experimentation in housing and living environments. Many of these positive examples have already made their way across the Atlantic and are gaining considerable momentum here. Shared-living arrangements, notably cohousing, have made considerable progress in this country, with Muir commons, completed in the early 1990s, representing the first such project. McCamant and Durrett reported (in 1998) more than 100 cohousing projects under way around the country. These American versions, however, are not always contributing to the green-urban vision advocated in this book. Some of the largest of these projects are located on greenfield sites and in places that make them extremely car-dependent. And the density of such projects is often not very high. Nyland, a cohousing project near Lafayette, Colorado, represents one such questionable model. Located outside of existing urban areas on a rural greenfield site, it is ostensibly car-dependent. While the homes are energy-conserving (a positive feature), the density is only about one unit per acre, in effect representing another form of sprawl.

Some American cohousing projects do, however, contribute to and strengthen the city fabric. Recent examples in Davis, California, and elsewhere suggest that the concept can apply equally in urban environments. The N Street cohousing project in Davis is one of the first examples of this application. Here, in an existing urban neighborhood, residents took down their fences and developed a shared backyard common space that now supports gardens, a chicken pen, a flagstone walkway that connects all twelve houses, and a common house. Other similar urban cohousing projects or "urban cooperative blocks" have been established in Portland, Sacramento, and elsewhere (see Norwood and Smith, 1995). These represent translations of European community design that are far superior to similar projects located in more suburban and exurban locations. Similar observations apply to the growing interest in ecovillages in this country. The challenge will be to make these ecological living ideas work in more compact, urban environments; and the European ecovillage examples discussed extensively in this chapter suggest that success is indeed possible.

Beyond its considerable design appeal, the cohousing movement represents the importance of continuing to look beyond the conventional single-family detached house on a suburban lot and the need to promote and encourage a host of housing and living options for Americans. The changing demographics—smaller household sizes, more single households, and especially the dramatic rise in the number of older Americans—suggests the importance of providing a variety of viable housing options, arrangements that permit an essential level of personal independence, privacy, and mobility, in addition to basic affordability. Many (other) European housing ideas are equally worthy of consideration given these demographic and societal trends. There are many opportunities to incorporate housing-over-shops and to facilitate or simply permit accessory residential units. Not only should these kinds of units be permitted, but American cities (and federal and state governments) should develop programs to financially underwrite or otherwise encourage them, as the Europeans have been willing to do. The European cities discussed here also illustrate dramatically the benefits of mixed-use urban environments in which there is a much greater acceptance of certain uses in close proximity to one another—activities and uses that in many (perhaps most?) American communities would be kept apart.

Perhaps most fundamental is the lesson of the importance, beauty, and functionality of cities themselves. For the most part, the cities examined here have managed to maintain and indeed strengthen their attractiveness as places to visit and live. City-center populations are substantial, and city-center economies are for the most part healthy. There is a strong commitment to cities that is worth emulating. Maintaining viable city-centers is, of course, made possible largely through strong planning controls and a land use system that emphasizes compact urban form, an ability and willingness to invest in urban infrastructure to support cities (especially public transit), and a system of favorable economic prices and signals. Many of the prerequisites for creating livable cities described here go fundamentally back to the land use policies discussed in Chapter 2.

In a number of American cities there are very positive signs of change, for instance a growing interest in living downtown. In few places are these trends more evident than in Denver, which has witnessed an influx of people and development, in particular in Lower Downtown or "LoDo" (Brooke, 1998). The reasons include proximity to a large (and expanding) downtown with amenities and entertainment attractions, from theaters to ballet, to shopping and restaurants; a growing number of "empty nesters"; changes in capital gains taxation; and perhaps most importantly a sharp reduction in the crime rate. Borne out by the experiences of European cities, many people are willing, indeed excited, to live in downtown and city-center locations if they feel safe there. The appeal of a walkable neighborhood, and of a lifestyle less reliant on the automobile, is greater in the United States than is probably thought. In Denver, a recent survey of downtown workers found that 70 percent were interested in living there as well (as cited in Brooke, 1998). The sentiments of one LoDo resident, recently quoted in the *New York Times,* are increasingly common: "We just got rid of one car. . . . We feel like we are on vacation the whole time" (quoted in Brooke, 1998, p. 1)

A special note is appropriate about the role of civic spaces and the pedestrian realm, one of the most impressive aspects of the European places studied. It has been commonly observed that American civic or public spaces take on a particular form: instead of pedestrian streets, plazas, and piazzas, we visit shopping malls, ballparks and other sporting arenas, and golf clubs (Southworth and Parthasarathy, 1997). It is often argued that the cultural importance given to work and the dominance of television (and now the Internet) in American culture tends to work against the use of civic spaces. To be sure, these are significant challenges, but they are not uniquely American. Clearly a number of American communities have been able to successfully create extremely vibrant popular pedestrian spaces. The relative success of pedestrian malls in cities such as Boulder (Colorado), Charlottesville (Virginia), and Burlington (Vermont)

Examples of pedestrianized urban spaces in the United States are fewer in number but do exist. The Pearl Street Mall, the centerpiece of a vibrant walking district of shops, restaurants, and offices in Boulder, Colorado, is one such example.

indicates that Americans are attracted to living, shopping, and visiting such spaces under the right conditions. Successful pedestrianized downtowns, or portions of downtowns, also exist in Minneapolis, Sacramento, and Portland (its downtown transit mall). These cities have succeeded for many of the same reasons European cities have—through making conscious land use decisions to keep civic and municipal functions in the center, creating highly attractive environments, and providing housing and population within and in close proximity to such areas. These are places where people want to go and where they have things to do and see.

Warren argues for looking for creative places where high-density, pedestrianized zones can be created—what she calls *urban oases*—connected to other centers and to major transit corridors through the use of automated guideway systems or people movers. These *compact pedestrian zones*, tree-filled and green and with cars pushed to the periphery, could be created at many different points in the more dispensed American urban/suburban landscape. As she describes the idea:

> Each cluster of development would ideally be focused on one or more vital humanist and social service functions placed directly at the station, such as branches of

libraries, educational, institutions, medical facilities, and museums. . . .

With green, compact pedestrian zones, each built around a cultural/commercial/educational core; a major portion of future new construction might thus be focused within the cities and inner suburbs of our existing metropolitan areas. Their construction could be undertaken on a project-by-project basis to gradually reclaim, recycle and relandscape to a maximum extent large portions of our already asphalted land—for example, the sites of abandoned neighborhoods, waterfront land that has opened up with the closing of obsolete industries and military bases, and the numerous commercial strips left behind in the ebbing tide of decentralization. . . .[2] (1998, p. 71)

It might be wondered whether Americans are truly ready to step out of their cars and to appreciate and value more pedestrian environments. The National Bicycling and Walking Study suggests that there is considerable potential here. It argues persuasively that there are tremendous health and environmental benefits to be realized, and it puts forth the very reasonable goal of doubling the number of trips made by walking or bicycling (from the current combined percentage of 7.9 percent to 15.8 percent).[3]

Under the right conditions, then, and using a package of design and planning strategies, the creation of delightful pedestrianized centers in American cities is possible. Key ingredients include the availability of good public transit service, a sufficient density of housing and a mix of activities, and the design of highly attractive places (such as Copenhagen) where people want to be. Especially promising for American cities is the prospect of creatively retrofitting the many car-dominated edge-city landscapes that have emerged in the last several decades. Plans are now under way to create a (pedestrian) town center in Tyson's Corner (Virginia)—an extreme edge city case—as well as to extend public transit. There will be many such opportunities in the future to creatively apply these urban design and pedestrianization lessons.

NOTES

1. These reopened streams coming into the city are referred to as the "Bachle," accordingly to Lennard and Lennard (1995). Dating back to the fourteenth century, they were largely covered over in the era of automobiles. "On hot days these tiny rivulets are very refreshing: many people paddle to cool hot feet; and children find the swift flowing water irresistible for all kinds of games" (p. 190).

2. Warren (1998) also describes some of the reasons why pedestrianized centers have been more successful in Europe than in the United States:

> In Europe, pedestrian zones have reinforced what was already an essentially centripetal urban system, with cities that were economically strong to begin with. . . . At the same time, there is a firm commitment in Europe at all levels of government to provide well-integrated systems of public transport for all levels of society, as a rational means of conserving fuel, urban space and air quality, in addition to the natural environment outside the cities; whereas in the United States, public transit is more commonly viewed as simply a social service for those unable to afford cars. (p. 64)

3. 7.2 percent of all trips are made by walking and 0.7 percent are made by bicycling, according to the 1990 Nationwide Personal Transportation Study (NPTS).

Part III

Transportation and Mobility in Green-Urban Cities

Chapter 4

Transit Cities: Public Transport Innovations and Priorities

High-Mobility Transit Cities

One of the more dramatic ways in which many of these European cities are more sustainable than their American counterparts can be seen in the creative approaches taken to transportation and mobility concerns. There is a strong recognition of the problems (environmental and others) and limitations of heavy reliance on the automobile, and a strong priority is given to finding other, environmentally friendly ways of enhancing mobility. Figure 4.1, which was prepared by the city of Münster, shows the environmental and space implications of these mobility choices.

In the cities studied, a high level of priority is given to building and maintaining a relatively fast, comfortable, and reliable system of public transport. The exact composition of the system varies from city to city, but includes some integrated combination of rail, tram, metro, and bus. Ridership levels are impressive, and the modal splits show how important public transport is in these communities In Stockholm, for example, some 70 percent of trips in the region during peak hours are made by public transit, as well as 40 percent of all trips in the region. In Utrecht, for trips to the downtown the modal split is an impressive 40 percent by public transit (and another 40 percent by bicycle). Berlin's current modal split is about 40 percent for public transit. Berlin has set high goals for the future, however, hoping to achieve an 80 percent public transit modal split for trips within the city and 60 percent for trips in outlying areas. In Helsinki, about 55 percent of all trips are made through environmentally friendly means (about 30 percent public transit, 16 percent walking, and 9 percent bicy-

Figure 4.1. Comparison of bicycles, cars, and buses

Shown is a creative visual comparison of the alternative modes of mobility available in cities. Prepared by the German city of Münster, these photographs show how the same number of people might be accommodated by bicycle, auto, or bus.

cle). In Zürich, public transit is used in about 30 percent of the trips to the city and about 40 percent of the trips within the city. In Copenhagen, about 31 percent of those working in the city commute by public transit (with about 34 percent riding bicycles).

For most American cities, with a few notable exceptions (e.g., New York City and Chicago), the percentage of trips made on public transit is rather low. In the Los Angeles region, about 8 percent of trips are made on public transit (Safdie, 1997). Nationwide, only about 5 percent of home-to-work trips are made on public transit, and only 2 percent of all urban travel (Warren, 1998).

In contrast, European cities have invested heavily in transit and have taken a host of other actions to promote and facilitate more environmental forms of mobility. Cities such as Utrecht, through a combination of urban form, land use decisions and policy, and transit investments, exemplify the high-mobility levels that exist in many European cities. In Utrecht, the main train station, providing both frequent community and inter-city service, is virtually in the center of the city—a major shopping mall adjoins the station (the largest in the country) and it is but a brief walk or bicycle ride to the city-center.

British planner Peter Hall argues that in recent decades substantial levels of new investment in public transit in European cities can be seen. He describes this investment as occurring in five "main forms": (1) Extensions of existing heavy rail system (e.g., the Paris metro); (2) new heavy rail sys-

Commitment to public transit is a key characteristic of many European cities. A typical scene in Linz, Austria, is that of trams sharing the urban space with pedestrians, bicycles, and autos.

tems in second-rank cities (e.g., Brussels, Amsterdam, and Vienna); (3) the "transformation of old tram systems into full-fledged light rail systems generally in third-order major provincial capital cities" (e.g., Hannover, Frankfurt, Stuttgart, Nantes, Toulouse, and Grenoble); (4) new express rail systems (e.g., the S-bahn trains in many German cities); and (5) high-speed inter-city rail (see Hall, 1995, pp. 69–70). Considered together, this level of collective investment in transit is impressive.

Public Transit Strategies and Solutions

There are a number of striking qualities about how public transit is planned and implemented in these cities. Public transport is viewed as a strong public good, an essential public service fundamental to the broader public welfare. Flowing from this perception is a willingness to subsidize public transport beyond what is collected at the farebox. Evidence of considerable new investments and extensions of public transit lines can be seen in almost all of the cities (with a few notable exceptions, such as the London Tube, which has witnessed a long period of disinvestment; see London First, 1997). Examples include a new light rail system planned in Stockholm to provide lateral connections between its otherwise radial-based transit system. The city of Bologna has recently adopted an ambitious new traffic and transport plan that calls for the construction of a new tram system within the city, along with substantial expansion of the metropolitan train system (including the addition of six new stations in the city and seven stations in the province). Dublin is also moving forward with a new light rail system.

Berlin is also significantly expanding its public transit system, with new

S-bahn and U-bahn lines under construction. It is even moving forward (with national government backing) with a pioneering maglev (magnetic levitation) train service to and from Hamburg (which will serve the city's new Lehrter Bahnhoff, northern railway station). Plans exist to extend the city's tram system into its western sections.

Cities such as Zürich have explicitly given priority to public transit and worked hard to bring these expansions about. Priority takes several forms. In Zürich, trams and buses travel on protected, dedicated lanes. A traffic control system gives trams and buses green lights at intersections. Numerous changes and improvements to the city street system have been made to minimize the interference of autos with transit movement (e.g., bans on left turns on tram line roads, prohibiting stopping or parking in certain areas, building pedestrian islands, and so forth). A single ticket is good for all modes of transit in the city (including buses, trams, and a new underground regional metro system). The frequency of service is high, and there are few areas in the Canton Zürich that are not within a few hundred meters of a station or stop.

These cities do many things to make transit a more attractive and viable alternative to driving. Real-time reporting of when the next tram, train, or bus will arrive is an example of the many small but cumulatively important improvements that have been made. Effective systems of real-time reporting can be seen, for instance, in Amsterdam, Linz, and Saarbrücken (at tram stations) and in Amersfoort and Dunkurque (at bus stops). Such design elements make a big difference to transit riders.

Coordinating Transit and Land Use

Importantly, transit investments complement, and are coordinated with major land use decisions. Virtually all the major new growth areas identified in this study have good public transit service as a basic, underlying design assumption. There is also a concerted effort to place major activities and large developments adjacent to or in close proximity to public transit stops. The cities studied here do not wait until after the housing is built; rather the lines and investments occur contemporaneously with the projects. The new community area of Rieselfeld, in Freiburg, already has a new tram line, even before the project has been completed. In Amsterdam, in the growth area of Nieuw Sloten, tram service began when the first homes were built (Oskam, 1995). The Ijburg growth district will be served by both a new high-speed tram and eventually an extension of the Amsterdam metro.

The Dutch government has adopted a national locational policy intended to strongly support public transit and reduce auto use. Called the A-B-C policy, it seeks to steer large institutional and commercial activities to sites where public transit can be utilized. Specifically, a distinction is made between three types of locations (see Elsenaar and Fanoy, 1993, p. 10):

A-locations. Public transit locations that are situated in city-centers close to the main railway station that are not easy to reach by car and that have limited parking facilities.

B-locations. Public transit locations that are easy to reach both by public transport and by car and that are often situated close to a suburban railway station or near other high-quality public transport modes.

C-locations. Locations that are situated on the outskirts of the city with a direct connection to the trunk road network and that are more difficult to reach by public transport.

Large facilities, such as hospitals and national government offices, are generally built in A-locations, and the national government has strongly implemented the policy. National standards also exist that limit the number of parking spaces depending upon the type of location, again with the intent to reduce auto reliance and promote public transit. When it comes to location of businesses, implementation of the A-B-C policy and parking restrictions is largely in the hands of local authorities, although the national government can intervene to prevent a project in a particular site. Some private businesses have clearly been located in more auto-oriented sites than needed and have been allowed more parking spaces than necessary, but on the whole the locational strategy seems to be working (especially in the Randstad). Understandably, the A-B-C policy is a key mechanism for implementing the compact cities strategy, and it clearly helps to strengthen cities and promote a denser, tighter urban form. One important recent example of the Dutch government's commitment to its locational policy can be seen in the location and building of its new central offices for the Ministry of Housing, Environment, and Physical Planning (VROM). This new structure is located directly across from Den Haag's main train station, and it consolidates the previously dispersed offices of the Ministry.

Multimodal, Integrated Systems

In these European cities, transit modes are generally integrated to an impressive degree, which means coordination of investments and routes so that transit modes complement one another. In most of the cities studied, for example, regional and national train systems are fully integrated within local transit routes, and it is easy to shift from one mode to another.

An impressive degree of attention is paid to making public transit attractive and comfortable. Cities such as Zürich and Freiburg are energetically working to speed trams and improve their reliability. Freiburg, along with many other cities, has recently begun purchasing low-carriage trams, which make it easier to board with a baby carriage or in a wheelchair, generally speeding boarding and disembarking of passengers. And, such improvements further enhance accessibility for the handicapped and the elderly.

One is impressed with the cumulative effect of many individual actions and design features intended to enhance the speed, comfort, and enjoyability of riding public transit in these study cities. In Stockholm, an emphasis has been placed on the aesthetic and artistic qualities of metro stations. The city's transit agency, AB Storstockholms Lokaltrafik (SL), spends a substantial amount of funds each year in support of public art and requires that a percentage of each new construction or renovation project be devoted to art. The results are dramatic. Consider, for example, the station at Kungstradgarden, which contains an amazing feast for the eyes—sculptures, wall and ceiling paintings, and a funky multicolor atmosphere make the station almost an attraction in itself.

A number of European cities, like their American counterparts, are rediscovering the merits of trams or streetcars. Saarbrücken is a good example of the benefits of streetcars. In 1997, it opened a new tram system, which runs through the center of town and was three years in the making. Saarbrücken had tram service up until the early 1960s, but discarded it in favor of the perceived-to-be-modern alternative at the time: buses. Buses have increasingly proven to be a problem for Saarbrücken. The downtown streets simply could not accommodate more additional bus traffic, with the city-center experiencing serious air quality problems (high levels of nitrogen oxide and ozone). Additional busses would cost more, as well (along with the need for additional drivers). The tram was seen as an elegant solution and, although merchants were unhappy about the disruptions to the streets during its building, almost everyone seems pleased with how it is functioning now, and it already carries some 25,000 residents each day.

The Saarbrücken tram has several unique design aspects. First, the decision was made to install a wide-carriage system so that the tram could operate on the tracks of the German rail system, Deutsche Bahn (DB). This was a very cost-effective strategy, and as a result the tram operates on 40–50 kilometers of DB rails, with a need to construct only about 3 kilometers of new rail. The DB rails tend to follow where the people and communities are, so the tram has considerable potential for expansion in directions that may help reduce auto-commuting into the city. (This is a serious problem as many cars now commute into the city daily.) The tram uses large cars; some trams are three or four cars long, with a single driver. They operate on tram-only lanes, with lighting priority at intersections.

Dunkerque is studying the construction of a new tram system that will make several important east-west connections in the region and will simi-

Saarbrücken, Germany, has recently opened a new system of wide-carriage trams that utilize the existing rail tracks and right-of-way of the Deutsche Bahn, the German national rail system.

larly utilize already existing rail corridors and lines. The current concept is to link the tram line to the existing lines along the Belgium coast (which run all the way to the Dutch border). This would, in theory, allow Dutch and Belgian residents easy access to the TGV high-speed train (Train à Grand Vitesse) with stops in Dunkerque (and fast, excellent service to Paris), and at the same time allow Dunkerque residents to connect to more direct Belgian train service to Brussels.

In Bologna, new traffic and transport plans envision a substantial expansion and improvement of public transit in that region. Several areas of new investment are planned, including the development of a metropolitan railway system and a series of new tram lines. Buses are currently the primary mode of public transit, covering about 40 percent of the trips from the province to the city-center. The city has identified the key commuting patterns into the city and plans to expand regional rail services along these specific corridors. The expansion plan involves adding six more train stations within the city and another seven new stations within the province (thirteen new stations in total). Frequency of trains would also be substantially increased, so that during peak hours, trains would run every ten minutes or so. Providing a number of smaller park-and-ride lots around closer-in stations is also part of the scheme. The bus routes, which are currently structured in a very radical direction, will be redesigned so that they more effectively feed passengers into the tram stations. An experiment on the northern line incorporating these routing ideas led to a 40 percent increase in rail ridership.

Building a tram system is the key element in Bologna's public transit strategy. The system as planned will consist of major lines from the north to the center, as well as from the east to the center (serving San Larrago, one of the first-ring outlying communities). The line will also be extended to the west (to serve the airport and the region's largest hospital), and a line will be extended to the northeast as well. Tram lines will converge in the historic center of town, at the Piazzi Maggone.

Bologna sees the new trams serving several important functions, including replacing inefficient, noisy, and polluting buses within the city. The trams will have a greater passenger capacity and will reduce substantially the number of vehicle movements on main streets in the city. The trams will be electrical, in contrast to the diesel buses that are run on most of the routes, resulting in a reduction of air pollutants in the center.[1]

Other European cities have similarly invested in new tram systems. These cities include the French cities of Grenoble, Strasbourg, and Nantes, and the city of Manchester in the United Kingdom. The city of Karlsruhe (Germany) has developed a creative tram system called the *Stadtbahn* or "city line," utilizing (as Saarbrücken does) existing train lines (European Commission, 1994).[2] In Stockholm, new tram lines are being planned that will connect existing radial transit lines to the south and west of the city (a leg of which would also serve the city's new Hammarby-Sjöstad development project).

Systematic Transit Priority

Few cities have been as strident in expanding and improving their transit systems as Zürich. The backbone of the Zürich system is an extensive network of trams and buses, which have been given priority, in some creative ways, over auto transport. The Zürich efforts have been gradual and long term, involving major improvements in the system over a twenty-year time period. A regional train system (the S-bahn) was added in 1990 and covers the area of the entire Canton Zürich (1,728 square kilometers). The S-bahn lines all intersect at the central train station in downtown Zürich. The entire transit system is under the control of the Zürich Transit Authority (or Verkehrsbetriebe Zürich). Together, the transit system provides 270 kilometers of line within the city (including 117 kilometers of tram lines). The total cantonal system includes 262 lines and covers some 2,300 kilometers.

The Zürich system of trams and buses is creative in its approach for several reasons. The first design feature is the explicit priority given to public transit—and indeed the public voted on and specifically approved this transit policy. The priority given to public transit is implemented in several ways. In many places trams and buses travel on exclusive, reserved lanes.

Few cities have been as committed to expanding and improving public transit as Zürich. One of its most important actions has been to officially give priority to trams on its city streets. Seen here is a tram-only boulevard.

A traffic control system is used to give trams and buses green lights at intersections (the city has the goal of "zero waiting time" at intersections), through the use of individual signal transmitters that allow each bus or tram to signal its approach to a traffic light. A central computerized control system monitors the location of transit vehicles (to within 10 meters), and bus and tram drivers are automatically given information about how close to schedules they are running. The control center can institute corrective responses when problems in the system arise, and in the case of breakdowns or other problems, there are always two trams and five buses strategically located to spring into action when needed.

The result of these many measures is an efficient, smooth-running transit system, one that citizens can count on for mobility. There are few areas in the Canton Zürich that are not within a few hundred meters of a station or a stop, and the frequency of service is quite impressive (most trams and buses in the city run every six to eight minutes). In addition, one ticket is good for all modes of transit in the city.

An equally important element of the Zürich transport policy is the control and restriction of auto traffic, which has been gradually accomplished through several means. The city has undertaken a number of traffic-calming measures. One technique involves managing and slowing auto traffic as it moves through the city. This is accomplished, again, through the centralized computer system and the control of traffic lights, with the intention of preventing excessive auto congestion that would interfere with the movement of transit vehicles. The city has also reduced speed limits in a number of areas and has instituted, through its Parking Ordinance, significant restrictions to parking in the city. Specifically, for all new or renovated buildings, the number of mandatory spaces has been cut in half, and no new spaces are permitted in the older historic portion of the city. Parking fees have also been increased substantially, approved by a public referendum in 1994 (City of Zürich, 1995). A number of other road and traffic measures have been undertaken to ensure that automobiles do not impede the movement of trams and buses (e.g., through left-hand turning or by pulling out in front of transit vehicles).[3]

As this list of improvements shows, Zürich has undertaken a systematic program, over a twenty-year period, to give priority in the road and traffic system to public transit. On nearly every measure, the Zürich transport system and policy are a success. Service has gradually expanded and improved. Getting around by tram, bus, or train is easy and pleasant and is usually faster than by car. Residents of cities such as Zürich will tell you that there is no sense that riding a bus or a tram is a second-class form of transport; as one interviewee told me, you will find even the richest residents of the city using the system to get around. Ridership is high, and the modal split is impressive when compared with many other cities. The transit authority has also been aggressive and creative in its public marketing, for example, by cosponsoring sporting and entertainment events in which the cost of transit is included in the price of tickets.

The Clear Benefits

During the course of this research, the author has ridden some thirty different public transit systems. The ease with which one moves around these cities and the mobility levels provided there are impressively high. It is also clear from these experiences that these systems provide mobility benefits to important segments of the population. The author witnessed numerous instances of older residents getting on and off and actively using all modes of public transport. The same was true for young people who clearly were too young to drive cars and might otherwise be stranded.

In Zürich, transit authority deputy director Ernest Joos heralds the transport policy as an economic boon for the city and region, and points to studies that show a high benefits-to-costs ratio for the transit investments (Joos, 1992). Other indicators pointed to include the very high value of land in Zürich, as well as Zürich's role in generating one of the highest gross national products in the world. The farebox does not cover all of the costs of the system, but it does cover a sizable 66 percent of operating costs.

Joos concludes, moreover, that the approach breaks the vicious transport circle of building roads, creating more traffic, and again building roads in response to this increase. The vicious circle, to Joos, is transformed into a rainbow, merging environmental and economic development goals. "The result is greater urbanity, better environmental conditions, increased economic strength (!) and stabilized private transport" (Joos, 1992, p. 2).

What explains the ability of Zürich to undertake such an aggressive public transit policy? Officials at the Zürich transit authority argue that much of the success has to do with the heavy emphasis in Switzerland on referenda and direct voting of the public on many public decisions, and specifically on all major infrastructure projects (required for any project costing more than 10 million Swiss francs [SF], or US $6.6 million). Survey data suggest that the general population is much more supportive of transit than decisionmakers and elected officials are likely to be. One explanation for this gulf is that decisionmakers tend to be males, between ages twenty and sixty, who are usually the biggest car-users (Joos, 1992). When the opinions of the broader public are considered, a different view emerges. "Expressed more simply, the quarter of citizens who travel by car at above-average frequency also make the decisions and, because they use their own needs as a measure of the needs of all citizens, they decide in favor of car traffic" (Joos, 1992, p 30).[3]

Different cities have adopted different approaches to financing public transit. In Stockholm, there are several primary revenue sources: the largest amount, or about 54 percent comes from the Stockholm County Council, and thus from county general tax revenue. About 44 percent in revenues come from the farebox. In the opinion of Börje Lindvall, secretary general of Stockholm's transit agency (SL), the fares are lower than many other transit systems and reflect, in large part, a feeling that public transit benefits everyone (not just daily riders) and so ought to be funded in this way. Although many counties in Sweden have established maximum caps on the public contribution (e.g., Uppsalla says no more than 35 percent of cost will be covered by the county), Stockholm has taken a different path.

The Tram City

Clearly one of the areas where Freiburg has excelled is in innovative transport and transportation planning. Understanding the city's efforts requires going back to the late 1960s and early 1970s. Like many innovations in Freiburg, the development of its policy and approach happened incrementally over a relatively long period. In 1972, the city's Parliament made an important decision to support and expand its street car–based system of public transit (which had been around since the early 1900s). Some were arguing at the time for a shift to buses; streetcars were viewed by many as being "old fashioned" and outdated. Ironically, according to Rüdiger Hufbauer, head of transportation planning for the city, it was the conservative members of the local parliament who strongly supported the trams—they were seen as the less-costly alternative.

Freiburg's current traffic development plan was adopted by the Parliament in 1989. Its four aims are as follows (Hufbauer, undated):

1. reducing motor car traffic in the town;
2. giving priority to environmental friendly traffic: bikes, public transport, and pedestrians;
3. promoting traffic calming everywhere, except for a few main roads; and
4. restricting parking for cars.

The Freiburg approach to transportation is very integrated and comprehensive, qualities that distinguish it from many other cities' efforts (e.g., Zürich has probably done more to improve its tram system, but it has not addressed bikes, pedestrians, and so forth to the same degree or in the same comprehensive way as Freiburg has).

Freiburg's system of trams is the heart of its public transit system. The current system covers much of the city, with major east-west and north-south lines. While the length of tramway lines is only about 27 kilometers, they carry the majority of riders in the Freiburg system. (There are another 170 kilometers of bus lines.) An extensive system of buses feeds into the tram line. The city's tram and bus systems are operated by the VAG (Freiburger Verkehrs AG). The current system is the result of expansion by the city in the mid-1980s when an important new line was added, extending service to the west (Landwasser), at a cost of 90 million deutsche marks (DM) (about US $50 million) (Hildebrandt, 1995) New extensions of the tram line are in the works, and a new line has just been extended to serve the new Reiselfeld development. (Incidentally, most people agree that the tram has done much to enhance the saleability and attractiveness of the Reiselfeld area, which used to be a sewage disposal area and so has a negative connotation for some.) At the end of these improvements, most of the city's population will be within a distance of 400 to 500 meters of a tram stop (most already are).

Grass has been planted between the tracks in a number of places (thus leading to the label "green trams"); it also has been found to reduce the noise from the trams. Trees have been planted alongside some of the tram lines, further greening these corridors. Often pedestrian and bicycle paths are provided alongside the tram routes.

The trams are by all accounts a great success. They are relatively fast (they take about half the time of buses), the routes are easy to understand, and they run with great frequency (trams come every 3 to 5 minutes at peak hours, thus usually not requiring riders to consult or memorize a schedule).

The trams are faster partly because in most areas of the city, they run in their own lanes, separate from cars. Like the Zürich system, traffic lights at intersections are electronically activated to give the trams a green light when they approach. The city has gradually been acquiring newer trams with lower platforms—which allow passengers to get on and off faster—further enhancing the speed of the trams.

The trams are also very clean, and the city places a premium on maintaining their cleanliness. The cars are returned each day to a depot where they are cleaned. One problem in the past has been graffiti. The city has sought to address this challenge through an interesting experiment. They decided to "give" one of their station houses (a building at the Paduallee stop, containing a newsstand and a rest area for tram drivers) to graffiti artists to paint. The design had to be approved in advance by the city, but the concept was that by allowing graffiti there, it would be discouraged elsewhere. The resulting building is a stimulating piece of graffiti art and does appear to have reduced the graffiti impulse in other places.

In addition to making public transit faster, the city has worked hard to make it easier and more attractive to use in other ways. Freiburg was the first city in Germany to introduce the *eco-ticket* (in 1985). The idea was to create a single-fare system, easy to understand, in which one ticket could be used to ride anywhere on the city's transit system. In the beginning, the price was set quite low to encourage participation (with a resulting increase in ridership of 23 percent, and an estimated 3,000 to 4,000 car owners converting to public transit; Heller, undated, p. 8). This ticket was also transferable (e.g., could be given to another family member to use), and on Sundays and holidays the ticket allowed an entire family to ride the system with a single ticket. The eco- or environmental-ticket was eliminated in 1991 and replaced with the *Regiokarte* ticket (now still fairly low—DM 64 per month (about US $35), less expensive than driving one's car). The same provisions apply, but passengers are now entitled to ride on the entire regional system, which provides access to some 2,900 kilometers of public transit (sixteen different transit companies in the region; ninety different lines). These innovations in the fare system, along with other improvements in service, have paid off with dramatic increases in ridership. Ridership has grown from 27 million trips in 1984 to about 65 million trips today.

One of the more interesting transit programs is the so-called "night bus." Many of the bus lines run well into the evening, and the VAG has embarked on a campaign to improve the security and safety of nighttime bus service. Different bus routes are named after planets (Venus, Neptune, and so forth), and bus drivers are allowed to make stops in front of specific houses when requested (the idea being to enhance safety for children riding the bus). The city has also actively and innovatively been involved in a public relations campaign for the transit system. This campaign has taken many forms, including film trailers in movie theaters and the creation of beer coasters and even condoms (in conjunction with AIDS awareness week) with public service messages.

The city's system is also integrated with the S-bahn train system. The central train station is the point of intersection for all tram lines, making transfers very easy. Additional plans are in the works to further connect train and tram lines. Increasingly, residents are using the Freiburg public transit systems to get to various recreational points. Several destinations in the Black Forest have become very popular, and demand has been so great on Sundays that services have had to be substantially expanded.

Freiburg has received significant financial help for building its public transit system from the *Länd* government. This state-level government pays for up to 85 percent of the cost of building tram lines (which comes primarily from taxes on car gasoline). Operating costs are largely covered by the farebox—about 70 percent, fairly high for public transit systems (plus revenue from advertisements on buses and trams). The yearly deficit is covered by a surplus (profit) earned by the city's energy and water company. (This is going to change in the year 2000, however, when the city will no longer cover the deficit.)

Other measures have aimed to make it more difficult and expensive to take one's automobile into the city, and to generally get people out of their cars. The city has virtually eliminated free parking areas in the old city, installing parking meters (with a cost of DM 4 per hour, or a bit over US $2, in the very center). The number of free parking spaces (on the street) has decreased from 6,774 in 1982 to some 409 today (the latter number is accounted for by parking for special visitors)—a dramatic reduction, to say the least. There are both public and private car garages available at a cost of around DM 20–30 per day (US $11 to US $16). The city plans not to allow or build any more garages (although this remains a contentious issue in the Parliament). The city has also implemented a parking sticker system for residents and has plans to extend this system further.

Another part of the city's strategy has been the provision of park-and-ride lots. There are currently 2,500 spaces at the end of tram lines, and a plan exists to expand this number by an additional 1,600 spaces. These lots are usually almost always full. At present, the parking is free, and the city is discussing the possibility of charging for this parking. The city has also created a new distinctive symbol for these lots.

The Special Feel of Trams

To fully appreciate the functioning and general utility of Freiburg's tram system requires riding around in it for several days. It is very easy to understand and to use. I encountered much evidence of how well the system works. On the last day of my visit, I saw a man in a motorized wheelchair, who was able to board and exit easily (given the new lower cars) without any assistance. With the car floor and station platform only a few inches apart, he was able to get on and off with little more than a mild bump. Riding around, one encounters a great many families with baby carriages getting on and off quickly. A couple of days into my visit, one woman with a carriage and a fully loaded backpack got on at a stop near the Altstad and got off at the main train station; it was easy for her to get around even with this considerable load. I was also struck by the number of older people using the tram system: they get on and off a bit slower, but the system clearly provides them with a level of mobility not possible in most auto-based transportation systems (these people were clearly beyond the age of driving).

I also saw kids traveling around, some quite young, both alone and in groups. I recall seeing one boy probably in his early teens, grasping a clipped newspaper advertisement, who looked as though he were off (without his parents!) to make an important acquisition of some kind. One comes away appreciating that these trams (and indeed the entire public transit system) must provide an incredible level of mobility and freedom for the younger residents of Freiburg.

Freiburg chose not to go the route of an underground subway system, and several interviewees commented to me about the importance of being able to see the trams. After riding around and experiencing them (from both the inside and the outside), I tend to agree with this assessment. It is hard to imagine the old section of Freiburg without the trams (and of course they have had streetcars since the early 1900s). Their presence contributes mightily to the vitality of street life there—the clanging of the tram bells as they approach a stop, the rolling sound as they move along the tracks, the blur of colors as they cross an intersection. Clearly, they contribute much to the energy and enjoyability of Freiburg streets, in addition to simply serving as a very effective and pragmatic way of getting around the city.

A variety of other traffic-calming measures have been put into place. On some major streets, the city has employed alternate-side parking, pedestrian islands, and other forms of traffic barriers. On those significant roads remaining—such as on the ring road that circles the Altstadt—the city is reducing the number of auto lanes (from four to two), creating a bus-only lane, and has been discussing extending the pedestrian zone even farther.

The result of all of these measures is a city that is very easy to get around in; one where automobile use is discouraged but where overall mobility is extremely high. The modal split reflects the general success of these different measures. While cars accounted for 60 percent of all trips by Freiburg residents in 1976, this percentage dropped to 46 percent by 1996. During that same period, bicycle use went from 18 percent to 28 percent, and public transit use from 22 percent to 26 percent. Moreover, this occurred during a period in which the number of automobiles per 1,000 people climbed from 350 to 480.

Mr. Hufbauer, of the city's transport office, thinks the transport policy is symbolic of Freiburg's general approach to planning. While other cities (such as Münster) may be more aggressively pursuing bicycles, there are few places in Germany that are putting all the pieces together the way Freiburg is. Freiburg is unusual in that, according to Mr. Hufbauer, it has "a system of all these elements and aspects in the whole."

High-Speed Rail, Green Transit, and Other Creative Mobility Strategies

Several cities have been developing mobility smart cards, which can be used on several different modes of transportation. Cities like Helsinki have been working to develop such a system. Especially promising is the idea that such a card could be used not only on public transit, but might also allow debits for taxi rides, car rentals, or bicycle rentals depending upon the user's specific needs that time and day.

Europeans are already more accustomed to using chip cards or smart cards, but the increasing use and experimentation with this technology in the United States will make the idea more feasible here over time. Indeed, Washington Metro and Chicago Transit Authority have both been testing the use of smart cards in their transit systems (Bigness, 1998; Reid, 1998). The idea of using a single debit card to provide access to or pay for several different modes of transport is not far away in American cities.

In many European cities, buses are also a key component of the transit mix. Admittedly, the European cities that rely almost exclusively on bus systems appear to be less successful in transit mobility (e.g., Leicester and Dublin). Partly, this appears to be the result of a stigma about riding buses (although probably much less than in the United States), and also of greater concerns about comfort, reliability, and permanence of routes. However, even in these cities there is both a considerable amount of looking ahead to the possibilities of other modes (e.g., light rail) and attempts at using buses in more creative ways. Indeed, a number of the cities studied (some where buses are part of a broader package of modes) have developed or are developing creative, promising bus strategies. Examples include Almere, which has developed a bus system running on a completely separate route and right-of-way from cars (essentially operating like a fixed-rail system). Buses traveling through the center of Groningen have been equipped with speed limiters, which prevent them from traveling greater than 15 kilometers per hour, thus reducing the safety concerns of bicyclists and merchants. A number of cities, including Utrecht, Groningen, Dublin, and Leicester, utilize direct bus (high-speed) routes, operating in bus-only lanes, in combination with the building of park-and-ride facilities (what Groningen calls a transferium). Leicester, in collaboration with local bus companies, is taking a number of other actions to improve bus service under its "quality bus" initiative (including bus-only lanes and increased frequency and quality of service).

One of the key transit planning issues faced by both American and European cities is the problem of suburb-to-suburb commuting patterns (see Hall, Sands, and Streeter, 1993). Several recent creative European initiatives to address these new community patterns are described by Hall (1995b), including Paris's new 175-kilometers transit system called ORBITALE (Organisation Regionale dans le Bassin Interieur des Transports Annulaires Liberes d'Encombrements), which is under construction and designed to laterally connect that region's dense inner suburbs (with numerous connections to the radial routes). But even this new addition will have its limitations: "completion of ORBITALE will, however, still leave the problem of connecting the outer suburbs and in particular the five new towns, which are located at an average of about 15 miles (25 kilometers) from the center of Paris. . . ." (Hall, 1995, pp. 76–77). A number of other cities, including Stockholm and Helsinki, are working on transit improvements to address similar commuting patterns.

Green urbanism suggests that there may be other ways in which transit should be ecological. Many of these European cities illustrate a concern with not simply improving and enhancing transit, but also providing it in the least ecologically damaging way. Several recent European examples are illustrative. In a number of these cities, there has been a push to replace conventional gasoline and diesel transit vehicles with more environment-friendly vehicles. In Stockholm, the transit agency (SL) operates (as of 1996) 130 ethanol and 6 hybrid buses (Stockholm Environment and Health Protection Administration, 1996). Leiden, as a further example, has recently introduced hybrid electric-diesel buses into its transit mix. These buses operate on diesel outside the city-center and then switch to electric when entering the downtown area. On the main city-center street in Leiden, Breestraat, some 60 buses pass by every hour. The city wants to make Breestraat a zero-emission street. Many other cities are moving in the direction of natural gas or electric buses.[4]

In Stockholm, its new metro line will be served by new Adtranz C2O trains, which are touted as "94-percent recyclable, extremely quiet" and consuming "one-fifth less energy than its predecessor" (Daimler-Benz, 1998). This is a direct reflection of the environmental priority given by

Stockholm's transit company SL. Among the energy-efficient features are a new braking system that recovers and stores energy from braking. A life-cycle evaluation was used in designing the cars, with a resulting emphasis on choosing of parts and materials that are recyclable.

Other innovative transit modes have also been pursued. Several European cities are experimenting with some form of "community taxi" (see European Commission, 1996a). In the Netherlands, the train-taxi is growing in use and importance. Train-taxies are shared taxis—up to four riders share designated taxis for a low fare (5 guilders or about US $2.50) purchased in combination with a train ticket.

Freight and goods transport is another important area receiving considerable attention in Europe, and some cities have developed creative strategies for addressing it at the urban scale. In particular is the issue of minimizing auto and truck traffic in city-centers. In this regard, Leiden has supported an interesting and unique goods distribution system using small electric trucks. The project ties back to the city's decision six years ago to make the center "auto-luw" or auto-minimal. A collaboration between a private transport company, an advising agency, and a city-owned company with responsibility for finding employment for the disabled led to the formation of the for-profit company Stadsdistributie Centrum (SdC) Leiden (with each organization having equal shares). Partly funded by a project grant from the European Commission (which covers about one-third of the cost of buying the trucks, as well as other expenses), the goods distribution system began operation in June 1997. The concept is a fairly simple one: large trucks deliver goods to the distribution center (in the adjoining town of Leiderdorp), which are then transferred to five small electric trucks for distribution to shops and stores in the center. In addition to deliveries, the trucks also pick up goods for distribution to other sites in the city and the region. The SdC essentially operates as a subcontractor to larger freight transport companies sending goods to the Leiden area. The SdC has had difficulties getting out the word to transport companies in the country about its services. It has raised its profile in recent months, and has now joined the national organization of freight transporters (of which there are about 40,000 members).[5]

The SdC, however, has been less than completely successful so far. After only a year of operation, the company was forced to approach the city for a loan (under threat of bankruptcy) and received 1 million guilders to keep the company going. Mr. Willard Brandhorst, director, estimates that the company is operating at only 20 percent of what is necessary for it to break even financially. A number of difficulties have been confronted along the way. The original site for the distribution center was to be much closer to the main north-south highway—the A-4—but opposition from nearby neighborhoods forced its temporary location in Leiderdorp. (There are

Small electric trucks distribute goods in compact city-center Leiden under a unique goods distribution system. The intention is to limit larger truck traffic in the center, as well as to reduce the air pollution, noise, and other negative impacts associated with them.

plans to move permanently to a site near the intersection of the A4/N206.) More fundamentally, the company was started in response to the city's stated intention of restricting larger truck traffic (all trucks over 7.5 tons in size) and preventing them from entering most areas of the centrum. The city has not yet implemented this plan, so larger truck deliveries are still possible in most places. The decision to buy more expensive electric trucks was also based on the city's stated intention to restrict access to environmentally friendly delivery vehicles only. The electric trucks, which are much more expensive than conventional diesel trucks, can only travel at 25 kilometers/hour, deemed acceptable in light of the city's stated intention to make the entire centrum a 30 kilometers/hour–restricted zone (which it also has not yet done). Ironically, hesitation in moving forward aggressively on the restrictions is in no small part a response to concerns about whether a small-truck distribution system will work (a kind of chicken-and-egg situation, and particularly what explains why the city is willing to financially support the company). Local politicians are watching to see how the SdC idea works before implementing these access restrictions. As Brandhorst says, "The city is waiting for us, and we are waiting for the city." Nevertheless, the small trucks distribution system is a creative response to the desire for more car-limited, compact cities and will be an important issue for Dutch and other cities in the future.

One of the most impressive aspects of the transport system in Europe is the ease with which travel is made from one city to another. Mobility

A comprehensive network of high-speed rail lines is emerging in Europe. Shown here is the X2000, Sweden's high-speed trains.

between European cities is largely the result of well-developed and generally well-funded (by American standards) national train systems. Most impressively, since the early 1980s, there has been considerable investment in and commitment to developing high-speed rail. High-speed rail systems in operation include France's TGV (Train à Grande Vitesse) (the first), Germany's ICE trains (Inter City Express), the AVE in Spain, and Sweden's X2000. Efforts are under way to connect and integrate these lines into a Europe-wide system (Ministry of Transport, Public Works and Water Management, undated). Many of these trains exceed 250 kilometers/hour and increasingly provide a competitive alternative to auto and air travel (up to 1,000 kilometers. They further strengthen the integration potential of urban transportation systems (allowing one to conceivably begin on a bicycle and end up, with ease and speed, in a city in another country).

Schiphol airport in Amsterdam in many ways illustrates well the benefits of train investments and the coordination between train service and other modes of transit. It is relatively effortless for passengers arriving by plane to travel down a set of escalators to the Nederlandse Spoorwegen (NS) station. Here, in addition to local and regional trains, an arriving passenger can board a high-speed train bound for Brussels or Paris.

Magnetic levitation trains (maglev), the newest technology in fast rail, with the capability to travel at 300 mph or greater, have also received serious attention in Europe. Germany is poised to operate (by 2005) the first commercial maglev train between Hamberg and Berlin, a trip that will take a mere one hour. While not without controversy (the cost is high and some are concerned about the health impacts of magnetic fields), the Transrapid Project may set the Europeans even further ahead in the area of train transport. Maglev is also being actively considered in other parts of Europe. A Transrapid proposal was unveiled in 1999 in the Netherlands that would provide maglev service to the main cities in the Randstad.

Lessons for American Cities

The tough reality today is that American cities must begin to offer a "radically better way of getting from A to B," as one Irish commentator notes. And the attack must be two-pronged—making it much more expensive to use one's private automobile and dramatically improving public transit: "Public transit will never be attractive unless it's fast and reliable" (Quinn, 1998, p. 18). The European cities profiled here offer many positive lessons for American cities. Perhaps most importantly, they offer tremendous inspiration for creating highly desirable, integrated transit and high-mobility living environments. Increasingly, many American cities appear convinced of the need to find ways to provide a more sustainable and balanced transportation system, one that provides meaningful alternatives to the automobile. The (re)emergence of light rail systems in a number of North American cities, although not without controversy and criticism from some quarters, seems a signal that many of the specific strategies pursued by European cities are increasingly relevant. The most significant lessons provided by cities such as Zürich, Freiburg, Stockholm, and Copenhagen are the need to constantly improve, enhance, and make attractive public transit systems; the importance of integrating and connecting different modes and elements of the transport system; and the importance of coordinating transit investments and major land use decisions (and the great merits of designing and putting in place meaningful mobility alternatives to the automobile before or contemporaneous with the development itself).

In part, the answer is about nurturing and growing a *transit ethos*, such as exists in European cities. The very real equity implications of relegating the poor, the young, and the old in our society to a second- or third-rung mobility class is perhaps the beginning point here of a societal discussion. Given that these members of the urban population typically hold the least political power, the dominance of a road- and car-based strategy to mobility is not surprising. There is little question that our current heavily auto-based form of transportation is simply inadequate for the environmental and social challenges we will face as a nation (and planet) in the future. Demographically and socially, especially as the numbers of elderly grow in the United States, the current transportation system represents a disaster of the first order.[6] The estimates of the number of older drivers are alarming, to say the least. By the year 2020, there will be 40 million drivers over age 70 (Rimer, 1997). As one child who had to take the car away from her elderly parent because of his dangerous driving notes in sadness: "It's demoralizing when it's your own parents. It's their last grasp of independence" (Rimer, 1997, p. A20). For an elderly person wanting to maintain freedom and mobility, this is fundamentally easier to do in the European cities described here.

In many ways, decent public transport becomes an equity issue, something that all citizens ought to have the right to expect. It is ironic that the powerful seniors lobby, which has been able to defeat state programs mandating more frequent driving tests for the elderly, does not seem to wish to throw its political weight behind improvements in public transit in American cities. Perhaps this represents an untapped political opportunity.

The tremendous dependence of our cities on fossil fuel–transportation represents an important reason, as well, to rethink mobility. Fairly compelling arguments have been made that oil discoveries have not kept up with the rate at which we are pumping reserves and that, in the not-too-distant future, absolute levels of oil production will decline. Remarkably, in February 1999, even the chairman and CEO of Arco Oil declared that we have "embarked on the beginning of the Last Days of the Age of Oil" (Bowlin, 1999, p. 2). And, given that about one-third of U.S. carbon dioxide emissions are transportation related, it becomes an environmental (and national security?) imperative to fundamentally move our cities in the direction of more green-urban mobility strategies, less dependent on non-renewable oil.

One of the clearest messages, then, is the need to expand and improve transit options, learning from many of the exemplary efforts of cities such as Zürich and Stockholm and Freiburg. As Bernick and Cervero (1996) document, there has been a renaissance of sorts in American public transit in the last decade, as a number of U.S. cities have installed and expanded new light rail systems (see also Cervero, 1994). And there have been a number of creative approaches taken. In San Diego, new light rail lines have been funded locally (completed faster and at less cost) and have resulted in substantial economic renewal of the central business district there. In Sacramento, a new light rail system has been installed at relatively low cost by utilizing existing rail corridors and constructing no-frills stations. In cities such as San Francisco and Washington, where heavy rail metro systems have been constructed, the emergence of new "transit villages" can be seen along transit corridors. One of the most promising examples can be seen around the Ballston metro station and other stations along the Orange line in Arlington County (Virginia). Here, through a combination of creative planning and regulatory incentives (e.g., density bonuses given to developments that agree to include at least 50 percent housing); and financial underwriting by local authorities, a vibrant transit- and pedestrian-oriented community is forming (Bernick and Cervero, 1996).

Although certainly controversial, these investments represent important steps in the direction of building (back) a transit society. Compared with the vast economic subsidies of automobiles, and the social and environmental costs associated with them, the relative cost of building and operating such systems is modest.

The European transit cities profiled here (e.g., Stockholm and Zürich) also tell the important lesson of constantly working to improve and enhance the ease of use and attractiveness of public transit relative to the auto. As Pucher and Lefevre note: "Germany, The Netherlands and Switzerland in particular, have lead the way in coordinating fare structures, timetables, routes and different modes of public transport. By integrating services more effectively, they have improved the competitive position of public transport vis-à-vis the automobile" (1996, pp. 208–209). Giving priority to transit and making transit rides faster and more enjoyable are part of what is necessary to get Americans out of their cars.

In looking to the future, American cities must learn from their European counterparts, and be sure to include the other essential ingredients that will make such systems work in the long term. These ingredients include a com-

Portland, Oregon's, light rail system, MAX, is one example of a number of recent efforts by American cities to invest in new public transit. Other notable American cities that have built new light rail systems include Sacramento, St. Louis, San Diego, and Dallas.

mitment to coordinating land use and development decisions with transit investments (which the Europeans have been especially good at doing); new corresponding controls on auto traffic and programs to reclaim streets and pedestrian areas; restrictions on the amount of parking in urban areas (and a move away from free or low-cost parking); efforts to encourage employers to adopt incentive structures to encourage public transit usage (as well as walking and bicycling) rather than auto use; and a host of other demand management strategies.

Undoubtedly, different local circumstances will require unique transit strategies. Improvements in public transit in the United States will necessarily need to address the problems of existing low-density residential environments and the problems associated with suburb-to-suburb or exurb-to-exurb commuting. Creative paratransit or mini-bus systems (such as Boulder's highly successful, high-frequency mini-bus transit approach) will necessarily need to be considered in many American communities. Reurbanizing and densifying currently low-density surbuban environments will also be a necessary ingredient in strengthening transit in the United States.

Smooth integration between the different modes of transit can do a great deal to enhance ease of use and attractiveness of public transit. One of the most impressive characteristics of the Dutch system is that by calling a single national phone information line, an operator can chart an entire trip for the caller from origin to destination, including necessary train-bus or other connections. If your ultimate destination is a rural locality where regular bus service is not available, a paratransit vehicle (mini-bus or taxi) can be reserved in advance and will likely be waiting upon your arrival. Although the Netherlands is admittedly a small, dense country, having such a degree of planned integration makes mobility by transit (especially intercity) exceptionally easy and desirable. American cities and transit authorities should work hard to make such transitions as available and easy as this system. If so, more Americans would be willing to leave the car behind, at least some of the time.

Particularly promising is the European lesson of thinking systematically about mobility options in advance of major new development areas, along with the powerful notion—as in the new Amsterdam Ijburg district—of presenting new residents with a package of mobility options from which they can choose. Asking new residents to think as carefully about how they plan to get around as they do about the color of the walls or carpeting or countertops in their new homes should be common practice. Developers of new housing should be expected to assemble, with the help of local governments and transit agencies, a package of options (e.g., discounted bus and subway passes, discounted rental car services, membership in a car-sharing company, or perhaps a discounted purchase of bicycles suitable for the community) to present or sell to new and prospective residents. Some arrangement could be established by which, depending on the packages purchased or chosen, developers could be rebated a portion of the impact fees they might be required to pay for such things as new roads and parking.

Greater attention to rail is another important lesson from Europe. The development of an integrated, high-speed rail system is especially promising, at least for significant population corridors in the United States. Indeed, as airport congestion continues and the frustrations of declining airline service and growing delays increase (e.g., witness the recent Northwest Airlines episode), rail travel and high-speed rail especially will appear much more attractive to Americans. Progress in a number of regions in developing high-speed rail can be pointed to, and the resources to follow through with them must be made available.

There is no question that special creativity and adaptation are needed to make these ideas work in the United States Officials in Chattanooga and Atlanta are moving forward on collaborative high-speed rail initiatives that will link these two cities; these initiatives may be a model for how strategic high-speed rail can occur in other U.S. cities. Specifically, the proposed high-speed link would travel the 115-mile corridor, linking the two cities and several smaller cities between them. The initiative (for which Congress has already appropriated $5 million for a detailed feasibility study) would accomplish several goals at once—an important lesson in the U.S. context. It would connect the two cities and the communities in between, but would also allow Chattanooga's underutilized airport to relieve some of the passenger pressure from Atlanta's burgeoning Hartsfield International (an airport that is expected to double its passenger miles served by the year 2015 and require a $6 to $9 billion airport expansion if this relief does not occur). Seen in this way, the high cost of investing in the high-speed rail connection could be largely offset by a reduced need for expansion of the Atlanta airport. And, the link could be later extended and expanded to other cities in incremental fashion. In addition, as advocate and Chattanooga councilman David Crockett believes, the system will strengthen other forms of public transit. "What sense will it make to go 185 miles an hour from Chattanooga to Atlanta only to rent an auto and go 24 miles an hour on a clogged freeway?" he asks (as quoted in Pierce, 1998). The "Chatlanta" high-speed rail initiative suggests the importance of strong intercity collaborations and alliances, the necessity of emphasizing multiple objectives in planning such projects, and the fact that high-speed rail investments are already feasible along many corridors and in many places in the United States, given the right forward-looking politics and the resources to support them.

One of the main lessons from Europe's more transit-oriented system is that cities (and state and federal agencies) must work to find ways to level the playing field between auto use and transit. Auto users should clearly be asked to pay for more of the cost of building and maintaining roads and highways, and although not likely to be politically popular, gasoline prices should be raised to reflect the true environmental and social costs of our auto-dominated society. Pucher and LeFevre (1996) note that total road user taxes are some five times higher in Europe than in the United States. They succinctly describe these differences:

> Overall, road users in the USA pay only 60 percent of the costs of road construction, maintenance, administration and law enforcement through taxes and user charges. The remaining 40 percent . . . is subsidized through government revenues. In contrast, road user taxes exceed government expenditures on roads in every European country. The ratio of road taxes to expenditures range from 5.1 in the Netherlands to 1.3 in Switzerland, but most European countries collect at least twice as much from road user taxes as they spend on roads. Thus, road users are heavily subsidized in the USA, whereas in Europe they pay such high road use taxes that they contribute significantly to overall government finance. (p. 28)

Gradually introducing higher gasoline and car taxes over a period of time is likely to be politically necessary, but this must begin soon. The extra revenues should then be pumped back into substantial improvements in local (and extra-local) public transit.

European transit systems—frequently rail—are also organized in ways that generally make it easier to reach major recreational destinations. This type of transit system arrangement holds promising application in many American cities. In Freiburg and many other German cities, the train systems take city dwellers to major destinations in the Black Forest and elsewhere. It is common for families to take the train for recreational day trips out of the city. In the Netherlands, high-demand beach resorts are well served by trains. Indeed, the NS (Nederlandse Spoorwegen) adds extra trains and more frequent service to coastal destinations such as Zandvoort during the peak of summer days and months. While driving remains possible, taking the train is quick, easy, and involves many fewer headaches.

As well, many of the national train companies offer package arrangements with destination amenities (e.g., lodging) and/or additional transportation upon reaching the main destinations. European train companies have been creative in devising transport-recreation packages. The Belgian national train company, for example, now offers something it calls the day-ticket (or "B-dag-TRIP") that offers customers a day's recreational package, all for a single price. One ticket allows the passenger not only to ride the train to a destination city, but it also provides passage on local bus, train, or metro, as well as entrance to the particular destination (e.g., a museum or a zoo). The Belgian company also offers a ticket called "trein en fiets" or "train and bike" that, for a single ticket, reserves a bicycle for use at the end destination (the company has 35 bicycle sites). Through such programs, it is possible to visit historic cities, bicycle in the countryside, or reach other destinations with ease for a relatively low cost and, perhaps most importantly, without the need for an automobile.

Considerable auto travel in the United States centers around recreation; thus, greater attention can and should be given to developing linkages with important parks and nature areas. Partly this may mean exploring new transit connections to existing natural areas (e.g., a train spur from Washington, D.C., to Shenandoah National Park) and partly developing new parklands and restored natural areas in close proximity to already established transit corridors. Moreover, Amtrak could follow the European lead and develop more creative partnerships—for example, with the National Park Service to transport visitors to national parks or with rental car agencies or newly formed car-sharing organizations. To Amtrak's credit, it has begun to develop such partnerships (see White, 1999).

Notes

1. Other planned improvements in the city's public transit system include the conversion of diesel buses to electric buses on certain lines; the use of electric mini-buses to improve the accessibility of train stations (e.g., by making the stations accessible from all directions and enhancing access for bicycles); and the creation of a single-ticket system that would allow riders to use all forms of public transit with a single ticket.

2. The EU Expert Committee on the Urban Environment describes other features of Karlsruhe's transport strategy: "Passengers benefit from the direct link, shorter train intervals, more stops and ease of a single-fare structure. The number of passengers per day has risen from 2000 to 8000, which has helped the different transport companies to recoup their investment. These measures are part of a comprehensive transport plan that also includes inner-city parking management and priority lanes for public transport" (European Commission, 1994, p. 143).

3. Ernst Joos, deputy director of the Zürich transit authority, describes some of the measures undertaken:

> . . . parking and stopping prohibited in 17 road sections. 41 bans on left turns in roads with tram routes. 72 "Give way" signs at intersections in roads carrying bus and tram traffic. 21 km of bus lanes. About 40 building projects, such as islands for bus and tram stops, separate tracks, pedestrian zones with trams and buses, multi-track systems, bus lanes, etc. 2 newly constructed sections for extending a tram line by 2 and 6.4 km, respectively, with a separate track throughout. (Joos, 1992, p. 4)

4. As Berger (1997) writes, the Europeans have been faster, as well, at embracing electric vehicle use. He estimates some 25,000 electric vehicles in use in Europe (eight times as many as in the United States), with some 2,000 in Switzerland (a relatively small nation) alone. Substantial public subsidies have been provided (as high as $4,000 per vehicle in France).

5. One thing that makes the SdC different from the typical arrangements in other cities is that it is simultaneously handling the freight of a number of different transport companies. This raises concerns by companies that competitors will gain insights about what kinds of goods are being sent and where. As a result, the SdC tries to the extent that it can to restrict the access of drivers and operators bringing goods into the center to the inside of the warehouse.

6. Consider the following example from a recent article in the *New York Times* (Rimer, 1997, p. A20):

> In Richmond, VA, Deborah Perkins, a geriatric nurse practitioner, recently advised a woman in her 80s with severe memory impairment to stop driving.
>
> "She burst into tears and said 'You might as well shoot me,'" Mrs. Perkins said in a telephone interview. "Its like telling a patient they have a terminal illness."

Chapter 5

Taming the Auto:
The Promise of Car-Free Cities

The Promise of Car-Free Cities

Automobiles—and the growth in their number and usage—are perhaps the single most significant sustainability issue for European cities, as evidenced in extensive interviews throughout Europe. This is not a surprising finding given the trends in much of Europe. The European Union (EU) as a whole is predicted to experience a 25 percent increase in kilometers traveled by car between 1990 and 2010 (European Commission, 1996). If current trends in the Netherlands continue, for instance, it is predicted that a 70 percent increase in car use will occur by 2010 (and a rise in the number of cars from 5 to 8 million). In many individual cities, such traffic increases can already be seen. As a dramatic case, Edinburgh has seen a 57 percent rise in traffic between 1981 and 1991 (Johnstone, 1998).

The costs associated with these trends in Europe are seen as high and rising. A recent EU-funded study calculated amazing extend costs associated with the automobile—estimated at more than $300 billion yearly, in the form of social, environmental, and other costs, or about 4 percent of the EU's GDP. Congestion costs in London have been estimated (in 1989) at £15 billion per year (Girardet, undated).

In spite of these trends (indeed perhaps because of them), European cities have undertaken a host of impressive measures to better manage the automobile. In virtually all of the cities studied, significant (and often dramatic) steps have been taken to restrict and curtail access for automobiles, in turn creating marvelous and highly attractive walking environments for citizens. There is now a network—called "Car Free Cities" and based in

Brussels—of about sixty cities working on these issues. Many participating cities have signed the so-called Copenhagen Declaration, making a symbolic commitment to finding ways to reduce the presence of cars in their cities. The network (launched by the European Commission [EC] in 1994) offers technical support to its members and has convened a series of conferences and seminars. Six working groups within the network have been established to address specific themes in moving toward car-free cities (Car Free Cities Coordination Office, undated).[1] As mentioned, in cities such as Vienna, delightful pedestrian environments have been created, with sculptures, fountains, and artwork, decorative tiling and brickwork, and the linking together of impressive civic structures. Many German cities, as we have seen, have developed extensive pedestrian areas. Virtually all of Freiburg's historic center is pedestrian-only (Boyes, 1997; Leonard and Leonard, 1997; BUND, 1995). In almost all Dutch cities, major portions of central shopping areas are pedestrian-only, with cities such as Amsterdam, Utrecht, and Groningen serving as excellent examples. Political and policy initiatives to control the growing influence of automobiles are, then, not surprising.

A number of European cities have taken measures to substantially limit auto traffic in their centers. Freiburg, Germany, shown here, has converted its center to a car-free district, essentially limited now to trams, pedestrians, and bicycles. Most of the rest of Freiburg has been designated a 30-kilometer-per-hour traffic-calmed zone.

The call for "car-free cities" is increasingly being made by a number of organizations in Europe, public and private. At a grass roots level, European environmental activists are increasingly aiming their attention at cars. In November of 1997, a conference called *Towards Car-Free Cities,* organized by activists, was held in Lyon, France. Among other things, conference participants explored techniques and strategies for effectively waging a public campaign against cars, and shared experiences and information. Future plans include the publication of a new magazine called *Car Busters* and a second conference and international day of protest against the automobile.

The conference received considerable media attention, in part because of its number of creative displays of opposition to the car. These displays included conducting an automobile funeral through the streets of Lyon, "car-walking" (walking atop cars parked on the sidewalk, and placing signs on windshields reading, "I walked over your car because I didn't want to slide under it"), placing police ribbons around cars, picking up and moving cars into the street so that traffic was blocked (called "car bouncing"), and distributing flyers asking drivers to consider giving up their cars. Those cars wrapped in police ribbon were left "'official' letters from the city explaining rationally why society can no longer bear the costs of private-car ownership. The letters concluded by giving drivers a choice: pay the true costs of your car with a hefty fine of 100,000 francs (US $16,000) or have your car crushed in exchange for a free bike" (Ghent, 1998, p. 13).

Hall (1995b) identifies three striking innovations in curtailing the automobile in European cities over the last two decades: (1) pedestrianization of central business cores; (2) traffic calming; (3) and especially in the 1990s, road pricing (pp. 70–71). To this list, several important innovations must be added: the development of car-free housing estates and car-limited development designs, and the emergence and phenomenal growth in car-sharing. Each of these innovations will now be discussed.

Traffic-Calming and Car-Limiting City Strategies

Short of complete pedestrianization, there are many creative examples of actions taken to restrict, discourage, or otherwise "calm" automobile traffic. Here again, European cities offer the best examples. A variety of specific traffic-calming strategies and technologies exist, virtually all of them extensively used in the case study cities. These strategies include the concept of the *woonerf* (or "living street or yard"), pioneered in the Netherlands, speed humps (or *drempels,* as the Dutch call them), curb and sidewalk extensions, raised brickwork, bollards and physical barriers of all types, and the creative use of trees (placement of trees in streets and parking lots). Traffic circles, or roundabouts, another calming measure, have become a popular replacement for conventional lighted intersections, and evidence suggests that fewer accidents result. One town in the Netherlands even uses sheep as a way of slowing traffic.

Many impressive individual projects point to big and small efforts to reconfigure neighborhood streets to create safer, calmer pedestrian environments. One of the best small examples (part of a larger systematic effort at calming) can be seen at the intersection of Skt. kundsgade, Alexandergade, and Fredensgade Streets, in Odense. Here, access for autos has been severely constrained to create a marvelous play area for children, with large trees and benches for sitting. Auto entranceways into the neighborhood are limited through narrowed, elevated stone roadways. Vertical wooden posts protect pedestrians and children from cars directed along a winding roadway leading around the sitting and playing area.

Many cities have designated large areas as 30-kilometer/hour zones, and installed a variety of traffic-calming measures. In Freiburg, for instance, some 90 percent of the population of the city now lives in 30-kilometer/hour speed-restricted zones. These measures can create enjoyable environments, much more suitable for children playing and outdoor socializing. One of the best examples of a successful residential traffic-calming project is the *Weststadt* district in Heidelberg. Through a combination of street narrowing, the installation of stonework around intersections, and the creation of bends and curves in streets, this area has become a much safer, more livable, and highly desirable neighborhood. At the same time, auto movement for residents (although restricted) is not prohibited.

Few compact cities in Europe have devoted more attention to reducing the role of the automobile in the center than Amsterdam. Residents here endorsed through a referendum in 1992 an ambitious program for reducing traffic congestion and car use, which includes: improvements in public transit, making parking in the central areas more expensive, road pricing (described later), and guiding land use decisions through the A-B-C locational policy (described in the previous chapter). Many of these actions have been under way for several years. What the Amsterdam approach suggests is that no single strategy or approach will be successful on its own—it is, rather, a series of interlocking strategies that will have some effect. To date, the city has in fact been raising the cost of parking and has substantially reduced the number of spaces available in the center. This is not always politically easy, and resistance by business interests has been considerable. Politics has also come into play in implementing the A-B-C policy. While the city has generally been aggressive at guiding high frequency/visitation activities to public transit or A-locations, there have been some concessions made to relocating businesses interested in enhanced automobile access. A recent example offered by Hugo Poelstra, head of the city's Traffic and Transport group, is the new ABN-Amro bank headquarters, to be located near the World Trade Center in the southern part of the city. Here, through negotiations, the company was able to extract permission for a higher number of automobile parking spaces than would normally be allowed at a public transit or A-location.

There are a number of examples of community-participation or community-based processes for identifying neighborhood improvements and improvements needed to enhance the quality and livability of an area. Leicester, for example, has involved the public in identifying areas where traffic calming is needed. Under its Feet First initiative, residents in the Highfields neighborhood identified changes needed to make streets safer, which led to the creation of several bicycle-only streets and the installation of traffic-calming measures. A similar initiative involved children in identifying safe routes to school, resulting in similar traffic-calming measures. Leicester's outcomes are impressive. In the Highfields case, 10 kilometers of streets were calmed, and the results have already been shown to be positive (a reported 20 percent increase in children walking to school and a majority of community respondents to a survey indicating that more people are walking and that the feeling of community there had improved; see Leicester City Council, undated). Surveys of residents in traffic-calmed areas have shown great support for the initiative and more demand from other neighborhoods than can be accommodated (Leicester City Council, undated-a).

The experience in other cities has been similar. Heidelberg witnessed more than a 31 percent reduction in accidents and a 44 percent reduction in casualties. Generally, studies of these and other European cities show consistent results: lowered accidents and fatalities, reduced noise levels, and greater pedestrian and outdoor activity (for a good summary, see Newman and Kenworthy, 1992). Interestingly, calming measures have also been shown to reduce air pollution (e.g., by reducing idling time, gear changing, and brake use).

There is no question that in the cities visited, calming initiatives have created spaces where children and residents feel safer and where greater walking, playing, and outdoor activity occur. Additional space for other nonauto uses is an extra benefit as well. In Leiceister, for example, extended sidewalks and curb extensions in the center have provided space for flower pots, benches, and bicycle racks. In Heidelberg, an outdoor cafe and small terrace have been created in Weststadt. One clear conclusion is that traffic-calming measures must be undertaken at a neighborhood or district level if they are to be successful. The best examples, such as Weststadt, have done this.

The Dutch have pioneered the idea of the *woonerf,* or living or shared street, which represents a powerful strategy for calming streets and neighborhoods. (*Woon* means "residential" in Dutch, and *erf* means "yard"). Specifically, the *woonerf* is a residential street where, through bends and curves in roadways and through tree plantings and brick and stone designs, car traffic is slowed significantly (cars are not to move faster than the walking pace of a pedestrian) and the roadways are shared with pedestrians, bicyclists, and children. Traffic lanes are intentionally narrow, just wide enough to allow a car and a bicycle to move by each other (Ten Grotenhuis, 1979; Royal Dutch Touring Club, 1978). Parking is strategically placed so that, when not in use, it becomes part of the pedestrian space. In the Netherlands, streets must meet certain conditions before receiving a *woonerf* designation (and the signage indicating such). Under the national Traffic Act, the legal relationship between cars and pedestrians and bicyclists actually changes in these designed areas. While on most streets, cars have priority over slower moving traffic, in a *woonerf,* each mode is considered equal. First appearing in the Netherlands in the mid-1970s, there were already some 2,700 *woonerven* (the plural of *woonerf*) by 1983 (Liebman, 1996). In 1999, there were an estimated 6,000 *woonerven* streets in the Netherlands (Quinn, 1999). To convert an existing *woonerf* requires approval by residents of the neighborhood (60 percent approval required).

Certain perceived limitations have arisen in using the *woonerf* idea, however. These limitations include the problem of too many parked cars and the diminution of the space which results; the problem of providing adequate access for fire trucks, garbage trucks, and other large vehicles (this has been solved in Delft by using stone hills at corners and through the use of smaller vehicles); the problem of the moped (higher-speed vehicles, although treated like bicycles); and public acceptance of the concept (Ten Grotenhuis, 1979). *Woonerven* also typically cost more to build and require some additional maintenance (e.g., the vegetation).

Delft was one of the first communities in the Netherlands to apply the *woonerf* concept, and this city represents an interesting laboratory for understanding the *woonerf's* evolution over the years. The Tanthoff district, in particular, demonstrates the shifting attitudes about *woonerven*. Tanthoff-east, built in the 1970s, is one of the largest areas of *woonerven*. It is an extensive network of low-rise, attached homes, connected by both its *woonerven* and an intricate network of paths and footbridges. While the spatial organization is exemplary in many ways, attitudes in Delft have shifted away from what some have called the "cauliflower" mazes, in support of straighter lines and more reliance on a conventional grid street layout. This shift can be seen dramatically in Tanthof-west, built in the 1980s. Although the street layout is based on a grid, it should be noted that many of the main traffic-calming measures typically found in a *woonerf* are found here also (such as extensive speed bumps and doglegs). The thinking in Delft, and elsewhere in the Netherlands, is a result of the perception of being a bit lost in large *woonerven*, and lacking a clear sense of relationship to other neighborhoods or the city-center (although connectedness is a necessary design element in any Dutch development). From the perspective of an outside observer and visitor, both sections of Tanthof appear to work well and to represent exemplary living environments. Perhaps more than anything, the Delft experience suggests the virtues of a wide repertoire of street design concepts and tools.

Other parts of Europe have embraced and applied similar calming ideas. Even in the United Kingdom, there has been a movement to create the equivalent of the *woonerf*—what are being called Home Zones. These would be similarly created, highly calmed streets, with a maximum 10 kilometers/hour speed limit. Advocated by the Children's Play Council, Home Zones are being touted as a strategy for making neighborhood streets safer for children (the United Kingdom has the highest child pedestrian mortality rate in Europe; Purves, 1998).

Many examples of aggressive parking strategies are also seen in the case study communities, and a key conclusion is that parking restrictions and pricing are an integral element of any effort to curtail automobiles. Bologna, for example, has developed an aggressive parking policy in which visitors by car must pay a relatively high hourly parking fee. As well, under the city's system of parking zones, certain streets have been designated only for residents, and in some areas even residents are required to pay hourly parking charges. Many of the other cities have taken a similarly aggressive approach to parking. Amsterdam has become infamous for its policy of "booting" parking violators. Berlin has imposed a similarly high parking rate to discourage cars (about DM 4 per hour).

Amsterdam implements a stringent policy of limiting parking (based largely on the national government's A-B-C policy) and encourages high visitation activity land uses near public transit stops (e.g., major new office complexes). Specifically, the city restricts the number of parking spaces new businesses are permitted to have in these transit-friendly locations. In the best transit locations (A-locations sites adjacent to train stations), new businesses are permitted no more than one space per ten employees.

Many European cities have been working hard to create car-free or car-limited centers. Creating car-free central districts is often the result of citizen-led initiatives and referenda, as was the case in both Amsterdam and Bologna. In Bologna, residents voted overwhelmingly to designate its historic center as a "car-restricted zone" (*zona a traffico limitato*). Under the new restrictions between the hours of 7:00 a.m. to 8:00 p.m., only residents of the center, business owners, taxis, delivery vehicles, and others with specific access needs are permitted to enter the historic core. The city has created a unique telemetric system for restricting access. At a limited number of entry points around the city, the telemetric equipment scans the license plates of entering cars to verify that they hold the required permit. (While the telemetric system is not in use at the present time because of a bureaucratic dispute between two national government agencies, it is expected to be restarted in the near future.)

The restrictions have, in the short time they have been in place, had the effect of significantly reducing car traffic in the center. One report estimates that the number of cars driving into the center daily has decreased by 62 percent (ICLEI, 1996). Nevertheless, Bologna is clearly not car free, and a large number of permits (82,000) have been issued. And the restrictions end at 8:00 p.m.: "Every evening 'leisure time traffic' pours out onto the streets and forms long car lines through the old center city and ruins evening walks" (ICLEI, 1996, p. 3). One answer is a more aggressive approach to promoting public transit, which Bologna has embarked on in recent months.

Bologna, Italy, through a citywide referendum, has designated its center a "car restricted zone" (*zona a traffico limitato*). General car traffic is forbidden from entering the center between 7:00 A.M. and 8:00 P.M. This is controlled through the issuance of permits and a series of telemetric-monitored gateways into the center.

Car-Free Developments and Housing Estates

Efforts are also being made to design new housing developments in ways that minimize and discourage the use of automobiles. The typical placement of new projects in close proximity to existing developed areas, and the incorporation of mixed uses, can reduce the need for residents to have or utilize an auto. Furthermore, the physical design of many new development projects is organized to de-emphasize the auto. An increasingly common development style is to cluster all parking on the outer perimeter of a development, not allowing cars to penetrate the interior areas (and not allowing residents to drive their cars right to their doorsteps). The number of spaces provided in these newer developments is also lower than with conventional development, and significantly lower than most American development.

The GWL-terrein project in the Westerpark district of Amsterdam is an example, providing a limited number of parking spaces, located only on the perimeter of the development, and actively discouraging residents from owning autos. The project provides only 110 spaces, plus 25 spaces for visitors, for a total of 135 spaces for a project including 600 dwelling units (see Figure 5.1). The use of these spaces is regulated through a system of parking permits. Residents who wish to have a car and to use one of the few available spaces must have a permit. There were more residents applying for permits (about twice as many) as spaces available, so a lottery is used to distribute the permits. According to the project leader, this meant that about 110 residents who moved to the project actually had to get rid of a car. One concern is that residents will often have cars anyway but will simply park them in surrounding neighborhoods. The parking permit system in Westerpark prohibits this because parking in the surrounding neighborhoods is also not possible without a permit.

The GWL-terrein project explicitly incorporates car-sharing services. Specifically, the company BAS (Buurt Auto Service) has on-site cars (there are 4 cars on-site all the time, and the company will bring more cars to the site when needed). There is also another car-sharing service with a computerized system just 300 meters from the project. In addition, all buildings have extensive storage facilities to accommodate bicycles. Another important feature about the GWL project is its location. Many destinations are within a close walking distance, including several schools, shops, daycare facilities, and a very large cultural center (an old gas factory). There is a shopping street about 150 meters away.

The education of residents in this project has been critical. In a number of ways, they have been informed that they are living in a special ecological project that is intentionally auto-limited. As residents move in, they are given several booklets about ecological housekeeping, for example. In addition, a full-time resident "housemaster" is available for helping residents

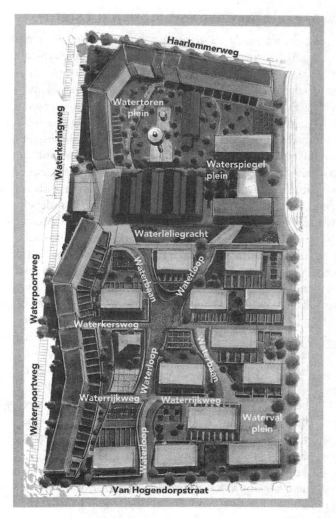

Figure 5.1. Map showing layout of GWL-terrein car-limited development (Amsterdam)

The layout of the car-limited ecological housing project called GWL-terrein in the Westerpark district of Amsterdam.

Source: Westerpark Stadsdeel, Amsterdam.

and taking care of problems. At several points, residents must sign disclosure statements acknowledging that they understand it is a car-free development. Such statements are included in all sales and rental contracts.

This particular development includes other important ecological features. Design features address four main themes: energy, water, green, and garbage. On the theme of water, a rainwater collection system has been employed, where water is collected in cisterns (below ground) and used for toilet flushing. There is no drainage infrastructure—rainwater is collected naturally and allowed to percolate. Also, the major high-rise buildings have green roofs, which also help reduce runoff. The green roofs are accessible to residents and have been planted in low flowering plants. Other features include low-flow shower heads, toilets that require only 4 liters per flush; kitchens fitted with separation bins for different types of garbage; the use of passive solar, with many buildings southern oriented; and good insulation in the walls and windows. A central cogeneration plant produces hot water for heating (fueled by natural gas) for the entire project. The interior of the project is car free; there is one hard surface road into the interior, to accommodate fire and heavy vehicles.

Much of the interior space of GWL-terrein is green. There are both private gardens and collective vegetable gardens, which include 120 common garden plots that are distributed with priority to those residents without their own backyard or terrace garden. The project planners asked the police to look at the design from a safety point of view, which led to the police's suggestion that the green be primarily in the form of trees and grass, with no bushes or shrubs. Fruit trees and endemic vegetation have been favored.

A number of lessons can be learned from the GWL-terrein project. The project leader recommends that in the future in such car-free concepts, no parking spaces at all should be provided. This eliminates the problem of how to fairly distribute the small number of spaces available. Another lesson is the importance of choice. At the same time that the GWL-terrein project was being planned, another project in Westerpark, one allowing cars, was also under way. In this way those looking for new homes in Westerpark had options and could choose. Giving residents something in exchange for limiting cars was also considered important. Thus, the project planners saw the need to emphasize the greenspaces and areas for children to play. The project leader reports that the interior spaces are well used and well appreciated. Interest in living at GWL-terrein has been very high. In fact, some 6,000 people have applied for apartments, which seems to demonstrate quite definitively that car-free or car-minimal designs have great potential.

Other car-free estates are being proposed around Europe, and as cities struggle with extreme growth in car use, these developments will likely be seen as an increasingly attractive planning option. At the moment, the GWL-terrein project in Amsterdam may be the closest realized project (really car-minimal, rather than car-free), but several others are in the works. One of the first proposed was the Hollerand car-free housing estate in Bremen (Germany). More recently, a £13 million car-free estate has been approved in Edinburgh, Scotland, a city that has, as noted earlier, seen a dramatic rise in car traffic in recent years. The estate will consist of 120 homes, in tenement style, located on a former railyard near the center of the city (Arlidge, 1997). It will incorporate a number of environmental features (e.g., solar panels, and waste and water recycling), but its most notable feature will be the lack of cars, and the lack of streets and parking that go along with cars (see Figure 5.2). Residents will be asked to sign an agreement that they will not own a car, but instead will join a car-sharing company (for £320 a year), which will provide an on-site pool of cars. The Canmore Housing Association, which is building the project, reports that interest in living in the development has already been high. As another example, Camden borough in London, has recently approved several similar projects; undoubtedly, other European cities will follow suit.

Short of car-free design, many examples were found of developments that have sought to minimize the position of the auto. In Zwijndrecht, in the Netherlands, several creative designs emphasize the pedestrian and de-emphasize the auto. In the De As development, residential units have been organized along a 500-meter pedestrian-only street. At one end of the pedestrian street lies an impressive greenspace in the form of a canal park, called de Devel ("the little water"). Cars here are relegated to several peripheral lots, as well as to parking behind the units. The street itself has several play areas incorporated into it, along with trees and vegetation.

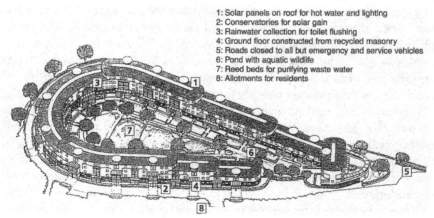

1: Solar panels on roof for hot water and lighting
2: Conservatories for solar gain
3: Rainwater collection for toilet flushing
4: Ground floor constructed from recycled masonry
5: Roads closed to all but emergency and service vehicles
6: Pond with aquatic wildlife
7: Reed beds for purifying waste water
8: Allotments for residents

Figure 5.2. Canmore car-free housing estate design (Edinburgh)

A car-free housing estate being built in Edinburgh, Scotland. In addition to access to an on-site car-sharing company, the project incorporates a number of other ecological design features, including solar panels, greywater recycling, and rainwater collection.

Source: The Statesman © 1999.

Front doors are oriented to the pedestrian street, which is described as "a social meeting place without cars" (Rabobank, 1995). The experiences of residents living there have been very positive—the pedestrian street has provided a safe play area and an area important for socializing. (Note also that the cohousing and ecovillage designs described elsewhere in this book offer similar advantages.) While experience with these car-free or car-minimal designs is mixed, the designs are creative and encouraging and reflect a clear effort to minimize the presence of the automobile. A recent promotional article describes the De As project as a "planning paradise for children and a social meeting place for adults" (Rabobank, 1995, p. 6). By all accounts, the design does seem to be functioning in this way. While the project does not include retail, there was a clear intention to mix the housing types and status of residents. The project includes patio homes for older residents, homes with offices below, both detached and attached homes, and some multi-family apartments. There is also a mix of owner-occupied units and rental units.

Another example of a car-limited development is the Het Groene Dak ("the green roof") development in Utrecht. As a result of reorienting the buildings in the project to maximize southern exposure, a beautiful, green "communal inner garden" was created—a wild, green, car-free area for children to play and residents to socialize. The residents also waged a creative battle with municipal officials to allow them to reduce the number of parking spaces in the development, which were to be provided in the form

Car-free or car-limited housing estates are a promising trend in European cities. Shown here is the new neighborhood "De As" in the Dutch city of Zwijndrecht. Cars are relegated to peripheral lots and the housing units face a pedestrian-only community street.
Source: Gemeente Zwijndrecht.

of street parking around the perimeter of development. While the normal parking standard in Utrecht was 1.1 spaces per housing unit, the city allowed a relaxing to .5, recognizing that these ecologically minded residents indeed had far fewer cars (a survey of prospective residents found an actual need for fewer than the stipulated 33 spaces). Interestingly, residents in surrounding neighborhoods raised objections to this lower parking standard, fearing Het Groene Dak residents would end up parking in *their* neighborhoods. The conflict was eventually disarmed when Het Groene Dak leaders sent letters to the surrounding neighborhood pledging not to park in their spaces and to (if ever necessary) park their cars in a nearby sports arena lot. A parking contingency plan was also mandated by the city—Het Groene Dak was allowed to convert what would normally be on-street parking into flowing extensions of greenspace. Under the required contingency plan, these areas would have to be converted to paved spaces should it be determined that residents own more cars than expected.

Many other green-urban projects seek to control or limit automobiles. Waldquelle, a new ecological development in Bielefeld, Germany, shows the possibilities of an incremental approach to creating car-free or at least car-limited settlements. Here, 130 homes are clustered together along a series of common spaces (backyards), connected by pedestrian pathways. Auto access to homes is provided through a limited network of narrow stone streets. Most parking in the neighborhood is very creatively provided in the form of permeable brickwork that abuts the stone roads and that for the most part has taken on the look of a natural green (grass) carpet. While cars are now accommodated in the interior of the project, longer-term aspirations (at least of the architect and some residents) are that the interior of the neighborhood become car free as soon as a common parking lot under construction (to serve a nearby commercial and market center) becomes available for use. Residents would park there, banishing cars from the interior neighborhood spaces. The stones used in constructing the narrow streets in Waldquelle are highly attractive and similar to those found in center-city pedestrian areas. The narrowness and winding nature of the roads suggest an ideal pedestrian environment should the plan to banish cars be realized. In the meantime, a delightful pedestrian-friendly neighborhood has emerged, with collective pathways and common spaces and extensive vegetation and gardens throughout.

Car-Sharing

In recent years, there have been a number of creative proposals for creating systems of shared cars and for moving away from the need to own one's own private vehicle (not to mention two or three of them). Architect

Mosha Safdie in his recent provocative book, *The City After the Automobile,* proposes the concept of the *utility-car* or *u-car.* Under such a system, cars would be available at certain collective depots to be picked up, used, and dropped off at other sites, much like luggage carts now provided at airports. His ideas are provocative, and although they have a very futuristic sound to them, there are now a number of tangible initiatives and experiments in European cities that are advancing this notion of collective cars or car-sharing.

Indeed, many of the leading applications of these ideas occur in Europe. One of the early experiments was undertaken in Amsterdam, the brainchild of Luud Schimmelpennink. Schimmelpennink has been a long time advocate for and inventor of "public" systems of mobility in cities. Most notably, he pioneered the idea of Amsterdam's white bikes. (Bicycle initiatives are discussed in detail in Chapter 6.) As a follow-up, Schimmelpennink created a experimental system of *witkarren*—or white cars—for Amsterdam.

Schimmelpennink's limited version of the *witkar* system was in use in Amsterdam for about a ten-year period between the mid-1970s and mid-1980s. It apparently worked quite well. There were four sites and thirty-five cars in operation (although the plans were for many more sites than this). While Schimmelpennink believes the *witkar* program was a modest success, the small number of stations limited its utility, and there was little move or interest at the time in expanding the system.

Interestingly, car-sharing has become a viable option in Europe, and a number of car-sharing companies have been formed (where residents can subscribe for an annual fee, entitling them access to a car on an hourly or per-kilometer charge basis). Indeed, there has been a real explosion in car-sharing in European cities, and an organization—European Car Sharing—has been established in Bremen to coordinate and represent these companies. Currently, 40 car-sharing companies are members, serving 300 European cities. There are now some 38,000 subscribers, and annual growth is impressive. (In 1991, there were only 1,000 subscribers.) There is no question that the conditions in many European cities favor the development of car-sharing. According to Joachim Schwartz, director of European Car Sharing, car-sharing will only work where residents have other viable options for their basic daily mobility: namely, either a good bicycle network and facilities or good public transit. Close proximity of shopping, daycare, and other basic services to one's home is also important. The main obstacle to further growth in car-sharing in Europe is a failure to fully assess car users for the costs of using cars. When this happens, car-sharing will boom. There is no question, though, that the costs of maintaining and operating a car in Europe are much higher than in the United

States, and that this has helped make European cities more fertile ground for car-sharing.

Certain cities have helped to facilitate car-sharing. Amsterdam has entered into contracts with car-sharing companies to designate on-street public spaces specifically for the cars. The ability to do this in Germany is legally difficult because public space on streets cannot legally be designated for a specific private company's use. However, some German cities, including Bremen, have made arrangements for designated parking on other publicly-owned property, such as school parking lots (which are not considered public space). Other cities have put money into starting up car-sharing programs and attempting to find companies willing to operate them. Edinburgh, Scotland, has taken this approach. Other cities, including Amsterdam again, have provided advertising assistance. In Berlin, the municipality has agreed to rent spaces to the company at the same rate as a monthly public transit pass. This is one way that car-sharing companies (and their subscribers) might be rewarded for reducing the number of cars on the street.

One recent conversation with a resident of the center of Utrecht confirms how car-sharing can work for many people. A member of Greenwheels, a Rotterdam-based car-sharing company, the individual related a recent story of hearing from a sick friend and needing a car on very short notice and for only a short period to visit the friend. He was able to collect a car at the centrum parking garage (one of Greenwheel's 25 collection points in Utrecht), make the trip, and later return the car—all fairly effortless.

A number of car-sharing studies further confirm the potential for in-

Greenwheels, a Dutch car-sharing company, places cars in many convenient locations, such as at the main train station in Utrecht, shown here.

creased use of these services and the potential to reduce the number of private automobiles on the street (see Lightfoot, 1996). Usually, car-sharing companies operate by charging an entrance fee or security deposit, a monthly fee, and a per-kilometer or per-hour usage fee. Reservations are made by phone, and studies suggest that subscribers rarely have difficulty securing a car when they need one. On average, car-sharing organizations have one car per eighteen subscribers, thus providing a more efficient and affordable form of automobility. Interestingly, promoting the use of car-sharing also appears to further strengthen local public transit; as the kilometers driven decreases, the use of public transit increases (Lightfoot, 1996, p. 12).[2]

One of the largest car-sharing operations is located in Berlin. Established in 1990, STATTAUTO is the largest car-sharing company in Germany. It currently has a membership of 3,100 and expects to have over 10,000 subsidies by the year 2000 (ICLEI, 1997). The company maintains 140 vehicles (including 2 electric cars and a solar charging station), with distribution points spread throughout the city (usually two to seven spaces per point). Typically, a car will be no further than a ten-minute walk, and subscribers have smart cards that allow access to car-key lockers, so cars can be collected twenty-four hours a day. Calculations by STATTAUTO suggest that the environmental benefits of car-sharing are considerable: a reduction of 510,000 car kilometers, an annual reduction of some 80 tonnes of carbon, and the taking of five cars out of circulation for every car-sharing vehicle (ICLEI, 1997).

Greenwheels illustrates the potential of newly emerging companies and the role of creative marketing in promoting car-sharing. Just two-and-a-half years old, the company now has more than 500 subscribers and provides cars in five cities, including Utrecht and Amsterdam. This company has been creatively making quid pro quo arrangements with a variety of different entities interested in having a car-sharing option available for their customers or employees. Greenwheels has an arrangement with the municipality of Rotterdam, for instance, to provide car-sharing services to several large departments. Departmental customer cards are given to departments, which then allow their employees to use the cars when needed. A recent agreement with the Nederlandse Spoorwegen (NS), the national train company, provides train passengers (with certain discount cards) to join the car-sharing service at a reduced price. Similarly, in two cities—Den Haag and Rotterdam—arrangements have been made with local transit companies to provide a discount for car-sharing members who wish to purchase yearly transit passes. Again, a major obstacle seen by Greenwheels is finding the necessary parking spaces. This has been helped by the local governments in this case. The city of Utrecht has, for example, designated two spaces in the taxi area at the central train station. (Interestingly, although these spaces are designated for Greenwheels, they technically remain public parking spaces, and the Utrecht police have no authority to fine people parking there.)

Representatives at Greenwheels feel that one of the most important lessons about successful car-sharing is that it must be made as easy and effortless as possible if it is to compete with private auto usage. One of the ways that Greenwheels does this is by reducing the paperwork and record-keeping involved in actually using a car. Subscribers are issued a smart card, a magnetized card with their picture on it, which they use to access key lockers at pick-up points. This card access, in combination with onboard computers in each car, means that the user needs to do very little when picking up or returning a vehicle. Subscribers simply use the cars when they need them and receive a monthly bill for kilometers driven and time used.

Call-a-Car and Demand Management

The Dutch Ministry of Transport has actively promoted car-sharing in that country, as well as several other "call-a-car" strategies. According to the ministry, these include: the subscription system, the coupon system, and what has been called the Family, Friends and Neighbors (FFN) system. (Bakker, 1996). A subscription system is one in which an individual signs up for a certain package of time and use of a vehicle over the course of a year (e.g., a certain number of days and kilometers) and pays a fixed monthly fee. This is closer to a traditional American leasing system, although reservations and collecting of the car are still required. The Dutch equivalent of AAA—the Algemene Nederlandse Wielrijders Bond (ANWB)—has started such a service (called "Auto-op-Afroep" or "Car-on-Call"), as have several car rental companies.

The coupon system is another version in which the user buys a book of coupons for a certain price, entitling similar occasional use of a car. Finally, a third variation is the "Family, Friends and Neighbors" system. Here, a car is shared between a limited number of friends and neighbors. Typically, the car is owned by one person or family and is shared by way of a contract, which stipulates costs and conditions for use. The call-a-car association (which the Dutch government has helped establish) has developed a standard contract to help. Bakker (1996) estimates there are now over 50,000 Dutch citizens involved in such programs. One problem has been the difficulty in getting car insurance companies to cover such arrangements, and the call-a-car association has been working with insurance companies on a special type of policy that would cover these arrangements.

KLM-the Dutch airline—has established its own creative system of car-sharing (called "Wings and Wheels") for its 12,000 employees working at

Schiphol Airport in Amsterdam. Cars are made available for employees to rent for a few days at a reduced rate, allowing them to take the cars home and to bring them back to the airport when they return (e.g., for their next flight). This seems to be a creative solution, especially well-suited for flight crews, where an automobile might sit in an employee parking lot unused for several days. KLM reports that as a result of the program, they now require some 300 fewer employee spaces at the airport (Bakker, 1996).

Together, some 15,000 Dutch were participating (by June 1996) in these various call-a-car schemes. This level of participation has been estimated to have resulted in a reduction of 5,000 cars, a reduction of 22 vehicle miles traveled by auto, and an increase in public transit travel of 11 million kilometers (Bakker, 1996). These are no small accomplishments, particularly in a small country where there are already too many private cars sharing a small space. The prognosis of the Ministry is optimistic—projections are that there will be 50,000 participants in various call-a-car schemes by 2001. This number is significant, although it is unclear how realistic the goal of 2 million participants by 2010 actually is. If this goal is reached, it will represent a serious tool in reducing auto traffic. Estimates are that such rates of participation would result in a 3-billion-kilometers reduction in car use and a 1.5 billion-kilometer increase in public transit (although this would still represent only 2.5 percent and 6 percent, respectively, of the total).

One of the most impressive actions by the Dutch government in this regard has been the establishment of a call-a-car association (called Autodate). This association is financially underwritten by the national government and performs a number of key organizing and coordinating roles, including holding meetings to share information between organizations, publishing a quarterly newsletter, and attending to the public relations and media aspects of the call-a-car concept. For example, the organization is about to embark on a major media campaign to promote the idea among the general public.

What is interesting in all of these programs is that they have the potential to reduce unnecessary travel by car. Evidence shows, not surprisingly, that owning a car is a stimulus to using it. Psychologically, this is exacerbated by the high amounts of money spent to buy, maintain, and insure vehicles. If the choice is to either run an errand by car or alternatively by foot or bicycle, the outcome will very often be the former.

Presenting residents of new housing projects with alternatives to autoreliance (from the beginning) is another important strategy. The new IJburg development being planned in Amsterdam represents the direction many cities are now taking. Here, the ANWB is working with the city to offer new residents a "mobility package," making it attractive to not have and operate a private automobile. New residents there will be able to purchase a package of transportation services for a single price, including membership in a car-sharing company and free public transit usage for a certain period of time (the project will be served by both a high-speed tram and eventually an extension of the city's underground metro system). Emphasizing mobility and a package of alternative measures to get from point A to point B is clearly an important trend in sustainable European cities.

It should again be noted that even in the most exemplary cities that have sought to control the automobile, trends show dramatic increases in automobile use. There are difficulties simply in implementing policies that seek to combat these trends. Considering these trends, the successful efforts of study communities to increase public transit ridership and bicycle use can be seen as even that much more impressive. Many of these cities have gone through (or are going through) wrenching disputes over road-building proposals. In Stockholm, for example, a major public controversy arose over plans to build a ring round around the city (the so-called Dennis-Package; most of it has been scrapped, at least for the time being). In Groningen, there has been a proposal to build a new underground parking lot near the Grote Markt in the city-center, in apparent contradiction to efforts to curtail the automobile there. Many other cities are facing similar pressures to further accommodate auto traffic.

Road Pricing

There is a growing recognition in many European cities that more fundamental economic adjustments will be necessary to affect change in the behavior of auto drivers and to cutback on the extent to which urban space is taken over by the car. Charging a financial premium for cars wishing to enter the city at particular times of the day—road pricing or congestion pricing—has been in use for a number of years in several European cities. Several other jurisdictions have recently instituted pilot projects or are otherwise looking seriously at this option.

The pioneers in road pricing have been the Norwegians, with pricing systems in place in several major cities, including Oslo, Trondheim, and Bergen. In Oslo, a system of electronic charges for cars crossing a ring into the center has been in place since the early 1990s. The toll, about US $1.70 per trip, is collected both electronically (through electronic tags) and manually at nineteen toll plazas. Each day, tolls are collected from about 230,000 vehicles, generating about 65 million pounds in revenue each year (Harper, 1998, Massie, 1998). Trondheim's system operates in a similar fashion, with twelve toll stations assessing highest fees in the morning and declining during the day until passage is free after 5:00 p.m. Drivers paying electronically—through smart cards—are assessed a reduced fee, compared with those paying by cash. The license plates of those attempting to escape without paying are photographed, and bills are sent through the mail. Toll plazas have been strategically sited to prevent diversion of traffic onto other local roads. Road pricing in Trondheim has reportedly resulted in an 8 percent reduction in car traffic entering the cordoned zone and a 7 percent increase in usage of public transit (Johnstone, 1998).

The reported effects of Oslo's system on reducing traffic are more modest: a 2 to 5 percent reduction in traffic passing the toll points, but "not negligible when related to the general growth of car traffic" (Euronet, 1996). Similar positive impacts on public transit have also been noted: "There was an initial increase in the use of public transport during the first months after the introduction of the system. Levels of public transport use have now stabilized which should be viewed as a positive outcome, considering the significant drop in public transport use that was evident before the system was introduced" (Euronet, 1996). Most of the toll system revenue has gone for road and highway improvements (about 25 percent for public transit, 5 percent for bicycle paths), including a series of road underpasses, which supporters believe have reduced pollution and enhanced attractiveness of the city-center.

Road pricing has been widely endorsed in the United Kingdom and has emerged as a major plank in the Blair administration's policy. In December 1998, a national government consultation document ("Cutting Congestion—Improving the Environment") was unveiled. The British proposal would give local authorities the right to impose road pricing under the condition that the resulting funds generated be invested in public transit improvements. Especially in the U.K. context, there is a consensus that for road pricing to be at all effective requires concomitant improvements in public transit. A limited number of road pricing experiments have already been undertaken, and the next step in the U.K. strategy involves expanding and extending these trials. A nationwide road pricing network is envisioned for 2001 or 2002.

Estimates of the income to be generated by U.K. road pricing are considerable and could produce a significant injection of needed capital into transit systems. According to David Begg, who heads Edinburgh's Transport Committee, an annual income of £500 million (about US $800 million) would likely be generated, "enough to build the best transit system in Europe" (Johnstone 1998, p. 15). Major plans are under way to impose road pricing for the 4 million autos driving into or through London each day, creating badly needed funds for maintaining and improving London's city transit system, especially the underground Tube. Groups such as London First have conducted their own studies of road pricing and are lending political support.

A second major prong of the U.K. government's strategy involves taxing free company parking spaces in town centers. There are an estimated 600,000 such subsidized spaces in London, and a modest annual fee (£750 per year) is predicted to generate £300 million per year (or about US $500 million) (Williams, 1998).

Nevertheless, there has also been substantial political objection to road pricing and a spirited debate about its merits and likely efficacy. Conservative city councilors in cities considering road pricing, such as Edinburgh, have objected to it as a new "hidden tax" that will "devastate the economy of the city" (Scotsman Publications Ltd., 1998, p. 9). It has also been suggested that road pricing will induce companies to move out of cities or regions where it is utilized (*The Economist*, 1998).

Leicester, in the summer of 1998, completed one of the initial road pricing experiments, with results that have given hope that such economic instruments could indeed influence driving decisions. Experimenting with a group of 100 volunteer communities over a twelve-month period, the study results provide insights into what level of fee would be needed to change commuter behavior. Specifically, it was not until the road fees rose to £10 per trip (about US $16) that commuters began to change their behavior. At that point, some 40 percent of participants shifted to a park-and-ride lot or otherwise found another way to reach the city-center. The results, according to the city's transport special projects officer Eddie Tyrer, were very encouraging: "All our findings indicate that around 30 percent of commuter traffic—our target figure—would switch to another effective mode of transport if it was in place. We would need £250 million up front to implement our plans, which include another dedicated fast-track bus lane and a tram system into the city center" (Gill, 1998, p. 8).

The Dutch Ministry of Transport has been developing a road-pricing program since 1994, after having been specifically given this charge by Parliament. While a number of the specifics of the scheme have not been decided, many of its features have already been substantially developed. The essential idea behind the Dutch approach is that any automobile traffic entering any of the four major cities of the Randstad—Amsterdam, Utrecht, Den Haag, or Rotterdam—during the congested morning hours would be charged a fee. Under the current scheme, the charges would apply between 7:00 A.M. and 9:00 A.M., and would be 7 guilders (about US $3.50), or 5 guilders for those who pay electronically. Drivers would pay each time they entered the metropolitan area, so that if a particular person's commute took him through, for example, three of these cities, he would be assessed the fine three times (see Figure 5.3). The toll would only apply going into the city in the most congested corridors. There is also the expectation that some graduated fare system would be applied to the earlier and later hours of the morning, for example, a smaller fee charged between 6:00 A.M. and 7:00 A.M. and between 9:00 A.M. and 10:00 A.M., but nothing has yet been decided on this.

Easy, electronic payment of charges is a key feature of the Dutch system. It is envisioned that most cars will be equipped with an electronic box that will allow the driver to insert a chip card. Chip cards, or smart cards, have

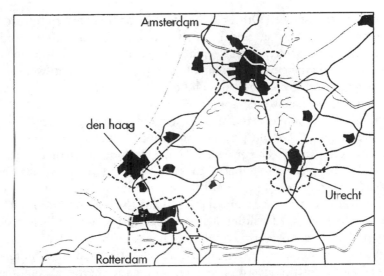

Figure 5.3. Dutch road-pricing scheme. Drawing showing zones around major cities of the Randstad

An extensive road-pricing system is under development in the Netherlands. Drivers crossing perimeters around the four largest cities in the Randstad—Amsterdam, Den Haag, Rotterdam, and Utrecht—would be charged a user fee, which would automatically be deducted by way of an electronic scanning device.

become very common in the Netherlands (indeed throughout Europe) and allow users to load them with money, which can then be used for a variety of functions, including making phone calls or paying for goods. The road-pricing system would work similarly. Drivers would insert the cards and the amount of the fare would be automatically deducted from the card as the cars pass under electronic scanning devices. The technology is apparently very reliable and the box would cost only about 100 guilders, suggesting that most users would find it cost-effective to purchase. For those without this equipment, the tolling stations would automatically videotape both front and rear license plates and the auto owners would receive a bill (at the end of each month) for the accumulated tolls. These systems work well even when cars are moving at high speeds (e.g., even at 200 kilometers/hour).

A unique feature of the Dutch system is that, in contrast to several of the Norwegian cities, the sole purpose of the fee is to reduce congestion, not to raise money to pay for road or auto-related infrastructure. Indeed, how to handle the revenue generated from the system has been a significant point of debate. Many believe the funds should be returned to car owners residing in the four cities, in the form of lowered car taxes. (This, by the way, is generally consistent with the Dutch government's push to move toward "variabilized" pricing for cars, giving breaks to those who drive their cars less frequently or less distance.) Others argue that the funds should go toward public transit or improving nonautomobile mobility options for residents. Returning revenues to residents becomes problematic when considering those who live outside the cities but commute into them each day, as well as those auto owners who live in the cities and do not pay the commuting fee, thus reaping what to some would appear to be an unearned benefit.

The proposed system has not been without its controversies. Concerns have been expressed about privacy and about the impact of steering traffic onto secondary roads. The project director responds to the first concern by noting that the piecing together of the data collected in the process of electronically charging the fare would require the involvement of several different government agencies, making it difficult, he believes, to invade one's privacy. The process of reading license plates and sending bills in the mail raises perhaps the most serious concerns. It is relevant to note, though, that this technology has already been in use in the Netherlands for a number of years without much concern. There are automatic speed-ticketing devices (which identify a speeding car, take a photograph of the license plate, and already numerous automatically send the offending vehicle owner a fine in the mail) on the main intercity highways in the country.

Concerning the potential generation of traffic on secondary roads as drivers look for ways to avoid paying the toll, the system planners are working hard to position tolling locations on many of these key secondary roads. The current plan envisions 100 tolling locations spread across the four cities, with 70 percent of them on secondary roads. So, it may in the end be quite difficult to avoid paying the fees. Nevertheless, the project director related the story of a tunnel toll in Rotterdam, which suggests the lengths to which many Dutch drivers may go to avoid paying a fare. In this particular case, the toll was only 2 guilders (about US $1), yet apparently people drove many kilometers out of their way to avoid the fee. Ironically, the project director notes that it may actually be this national character trait of frugality that makes these kinds of road-pricing systems so appropriate there.

One other problem involves how to handle autos licensed outside the Netherlands. How does the Dutch system handle a car with a German license plate? Dutch planners expect to be able to work with the other European countries to send out bills (albeit more infrequently than every month; perhaps even once a year) to these car owners. Another concern is the impact such a pricing system might have on discouraging business and employment activity in the city-centers. Will such a system further push economic growth, as well as population and housing, to outer, peripheral locations and to cities and towns outside of these four urban areas? Economic analyses prepared by the Dutch transport ministry show such impacts are unlikely, however.

This bold Dutch scheme was to be fully functional by 2001, but because of opposition by road-user groups and national elections, momentum has slowed. Rather than full implementation of the scheme, it is now expected that road pricing will first be tried in only one city in the Randstad (yet to be chosen).

Many other cities (and national governments as well) believe that some form of road pricing will eventually be necessary to address the increases in traffic. Currently, few European cities are using it (e.g., Bergen and Oslo), but a number of cities are experimenting, or soon will be experimenting with this technology (e.g., Leicester and Amsterdam). The success and functioning of road pricing remain to be seen, but clearly it could help to reduce car traffic, especially during peak hours.

Lessons for American Cities

These European cities represent an important laboratory for a variety of ideas and strategies for taming the automobile. A number of the traffic-calming techniques pioneered in European cities, for example, have already been extensively applied in many American communities. This trend will likely continue. A number of Americans have strongly embraced the notion of the Dutch *woonerf*, or shared streets, and its Danish, German, and British counterparts. Liebman (1996, p. 72) argues for the concept as one of several "good community-building ideas from abroad," and offers some suggestions about how shared streets might be created in American cities (see Masser, 1992; Southworth and Ben-Joseph, 1997). "If *woonerven* are to be accepted in the United States," Liebman observes, "they must be presented as an expansion of the legal rights of property owners" (Liebman, 1997, p. 72). He suggests that allowing for their creation by neighborhood petition could help to strengthen social cohesiveness.[3]

Ben-Joseph (1995) argues that the *woonerf* concept is adaptable to many suburban development settings and notes the high number of American cities that have already taken actions (or are in the process of doing so) to calm traffic along residential streets. He points to particular promise in applying the shared-street concept to neo-traditional or new-urbanist designs, arguing that it may serve as an important design modification to the grid street pattern typically argued for in such communities. "Shared streets in a connected system can eliminate the deficiencies of the grid. Speed will be reduced and through traffic by non-residents discouraged, yet connective factors such as access points and route choices will be much more numerous than in the typical hierarchical, discontinuous street systems. This design would thus combine a high degree of livability and safety in the residential streets while maintaining links to the larger neighborhood" (p. 512). *Woonerven*, then, might in many places be creatively used to promote and allow development connectedness (strongly argued for in

Chapter 2), at the same time that space is more efficiently used and the dangers of auto traffic reduced.

In addition, there is no question that many American communities are ripe for further traffic calming, and in many cities around the country the full array of European calming strategies are in use. There is every reason to think that these techniques will gain even further acceptance and application as more American neighborhoods clamor for protection from automobiles.

Cities such as Portland and Seattle, for example, have already been implementing fairly aggressive traffic-calming programs. Portland has a traffic calming section within its Bureau of Traffic Management and undertakes a number of initiatives, including a neighborhood traffic management program. It also maintains a citywide ranked list of streets, which it uses to guide traffic-calming improvements and investments. This city has made numerous traffic-calming investments already, including the installation of more than 60 traffic circles and some 500 speed bumps on many neighborhood streets (City of Portland, 1999). Similarly, Seattle has installed more than 200 European-style traffic circles and many other calming devices. Studies in these cities suggest that these investments can substantially reduce traffic speeds, reduce accidents, and enhance the livability of neighborhoods (City of Portland, 1999).

One uniquely American adaptation can be seen in Portland's Residential Speed Bump Purchase Program, which allows neighborhoods with streets low on the citywide list to fund their own traffic calming. Under this program, residents of a street pay for the cost of the speed bumps, going through a process in which the city's Traffic Calming staff prepare the project design, estimate the costs, and present and discuss their design work through a series of neighborhood open houses. A petition signed by two-thirds of the residents must be submitted to the city before the project can be built, and payment can be made through the formation of a local improvement district (or in any other way acceptable to the neighborhood; all residents need not contribute). Such a program (like the process for setting up Dutch *woonerven*) allows residents to take direct action and provides them with an option for bringing about traffic-calming measures when the local government may have insufficient resources.

Other American cities that might be offered as positive examples of traffic calming include Berkeley (California), Palo Alto (California), and Eugene (Oregon) (for a review of a number of American traffic-calming initiatives, see the National Bicycling and Walking Study, 1994). West Palm Beach (Florida) has undertaken a host of calming measures, using these improvements as effective techniques for revitalizing depressed neighborhoods in that city (Public Technology, Inc., undated). New York City has recently announced a major $80-million, four-year project to calm traffic near and around schools (Tri-State Transportation Campaign, 1998). Also, for the first time, under the new federal transportation bill ("TEA 21"—a reauthorization of ISTEA), federal funds will now be available for local traffic-calming projects. American cities may have new opportunities, then, for undertaking creative strategies for reducing the impact of cars.

In the American context, clearly it is difficult, for many reasons already discussed in this book, to break out of the automobile-dominated mind-set. Perhaps uniquely American is the extent to which the movement of cars and vehicular traffic is seen as the almost singular legitimate form of transportation and mobility policy. A careful examination of the language of transportation planning demonstrates this. Creatively, one recent impressive example of an attempt to modify language (and thus attitudes and perspectives) can be seen in the unusual "City Transportation Language Policy," adopted by the city of West Palm Beach. The policy states the city's intention to change official uses of language as a step toward becoming a more sustainable community. The policy attempts to replace pro-automobile language with language that is more "objective" and more "inclusive of all of the constituents and modes of transportation" (City of West Palm Beach, 1996, p. 1). The word *improvements* is often attached to descriptions of road projects, for example, and will be replaced with more neutral and descriptive words, such as *modification*. *Upgrading* (as in upgrading streets) will be replaced with *widening* or *changing*. *Enhanced level of service* will be replaced by *changed level of service*. *Traffic demand* implies a "sense of urgency" and will be replaced by *motor vehicle use*. Common references to bicycles and walking as *alternative modes of transportation* imply that they are nontraditional or nonconventional (and thus of less importance or value) and will no longer be made. This is one very thoughtful window of analysis into the many pervasive ways in which unsustainable behaviors and policies are often reinforced through language.

The European inroads and innovations in road pricing may be particularly applicable to the American market approach taken to planning and public policy, where guidance by economic signals and incentives is often preferred to direct regulation or intervention. Some American cities are already using road pricing, albeit to a more limited degree than envisioned in Europe (we tend to refer to it as "congestion pricing" in the United States). In fact, road pricing—or congestion pricing—got a major push from ISTEA (the Intermodal Surface Transportation Act of 1991), and more than $30 million has already been spent on a series of congestion-pricing pilot programs. Pilot initiatives have been under way in a number of cities around the country, including San Diego, Houston, Minneapolis, Portland, and Boulder (CO), among others. For the most part, these programs have been successful, and they demonstrate the considerable potential of road pricing as a traffic management tool in the United States (see

Wahrman, 1998). A number of these pilot efforts have created "HOT" lanes—high-occupancy/toll lanes—that permit either ride-share cars or single-occupancy cars for a fee. In Orange County (California), Express Lane tolls on State Road 1 operate in this way. A major communting route, these lanes have been popular and have significantly reduced commute times and improved traffic flow.

San Diego has gotten much attention for its dynamic road-pricing arrangement on a stretch of Interstate 15, where during certain high-volume times of the day drivers can pay a premium fee (which can be adjusted every 6 minutes) to utilize special Express Lanes (*The Economist,* 1998). Like the European systems described here, on-car transponders automatically deduct the toll charge, which normally ranges from 50 cents to $4.00. An Express Bus service has also been created as part of the scheme (see Federal Highway Administration, 1998).

Particular U.S. cities and regions may be more ready for congestion pricing than others. As Wahrman (1998) notes, acceptability will likely be high where bridge and road tolls are already in use (e.g., as in the Houston area). Nevertheless, congestion pricing will be viewed by some as an additional tax and as an interference with personal freedoms associated with unfettered auto use.

Congestion pricing met a political death in Minneapolis, and the experiences there illustrate both the obstacles faced in applying this idea and some strategies necessary for overcoming opposition. The experiment in that city—an express pay lane on Interstate 394—was cancelled in response to overwhelming negative public opinion. One of the local proponents of the experiment there, reflecting on the opposition, believes the lessons learned are clear: build support with business and political leaders, make a compelling case for the pricing scheme, address the perceived equity issues (the project was seen as benefiting the rich), and choose an appropriate road or highway on which to demonstrate the idea (I-394 presented different enforcement issues) (Blake, 1998). Starting with a relatively expensive monthly fee was also viewed as a detriment in Minneapolis.

These experiences, along with other road and bridge tolls applied around the United States, suggest that American drivers would be willing to pay the requisite fees. It is unlikely, though, that limited experiments such as those in San Diego and elsewhere will by themselves significantly reduce overall traffic or car use. More comprehensive urban (and regional) schemes will be needed, and road-pricing represents a potentially significant traffic management tool only when coupled with other elements of a sustainable mobility strategy. A key element must be the availability of alternatives to driving at all, again raising the importance of safe, attractive, fast public transit.

Another important mobility option Americans should have is the ability to join a car-sharing company or club. We know that when individuals own cars, there is a tendency to want to use them. By providing the option of using a car only when really needed (and in the face of rising costs associated with roads and highways), there will tend to be fewer cars on the road, and public transit, bicycling, and other mobility options will likely be strengthened. While car-sharing has not yet caught on in North America, there is tremendous potential here. Wagner and Katzev (1996) argue that "there has never been a better time to initiate a car sharing organization [like ATG, the Swiss car-sharing company] in the U.S." (p. 13). Car-sharing has been quicker, albeit still limited, to establish itself in Canada. Two such organizations have existed in Quebec City and Montreal, with a small combined membership (in 1996) of about 200. More recently, car-sharing experiments have been started in several other North American cities, including Portland (Car Sharing Portland), Seattle (Seattle Car Sharing Project), and Victoria, B.C. (Victoria Car Share Co-Op). One possible adaptation to American circumstances includes the range and type of vehicles made available. Car Sharing Portland has recently added a pickup truck to its fleet of vehicles, perhaps a necessary concession to the American penchant for hauling large things from place to place. With Swiss consultants, the Portland pilot program appears to be well-modeled after European ideas. Its car locations include spaces near MAX light rail stops, as well as near important destinations and a downtown location within Portland's so-called "fareless square"—an area where transit services converge and where riding transit is free (Car Sharing Portland, Inc., undated).

NOTES

1. The six working groups include the following: cycling and walking, commercial traffic, commuting, public transport, practical alternatives to the car, and use of less polluting urban vehicles. Each working group is chaired by a specific European city.

2. Lightfoot (1996) concludes that car-sharing potential is high, "particularly in overcrowded regions with well-developed public transportation" (p. 8). Proximity to a car-sharing location appears to be an important factor to potential subscribers. An obstacle to be overcome is the fixation on the materialistic ownership of cars. As Lightfoot notes, "The transition from the passion for car ownership to the emotionally less binding car usage . . . does not come easily to many in a society which feels obligated to materialistic possessions" (p. 16).

3. Liebman (1996) identifies several mechanisms that might be used. A *woonerf* could be created through petition, through residential community associations, or through street privatization. "In the short run, the Dutch mechanism [of petition] is simplest and results in 'stronger social cohesiveness, much brought about by the involvement of the residents themselves in a sophisticated process of planning their own surroundings'" (p. 72).

Chapter 6

Bicycles: Low-Tech Ecological Mobility

Bicycles as a Legitimate Form of Mobility

There are few mobility options more environmentally-friendly than bicycles. They are zero emission, take up relatively little space, are inexpensive, are available to the young and old alike, and provide their users with important physical exercise. In the United States and many other developed countries, we have ignored or forgotten this relatively low-tech mobility option. Yet, in many northern and western European cities, bicycles are a significant and legitimate mobility option and an increasingly important part of the transportation mix there.

Bicycle use as a percentage of the modal split is consistently much higher in most of the cities examined in this study and vigorously promoted as a more environmentally friendly mode, which provides greater mobility than the automobile (especially for shorter distances). Most of the cities studied here have developed, and continue to develop, extensive and impressive bicycle networks. Berlin has 800 kilometers of bike lanes, and Freiburg has 410 kilometers. Vienna has more than doubled its bicycle network since the late 1980s and now has more than 500 kilometers. Copenhagen has about 300 kilometers of bike lanes and now has a policy of installing bike lanes along all major streets. Bicycle use there has gone up 65 percent since 1970. These cities show commitment to making bicycle use easy and safe, and they reveal the key ingredients to building bicycle-friendly cities.

Bicycle use in these exemplary cities is a year-round proposition. Summer use of bicycles is usually higher in northern cities such as Copenhagen, where some 40 percent of work-commutes are by bicycle during these months (Bjornskov, 1995; Murphy, 1996). Nevertheless, in Copenhagen

Delft, Netherlands, has created a fine-mesh system of bikeways and lanes throughout the city that connects all neighborhoods and major destinations. To create this system, the city undertook a series of bridge and underpass improvements (such as shown here).

some 70 percent of those normally bicycling also bicycle to work during the winter months. Similar experiences can be found in Finnish cities, suggesting that the notion that bicycling is feasible or acceptable only in ideal weather conditions is untrue. That such high rates of usage can be achieved in northern European cities suggests great promise for American cities. And, while bicycles are especially promising for shorter distance trips, it is clear that many people are prepared to ride their bicycles considerable distances. It has been estimated that in Copenhagen, an average bicycle commute is 7 kilometers, or about 20 minutes—many commutes are longer, which indicates that many residential areas will, given facilities and safe routes, be within a reasonable bicycle commuting range.

Bicycle-Friendly Cities

The cities studied here have achieved impressive rates of bicycle use. In Freiburg, bicycle use accounts for 28 percent of all trips (an increase from 18 percent in 1976), and in Münster 34 percent of trips made daily by residents occur on bicycles. In many cities in the Netherlands, it is not uncommon for the bicycle share of the modal split to approach 40 percent and even higher for shorter distances. In Groningen, a university city in the north of Holland, the percentage of trips by bicycle in the city-center is about 60 percent, and about 50 percent for trips between 2.5 to 5 kilometers (Ministry of Transport, Public Works, and Water Management, 1995; Welleman, 1996).

What explains the ability of these cities to achieve such high bicycle use? First, these cities have shown a willingness to make the basic investments necessary to make roads and the urban environment accommodating to bikes. Many Dutch cities, such as Utrecht, Amsterdam, and Leiden, rely heavily on bicycle mobility and have taken many actions to promote and facilitate their use. These actions typically include extensive bicycle trails and separated bicycle lanes, often with separate traffic signals. The city of Delft has undertaken a comprehensive program for creating a fine-mesh bicycle network, linking virtually all major destinations in the city. Over a five-year period, the city undertook a series of improvements and investments, including creating new cycle lanes and constructing bridges and tunnels to connect routes (Municipality of Delft, 1984). Bicycle usage went up (now at about 43 percent of trips), trip length went up, and injuries and fatalities went down (see Ministry of Transport, Public Works and Water Management, 1995).

Few developed nations place as much emphasis on bicycles as does the Netherlands, of course, and from this country much can be learned. There are 17 million bicycles nationally: more bicycles than people. And, among European nations, the Netherlands has the highest proportion of bike lanes and paths, some 20,000 kilometers (out of a total of 110,000 kilometers of streets and roads; Welleman, 1996). Nationally, about 27 percent of all trips are made by bicycle and about 40 percent for trips shorter than 2.5 kilometers. The Dutch government has embraced the bicycle as a major element in solving its mobility programs in the future, and the Second Structure Scheme for Traffic and Transport set down the goal of increasing bicycle use by 30 percent by 2010. A national bicycle plan has been prepared, and significant national subsidies have gone toward improving bicycle facilities and enhancing bicycle safety.

One can very quickly appreciate the ease of bicycle-based mobility by spending time in virtually any Dutch city. My own freedom of movement, speed, and ease of getting about in Leiden demonstrated this. Bicyclists there, as in most Dutch cities, have their own lanes and signaling, and direct routes to all major destinations in the city. Traveling by bicycle is clearly the fastest and easiest way of getting somewhere, and extensive bike connections between cities (and between cities and surrounding countryside) make bicycle mobility a realistic option even for longer distances.

Dutch cities like Leiden also have an impressive degree of spatial connectedness between the city-center and outer suburban areas. From this city's residential suburbs to the south, for instance, it is a quick bicycle ride by way of separated bicycle paths to the historic core, with separate bicycle signaling and protected lanes even around traffic circles or roundabouts, which are common in the Netherlands. Virtually all of the city's residential areas are similarly connected by such bikeways. Traveling from the doorstep of one's home, through one's neighborhood, to a main bike thoroughfare, and then arriving at a center-city office or store, is relatively fast and effortless.

In Leiden's outer residential areas (built to much higher densities than American suburbs), extensive bicycle and pedestrian connections have been designed into the spatial fabric from the beginning. A primary spatial planning feature of such neighborhoods is the high degree of pedestrian and bicycle connection and integration. There appears a conscious effort not to block or close off pedestrian/bicycle movement between housing blocks and neighborhoods, but to permit and encourage it as a general planning rule.

Extensive bicycle parking facilities are common in the Netherlands (e.g., at train stations and public buildings), as are facilities where bicycles, for a minimal fee, can be left in a protected and locked facility (something like valet parking for bicycles). One of the most creative new bicycle facilities can be seen in Tilburg, where a modern underground facility has recently been built. Providing a secure parking area (for 50 cents a day, or a very modest 40 guilders a year [about US $20]) and even a walking sidewalk to the lower level in the very center of the city, it is but a few meters away from shops, stores, and restaurants. This new bicycle garage has a capacity of 3,000 bicycles and also provides needed employment for residents. In Groningen, there are a large number of indoor bike parking facilities—some twenty facilities (most of them operated by the same organization) allow customers to pay a small yearly fee (25 guilders), entitling them to park at any of the locations. Many cities are gradually converting spaces for auto parking to spaces for bicycles. Utrecht has discovered that it can fit six to ten bicycles in the same space it takes to park one automobile. It has begun installing new bike lockers, using car spaces to do it, and has already installed ten such lockers in an area north of the old city.

Considerable bicycle investments and innovation can be found in Danish cities as well. Odense has been experimenting with some interesting strategies for bike parking, including several types of bike racks, including one which incorporates clinging vegetation and one which gives the option of a ring-chain that ties into the typical built-in rear wheel lock present on most European bikes.

There are examples of cities that have substantially retrofitted the urban landscape to better accommodate bicycles. Århus has undertaken an impressive reorganization of traffic flow in and around its center to give bicycles greater space and more priority (Århus Kommune, 1997). Specifically, it has created a network of streets where auto traffic has been restricted to one way and where bicycles are given priority and allowed to travel in both directions (See Århus Kommune, 1998). Auto traffic along these one-way streets has also been significantly calmed, with speeds

Safe, secure places to park bicycles are essential and Dutch cities typically provide extensive parking facilities. Shown here is a new underground bicycle parking facility in the Dutch city of Tilburg.

restricted to 15 kilometers/hour. On these bicycle-priority streets, a special protected lane has been created for bicycles moving against the direction of cars. What results is a bicycle-priority circle around the center, and a series of six gateways into the center. New bicycle-priority logos have been installed on the surface at intersections marking the beginning of the bicycle-priority streets, as well as crossbands at certain intervals (the design is essentially a concrete slab with a circle and an "X" in the middle of it). Other elements of the redesign include taking away some auto parking on the one-way streets and increasing parking facilities for bicycles. Signage marking the new bicycle routes has also been installed, showing (among other things) connections to regional bike routes.

Not only are many of these cities doing their best to make the existing urban environment bicycle friendly, but great sensitivity is also typically given to incorporating bicycles from the beginning into the design of new developments and housing estates. This is especially apparent in the Netherlands, where new VINEX sites typically include in their spatial designs both extensive internal networks of bikeways, and direct bicycle connections with the existing city. The importance placed on connections can be seen most clearly in the new Leidsche Rijn development in Utrecht. Here the design includes an extensive system of bike lanes throughout the new district and a bicycle-only bridge linking the district to the Utrecht city-center. These features are common in Dutch developments. As another example, the new growth district of Nieuwland, in Amersfoort, gives similar prominence to bikes, including a bike and pedestrian–only bridge providing a direct route to Amersfoort centrum.

Many of the other new Dutch districts discussed at other points in this book further exemplify this designing-in of bicycles from the beginning, including the new town of Houten and the Amsterdam district Nieuw Sloten, among many others. Again, many community sustainability features—such as greater emphasis given to bicycle use—are made considerably easier because of the emphasis given in Europe to creating more compact urban forms.

In the Netherlands and in Denmark, most major public facilities or destinations, such as train stations, provide large amounts of bicycle parking (although it never seems to be enough). In many of these cities, large percentages of people riding public transit ride their bicycles to the station. In Copenhagen, for example, about half of the train commuters do this. Even higher percentages are evident in other Dutch cities, making the provision of safe and convenient places to park bicycles essential. A number of cities have also placed bike facilities at key bus stops (these facilities include bike lockers; users rent them for a monthly fee and have their own key). This is another demonstration of the importance of integrating transport modes and the need for smooth transition from one mobility mode to another.

A sea of bicycles are parked outside a Copenhagen train station. Multimodal trips are common in European cities. Extensive bicycle parking facilities provided at train and transit stations help to make this possible (though there never seem to be enough spaces).

Many German cities have made impressive strides in promoting bicycle mobility. Münster is one of the clear leaders. The city has implemented one of the most aggressive and successful programs for expanding bicycle use. Following the war, bicycles fell out of favor in Münster and the auto gained considerable ground. Interestingly, bicycles were seen more as an impediment to the smooth and efficient flow of auto traffic, and a less-than-supportive attitude characterized city decision makers during that period. During the late 1970s and early 1980s, the bike went through a bit of a renaissance in Münster, marking the beginning of the city's support of bikes and consideration of them as key component of the mobility equation. By the 1980s, the city had developed a real bicycle program.

Münster's efforts to lure people out of their cars and back onto bikes are impressive. Generally, the city's program can be characterized not as one single action—no silver bullet—but rather as a series of many steps taken over a considerable period of time. Many improvements in the bike system have cumulatively added up to make Münster an extremely bicycle-friendly city.

Several creative strategies have been used by Münster to strengthen and promote bicycle use. Much attention has been made to gradually and impressively expanding the facilities and network available to bicyclists. Münster has 250 kilometers of bike lanes within the developed city and another 300 kilometers of agricultural bikeways outside the urbanized area. The city has a marvelous bicycle/pedestrian-only ring-promenade, which circles the city and permits bicycles to reach the city-center quite easily. Together, these improvements have resulted in a "network of integrated bicycle paths" (Pucher, 1997, p. 26).[1] Efforts at traffic calming have clearly helped as well. Many of the residential areas in Münster has been designated 30-kilometer/hour restricted speed zones, and there are plans to expand the area substantially in the future.

The city provides several types of bike lanes and routes. One type is a lane, essentially carved out of the public sidewalk, with a vivid brick pattern that alerts pedestrians to it. This seems to work quite well and to maintain sufficient sidewalks for the pedestrian traffic. In many places, bicyclists have their own traffic lights, and in some places double red (stop) emblems appear for added effect and safety. At some intersections, bicyclists are given priority in the form of an advance green light, allowing them to comfortably start out through the intersection before worrying about cars from behind. In addition, some intersections are designed to allow bikes to move ahead of cars, with cars being required to stop further back from the intersection.

In the future, the Münster bicycle planners see the need to funnel traffic along major bike roads, feeding into the bike and pedestrian promenade, which circles the city. The promenade will (and does) act as a kind of ringroad or expressway for bikes entering the old city. Bicycles enter from a number of feeder routes and then use the road to move circularly around the city.

One issue has been whether a mixing of bike and bus traffic should be permitted. There is a recognition that there is simply not enough space in the city to allow buses to have their own lanes. So, in the Münster tradition, a period of experimentation ensued—for one year, it was tried on several streets and a study was conducted. The idea was found to work, so the mixing of buses and bikes has occurred on certain roads for about five years now. Under this scheme, on certain four-lane streets there is a lane of car traffic on each side and a lane for both buses and bikes (buses basically are allowed in bike lanes).

In Münster, increasing the use of bikes is seen as an effective strategy for getting people out of their cars. This increase in bike use, rather than expanding or promoting greater bus ridership, is seen as the answer. The reason? As one of the city's bike planners explained: bikes and cars are more interchangeable in the sense that each is a freedom-enhancing kind of vehicle—each can allow the individual to go when and wherever they wish. The bus, the major form of public transit in Münster, is simply not perceived in that way.

Another important strategy has been to give bicyclists flexibility that car drivers do not have. One of the important initiatives has been a program to provide bikes with short-cut routes. The basic idea here is to provide bicyclists with as attractive and short a route system as possible. To do this, the city has taken a number of actions, such as allowing bikes to go down one-way streets in the opposite direction and allowing bikes to continue beyond dead-end streets. Many streets have signs showing certain restrictions on motorized traffic, which are followed by an emblem of a bike and the word *frei*—indicating that bicycles do not have to abide by that particular traffic restriction. Bikes, for instance, do not generally have to pay attention to one-way streets (e.g., they can go down a one-way street the wrong way; this is called *Unechten Einbahnstrassen* or "unreal one-way streets").

In Münster, development regulations now require bike storage facilities for new multi-family developments. Specifically, such new developments are required to incorporate a minimum number of bike spaces: one bike space required per 30 square meters of housing area. The city has also issued guidelines to developers educating them on where and how to build the parking facilities.

Parking for bicycles has been a significant problem in Münster, and the city is looking for ways to increase bike spaces. It has several large projects in the works, including a plan to build a 3,000-space facility at the main train station. The city also tries to get the word about bicycles out to new residents and to interest them in using this mode of transport. Among these residents are the some 6,000 new students who come to town each year. The city sends these new residents a brochure touting the benefits of bikes. Other bike-supportive activities of the city include the convening of "bicycle days": a bicycle congress and exhibition that convenes every two years.

Münster is also helping other cities and towns in its region develop their own bicycle systems. The *Länd* (state) in which Münster is located, North-Rhine Westfalia, has implemented a program called "bicycle-friendly towns" through which Münster was asked to share its experience with bicycle planning and to assist other jurisdictions in developing bike programs. Among other actions, this länder program provides a subsidy for communities wishing to build bike lanes.

Other German cities have made similar progress, although few can match Münster's efforts. Promoting and facilitating bicycle use is another key component of Freiburg's transportation strategy. Indeed, just as Freiburg sees itself as the solar city (see Chapter 9), the bicycle also seems intimately linked to the city's self-image. This city has also dramatically expanded its bicycle network since the 1970s. The mid-to-late 1980s especially saw the development of a comprehensive system of bike lanes and facilities. This system includes separated bike paths, bike lanes on streets, and large areas of the city that have been traffic-calmed (a very high percentage of the city has been converted to 30-kilometer/hour speed restricted zones—some 90 percent of the city's population now lives in these areas). There are currently 410 kilometers in this bike system.

Freiburg has similarly suffered from insufficient places to park bikes. Over time, the city has converted auto parking into bike-rack areas. The city has expanded the number of bike spaces from 2,200 in 1987 to 4,000 in 1996. The city has also started a bike-and-ride program by providing bike racks, some with roofs, at tram stations (bikes are not permitted on trams because of limited space, although this was tried for a time).

One of the more interesting bike projects in Freiburg was the special addition of a bike path along the Dreisam River, connecting peripheral areas to the city-center. A significant engineering feat, the paths are even subject to occasional flooding. Some 15,000 bicycle journeys per day have been recorded on this path. Other projects include a major city bridge that has been converted from auto use to bicycle and pedestrian-only use, and

In Münster, Germany, bicycle mobility is enhanced through a bicycle-expressway that circles the city.

the design of the city's new train station, which will incorporate important bike-friendly design features including valet-checking for bikes (they admit that this idea came from the Dutch!). The station will also include a bike repair shop, a tourist office for bicyclists, and a café and meeting place.

The city has also created a special bike fund. Much (about 50 percent) of the funding of new bike lanes and facilities has come from the länder government (although this funding ended about three years ago). Freiburg officials are understandably proud of what has been accomplished in a relatively short period of time (Heller, 1997):

> One main finding to emerge from twenty years traffic planning in Freiburg is that the role of cycle traffic in reducing individual traffic in urban areas is being underestimated. On a well laid cycle path network, for distances under five kilometers, cycles are a serious competitor to cars. In Freiburg the cycle path network has been continually expanded since the seventies, an investment of 30 million DM has enabled an extension of the cycle path network from about 30 km in 1992 to about 150 km bituminized cycle paths today. In addition, there are 250 km graveled cycle paths, which are being used increasingly by commuters from small towns to the east and west for the daily journey from home to work. The funds allocated to

the maintenance and extension of the cycle path network come to about 5 million DM per year. In order to solve the special parking problems for cyclists, approximately 3000 new bicycle parking spaces have been made available, and a special cycle port is under construction at the railway station to enable train passengers a direct transfer. Whereas the city LCTS (local commuter transport system) projects require a long preliminary planning period and involve substantial investment costs, even in the inner-city area, the new construction and improvement of cycle paths is possible with considerably lower costs which, in terms of cost-benefit, can hardly be surpassed. (p. 8)

American transportation researcher John Pucher reports dramatic increases in bicycle ridership in a number of German cities, including Bremen and Munich, as well as the more notable examples of Münster and Freiburg. He concludes that conscious public policies explain the increasing use of bicycles in these cities. German cities are doing many things: building integrated networks of bikeways (many are grade-separated from auto traffic) and bike paths, providing extensive new bicycle parking facilities (in city-centers and at train stations), improving bicycle signage, and giving bicyclists priority over cars, among other actions. "The German lesson is that bicycling can be increased even under quite unfavorable circumstances, provided the right public policies are implemented" (Pucher, 1997, p. 44).

Pucher argues that corresponding efforts to calm auto traffic and discourage use of cars have been equally important to creating bicycle-friendly environments in German cities. Extensive traffic calming, higher costs imposed on using automobiles (e.g., higher parking costs and high gasoline taxes—more than $4 per gallon in Germany), and restrictions on new road building are important ingredients: "The end result of all these auto-restraint policies is to make auto use more expensive, more difficult, less convenient, and slower than it used to be. That has increased the competitiveness of alternative modes such as public transit, walking, and bicycling" (Pucher, 1997, pp. 43–44). And there is no question that the large college student populations in cities such as Münster and Freiburg have made it easier to bring about higher levels of bicycles use because students are more likely to use bicycles and to support political candidates who support bicycle investments.

Interestingly, even those cities among the study group that are most auto dependent, are increasingly viewing bicycles as a significant part of the solution to future mobility needs. In London, for example, a London Cycling Campaign and the development of a London Cycle Network have been under way for some time. Even business groups such as London First are calling for a significant increase in bicycle use. Efforts continue to build the London Cycle Network (an idea dating back to the Greater London Council). Originally, the concept was to include a star-shaped network of 1,000 miles of bikeways. The concept has recently been resuscitated and expanded to 1,500 miles of a strategic network (a connected regional network). (Significant new funding for the boroughs for this purpose was provided in the mid-1990s.) The network remains incomplete and uncoordinated in many ways, but considerable new interest in bicycles as a legitimate mode of transportation in London is encouraging.

Dublin has recently completed an ambitious new cycle plan, calling for, among other things, the creation of a 130 kilometers bicycle network, with major new commuting routes leading into the center of the city, and a modal split target of 10 percent (from its current 5 percent; see Dublin Corporation, 1997). Already, the city has taken a number of steps to promote greater bicycle use (e.g., the provision of cycle parking in car parks and shower and changing facilities at civic offices). These cities show that bicycles can in fact represent a viable (and significant) mode of transportation and that cities can take a host of actions (many not very complicated) to entice their use.

Leicester has established the goal of increasing the percentage of home-to-work trips by bicycle to 10 percent (from the current 3 percent). While the modal split for bicycles is still low, bicycle use is reported to have risen by 50 percent from the late 1980s. Leicester has also gradually tried to expand bike facilities. One of the most dramatic recent examples is the near completion of a bicycle facility at the city hall. This underground facility will have places to store bikes, as well as changing and shower rooms for those riding into town. The city also provides some innovative incentives for riding one's bicycle. It is now the city's policy to encourage the use of bicycles for official council business; to that end, the city provides its employees with the same per-mile rate of reimbursement for bicycle use as for auto use. The city's bicycle-friendly employers program provides businesses with grants of £1,500 (about US $2,400) for the construction of bicycle facilities, and six employees have already received such grants (see Leicester City Council, undated-a). Environ, the environmental charity in Leicester, also sets the lead on this issue, providing its employees with, among other things, a £50-per-year (about US $80) bicycle maintenance payment.

Public Bikes Programs

The idea of public bicycles—bicycles that might be picked up and used by anyone who needs one then deposited back where it was found when the user is done—was born in Amsterdam in the 1960s. It was the brainchild of Luud Schimmelpennink, who had written a provocative magazine article proposing that 25,000 free bikes be made available as part of a strategy for making Amsterdam car free. He dubbed them "white bikes" or *witfietsen.* Schimmelpennink and others simply painted some bikes white and put them out on the street for public use. The year was 1965, and relationships with local police were not so good. The experiment never really had a chance to work because most of the bikes were confiscated by the police before the idea could be tested. Schimmelpennink has never forgotten this idea and has, as discussed later, developed yet another, more sophisticated version.

There has indeed been a resurgence of interest in the white bike concept in Europe, and a number of cities have developed programs, including cities in Scandinavia (Copenhagen; Sandiness, Norway), Germany (Mannheim, Hannover, Berlin), the United Kingdom, Austria (Vienna has indicated its intention to establish a 3,000-bike program), France (La Rochelle), and the Netherlands.

Taking the original lead from Amsterdam, the city of Copenhagen has been operating for several years a program it calls City Bikes. More than 2,000 public bikes are now found at 150 locations around the city and can, with the deposit of a 20 kroner coin (about US $3), be used within the city-center. The bikes are brightly painted, with companies paying for the bikes in exchange for the right to display advertising on them. The bikes are geared in such a way that the pedaling is difficult enough to discourage their theft. The program has been a success, and the number of bikes has been gradually expanded each year. On any given day, a visitor will find the bikes in heavy use. A Danish newspaper monitored one of the public bikes for a twelve-hour period and found that it was idle in a rack for a mere eight minutes (O'Meara, 1998). An initial problem encountered was the considerable pounding the bikes took, which surprised city staff. In the words of Nicolae Plesner, the program coordinator, "We expected people to treat them better." Over time, the bike frames have been strengthened (Knowlton, 1995; Murphy, 1996; City of Copenhagen, 1996).

The advantages and limitations of the Copenhagen approach were demonstrated on a recent trip to the city. One morning, late for a train that I needed to catch at the Central Station, I hurriedly used one of the public bikes at a stand near my hotel. Depositing the 20 kroner coin, I took a bike, which got me to the train in the nick of time. Especially for this kind of trip, the bikes are very effective, providing a kind of instant mobility that no other mode can offer.

The downsides of the Copenhagen program are also evident. The most significant limitation is the frequent inability to find a bike when you need

Copenhagen's public bikes program, called "City Bikes," has been highly successful. A recent tracking of one of these bicycles found that it sat idle a mere 8 minutes over the course of a 12-hour period.

one. The sight of people riding or walking with the brightly colored bikes is ubiquitous, but their popularity means that they are very hard to find, at least during the tourist season. A second dimension is the fact that many of the bikes that one does find are often in some state of disrepair. I found that the seats are particularly prone to being broken, and there is the real sense that the bikes are subjected to some rough treatment in their daily and nightly use.

Several problems also relate to the deposit stands, where one can pick up and return the bikes. At a number of these stands, vandals had broken off the ends of the locking chains, which are inserted into the returned bike to get back the 20 kroner deposit coin. Also, in a number of places, the high volume of bike traffic meant that private bikes were being locked to the public bike racks. Perhaps this is as much a positive as a negative, yet in places there was often little room to park the public bikes once they had been returned.

These problems point out the importance of reliability. If the system is to work, especially if auto drivers are to leave their cars at home, there needs to be some reasonable assurance that a public bike can be found. On my recent visit, the continued lack of locating an available (unbroken) bike did adjust my expectations and behavior about getting around the city. If bikes are never available, people will tend not to rely on them, and other mobility options will be taken (including autos). Nevertheless, the Copenhagen experience demonstrates convincingly that public bikes (with perhaps more bikes rather than fewer) can enhance tremendously personal mobility.

Other impressive public bikes initiatives exist. The Dutch have been creatively using a similar public bikes strategy for mobility within parks. One impressive example is the Hoge Veluwe national park near Arnhem. Here, access to the interior of this 5,500-hectare park is not possible by car. Rather, free white bikes are provided, and visitors travel through the park on a network of low-impact bike paths. Upon arriving at the park by car, visitors have no choice but to shift to bicycles if they want to experience the natural interior of this beautiful landscape. Riding the white bikes around the park is a marvelous experience. The park's wide vistas, heather, dunes, and quiet solitude are complemented well by the bikes. They are quiet, they encourage a slower appreciation of these surroundings, and they allow for stopping, resting, and wildlife watching along the way. The impact on the parkland itself is minimal—a series of narrow bike paths, with a limited sense of intrusion on this ecosystem. At the same time, visitors are encouraged to get some exercise.

Luud Schimmelpennink, the white bikes guru from Amsterdam, has never really lost his interest in promoting the public bikes notion. The most recent and fascinating reincarnation is seen in the Depot concept that

The only way to see the Hoge Veluwe National Park in the Netherlands is on bicycle. Visitors arrive by car and must shift to one of these free white bikes.

Here, children and adults alike enjoy the quiet (car-free) environment of the Hoge Veluwe National Park.

Schimmelpennink and his Y-tech company have been working out for Amsterdam. The Depot idea is to provide a series of bike depots or stations, strategically placed around the city, with each holding an average of seventeen bikes. The user arrives at an electronic kiosk, with a map indicating the locations of other depots in the city, and books a reservation to use a bike to travel to one of these other locations. If there is a spot available to park the bike at the destination depot, the ride there is free. If not, the cost is 2 guilders (about US $1)—the necessary charge for Y-tech to ferry the bike to another depot where it is needed. To release the bike, the user must insert a chip card or smart card, and the required fee, if there is one, is deducted from it. No trip should be longer than thirty minutes—if it is, then an additional charge of 5 Dutch cents per minute is applied.

For the last two years, the Depot system has been in pilot trials in Amsterdam. The depots have been functioning with about twelve bikes in use. The pilot efforts have generally been successful, although there have been thefts of some bikes, requiring some additional redesign of the depot locking mechanisms. The system is now being installed, with 45 depot sites and 750 bikes in use by the end of the year 2000. Eventually, the sites will be distributed throughout the city and will involve perhaps 5,000 bicycles in total.

The bikes are very sturdy and relatively easy to pedal. They are equipped with an easily adjustable seat and front and rear lights (the lights come on automatically, and the rear lights flicker when a kiosk booking is completed to show the user which bike to take). The cost of the bikes is about

A new white-bikes system is currently being tested in Amsterdam. The Depot system shown here will allow a rider to take a bike from one depot or bike station or another, either free of charge or for a small fee, depending on the time taken for the trip and the number of bicycles already at the destination station.

Luud Schimmelpennink, shown here, is the creator and driving force behind the depot public bikes initiative in Amsterdam. Schimmelpennink initiated the original white-bikes idea in Amsterdam, and so the depot concept is a natural extension of his ideas and work.

1,200 guilders (US $600) apiece and are specially made by a company in Eindhoven.

One interesting idea is how these Depot bikes can be integrated with other modes of transportation. Arrangements have already been made with a car-sharing company (and with the city to provide the car spaces) to provide car-sharing cars through the Depot kiosks. In fact, the electronic kiosks are equipped with a series of circular key-holding devices that will actually dispense car keys. The cars will be located at each depot site. The city has already given permission to designate two car-sharing spaces at twelve depot locations. The depot idea has been supported financially by the national government and has received strong political support from the city. The city's transit agency also views the bikes as an extension of public transit services.

Building a Bike-Riding Culture

In many ways, these bicycle-promoting cities have also helped to nurture a culture that values the bicycle and sees it as a legitimate form of mobility. One interesting pilot program called Cykelbus'ters was undertaken in Århus, Denmark, with funding from the Danish Transport Council and the Danish Environmental Protection Agency. The city offered a series of incentives to a selected group of 175 city residents in an effort to induce them to change their mobility behavior away from automobile use to bicycles and public transit. Specifically, under the pilot program these participants were given a new bicycle, which they could select from a local shop, and which they had the option of purchasing later. Bikes could be valued to 4,000 Danish kroner, or about US $570 (with a 1,000 kroner deposit required of each participant), and participants would also receive unlimited maintenance, rain gear, and a one-year public transit pass. The initial pilot project lasted a year (from April 1995 to April 1996). Participants agreed to try to use their bicycles and take the bus as much as possible (signing a contract with the city), and agreed as well to keep trip diaries and to monitor and record travel by different modes (each bicycle was equipped with a computer and participants were asked to send in readings each week, as well as car odometer readings and used bus passes; see Bunde, 1997).

By all measures, the experiment has been a success. The 175 participants, described as "habitual car drivers" and chosen from 1,700 interested people, have substantially changed their behavior and lifestyle. Most finished the program (only sixteen dropped out because of a change in location of home or work). Evidence at the end of the year suggests that bike ridership grew dramatically (six times the average summer biking rate, three times the average winter biking rate), public transit use grew sharply, and the use of automobiles was reduced by half (Århus Kommune, 1997). Big questions remain, of course. Will the change in behavior last over time, and what are the city's next steps to extend the idea beyond this small group of volunteers? This remains to be seen.

There are a number of lessons apparent from Cykelbus'ters. The first is that people may need incentives to change their lifestyles and that it is not just a matter of issuing lofty pronouncements. In the words of the project director: "It has been no use telling people to go buy bikes. Our idea then was to make cycling to and from work as attractive as possible and thus create an example for others" (as quoted in Århus Kommune, 1997, p. 5). Another lesson is that working to improve the city's environment to make it more friendly to bicycling is an important corresponding step, and the city has taken some impressive steps in this regard as mentioned earlier.

A number of cities and local authorities have developed programs to work directly with employers and businesses to encourage bicycle commuting. The London Cycling Campaign has implemented, for example, an "Employers Campaign" in which a small number of employers helped to identify obstacles to bicycle commuting.[2]

A number of communities in the Netherlands are also implementing "Cycle to Work" campaigns, but with an interesting twist. In the Southern Province of Zeeland, about 100 companies (and some 3,000 individuals) are participating in such programs, with considerable benefits both in terms of car traffic reduction and reduction of carbon dioxide emissions. The program has resulted in an estimated 800 fewer tonnes of carbon dioxide being pumped into the atmosphere (in 1997). Another powerful twist to this program is that about one-third of the companies are also contributing to a Climate Fund, their contributions based specifically on the amount of bicycle commuting done by their employees. The fund is managed by an environmental organization called Ecooperation, which funnels the funds to several Third World countries to finance projects that help to compensate for the excessive carbon dioxide emissions of northern countries. In 1997, 60 million guilders were generated from the program (about US $30 million), and the program is viewed as an important mechanism "to compensate for the inequitable distribution of the environmental space" (VROM, 1998, p. 8).

Lessons for American Cities

How many of the bicycle ideas discussed in this chapter could actually be applied with success in American cities, and how feasible is it to expect

American cities to significantly increase their reliance on bicycles for mobility? Pucher, in his study of the rise in bicycle use in many German cities, concludes that the main explanation is a matter of public policies and conscious commitment to bicycle improvements (Pucher, 1997). He refutes many of the conventional reasons offered for why bicycles will not be used or ridden. He observes, for instance, that the weather conditions are often the worst in those cities where bicycle use is the highest (worse conditions than in most American cities). Flat topography certainly helps in countries such as Denmark and the Netherlands, but he notes much higher rates of bicycle travel even in the more mountainous European countries such as Switzerland and Austria. It seems clear that there are few compelling reasons why American cities cannot also achieve similar results. His conclusions are important to keep in mind:

> The main reason for differences in the level of bicycle use is public policy. In the United States, very little has been done to promote bicycle use. . . . In the Netherlands, Denmark, Germany, and Switzerland, by contrast, various levels of government have constructed extensive systems of bikeways and bike lanes with completely separate rights of way. . . . In short, bicycling has been thriving precisely in those countries that have adopted policies to make bicycling, faster, safer, and more convenient. . . . Bicycling remains at low levels in U.S. cities because cyclists are treated as second-class travelers, somehow not worthy of their legal right to share streets with cars. At the same time, there are few separate bikeways where bicyclists would be better protected from inconsiderate motorists. (p. 44)

Along with important improvements in bicycle networks and facilities, another important European lesson is the corresponding importance of controlling auto usage and taking actions to discourage or make more costly the continued reliance on this mode of transport. Indeed, increases in gas taxes and other auto-restraints (already discussed in other chapters) may not be politically popular, but they clearly would help to level the mobility playing field and make bicycle mobility a more attractive option. Pucher, in his study of German cities, emphasizes the important role of such restraints:

> Without restricting auto use, policies to encourage walking, bicycling, and taking transit would have been far less effective. Conversely, only restricting auto use would not

have worked either, since travelers obviously need an alternative mode of travel if they are expected to drive less. The combination of the carrot-and-stick approaches has produced very impressive results in German cities. Not only has it shifted modal split in favor of public transport and bicycling, but the increased taxes on auto drivers have been the ideal source of revenues for financing improvements in public transport, bicycling, and pedestrian facilities. (1997, p. 44)

How bicycles can become a more significant part of the daily lives and lifestyles of Americans is a complex question to answer. It is perhaps useful to remember that a number of American cities, especially smaller and medium-sized university towns, have had long bicycling traditions. While the experiences of such cities—places such as Davis, Eugene, and Boulder—are easily dismissed as unusual, they do demonstrate that given the right circumstances and the right investments in bike infrastructure and facilities, considerable utilitarian bicycling can occur in American cities.

Many larger American cities have begun to make significant new commitments to bicycle mobility. Cities such as Portland have made significant progress toward creating a bicycle-supportive city. In Portland, there are now 240 kilometers of bikeways and the city has also adopted minimum requirements for bicycle parking in all new commercial parking garages (one bicycle space for every twenty auto spaces; O'Meara, 1998).

With the impetus and stimulation of the Intermodal Surface Transportation Efficiency Act (ISTEA) of 1991 there have been tremendous new bicycle improvements and initiatives undertaken around the country. In many ways, the case can be made that American cities are on the verge of major advancements in bicycle use. The amount of nonrecreational bicycling that already occurs in American cities in the face of poor facilities and an unsupportive culture is remarkable. A recent survey of residents of Washington, D.C., for instance, found that an incredible 20,000 of them commuted to work each day by bicycle.

Incredibly, even cities such as Houston have developed and are implementing impressive plans for creating citywide bicycle networks. In Houston's case, it broke ground in the fall of 1997 on an ambitious 360-mile system. As the *Houston Chronicle* reported, "A cyclist will be able to pedal the entire length and breadth of the city, largely avoiding the worst traffic dangers" (Feldstein, 1997, p. A37). The system includes a mix of bike/hike trails (63 miles) along abandoned railways and bayous, designated bike lanes, and bike routes. Chicago, as well, has made great strides, including

Several U.S. cities have made great strides in becoming more bicycle-friendly. Boulder, Colorado, is one such city and has been building impressive bicycle underpasses, such as the one shown.

hiring a bicycle coordinator, adding new bike lanes (38 new miles in 1996 alone), connecting abandoned rail lines, and adding some 650 new bike racks each year (with a total of 5,240—more than any other U.S. city; Gregory, 1996). And cities such as Washington, D.C., are beginning, through grassroots works by bicycle advocates, to develop a system of bicycle trails and routes, albeit still in a rudimentary stage.

Some of the lessons of European cities—the importance of connectedness and the designing of new developments from the start to accommodate bicycles—are ripe for learning in the United States. New housing developments in outer Virginia suburbs in the Washington region (e.g., in Loudoun County) are failing even to provide direct bicycle connections *where trails already exist!* Such connections could and should be both required during local planning permit review, and seen as a feature that new residents will appreciate and value. And, ideally, there must be leadership at regional levels to ensure that a logical, workable system of trails and bikeways exists to which connections can be made.

Only a handful of American cities, typically smaller cities, have achieved conditions of bicycle ridership and mobility approaching the European examples described here. Bicycle use has reached impressive levels, for example, in Davis, California, with an estimated 20 to 25 percent of daily trips made on bicycles, an extremely high percentage by American standards. Davis, helped by its large student population, has incorporated bicycles into its planning in some very important (and European-like) ways. Davis requires all new developments to be connected to one another and to a greenway/bikeway system that extends through much of the city. An important objective is that elementary school children be able to travel by bike from their homes to schools and parks without having to cross major roads (or generally deal with car traffic). In building a connected system of bikeways and bike routes, the city has taken a number of fairly aggressive actions, including buying and demolishing a home in order to create an important bicycle linkage to an elementary school. The city has constructed a number of bicycle underpasses and intersections with separate bicycle turning lanes and lighting. There are extensive bicycle racks located at virtually any major building or street location, and the city now imposes a minimum bicycle parking standard for new development. Several bicycle-only bridges have been built, along with a number of bike tunnels from the main city core. One problem area has been Interstate 80 (a six-lane interstate highway), which separates the southern part of the city. Already, a major bridge over the highway has included both a generous bike lane and a separated pedestrian bikeway. Additional I-80 bike overpasses are also planned (one of which will be bike-only, at a cost of $2 million).

The cultural dimension must not be overlooked, of course, and riding a bicycle to work is still perceived by many in the American general public as difficult and/or something done by a bunch of environmental crazies. In the United States especially, it seems that businesses must play an important role if bicycling is ever to seriously gain importance. So much of American life is focused around the work environment, and the importance of signals sent by employers should not be underestimated. While some examples can already be cited of companies taking the lead, a major push will be needed in every locality to enlist the enthusiasm and active participation of the business sector.

Especially on the mean and pervasive streets of the United States, it seems, citizens are understandably intimidated by the hazards and difficulties of bicycling. We must accept that major increases in bicycle use will not occur simply through the installation of bike lanes and trails alone, but like many of the sustainability ideas discussed in this book, they will require citizens to learn new skills. Consequently, and especially in the absence of a strong bicycling culture like that in the Netherlands, American cities must spend considerable energy helping citizens to learn these new skills of a more sustainable lifestyle. One creative idea has been implemented in Washington, D.C. There, many residents would like to commute to work by bicycle but find the challenge of doing so to be too daunting. A call to the Washington Area Bicyclists Association, however, will result in getting hooked up with one of their 100 bicycle mentors, who will provide advice, technical guidance about strategies for navigating the car-dominated land-scape, and moral support. This kind of sustainable lifestyle mentoring, in which people learn the skills to live differently (and to do things they often already want to do), is probably essential to overcome the inevitable feel-ings of uncertainty, inertia, and even fear. Of course, many other changes are needed to promote bicycle commuting, and many other policies and actions can be undertaken to enhance bicycle use (from subsidies to park-ing to bicycle-friendly businesses).

It is, however, a legitimate question whether Americans and American culture will ever see the same level of bicycle ridership as in these most impressive European cities. I am optimistic, despite the cultural circum-stances of the United States that tend to work against bicycle use: heavy dependence on the auto, a high percentage of the population overweight and out of shape (more reason to emphasize bicycles), an emphasis given to convenience, and a heavy cultural emphasis on work (and getting to and from work in the most seemingly expeditious manner), among others.

Obstacles to bicycling are often greatly overstated. Safety is certainly a significant concern—both to policymakers and to bicyclists themselves—and localities must continue to enhance both the actual and perceived safety of bicycling. And it should be kept in mind that studies show that the health benefits of increased ridership and increased life expectancy more than outweigh the dangers (see National Bicycling and Walking Study, 1994).

In the U.S. context, it may also be politically necessary to emphasize the public cost savings of shifting (partially) to bicycle use. Providing new parking facilities for bicycles is dramatically cheaper than providing new parking spaces for cars (an estimated bike cost of $50 to $500 per parking space compared to $12,000 to $18,000 per car space in a parking garage; World Watch Institute, 1999). Tremendous public cost savings ($100 bil-lion) from even modest shifts to bicycle use (a 5 percent shift in miles) have been estimated (see World Watch Institute, 1999).

Particularly promising are the possibilities of shifting from car to bicy-cle for shorter trips and for linking bicycle and transit usage. As the National Bicycling and Walking Study indicates:

> . . . more than a quarter of all travel trips are one mile or
> less, 40 percent are two miles or less, almost half are three
> miles or less, and two-thirds are 5 miles or less. Moreover,
> 53 percent of all people nationwide live less than two

miles from the closest public transportation route, making a multimodal bicycle- or walk-transit trip an attractive possibility. (National Bicycling and Walking Study, 1994 executive summary, p. ix)

The white bikes, or public bikes, idea also holds promise. Already, a number of American communities have started public bike programs, an idea that seems to have considerable appeal and attractiveness. The actual implementation of public bike programs has had a checkered experience so far in the United States. The yellow bikes program in Portland was by most accounts a disaster—most of the completely free bikes were vandalized, abandoned, or stolen (Mudd, 1998). The program has started up again, however, now with more than 1,000 bikes and with some important changes, including bikes using women's frames and welded parts: "The theory being that most thieves are men who would rather not be seen riding a girlish bike" (Mudd, 1998, p. 52).

Boulder (Colorado) has had the largest of such programs, and by many accounts the most successful to date. Its program, called Spokes for Folks, which began in 1994, involves putting out each spring about 125 lime green bicycles, equipped with functional baskets in the front, which carry the rules of the program. The cost of the effort is minor, as the bikes are mostly donated and local high school students restore, paint, and maintain them. Because of the winter weather in Boulder, the bikes are collected in late fall, with few of them lost or stolen. Interestingly the city also maintains an informal policy of finding a bicycle for any citizen who needs one. Jan Ward, the city's coordinator of Spokes for Folks, maintains a storage area where such bikes are collected and dispensed.[3]

The American and European approaches to public bikes programs, then, are quite different. There is simply no real comparison between, for example, the Copenhagen City Bikes program and any of the American programs. The American efforts involve older bikes, generally fewer in number, and simply placed in prominent places for the taking with no deposit required, no real system of depots, and no clearly understood arrangement for where to find the bikes. In short, a well-designed experiment, with specially designed bikes, a meaningful deposit, and a significant number of available bikes has yet to be tried in an American city. The interest in public bikes expressed by so many cities suggests there is considerable political and popular support for this idea.

Some argue for collective bike programs more uniquely adapted to an American culture "short on trust." As one organizer suggests: "Perhaps we should adopt a more American version of a community bike program, with controlled sign-out and deposit points" (Mudd, 1998, p. 52). Minneapolis/St. Paul has indeed initiated such a program where public bikes are

A public-bikes program called "Spokes for Folks" has been successfully operated for several years in Boulder, Colorado.
Source: City of Boulder.

checked out of specific, controlled locations, such as banks and bookstores. Participants are issued a yellow bike card and a key when they submit a liability waiver form and a $10 refundable deposit. This would seem a sensible adaptation in many places.

One issue that may be unique to American cities has to do with legal liability. City attorneys in Boulder argue that requiring even a small deposit would open up the city to liability claims should users be injured or killed. Thus, the bicycles must be completely free. The legal arguments, however, are unconvincing, and the issue is worth further study. More limited bicycle-lending initiatives, where a bicycle can essentially be "checked out" of a library or other public place in exchange for some form of deposit, is one way around this. At the same time, borrowers can be asked to sign a liability waiver form.

In adapting bicycle transport to the American scene, one potentially powerful idea is to more effectively promote the use of electric bicycles. The electric bicycle has the advantage of overcoming many of the real (or perceptual) problems of bicycle use in the United States. They would allow many Americans to overcome the limitations of topography, distance, and weather. They provide a partial answer to the problem of those needing to wear office attire and the desire not to arrive at work as a bundle of perspiration (shower and changing facilities would also address the problem, of course). Significant technical improvements in electric bikes have been made, and now several major manufacturers make them.

One of the most interesting local electric bicycle programs can be found in the city of Palm Springs, California. Here, funding for the Electric Bicycle Demonstration Program (its formal title) has come from a grant from the South Coast Air Quality Management District. Under the program, the city has made available about thirty electric bikes to residents to borrow and to try out for a month. To borrow one of the bikes, a citizen must put down a small deposit, go through a brief training program, be willing to maintain a daily trip log, and at the end fill out an evaluational questionnaire. The program uses bicycles from four different manufacturers. Creatively, the city has installed four solar charging units (including at the regional airport and on the roof of city hall); thus, the bikes have become known as "solar bikes."[4]

The demonstration project has recently ended, and the last group of participants finished their time on the bikes. City officials feel the program has been successful, and indeed it has already been emulated in several other places. Interest in the bikes has been high, and participants have ranged in age from 18 to 80 (City of Palm Springs, 1998). Experience in Palm Springs shows that even in this very hot climate, bicycling is possible, at least with the power assist given by electric bikes. In the words of one participant: "I

Palm Springs, California, completed an unusual Electric Bicycle Demonstration Program, under which citizens can borrow bikes and try them out for a month. A series of solar-electric charging stations, such as the one shown here, have also been installed in key locations around the city. Shown here are Angelo Pappas and Marjorie Kossler, participants in the program.
Source: City of Palm Springs, Electric Bicycle Demonstration Program.

have a very short commute, and in the hottest parts of the day you just use the electricity and a little less pedaling" (Haberman, 1997, p. B3). The electric boost helps solve the problem of arriving at work drenched in perspiration. And, it provides an important mobility option to elderly residents and those with health problems. Similar electric bike initiatives, then, may represent an important adaptation to the American cultural context, as well as to the weather and topographic conditions in many American cities.

These and other promising experiences suggest that American cities and towns can and should be much more bicycle friendly. Bicycle travel can become, as it has in many of the European cities examined, a legitimate and important mobility option and part of a sustainable healthful lifestyle.

NOTES

1. Pucher (1997) elaborates on the elements of this network: " . . . with most paths separated from both auto and pedestrian traffic. Münster even has a tree-lined bicycle expressway (7 meters wide, 6 km long) that encircles the city along the route of the medieval city wall. It provides direct connections with 16 major bike routes radiating to outlying portions of Münster, its suburbs, and the surrounding countryside, which is also crisscrossed by a dense network of integrated bike paths. The same bicycle expressway also connects with 26 bike paths leading inward toward the town center and the Cathedral Square. In addition to 252 km of separate bike paths, bicyclists benefit from over 300 km of bike routes over lightly traveled roads restricted to local traffic. Finally, most residential streets in Münster can be safely used by bicyclists, thanks to traffic-calming measures that give pedestrians and bicyclists right-of-way priority and restrict auto speeds to 30 km per hour (19 mph)" (p. 26).
2. Interestingly, a survey of potential riders was conducted with results suggesting that there are some misimpressions about the pros and cons of bicycle commuting. The survey found that the weather was overestimated as a likely problem in bicycle commuting. Even though local weather data suggest that riders can be expected to get very wet from rain on an average of twelve days a year, the survey respondents estimated this number to be much higher. By far, the most significant obstacle preventing bicycle use identified in the survey was "dangerous roads" (cited by 62 percent of respondents).
3. From an interview with Jan Ward, Spokes for Folks coordinator, July 1998.
4. The solar charging units were funded through a grant from Sun Utility Network, Inc. In conjunction, the city has also installed twenty-four fully enclosed coin-operated bike lockers.

Part IV

Green, Organic Cities

Chapter 7

Urban Ecology and Strategies
for Greening the Urban Environment

Cities like Forests

Cities can be fundamentally greener and more natural. Indeed, in contrast to the historic opposition of things *urban* and things *natural*, cities are fundamentally embedded in a natural environment. They can, moreover, be reenvisioned to operate and function in natural ways—they can be restorative, renourishing, and replenishing of nature, and in short like natural ecosystems: cities like *forests*, like *prairies*, like *wetlands*. The urban greening and urban ecology initiatives in many European cities provide positive and creative examples of ways in which cities might aspire to this reconception.

It is, perhaps, surprising how much nature already exists within relatively dense European cities. In cities such as Berlin and Heidelberg, there has emerged a significant diversity of plant and animal life. In many derelict or abandoned sites, complex plant and animal communities and unique biotopes have emerged. Nature emerges between buildings in interior and courtyard spaces and on rooftops.

A number of strategies for protecting and promoting green have been pursued by the European cities studied here, many of which could be applied in American cities. One approach has been to mandate a high degree of green and nature-enhancing features as part of new development or redevelopment schemes. Many examples can be cited of new development projects that will incorporate, or have incorporated, extensive natural areas in close proximity to residents, while at the same time accommodating a relatively high density of people and development. In part, this is

Many European cities own large forests and greenspaces, such as the Vienna Woods shown here. These are often easily accessible through public transit (the area shown here is a few minutes walk from a Vienna tram stop).

made more feasible by the higher degree of control the public exercises over the design and planning of new development and redevelopment projects (down to the point of specifying the number and location of trees and vegetation on a building plan).

Natural Capital of Cities

Many of these European cities have a long history of protecting extensive systems of open space, woodlands, and natural areas in close proximity to urban areas. Many are structured around the notion of open space fingers, or wedges, that penetrate (or nearly so) urban centers. Another important point is that largely as a result of the density, compactness, and design of European cities, residents have phenomenal access to large areas of open space and nature. As already noted, it is a relatively easy and quick trip by public transit to major areas of greenspace in cities such as Vienna and Stockholm. Helsinki also has an extensive system of greenspace, with the large Keskuspuisto central park penetrating into the heart of the city. This park extends in a mostly unbroken wedge, from the center to an area of old growth forest to the north of the city. It is 1,000 hectares in size, and 11 kilometers long (Association of Finnish Land Authorities, 1996).

In many cities, the percentage of land area that is open and serves as greenspace is quite high. In Vienna, some 50 percent of the city's land area is in greenspace, with 18 percent in forests. About one-quarter of Zürich's land area is in forests. In Graz, 53 percent of the city's land area is in forest or agricultural use. Of Heidelberg's 108 square kilometers of land area, only 29 square kilometers is actually built up, with most of the remaining land consisting of open uses of forests and agriculture (about 40 percent of the total land is in forests). Bologna has set aside its large southern area of hills as a protected greenspace and has delineated an extensive greenbelt on the northern side as well. Less than half of Berlin's 890 kilometers of urban area is built upon. Berlin owns some 10,000 hectares of woodland, or about 18 percent of the land area of the city. These areas are strongly protected under the Berlin Forest Act (City of Berlin, 1996). Leicester's land use plan protects nine open space wedges (which include farmland, wetlands, and public recreational areas; Leicester City Council, 1994).

To be sure, many of these cities have taken special efforts to understand and live within their regional ecological conditions. Scandinavian cities such as Stockholm are highly water dependent and have in the past caused substantial water quality degradation. Rejuvenation of Lake Mälaren, the city's main source of drinking water, is a great success story, in large part because of significantly increasing the treatment by the city's waste treatment plants (especially reducing emissions of phosphorous). The city has also prepared a comprehensive plan for lake restoration and management and uses this plan in making local development decisions.

A major part of Berlin's ecological context is its dependence entirely on a local groundwater source. The city has taken great strides to protect and safeguard this source, including careful monitoring of groundwater, provisions to safeguard groundwater (e.g., during construction, such as that occurring at Potsdamer Platz), and programs to gradually remove impervious surfaces in the city as well as to promote conservation and rainwater use, among others.

Ecological Networks: National and Urban

Many European cities are attempting to bring nature into the city-center and to develop physical and ecological connections between built-up areas of the city and surrounding natural areas and greenspaces. Corridors and ecological connections can be found to various degrees in a number of these cities. Helsinki's central park, as one important green finger, penetrates well into the city-center, and Stockholm's Royal Ecopark (former royal hunting grounds)—a 10-kilometer long greenbelt around and within the city-center—provides significant "wildness" in close proximity to urban residents (City of Stockholm, 1997). In 1995, the ecopark was designated through an amendment to the Natural Resources Act as the country's first national city park (and possibly the first in the world).

There is also a trend in the direction of creating and strengthening ecological networks within and between centers. This is perhaps most clearly evident in Dutch cities, where extensive attention to ecological networks has occurred at the national and provincial levels. Under the national government's innovative nature policy, a national ecological network has been established (see Phillips, 1996), which must be more specifically elaborated and delineated at the provincial level. Cities, in turn, are attempting to orient their own planning and development decisions in order to tie into this network and build upon it. At a municipal level, such networks can consist of ecological waterways (e.g., canals), tree corridors, and connections between parks and open space systems. Dutch cities such as Groningen, Amsterdam, and Utrecht have a full-time urban ecology staff and are making concerted efforts to create and restore these important ecological connections and corridors. The new Dutch town of Almere has made some of the most significant progress at building ecological networks, with most residents in this new town only a few hundred meters from extensive greenspaces and a short bike ride from large restored areas of wetlands and wildlife. Similar urban ecological networks have been developed or are under way in German and Scandinavian cities. Many of these cities are recognizing the need to view urban parks and nature in a more integrated, connected fashion.

At the national and continental levels, Europe provides other important examples of the visualization and creation of broader ecological networks. There are a number of efforts under way to protect and restore biodiversity in Europe (see Phillips, 1996). These efforts include the Pan-European Biological and Landscape Diversity Strategy and the development of a European Ecological Network (a concept known as "EECONET"). In addition, under the European Union's Birds directive and Habitat directive, member states are required to set aside protected areas that will comprise Europe's "Natura 2000" (a "representative network of protected sites"; Phillips, 1996, p. 82). A number of European nations have developed, or are in the process of developing, their own national ecological networks (see Jongman, 1995), which would ideally fit within these broader continental "visions."

The most developed of these networks is the national ecological network adopted by the Netherlands as a key component of its Nature Policy Plan (see Van Zadelhoff and Lammers, 1995). As a densely populated nation, the Netherlands has experienced tremendous stresses on its natural environment and indigenous biodiversity. To address this situation, it has taken the tremendously impressive step of preparing a national Nature Policy Plan. At the heart of this plan—based on preserving and connecting large blocks of remaining natural land and representative sets of ecosystem types of regional, national, and international importance—is a *national ecological network* (see Figure 7.1). Based on extensive background studies, a map delineating a "coherent and robust" ecological network was prepared, which serves as the framework for national regional and local conservation actions. Several categories of designation are included on the map. "Core" areas are existing natural areas of at least 500 hectares in size that are viewed as biological "hot spots, capable of recolonizing surrounding smaller ecosystems" (van Zadelhoff and Lammers, 1995, p. 80). "Nature development" areas are areas suitable for ecological regeneration or restoration, often farmlands that can be converted to wetlands or woodlands.

Ecological corridors intended to provide connections and migration opportunities between core areas are also included on the network map. In practice, these corridors are likely to be "hedgerows, dikes, banks of waterways and roads, etc." (p. 84). Buffer zones are also viewed as an important part of the network but are not delineated on the national map. For each category, the map delineates more land or area than the final network will include. This is to allow flexibility in acquiring or redeveloping lands, and it anticipates the working out of greater detail at the provincial and local levels. Indeed the network has provided important input to provincial and municipal land use plans. The Dutch Parliament adopted the Nature Policy Plan (with the ecological network) in November 1990 and has substantially increased national funding for its implementation (shortening the implementation time to twenty years and doubling the annual funding allocation).

In mapping the national ecological network, it is understood that more land is included at this national scale than will actually be secured and protected. For nature development areas, about three times the actual target is contained on the national ecological network map; for core areas, about twice as much land is indicated. Under the Dutch scheme, it is in more detailed provincial plans that decisions about which actual lands will be secured and what specific boundaries will be set are to be made. About 10 percent of the network will be made up of land currently in agricultural use (Van den Brink, 1994).

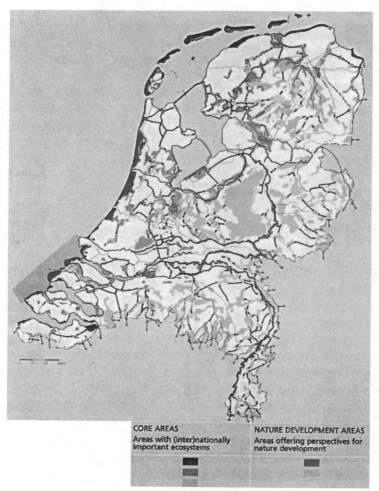

CORE AREAS
Areas with (inter)nationally
important ecosystems

NATURE DEVELOPMENT AREAS
Areas offering perspectives for
nature development

Figure 7.1. Dutch national ecological network

The national ecological network for the Netherlands. Arrows represent ecological corridors to be developed; those having dashed lines are concerning transboundary nature areas.

Source: Møller, M.S. 1995. *Nature Restoration in the European Union*, Ministry of Environment and Energy, Denmark.

Implementation of the Nature Policy Plan, and realization of the national ecological network, will require a variety of public actions and projects, including acquisition of lands, agreements with farmers willing to support nature values, and other implementation instruments (Van den Brink, 1994).

Van Zadelhoff and Lammers insightfully note the considerable political benefits of concretely delineating such an ecological network on a map and providing defined ecological targets. They identify the following political benefits:

> The concept of a coherent network, visualized in a clear, attractive map appears to be a unifying and stimulating concept in several ways:
>
> - to politicians as a clear, offensive strategy with not only problems but also solutions.
> - to the public as a clear message: the ecological network or a social feedback to a nature-hostile society.
> - to scientists as a stimulus for cooperation and to present scientific information in a way that can be effectively used in decision making by politicians.
> - to local initiatives, lifting local plans to a higher level as part of a national network.
> - Network ideas are now being developed and implemented at European scale. (p. 86)

The national ecological network places clear spatial parameters on planning and development at lower jurisdictional levels. Each provincial government must work out the more precise details in its own provincial nature policy plan, and local planning must build upon these regionally specified networks. Under the national nature plan, most development or alteration of lands within core areas or development areas is prohibited.[1]

Reimagining the Built Environment: Organic, Living Buildings and Urban Landscapes

European cities offer many positive examples of efforts to incorporate green features and nature into the design of the built environment. One of the key notions behind rooftop gardens, greenroofs, greening courtyards, and other urban green strategies is necessary compensation for the loss of greenspace brought about through urban buildings and development. In Europe, one of the early advocates of this kind of ecological compensation through greenroofs and green buildings was Austrian Friedensreich Hundertwasser. An ecological architect and artist, his wild designs remain exemplars of how otherwise gray and brown urban landscapes can be fundamentally transformed (see Rand, 1993). The most significant and widely seen built example of his work is the Hundertwasser Haus in

Vienna. A building of social flats owned by the city of Vienna, Hundert-wasser has transformed it into a green flowing piece of urban nature. The building reflects Hundertwasser's basic belief that there exists an obliga-tion to replace every bit of nature taken in the process of construction and city building. The result here is an extensive set of roof gardens and ter-races, and windows overflowing with trees and vegetation. In Hundert-wasser's words: "Everything horizontal under the sun, under the open sky belongs to nature. Roads and roofs should be planted with trees. It must be possible to breathe forest air in the city again . . ." (Rand, 1993, p.146).

Other key concepts in the Hundertwasser philosophy include the notion of *tree tenants*—the idea that every window ought to have a tree growing out of it. In the Hundertwasser Haus design, every flush of the building's toilets waters these trees. Another of his ideas is the *window right:* the right that each tenant has to change the facade of a window (as far as they can reach out and around the window). (The latter is actually included in apartment leases, although such modifications apparently also require city approval). Other features of the Hundertwasser Haus include a winter gar-den, which is common space in the building, an adventure room with an undulating floor (popular with the children in the building), and the exten-sive use of recycled materials (such as bricks from demolished buildings and recycled tiles). The exterior of this and other Hundertwasser buildings are colorful and daring, including the extensive use of colored tiles, upside-down cones and columns, and windows of many different shapes and sizes. The result of Hundertwasser's work is a unique and stimulating mix of the natural and the artistic. The house remains an early example of how build-ings and urban structures can contribute to the greenness of cities rather than detract from them.

The tangible forms that greenness and strategies for naturalizing cities take are varied and diverse. Many of the cities examined have, for exam-ple, made impressive efforts at urban tree planting. There are some 400,000 trees in Berlin alone. Indeed, flying into Berlin one gets a feeling (at least in spring and summer) of descending into a green oasis, not a heavily urbanized city. Freiburg has substantially increased its number of trees in the last ten years, now numbering about 25,000. Erlangen has planted some 30,000 trees since 1972 (Deutsche Umwelthilfe, 1991). Cities are also implementing a variety of landscaping and greening stan-dards. Many of the cities have specific tree planting standards. In Graz, for example, new parking areas must include trees at the rate of one tree per every three spaces.

Many positive examples can be cited of new housing projects that incorporate trees and vegetation as major design elements. One example is the GWL-terrein project in Amsterdam. Here, the trees are planted in main courtyards, surrounded by a shallow layer of brick, and given ample room for aeration and water. The design and planning of streets and roads can also offer many opportunities to incorporate trees and greenness. The Dutch have been especially creative at planting trees in the streets. In this way, trees have both a greening and a traffic-calming function.

The *woonerf* concept, or shared-street concept (discussed in Chapter 5), utilizes trees and vegetated areas as a technique not only for slowing traffic, but also for greening the street. Many examples of streets in cities such as Den Haag (e.g., Statenkwartier) can be cited where trees have been planted a few feet into the street and between on-street parking. In Utrecht, the Het Groene Dak housing project has taken a creative approach by planting trees and vegetation in a certain number of on-street parking spaces. By determining that fewer cars than average were owned by residents of the project, and by convincing the municipality to reduce the parking required, these unneeded spaces became green areas instead. Projects such as Het Groene Dak illustrate the potential for accommodating substantial urban density (sixty-six units per hectare in this case) while minimizing paved surfaces and creating delightful green and wild spaces in an inner communal garden.

Efforts have also been made in many of these cities to avoid large areas of paving or hard surface without trees and vegetation. Unlike many typical American parking lots, for example, the parking lots in these cities typically include tremendous trees and shading. Notable examples of city parking lots with a high tree density can be seen in Odense and Saarbrücken. Very often permeable brick or paving material is also emphasized. A positive example of green parking lot design is found in Leiden along the street Hooglandsekerkgracht, a very urban street with a center island devoted to about fifty parking spaces. With wide crowns and strategic spacing, virtually all of the parking is shaded by eighteen relatively large trees during the summer, which provides another important element of green in this otherwise dense urban environment.

Greenroofs: Creating Meadows in the Sky

Greenroofs, or *eco-roofs* as they are sometimes called, have become increasingly common in Europe, especially in Germany and the Netherlands, and provide many benefits over conventional roofs. Among their key advantages are the protection they provide from UV rays and the ability to extend the life of a roof, the ability to cool the urban environment (addressing the urban heat island effect), carbon dioxide sequestration, the control of stormwater runoff, and the provision of significant habitat, especially for plants, invertebrates, and birds. Butterflies have been found in U.S. studies to visit rooftop gardens as high as twenty stories. German studies have demonstrated a considerable biodiversity on greenroofs there (Mann, 1996). While the short-term cost of a greenroof may be higher, these costs can be more than outweighed by the added life of the roof.

Greenroofs can also provide extensive added insulation (as high as a 10 percent increase, according to Johnston and Newton, 1997). There are also public relations benefits to be had: "Green roofs clearly attract interest and usually result in a positive image for those organizations that instigate them" (Johnston and Newton, 1997, p. 50). It has been estimated that a rooftop garden in Britain may add between 10 percent and 30 percent to the market value of a building (Letts, 1998). A more complete set of advantages (and disadvantages) is presented in Table 7.1 (from Johnston and Newton, 1997).

Traditionally, two styles or types of greenroofs are distinguished—*intensive* or *traditional* roof gardens, and *extensive* or *ecological* rooftops. The former—typically referred to as *roof gardens*—include structures that can accommodate deep soils, trees, and shrubs, and deeper-rooted vegetation. Because of the depth of the soil cover required for intensive roof gardens, additional structural reinforcement is typically needed, as well as more active and intensive management. Extensive rooftop systems—or *ecological roofs*—typically involve coverage of the entire rooftop with a relatively thin covering of soil and vegetation. These kinds of rooftops are generally designed to involve little maintenance and few inputs and can even be installed on rooftops with a considerable pitch to them (roofs of up to 30 percent slope, according to Thompson, 1998).

The aesthetic benefits should not be underestimated. Several recent German examples visited by the author illustrate the visual difference such roofs can make. In the Cosmos building in Saarbrücken, a simple linear greenroof can be impressively viewed by offices on several higher floors. There is a remarkable feeling of looking out over a farm field or pasture, in this example. Green roofs have the potential to make a tremendous difference in the visual landscape and qualities of cities. As one British observer notes "It's depressing to look round a city and see so many grey spaces. People are starved of greenery. This puts a little back" (Ambrey, 1994, p. 3). The Saarbrücken energy company building ("the building of the future") also has a green rooftop, largely planted in flowering plants.

Table 7.1. Roof Gardens and Green Roofs: A Comparison

ROOF GARDEN INTENSIVE *traditional* Deep soil, irrigation system, more favorable conditions for plants.	GREENROOF EXTENSIVE *ecological* Thin soil, little or no irrigation, stressful conditions for plants.

ADVANTAGES
• allows greater diversity of
  plants/habitats
• good insulation properties
• can simulate a wildlife garden
  "on the ground"
• can be very attractive visually
• more diverse utilization of roof
  (e.g., for growing food) as open
  space
	ADVANTAGES
	• lightweight roof generally does
	  not require strengthening
	• suitable for large areas
	• suitable for roofs from 0°–30°
	  slope
	• low maintenance
	• often no need for
	  irrigation/drainage system
	• relatively little technical expertise
	  needed

DISADVANTAGES
• greater weight loading on roof
  spontaneously
• need for irrigation and drainage
  systems (greater need for energy,
  water, materials, etc.)
• higher cost
• more complex systems and expertise
  required
	• often suitable for refurbishment
	  projects
	• can leave vegetation to develop
	• relatively inexpensive
	• looks more natural
	• easier for planning authority to
	  demand greenroof as a condition
	  of planning permission
	
	DISADVANTAGES
	• more limited choice of plants
	• usually no access for recreation, etc.
	• unattractive to some, especially in
	  winter

Source: Johnston and Newton, 1997.

Many of the company's offices actually front on this delightful and color-ful green garden. In these cases, the difference between the views workers of this kind of lush roof experience and a conventional (at least in the United States) rooftop is remarkable. The benefits, although difficult to document, are likely to be substantial in terms of happier, healthier, and ultimately more productive employees. There is clear evidence of lower absenteeism and increased productivity in ecological buildings that include green features (such as the ING bank headquarters in Amsterdam, discussed in Chapter 10), and it is highly probable that similar benefits from greenroofs occur as well.

The use of extensive greenroofs has become increasingly common in the Netherlands, and a number of creative applications there can be cited. Examples of relatively large grass roofs include the terminal building at Schiphol Airport in Amsterdam, the new main library at the Technical University in Delft, and the GWL-terrein housing project in Amsterdam. The renovation of a housing complex for the elderly in the Dutch city of Zevenaar is being fitted with a green roof (the Pelgromhof; a design by green Dutch architect Frans van der Werf). There have been some very creative recent incorporations of grass roofs, including one integrated as a layer into the recent eco-Kantoor (ecological office building) in Bunnik. And in Leiden, even the main train station incorporates a greenroof.

The greenroof used in the GWL-terrein project in Amsterdam is an exemplary design. The plantings have been carefully selected so that, for example, plants that die in summer serve as food for winter plants. When

Greenroofs or eco-roofs are now common in Europe, especially in Germany, Austria, and the Netherlands. Shown here is a multilevel greenroof at the GWL-terrein housing complex in Amsterdam.

visited during the month of June, the roof was spectacularly green and healthy. The roof is an interesting design in terms of water management. The building itself has a tapered form, from seven stories at one end to three at the other. The rooftops are slanted so that excess water draining from upper levels is guided to lower levels of the greenroof, and at the end any remaining water flows to the open ground below. This overflow from level to level occurs though two pipes extending at the end of each roof level. The outer walkways are also rainwater collection points leading to the next lower greenroof level. The GWL rooftops are not really accessible or directly usable by most residents of the building, but all residents are entitled to visit the rooftop area, and there are small areas where residents might bring chairs and sit. The greenroof itself is off limits for walking. The roof has the most direct visual impact for several apartments on the top floors, which have private gardens facing the greenroof. The grass roof is actually quite shallow with substrate extending perhaps 10 centimeters deep. One layering material used in the roof is a kind of lava rock, which absorbs and retains water and helps the plants survive during dry periods. A firm specializing in greenroofs—Ekogras—designed and built the roof.

Several of the early pilot projects in sustainable building in the Netherlands have incorporated grass roofs, notably a section of Ecolonia (in Alphen a/d Rijn), and the Romolenpolder in Haarlem. Haarlem's Romolenpolder neighborhood is one of the most intriguing applications of greenroofs. A part of this neighborhood, consisting of about thirty-five two-story attached homes with flowing grass roofs, shows convincingly the difference eco-roofs can make in greening even low-rise, more suburban-style development. The green rooftops are a visually distinctive feature in the neighborhood and in combination with grass and other forms of vegetation interspersed throughout the neighborhood, give one the impression of being enveloped by green. The residents there are quite fond of the rooftops—they talk about how their homes are cooler in the summer and warmer in the winter, and they appear to be very proud of the distinctive look of the place. The larger Romolenpolder neighborhood, completed in the mid-1990s, was designed and conceived with the environment at the center (see Ministry of Housing, Spatial Planning and the Environment, 1996). Other elements of the neighborhood include a children's farm and education center, an integrated waste collection system, and an emphasis throughout the district on ecological landscaping. The latter adds distinctively to the look and feel of the neighborhood. Where greenspaces in the center strips between roads, along sidewalks, and beside homes would normally be frequently mowed and trimmed, in Romolenpolder, these areas have been allowed to grow and become largely wild. Many residents of the

Greenroofs are also beneficial in more suburban settings, such as in the Romolen-polder neighborhood in Haarlem, the Netherlands.

low-rise homes have continued this theme in their own backyard gardens, with wild assemblages of flowers and shrubs.

A number of cities promote and/or require the installation of greenroofs on new buildings. The city of Linz in Austria has one of the most extensive greenroofs programs in Europe. Under this program, the city frequently requires building plans to compensate for the loss of greenspace taken by a building. Creation of greenroofs has frequently been the response. Also, since the late 1980s, the city has subsidized the installation of greenroofs—specifically, it will pay for 35 percent of the cost. Since the program has begun, the city has spent an estimated 35 million shillings (nearly US $3 million) on this subsidy. The program has been quite successful, and there are an estimated 300 greenroofs scattered around the city. They have been incorporated into many different types of buildings, including a hospital, a kindergarten, a hotel (e.g., the Ramada Inn), a school, a concert hall, and even the roof of a gas station. Linz's experience suggests that these new areas can be seen as an important element in promoting urban biodiversity. A recent analysis of a number of the Linz greenroofs found that they harbor a high degree of biodiversity. A number of other cities, especially in Germany, have similar roof garden programs and have in place similar combinations of financial subsidies and regulations requiring them.

Greenroofs have been slower to make their way into British building designs but are now becoming popular there as well. Recent examples of new buildings that incorporate extensive greenroofs can be cited there, including a housing project in Brighton, the London Wildlife Trust's Visitor Center, the Scottish Widows Insurance Company, the Sainsbury Center for the Visual Arts at the University of East Anglia, and a new addition to the offices of the Women's Pioneer Housing Association, among others. Extensive greenroofs can be found on a wide range of building types now, including schools, a community center, a new theatre and arts center, and a new bus station. Several new British companies offer greenroof design and installation services. One company is utilizing a new installation technique called *hydroplanting* (or "spray greening"). Under this system, "Seeds, nutrients and a soil substitute are mixed together into a kind of gel and then sprayed directly onto the roof" (Letts, 1998).[2]

Greenwalls and Green Streets

There are many other positive and creative examples in European cities of efforts to green existing and new buildings, including balcony gardens, greenwalls, nestboxes, and other habitat enhancements, as well as greenroofs. (For a discussion of many of these examples and a review of the benefits and technical aspects, see Johnston and Newton, 1997). European cities and towns offer many other examples of creative urban greening. Greenwalls are especially common in German cities, and increasing efforts are made to design structures such as outside stairwells of apartment buildings and parking garages with trellises and vine-climbing frames to provide space for clinging plants. Common species used include Virginia creeper and wisteria. Interestingly, greenwalls provide many of the same benefits as greenroofs. Although our tendency in the United States is to view ivy and other wall clinging plants as destructive to building facades, their effects are generally just the opposite: wall vegetation shields against UV rays, provides shading and cooling during summer months and insulation during winter months (as much as 30 percent, according to Johnston and Newton, 1997), and provides protection against chemical weathering. Health benefits of greenwalls include the filtering of air pollutants, the minimizing of noise, and positive humidifying effects. Spitthover (cited in Kennedy and Kennedy, 1997) cautions, however, that the presence of "deep crevices and fissures," and high moisture, can lead to root damage. "A completely intact surface is thus an absolute requirement for planting with genuine climbers such as ivy and Virginia creeper" (p. 49). As Spitthover notes, it is important to choose carefully the type of vegetation planted. Deciduous plants such as Virginia creeper are appropriate for south or southwest facing walls, where shading in summer is desired but heat gain during the winter months is also desired. On north facades, shade-tolerant, evergreen climbers are more appropriate.

The visual benefits, of course, are tremendous, and as with greenroofs, there may be significant ecological benefits too (e.g., providing important habitat for birds and insects). (Kohler, 1998, as cited in Johnston and Newton, 1997). Policy in a number of European cities, including Kassel, Munich, Berlin, and Frankfurt, supports the installation of greenwalls (Johnston and Newton, 1997). Numerous examples of greenwalls can be found in the study cities, some planned but many that appear to have emerged naturally over many years. These examples include the entire wall of a factory building in Dunkerque. Ivy is now being designed into some buildings from the start. A recent example is a new police station in Leusden, in the Netherlands. Not only is the ivy seen to provide important protection from weather and the creation of a new biotope, but it is also viewed as a measure to prevent graffiti (Government Buildings Agency, 1997).

Green Courtyards and Ecological Living Spaces

Many of the newer development projects visited and studied by the author demonstrate a remarkable ability to create greenspace—often quite wild and untamed—at the same time that fairly high densities are achieved. A number of examples can be cited, including, for example, the interior courtyard space of the Fredensgade ecological urban renewal project in Kolding (Denmark), which includes an extensive play area and a flow form/stream that constantly pumps and circulates recycled water from the project. The lake and surrounding environment at Ecolonia (in the Netherlands) provides similar benefits. The Het Groene Dak project in Utrecht (in the heart of the city) involved the reconfiguring of the housing to create a wild interior courtyard space, which includes a pond, a common house, and other amenities. Interestingly, residents of the surrounding neighborhoods are rumored to have complained that the development was permitted more greenspace than their own projects. According to city staff, this is not the case at all, but Het Groene Dak's design simply seems to contain more greenspace because of its efficient placement and spatial organization. These projects, it should be emphasized, are at considerably high densities. Kennedy and Kennedy (1997), in their study of European ecological settlements, observe the positive qualities of many of these projects for children and the provision of impressive natural play spaces:

> Ecological settlements with diverse automobile-free open
> areas offer an ideal opportunity to develop this kind of

play environment around the residences—alleys, paths, courtyards, lawns, and spaces surrounding tenant gardens and community facilities—constitute a coherent play scape, which no longer requires any need for specially designed playgrounds. Individual activity and creativity is enhanced by further ecological measures like the rainwater collecting ponds at "Ecolonia." . . . If there is an opportunity, children will play in or around water. Puddles, hoses, pumps, and the like are welcome play opportunities, especially in combination with sand and mud.

In contrast to conventional settlement projects which are often marked by an unnecessarily high degree of sealed surfaces and "manicured" green spaces, which hardly enhance children to play. On the other hand ecological settlement projects have play areas, which are usually characterized by minimum paving, plenty of vegetation, and porous surfaces, e.g., gravel areas with spontaneous vegetation, rather than by "manicured" landscaping. (pp. 45–46)

One of the most impressive design features of the Het Groene Dak is its greywater treatment system. Reusing greywater from ten of the homes, once it goes through a settling and aeration process, it is pumped to a surface reedbed for final filtration (and then sent to a pond in an interior courtyard for percolation back into the ground). Creatively, this reedbed composes an entire side of one of the project's buildings, in effect utilizing space to create an element of ecological infrastructure where turfgrass or other typical landscaping would be placed. This reedbed, then, has become a prominent visible element in the project, hard to miss by those walking by on the adjacent sidewalk (see photo).

Many municipalities financially support the development of these kinds of green-urban features. The city of Vienna, for instance, has for many years provided financial subsidies for greening courtyards. Started in 1982, the Green Courtyards program has resulted in green improvements in more than 2,400 courtyards (by 1990; City of Vienna, 1992).

Eco-Bridges

Another greening strategy is to build ecoducts or ecobridges that seek to tie together urban habitats. The Dutch have a history of building impressive eco-bridges that provide natural connections passing over highways and roads. The Dutch Rijkswaterstaat (water management agency) has been, since 1998, building wildviaducts—wildlife viaducts or highway over-passes—in the Veluwe region. Studies suggest that these green viaducts do work in practice, with wildlife using them (e.g., the wildviaduct Woeste Hoeve; see TROS video, 1998).

Other notable examples of the use of wildviaducts or "ecoducts" in the Netherlands include a wild connection across the A-1 near Kootwijk (50 meters across), one in the Midden-Brabant area connecting two nature parks, and important wildviaducts across the A-50, near Arnhem. These bridges and ecoducts are not without controversy. First, they can be fairly costly to build: for example, the A-1 ecoduct cost about 6 million guilders (US $3 million to construct). Some in the natural and biological commu-nity question ecoducts' ability to actually enhance nature, noting that in some cases the wildviaducts provide connections that do not lead to signif-icant areas of habitat, and that the general trends (these efforts at building ecoducts notwithstanding) are in the direction of declining nature (see Bra-bants Dagblad, 1997; Rigter, 1997).

Other more urban examples can be found. In the new Utrecht (the Netherlands) growth district of Leidsche Rijn, dramatic plans are to move and "cap" the A-1 highway for a length of 2 kilometers. This strategy of highway roofing will allow pedestrian and bicycle connections to the center of Utrecht for the 30,000 new residents. This is a bold plan that will create new land and overcome the typical spatial obstacles presented by major roads and highways (see Gemeente Utrecht, undated; 1992). More Dutch and European cities will likely be doing this in the future.

City Farms and Ecology Parks

Other creative examples of injecting nature into the city include the creation of *ecology parks* (as in London) and *city farms* (municipal-owned farms, often on the outskirts of cities, for educational functions) (see Goode, 1989).

Many of the cities studied own and operate working farms—city farms—that serve a variety of recreational, educational, and other benefits. In many ways, this is a distinctively European idea. The city of Göteburg, for example, owns sixty farms, encompassing some 2,700 hectares of land. The land, acquired as sites for future urban expansion, is currently utilized for a variety of agricultural and recreational purposes (the bigger proper-ties are leased to farmers). A number of the smaller farms are open to the public and are utilized for a variety of social functions. Examples include public stables, pick-your-own berry and vegetable farms, a visiting or pet-ting farm, and a riding stable for disabled persons, among others (City of Göteburg, undated). Another example, the Aspö city farm in Skörde, Swe-den, was established adjacent to several residential areas. Its workings are detailed in the *European Sustainable Cities* report:

The city farm has cows, pigs, chickens, and small fields of grain and other crops. Day nursery and school classes frequently visit the farm, and everyone interested may join in the work. Children can help look after the animals, although the animals are sent to the slaughterhouse as with normal farming practice. The services of a farmer are hired for the management of the farm, and a recreational teacher is hired to lead the study tours and other activities. The farm makes a small profit.

Countries like the United Kingdom have their own well-developed network of city farms, and even a National Federation of City Farms, located in Bristol, with sixty members. Typically, these farms receive core funding from local governments, but they are also required to supplement these funds through the sale of agricultural goods and products. City farms are often tucked in between development and in fairly urban environments. The Freightlines farm in Islington Burough illustrates the important role such parks can play in an urban setting. Some 40,000 visitors come to this farm yearly. A variety of workshops, tours, and educational programs are offered, largely aimed at schoolchildren. It is also a commercial working farm, supplying eggs, honey, and other products to local residents. Farmyard manure is also sold for yard use to local residents (Farmers Weekly, 1998).

Dutch cities have been particularly effective at integrating city farms into new development. Small areas of pasture, livestock, and farm buildings are often sited at the core of green areas around which housing is clustered. Good examples can be seen in Leiden in the Stevenshof and Merenwijk neighborhoods.

Ecology parks have been created in United Kingdom out of small areas of leftover land, often former industrial or previously developed lands. Such parks typically entail the restoration of habitat along with the creation of an educational center and environmental education programs aimed at urban schools and children. One recent example in London is the establishment of an ecology park in the docklands area (see Lucas, 1994).

Green Schools

Another promising idea found in European cities is the notion of greening of schools. Several examples can be found of efforts among the study cities to make schools and school grounds more green and to take advantage of the opportunities to promote environmental education there. Zürich, for example, has been implementing a *Nature around the schoolhouse* project, including measures to educate students about environment in the city, to change the way school grounds are managed, and in certain cases to "structurally redesign" schoolhouses (Berger and Borer, 1994). The last measure includes actions to break up and take out impervious surfaces around the schools and to plant trees and vegetation. Nine schoolhouses so far have undergone this form of restructuring, and another forty have had special core measures applied. The students in these schools have been directly involved in carrying out these changes.

The schools built in the new development area of Nieuwland, in Amersfoort, also include some interesting measures for educating and involving students. De Wonderboom primary school, for instance, includes both a greenroof and extensive photovoltaic panels. As a result of extensive daylighting in the design, students can, through an interesting mirror system, directly see and monitor the greenroof. In the main entrance to this school, moreover, is an energy panel, which allows students (and teachers) to see daily, monthly, and yearly energy consumption as well as the production from the photovoltaics.

Desealing and Natural Drainage Strategies

Many European cities are working hard to minimize the presence of concrete and hard surfaces. Berlin has been implementing a program to deseal or remove concrete and paved surfaces throughout the city. Under its landscape plan, the city has spent DM 30 million over twelve years (about US $16 million) to remove pavement and plant vegetation. This has taken place on some 1,400 sites in the city.

Saarbrücken has one of the most interesting programs for encouraging green development in the city, particularly aimed at rainwater management. The city's program for encouraging rainwater retrieval and percolation is literally translated "rainwater is so valuable for the canal" (*"Regenwasser ist zu kostbar für den Kanal!"*) (Landeshauptstadt Saarbrücken, 1997). It is actually part of a broader program of the German Länd (state) of Saarland. Saarland has made several million deutsche marks available to communities, and some fifty communities have developed programs. Saarbrücken's program is essentially one of providing small financial subsidies for citizens (and businesses) who wish to undertake some sort of project or action that conserves water and reduces stormwater runoff.

Specifically, these proposed actions can qualify for grants from DM 5,000 to DM 10,000 (US $2,700 to US $5,400) for one of several types of actions: (1) projects for collecting and using rainwater in or around the home, for example, for toilet flushing or plant watering, (2) projects for desealing, or taking up impermeable pavement and replacing it with vegetation or permeable bricks, and (3) the installation of greenroofs. The actual grant award is based on a per square meter calculation, ranging from DM 15/square meter (about US $8) for rainwater use (based on the area of the rooftop) to DM 30/square meter (about US $16) for desealing and rainwater diversion projects, to DM 60/square meter (about US $32) for installing a greenroof. Desealing projects qualify for a maximum DM 5,000 grant (about US $2,700) and greenroofs for a maximum DM 10,000 (about US $5,400), the highest award. The program, although only in its second year, has been quite popular with the public.

About forty projects have been funded so far, most for rainwater using and desealing and just a few for the installation of greenroofs. The municipality's environment department has received a great many requests for information about the program. In the first year, it had about DM 100,000 to distribute (about US $54,000), with the goal of spreading it around in small amounts for a number of different projects. In most cases, the grants do not cover the entire cost of the proposed action or project, and it might be wondered whether the funds are going to pay for improvements that homeowners might be planning to undertake anyway. However, there is good indication that the program, even though the grants are not large and the number of participants is currently small, does have an important catalytic effect in encouraging these kinds of greening and ecological investments. Interestingly, the administrator of the program believes that interest in the program is not driven so much by stronger environmental ideology as a genuine interest in making homes nicer. She believes that even greater interest will result when, in the near future, the Stadtwerke begins to charge residents not only for wastewater but also for the stormwater generated from one's property.

In many projects, rainwater collection and use, greywater recycling, and water conservation are key design elements. The GWL-terrein project in Amsterdam, for example, is making extensive use of rainwater for toilet flushing. In combination with water-conserving toilets, very little water is used for flushing (only 4 liters per flush, compared to 9 to 10 liters for an average Dutch toilet). Rainwater is collected from rooftops, stored in cisterns, and used for toilet flushing. A float mechanism triggers a filling up of the cisterns with tap water when they become too low.

There are many examples in these cities of projects incorporating natural drainage as a key design element. The Dutch now frequently utilize what they call *wadies*—or natural drainage ditches—and these are key ecological features in a number of recent residential projects. In *Oikos*, an ecological project in Enschede, the wadies are a main feature. Here, instead of conventional storm sewers, water is directed into these green swales from sidewalks and rooftops. Within these linear swales is a perforated drainpipe, surrounded by a fabric cocoon of clay pellets. The pellets actually accommodate the growth of bacteria, which provide a treatment function for collected stormwater. In the Enschede area, groundwater levels have been gradually declining, with serious impact on heather plant communities. So, in this western region of the Netherlands, there is special emphasis on allowing as much groundwater percolation as possible.

Much of the parking in *Oikos* is in the form of permeable bricks, which allow water to percolate into the ground and a green carpet of grass to grow around the bricks. Creatively, roof spouting guides water across the sidewalks to these permeable parking and street spaces. Project planners like the notion that residents can see directly what is flowing into these wadis and permeable spaces. (In the past, problems have arisen from residents pouring unwelcome things down the storm drains.) In a central area in the development, a common car-washing area has been created. Here, the water from washing cars does not go into the wadis (and thus into the groundwater), but into the city's sewage system for treatment instead. Rainwater is used for this purpose and is collected and stored in an underground cistern. The washing pump is solar powered.

Planning for Local Climate

There is a much greater sense by the cities in this study of their climatological and meteorological context and the need to manage development and growth in ways that protect favorable climatic conditions.

A detailed climate study serves as a major environmental basis for the land use plan for Graz (Stadtklimaanalyse Graz), for example. This city has pollution problems that are the result of a combination of topographic conditions (700-meter mountains immediately to the west of the city; hills to the east), and inversions that occur in certain months of the year. Climatopes and wind circulation patterns have been extensively mapped, and problem areas identified. Policies flow directly from these conditions, including mandating that certain areas of the city must convert to the city's district heating network by a certain date, as well as the preparation of a new landscape plan that will better protect greenspace in and around the city.

Berlin also experiences higher-than-normal urban temperatures in summer and views its regional landscape as an important factor in addressing this situation. (see City of Berlin, 1996). Berlin's woodlands—comprising 18 percent of its land area—are seen as important "climate lanes," allowing for the flow of cool air into the city during hot conditions. Under the city's Landscape Programme, "climate protection priority areas" are delineated, which must be protected, as well as problem areas where greening and removal of concrete and asphalt surfaces should occur. Climate zonation is also used in the Heidelberg and Münster plans.

Freiburg's planning also reflects a strong concern about protecting positive local climatic conditions. Specifically, it tries to prevent obstruction to the cool winds that flow down each evening from the Black Forest. The city implements a concept of *transparent construction*, requiring buildings in certain wind zones to be designed (with the use of a university wind model) to allow winds to flow through. The city's new soccer stadium, for example, was designed and oriented to allow this.

Saarbrücken prepared and published its first climate zone plan in 1997. It looks like many similar plans that identify important dynamic processes and climate zones in the city (the larger regional jurisdiction has prepared a similar map), barriers to air movement, forests, and other climatically important areas. The map and plan are the bases for making climate-friendly land use decisions. In particular, the stream valleys leading into the city (which represent important fresh air flows) and the agricultural areas to the west of the city are viewed as important climate regulation zones. Most of these areas have now been placed off limits for development in the city's development plan.

Ecological Regeneration

There are also examples of cities that have undertaken serious and substantial ecological restoration or regeneration work. The city of Leicester, for example, has taken extensive actions to restore the river corridor that runs through the city. Riverside Park, a 2,400-acre, 12-mile-long park, has been created out of what was largely derelict land in the early 1970s. Under the Leicester Ecology Strategy, and through partnerships with organizations such as British Waterways, the National Rivers Authority, and the Countryside Commission, as well as with landowners, significant resources have been directed to restoring and cleaning up the corridor. Riverside Park has now become one of the city's most important ecological and recreational resources (see Environ, 1996).

A number of cities are attempting to restore the natural qualities of streams and creeks, many of which had been channelized or put underground. Such programs exist in Zürich and Heidelberg, for example. In Zürich, some 100 kilometers of streams have been placed underground and "canalized." Zürich has embarked on a program to eventually open up, or bring to the surface, 40 kilometers of these streams, and it has already done this for 25 kilometers (Villiger, 1989). The placement of these new "opened" streams is based on historical records of where the streams originally existed, a route where they can be kept open and unbroken, and where they tie into and connect with existing footpaths and open spaces. The resulting streams are intended to accommodate native trees and vegetation and contribute to the greenness of urban areas. As Villiger (1989) describes their purpose:

> On their way down from the wooded hilltops into the valleys, the streams have a linking and structuring function. Together with the appurtenant vegetation, they can have a noticeable effect on the climate, bringing fresh air into the built-up area along their line of descent. Provided they have an almost natural bottom and do not descend in a step-like manner, they can accommodate a rich flora and fauna. (p. 8)

Ecological Urban Restructuring

One of the most interesting model projects for greening the urban environment, yet to be implemented, was prepared for the former East German city of Leipzig. An effort to demonstrate the concepts of "ecological urban restructuring," the model project was the brainchild of Ekhart Hahn and was funded through the European Union program LIFE. The project sought to "green" a major slice or cross section of the city—specifically its eastern district (Leipzig Ostraum). A central design element was to be the creation of a *Green Radial,* which would connect the surrounding countryside with the very center of the city, specifically an abandoned railyard (the Eilenburger Bahnhof) (Hahn and LaFond, 1997). The two-kilometer radial would be redesigned to include bicycle paths and pedestrian greenspaces (connecting city and countryside) and recreational facilities.

Mixed-use new neighborhoods would surround the radial and would be greened through new community gardens, recycling and composting facilities, and other "ecological restructuring." A new residential ecological community is envisioned, and connections at the edge are to be made with an organic farm and municipal farms, which will grow and market local ecologically produced agricultural products. In about the middle of the Green Radial would be an innovative neighborhood ecological center—dubbed an "ecostation." To be housed in a former locomotive barn, the ecostation would be the center of energy and activity, a place where ecological training and workshops could be held, where equipment and tools could be borrowed, where public meetings and conferences could take place, where information about ecological services and products could be found, and where a variety of ecological demonstrations could occur. More specifically, Hahn and Lafond list some of the likely activities and functions to be served by the ecostation (Hahn and LaFond, 1997, p. 46):

- Exhibition, seminar, and event spaces
- Environmental library with reading cafe
- Natural foods restaurant with ecological nutrition counseling center and teaching kitchen
- Coordination office for "Local Agenda 21"
- Information and advice for ecological neighborhood renewal
- Energy office for implementation of neighborhood-based energy concepts
- Water and waste agencies
- Mobility service bureau (car-sharing, car-pooling, bicycle center with rentals and self-help workshop, coordination of "Job-ticket" concepts, support of "auto-free" communities, etc.
- Environmental measurement station for taking and analyzing readings of air, water, and soil quality
- Information regarding "municipal farms" and rural initiatives
- Green Workshop for the practical realization of the Green Radial.

While the Leipzig demonstration met with certain difficulties, and the Green Radial concept and the ecostation have not yet been implemented, these ideas represent powerful new ways of reconsidering the spatial relationships between city and countryside.

Urban Gardens

Many of the European cities studied here maintain extensive allotment gardens—areas of small garden plots, rented or assigned to the general public and used for recreational flower and food gardening. There is a long tradition of allotment gardens in Europe, and they are a significant element of green in many of the European cities. Extensive allotment gardens exist, for instance, in Copenhagen, Amsterdam, and Berlin (80,000 in Berlin alone with some 16,000 on a waiting list), and these further contribute to providing greenspace and improving the quality of life experienced by residents (United Nations Development Programme, 1996). Some cities have been gradually expanding these gardens. Freiburg has about 4,000 *Kleingarten* (small gardens), adding another 300 or 400 per year. (There is also currently a waiting list there.)

An important and consistent feature in many of the new development areas planned in these European cities is the provision made for new allotments or community gardens. Indeed, perhaps a reflection of the historical importance of such gardens, even very urban sites are making provisions for them. In Helsinki, the Viikki ecological neighborhood, for example, envisions the creation of a horticultural center that will "rent out allotments to residents, give information, lend and hire gardening tools and maintain model plots" (City of Helsinki, undated, p. 4). In the design of Oikos, an ecological housing project in Enschede (Netherlands), a series of community gardens interspersed throughout the residential areas is a main feature of the project's masterplan. Similarly, much of the interior space of the GWL-terrein project in Amsterdam is organized in the form of allotment gardens.

Urban Wildlife and Habitat Conservation

The case cities also provide good examples of efforts to identify important areas of wildlife habitat in and around cities and to protect and enhance these areas. For many of the study cities, extensive biotope and habitat mapping and protection programs have been established. In London, many of the boroughs have prepared detailed habitat studies and plans. There has been a significant effort to protect important nature and habitat sites in the London area. Beginning in the 1980s, and with the biological and technical assistance of the London Ecology Unit, individual boroughs prepared nature conservation strategies and incorporated these into their Urban Development Plans (UDPs). Today, nineteen boroughs have published strategies, with another six strategies in preparation (of thirty-two boroughs). At the heart of these strategies is a system for mapping and classifying local natural areas, as well as for identifying areas of nature deficiency (spatial gaps where it is farther than a kilometer to a nature site). Local sites are classified according to whether they are of metropolitan significance, borough significance, or local significance (see, for example, Yardham, Waite, Simpson, and Machin, 1994).

Local borough plans (where these strategies have been prepared) incorporate these designations, and, according to David Goode, director of the London Ecology Unit, are generally placed off limits to development (although the loss of some brownfield or derelict sites has occurred through redevelopment). The most recent nature conservation effort has been the initiation of a new London Biodiversity Partnership, bringing together a diverse array of groups and actors and land users to develop a strategic action plan for preserving habitat and species in Greater London (many other local jurisdictions are or will be preparing Biodiversity Action Plans in the United Kingdom).

Leicester was one of the first cities in the United Kingdom to develop a comprehensive ecology strategy. As a first step, it conducted an extensive, and at the time unusual, Habitat Survey. The survey rated all vacant lands and sites in the city (including such areas as churchyards and garden allotments) according to their habitat value, applying a letter grade to each. Some 1,800 sites were surveyed and classified. The result was a truly impressive, comprehensive picture of the extent and quality of habitat within the city (Leicester City Council, 1989). The survey's results show an urbanized environment with considerable wildlife and important natural habitat, including "189 miles of linear habitats, such as the canal, rivers, streams, railways, road verges and hedgerows, which provide homes and corridors for a great variety of wildlife" (p. 19). This survey and classification led to the development of the Leicester Ecology Strategy. The strategy identifies ways in which this urban ecology can be protected and restored and sets forth a series of ecology policies for the city, as well as more detailed conservation and management proposals for various areas and parts of the city. For example, policy E2 states that the council will define and protect "a 'green network' of wedges, corridors, and other vegetated areas and features, so as to conserve an integrated system of wildlife habitats and will resist development of these sites" (Leicester City Council, 1989, p. 59). These habitat protection goals and targets have been incorporated into Leicester's land use plan and are reflected in specific initiatives, such as Riverside Park, which was discussed earlier.

In Bologna, the province has developed an exemplary plan that delineates natural and sensitive lands. Protected areas include natural parks (there are five in the province), rivers (including a zone of 150 meters on either side), and hills and woods. Most of these areas have strong protection and are generally off limits to development.

Many German cities, including Berlin and Heidelberg, have had comprehensive biotope mapping initiatives (see Sukopp, 1980). Heidelberg has taken a number of, albeit small, actions to construct new habitat (e.g., new parks and lakes for amphibians; bat habitat). The city is also subsidizing farmers to maintain and restore certain habitat types, and it operates a "rent-a-sheep" program, which helps to maintain certain grassland habitats (and also provides jobs for the unemployed in the city). These are but a few examples of a rich set of ideas and strategies for greening and naturalizing European cities.

Lessons for American Cities

Urban environments can and must become more fundamentally green and natural. Cities ought to be, as discussed in Chapter 1, like forests—enhancing, improving, and restoring the natural environment and condition of cities. These European cities (and countries) taken together provide a tremendous variety of creative and inspirational ideas for greening the urban landscape. These ideas range from strategic tree planting, ecological roofs, and the de-sealing of urban pavement, to the incorporation of a range of ecological features into new development projects and renovated urban districts. Virtually all of these ideas have potential application in American cities.

An important lesson from many of these European cities has to do with the very perception we have of cities. In many of the greenest of these cities, and in places such as Berlin where much of the early work of urban ecology occurred, there is a sense that cities *are* and ought to be places where nature occurs. In the United States, a challenge remains to overcome the polar distinction between what is *urban* and what is *natural*. Perhaps because of the expansiveness of our ecological resources and land base, we have tended to see the most significant forms of nature as occurring somewhere else—often hundreds of miles away from where most people actually live—in national parks, national seashores, and wilderness areas.

The emphasis, especially in the Netherlands, on developing ecological networks—an integrated coherent strategy for protecting and restoring natural landscapes—is one of the most important lessons to be learned. In the Netherlands, it begins at the national scale and cascades down to the regional and municipal levels, with each higher level providing a coherent framework in which to make conservation and restoration decisions. While a national ecological network in the United States is probably unlikely (although highly desirable), it is clear that regional, bioregional, and metropolitan-scale greenspace conservation strategies are needed. Indeed, without them, it is not at all clear that discrete isolated greenspace conservation actions will in fact add up to very much. Some promising regional greenspace strategies are emerging, and their examples are worth emulating and extending. The Portland Greenspaces program is one example. Here, a regional greenspaces plan, adopted in 1992, calls for the creation of a "regional system of parks, natural areas, greenways and trails for fish, wildlife and people." The system will include fifty-seven urban natural areas and thirty-four trail and greenway corridors. A 1995 bond measure ($135 million) will allow the acquisition of 6,000 acres, much of which has already been purchased (Howe, 1998). In the Twin Cities region of Minnesota, another such example of a collaborative program for developing a regional greenway system has been under development since 1996, and a Metro Area Nature Resources Map has recently been prepared (Pfeifer and Balch, 1999).

There is no question about the need for such regional-level strategies. However, to date even the most advanced initiatives are modest in scope. The proposed Twin Cities plan, for instance, would secure but 4 percent of the 2 million acres in that region. Setting aside larger amounts of green-spaces (taking the European lead) is necessary, and concepts for bolder regional ecological networks are needed. The problem of speculative land values in American cities and the high cost of land acquisition here make the establishment of such regional systems more difficult. Steady, dedicated sources of revenue are essential, for example, drawing from Boulder's example of an open space sales tax (already resulting in the acquisition of some 27,000 acres).

One promising line of argument in the U.S. context is the recent call for *green infrastructure*. The key idea here is that elements of the natural environment—wetlands, forests, groundwater recharge zones—are equally essential forms of infrastructure to those other "built" forms that we more typically fund—roads, sewer lines, schools. There is considerable rhetorical power in green infrastructure, and coupled with a heightened sense of the ecological services provided by the environment (e.g., natural wetlands provide important flood retention benefits), it may serve as an effective banner under which to argue for greenspace protection. As a small example of the currency of green infrastructure, the current governor of Maryland, Parris Glendening, made prominent mention of it in his 1999 inaugural address (Glendening, 1999).

Several other ideas discussed in this chapter warrant special mention here. There is no question, for example, that there is tremendous potential for greenroofs or eco-roofs in the United States. To date, however, there have been few buildings in the United States that have incorporated extensive eco-roof designs. One recent example, however, is the newly opened Gap headquarters building in San Bruno, California (see Photo 7.6). Designed by William McDonough and Partners, it incorporates a green roof of "native grasses and wildflowers . . . which undulates like the surrounding green hills" (Templin, 1998, p. 8; *Interiors*, 1999). McDonough is fond of noting that the birds do not know there is a building there. Integration of the structure into the existing natural site was an objective from the beginning. While this building is a positive sign of the potential appeal of greenroofs, more experimentation should be encouraged.

Promoting greenroofs in an American context will likely require some adaptations in strategy, of course. In many European cities, as mentioned, it is common to offer public subsidies for such private greening investments (such as in Vienna and Linz), but this has not generally been a role local governments have played in the United States. Greening as a mitigation requirement under development regulations is certainly a possibility, and technical assistance is also needed. Encouraging greenroofs and courtyards in the American context may more appropriately be promoted through incentives and density bonuses. Indeed, Portland and Seattle already have such measures on the books, and other cities could follow suit. And, as Thompson (1998) notes, more technical literature in English on greenroofs is needed, and the development of a greenroof industry will be necessary in the long term. Some collaborative ventures between U.S. and German firms are already beginning though. There are also signs that some U.S. cities are understanding the value of greenroofs, and several have already developed initiatives to explore and to encourage them. Portland's Bureau of Environmental Services has joined with Portland General Electric to research the potential of greenroofs, and the Bureau is itself designing and building a structure with an eco-roof, largely to demonstrate the stormwater retention potential. Such greenroofs can retain large amounts of rainwater—studies have documented up to a 75 percent retention (Johnston and Newton, 1997).

A group of graduate students at Portland State University (calling themselves "Green Roofs Unlimited") has prepared an interesting analysis of the potential application of greenroofs in Portland. This analysis, while crude, demonstrates the amount of unused rooftop space typically available in the downtowns of American cities. For Portland's downtown, an area encompassing about 723 acres, it was determined that there were 219 acres of roof space—or about one-third of the area of the downtown available for greenroofs. The group also calculated the potential of these areas to capture rainfall and to help the city in dealing with its combined sewer overflow problem (the city is currently spending $700 million to address this problem). This rooftop area, if comprised of greenroofs and assuming that 60 percent of the rainfall is captured by the roofs, would serve to retain an estimated 67 million gallons per year and reduce the volume of combined sewer overflow by between 11 and 15 percent (Beckman et al., 1997, p. 25).

This is no small reduction in stormwater, and it represents a tremendous economic value (savings) to the city. These PSU calculations demonstrate the public economics of these types of greening initiatives. It seems prudent to provide European-style subsidies for the installation of greenroofs when the economic (and other) benefits are clearly significant. And many other green-urban features could be encouraged and sponsored by American cities with small grants or subsidies with much larger long-term paybacks.

In some European cities, greenroofs have been installed on the rooftops of shopping centers, and here there is considerable potential for retrofitting American buildings. The American low-density suburban landscape, especially, contains numerous buildings with large expansive rooftops, which otherwise simply add to the extent of impervious surfaces and contribute further to the urban heat island effect. Perhaps the place to start is to undertake one or more pilot rooftop retrofits, which could be studied and which would likely stimulate considerable further interest in and enthusiasm for this idea. (Perhaps an organic-oriented grocery chain would be the most promising sponsor?)

Moreover, greenroofs, green walls, green streets, and many other urban greening programs will become increasingly important in those American cities where compact, denser development patterns are given priority. Such strategies may be particularly relevant in cities such as Portland, San Jose, Seattle, and elsewhere, where serious containment of growth has occurred and is still occurring. The PSU study group makes this point well:

> The City of Portland is at a crossroads. We are pursuing a dense urban form which will create a walkable and efficient city while protecting valuable natural resources and farmland on the periphery. However, density does not come without negative impacts on the health of both the natural and social environment within our community. Increasing the intensity of development means that there will be less room for the natural spaces that enhance our quality of life. . . . By adding more greenspace to urban areas, green roofs have the potential to bring substantial benefits to our community through mitigating some of the negative impacts of development. (Beckman et al., 1997, p. 1)

The PSU study also documents the existence of a number of mostly conventional roof gardens in primarily northwestern cities and existing development regulations that might serve to encourage greenroofs. Portland, for example, already implements a floor-area bonus for buildings that include rooftop gardens (at a 1:1 ratio).[3] The bonus is available only to buildings in high-intensity zones (e.g., basically high-rise structures) and has not been used very often. Seattle has in place a similar density bonus feature, providing a maximum bonus of up to 30 percent of lot area (for interior accessible gardens). Under the Seattle regulations, to receive the bonus the rooftop gardens must be open to the public (considered a public amenity or benefit). Such a condition may limit the attractiveness of such bonuses, and fails to acknowledge the many public benefits provided by such greenroofs or eco-roofs, regardless of whether they are physically accessible to the public.

Positive examples of higher-density urban neighborhoods and districts that incorporate gardens, streams, urban forests, and permeable pavements are needed to demonstrate the real potential of this fusion of urban and environmental. And, as argued in several other chapters, it may be necessary in the American context to emphasize the clear economic benefits and cost savings associated with these greening strategies. The environmental group American Forests has, for example, through very helpful computer modeling, estimated the stormwater management and retention benefits of tree planting. The numbers are impressive: in the city of Atlanta, for example, the stormwater and flood management benefits of trees in that region have been estimated to provide the equivalent of a $2 billion reservoir.

The emphasis on urban designs and projects that incorporate natural drainage is another striking trend in Dutch and other European cities. Here, some positive American examples can indeed be cited, which show both the considerable benefits—environmental and economic—and the fact that such designs are feasible and saleable. Probably the most successful American example, and indeed an inspirational one, is Village Homes in Davis (California). The inspiration of husband-and-wife team Michael and Judy Corbett, this development of 240 solar homes is organized around a series of interlocking green fingers. Green drainage swales collect stormwater and, in combination with a series of check dams, made it unnecessary to install conventional storm drains. The Corbetts ran up against a common obstacle: the objections of public works officials who did not think the natural drainage system would work (overcoming a traditional engineering mentality certainly remains a serious impediment in

Natural drainage has also been a key design element in several American ecological developments, most notably as shown here in Village Homes, Davis, California.

the United States). In the end, the system was allowed only after a guarantee bond was provided (see Beatley and Manning, 1997). In addition to working quite well, the natural system saved about $800 per household (what the installation of storm drains would have cost).

Natural drainage strategies applied in the American setting will, however, often run up against other unique American values about yard and lawn. This can be seen in the checkered history of natural drainage employed in The Woodlands, an Ian McHarg-designed new town north of Houston. Here, homes in the original neighborhoods were built with natural swales and ditches and without conventional stormwater drains (see Girling and Helphand, 1994; Middleton, 1997). Although by all accounts these natural drainage features have worked well, the development company has since abandoned the idea in its more recent neighborhoods, based on what they perceive housing consumers want and expect. Water-retaining ditches and soggy lawns are viewed as too rustic and unkept for contemporary housing consumers. This is a disappointing conclusion, but perhaps it suggests that for natural drainage designs to be acceptable in mainstream America, a concerted reconceptualizing of the traditional aesthetic of the American lawn or yard may be needed. This reconception certainly is possible.

Another important greening strategy that American cities could easily implement, with considerable environmental and economic return, is to ensure a minimum tree cover in all new parking areas. The city of Davis has adopted a minimum parking lot shading standard that requires (through the submittal of a shading plan) the achievement of at least 50 percent shade cover within fifteen years. The city has also prepared a set of parking lot shading guidelines, which provide more specific advice about how to calculate shade cover, minimum specifications for planters and tree irrigation, and a master parking lot tree list providing information about the crown diameters of different species after fifteen years of growth (City of Davis, undated). Within the city of Davis, efforts have also been made to reconceive and design stormwater retention pools into wetlands, again adding important habitat to the Pacific Flyway. Ponds and drainage ways have become habitat, while also serving as important natural and open space for residents and part of an integral community bikeway and mobility system.

Designing-in community gardens is another compelling idea. In new projects, such as the GWL-terrein (Westerpark) project in Amsterdam, Oikos in Enschede, or Viikki in Helsinki, there is an explicit attempt to include such gardens. These designs show convincingly that density and urbanity can be achieved alongside food and flower production and generally greener environments. Some recent American examples also certainly begin to indicate that these ideas are possible here. Prairie Crossings, an

Many new housing estates in Europe are incorporating community gardens into their designs. The gardens shown here are located in the car-free center of the GWL-terrein project in Amsterdam.

ecoburb development in Grayslake, Illinois, has been receiving considerable attention. The development consists of 317 homes clustered to leave about two-thirds of this site permanently undeveloped, setting aside land as a nature prairie. It is adjacent to the larger 2,500-acre Liberty Prairie Reserve and contributes to its protection and restoration through a fee assessed at the time of home sale (.5 percent of the home sale price, averaging about $1,500 per home; Brown, 1998; Beatley and Manning, 1997). The development includes an organic farm, and residents have the option to receive through subscription a basket of fresh produce and flowers during the growing season. Gardening plots are also available to residents who wish to grow their own food. The basic difficulty with this development is its exurban location, some 40 miles north of Chicago, although limited train service will be available to residents. Despite its conservation focus, the development still contributes to a landscape of rural sprawl. To be effective examples, these green American developments must (as I will argue elsewhere) be located in places that contribute to and strengthen the existing urban fabric of cities. There are few actual examples of new American developments—especially those in more urban locations—that explicitly incorporate features such as community gardens into their designs. The European examples show that it can be done and that it can greatly contribute to enhancing the quality of life in a new urban neighborhood. In many creative ways, as we have seen, urban development can incorporate not only gardens, but greenroofs, trees, wetlands, and wildlife habitat, which all enhance nature and human livability.

One important step in the U.S. context, and one we must continue to build upon, has been the recent directing of scientific research and monies to understanding the natural ecology of cities. Specifically, the National Science Foundation (NSF) has now designated two urban sites as part of its Long-Term Ecological Research (LTER) network, mostly consisting of relatively primitive natural ecosystems. Under the LTER program, significant NSF research monies are devoted over a considerable period of time to understanding the ecological dimensions and functioning of, in this case, the two cities of Phoenix and Baltimore (Jensen, 1998). The knowledge learned from this research, still in the very preliminary stages (sites were only designated in 1997), will be extremely helpful both in reconceptualizing American cities and in guiding planning and policy to make them *more* natural and nature-enhancing. And the interdisciplinary nature of these projects is also promising. As it stands, though, only two of these LTER sites out of twenty are urban; over time, additional cities should be added and research funded. Americans clearly have a long way to go to begin viewing cities and urban environments as ecosystems and places of nature.

NOTES

1. "New housing, motorways and other infrastructure, industry, and large building complexes will be excluded from these areas. In principle, interventions such as water management systems that cause irrevocable damage to the structure of the soil will also be excluded from these areas. Other interventions that affect the soil structure (for example, deep ploughing) and water catchment or infiltration systems, must be avoided as well" (van Zadelhoff and Lammers, 1995, p. 95).

2. "Benefits of hydroplanting include the acceleration of the germination process by steeping the seed and seedlings in the sprayed mass which is exacerbated by the high pressures in the pipes. Hydroplanting also tends to improve the substrate's properties, particularly with regard to water capacity, substrate invigoration and capillary action" *Building Design,* 1998.

3. More specific requirements are summarized by the Portland State University study group: "To qualify for this bonus, the garden must cover at least 50 percent of the roof area of the building and at least 30 percent of the garden area must be landscaped. The roof area from which the 50 percent garden coverage is calculated includes the terraces created by setbacks and the top of the tower" (Beckman et al., 1997, p. 61).

Chapter 8

Urban Ecocycle Balancing: Toward Closed-Loop Cities

Urban "Ecocycles" and the Metabolism of Cities

Sir Richard Rogers argues in his book *Cities for a Small Planet* for the need to replace our linear approach to pollution and resource use in cities with ones that emphasizes circular systems. What is needed, he argues, is "a new form of comprehensive holistic urban planning" (Rogers, 1997 p. 30). An extension of our view of cities like forests is to appreciate that they are ultimately composed of a complex flow of inputs and outputs—of energy and resources flowing in, and waste and pollution flowing out. Among European cities, there is a growing body of experience and experimentation in support of a circular view of urban metabolism. This chapter examines some of the most important emerging examples. While no European city (or a city anywhere for that matter) has succeeded in fully implementing a circular vision, there are many exemplary beginnings that offer inspiration.

There is an explosion of interest in the idea of ecocycles within European cities and the potential of reorienting production and consumption processes so that these ecocycles are in (better) balance. Thinking in terms of the inputs (e.g., energy and food) and outputs (e.g., waters and carbon emissions) has become a useful frame of reference for local sustainability. The rough calculations for London illustrate the magnitude of these input/output flows and suggest opportunities for reducing throughput and more directly tying inputs and outputs (see Table 8.1). London requires an astounding 2.4 million tonnes of food each year and generates some 60 million tonnes of carbon dioxide (Sustainable London Trust, 1997). In the

Table 8.1. The Metabolism of Greater London and London's Ecological Footprint

THE METABOLISM OF GREATER LONDON
(population 7,000,000)

These figures quantify London's resource use. They are listed here to emphasize the huge potential for greater resource efficiency. London's waste output could be used as a significant resource for new recycling and energy efficiency industries.

1) INPUTS	tonnes per year
Total tonnes of fuel, oil, equivalent	20,000,000
Oxygen	40,000,000
Water	1,002,000,000
Food	2,400,000
Timber	1,200,000
Paper	2,200,000
Plastics	2,100,000
Glass	360,000
Cement	1,940,000
Bricks, blocks, sand, and tarmac	6,000,000
Metals (total)	1,200,000
2) WASTES	
Industrial and demolition wastes	11,400,000
Household, civic, and commerical wastes	3,900,000
Wet, digested sewage sludge	7,500,000
CO_2	60,000,000
SO_2	400,000
NO_x	280,000

LONDON'S ECOLOGICAL FOOTPRINT

London's ecological footprint, following the definition by Canadian economist William Rees, consists of the land area required to supply London with food, fibre and wood products, and the area of growing vegetation needed to reabsorb London's carbon dioxide output:

	Acres
London's surface areas:	390,000
Farmland used: 3 acres/person:	21,000,000
Forest area required by London for wood products = 0.27 acres/person	1,900,000
Land area required for carbon absorption (equal to acreage required for fuel production from biomass) = 3.7 acres/person	26,000,000
TOTAL London ecological footprint: = 125 times London's surface area	48,900,000
Britain's productive land:	52,000,000
Britain's total surface area:	60,000,000

Source: Herbert Girardet, 1995 and 1996; sources available.

words of a study by the Sustainable London Trust: "London has become used to a linear throughput of resources, utilizing raw materials and then discarding them as waste when we are finished with them. To become more sustainable, London needs to reduce its excessive energy consumption, pursue linear resource flows and in the process reduce its waste output" (Sustainable London Trust, 1997, p. 10).

London has far to go in balancing these ecocycles, but other cities in Europe have done more. One of the most impressive cities in this region is Stockholm, and indeed the ecocycles idea has an especially high degree of currency in Sweden. The key idea here is that cities must begin to look for ways in which, as in nature, wastes represent productive inputs, or "food," for other processes. The city of Stockholm has made some of the most impressive progress in this area. As Figure 8.1 illustrates, the city, and its various companies dealing with elements of the cycles, are moving in the direction of a more coordinated framework. A number of actions in support of ecocycle balancing have already occurred. These include, for example, the conversion of sewage sludge to fertilizer and its use in food production, and the generation of biogas from sludge. The biogas is used to fuel public vehicles in the city and to fuel a combined heat and power plant. In this way, wastes are returned to residents in the form of district heating.

Stockholm's production of heat and energy takes an ecocycle approach in other ways. Several of its combined heat and power plant are fueled by waste dust from a sawmill in the north of the country, first converting the dust into pellets at a compressing plant (owned by the city) and shipping them by boat (also owned by the city) directly to the plant. The result is the use of a renewable energy source and the conversion of a waste stream into a productive good.

In the administrative organization of the city of Stockholm, an ecocycles division was created and headed by Green Party vice-mayor Krister Skånberg. It includes the companies dealing with energy, water, and waste. Skånberg explained how the label just seemed to fit. Concern for promoting more balanced ecocycles in the city aptly describes many of its initiatives. Few cities anywhere in the world are doing as much in this area.

Skånberg has also been spearheading efforts to incorporate the principles of the Natural Step program into Stockholm city government. Natural Step, the brainchild of Swedish cancer researcher Karl-Henrik Robèrt, lays out a series of four system conditions that all companies and organizations concerned with sustainability should strive to respect. Complementary to and supportive of ecocycle balancing, these conditions include the following: (1) that substances from the earth's crust must not be allowed to sys-

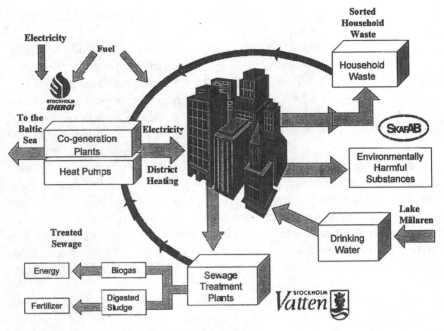

Figure 8.1. Ecocycle balancing in Stockholm

The city of Stockholm is beginning to develop a comprehensive ecocycle balancing strategy in which wastes of one activity become productive inputs for other activities. Shown here are some of the key interconnections being made in Stockholm between the city's energy company, waste management agency, and water department.

Source: City of Stockholm, ecocycles division.

tematically increase in the ecosphere; (2) that substances produced by society must not be allowed to systematically increase in the ecosphere; (3) that the physical basis for productivity and diversity of nature must not be systematically diminished, and (4) that there should be fair and efficient use of resources with respect to meeting human needs (The Natural Step, 1996). (The history and background of the Natural Step is discussed in greater detail in Chapter 11.) Skånberg has been successful in Stockholm, and the system rules of Natural Step have been included word for word in the city's new environmental policy. It is not clear what status this policy will actually have, but Skånberg believes it will be frequently referred to and will help to shape and guide the council's decisions in the future. In his words "Of course the council could decide to forget what it decided, . . . but words have an enormous impact once printed." Skånberg admits that people have been skeptical about the Natural Step program. "Some ask 'Is this a religion or what?'" he says. While the concept has been more often adopted by businesses and corporations, he sees no reason why government should not also embrace it.

Specific evidence of implementation of a Natural Step agenda is premature, but Skånberg points to several recent initiatives that move the city in this direction. One involves his efforts to reform purchasing policies and practices in the city. The companies and offices over which he has some control amount to about 2 billion Swedish kroner, and he believes there are many ways in which these purchase decisions could be made more in line with ecocycle ideas. A set of environmental guidelines has already been prepared to guide purchasing contracts, which lays out both unacceptable impacts or practices, as well as the things that should be discouraged. These guidelines have been given to potential contractors, and Skånberg feels that the message is getting out that those who do business with the city will be scrutinized and held to a high environmental standard.[1] The entire city government is now in the midst of examining and inventorying its environmental impacts with the goal of certification under the EU's Eco-Management and Audit (EMAS) program.

One interesting recent pilot program in Stockholm that further shows the potential of the ecocycle idea is a program called "from table to soil" (translated from the Swedish *"från bord till jord"*). Under this pilot program, organic wastes are collected from participating restaurants and certain kitchens and are processed through a digester, generating biogas (fertilizer). The fertilizer has been used on farm fields in the production of crops. An evaluation study of the pilot's first year indicates generally favorable results. The study found low levels of contamination in the fertilizer and a high production of biogas. The feeling is that with the results so positive, the program will be extended to the entire community. And, Skånberg would like to have a similar process for household organic wastes (although these wastes are not usually as clean).

Can Vice-Mayor Skånberg ever imagine these kinds of initiatives really and fundamentally bringing the city's ecocycles into balance? In the short term probably not. But in the longer term, he is more optimistic. He predicts that in fifty years the situation will have changed dramatically— instead of 10 percent of the city's cycles in balance and 90 percent out of balance, the reverse may be the case.

Stockholm's experience shows the strong importance of cooperation between and among the different agencies, companies, and branches of city government. Skånberg notes the remarkable transformation in thinking since the green-red coalition came into power in his city. He believes staff in all the departments feel freer and more inclined to think green. A main obstacle in the past has been a kind of conservatism—staff afraid to bring up things, to look for interconnections, to think creatively especially if they expected that their ideas would not be appreciated or met with a positive reaction. There is clearly a new, more positive climate in Stockholm city government, and Skånberg says he gets calls all the time to come and visit the departments and to discuss new ideas.

Stockholm is not the only Swedish municipality pursuing an ecocycles approach. Göteburg, for example, has also received well-deserved attention for its efforts in this area. This port city took an explicit ecobalancing approach to preparing its structural (comprehensive) plan in the early 1990s. Specifically, it prepared "material cycles" (analyses) for water and nitrogen, and later carbon dioxide (Berggrund, 1996). These analyses showed the interconnections and linkages between different community sectors and activities, and the major sources of emissions (in the case of nitrogen). Information about these cycles and elements of the metabolism of the city were then used in engaging citizens and politicians in consultations about the structure plan. "Eco-balancing studies . . . have increased awareness about linkages between land development and material flows and cycles in the city and the local environment. They have educated policymakers and residents about the metabolism of the city and about the imbalances in the city's imports of materials and exports of wastes. These studies have mobilized support for work on sustainability and have provided the opportunity for consideration of ecological cycle issues in urban planning. The future challenge is to develop an eco-balancing tool or model that will have more direct input into the structural planning process" (Berggrund, 1996, p. 96).

The Swedish municipality of Ystad has undertaken its own ecocycles program to create more sustainable relationships between the city and the surrounding countryside, and to identify where it can promote local decentralized approaches to dealing with necessary inputs to and outputs from the city. The ecocycles project there yielded a host of projects, ideas, and planned changes in local practice, including a move toward organic waste treatment, the restoration of biodiversity on municipal lands, promoting and encouraging local food production (including a study of patterns of food production and consumption in the city), and investigation of local farmland producing bioenergy (already 60 percent of the fuel for its district heating system comes from energy crops). Much of the early effort here has been focused on studying these issues and engaging the public in a dialogue about the possibilities for the future (European Academy of the Urban Environment, 1996). So far, a major achievement here has been a "new way of thinking among public officials and a large section of the population . . ." now "tries to integrate ecological and environmental aspects and takes a more holistic viewpoint of issues" (European Academy of the Urban Environment, 1996, p. 5).

Examples of other Scandinavian cities pursuing ecocycle balancing strategies can be cited, although few rise to the level of Stockholm's effort. The Swedish town of Eslöv, for example, also extracts biogas from sewage and organic wastes and sends this as fuel for a neighborhood heating system. As a result, the cost of waste treatment here is paid for from the sale of the gas. (And, the amount of sewage sludge generated in the process has been dramatically reduced [European Commission, 1996].)

Connections between City and Hinterland

An important role played by the concepts of environmental space and ecological footprints is that they help to highlight the inherent interconnections between a city and its hinterland—a hinterland that is both regional and global. Many cities are beginning to calculate and be committed to understanding their regional and global impacts. The Sustainable London Trust, for example, in their recent report *Creating a Sustainable London,* begins with the premise that London exerts tremendous resource demands on the world and then recommends a host of actions to reduce those demands. Indeed, London's ecological footprint is calculated to be some 50 million acres, or an area some 125 times the size of the city itself. Greater resource efficiency, promoting circular resource flows, and protecting and promoting local and regional food production are advocated. "Links between consumers and growers in the surrounding rural belt should be encouraged to provide fresh, safe food for city dwellers. Secure local markets for farmers reduce energy needed in food transport and also create a useful setting for environmental education for city people" (Sustainable London Trust, 1997, pp. 10–11). The report continues:

> Of London's own 400,000 acres, nearly 10 percent are classified as farmland, yet only a small proportion is actually used for growing food. Enhancing local food production could be the basis for developing a positive interdependence between city and country, the one providing a secure local market for agricultural produce, the other a place for city-dwellers to enjoy outdoor activities." (Sustainable London Trust, 1997, pp. 7–8)

There has been considerable thinking and writing in Europe about the need to reconnect the city with its hinterland as a primary element in moving toward a more ecocycle-balanced, circular metabolism. In a recent Swedish publication, *Urban Development in an Eco-Cycles Adapted Industrial Society* (Boplats, 1996), several authors argue for clearer, environmentally sustainable connections. Figure 8.2 is one helpful product of this work, graphically illustrating how the surrounding countryside of a city can provide important direct inputs (such as food and energy fuels) and can also serve to recycle the wastes and pollution generated by urban populations and indeed convert these to useful inputs (e.g., ashes applied to forests and organic wastes as fertilizer for farmland). As Husberger (1996) notes: "Town and country are mutually dependent. . . . In the landscape mosaic which evolves out of this inter-dependence, green areas on the urban periphery, will take on a triple function: for peoples' well-being, for the health of the town and for biological diversity" (p. 38).

Thinking critically about a city's reliances and impacts on its hinterland, then, and taking actions to minimize impacts or formalize relationships will be a major challenge for sustainable cities in the future. Many of the cities

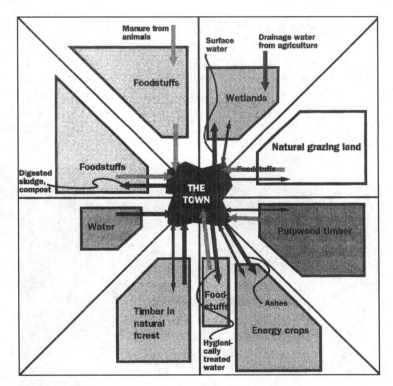

Figure 8.2. Connections between city and countryside

This illustration from a publication of the Swedish Council for Planning and Coordination Research depicts a new way of thinking about the interconnectedness of city and countryside. The countryside ideally provides food and energy for the city and treats and recycles the wastes that urban populations generate.

Source: Husberger, 1996.

examined here are at least beginning to explore these interconnections and to make (albeit modest) efforts to develop more harmonious and sustainable relationships. Münster, Germany, for example, has begun a dialogue with farmers in surrounding areas about the possibilities of more environmentally sustainable food production and the development of a local market for these foods. Utrecht has been working on a similar initiative to help strengthen local organic farming through a subscription farming service. A number of other local governments around Europe have been working in a variety of ways to promote and facilitate organic production (e.g., see Association of Finnish Local Authorities, 1996).

European cities have been leading the way in the composting and recycling of organic wastes. About 100 French cities and many Swiss, Austrian, and German cities have developed comprehensive composting programs and facilities. "In German towns and cities, at this point in time, 17 composting plants are under construction with a combined annual capacity of 600,000 tonnes" (Girardet, undated, p. 44). Through these programs, organic wastes are typically separated at their source (such as households, restaurants, and kitchens) and returned to farms or used in gardens.

The city of Graz has entered into contracts with twenty farmers to accept and compost (source-separated) organic and lawn wastes collected from homes in the city. The farms, located within a 60-kilometer radius of Graz, receive the premixed organic material from the city, actively compost

Public markets such as this one, which help to establish connections between city dwellers and area farmers, are a common feature in European cities.

it for typically between ten and twelve weeks, and then apply the waste to their fields. Farmers are paid by the metric ton and the program is viewed both as a way of providing an additional source of farm income, as well as a way to substantially reduce the city's composting costs. "Overall the project operates as a symbiosis between town and country. Graz residential waste is composted and applied, . . . to the benefit of agricultural land surrounding the city" (Hayes, 1997, p. 35).

Since the early 1990s, Helsinki has undertaken an aggressive biowaste separation and recycling program, which is intended to move this metropolitan area in the direction of "closing the nutrient circle." Under its waste management regulations, all housing blocks of more than nine units must provide separate biowaste collection containers (or provide their own onsite composting). The program is administered by the Helsinki Metropolitan Area Council, which has responsibility for waste collection and management in this metro area of about 1 million. To encourage separation of biowaste, the collection charge for it is half that applied to mixed garbage (see Helsinki Metropolitan Area Council (YTV), 1993; European Commission DGXI, 1996b). Helsinki's goal is to recycle 60 percent of its biowaste by the year 2000 (it has already achieved an overall recycling rate of 40 percent).

In Dutch cities, organic household wastes are typically separated and the resulting so-called "GFT" ("groente, fruit, en tuinafval," or vegetable, fruit, and yard waste) is commonly digested and used to produce biogas. An impressive example of this is the biogas plant in Tilburg. This plant opened in 1994 and now processes about 52,000 tonnes per year of organic wastes (along with some paper and cardboard). After purification, the resulting gas is fed into the city's natural gas network and provides enough gas each year (about 7.5 cubic meters) to meet the needs of 1,200–1,500 homes (Brouwers et al., 1998). Some 28,000 tonnes of high-quality compost are also produced for use in agriculture (NOVEM, 1999).

In Denmark, the municipality of Herning operates a similarly sized facility that produces biogas from both household wastes and agricultural wastes (cattle and pig manure). The facility, which is able to process the entire food waste of Herning, prevents about 1,000 tonnes in carbon dioxide emissions each year (Herning Kommunale Vaerken, undated). The separation and reuse of household organic wastes is a significant example of how many European cities are closing the resource loop.

In countries, such as Finland and Sweden, where there are extensive forests, there is considerable potential for cities to develop energy systems mostly or entirely fueled by these renewable biomass sources and tied to sustainable regional production. In Finland, for example, the municipality of Kuhmo has constructed a power plant (tied to district heating systems), in which wood waste (wood chips and such) provides 95 percent of the fuel (Association of Finnish Local Authorities, 1996). A number of other Scandinavian cities have developed similar renewable energy relationships. Collier and Löfstedt (1997) describe the Swedish city of Eskilstuna, whose local energy company has signed long-term contracts with local farmers who are willing to grow willow to be used to fuel the city's district heating system. The city of Växjö has similarly emphasized biomass energy sources (currently 80 percent of the city's heating needs are provided through biomass).

Many of the study cities also provide examples of exemplary recycling and reuse of household wastes. Leicester, for example, has opened a materials recovery facility called Planet Works (a recycled printing factory). Among the interesting features of this facility is the establishment of what it calls "green accounts." Under this initiative, groups in the community can receive cash credit for bringing in recyclable materials. So far, some 1,000 green accounts have been established. This facility also includes a community resource center, where schools and community groups are entitled, for a small annual membership fee, to take materials (such as textiles and paper) donated to the center by local factories. There are some 400 member groups.

The Mikkeli Region Environment Center in Finland (an association of five municipalities) has set the goal of recycling 70 percent of its wastes, and it recently embarked on a unique pilot project for collecting recycled paper. Residents of sparsely populated areas were given cloth bags in which to place paper waste, which were then collected by post carriers (Association of Finnish Local Authorities, 1996). European cities and regions provide many such creative approaches to waste recycling and reuse.

Closed-Loop Economies: Industrial Symbiosis in the City

Local economies can also contribute significantly to helping a city achieve a circular metabolism through industrial symbiosis, or the connecting of the wastes and inputs of different businesses and industries. Under such schemes, wastes of one industry become the productive inputs to another. The most notable example (in the world) of industrial symbosis is the industrial complex at Kalundborg, Denmark. Here, truly symbiotic relationships have been developed between a power plant (the Asnæs Power Plant), an oil refinery (Statoil), a pharmaceutical company, a plasterboard maker, and the municipality of Kalundborg. The extent of symbiosis is impressive: the power company provides excess heat energy to the municipality for use in its district heating system, provides heat to a fish farm, sells steam to the refinery, and provides gypsum from its SO_2 scrubbers to the plasterboard maker. It also sells flyash to local construction firms. The refinery in turn sells its excess flare gas for fuel to the power plant and the plasterboard maker, provides cooling water to the power plant, and sells sulfur (from its desulphurization process) to a maker of sulfuric acid. The pharmaceutical company, which receives steam heat from the power plant, sends its treated sludge to local farms (see Figure 8.3).

The environmental and economic advantages of developing these types of symbiotic relationships are clear in the Kalundborg case. As Gertler and Ehrenfeld (1994) note, "[T]he linkages at Kalundborg have reduced the material and energy through-put of the participating firms without hindering their production and expansion" (p. 2). Environmental benefits include significant reductions in the amounts of water, oil, and coal consumed, and in pollutants emitted (nearly a 60 percent reduction in SO_2), as well as a significant reduction in the virgin materials used in manufacturing processes (e.g., two-thirds of the gypsum needed by the plasterboard company is provided by the power plant) and the recycling of materials such as sulfur and flyash, among others. There are many specific reasons that help to explain why and how the Kalundborg symbiosis occurred (including a more flexible and cooperative Danish regulatory system and higher background concern about and awareness of the environment), and some specific conditions that are necessary for or at least strongly facilitate these interconnections (e.g., a necessary fit between industries, geographical proximity, and trust and openness between the different parties). Yet, the model is a powerful one, and there is no clear reason why similar closed-loop ideas cannot work in U.S. cities as well.

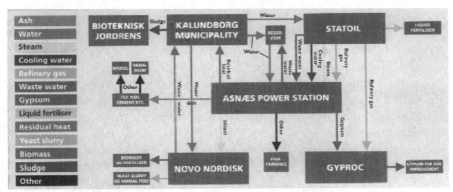

Figure 8.3. Kalundborg eco-industrial complex (Denmark)

The industrial complex in Kalundborg, Denmark, provides one of the few working models of industrial symbiosis. As the illustration shows, a number of different symbiotic interconnections have been developed, with a power plant at the center.

Source: Kalundborg Symbiosis Institute.

The process of developing these impressive symbiotic relationships has been gradual and evolutionary. The first symbioses revolved around reusing water in the 1960s. Clearly, one important key in Kalundborg's success is the ongoing structure for coordination and communication between the companies and other actors in the area. An important structure has been the convening of an environmental committee, or an environmental "club," as its chairman Valdemar Christenson calls it. This group, started in 1989, meets four times a year to discuss future opportunities for expanding symbiosis. Represented in this group are the major companies in the region, the local government (both politicians and municipal officials), and local environmental groups. Here, through discussion and some brainstorming, ideas for expanding symbiosis are hatched. As a recent example, Christenson, who represents the power company, brought to the table their plans to use a new kind of oil to enhance its desulfurization process. Another company, upon hearing this, was interested in using the waste for one of its own processes. A number of other new symbiosis initiatives have been started or discussed in recent years.

Other factors help to explain why the Kalundborg experience developed and has been so successful. Many of the energy efficiencies were prompted by the energy crises of the 1970s and 1980s. There is no question that many, perhaps most, of the symbiotic arrangements have occurred as a result of the leadership and initiative of the Asnæs Power Company. Without their foresight and coordinating role, few of the programs would probably exist today. As the chair of the "environmental club" argues, it is a matter of good economic and business sense to be involved in these arrangements because, ultimately, they save money and enhance profitability. Many of the companies are also benefiting from an enhanced environmental image, which Christenson believes also is valued in terms of its worth in enhanced profits. Environmental altruism, to listen to him, has little to do with the symbioses that have developed. The trend in Denmark toward gradually increasing taxes on waste should also help, he believes, to create further incentives to seek out these kinds of relationships.

Physical proximity surely helps to partly explain these arrangements. The main companies are situated in a kind of semicircle, only about 2 kilometers across and about 4 kilometers around. Christenson believes the "short mental distance" is an extremely important ingredient in Kalundborg's success. Because the town is small, industrial managers and their families tend to know each other, their children go to the same schools, they belong to the same tennis clubs, and so on. This certainly facilitates collaboration and makes it easier to share thoughts of future development.

Another compelling example of symbiosis, although more limited in scope, can be seen in the RoCa3 power plant near Rotterdam, in the Netherlands. Operating since 1996, the plant provides electricity, heating, and carbon dioxide to 130 greenhouses in the area (about 250 hectares of greenhouses). This combind heat and power plant (CHP), then, provides hot water for heating in a way similar to the residential district heating schemes discussed earlier (see Figure 8.4). One unique aspect is the delivery of carbon dioxide (in a separate pipe). Maintaining elevated carbon dioxide levels in Dutch greenhouses is a typical practice (to spur plant production), and the carbon dioxide is usually generated on site. The RoCa3 plant siphons off part of the exhaust stream from its burning of natural gas to pipe to the greenhouses (this is further enriched by burning additional natural gas so that maximum concentration levels are achieved and compressed). Distribution to the greenhouse area occurs through a set of three pipes—one for carbon dioxide, one for outgoing hot water, and one for returning cool water (thus, the heating system is a closed one) (see photo). The pipes travel a distance of 10 kilometers.

Electriciteitsbedrijf Zuid-Holland (EZH), the company operating the plant, reports significant environmental benefits. The central heating system, along with the combined production of heat and power, has a much greater energy efficiency when compared to individual greenhouse boilers. EZH estimates a 20 percent increase in efficiency, the equivalent of the natural gas consumption of 40,000 households (Electriciteitsbedrijf Zuid-Holland [EZH], undated). Reduction in carbon dioxide emissions is primarily a result of reduced burning of natural gas, and EZH estimates an annual reduction of 130,000 tonnes, or about 25 percent less ("equal to that of 20,000 cars each driving 35,000 kilometers per year" [p. 3]).

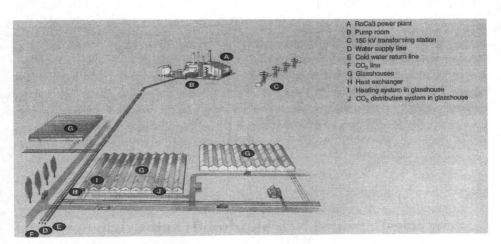

A RoCa3 power plant
B Pump room
C 150 kV transforming station
D Water supply line
E Cold water return line
F CO_2 line
G Glasshouses
H Heat exchanger
I Heating system in glasshouse
J CO_2 distribution system in glasshouse

Figure 8.4. RoCa3 power plant and greenhouses

The RoCa3 power plant near Rotterdam provides heating (hot water) and carbon dioxide to a large area of greenhouses.

Source: Electriciteitsbedrijf Zuid-Holland.

The RoCa3 power plant, in Rotterdam, provides hot water for heating and waste carbon dioxide to a large area of greenhouses. Shown here are the two (larger) hot water pipes (one for outgoing hot water, the other for returning cooler water) and the carbon-dioxide transmission pipe.

The RoCa3 plant and greenhouse heating/carbon dioxide project has been officially supported by the Dutch government through the use of green funds, which offer tax-free interest on returns (see Chapter 10). Specifically, EZH was able to secure a loan at a substantially lower interest rate (for the required 176 million guilders, or about US $90 million). EZH believes that, at least in the Netherlands, there is much more potential for these types of arrangements. They have reached their current capacity to provide the greenhouse area with heat and carbon dioxide and can take no more customers at the moment. Plans exist to build another plant, which will expand capacity and provide the other 250 or so hectares of greenhouses in the area. Even larger greenhouse areas exist in the Netherlands. In the famous Westpark district, for example, there are some 5,000 hectares of greenhouses, and EZH believes the idea could be applied there as well. Other collaborative arrangements are also possible, and EZH has just signed an agreement with Arco Chemical to provide CHP services to one of their new plants soon to be located in Rotterdam.

Ecocycle-Balanced Neighborhoods and Urban Development

Closed-loop or circular metabolism can also be implemented at a neighborhood or development level, and increasingly there are many good examples of this in European cities. The new collaborative spirit in Stockholm in support of closed-loop solutions is also finding positive expression in the planning now under way for Stockholm's new urban growth district—Hammarby Sjöstad. This district, eventually to house 15,000 residents, is being designed from the beginning "with the principle of natural cycles in mind." Throughout its design, from how waste will be treated, to transportation and mobility issues, to how the homes and businesses will be heated, a circular metabolism is a primary objective. A set of ambitious project goals have been established, which lays out more specifically the circular relations to be developed (City of Stockholm, undated-a, -b). All energy needed for heating the buildings in Hammarby Sjöstad, for instance, is to be generated from waste or with other renewable energy sources. Biogas will be extracted from sewage and organic wastes and used in heating. Fertilizer for agriculture will also be produced. A goal of reclaiming more than one-half of nitrogen and water and 95 percent of the phosphorous in wastes has been established (to be used in agricultural operations; City of Stockholm, undated-a, -b).

Vehicles powered by biofuels or electricity will make up at least 15 percent of transport within the project. Other key environmental features will include the local treatment of stormwater and wastewater, the use of rooftop photovoltaics, the establishment of a maximum allowable energy consumption standard, a water consumption rate one-half of what is typical, and the goal of 80 percent of commuter trips to be made on public transit. These goals are to be met in the context of a compact urban community, composed of buildings five- to seven-stories in height. Shops, offices, and light industry will also be included in the district. The neighborhood will be served by a fast train and will provide a pedestrian- and bicycle-friendly environment.

Planning these symbioses and circular flows of inputs and outputs in Hammarby Sjöstad has required a close working relationship between the main municipal agencies. A joint proposal for provision of energy, water, and the treatment of waste has been developed by the lead agencies: Stockholm Energi, Stockholm Water, and SKAFAB (the city's Waste Recycling Company). The Hammarby Sjöstad vision emphasizes the importance of collaboration and integrated thinking among and between those agencies and offices that (typically) have responsibility for different pieces or segments of a closed-loop system (City of Stockholm, undated-a, -b).

The vision of Hammarby Sjöstad, then, is one of a closed-loop urban neighborhood. Throughput—or the amounts of energy, water, and other resources used and consumed by residents—will be, first of all, kept to a minimum. Second, wastes generated from within the project will serve as productive inputs to other activities—to provide heating, energy, and inputs for agricultural production.

Near the Dutch city of Dordrecht, an innovative symbiosis development called City Fruitful has been under discussion and development since the early 1990s. The idea here was to plan a new neighborhood that would integrate residential uses with greenhouses. The neighborhood as envisioned would include 1,700 homes on 56 hectares (with 22 hectares of greenhouses). Living spaces would be closely integrated with the greenhouses. The homes would be "above, under, between, and next to" the commerical greenhouses (Kuiper Compagnons, undated). The greenhouses would provide employment for residents, and would be managed and operated in a closed-loop manner. Fruits and vegetables would be grown for residents in more ecological ways, while the greenhouses would recycle wastewater and organic wastes. The compact design (considerably less land is needed by combining the uses than would conventionally be needed if kept separate) would be largely car free, with great reliance on a system of pedestrian and bicycle paths that would permeate the greenhouses and winter gardens. Forests, fields, and fruit orchards would also be interspersed throughout the circular neighborhood (see Kuiper Compagnons, undated; Municipality of Dordrecht, 1994).

Despite the excitement behind these new symbiotic living ideas, City Fruitful is not likely to be built (at least not any time soon). Several problems have been encountered, including controversy over finding a location, lack of sufficient investment monies, and a less than enthusiastic reaction from the greenhouse industry (see Benjamin, 1997; De Dordtenaars, 1997). Nevertheless, one of the important concepts implicit here is the bringing closer together of a typically polluting industry—one that is often pushed away from where people live. Bringing people and greenhouses together, the proponents of City Fruitful note, would in turn require fundamentally more ecological and safer forms of greenhouse production; the techniques and technologies for which do now exist. "Out of sight, out of mind," would be less possible in symbiotic developments such as this one.

One of the most interesting examples of ecocycle balancing within a housing block can be seen in the ecological renovation of the Fredensgade complex in Kolding (Denmark). This series of 4- and 5-story buildings consisting of 140 flats, with an interior courtyard, was fully renovated in the mid-1990s. A number of new ecological features were incorporated at that time, including a rainwater collection system and the extensive use of passive and active solar energy systems. But the boldest move was to disconnect the housing project from the city's wastewater treatment system, and to begin to treat its own wastewater, circulating it through a very interesting urban living machine—a pyramidal structure called the bioworks, situated for all residents to see in the interior courtyard.

The stages in the process of the treatment of wastewater in the bioworks are shown in Figure 8.5. First, the wastewater is deposited in a series of

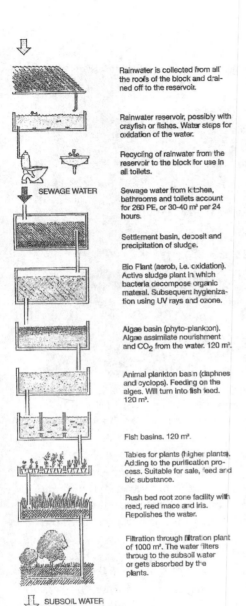

Rainwater is collected from all the roofs of the block and drained off to the reservoir.

Rainwater reservoir, possibly with crayfish or fishes. Water steps for oxidation of the water.

Recycling of rainwater from the reservoir to the block for use in all toilets.

SEWAGE WATER

Sewage water from kitchen, bathrooms and toilets account for 260 PE, or 30-40 m³ per 24 hours.

Settlement basin, deposit and precipitation of sludge.

Bio Plant (aerob, i.e. oxidation). Active sludge plant in which bacteria decompose organic material. Subsequent hygienization using UV rays and ozone.

Algae basin (phyto-plankton). Algae assimilate nourishment and CO_2 from the water. 120 m².

Animal plankton basin (daphnes and cyclops). Feeding on the algae. Will turn into fish feed. 120 m³.

Fish basins. 120 m³.

Tables for plants (higher plants). Adding to the purification process. Suitable for sale, feed and bic substance.

Rush bed root zone facility with reed, reed mace and iris. Repolishes the water.

Filtration through filtration plant of 1000 m². The water filters throug to the subsoil water or gets absorbed by the plants.

SUBSOIL WATER

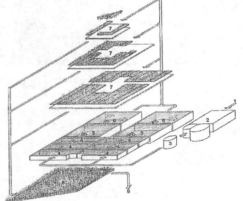

1: Sewage water from the flats
2: Sludge deposit and pre-treatment by means of bacteria.
3: Hygienizing (UV-rays/ozone).
4: Algae basin with algae feeding on the nutritive salts of the water
5: Animal plankton feeding on the algae.
6: Fishes and mussels feeding on algae and animal plankton.
7: Horticultural area with the plants being nourished by the nutritious matters of the water.
8: Root zone facility for final treatment of the water.
9: Filtration plant from where the water is filtered to the subsoil water.

Figure 8.5. Fredensgade bioworks diagram

Wastewater is treated and passes through several stages in the Fredensgade "bioworks," shown here. Within the pyramid, wastewater is first broken down by passing through a series of basins where bacteria is eaten by algae, plankton, fishes, and mussels. Then the water is pumped to the top of the pyramid where it filters through a series of plant-production levels where wastes become productive nutrients to this commercial horticultural operation. In the final stage, wastewater is filtered through an outside reedbed and allowed to percolate back into the ground.

Source: Municipality of Kolding.

The "bioworks" pyramid, located in the interior of the Fredensgade development in Kolding, Denmark, treats and recycles wastewater from the complex and makes this natural process a visually prominent element in the neighborhood.

underground tanks, where organic materials are removed and bacteria is killed through the use of ultraviolet rays and an ozone treatment (Kolding Kommune, 1995). The wastewater then enters the bioworks pyramid and is processed through a series of biological tanks on the ground level. Each tank (there are two independent systems) represents a different level of biological breakdown (from algae to plankton to fishes and mussels), and a simulated food chain. After leaving the last chamber (fishes and mussels), the water is pumped to the top of the pyramid and used for irrigating and fertilizing platforms of plants. As the effluent makes its way down the pyramid, the last stage involves pumping it to an outside reedbed and then finally to an underground filtration bed. The water is then allowed, in the final stage, to percolate back to the underlying groundwater aquifer.

The pyramid is an impressive visual presence in the development—really a piece of ecological architecture. Unfortunately, the inside of the pyramid is off limits to residents of the neighborhood (mainly because it is considered a kind of industrial work environment); once inside, it is easy to see why access to the public needs to be controlled. Nevertheless, there is considerable public space around the pyramid, including a children's play area, and quite a bit of greenspace. Ground-floor residents also have their own private gardens, which open up to the common area. A portion of the collected rainwater on the site is pumped to a flow form, and a small human-made creek trickles down to a small pond (rainwater reservoir).[2]

The bioworks have been operating for about five years, and no problems have been experienced. The water percolating into the ground is apparently quite clear, and local health authorities are happy with the way the system works. One issue that has arisen is whether the residents will be willing to take over management of the facility. This was the original plan, but residents have expressed reservations about this. Some want to wait longer to make sure that no problems with the wastewater system develop. Currently, residents do not pay any type of wastewater fee to the city (because there is no wastewater), and as these fees continue to rise it is believed that residents may further appreciate the benefits of not being connected to the public sewage treatment system.

Interestingly, the bioworks pyramid has actually one tenant: a commercial plant grower, who pays rent for the space to the city. While there are fish in the lowest level of the structure, they are currently not harvested. Moreover, the health department has forbidden the growing of vegetables or fish harvesting that would ultimately be for human consumption. The city would like to see this use happen eventually, but it may take some convincing of health officials before it is allowed. It was also originally envisioned that at the final stage of purification, the wastewater would be directed to the rainwater pond for reuse again in the buildings. This raises additional health concerns and has not yet been allowed to occur.[3]

There are a number of other positive examples around Europe of housing projects and urban neighborhoods that are promoting some form of closed-loop strategy. For example, in Morra Park, an ecological housing project in Drachten, Netherlands, a main design feature is a closed-loop canal system that circulates and cleanses water. Rainwater is collected in the canals and circulated by pump through a constructed wetland. Other design features include southern orientation and solar rooms (serres), efforts to minimize hard surfaces, and the use of nontoxic building materials. The result has been a positive one in several ways. Unlike the typical canals in surrounding agricultural areas, the water quality in the closed system is very high, and in fact residents can and do swim in the canals. As well, the canals are an aesthetic and recreational amenity for residents in other ways. On any given day, children can be seen launching toy boats or paddling about in canoes. Evaluation studies show residents are quite pleased with the resulting quality of the environment.

Another Dutch illustration is the centralized greywater recycling system in Polderdrift (in Arnhem). This is one of the first examples of an entire residential complex connected to such a centralized system. Water from sinks and showers is processed and treated through a reedbed filtration system in the very center of the complex and then is recirculated to the apartments and used again for toilet flushing. As with Fredensgade and Morra Park, the treatment system is itself a central part of the visual and aesthetic experience of living in the project. It is a visible kind of ecological infrastructure that demonstrates on a daily basis how and where residents' greywater wastes go and are treated. These are but a few examples of a large and growing number of European projects that demonstrate closed-loop ideas and technologies.

Encouraging Ecocycle Balancing: The Role of Green Taxes

There is little question that many of the ecocycle balancing initiatives described here, and a greater emphasis on biomass and renewable energy sources are encouraged and fostered in part because of the existence of *green taxes* or *environmental taxes,* in European counties.

A wide range of green taxes are used in Europe, and expansion of green taxes has been especially apparent in the northern European counties. A variety of such taxes exist, including those that impose charges on sulphur, nitric oxides, household wastes, water pollution, and carbon dioxide emissions. A recent study commissioned by the European Environment Agency concluded that these systems have generally been successful at achieving their environmental goals, without apparent impacts on competitiveness (the main complaint) (see European Environment Agency, 1996). Countries like Denmark, moreover, are gradually shifting the tax burden from labor and income to energy consumption and pollution.[4]

Sweden has an extensive set of green taxes (e.g., on sulphur, nitrogen oxide, carbon), and a recent evaluation report there concludes that the taxes have resulted in significant reductions in pollution, with relatively small administrative costs (less than 1 percent in the case of the nitrogen oxide tax; Swedish Environmental Protection Agency, 1997). The carbon tax imposed there has resulted in a major shift to using biofuels in municipal district heating systems.

The Netherlands has also made great strides in the area of environmental or eco-taxes. It now levies extensive energy taxes, taxes on groundwater withdrawal, and a per-kilogram tax on waste (see Vermeend and Van der Vaart 1998 for a full discussion of Dutch green taxes). The national government's tax system has also been modified in important ways to promote more sustainable mobility. For example, companies are allowed a tax-free reimbursement for employees who use public transport while similar benefits are restricted for auto usage. Employers are also permitted to give each employee one 1,500 guilder bicycle (about US $750) every three years, while the employee is taxed for only 150 guilders (about $75). Employer payments for rain gear and bicycle insurance are also tax free. The Netherlands has also adopted a program of accelerated depreciation for investment in sustainable technologies and has declared that money placed in green investment funds are also tax free. These taxation policies and priorities have done much to encourage a wide range of ecological projects and investments and certainly help move the country in the direction of becoming a closed-loop society.

Germany's 1991 packaging law (Avoidance of Waste Ordinance) requires companies either to directly take back their packaging waste or to make arrangements for its collection and reuse. Girardet (undated) describes the positive results of this law:

> Customers have the right to strip packaging off products at the check-out til and to leave it there. This has led supermarkets to put pressure on producers to reduce their packaging. Companies are increasingly organizing their own waste collection and recycling systems. Overall, the Ordinance, together with high charges for dumping waste, has caused a massive increase in waste recycling in Germany. After initial oversupply of waste materials, recycling capacity in the country is now greatly increased, with considerable long-term benefits for the national economy. In other European countries, such as Austria, Switzerland and Denmark, similar situations exist. (p. 26)

Germany has also recently put into place considerable new taxes on energy use that will be used to reduce social security taxes there. There is little question that this growing emphasis on ecological tax reform in Europe helps create a supportive climate for ecocycle balancing.

Lessons for American Cities

There are many ways in which American cities and towns can move in the direction of supporting a more circular, ecocycle-balanced metabolism. An inital observation is that it is difficult to develop either a sense of concern about the resource inputs needed and wastes generated by a community or an appreciation of what the opportunities might be without first having some basic information and knowledge. As a first step, American cities should prepare an analysis of their metabolisms and metabolic flows. This might be modeled after Girardet's study of London. As it has become common in the United States for each local government to prepare a comprehensive plan, urban metabolism should become an important new element in these plans. Regional governments (e.g., COGs), moreover, could take the lead in documenting, analyzing, and promoting discussion about the *region*'s urban metabolism. These would be modest, though important, steps in the direction of green-urbanism.

There are currently a number of ecoindustrial parks, or industrial symbiosis complexes, in some stage of development around the United States. The USEPA has been influential in their sponsorship, and they include parks in development in Baltimore, Brownsville, Cape Charles (Virginia), Chattanooga, and elsewhere. So far, however, the progress has been limited. Nevertheless, the idea must continue to receive strong support (financial and other forms). Chattanooga's project illustrates the potential of this idea as an integral part of any urban sustainability program. As part of the city's redevelopment plan for its Southside Business District, it has proposed a SMART Park that will connect a series of resource and waste flows from industrial and nonindustrial activities. Key elements of this Chattanooga "zero emission" park would be a central energy plant, a working foundry, a food processing plant, Findley Stadium, and the city's trade center, among others. One waste stream would capture ethanol that would be used to fuel the city's hybrid-electric buses (Chattanooga Institute, undated).

When it comes to balancing urban ecocycles, other promising beginnings in American communities can also be identified. A number of American communities have applied some form of the "living machine" technology in treating wastewater, for instance, and in turn at least a partial ecocycle-balanced approach to this form of waste. The town of Arcata, California, has received much (well-deserved) attention for its early and innovative effort to develop a natural wetland for treatment of its wastewater. The result is the Arcata Marsh and Wildlife Sanctuary, which provides important wildlife and bird habitat while effectively treating wastewater without the large infrastructure and chemical-intensive approach of most conventional municipal treatment plants (Curtius, 1998a). Using a more natural design was also significantly less costly than the price of the city's share of a planned regional wastewater plant—to the tune of half as much. It is claimed that as a result Arcata's local sewage bill's "are the lowest in the country" (Curtius, 1998a, p. A3). Curtius describes how this system works:

> Sewage flows into the collection area, where wastewater is separated from sludge. The sludge is kept in huge tanks, where it is 'digested' for a month before being drained into drying trays. The dried sludge then is broken up and

mixed with plants harvested from the marsh and wood chips in a compost pile. High temperatures in the pile kill off harmful bacteria. Within a month, the compost is ready to spread across the town's soccer fields, its forest and on flower beds.

The water, meanwhile, sits in an oxidation pond, where sunlight kills most microbes. It is chlorinated, then allowed to flow into a series of three marsh ponds. There, it mixes with the brackish water of the bay. Two weeks to a month after it first enters the plant, the water is rechlorinated, then dechlorinated and discharged into Humboldt Bay. (p. A3)

Other cities have at least partially adopted the Arcata design, including cities such as Davis (California) and Burlington (Vermont), among others. Arcata's ownership and sustainable management of a community forest also puts it in a unique category. The forest, a productive town amenity, figures clearly into an ecobalanced strategy for this small town. The concept of a *sewage forest*—where a city's sewage is treated through application to a living, growing forest—holds particular promise. Such forests, already applied at a small scale by several other American communities, hold potential for naturally treating sewage and at the same time sequestering large amounts of carbon. Wickham (1999) estimates that the annual carbon reduction potential of this technique is an astounding 740 million tons (some 15 percent of U.S. emissions) when the carbon expended in the process of conventional sewage treatment is taken into account.

The Davis Wetlands Project is another exemplary effort to recycle wastes and to restore and replace wildlife habitat. Here, the city of Davis, in collaboration with the U.S. Army Corps and others, has planned and constructed a 400-acre system of wetlands and ponds. The constructed lagoon and pond system receives the city's stormwater and treated wastewater (at tertiary treatment levels), which is further treated as it moves through this system before being discharged into the Yolo Basin (and eventually the Sacramento River). In addition to permanent wetlands, the project also creates significant seasonal wetlands, as well as new riparian woodlands and grassland habitats. Only native vegetation has been planted. Water levels in the lagoon system are managed seasonally to maximize their habitat potential. During the winter months, higher water levels are maintained to support winter waterfowl. During the spring, water levels are lowered to increase habitat for wading shorebirds.

The Davis Wetlands Project is an effort to replace some of the nearly 95 percent of the wetlands lost to agriculture in the Central Valley. In the past, large areas of Yolo County were allowed to seasonally flood, providing important habitat for waterfowl moving along the Pacific Flyway. Significant about these kinds of projects is the recognition of an important habitat-restorative role for cities, as well as the fact that such projects can at once enhance biodiversity and creatively treat and recycle urban waste. Such projects help to move us in the direction of creating circular wastestreams and balanced urban ecocycles, as well as creating important new habitat areas. Another result is to create ecological places of significance for the community—important recreational and educational resources for residents. Already, for example, the Davis project has become an important educational and civic project for the community.

American communities, taking the lead from European cities, should also be more aggressive in directly securing and managing surrounding hinterlands as important elements of their local ecological capital. Already discussed in Chapter 7 is the need for ecological networks and regional greenspace strategies. Part of such networks could be productive farmlands, which provide food for the region (delivered through farmers markets, subscription farming, and arrangements for connecting farmers with restaurants and grocers) and energy crops for decentralized energy production facilities, among many other possible ideas.

Finally, there is much to recommend green tax reform in the United States, although the political feasibility in the short term is questionable. Especially if such taxes can (as in countries like Denmark and Germany) be linked to reductions in other taxes, including taxes on income, their acceptability will be enhanced considerably (Burke, 1997). However unacceptable in the foreseeable future, the importance of a shift in taxing structures is a major lesson to be learned from the Europeans.

There are, in fact, signs that environmental tax reform is beginning to receive serious attention in several states. Environmental tax-shifting proposals have been floated or are under review in Vermont, Oregon, Maine, Michigan, and Minnesota. Minnesota's proposed Economic Efficiency and Pollution Reduction Act of 1998 has been by far the most ambitious. It demonstrates the considerable combined fiscal and environmental benefits of such strategies. Under the proposed law, a US $50 per ton tax on carbon would have generated some $1.3 billion in tax revenues, in turn allowing for a reduction of property taxes by about 25 percent. Renewable energy sources would be exempt from the tax. Generated funds would also have been used to pay for investments in energy efficiency, as well as for public transit and bridge repair (Sustainable Minnesota, 1998). The proposal would have reduced energy use and pollution, while at the same time creating an estimated 12,000 new jobs. Recent opinion polls actually suggest that Americans favor such tax-shifting proposals (e.g., Friends of the

Earth, 1998; Vermont Fair Tax Coalition, 1999). Such tax shifting has tremendous promise, and within the U.S. framework it appears to be an especially appropriate and supportive role for states to play.

NOTES

1. He relates a story about going through the process of choosing a gasoline contractor and raising concern about Shell Oil. Eventually Shell was chosen, but in the process the company voluntarily agreed to take a number of actions to promote alternative-fuel vehicles in the city. He believes the guidelines and new expectations have helped to encourage and push along their new attitude.
2. The flow form and creek have not been running of late, however, apparently because of problems with the pump and circulation system.
3. Interestingly, only about 5 percent to 10 percent of the effluent water actually enters the pyramid. Most of the wastewater is treated through the below-ground septic tanks and reedbed system (see Kennedy and Kennedy, 1997).
4. From 1994 to 1998, Denmark is reported to have reduced its income tax by 8 percent to 10 percent, while increasing taxes on gasoline, water, energy, and waste (Burke, 1997).

Chapter 9

Renewable Energy Cities: Living on Solar Income

Low-Energy, Renewable-Energy Cities

Cities, and the populations and economic activities supported within their boundaries, use tremendous amounts of energy. There are, consequently, great opportunities to redesign, reconfigure, and reimagine the way these energy needs are satisfied, to reduce waste, increase efficiency, and greatly reduce environmental impacts (including, importantly, emissions of carbon dioxide and other greenhouse gases). Green-urban cities move on several energy fronts simultaneously: they reduce energy waste and increase energy efficiency, and they move in the direction of satisfying energy needs through renewable sources. There are many positive examples from European cities that have ranked energy high on the local agenda. Especially impressive are the efforts to promote and facilitate solar energy in many of these cities. The sections that follow describe and evaluate a range of local energy programs and initiatives.

Municipal Energy Planning and Conservation

There are a number of obvious energy features of green-urban European cities. Generally, these cities tend to use much less energy and thus produce less carbon dioxide than American cities. Similarly, they generally place much greater importance on promoting energy conservation and renewable energy sources. A number of reasons help explain this, with important lessons and ideas for American cities. One reason is the typically more efficient form of heating and power generation in place in many European cities. Many European cities have long histories of providing a large percentage of their heating needs through district heating systems, typically through the combined generation of heat and power (CHP plants) (see Nijkamp and Perrels, 1994). These systems have in turn been encouraged and financially supported at the national government level.[1]

The energy and environmental advantages of combined heat and power (CHP) production are considerable, and the use of this method is one of the clearest environmental technology stories from Europe. Efficiency in fuel conversion is much higher (typically close to 90 percent) than from separate production of electricity and heat (typically around 40 percent or lower). This type of production can result, moreover, in significant reductions in nitrogen oxides (NOX) and other air pollutants and in overall carbon dioxide production. There are many different sizes and scales of CHP plants used, from large-scale (serving major cities and larger district heating systems) to small-scale industrial and municipal users typically producing less than 1 MegaWatt (MW) (including block and mini CHP plants) that are not connected to a district heating network. There are many ways of utilizing CHP and district heating technologies, and these European cities provide abundant practical illustrations.

The city of Helsinki has one of the most extensive and successful district heating systems and has won an United National Environmental Award for it. Although only dating back to the late 1950s, district heating is now provided to more than 91 percent of the buildings in the city (see Figure 9.1) (Helsinki Energy, undated). Fueled by combined heat and power plants owned by the city, the result has been a significant increase in fuel efficiency (from 40 percent to up to 80 percent), as well as substantial reductions in local sulfur dioxide and nitrogen oxide levels (as the result of desulfurization and replacing individual house chimneys). The city has further worked to reduce average energy consumption through a program of consumer education, building insulation, and installation of new heat recovery and thermostat systems (Helsinki Energy, undated). Cities such as Helsinki illustrate the great potential for district heating (though it should be noted that in this particular city there is heavy reliance on a high carbon, nonrenewable energy source, namely coal).

Many of the case cities are working to increase efficiency and expand the use of district heating. Only 64 percent of Stockholm's heating needs are provided through district heating, and the city is taking action to expand this percentage (to a potential of about 80 percent). Vienna only started district heating in the 1990s but has now converted 100,000 flats and many institutional buildings, such as hospitals (costs of hookup to the system are subsidized by the city). There is also a clear effort to promote renewable energy sources, and already some 50 percent of the energy sup-

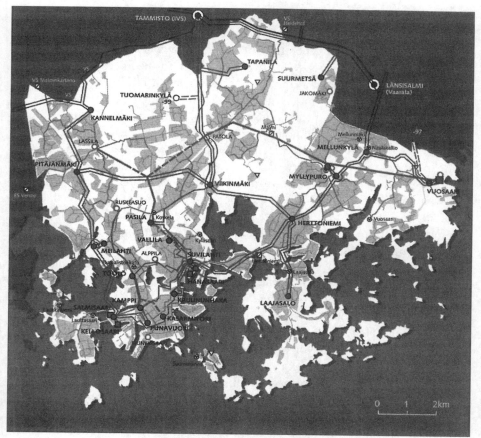

Figure 9.1. Map of district heating network (Helsinki)

Electricity and district heating transmission networks in Helsinki. Shaded areas indicate the coverage of the district heating network.

Source: Helsinki Energy.

ply for district heating comes from renewable sources. (One of the city's CHP plants uses only biofuels.)

Stockholm Energi, the city's energy company, has also been gradually expanding the city's district cooling network. Under this system, cooling water is collected from seawater (80 percent from Lilla Vartan) and supplied to 35 percent of the downtown buildings needing summer air conditioning. Estimates suggest that district cooling will result in a considerable reduction in the use of environment-damaging refrigerants (Stockholm Energi, 1997).

There are few European countries where district heating is more prevalent than Denmark. In total, there are 400 district heating companies in

Denmark.[2] Currently some 50 percent of heat demand in the country is provided through district heating, a dramatic increase from only 5 percent in 1952 (Danish Energy Agency, 1998). The percentage rates are much higher for the larger Danish cities, such as Copenhagen, where district heating coverage is typically 95 percent to 98 percent. The heating system at Århus is illustrative. Here, 98 percent of heat for the city is produced through a network that includes a central CHP power plant (waste energy from the large Studstrupvaerket power plant), a waste incinerator plant, and three peak load boilers (used when needed). The 100-kilometer distribution system circulates 40 million cubic meters of heating water per year, with a reported heat loss of only 1.5 percent (although this loss may be as high as 20 percent in rural areas) (Danish Energy Agency, 1998). The expansion of CHP and district heating in Denmark has in large part been the result of national government financial incentives and support. The national government has provided a series of significant investment subsidies and grants heavily funded in recent years from the proceeds of its green taxes (for a chronology and summary of recent incentives, see Danish Energy Agency, 1998).

Decentralized Energy Production

The use of more localized, smaller-scale CHP plants brings power production down to the geographical scale at which it can be seen in the community and have an important visual presence. There are many examples of such plants that are architecturally striking, a characteristic that represents an opportunity for such community facilities to not only enhance appreciation of and education about the source of power generation but also to produce new important elements of the civic infrastructure in the community. Some good examples can be found in Danish cities. The CHP plant in Viborg, Denmark, is one such example. The building is visually striking, and as a recent case study of the plant notes, "The beautiful design of the plant as such is a source of pride to the citizens of Viborg" (Danish Energy Agency, 1998, p. 29). Another impressive example is the district heating plant in the Spittelau district of Vienna. A dramatic retrofitted designed by architect/artist Hundertwasser, it is an example of civic art as much as it is a functional building. Its gray industrial exterior has been transformed into a colorful mosaic of tiles and curves and gold spheres. The truck loading dock even has a plush green roof covering it (Rand, 1993).

A decentralized energy strategy was embarked upon by the city of Amsterdam in the late 1980s. The city's municipal energy company is implementing a system of more than thirty decentralized cogeneration units. "The locally produced electricity is distributed to the grid belonging to the

Use of decentralized combined heat and power plants to provide heat to district heating systems is a common practice in many European cities. Shown here is a CHP plant in Vienna that has been artistically redesigned by Friedensreich Hundertwasser to become an important piece of civic architecture, as well as a utility structure.

municipal energy company, whereas the heat is used on site in council housing, hospitals, hotels and other large buildings" (European Commission, 1996, p. 120). Significant energy savings have been reported from this program.

In Saarbrücken, a municipal-owned utility company—Saarbrücken Stadtwerke—is responsible for providing water, gas, electricity, and block heating. Unlike most other cities, some 97 percent of the energy needs of this city are produced locally. Much of this production comes from conventional electric power generation, which is fueled by coal waste (Saarbrucken is in a major coal-producing region). This method is seen by the company as a more environmentally responsible form of production, because it uses waste dust and also results in clearing spoil sites that can be later used for industrial redevelopment. Extensive district heat is also produced in the process, and about 50 percent of the homes in the city are now connected to this system.

While CHP production and district heating systems are more commonly used in Scandinavian and northern European cities, new application of this technology can be increasingly found in other parts of Europe. Although currently supplying only a small portion of its power needs through CHP, the U.K. government has developed a national strategy for promoting the technology, and its growth there in recent years has been substantial. The U.K. strategy has set the goal of 5,000 MW by the year 2000 (3,500 MW

Solar-powered parking lot lights are seen here in a new ecological housing estate in Gouda, the Netherlands.

at 1,300 sites had already been achieved by 1996) (U.K. Department of the Environment, undated). It has attempted to set the stage by installing a CHP/district heating system for its Whitehall government offices, which is estimated to result in a reduction of 5,000 tonnes of carbon emissions each year and produce a sizable savings of £750,000 (US $1.2 million) in public energy expenditures (U.K. Department of the Environment, 1996).

In Dublin, a new CHP system has been installed in the Civic Offices of the Dublin Corporation, and it serves the heating needs of the municipal offices, a church, five nearby hotels, and fifty-three apartments (Conservation Engineering Limited, undated).[3] Plans exist to connect new apartments in Temple Bar to this system in the future. A natural-gas-fired generator produces 922 kW of output, and during peak winter heating and energy loads, supplemental gas boilers can be brought into service. Excess electricity production is sold to the national power grid. Supported by the EC Thermie program, the arrangement takes advantage of complementary heat-energy local schedules (high daytime, weekday needs in the offices, higher nighttime and weekend needs in the hotels and apartments). Other small-scale CHP systems have also been built in Ireland in recent years.

One of the most exciting combinations of energy technologies developing in Europe is the concept of solar-assisted district heating networks. Here, extensive solar panels generate, during summer months, much of the heating of the water circulated in the district network. Seasonal storage of energy is also provided. Recent examples include large-scale systems in Friedrichshafen (Germany) and Marstal (Aeroe Island, Denmark) (see Kunz, 1999). In the latter (described as the "largest flat-plate solar heating system in the world"), the solar collectors provide about 12.5 percent of the annual heating needs of the district heating system (serving a town of

5,000 people and 1,250 connected homes).[4] During the summer months (June, July, and August), 100 percent of the heating needs are satisfied through the collectors (Kunz, 1999). Efficiency is improved through a system of variable water flow and temperature-regulated circulation pumps, and water from the 640 solar collectors is stored in a 2,100-square-meter tank. The environmental benefits of such a system are considerable, including a major reduction in yearly carbon dioxide emissions (933 fewer tonnes), and the cost of producing the energy in this way is competitive with conventional power (CADDET, 1997; Brouwers, et al., 1998).

Strides in Energy Efficiency

Many examples exist of communities that are taking a much more aggressive stance toward promoting energy efficiency and demand reduction. Often, this starts with improvements in the energy efficiency (and resource efficiency more generally) of public buildings. Saarbrücken, for example, which has made tremendous strides at reducing energy consumption in the city, first undertook a significant effort to enhance the efficiency of its own buildings and reduce its own consumption of energy. It saw this as an area where it had immediate control, and it recognized that such actions would set positive examples for citizens. It did a number of things to reduce energy consumption. One important step was to give clear direction to housekeepers and building managers about the appropriate levels of heating (e.g., in offices, school rooms, and so forth, heating was to be set at 20° C and at 12° C for stairwells) during the day, with adjustments to be made for the time of day. The housekeepers and building managers were asked to monitor consumption and to record meter readings for heating, and later electricity and water consumption. A program of building improvements was also undertaken, with about DM 1 million spent each year to increase insulation (about US $540,000), install more energy efficient windows, and perform a host of other actions. The city also made it a policy to gradually replace oil-burning and coal-burning heating systems in its larger buildings with connections to the city's district heating system.

The combined results of these actions by the Saarbrücken Stadtwerke, (the city's municipal energy company) have been dramatic. Between 1981 and 1996, consumption of heating in city properties was reduced by 53 percent. Corresponding reductions in carbon dioxide emissions have also been considerable—a reduction from 65,000 tonnes in 1981 to 35,000 tonnes (in 1997). The investments have also proven to be highly cost-effective for the city. The DM 1 million yearly investment has yielded a DM 10 million return (about US $5.4 million) in the form of power savings. Freiburg has aggressively sought improved energy efficiency in its own municipal buildings since the late 1970s. It invested DM 6.3 million in energy efficiency improvements (about US $3.4 million) between 1979 and 1991, which have been estimated to save the city nearly DM 25 million (about US $13.5 million) (Von Ungern-Sternberg, 1996).[6] Freiburg is also promoting energy conservation through the electricity rate structure it imposes on customers (through the utility company it partially owns). In 1992, Freiburg adopted an innovative system of "linear time-variable electricity charges," in which consumers are charged according to the time of day their consumption occurs. (The result is an overall reduction in consumption and a shifting of consumption to low-peak times; Heller, 1997.) Other cities, including Odense and Charleroi (Belgium) have undertaken similar programs aimed at substantially reducing energy consumption in municipal buildings (European Commission, 1996).

Heidelberg has taken a number of actions, many quite creative, to reduce energy consumption in its own public buildings. Most creative perhaps are the incentive-based contracts the city has entered into with private companies. Under these arrangements, private companies are allowed to keep a high percentage of the financial gains that can be reaped through energy-conservation measures and energy retrofitting measures (20 percent of any reduction, however, goes back to the city). This arrangement is being made for half of the city's buildings, while the city is undertaking its own retrofitting program on the other structures. The city has also set up partnerships with its schools, encouraging them to take actions to conserve energy and creating positive economic incentives for doing so by allowing them to keep 40 percent of the resulting savings (40 percent goes to retrofitting the building and the other 20 percent to the city's general revenue).[7] The city provides the schools with monitoring equipment and technical assistance, and the schools agree to form "E-teams" (energy teams) to guide the project. In this way, an evaluation function is also served. Municipal energy agencies frequently form their own "E-teams," which provide advice to homeowners and businesses about ways to reduce energy consumption (and at the same time provide needed local employment). Often, this advice involves the preparation of an energy audit.

Many of these cities illustrate, as well, a willingness to subsidize energy efficiency improvements in private homes and businesses. The Saarbrücken Stadtwerke, for instance, has implemented a series of below-market energy conservation improvement loans to homeowners, allowing investments in such things as insulation and district heating hookups. The energy company also provides rebates for the purchase of energy-efficient appliances and for the conversion of water heating from electric to gas (Results Center, undated).

Cities are attempting to promote high energy-efficiency standards in businesses and homes in their communities. Leicester, for example, has been emphasizing a very useful system for evaluating and rating the energy efficiency of homes. Under the National Energy Rating System, buildings receive a rating of between 1 and 10 (with 10 the most energy-efficient). The city uses this rating system as a mechanism for setting minimum energy standards for the city. Specifically, for the city as a whole a target of 6 has been established, but for buildings on city property a minimum score of 9 is required.

Some cities, such as Leicester, have sought to understand and address energy-consumption citywide. To do this, an energy model was developed that estimates and projects, under different scenarios, the energy consumption of all sectors in a city (commercial, housing, and transportation).[5] The model—the Dynamic Regional Energy Analysis Model—was developed by researchers at the Open University in Milton Keynes, and its development was funded through the EU. It estimates the total energy consumed and the carbon dioxide generated, given such inputs as weather, population, and housing characteristics, and the efficiency of appliances and heating plants (see Titheridge, Boyle, and Fleming, 1996; Green, 1995). A key goal was to begin to identify the type and magnitude of local actions that would be necessary to reach the city's carbon dioxide reduction goals (50 percent reduction by 2025). A *green scenario* indicated that a reduction in energy use of 65 percent was possible, through a series of technological and lifestyle changes (Environ, 1996).

In Leiden, similar collaborative programs to promote energy and resource conservation between the city and the energy company have been undertaken. Recently, customers were offered a package of equipment, including a low-flow shower head, low-flow faucet, and water-conserving toilet. Customers were offered the package at a subsidized price, with the city and energy company providing the subsidy. The availability of the conservation equipment was advertised in local papers, through the distribution of brochures, and with exhibits at special local events. The six jurisdictions in the Leiden region combine to pay the salary of a sustainability advisor who attends local events (such as summer fairs), as well as advises local governments about incorporating sustainability concerns into housing project designs and other local matters. A number of other cities operate energy advice centers or services to assist customers in undertaking energy efficiency improvements.

In Saarbrücken, the municipal energy company operates an extensive and impressive energy Information Center. The Info Center staff help residents with energy issues in a number of ways. They distribute free electricity consumption meters and help citizens calculate the energy consumption of their homes. One of the first things that catches the eye when entering the Info Center is a full-scale miniature model of a town, visually depicting the various renewable energy options available and giving, in a tangible physical model, a sense of what some of these options might look like—including homes with solar panels, grocery stores with PV arrays, wind turbines, and a biomass forest. What is missing, of course, are the many other elements that might make up a sustainable place, but the model town is a good heuristic devise for an energy company lobby.

Energy Standards for New Development

Many of these cities have sought to ensure that the new housing constructed in their communities is designed and built in ways that greatly minimize the energy consumed. Especially for German and Dutch cities, minimum energy consumption standards are commonly established as a condition for development that takes place on city-owned land. Heidelberg, for instance, has set a minimum energy standard for new homes built on city-owned property: 65 kWh/square meter per year for single-family homes and 50 kWh/square meter per year for buildings with multiple flats. Freiburg implements a similar low-energy concept, requiring a standard of 65 kWh/per m2 per year for projects such as the new Rieselfeld development (where the city owned the land and could impose this condition). Münster has adopted similar policies. Vienna, through its construction ordinance, imposes a standard of 60 kWh/square meter per year for all new buildings.

Many of the cities have taken proactive stances by building demonstration projects that show the feasibility and practicality of energy-efficient housing. To demonstrate that very low per-household energy use is possible, for example, Heidelberg recently experimented with designing a new social housing project to a very high standard. Specifically, the project, called Am Dorf, involves social flats built to the very low energy standard of 47 kWh/square meter per year. The project of sixty-eight units, built by a city-owned social building company, demonstrates a number of design features, including good insulation practice, reduction of thermal bridges, solar orientation (large windows on the southern side, small windows on the northern side), solar panels for hot water heating, and rainwater collection for toilet flushing (providing about a third of the water required for flushing).

Many new Dutch housing districts have energy conservation and low-energy usage as central design themes. Energy conservation elements of the GWL project in Amsterdam are considerable. A power generator is located in the center of the project, which produces electricity and also provides centralized district heating (hot water) for all units in the development. As a result, none of the new homes has its own separate heating unit. A separate line for clean hot water runs to each unit as well, for bath and other hot water needs. Hot-filled washing machines can also be used in the project. Together, the energy savings for residents is considerable.

Urban Policies to Promote Renewable Energy

Renewable energy sources are receiving substantial attention in these European cities and are being promoted by local governments in a variety of ways. Stockholm Energi fuels its district heating system in several different ways, including through the use of biofuels, the extraction of heat energy from wastewater using heat pumps, and the extraction of bio-oil from pulp and paper mills, among other sources. The city's energy company has plans to increase the use of these kinds of biofuels (with a target of about 50 percent from renewable sources). A relatively high percentage of the city's electricity production also is provided through hydroelectric sources.

Some of the cities are actively pursuing wind energy. The city of Bologna, for example, has invested in a 3.5 MW wind park. The city of Heidelberg has developed several renewable energy projects, including a hydroelectric power plant on the Neckar River and plans to build three wind turbines on a high spot not far from the old section of the city (to provide 600 kW of power).

Wind energy has been of considerable interest in Saarbrücken, and this city has invested (about 24 percent ownership) in a windpark in Ensheim, in the northern part of the länder (state). Saarbrücken has basically given up on the notion of supporting wind within its city borders, in part because the city lies in a valley but also because it sees few opportunities to accommodate wind turbines without the noise and aesthetic objections it believes residents will have to them. The Stadtwerke in Saarbrücken has also been exploring a number of renewable energy sources. An experimental biomass project has been started in Bliestal, involving the planting of 10 hectares of biomass plants to be used as fuel.

To be sure, much of the growth in renewables in European cities can be accounted for through extensive central government subsidies and development monies. Moreover, a growing number of European nations, such as Denmark and Sweden, have adopted carbon taxes that facilitate this shift. The dramatic rise in the use of biomass energy in Sweden, for example, is in large degree a result of its carbon tax (*The Economist*, 1998). The cost of renewables—especially wind, but also photovoltaics—has gone down sharply as result of government subsidies (e.g., wind is now reported to be competitive with fossil-fuel-based power in the United Kingdom; the costs of wind have gone down markedly since 1990, with a reported fifteen-fold increase in production in Germany and elsewhere; *The Economist*, 1998).

Denmark has a long history of national energy planning and has adopted (since the 1970s) a series of increasingly ambitious national energy plans. The most recent version, Energy 21, sets ambitious carbon dioxide reduction targets: 20 percent reduction by 2005 (from 1998 levels) and halving its carbon dioxide emissions by 2030. Key components of Energy 21 are an increased promotion and development of CHP and a greater emphasis given to renewable energy sources, especially wind and biomass (as well as the goal of increasing their share of the power mix by 1 percent per year).

Denmark has taken impressive steps to promote wind energy and to treat it as such a significant part of its energy mix. Wind energy has received special attention and priority in Denmark, where the national target of providing 30 percent of its energy supply from wind by the year 2020 has been embraced. Wind already represents an impressive 8 percent of its energy supply. Here, planning for wind energy has also been integrated with spatial planning. A national atlas, based on wind patterns, separation from telecommunication corridors, and location of sensitive environmental areas, has been developed. Municipalities use this atlas as the basis for their own planning. Under the Danish planning system, all municipalities must delineate appropriate sites for future wind parks in their structure plans.

In the fall of 1997, Denmark unveiled an impressive Marine Windmill Action Plan, which calls for the building of 500 marine windmills intended to produce 750 MW of power in the next ten years and an amazing 4,000 MW by 2030 (Engelund, 1997). This will increase Denmark's percentage share of wind energy near 50 percent. Marine windmill parks are seen to have significant advantages over land sites, including the ability to take advantage of windier sites and a reduced impact on the landscape. The amount of marine space necessary will be quite small—an estimated 1 percent. Some environmental concerns remain, especially concerns by the ornithological community about the impacts on birds. Some controversy has also already arisen about the initial site choices, which environmentalists believe are too centered on shallow locations (marine windmills can now be sited on marine locations as deep as 15 meters and perhaps deeper). The windmills will be funded through an increase in electricity rates, although the energy costs compared to traditional coal-fired power generation are already fairly competitive (5 to 5.5 U.S. cents compared to 3.2 to 4.0 U.S. cents). These initiatives are also wisely viewed by the Danish government as an opportunity to advance the technology and commercial interests of the country.

Installation and production of wind energy in European countries has seen dramatic growth. Of the 1,510 MW installed worldwide in 1997, a very high percentage is accounted for by European nations, especially Germany, Denmark, and most recently Spain (Rackstraw, 1998). Germany, which saw the installation of some 532 MW in 1997 alone, provides significant financial support for wind energy, including the implementation of an electricity feed law (which requires utilities to buy wind production and sets a minimum price based on average electric rates). Other capital and operating subsidies are provided as well, some at länder level. As Rackstraw notes, the "political dynamic" in Germany in large part explains this level of support. A strong political lobby and popular support for renewables are important explanations. "There is broad and deep support for wind energy (and environmental causes in general) in Germany, which insulates the German wind policy approach from attack" (Rackstraw, 1998, pp. 23–24). The Danish public has even stronger support for wind, and in both countries, the employment generated from this industry (Denmark supplies 75 percent of the wind turbines in the world) is also highly valued.

Emerging Solar Cities

Solar has gained considerable ground in Germany, the Netherlands, and the Scandinavian countries and is now commonly incorporated into new construction and redevelopment projects. Several cities in the study are even beginning to describe themselves as *solar cities,* most notably Freiburg, Berlin, and Saarbrücken.

Freiburg is promoting solar in several ways, including by incorporating solar technology in new public buildings and facilities and by subsidizing private solar buildings. For a medium-sized city, Freiburg has an amazing number of buildings and development projects that incorporate solar technology. Examples can be found of both private and public buildings. Solar energy is (or will be) incorporated into both the Vauban and the Reiselfeld developments (major new housing areas). The entire rooftop of the new addition to the city's soccer stadium (Driesam-Stadion), built in 1994, is covered with photovoltaics, which generate energy beyond the needs of the stadium, sending it back into the local electricity grid. Impressive private designs include the Solarhaus Heleotrope (designed by local architect Rolf Disch), and the Solarhaus Freiburg—known as the self-sufficient solar house—which is one of the best known demonstration projects in the city (discussed later).

The city has also actively promoted solar energy and solar technology as an economic development strategy. Freiburg city is proud of attracting the International Solar Energy Society (ISES) to the city. The city provided ISES with a city-owned building to house its offices (an old villa—the Villa Tannheim) rent free for a period of five years. The villa is itself a solar demonstration project. The renovated Villa Tannheim incorporates and demonstrates a number of energy-conserving technologies. "The aim of the renovation was to reconstruct the outer appearance of the patrician building using renewable energy sources" (International Solar Energy Society [ISES], undated, p. 22) A number of specific energy measures were incorporated into the renovation, including new wall and roof insulation (spray-blown material made from recycled paper); transparent insulation on the western facade of the building (reducing thermal loss and capturing solar radiation gains), triple-glazed, low-emissity windows, the replacement of an oil-fired furnace with one fueled by natural gas, and the installation of 7.5 square meters of solar collectors (ISES, undated). Villa Tannheim both symbolizes the city's (and ISES's) commitment to renewable energy technologies and serves as another important demonstration building in the community. Freiburg is also home to the Fraunhofer Institute for Solar Energy Systems, a major solar research and development organization.

The extent of the solar industry that has emerged in Freiburg is impressive. It includes an estimated 450 companies, including 10,000 workers and generating DM 2 billion (about US $1 million) in income (Stuchlik and Heidler, 1998). Interestingly, a kind of solar ecotourism has developed along with these many solar initiatives in Freiburg. It is reported that each year some 120 groups of Japanese citizens visit the city to see and understand these solar initiatives firsthand (Stuchlik and Heidler, 1998). The most recent solar initiative by the city, "Freiburg Solar Region," will involve highlighting a series of solar projects in the city. A solar manager has been hired to coordinate the activities, and a solar pavilion will soon be installed in the city-center to further promote and educate about solar.[8]

Many of these cities place clear priority on promoting and funding solar energy. Cities such as Freiburg, Berlin, and Vienna are actively promoting solar energy through the provision of subsidies. Freiburg, for example, provides a public subsidy for solar, paying DM 2 per (about US $1.10) kilowatt hour produced from solar panels in private structures (Heller, 1997).

Few cities have done as much as Saarbrücken to promote and nurture solar power. The financial incentives offerred by this, in combination with those provided by the state, are substantial. For the installation of PVs, the Stadtwerke provides DM 1,000 per KW installed (about US $540), beyond the already generous länder subsidies. Together, these installation subsidies for a 50-square-meter rooftop system will likely total about DM 28,000 (about US $15,000), or about 50 percent of the market cost. As well, the Stadtwerke offers an operating subsidy of 55 pfennings per kWh produced (a two-meter system is used). To date, about thirty-nine homes have installed PV systems and taken advantage of the subsidies, amounting to 276 kW installed. Through a cooperative arrangement between the Stadtwerke and a city-owned bank, low-interest loans (2.9 percent for five years) can also be secured to cover the remaining costs of installing PV systems. As part of this rooftops initiative, the Stadtwerke has also supported a solar demonstration house in Ensheim. It demonstrates how PV rooftop systems might be integrated into a typical subdivision (Results Center, undated).

Although the subsidies to promote solar have been reasonably successful (the Stadtwerke staff believe that on a per-capita basis Saarbrücken leads German cities), the Saarbrücken experience shows the difficulties and slow process of promoting this technology. The region is an economically poor one, and people are still, according to Dr. Thomas Rohrback of the Stadtwerke, thinking too often in the short term. There is an emphasis on justifying all solar investments according to their "payback," a standard we seem to apply only to solar energy.

One important ingredient in promoting solar energy in Saarbrücken has been the creation of a nonprofit technical assistance and solar promotion company called ARGE Solar. The company, with a considerable staff, was created in 1989. The bulk of its funding (about two-thirds) is provided by contributions from the major municipal and regional energy companies. Some funding comes from other organizations as well, including universities and the Saarland Ministry of the Environment. The company's function is an important one. It serves a dual role of providing technical assistance to solar consumers and promoting and making solar energy visible in Saarland. It helps consumers in dealing with technical questions about the kinds of solar energy systems and products that are available, and it will help consumers take advantage of the different subsidy programs available at various jurisdictional levels. Its public relations function leads it to trade fairs and exhibits around Saarland.

What is most impressive in Saarbrücken is the development of a seemingly large number of private solar energy companies working in the area— mostly installation firms but also some producers. In the beginning there were only three firms, and now there are about fifty major producers and sellers, and an estimated 200 companies that install solar systems working in Saarland. This has meant competition, diversity and choice in products, and some assurance to average homeowners that the idea of investing in solar is neither radical nor experimental. Dr. Alexander Dörr, who leads ARGE Solar, believes that the subsidy programs have made a big difference and that they explain much of the expanding solar market. The picture for growth in solar energy systems has been stronger where Saarland as a whole is considered. Here, the number of applicants for subsidies and the number of systems installed have grown steadily. There are now some 500 installed solar hot water systems in Saarland and 350 grid-connected PV systems.

There are a number of examples in European cities of public buildings and facilities that have creatively integrated photovoltaic (PV) panels. Freiburg, as mentioned, has incorporated extensive photovoltaics (PVs) on the rooftop of a new wing of a soccer stadium. Other cities, including Berlin and Heidelberg, provide numerous examples of efforts to include solar in new public building projects. In Berlin, for example, designs for the new parliament building, ministry of finance, and main railway station all include PV panels.

Similar projects are being developed in the United Kingdom. Plans for the world's largest solar football stadium have been announced. A joint project of British Petroleum and Newcastle United, the stadium (with a capacity of 51,000) will include 350 kW of PVs in the St. James Park facility in Newcastle. The grid-connected PV system will cover an estimated 10 percent of the power needs of the stadium and is intended to help further Newcastle's goal of satisfying 1 percent of its power demand through solar by 2010) (see "World's largest solar-powered sports stadium," 1998). (The chief executive of Newcastle United has also indicated the club's intentions to encourage fans to use public transit in traveling to the stadium.)

Solar power is increasingly applied in a host of smaller (though cumulatively important) ways. A number of the study cities are extensively using PVs to power parking meters. These are seen extensively, for example, in Freiburg. In Leiden, the city has utilized them in two forms: it has about thirty-five solar-powered centralized meters (where a person purchases a ticket from a centralized box to display on the dash) and some 200 individual solar meters scattered throughout the city. A visually dramatic example of this kind of PV-use can be seen in a new residential area in the Dutch city of Gouda (Achterwillens-noordoost). Here, an extensive area of parking lot lighting is powered by south-oriented PV-panels, mounted in dramatic fashion on top of the light fixtures (see photo). The PVs act as a prominent visual statement of the ecological principles underlying this new residential area.

Another creative use for PVs is their integration into road and highway noise barriers. Under a EU-sponsored program called "highways to the sun," the Dutch government has been placing PV panels on sound barriers along several major highways, include the A-12, near Utrecht. The panels are visually dramatic and so, in addition to generating electricity, they serve to dampen the negative visual effect of such barriers.

Recently, an alliance between noise barrier companies and PV production companies in Germany has led to a design competition and the construction of some promising designs (mostly in Germany, but also in Switzerland). What is different in these pilot projects is the attempt to go beyond simply placing PVs on top of noise barriers to designing structures so that the PVs constitute the barrier itself (Reich et al., 1998). A number of benefits to integrated PV noise barriers include the free advertising of PVs that occurs ("Highways are the best 'shopping window' PV can get"), a fairly large new market, the ability to in effect reduce the cost of PVs (i.e., "buy one, get two functions"), and the benefit of bringing on board a new group of actors (public highway authorities). A recent study by the Fraunhofer Institute for Solar Energy Systems also shows considerable energy production potential. Analyzing the noise barriers likely to be needed for the next five years of road construction in Germany alone leads to an impressive 115 MW capacity ("equivalent to twice the number of PV modules sold in Europe from 1985 to 1995") (Reich et al., 1998, p. 66).

Solar Urban Development

Europe provides a number of very positive examples of new towns and larger urban developments conceived and designed with solar energy at their core. Indeed, these examples (increasing in number) demonstrate clearly that solar energy can be a central design element in new urban developments. Nieuwland, a new urban growth district in the Dutch city of Amersfoort, for example, has been designed and built to integrate solar energy in a number of ways. Most impressively, a large number of the buildings in the development include active and passive solar features. Through a collaboration with REMU, the regional power company, PVs are used extensively, and when completed Nieuwland will be the largest residential PV project in Europe. The evidence of this solar emphasis can be seen throughout the project—including many homes utilizing passive solar, with the extensive use of glass rooms, or *serres,* and solar hot water heating systems. One of the most impressive projects there is a fifty-unit social housing apartment building, which includes a unique roof-integrated PV and hot water heating system. There is also a visually dramatic area of single-family (duplex) houses with PV rooftops (see photo). These PV roof systems are paid for (and continue to be owned and maintained) by REMU.

There are few new residential districts anywhere in the world (Nieuwland is really a small new town) where one can find such a high percentage of new homes incorporating solar. Of the total 4,400 new homes in Nieuwland, about 1,100 will include thermal solar and 900 will include photovoltaics. The newest quarter of Nieuwland (not yet completed) will have an even greater active solar presence. PV systems will be placed on a number of community buildings, including a sports hall, community center and crèche, additional residential units (PVs on 500 new single-family homes and vertical solar walls on new apartments), and school buildings. Together these buildings are expected to produce 1 MW of power (including some 10,000 square meter of PV panels). The installation of solar in the innovative project is heavily subsidized, with about half of the cost of the PVs paid through a combination of NOVEM (Dutch Energy Agency) and EU (THERMIE) subsidies.

Two of the three main school buildings to be built in Nieuwland will incorporate PV roof systems and contribute to the community's generation of power. De Wonderboom primary school has already been built and includes 196 PV panels, as well as a greenroof (see photo). This is a special school; one feels immediately when entering it that there is something unique about it. First, the building incorporates extensive use of daylighting, with light shelves bouncing sunlight into each classroom. Second, a number of building features have been included to reduce overall energy consumption, including extra insulation, high-efficiency window glazing, the use of

Solar homes in the new growth district of Nieuwland in Amersfoort, the Netherlands. The photovoltaic rooftops are installed and will continue to be owned and maintained by REMU, the regional power company.

energy-conserving lighting (including a system that moderates light frequency according to daylight conditions), and a heat recovery system.

Perhaps the most creative design feature of this school building is a series of mirrors that projects a view of the greenroof into the classrooms. The condition and health of the eco-roof then becomes a subject for class attention. Indeed, the energy and other features of the school are integrated into the teaching curriculum. A set of meters that monitor energy consumption and show the energy production of the PV system assumes a main position in the entranceway to the school, and the students are directly involved meeting energy targets for the building.

In Linz, an entirely new solar city is nearing the construction stage and will be located in the southern district of Pichling. Planning for this project has been under way since the early 1990s, and project planners now predict the first residents will be living in this solar city by 2001. Intended to eventually consist of 25,000 residents, the community will be organized into a compact south-facing, mixed-use village. In addition to passive and active solar, the initial plans also include extensive pedestrian and cycle paths and greenspaces (including allotment gardens, natural drainage areas, and a restored stream). An energy standard has been set (< 40

The Wonderboom school in Nieuwland (Amersfoort), has both photovoltaic panels and a greenroof. These sustainability features are incorporated into the curriculum of the school.

Photo commissioned by REMU, Jan Van Yken, photographer, Amersfoort.

kWh/square meter per year), and the homes will incorporate natural ventilation, daylighting, and heat recovery systems (Amesberger, 1998).

The first 750 homes have been designed by a distinguished team of architects, including Sir Norman Foster, Sir Richard Rogers, and Professor Thomas Herzog (from Germany), with another 750 homes designed by Austrian architect Martin Trebersburg. These homes, with funding subsidies from the province of Upper Austria and the EU (research and development monies), are intended to serve as models of solar architecture design. The density of the village is considerable (the first 1,500 units will be placed on 34 hectares).

A distinguishing feature of the project is its comprehensive consideration of energy and other ecological design issues. Its layout is intended to give preference to pedestrians and bicycles and will be served by rail and tram. Electricity will be generated for the project through renewable energy sources—a cogeneration plant to be fueled from biogas and vegetable oil. Closed-loop systems will be emphasized, with organic wastes and sewage used to generate biogas, which will in turn be used to generate electricity. Greywater recycling and rainwater collection systems are also planned.

An even more ambitious solar project is in the planning stage in the city of Heerhugowaard, northwest of Amsterdam. Here, *De Stad van de Zon,* or the "City of the Sun," is being planned as a solar community of 2,500 homes, a piece of a larger compact growth area for this region of the Netherlands. The most recent town design envisions a south-oriented square town configuration; an island set amidst a water backdrop, with much of this old polder being reflooded. The plans set the ambitious goal of the new town being entirely free of carbon dioxide emissions and generating 5 MW of electric power from rooftop PV systems. An east–west road grid and south-facing homes will characterize the southern half of the island–city (the northern portion will preserve the rural elements and lines of the existing polder), and extensive use of passive solar in building designs will be made. In addition to the generation of power from PVs and the use of passive solar designs, other measures will be necessary to reach the goal of a zero carbon dioxide-emission town, including discouraging the use of autos (preference will given to pedestrian and bicycle mobility and to travel by bus), extracting energy from household wastes, and planting 100 hectares of forests as compensation for what carbon dioxide is emitted (Gemeente Heerhugowaard, 1999).

Interestingly, cities and towns in the Netherlands are increasingly trying to outdo each other when it comes to the use of solar power specifically, and to the practice of sustainable building and community planning more generally. In the case of Heerhugowaard, innovative solar town planning is partly explained as an important economic-development strategy—a way to "put Heerhugowaard on the map," in the words of one city official. Such projects are seen to distinguish the city as innovative and forward-looking, and in turn as a desirable place for businesses to locate. This is important, in addition to the financial support provided for such energy projects by NOVEM, the Dutch energy agency, and the positive examples provided of creative solar and sustainability projects under way in many other Dutch cities. What has emerged is a culture of support for solar power and an environment in which creative energy ideas and accomplishments are recognized and rewarded. A national PV competition, for example, led to the Heerhugowaard plan receiving a special prize, for which the city has been understandably proud. The precise impact of such an award is hard to know, but their importance in helping to support and stimulate projects like De Stad van de Zon should not be underestimated.

Zero-Energy Building and Energy-Balanced Homes

Europe has been a leader in the development of low-energy housing and in the integration of energy conservation and renewable energy sources into large-scale housing developments. There have been a number of interesting and innovative attempts in various study cities to develop the notion of an energy autonomous or energy self-sufficient house. These attempts have included, for example, the "Jenni house" in Switzerland and, more recently, the "self-sufficient" solar house in Freiburg, Germany, developed by the Fraunhofer Institute for Solar Energy Systems. The Freiburg house was intended to be unplugged from the conventional power grid, generating all of its own power. The intent was to "demonstrate that the entire energy needed in a single-family home can be supplied by the solar energy incident on the roof and walls, even under Central European climate conditions" (BINE, 1994, p. 1). Solar radiation intensity in Germany is limited, and production during the winter months is quite small, making the goal of independence from electric or gas connections a challenging one.

The Freiburg house, a two-story, 145-square-meter home, incorporates a number of technological innovations. Most important is its hydrogen/oxygen fuel cell system, which permits the long-term storage of summer solar gain. Other important features include its southern orientation, high levels of insulation, use of transparent insulation, small northern window area, airtight-building envelope, and heat-recovery ventilation system. A system of roller-blinds can be extended over the thermal insulation and windows. The active solar components include hot water solar panels (with a 1,000-liter storage tank) and PV panels. The house, with the exception of winter months, generates sufficient electricity for itself. Winter is when the hydrogen/oxygen storage system becomes critical. The system works in this way:

> In summer, photovoltaically generated electricity is used for the electrolysis of water to hydrogen (H_2) and oxygen (O_2) which is stored in tanks. Flameless combustion of the hydrogen is the source of heat for cooking and it is also used to heat the inlet air in the ventilation system on particularly cold days. If additional electricity is required, it is gained from the reaction of hydrogen and oxygen in a fuel cell. As it is only operated during periods with little sunshine, the heat losses from the fuel cell of about 40 percent (at a temperature of about 70° C) can be used to heat the hot water via a heat exchanger (heat/electricity conservation). (BINE, 1994, p. 2)

The building structure is designed for heat storage. Glass foam insulation is used in upper-story ceilings, and triple-glazed windows used on the northern facade. The ventilation system (with an air exchange rate of .5 per hour) is designed so that warm exhaust air heats incoming fresh air (a hydrogen burner provides additional pre-heating during the winter months).

This grid-connected zero-energy home in the Dutch coastal resort town of Zand-voort produces, over the course of a year, as much energy as it uses.

The experience with the house so far has been moderately successful. Completed in 1992, it was occupied for a period by a small family (its intended use). During its first two winters, the house did not achieve energy autonomy and had to be connected to the grid. Since then, the use of the building has changed, transitioning from a residence to an office. The Fraunhofer Institute, which built the structure, has also changed its moniker from the "self-sufficient solar house" to simply the "solar house." Although it is not clear that the house successfully illustrates self-sufficiency (and many have expressed safety concerns about the hydrogen fuel cell), there is no question that the house exemplifies many impressive solar and energy conservation features, including a high degree of thermal performance.

REMU has also sponsored the construction of two energy-balanced homes in Nieuwland. These homes are grid connected and gas connected, but through a combination of energy efficiency and solar features, they are designed to produce as much energy as they consume over the course of a year. Among the key features of these homes are extensive rooftop PVs, ground-source heat pumps, a high efficiency wall-warming system, a heat recovery ventilation system, and other environmental features, including rainwater collection. Each structure also incorporates a second-floor atrium, utilizing transparent PV, which permits daylight to enter the homes at the same time that electricity is produced. The PV panels are expected to generate about 7,500 kWh per year, sufficient to provide electricity for the home and to operate the electric heat pump.

Another early zero-energy house, what the Dutch call *nul-energiewoning*, can be found in the Dutch beach town of Zandvoort. Here, a single-family home was designed and built from the beginning to use no more energy than it produced in a year. It was, and continues to be, the hobby and personal project of its owner and occupant, Peer Kamp, an engineer with no formal training in energy technology and design who has taken on the project as almost a kind of personal mission. The house, completed in 1995, is connected to the electric grid, but it does not have a natural gas connection, which is usual for Dutch homes. Kamp's goal from the beginning has been to, through a combination of energy efficiency and energy production, consume in a given year no more than the home produced (or gave back to the energy company). The home has two meters—one for outgoing energy from its roof array of PVs and one for purposes of buying energy from the regional energy supplier.

The basic design of the home is rather simple, and Kamp holds simplicity as a key design assumption behind the house. He likes to recite Winston Churchill, who once wrote to a friend "I write you a long letter, because I don't have the time to write a shorter one." The simpler solution is the better one in his mind, and in most respects this simplicity finds expression throughout the house.

The basic features of the house include a southern orientation, 32 square meters of PV panels, which take up the bulk of the south facing roof, 7 square meters of hot water panels, and considerable energy efficiency components, including extensive additional insulation (compared to the average Dutch home) and low-emissity windows. The 64 PV panels of the roof-integrated system have a peak power production of 3.3 kilowatts (using two inverters). Other features include a ground-sourced heat pump, low-energy lighting and kitchen appliances, a hot-fill washing machine, and hot-fill dishwashing, among others.

One of the most innovative features is a system for heating the upper floor of this three-level home. Designed and conceived by Kamp himself, it involves dedicating five of the south-facing vertical window panels for solar heating and circulating this warm air through the floor structure. Electrically operated window shades come down during the summer when this additional heat gain is not needed.

The energy features of the home were heavily subsidized by NOVEM, the Dutch Energy Agency. The PV panels, at the time, cost about 80,000 guilders (about US $40,000), but Kamp paid only 5,000 guilders for them (and now owns them). He believes they would cost half as much today, but these solar features certainly add significantly to the cost of the home.

The extensive insulation and tight building envelope have also meant special attention to ventilation. A modest, though effective, ventilation system, powered by two motors and utilizing an innovative cross-flow heat recovery device, has been installed. One interesting feature is Kamp's strategy of routing the ventilation airflow through a laundry drying area, where the family's washing machine is located. Instead of a conventional dryer, the Kamp family simply hangs their clothes to dry, and apparently the drying time is quite fast.

The interior spaces of the home, particularly the south-facing living room, are bright and sunny. Most of the interior is finished in light-colored wood and light paints and other finishings. The taking over of the south-facing walls for PVs has meant that careful consideration had to be given to room layout on the upper floor. Kamp's solution was to place the bathroom in these angled spaces, as well as to use them for creative closet and storage areas.[9] The angle of the roof—45 degrees—was a space-energy compromise as well.

From an energy conservation point of view, the home has been extremely successful. In most years, the home produces at least as much as it consumes. Monitoring in 1995 showed electrical production from the PVs of 2,876 kWh and electric consumption of 2,582 kWh (NOVEM, 1996). In 1997, production did not exceed consumption, a result of an especially harsh winter. But on average, Kamp believes the home will reach its net energy goal. Interestingly, and an important point to Kamp, although the PV panels are the most dramatic feature of the home, the major contributions toward making it a zero net energy house are the home's insulation and other energy efficiency features. In this sense, the home demonstrates the not very radical benefits of incorporating these kinds of efficiency features into all new homes.

The aesthetic issues surrounding the Zandvoort house are interesting and perhaps somewhat debatable. A NOVEM evaluation report concludes that the roof integrated system "is completely successful from both the technical and the aesthetic point of view. . . ." (NOVEM, 1996). However, not all residents of a conventional residential neighborhood will likely find it attractive or pleasing to the eye. Interestingly, the building's dramatic south face points outward from its residential surroundings and is essentially surrounded by a nature preserve. So, at least in this case, few people will have the chance ever to glimpse the PVs or to have any sense that the house is in some way special or different when compared with the other homes in this residential area. One would really have to almost trespass to see the roof. This may be a good thing because Kamp has raised the ire of his neighbors by letting his lawn grow unmowed and uncontrolled—resulting in luxurious bushes and flowers, but some unhappy neighbors.

Carbon Dioxide Reduction Strategies

A distinctive environmental theme in the cities studied is the attention paid to global climate change and the development of local strategies to reduce carbon dioxide and greenhouse gases. Indeed, as mentioned in Chapter 1, there are several European initiatives that have encouraged cities to develop carbon dioxide reduction strategies. These include the ICLEI-sponsored Cities for Climate Protection and the German-based Climate Alliance (see ICLEI, 1997). Participation has been impressive, with some 400 cities participating in the German-based Climate Alliance.

These local strategies typically set ambitious emission reduction targets and use a variety of measures to achieve them. Den Haag has set a target of reducing emissions by 50 percent by 2010 (a reduction of 300,000 tonnes). It hopes to accomplish this through a package of measures, including extending district heating, promoting energy savings in offices and existing buildings, promoting greater energy efficiency in new construction areas (e.g. the Wateringen VINEX site), and implementing a more aggressive traffic plan, among other measures. This will be a challenge because the council predicts that carbon dioxide emissions will rise by 34 percent if current trends continue. The Helsinki Metropolitan Area Council has prepared a regional carbon dioxide reduction strategy, which sets the goal of a 17 percent reduction overall by 2010 (compared to 1994 levels). Reductions are to occur through a comprehensive set of measures, including an increased use of natural gas, various traffic measures (e.g., an increased public transit use), and waste management measures (e.g., gas recovery from landfills) (Helsinki Metropolitan Area Council (YTV), undated).

The city of Bologna is one of the few Italian localities to develop a carbon dioxide reduction plan, and has also been participating in the Urban CO_2 Reduction Project. Preceded by a detailed energy study—Bologna Energy Study (BEST)—the Bologna Council approved its carbon dioxide reduction strategy in 1995 (Municipality of Bologna, 1996). The strategy adopts the target of a 16 percent reduction (from 1990 levels) in carbon dioxide emissions by 2005, as compared with a trend scenario that predicts a 15 percent increase. Reduction measures are identified in six major sectors: efficiency in energy use and distribution (cogeneration); urban transport system; recycling; increase in vegetation; renewable energy use; and incentives for reducing energy consumption. Although it is unclear how much progress has precisely been made in reaching these targets, notable actions taken in support of the strategy include the creation of a new Bologna Agency for Energy and Sustainable Development, a new aggressive traffic and transport plan, and a variety of energy conservation projects (including, for example, new cogeneration plants and the extension of district heating; a biogas recovery plant; conversion of municipal vehicles to use of natural gas, including garbage collection trucks and energy company service vehicles; and development of wind energy).

The Stadtwerke in Saarbrücken joined ICLEI's Urban CO_2 Reduction Project in 1991, and by 1993 had a carbon dioxide reduction program approved by the local city council. It adopted the goal of a 25 percent reduction in emissions (compared to 1990) by 2005. Saarbrücken is on the way to meeting its goal and has experienced a 15 percent reduction already (between 1990 and 1996). Two main reasons are responsible for the reduction: the many different energy programs of the Stadtwerke itself, already discussed, and substantial improvements made in a local steel foundry (for which the city admits it cannot really take much credit).

The city of Münster has also developed a carbon dioxide reduction strategy. One of the key ways it seeks to implement this strategy is by seeking improvements in energy conservation in the city, and this effort applies both to city properties and to the private sector. One of the ways that it promotes energy efficiency is by financially supporting homeowners to install insulation in their homes (similar to Saarbrücken and other cities discussed). Specifically, the city assumes a percentage of the cost for existing structures, from 10 percent to 15 percent, depending on the energy reduction brought about (i.e., the greater the reduction, the higher the percentage assumed by the city). To get the subsidy, the homeowner must have an "energy passport" prepared; this is essentially a calculation of the energy savings that could be expected if improvements were made. The city allocated DM 1 million in 1997 for this program (about US $540,000) and plans to expand funding in the future.

Linz also has an active carbon dioxide reduction program. It is a signatory of the Climate Alliance Treaty and has set an ambitious carbon dioxide reduction goal: to cut carbon dioxide emissions by 40 percent (from 1987 levels) by 2010. They have set an intermediate goal of 20 percent reduction by 1998. Several key measures are part of the strategy, including: (1) improvements in emission controls for local steel production; (2) reductions in local heating oil use, through a combination of district heating and conversion to gas heating; (3) the solar city, described earlier; and (4) a series of traffic and transport improvements. Together, these measures should substantially reduce carbon emissions. There are many other examples. These European cities show an impressive commitment to understanding their carbon dioxide emissions and to developing credible and serious proportions for reducing them.

Lessons for American Cities

There is no question that American society—and its cities and communities—will need to place greater emphasis in the years ahead on renewable energy sources if it is to seriously seek to achieve its Kyoto obligation of a 7 percent reduction (from 1990 levels) in carbon dioxide emissions (by 2012). Ironically, the United States. has in the past been a market leader in the area of wind energy. U.S. production constitutes a considerable share of global production (1,805 MW in 1997, out of a total production of 7,763 MW), second only to Germany. While the U.S. annual installation of wind is now very small, there are encouraging developments on the horizon. The American Wind Energy Association reports that there are a number of sizable wind projects recently completed or soon to be completed, and the marketing of green energy packages to energy customers under power company restructuring plans offers some considerable promise (Gray, 1998).[10] The continued low price of power from traditional coal-fired power plants remains the main obstacle.

In his book *Going Local* (1998), Shuman concludes that American communities have tremendous potential to decentralize energy production. As he rightly notes, the precise configuration or package of local production possibilities will vary from place to place and from region to region (Shuman, 1998, pp. 66–67):

> Communities on open plains, mountainsides, or coastlines have wind resources that can be used either for pumping purposes or for making electricity. Southern communities are bathed in solar energy usable for heating, cooling and electrical generation using both photovoltaics and solar-thermal-electric power technology. Western communities can tap geothermal resources. Landlocked communities can harness the power of rivers through small-scale hydro-electric dams. Rural communities have a surplus of agricultural, forestry, and animal wastes that can be used as or converted into combustible fuels. Urban areas may have a

high enough population density to construct an economical district heating system in which a central heating unit
pumps hot water and steam to nearby houses and factories. Technological innovations of recent years are steadily
improving the ability of communities endowed with
renewable energy resources to tap them economically.

American cities can and should be much more fundamentally reliant on
renewable energy sources. Indeed, there are many regions and metropolitan areas in the United States that could fundamentally reorient their
energy situations in the direction of more sustainable, renewable techniques and technologies. Several provocative proposals for reorganizing
American regions and towns around more renewable sources of energy
have been made and are worthy of discussion. Callenbach, for example,
believes the Great Plains region is particularly suited for a transition to a
renewable-energy society. Conditions for tapping wind energy are especially strong here, and he believes that in combination with the rich potential for biomass production (poplar and switchgrass), the region could supply all of its energy needs through these renewable sources (Callenbach,
1996). Each American region or bioregion will have these types of unique
renewable energy opportunities that could and should be explored (see also
Berger, 1997).

The European examples profiled here show convincingly what a clear
difference municipal and local government leadership can make. What
cities such as Saarbrücken and Freiburg illustrate is that through a combination of vigorous leading by example, modest financial underwriting, and
technical assistance and education, renewable energy businesses (and culture) can be nurtured and grown. This is made easier, of course, through
the existence of municipal energy companies, but nevertheless even where
these do not exist, U.S. local governments may be able to engage in creative
partnerships with regional distribution companies to promote renewable
energy and may be able (especially under the new climate of deregulation)
to exert considerable influence through their own energy purchasing decisions.

The European cases, furthermore, suggest the potential use in American
cities of a number of more efficient, environmentally benign energy technologies. Combined heat and power production (CHP) and district heating
schemes are important technologies that can be applied in many American
cities (and developments). Micro-CHP plants are especially appropriate for
industrial and government complexes (e.g., government office complexes
and hospitals), and there are undoubtedly many creative opportunities to
link together residential neighborhoods with these industrial and govern-

mental networks. In the American context, citywide district heating (and cooling) networks are less likely or feasible, but smaller networks, perhaps fueled by biomass or other renewable fuels, could satisfy significant portions of future energy needs in cities. Particularly promising are integrated solar/CHP systems, such as those described here and being used increasingly in Europe.

Solar energy must become a more central part of the mix of energy sources that cities depend upon and ideally must be integrated into the city's very fabric and texture. Many European examples—innovative solar building designs and emerging solar cities—point to technical and public policy directions. Indeed, the fact that solar is given such emphasis even in northern European cities ought to show that it is highly feasible for many sunnier areas in this country. Shuman (1998) concludes that the economics of PVs "is rapidly improving" and points to production of PV power by the Sacramento Municipal Utility District (SMUD) at 17 cents per kWh— already beating the peak kW cost in some thirty-five American cities. Global sales of PVs are predicted to reach an impressive $100 billion by the year 2030.

This is not to say that we are building a solar society from the ground up; there are indeed many promising American initiatives. It has been estimated that there are already some 100,000 buildings in the United States incorporating solar energy. At the building level, there are increasingly positive examples of PV-integrated designs, which better fit American aesthetic sensibilities (e.g., a recent townhouse project in Bowie, Maryland). While so far there has been little attention paid to designing or encouraging zero-energy housing, there are some examples that come close, including the Toronto Healthy-house and a number of U.S. homes that, because of their remote locations, are "off the grid" (not connected to electric service). And, as elsewhere, there are increasing uses of PVs in circumstances where extending power lines is too costly (such as to power road signs).

Although there are few examples of American cities that have fully or wholeheartedly embraced the solar agenda, there are some positive examples and promising trends. Perhaps the most impressive of these is Sacramento, and specifically the solar (and other sustainable energy) initiatives of the Sacramento Municipal Utility District (SMUD). The SMUD has undertaken several major programs to expand the use of solar energy. One example is its "PV Pioneers Program," in which it installs 400-square-foot rooftop PV systems on private homes, turning them into "miniature power plants." Customers must apply for the privilege, and their rooftops must meet certain conditions.[11] Through this program some 1.5 MW of power are fed into the SMUD system. The SMUD's calculations of the environmental benefits of each system over a 30-year period show dramatically the potential of such systems (including sizeable reductions in carbon emissions).

The SMUD has also been pioneering the notion of strategically incorporating PVs into civic projects, in a way much like several of the European cities profiled here. This has already included the installation of a 130 kilowatt system above a parking lot at the Sacramento airport and a proposal to incorporate PVs into a new building at the Sacramento Zoo. These efforts illustrate the many creative ways in which American cities can begin to satisfy at least a part of their power demands from renewable sources.

What is perhaps most impressive about the European approach to solar, and renewable energy sources in general, is a willingness to put into place significant financial supports and subsidies at EU, national, state, and municipal levels. Similar financial incentives will be needed if American communities are to become less fossil-fuel dependent. The recent tax credit for installation of solar energy systems proposed by the Clinton–Gore administration, as part of its 1 million solar roofs initiative, is surely a step in the right direction, but frankly it is only a modest beginning. As the number of green energy pricing programs increases (options that allow consumers to pay a higher premium to ensure that their energy comes from renewable sources) with the deregulation of the energy industry nationally, additional financial support for renewables of all types will most likely result. Greater financial resources and subsidies will be necessary, and cities themselves must help as well.

Every new community or civic building should be viewed as an opportunity to produce sustainable energy, a chance to reduce the community's carbon footprint and to reduce our collective dependence on fossil fuels. Every new school should be thought of similarly, with the installation of solar power viewed as an important opportunity to teach the next generation of citizens and leaders about alternative energy options. States and cities should take the lead. Every school building should be an opportunity to learn about the possibilities of becoming a green and sustainable community. One creative U.S. example of underwriting PVs is Colorado's Rooftop for Schools Program. Under this program, the state provides grants to schools to cover about half of the cost of installing a (2-kW) rooftop system (with a maximum grant of $7,500). To receive the grants, schools must also incorporate solar education units into their curricula. The state's largest utility (Public Service Company of Colorado) has developed its own similar solar school rooftops program. Communities (and states) in the United States should recognize the tremendous educational value and opportunities to help grow an energy-aware citizenry through such programs.

There is no question that American cities, with the right leadership and the creative application of technology and incentives, can become funda-mentally less dependent on nonrenewable fossil fuels. American cities can, as these green-urban European examples effectively demonstrate, become fundamentally more energy efficient at the same time that they shift toward renewable, solar-based societies and economies.

Notes

1. The Results Center (undated), for example, reports that a German national grants program paid for 42 percent of the construction costs associated with Saarbrücken's district heating system.
2. Most are either owned by municipalities or by consumer cooperatives.
3. Conservation Engineering Limited (undated) provides the following useful description of how excess heat is extracted: "The engine is cooled by a number of heat exchangers that extract heat from the engine lubricating oil, the jacket cooling water and the exhaust. These heat exchangers trans-fer practically all of the heat from the engine to the water circulating through the district heating system. Each building connected to the district heating system is fitted with a plate heat exchanger capable of meeting both heating and hot water loads. During peak winter conditions, the input to the district heating system is increased by transferring heat to the system from the existing gas boilers in the Civic offices" (p. 1).
4. In addition to the collectors, the system includes a 74,000-cubic-foot water storage tank.
5. More specifically, energy use is calculated in the following way: "Monthly energy demand is calculated using such parameters as mean monthly air temperature, population, housing size and type, the number of people in each household, car ownership, the floor areas of domestic and non-domestic buildings, appliance and plant efficiencies, the market shares of fuels, indices of economic activity, mean monthly temperature, solar radi-ation, wind speed and other relevant factors" (Titteridge, Boyle, and Flem-ing, 1996). Estimates put total energy usage for Leicester in 1990 at 36 PJ and carbon dioxide emissions at 3 million tonnes.
6. In some German cities, including Hannover and Hamburg, an even higher percentage of the savings—50 percent—is allowed to be kept by the schools.
7. Another DM 2 million has been invested in recent years ". . . in energy-saving burners and boilers, heat recovery plants, improved insulation, thermostat valves and solar-energy plants."
8. The following main projects are included in the Freiburg Solar Region ini-tiative:
    — Workplace of the Future: SolarFabrik
    — Civic Initiative: Communal Solar Energy Facility
    — Tourism and Leisure: Solar Cable Railway
    — Future Living: Solar Settlement Schlierberg
    — Research and Development: Solar Funding Initiatives

— Education and Training: Solar Tower and Solar Education Centre-Euregio

9. This is not a happy solution to those homeowners who really enjoy windows in bath and shower areas.

10. Restructuring of the power industry also represents a potential negative to renewable energy sources if it pushes the price of electricity down further as many predict. Some argue for the need for a Renewables Portfolio Standard (RPS), which would require all companies to produce a certain percentage of their power from renewables. The American Wind Energy Association recently issued a white paper that puts forth an ambitious set of proposals for the future, including a proposed Strategic Wind Energy Initiative.

11. The rooftop must meet the following conditions: it must be sloped and facing south, southwest, or west; it must be made of asphalt composition shingle, in good condition; and it must be large enough to provide 400 square feet of shaded area. Customers must also pay an additional $4 per month, which is added to their power bill. After ten years, the homeowner has the option of purchasing the system. Despite the lack of clear financial incentives—and indeed the increased costs to the homeowner—the program has been successful. Since its start in 1993, 420 homeowners have agreed to host the PV systems, as well as more than twenty churches and commercial buildings (Sacramento Municipal Utility District [SMUD], undated).

Chapter 10

Building Ecologically: Designing Buildings and Neighborhoods with Nature in Mind

A Revolution in Ecological Building

It is a commonly cited statistic that some 40 percent of the world's energy consumption results from the construction and operation of buildings, and a high percentage of the resources that enter the global economy end up in the form of buildings or structures. The green-urban city views this continuous process of building, renovating, and managing of structures—homes, businesses, civic architecture—as important opportunities to reduce its ecological footprint. European cities (and countries) have made tremendous progress in this area, and they provide a wealth of project examples and program ideas from which to learn.

Especially in the Netherlands, Denmark, and Germany, there is now extensive experience with ecological or green neighborhoods and buildings. Indeed, this situation might be characterized as a revolution because there is so much activity in this area now, especially in countries such as the Netherlands, where ecological building features have become common practice. A number of these projects were visited, and together they represent a clear demonstration of the potential of significantly reducing resource demands through building and neighborhood design. These European countries have arrived much sooner at the conclusion that new development can and must be different if environmental consumption is to be reduced. The attributes and specific designs featured in these projects vary, but they tend to have in common an emphasis on minimizing the ecological footprint of their residents, and they tend to include high energy conservation standards, low water usage, the use of sustainable building materials, an emphasis on recycling and material reuse, and the incorporation of solar energy in the form of solar panels and photovoltaics, among other features, These projects also emphasize minimizing the role of, or doing without, the automobile. Most are sited in close proximity to public transit, emphasize walking and bicycling as mobility options, and typically restrict the number of spaces provided for automobiles.

Many Examples of Ecological Building Projects: The Dutch Leading the Way

Many specific examples can be cited that show the potential gain—environmental and social—from these building strategies. In the Netherlands, significant experimentation with sustainable development projects began in the early 1990s, partially funded by the Dutch government. Three projects are frequently cited as the important examples of the first wave of experimentation: Ecolonia (Alphen a/d Rijn), Morra Park (Drachten), and Ecodus (Delft). The author has visited and studied each of these early ecodevelopments, as well as more recent projects, and together they provide important inspiration and guidance.

One of the first ecological demonstration projects in the Netherlands was Ecolonia. Located in Alphen a/d Rijn, this residential neighborhood was an important testing ground for many ecological ideas and technologies that are now more commonly used throughout the country. Specifically, the neighborhood includes 101 residential units, clustered around a pedestrian common area and a lake. The overall masterplan for the neighborhood was the work of Belgian architect Lucien Kroll. Sponsored by the Dutch energy agency (NOVEM), the design of the actual structures was assigned to nine different architects (each designing for groups of ten to eighteen homes). The architects were in charge of creating their own unique design aesthetic and whatever combination of ecological design features they deemed appropriate. They were given broad environmental parameters that they had to design within, including an energy standard (200 megajoules/square meter) that buildings could not exceed.

Ecolonia demonstrated a wide range of ecological building ideas and techniques, including greenroofs on some units, many energy-conserving features (e.g., added insulation), the use of recycled building materials, solar hot water heating units, rainwater collection and its use in toilet flushing, car washing, and garden watering. Ecolonia provided a wealth of practical insights about what ideas and techniques worked and which ones

Ecolonia, one of the first ecological housing projects in the Netherlands, helped to demonstrate and test a host of ecological-design and building measures.

were less successful. On balance, and despite certain problems, the project was successful at achieving its goals. As Edwards (1996, p. 195) notes:

> Ecolonia does demonstrate that significant savings in energy use and environmental impact can be achieved by optimizing building materials and methods. By paying particular regard to orientation (south, east and west facing housing—not north), to differential window areas according to aspect, to increased levels of insulation and efficient boiler systems, Ecolonia has met the target in the NMP [National Environmental Policy Plan] of a 25 percent reduction in household energy use.

Ecolonia has played a significant role in the promotion and advancement of ecological buildings in the Netherlands—indeed, its mainstreaming. NOVEM, the Dutch national energy agency, has undertaken a series of detailed evaluation studies, with a number of important conclusions and ecological building insights. These studies concluded, for example, that sunboilers and solar heating units were successful and ready to incorporate into mainstream construction (NOVEM, undated).[1] For many months, a visitors center existed on site (which has itself been recycled and is now the visitors center at Nieuwland, the ecological housing project in Amersfoort), and hundreds of architects, builders, and community officials have toured the project. Ecolonia, aside from its benefits from a technical learning point of view, has had an important catalytic effect in the country.

Morra Park is a 125-unit development in the southern part of the city of Drachten, in the Friesland region of the Netherlands (see Figure 10.1). It incorporates a number of sustainability features, including a southern orientation, solar glass rooms attached to each unit, and the inclusion of solar panels on each unit (VROM, undated). The glass sunrooms (called *serres*) collect warm air at the top that is then blown into the wall space between the attached homes. Water is a key feature, and the development incorporates a closed-loop canal system, which collects stormwater runoff

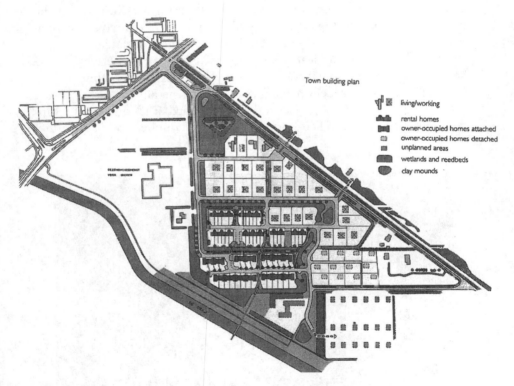

Figure 10.1. Morra Park: diagram of closed-loop canal circulation

In Morra Park, an ecological housing project in Drachten, the Netherlands. A key design feature is a closed-loop canal system for collecting and naturally treating stormwater runoff. The water in the canals is dramatically cleaner than in neighborhood farming regions and is clean enough for residents to swim in.

Source: Municipality of Smallingerland, Drachten, the Netherlands.

and circulates and filters water through a constructed wetlands. Water is circulated through the canal by way of a windmill-powered pump. Parking is restricted to certain areas, which utilize permeable tiles to allow water percolation. Indeed, the project does not use asphalt and has very few hard surfaces. An interesting feature of the project is that one area of houses is devoted to combined home/work arrangements. In these structures, 30 percent of the floor area must be devoted to the occupants' primary economic livelihood. Home businesses that have located here include an architect, an accountant, and a photographer.

The project includes a mixture of housing types and income levels (as with most Dutch housing). One result of the Morra Park design has been the creation of impressive greenness. Efforts were made to preserve existing natural site features (e.g., including older trees along the canals). Several wooden footbridges, footpaths, and bike trails are included in the design. Common vegetable gardens and composting areas have also been provided. An effort was also made to build with more sustainable materials. For example, no tropical woods, no zinc, and no PVCs are used. The homes are designed to facilitate separation of wastes and recycling.

The project is almost entirely built out and is generally considered a success. As one planner and project resident explained, it is considered a very desirable place to live. The home designs have resulted in a substantial

Morra Park, an ecological housing project in Drachten, the Netherlands, utilizes a closed-loop canal system that collects, circulates, and cleanses stormwater.

reduction in energy usage, using an estimated 40 to 50 percent less energy than conventional homes in Drachten.[2] The project has not been a complete success, however, because certain elements of the design have not worked as well.[3] In particular, the glass sunrooms have been too hot in the summer, and during the winter they have been wastefully heated by some residents.

The project Ecodus (short for Ecological building plan on the vander DUSsenweg) is another of the first-generation sustainable developments. Located in Delft, the project consists of about 250 dwelling units, built through a collaboration between the local housing society, the municipality, and a private developer. The development is a combination of privately owned and rental houses. Sustainable design features include a south and southeast orientation, solar panels (all units have them for hot water), the protection and incorporation of existing natural features of the site (including waterways and poplar trees), and high energy efficiency (high-value insulation, in combination with high-insulating glass). As well, Ecodus includes other features: the design of the block of flats on the west end to serve as a noise barrier (with bathrooms and kitchens facing the street and living quarters and bedrooms located on the quiet side); a concentration of parking in certain areas (and a fairly low parking ratio of 1:1); ready access to Delft's extensive bicycle network; narrow roads and keeping to a minimum the paved surface; rainwater collection in the canals and a natural wetlands purification system (like Morra Park's); extensive gardens for residents and a neighborhood orchard; the use of sustainable materials (e.g., glazed stoneware sewage pipe, avoidance of PVC pipe, limits on use of tropical hardwoods, use of water-based acrylic paint, vegetable-based sheet piling, recycled brick and oil); the use of 20 percent recycled concrete; house-to-house waste collection (including organic wastes and household chemicals); free composting bins; no chemicals permitted in gardens and green areas; and water-saving devices on toilets and showers (Delft, 1996).[4]

With construction completed in 1992, the goal of this project was somewhat different from other demonstration projects in the sense that the city specifically wanted to apply ecological principles to a typical or "normal" development (as one city environment department staff says, a "normal project for normal people"), and within typical financial limitations. There is little architectural experimentation, and in most respects Ecodus looks like a conventional development. The municipality has viewed Ecodus as a model for how all future development in the city should be constructed.

Several evaluations of the project have been completed, and some features have been found to work quite well and others not as well. One problem area includes the interior separation of kitchen and living quarters, a feature important for energy efficiency. Many Dutch families are opting for open kitchens and are taking out the separation wall (the Dutch in general tend to place importance on improving and modifying their homes). Parking and car usage are additional problems, as more residents have cars than originally expected and hoped (resulting in residents parking in places they should not). The idea of creating a car-free area was scrapped because of a need for access for waste collection trucks.

The solar and energy-efficiency features have generally worked well. There have, however, been conflicts over the desires of some residents to add an additional floor to their homes. These proposals have not been approved by the city because they would interfere with solar access for other units. To some, this represents the thorny issue of how to design affordable housing that residents can live in throughout the different stages of their lives. Forcing those who wish larger units to move out is seen by some as contrary to the goals of sustainability.

In the most recent city evaluation, an effort was made to determine how residents actually enjoy or value living there. The study concludes that indeed residents are happy living there and are especially pleased with the greenery and gardens, and the small homes and walkways throughout the project.

Since these initial demostration projects, there have been a host of more recent innovative ecological developments throughout the country. Oikos, near Enschede, is one of the more impressive of the latest generation of ecological building projects in the Netherlands. Located within a larger VINEX development site, the project incorporates a number of significant ecological features. These include the extensive use of *wadies,* or natural drainage areas (described in more detail in Chapter 7), the minimization of hard surfaces and the use of permeable bricks for parking spaces, extensive solar orientation (some 75 percent of the units are oriented to the south), and the extensive incorporation of natural areas and public gardens between the buildings (see Figure 10.2).

In the southern portion of the site (called the "outer Oikos"), new development will occur in development clusters, with extensive natural spaces—referred to as *eco-tuinen,* or natural gardens, between and around them. In addition, areas will be specifically identified in advance for community flower and vegetable gardens. Everywhere there is an emphasis on promoting natural drainage.

Other sustainable building features include high-speed bus service (to the center of Enschede), provided through a bus-only lane penetrating to the center of the community; good bicycle connections (there is a very high rate of bicycling in Enschede); restrictions on the building of wooden fences (only natural green fences will be permitted); and the building of a network of green hedges through the community. The buildings will not use tropi-

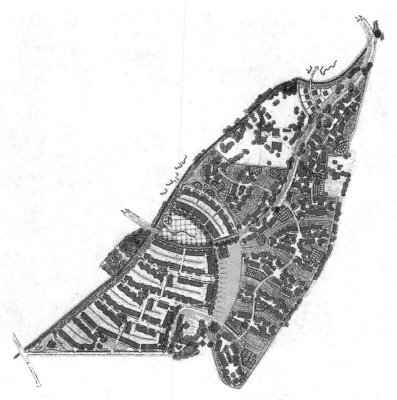

Figure 10.2. Plan diagram for Oikos ecological development

Oikos is a new ecological community in Enschede, the Netherlands. As the building plan shows, the design includes extensive green areas intermixed with housing. These green areas take many forms, including *wadies,* or natural drainage ditches, and community gardens (small cross-hatched areas on the map).

Source: BMD Enschede and Bureau Zandvoort.

cal woods; instead, they will use more sustainable woods and water-based paint (the lumber for the much of the buildings is western red cedar, which requires no treatment. It does come from Canada, though, raising questions about the environmental and energy costs of transportation).

Oikos will include a community center, where commercial and retail establishments will be located on the ground level with apartments above. At the very center will be a small public park with an interesting wishbone-shaped fountain. The fountain's pump will be powered by PV panels and will create the effect of a constant rainbow.

The physical design of Oikos is intended to facilitate interaction between residents. There are a series of crosswalks, each with a small public space,

Passive solar energy is an important design feature in many of the buildings in Oikos, an ecological development in Enschede, the Netherlands. About 75 percent of the homes are oriented to the south to take advantage of passive solar.

that eventually leads residents to the center of the community. As with many Dutch projects, the designers intended to de-emphasize the automobile. The direct route of the bus-only corridor has been described as the "front door" of the community, while the entrance for cars is considered to be the "back door." Nevertheless, there will be a considerable number of cars there and a considerable amount of commuting (although only 1.3 auto spaces per unit are to built).

In Oikos, there has also been a great emphasis on educating the new residents about living ecologically. Municipal officials have convened a series of informal meetings with new residents to educate them about the ecological features of the project, giving them ideas about how they might maintain their homes in a consistent fashion. For example, new residents are given a list of native species of plants, trees, and vegetation, along with advice about how to maintain their gardens and outdoor areas in more ecologically sensitive ways.

In Amsterdam, the largest new development site, the IJburg project, incorporates many sustainable features. Although controversial because it involves creating islands in the IJmeer (with a resulting loss of shallow-water aquatic habitat), the development incorporates a number of both basic and innovative features to minimize its ecological footprint. Supporters of the project (the project was just endorsed by a citywide referendum and is moving forward) argue that its close-in location, dense and compact design, and ability to provide good public transit serve to make it, from the beginning, a relatively low-impact alternative for addressing the city's housing needs. Its density will average about 60 dwelling units/ hectare, but will be as high as 110 dwelling units/hectare in certain areas. It will be served first by a high-speed tram and later by an extension of the city's underground metro system. In addition, several sections of the first island to be developed will be designed as car-free zones, and the number of allowable parking spaces for the entire project will be kept lower than is typical. The city, in collaboration with the national auto club (ANWB), is working on developing a set of mobility packages or options that will be offered to prospective homeowners (e.g., combinations of discounted public transit, membership in a car-sharing service, and so on). Other sustainable design and building ideas will be used in Ijburg, including utilizing district heating, high standards for insulation, restrictions on the use of certain building materials, and the use of active and passive forms of solar energy. Consideration is also being given to using a dual-line system for provision of water, in which a separate line brings less-than-potable water (e.g., from sewage treatment) to be used for toilet flushing, garden watering, and so forth. IJburg will also take advantage of the Netherlands' special green investment funds, which will allow homeowners, once the project is certified as a green project, to obtain below-market mortgage rates.

Other environmental aspects of the project include the restoration of a former chemical dump to the south of the site (the plan includes building a containment barrier and a soil cover) and conversion to a park. A compensation package has also been negotiated with environmental groups and will include an expenditure of 40 million guilders (about US $20 million) to create and/or restore shallow habitat along shorelines north of Amsterdam and to create a bird island immediately to the east of IJburg.

Other ecological innovations can be found in many other Dutch projects. One interesting design idea in Nieuwland, in Amersfoort, is the concept of *school houses*. There are fourteen of these structures planned. They are small school structures designed so that later, as the community matures and the numbers of school-age children decline, they can each be divided and converted into two single-family attached residential units. (These units will also accommodate PV panels on their rooftops.) These examples represent forward-looking architecture and community design, which recognize the fundamental need for flexibility and modification in interior spaces and even the uses of buildings over time.

Another variation on this theme are buildings designed from the beginning for dismantling and reuse. One such recent example is a new (so-called) *dismountable* police station in the Dutch town of Boxmeer. This is the result of a study (commissioned by the Dutch National Building Agency) of the concept of the *fast-office*, or a "lightweight, easily dismountable building which can be completely reused." As the National Building Agency explains, such a design provides badly needed flexibility: "Changes are always taking place in the police force and the situation twenty years from now is likely to be completely different to today's situation. The two-level building can be reassembled elsewhere, possibly with a different appearance" (National Building Agency, 1997, p. 38). Other important environmental features of this police station are an emphasis on natural ventilation ("electronically-controlled ventilation grilles"), day-light-controlled lighting, and double sliding windows (as an alternative to potentially leaking double-glazed windows).

Newer generation ecological or sustainable building projects are numerous, with creative examples in virtually all of the case study cities. Other impressive Dutch ecological projects under way in study cities, include the CiBoGa project and Piccardthofplas in Groningen; DeWijk in Tilburg; Nieuwland in Amersfoort; and Polderdrift in Arnhem, among many others.

Scandinavian Exemplars

Many exemplary Scandinavian projects and designs can also be cited. Indeed, for the major Scandinavian cities studied—Copenhagen, Stockholm, and Helsinki—the major new development areas in each are being planned and designed according to sustainability principles (and in fact the three cities are beginning to work together, to share information, and to collaborate on proposals for funding certain aspects of the projects). These projects are Viikki in Helsinki, Ørebro in Copenhagen, and Hammarby Sjöstad in Stockholm.

In Helsinki, the municipal government's new development area (called Viikki), which will accommodate a new science park, will also include an interesting ecological housing district that will eventually be home to some 1,700 residents (City of Helsinki, undated). The preliminary design involves, among other things, an "ecological day care center and school," a wood industry activity center (to demonstrate how Finnish woods can be used in building), and a horticultural and gardening center that will provide residents with information about the environment and advice about gardening. A large conservation area lies to the south and east of the new community, with a large portion in protected wetlands. Other lands will be available for allotment gardens and walking trails, and some areas will remain in farm use. Interestingly, the intention behind the horticulture center is to in part, "rent out allotments to residents, give information, lend and hire gardening tools and maintain model plots" (City of Helsinki, undated, p. 4).

The area designed for ecological housing, although not built yet, has been designed. The design was generated through a competition and resulted in a basic layout of south-facing homes with dwellings "grouped along 'courtyard' streets, with green strips penetrating the gaps between the blocks. These green strips promote the utilization of rainwater, composting and allotment gardens" (City of Helsinki, undated, p. 2).

Interest in promoting sustainable building in the district has already resulted in the construction of an apartment complex made of Finnish timber. Ironically, wood construction has been rare in this land of abundant forests, largely a response to the perceived fire potential of such construction. New interest in utilizing Finnish wood resources led to this important demonstration project.

In the Copenhagen region, there are many examples of ecological building. One of the more notable is Skotteparken, a low-energy housing project in the community of Ballerup. This project consists of 100 residential units, partly funded through the EU's THERMIE program, which are intended to demonstrate and support new energy technologies. The project consists of six blocks, organized in a horseshoe pattern, with a small lake and a recreational area at the center. Heating for the project is provided through a combination of a small CHP (located in an adjacent school and fueled with natural gas) and solar collectors incorporated in the rooftops of the structures (100 square meters of solar collectors in each building). The CHP will operate on a pulse basis, providing energy to each of the building's boilers when solar heating is insufficient and boiler temperatures fall below a certain level. It is expected that the solar collectors will provide sufficient room heating except during the winter months, as well as 65 percent of the hot water needs over the entire year (Building and Social Housing Foundation, 1996).

Other energy features of this project include extra insulation, low-emissivity window glass (U-value 0.95), heat recovery of forced ventilation air (80 percent recovery), and low-energy lighting and appliances. Water-saving measures include low-use kitchen and bathroom taps and the collection of rainwater in the small lake. The projected energy and waste savings are substantial (predicted reductions are 60 percent in gas use, 30 percent in water, and 20 percent in electricity (Building and Social Housing Foundation, 1996). The project won a World Habitat Award in 1993.

Ecological Buildings and Institutional Structures

Examples of a number of larger institutional structures designed and built according to sustainability principles also exist in the case study communities. These include the Queens Building (in Leicester), the ING-headquarters building (in Amsterdam), and the SAS-headquarters building (in Stockholm), among others. Examples of mixed residential/office buildings designed around green principles can also be cited, including the "green building" in Temple Bar (Dublin).

Even major new city-center development projects, including major office and institutional uses, are being designed and conceived of as sustainable building projects. One of the clearest examples of this is in Berlin, with the massive new development occurring at Potsdamer Platz, as well as the new federal government complex. The buildings will be heated by a central heating and power plant and cooled by a central plant. Mobility will be heavily public transit oriented, with the target modal split set at 80 percent public/20 percent private. This is possible because the area will be served by the metro system, and there are plans to construct a new main train terminal at which major transit modes will intersect.

Especially unusual is the extensive planning and care that has gone into organizing the actual construction in ways that minimize impact on the natural environment. To minimize disruptive truck traffic, construction logistics are largely occurring by rail. Great attention is being paid to impacts of the project on groundwater, with special concern about the impacts of a lowering of the groundwater table on the adjacent Grosser Tiergarten. As a result, an extensive groundwater monitoring and management system has been developed. Among other measures, groundwater extracted during excavation will be returned to the aquifer. Other environmental measures include the designing and configuration of the buildings to reduce winds and the implementation of an environmental mitigation package (including the creation of a new 20-hectare park).

The ING-bank headquarters building (formerly the NMB bank) in Amsterdam is one European ecological design that has actually received considerable attention in the United States. It is a large building—some 50,000 square meters, housing 2,400 employees—designed in a distinctive S-shape, accentuated by a series of ten slanting towers. Designed by Dutch architect Ton Alberts, the building has a strong organic look with natural colors and shapes—a building that seems to grow from the very ground itself. In contrast to a skyscraper, it is often called a "groundhugger." The entire building is designed around a main corridor—or "mainstreet"—along which major functions and activities, including canteens, theaters, and meeting rooms, are located.

An emphasis in the building is given to energy conservation, which is accomplished in several significant ways. The building is angled toward the sun and emphasizes daylighting throughout. No workspace is more than 23 feet away from a window, and windows are fully operable. The interior spaces are mostly painted in light colors, and the atrium towers contain extensive "sun paintings"—metal sculptures that help to further bounce sunlight into the interior of the building. There is considerable vegetation along the mainstreet, including hanging plants that drape luxuriously from the upper floors of the atria. Water flow forms are used extensively, with some handrails transformed into gurgling brooks. Water for these flow forms comes from a rainwater collection system. Other energy features include double-glazed windows, a high-efficiently electric generator, an energy retrieval wheel, and other heat recovery systems. Again, there is a heavy emphasis on daylighting and a heavy reliance on task lighting.

Nature is visually close, and the building has a series of impressive gardens and green courtyards surrounding it. The effort to create these greenspaces included the unusual step of helicoptering in several large trees to be planted in one of the courtyards (ING Bank, undated). Perhaps the only negative about these gardens and courtyards is that they provide largely visual (but not physical) access, and the interior building spaces seem little connected to this marvelous green exterior. The location of this bank headquarters expresses its sustainability impulses as well. It is located on a main pedestrian square and shopping area, a few feet away from a bicycle-only path and just a few blocks away from a major metro and train stop. The front of the building is also accentuated by a group of some fourteen older trees that were transplanted from another location where they were going to be cut down.

The results of this early design are spectacular. Energy consumption has been dramatically reduced (estimated to be only 10 percent of what it was in the previous building). The estimated payback period was extremely short.[5] Employee absenteeism has been reduced considerably as well, and employees clearly enjoy working in this structure. Increases in productivity have surely occurred because the office is both a delightful, humane space to work in and one of which the bank (and its employees) can actually be proud.

The new Queens Building at De Montfort University in Leicester represents another significant example of large-scale European ecological building. Designed by Short Ford Architects, the most significant design feature of the building is its emphasis on natural ventilation. More specifically, this feature is achieved through its orientation, a narrow profile facilitating cross-ventilation, and the use of "ventilation chimneys" that cool the building through a stack effect. This is no small accomplishment given the heat loads generated by computers and the more than 1,000 students and faculty members that occupy the structure at any given time. Other environmental features include the incorporation of a combined heat and power plant, the use of CFC-free insulation for piping, and the creation of more flexible, adaptable spaces within the building (De Montfort University, 1993). The building also makes extensive use of daylighting through "rooflights and glazed gables," which bring light deep into laboratory spaces that in a conventional building would not experience much natural lighting (Steele, 1997). Steele describes the building as "the largest naturally ventilated building in Europe," and one that sets "a significant precedent" for future building (p. 68). The use of natural stack effect as a main design feature is impressive:

> The cooling action works by a wholly passive natural stack effect unaided by fans or other mechanical means, a kind of thermosyphon operable in still air conditions, enhanced further by a moving air stream across the roof. The building is compartmented to keep air flow routes relatively intelligible and more locally controllable. The fire regulations are satisfied simultaneously and acoustic privacy is maintained. (De Montfort University, 1993, p. 11)

In this way, the Queens Building utilizes natural principles to cool the building, which reduces energy consumption substantially and fosters a pleasant working and learning environment.

Ecological Urban Renewal

Another important trend evident in several of the study cities is the incorporation of ecological or environmental design features when buildings and neighborhoods are restored or renovated. Numerous examples of ecological renovations in Denmark, the Netherlands, Germany, and elsewhere can be cited (see Danish Town Planning Institute, 1996). A number of such ecological renovations have taken place in Berlin, including pilot projects at Unionplatz (see Mega, 1996) and the now well-known Block 103 project (Berlin-Kreuzberg; see European Academy of the Urban Environment, 1997). These projects typically involve greening initiatives (greenwalls, roof gardens, tree planting, and the replacement of pavement with green), rainwater collection systems with rainwater treated through a vertical biological filter and used for toilet flushing (in the case of Block 103), the use of environmental building materials, and solar energy systems (180 square meters of photovoltaics in Block 103), among other improvements. Block 103 also involved a social dimension, incorporating a community kitchen that served residents organic meals on a weekly basis (see

Kennedy and Kennedy, 1997). The results of this pilot project have been quite positive.

The urban regenerative project at Fredensgade in Kolding is one of the most spectacular ecological urban renewal projects for several reasons. Comprising about 140 flats, the blocks of four- and five-story buildings were creatively renewed and renovated, incorporating a number of ecological features. Two older buildings were demolished, with two new buildings constructed (with one made entirely of recycled building materials). (Construction was completed in 1993.) Parking has also been limited in the development. Most of the interior courtyard space is off limits to cars, but there are about fifteen spots. A beautiful green courtyard and play space were created.

By far the most impressive aspect of the Fredensgade project is the glass pyramid greenhouse and wastewater treatment facility, which is known as the "bioworks," situated in the center of the interior courtyard. It comes into sight spectacularly as one enters the courtyard from one of several street entrances. The project was built in a collaboration between the city of Kolding and the social housing company Byfornyelsesselskabet Denmark, and funding for the bioworks project comes from the Danish Green Fund (which provides monies for a variety of pilot environmental projects). (The functioning of this urban "living machine" is described in further detail in Chapter 8.)

Rainwater is also collected in a below-ground cistern, purified in a pond, and then pumped to the flats for toilet flushing and for use in washing machines. Some of the units have added solar hot water heaters, and many have installed passive solar winter gardens and glass rooms. Additional insulation, energy-efficient glass, water-saving fixtures and toilets, and extensive recycling and composting facilities were also added. Extensive use was made of recycled brick and other materials. There is at least one section of rooftop that has been converted into a glass solar terrace. A series of photovoltaic panels in the interior provides most of the power to run the pumps and motors in the bioworks. The PV panels also power hookups for charging electric vehicles.

The Solgården urban renewal project, also in Kolding, illustrates how older buildings can be effectively retrofitted to incorporate photovoltaics and solar energy. Just completed, this project (its name means "sun court") includes "architecturally integrated" photovoltaic panels in four curving arrays on the rooftop and on the exterior walls of new enclosed balcony sunrooms (Municipality of Kolding, 1996). The explicit objective in the renovation of this late 1930s apartment building is a 50 percent reduction in the fossil fuel consumed by residents of the building.[6] In total, the building includes 846 photovoltaic modules and will provide more than half of the electrical demand of the buildings. A number of other environmental improvements have been made to the building (e.g., additional insulation, use of water-conserving bathroom and kitchen fixtures, and the installation of energy-efficient appliances), along with other general enhancements (such as the installation of elevators). The photovoltaics in the structure have been heavily subsidized by the Danish Ministry of Housing, with one of the key objectives of the project being to demonstrate how photovoltaic technology can be applied in urban renewal and renovation projects. The result of this creative integration of photovoltaics, is the use of otherwise wasted rooftop space, and the creation of a most visually distinctive building, strikingly visible from many street-level vantage points around this particular neighborhood.

In Germany, other notable ecological renovation projects include the redevelopment of 167 units in the Unionplatz area in Berlin, incorporating new greenery, composting facilities, and solar hot water units, among other improvements (Forum for the Future, 1997b). In Denmark, other ecological renovation projects include an eight-block renovation in Slagelse (including the incorporation of active and passive solar, a waste-sorting initiative, and traffic enhancing measures) (Ministry of Environment and Energy, undated).

Many European cities contain remnants of Corbusier's ideas of the radiant city—especially the 1960s large high-rise residential blocks, set in a green sea of open land. Increasingly, there are efforts to redesign or reconfigure these estates to make them more green and to incorporate ecological features. The Bijlmermeer district in Amsterdam is one example, dating to the mid-1960s. These flats were seen as a desirable alternative to overcrowded living conditions in other parts of the city, and their average size tended to be substantially greater. Over time, the area acquired the perception of undesirable housing: buildings seen as oppressive in scale, concerns about crime and safety, open spaces that could not be socially managed or controlled. (Interestingly, the density of the Bijlmermeer is only about 40 units per hectare, and the same density could easily be accommodated through a more traditional urban street pattern and thus at a much more human scale.) The city is now working to reconfigure the space and to include new green features, such as a lake and small stream.

The efforts of Berlin to green its large housing blocks, especially in eastern Berlin, is another example of this effort. Here, the city has undertaken a variety of measures to make these housing areas more visually attractive and to enhance the quality of living there. Specific actions taken include the tearing up of asphalt and concrete and their replacement with trees and shrubbery, the building of green play areas for children, and extensive painting and structural upgrading of the buildings. Interestingly, the experience of high-rise block housing, although not a very positive one in most western European cities (e.g., in Amsterdam), has been much more favorable in eastern European countries, where it has been viewed as desirable housing (and not stigmatized as places of crime, drugs, and low-income residents, in the same way as in western European cities). In Berlin, enhancing the attractiveness of these housing areas, checking physical or social deterioration before it occurs, is seen as critical to preventing the exodus of middle-income residents from these areas. This strategy is considered an important partial solution to Berlin's housing problem (e.g., the most effective and sustainable strategy is to try to keep residents of these housing estates where they are and make it attractive for them to stay there).

Strategies for Promoting Green Buildings

The European enthusiasm for ecological building is reflected in a number of programs, incentives, and investments. The Netherlands has perhaps done the most to promote green or sustainable building. To its credit, the national government of the Netherlands has given a high priority to promoting and facilitating sustainable buildings. It has now prepared its second National Action Plan for Sustainable Building. These action plans establish national goals and targets and identify a number of key programs and actions that will be taken, typically in a two-year period.[7] The elements of the Dutch national sustainable building strategy are summarized in Box 10.1.

The national government provides financial subsidies, has sponsored national pilot demonstration projects (such as Ecolonia), and has orchestrated agreements with the building industry that set sustainable building targets. The government has recently established a national center for sustainable building (in Utrecht), and the incorporation of sustainable building practices is now typical for all new national building sites (the VINEX sites—building areas approved in the fourth national memorandum on planning, where some three-quarters of the homes built in the Netherlands occur). Development occurs here through agreements between the central government and regional authorities, which now commonly include provisions dealing with sustainable building. Also, more than 60 percent of municipalities have chosen sustainable building as an area of future work under a scheme providing them with additional environmental monies. It has been estimated that some 14,000 homes in the Netherlands were built incorporating some sustainability features between 1991 and 1995 (VROM, 1995).

The promotion of sustainable building has been greatly aided through the development of the "National Sustainable Building Package." This package is essentially a comprehensive set of sustainability measures that

---

Box 10.1. Elements of the Dutch Strategy for Advancing Sustainable
Building

- National Sustainable Building Action Plan
- National Sustainable Building Packet
- Sustainable Building Information Center
  ("Dubo Centrum")
- Demonstration Projects
- Covenants with Social Housing Associations
- Green Funds and Green Mortgages
- VINEX Contracts between Municipalities and National
  Government
- National Government Building Agency (applying concepts to
  government buildings and facilities)

---

could be used by builders and developers. Although not a national code per
se (there are in fact also minimum mandatory national standards for areas
such as energy conservation), it provides significant guidance for going
above and beyond the minimum building and construction standards. The
package is, moreover, being used in certain mandatory ways. For instance,
many cities (some 75 percent of them) reference the package and commonly stipulate that projects must contain a certain percentage or number
of measures from the national package. The package itself is distributed for
a modest cost by the national construction association, which entitles a
subscriber to subsequent updates and additions.

The Dutch government has a long history of funding and sponsoring
demonstration projects, even well before its national action plan. These
projects have included, for example, the highly influential Ecolonia project
(described earlier), which served to demonstrate and illustrate the use of a
variety of suitable building materials, techniques, and technologies. The
current national plan contains funding for some thirty-four deconstruction
projects, including housing, offices, schools, and other utility buildings.

Another leverage point involves covenants entered into by social housing associations and the national government. Although the percentage of
social or assisted housing in the Netherlands is declining, it still represents
about 30 percent of new homes. As part of these covenants, the national
government has been of late stipulating a minimum expenditure by these
associations on sustainable housing.

Another important element of the Dutch strategy for promoting sustainable building is the commitment to lead by example. An important
prong of the national action plan is for the national government to
demonstrate and incorporate sustainability principles into its own build-

ings. Coordinated by the national building agency within the Ministry of Housing, Spatial Planning, and Environment (VROM), there is now a variety of impressive demonstrations of sustainable building in these new government facilities. The new shared workspace building in Haarlem is one such example (described in Chapter 12). Other examples include a tax office in Enschede with impressive daylighting features, a hotel office in Den Haag (a government office that agencies can rent for short periods of time), the building of the new National Institute for Nature Research (IBN) (which will employ a system of natural ventilation), a new police station in Leusden, and the "dismountable" (recyclable) police station in Boxmeer (already mentioned), among others (Government Buildings Agency, 1997).

The national sustainable building center—or DuboCentrum, as it is known—is the first of its kind in Europe and demonstrates the commitment given to sustainable building by the national government there. Although it is a private information and technical assistance center, it receives about two-thirds of its funding from the national government, with the remainder provided by private sources. The center responds to the needs of builders, developers, and others who are interested in building more sustainably, providing practical guidance about how to actually go about it. The center's advice-giving and information-distribution functions are especially helpful for smaller contractors and architectural firms that simply may lack the internal resources to do the research and learning necessary to put these ideas into practice. The organization of the center is important. Because it is industry run, it appears to have considerable credibility. In addition to its advice-giving and clearinghouse functions, the center also sponsors field visits and tours of sustainable buildings and projects. It also produces an extremely timely monthly magazine on sustainable building, which has become a widely read journal within the country. The center has also produced a series of detailed case reports on the many sustainable building projects that have been completed.

Green Mortgages

A unique system of green funds is also maintained in the Netherlands and is a major source of private funding for a variety of ecological projects and investments. The funds are operated by private banks, but the projects are certified and approved by the national government. The main financial incentive behind the program is that interest income for those investing in green funds is tax free. While an investment return of around 6 percent is normal, the 2 to 3 percent return from green funds is made quite attractive because of its tax-free status. The banks are required under the program to invest at least 70 percent of these funds in certified green projects. Projects must have a minimum value of 50,000 guilders (US $25,000).

The program only began in 1995, but it has already been extremely successful. The government's initial target was to stimulate the investment of 1 billion guilders within 10 years, but investment in green projects has already reached 3 billion guilders. There are now six funds (there were formerly eight, but one bank consolidated three different funds into a single fund), and the country's major banks are all actively participating (including ING, Rabobank, and ABN-Amro). A variety of different ecological projects are being underwritten through the funds. Large amounts of funding have gone to support the development of district heating, organic farming, ecological landscape and nature restoration projects, the construction of windmills, as well as sustainable building projects.

Clearly, one of the most creative applications of the Dutch green funds can be seen in the funding of ecological building projects. Ecological homes and buildings became eligible in November 1997. Already, some 3,000 homes have been certified for green mortgages under the program. To qualify, a home must meet two sets of ecological building standards—a mandatory list of requirements (known as the "basic" requirements) and the achievement of a minimum number of points (60) from another list of design features. Houses are certified by NOVEM, the Dutch national energy agency, and staff there point out that the basic standards are quite stringent. For example, the energy standard that must be satisfied is substantially higher than the already high national standard, and buildings must be designed so that they are flexible enough to be used later for senior housing, among other requirements. Under the point system, for example, high points are given for projects that incorporate photovoltaics.

Once a green certificate is issued for a home, the buyer then qualifies for a below-interest mortgage. The typical reduction in one's monthly mortgage payment is admittedly modest (averaging about 100 guilders, or about $50 USD), but it is viewed by builders and developers as making it easier to sell their homes, as well as providing an improved public image.

Green House Numbers

Die Grüne Hausnummer, or the green house number, is a creative program created by the Saarland (Germany) Ministry of Environment, Energy and Transportation. It represents another creative idea for promoting sustainable building. The brainchild of the current Minister of the Environment, Willy Leonhardt, the idea is to give the owners of buildings a psychological incentive and encouragement for doing more to build and renovate their homes with green features. Leonhardt got the idea from the Swiss, who had developed a similar program for low-energy homes. A point system has been established, and participants must amass a total score of at least 100 points, based on a variety of possible green features, including greenroofs, solar energy, energy conservation features, and so on. Once the points have been reviewed and certified by a ministry inspector, the building owner is awarded a framed certificate, and, perhaps most importantly, given a green number address placard, which is displayed at the front of the home or building and which becomes the address plate for the building. The number is in distinctive green, against a cream background, and declares the achievement of *Die Grüne Hausnummer*.

The program began in June of 1996 and has been quite popular. There are now more than seventy buildings that have been awarded the green house number. And increasingly, the buildings are not just residential properties. Recently, the first hotel was certified (getting a fairly high score of 120 points). Renovated buildings qualify as well. A recent renovation of a 1718 structure gained certification for features that included, among others, composting facilities, a rainwater collection system for toilet flushing, and a modern, more energy-efficient heating system.

The minister's basic idea was to find a way to redirect some of the impulses that home buyers have to spend money on extras and to obtain the status value these extras seem to convey. Why not encourage some of these investments to be green ones, and why not facilitate a sense of pride and status and public recognition from green expenditures? Why not direct some of these impulses "to impress" into ecological features and improvements? As Bern Dunnzlaff, of the Saarland Environment Ministry, observes, the program is popular in large degree because it provides an opportunity for individuals to directly do something to improve the environment and to reassure themselves that they are actually doing something. It seems to be working, and there is also a sense that the green house number bestows some additional economic value on the home or building. The placard is quite attractive; in a way, it reminds one of a historic marker or monument placard. One wonders whether it would not be a fitting extension of the idea to tell (in brief words, similar to a historic plaque) the story behind the building, such as the special characteristics of the building that distinguish it from the average or run-of-the mill home or building.

The program has received considerable press around Saarland, which seems to be a key ingredient in making the idea work. Much has been made of the awarding of the green house number status, and the minister himself often shows up to hand out the certificates and placards. A sense of pride is conveyed in the newspaper reporting in the smaller towns and cities when a high point score is obtained. A sort of snowball effort has occurred as a result. The program has also gotten attention outside of Saarland, and the Ministry has even received requests for green house numbers for buildings outside of the state.

Other Important Strategies

Understanding of the actual long-term results or accomplishments of ecological developments or urban ecological renewal remains limited, and is a potentially important area for future research. Substantial savings in energy and other environmental results are well documented. The broader social implications of settlement patterns are interesting, although less documented. Enhancing the environmental qualities of a neighborhood does appear to reinforce its social stability and create feelings of commitment to place. In Albertslund, for example, the Agenda 21 activities, which were focused on one particular housing area, have resulted in substantial reductions in the turnover rate for social housing in that area (from 30 percent to 15 percent, in comparison with other housing areas in the city).

It is possible, as well, that living in a sustainable neighborhood may result in other changes in personal and family behavior that are supportive of the environment. A planner and resident of Morra Park expressed the view that the obvious environmental features of the homes there (e.g., solar panels on each residence) have the effect of causing residents to be generally more conscious of environmental issues. The spatial organization of developments, with an emphasis typically on clustered housing and shared environmental and community spaces, may tend to encourage greater interaction between residents.

And in ecological housing projects such as Het Groene Dak ("the green roof") in Utrecht and Polderdrift in Arnhem (both in the Netherlands)— both projects that emphasize environmental concerns—visits and interviews with residents suggest a stronger cohesion and sense of community.

Educating new residents about how to live more ecologically and how to properly use the ecological features of one's new home is a common feature in many of the projects visited. In Het Groene Dak, for example, an environmental booklet was specifically prepared for, and distributed to, new residents. It covers topics such as how to equip the homes in ways that minimize environmental impacts (e.g., the kinds of wood, carpeting, and other materials used to finish the home, and the kinds of appliances to purchase). All new residents of GWL-terrein in Amsterdam are given an extensive environmental packet that provides information on car-sharing services and environmental housekeeping (Stichting Natuur en Milieu, 1994).

Industry-sponsored exhibitions of ecological building products, materials, and services are another effective strategy. In the Netherlands, VIBA (Vereniging Integrale Biologische Architectuur, or the association for biological architecture) has organized a permanent exhibition of sustainable building materials and technologies in the city of 's-Hertogenbosch. Contained in two large halls, examples of virtually every imaginable ecological building product or service—from rooftop photovoltaic systems to windows to alternative insulation materials—is displayed with technical specifications and contact information (see VIBA, 1996). A contractor or architect (or even a member of the general public) interested in ecological building would find tangible information and guidance about how to go about it, as well as a hands-on, visual impressions of how these systems and materials will look and function.

Amsterdam has developed a "DuBo-kaart," or a map of sustainable building projects, which is likely to be a very useful information tool for educating builders, planners, and the general public there. It impressively identifies some forty-two projects around the city, from single buildings to large housing developments (Berents, 1998).

Lessons for American Cities

One of the clearest conclusions is that, compared to many of the European initiatives profiled, there is simply not enough attention given in the United States to aggressively promoting ecological design and building. The northern Europeans especially have made major national commitments to advancing ecological building, often with substantial and creative financial underwriting and through other important forms of national (and municipal) leadership. The priority given by northern European countries to promoting ecological construction and building is impressive—and is a direction the United States should emulate. The sheer magnitude and amount of ecological building (as a relatively high percentage of total building, especially in the Netherlands), the comprehensive policies and concerted action plans and financial and other incentives taken to implement them, the importance placed by government on funding demonstration projects, and the very creative design features of these projects, are all exemplary elements of the European approach.

Instead of a serious commitment to ecological building and design, however, the American situation (in contrast) can best be characterized as a haphazard, scattered set of buildings and projects (many very impressive), which is driven more by enlightened clients and specific designers than by strong public policy. To be sure, there has already occurred a significant and growing body of ecological design and building, and design organizations such as the American Institute of Architects have given the subject serious attention in recent years. Yet, although we do increasingly have examples of ecological housing and design projects, many of the more highly visible projects raise real concerns about how truly green or sustainable they actually are. Recent American examples include what some have called "ecoburbs," or ecological suburbs, reflecting the observation that they tend to be located in suburban (often exurban) locations, and typically on greenfield sites. These developments include, for example, Prairie Crossings (about 40 miles north of Chicago), Haymount (on the banks of the Rappahannock River near Fredericksburg, Virginia), and The Woodlands, Texas. The Woodlands, an Ian McHarg–designed ecological new town (near Houston), reflects the suburban low density of about two units per acre (18,000 homes on about 10,000 acres). While projects such as these often involve major provisions for the conservation of open space, their low density and fundamental car dependence suggest they are less than ideal from the perspective of reducing society's ecological footprint. And some, such as Dewees Island (South Carolina), are located in extremely sensitive environmental locations. The density of these projects also raises questions.

Civano, a new (highly touted) ecological community in Tucson, incorporates a number of significant features for reducing the ecological footprints of residents. The positive elements of this new community are many, including very energy efficient houses, large areas of protected greenspace (including a community orchard), and an Environmental Technologies Business Center. But here as well, the proposed density is relatively low (2,600 homes on 1,132 acres), the project is located at the urban periphery, and the development includes some puzzling features, including an "environmentally sensitive" eighteen-hole golf course. Nevertheless, projects like Civano are certainly a good start on the way to more sustainable forms of settlement in the United States.

In contrast, the European ecological projects profiled here are (for the most part) built at substantially higher densities, often on brownfield or urban sites (e.g., GWL-terrein in Amsterdam), with transit and walkability/bicycles as key design features. Indeed, the projects highlighted in this book illustrate well that ecological design and building can help to strengthen the existing urban fabric and promote more efficient use of land and a compact regional urban form. American ecological building must learn these important lessons, and it must follow the important examples showing that a sustainable *location* is as important as the building material or the embodied energy of the structure itself. Sustainable living requires that attention be given to all of these considerations.

The so-called "green building" in urban Dublin and the Solgarden renovation project in Kolding, among many other examples, illustrate well that impressive ecological design features can be accommodated in very urban environments. We have few such examples in U.S. cities, and here a few prominent demonstration projects could be extremely influential. One such creative example can be found in Toronto. The Toronto Healthy House does effectively illustrate the potential of sensible ecological building in the heart of a city. Located on an infill lot in the highly walkable Broadview and Danforth neighborhood, the Healthy House illustrates many of the technologies and building strategies currently available that can fundamentally reduce the ecological footprints of homes. Sponsored by the Canada Mortgage and Housing Corporation, the home is really a duplex—two connected three-bedroom homes. The Healthy House is independent of urban services and is not connected to the city's wastewater treatment system or water or power network. A rainwater collection system provides water to the house, and through a combination of water-conserving fixtures and appliances, water use in the house is estimated to be one-tenth of the usual amount. Heating of the house occurs through passive solar, supplemented by a radiant hot-water floor heating system when the solar is insufficient (see Canada Mortgage and Housing Corporation, undated). Electricity is supplied through a 2.3 kWh array of photovoltaic panels, and a backup generator when needed. Some other basic energy features include low-energy appliances, extra insulation, the structure's four-floor vertical orientation, and high-efficiency triple-glazed windows. A biological wastewater treatment system is contained in the basement, and the home recycles much of its water. An emphasis is also given to the use of low-toxic materials. Moreover, the house illustrates the potential of a modestly sized home: the house is 1,700 square feet in size, and total operating costs for a year have been estimated at less than US $200 (Canada Mortgage and Housing Corporation, undated). Toronto's Healthy House illustrates the potential of green-urban residential building, even in a cold

The Healthy House in Toronto demonstrates convincingly that ecological design features can be successfully applied in urban settings. Among its considerable ecological features, this home is independent of both the electric power grid and public sewer and water.

northern climate. It is a home that shows well how it is possible to minimize the ecological footprint of lifestyles through building design, achieve affordable housing, and create more healthful living environments—all at the same time. In the United States, our own Fannie Mae should take the lead by sponsoring and financially underwriting similar demonstration homes, perhaps one in each major climatic zone of the country.

Nevertheless, these are some promising beginnings—programs and initiatives that represent important policy directions but that will require significant expansion in the future. Not surprisingly, many of the U.S. approaches entail a heavy free-market orientation: an emphasis on creating incentives and a strategy of ecolabeling homes to encourage buyers to be more conscious of the choices they make concerning, in particular, the energy-consumption attributes of their new homes. At the federal level, USEPA and USDOE have jointly initiated the Energy Star Homes Program, which seeks to encourage and reward home construction that exceeds national energy standards. Specifically, new homes qualify for certification if their projected energy consumption is 30 percent lower than that called for by the national energy code (as determined by an independent verifier) (USEPA, 1998). If the homes satisfy this standard, builders and developers are then permitted to use the Energy Star logo in selling and marketing their homes. One of the clear advantages of the program for homebuyers is that it may qualify them for an energy-efficient mortgage, and there are now a number of mortgage lenders participating in the Energy Star initiative. Because buyers have lower monthly energy costs, these mortgage companies are able to qualify borrowers for larger loan amounts and other financial benefits.[8] Typical design features in Energy Star homes include greater insulation, the use of high-performance windows, tight construction, and more efficient heating and cooling systems.

Advocates of Energy Star homes, including USDOE and USEPA, argue that the small increases in the cost of the home due to these energy investments are more than outweighed by the reduced energy costs associated with operating the home. USEPA estimates that Energy Star homes will save an average of $400 per year in reduced energy costs (USEPA, 1998). The higher energy standards are also believed to improve the saleability of the home. Since the initiation of this program, more than 4,000 Energy Star homes have been built, and some 780 builders and developers have participated. USEPA has estimated that the program will result in a 4 million metric ton reduction (by 2010) in carbon emissions.

There are also an increasing number of office, commercial, and industrial buildings in the United States that reflect ecological design principles and have begun to set a higher design standard for these types of structures.

Several recent projects by William McDonough and Partners provide compelling examples of the possibilities here. The new Gap headquarters building in San Bruno (California) and the Herman Miller factory in Holland (Michigan) are two of the best. The Gap building includes an undulating greenroof, uses nontoxic materials and sustainably harvested woods, includes extensive daylighting throughout the building, and contains other energy conservation features that add up to substantially lower energy consumption than required under California's already tough codes (*Interiors*, 1990a).

The Herman Miller furniture factory has many of the same ecological features, including a constructed wetlands system for collecting and treating stormwater runoff, a circulation street connecting the factory space and offices (reminiscent of ING's mainstreet), and extensive daylighting throughout the building. Indeed, like the Ecover factory in Belgium (described in Chapter 12), the production areas of the building receive extensive daylight through an angled glass roof and system of light monitors (Interior Architect, 1999b). McDonough, and other American ecological architects, have made convincing arguments that such working conditions—fresh air, daylight, visual connections to greenery—can raise productivity more than enough to pay for any additional costs associated with these design features.

Perhaps most ambitious of all is the new Adam Joseph Lewis Center for Environmental Studies, at Oberlin College in Ohio. The brainchild of environmental studies professor and national proponent of ecological literacy, David Orr, the building (when completed) will set a new environmental standard for educational and other institutional structures. It will include a living machine that treats its own wastewater, a rainwater collection and recycling system, and, most impressively, it will be energy independent. The building will not be connected to the power grid but will generate its own power through a combination of southern orientation, rooftop photovoltaics, geothermal pumps, and energy conservation measures. The energy consumption of the building is projected to be about 20 percent of that typically seen in that part of Ohio. The building also demonstrates the concept of "product of service," in that the carpet tiles will continue to be owned by their manufacturer (Interface) and will be returned and recycled at the end of their useful life (Interior Architecture, 1999c). The Oberlin building, then, may become the American building that comes closest to achieving the metaphor of a structure functioning like a tree. Orr is fond of emphasizing the point that we are shaped as a culture by what we build and that our design and building choices make important symbolic statements about what we value and think to be important. "Architecture as Pedagogy," Orr would argue, and these American exemplars, as with their European counterpoints, begin to change and alter what we teach to be important (see Orr, 1994).

An important lesson from the European experience is the potentially powerful role government can play as a facilitator and catalyst for sustainable building. Many of the European initiatives discussed could easily be adapted to the American context. One particularly promising idea is the notion of a green mortgage. In fact, such an idea could effectively build on the existing notions of energy-efficient mortgages (already provided by a number of mortgage companies and lending institutions, typically in combination with participation in the EPA Energy Star Homes program), and location-efficient mortgages (which Fannie Mae has experimented with and appears to be gradually embracing). Green mortgages are the next logical step.

And, as the efforts of the Dutch national building agency effectively show, we should view every new public building project as an opportunity to demonstrate and promote new ecological building techniques, ideas, and products. Governments at every level in the United States have similar opportunities, although public building design and construction is rarely seen in this way. One impressive exception can be seen in the recent efforts of the U.S. Postal Service, which has, to its credit, been attempting to lead by example and to promote green building concepts in its postal service buildings. The first such green post office was opened in January 1999, in Fort Worth, Texas. It includes an impressive array of green design features, including a rainwater collection system, the extensive use of daylighting, low-VOC (volatile organic compounds) materials, the use of local stone and large amounts of recycled materials (e.g., recycled stone/concrete, waste fly ash in concrete, recycled tires and plastics in dock and wall bumpers), the use of certified sustainably harvested wood throughout the building, the use of native plants, and a compressed natural gas fueling station (the Postal Service has already converted some 1,500 of its vehicles in the Dallas/Fort Worth area to compressed natural gas as part of a national program to shift to alternatively fueled vehicles). One of the most interesting design features of the building is the use of straw—a local agricultural waste product—in the building's exterior wall panel system (Environmental Building News, 1999; U.S. Postal Service, undated).

To its credit, the U.S. Postal Service sees the tremendous opportunity it has for making a difference here. It states this clearly in a recent press release: "The United States Postal Service is committed to sustainable principles. It recognizes the positive role that it can perform in environmental leadership, both as a public agency and as one of the largest builders in the nation. By taking a proactive approach . . . the Postal Service is helping to protect the environment, providing a healthy indoor environment for its customers and employees, and setting a standard for others" (U.S. Postal Service, undated, p. 1). Perhaps other federal (and state and local) agencies will take this important lead and also begin to view new buildings and renovation projects as opportunities for green innovation and a reduction of their overall ecological footprints. Indeed, each year some 500 to 700 new postal buildings are constructed nationwide. And, because of its "semi-private federal agency" status, the Postal Service is not constrained by local building and health codes and thus has more flexibility in experimenting with and demonstrating new ecological building ideas. In addition to the Fort Worth facility, other green post office designs are in the works in Raleigh (North Carolina) and for a site in the Northeast.

Several U.S. cities have also taken impressive steps to promote ecological building, showing the potentially significant role to be played by cities and local governments. The green builder idea found its beginnings in Austin, Texas. The basic idea is that the city of Austin seeks to promote more sustainable and ecological building and construction through a combination of builder and consumer education, and especially through a certification process that awards green builder "stars" to homes and buildings that meet certain green criteria. Participating builders must attend training in green building (both an initial basic program and ongoing seminars).

The Green Builder program in Austin, Texas, has done much to educate and promote environmentally friendly building. Shown here is a green-builder certified home under construction in east Austin.

(For a more extensive discussion of the Austin program, see Beatley and Manning, 1997.)

Boulder (Colorado) is another example and has established a unique mandatory green building point system called greenpoints. Under this initiative, all new construction must satisfy a minimum number of green building points. The city does not tell builders precisely what must be incorporated; rather, builders are given a choice of design features and technologies from which they must amass a minimum number of greenpoints, depending upon the square footage of the structure (see Box 10.2).[9] The greenpoints guidelines provide more detailed information about green building techniques and the range of points available under each. Major groupings or categories under which points are assigned include land use (e.g., enhanced solar access); framing (e.g., recycled content roofing); plumbing (e.g., hot water pipe insulation); insulation (e.g., high R-value wall insulation); HVAC (e.g., high-efficiency furnaces); solar (e.g., passive solar heating); and indoor air quality (e.g., low-VOC interior paints). Under the solar category, as one example, new buildings can gain between two and ten points depending on the extent to which the home will be heated through passive solar (see below). Other cities, including Los Angeles County (California) and Scottsdale (Arizona), have followed Boulder's lead and have either established or are in the process of establishing similar greenpoints programs. The Boulder greenpoints program is viewed as a success by local officials. Additional construction costs resulting from the greenpoints features are estimated in the range of 1 to 3 percent (seen as modest) and are often paid back in other long-term savings (such as reduced energy consumption). In addition to its mandatory greenpoints, Boulder is also attempting to educate builders about green building practices in ways similar to Austin. It offers a free training program to builders, which upon completion awards them a certificate and recognizes them as "gold level builders," a designation with some considerable marketing appeal. To date, some twenty-two builders have been certified, and the city is now working on recognizing and certifying suppliers and retailers who stock "greenpoint building supplies." A voluntary greenpoint remodeling program has also been established. A booklet describing green remodeling techniques and ideas was advertised in a utility bill insert, resulting in some 2,500 requests for the booklet.

Still, getting American homebuyers interested in, and excited about, energy and other sustainable design features is a tough challenge. Recent surveys of homebuyers suggest that other home features are of much greater importance to them. Indeed, to achieve significant ecological building in American cities will require a major public awareness and attitude-shifting campaign. Presently, most social norms concerning homebuying

Box 10.2. Points Assigned for Passive Solar Space
Heating: Boulder Greenpoints Program

   2 points: 20–39% passive, solar heating
   6 points: 40–59% passive, solar heating
  10 points: 60% or greater passive, solar heating

Source: City of Boulder, undated, p. 18

place importance on such things as curb appeal, the size of rooms, the types of countertops, and other features that are the most visible and that clearly serve to enhance the investment or resale value of one's home. A recent survey of a sample of Americans conducted by the National Home Builders Association (NHBA) (not an unbiased organization, of course) paints a remarkably different portrait of Americans and highlights these contradictions. The results of this survey make clear that while most Americans may abstractly support environmental protection, few see it as a priority when purchasing a home. An amazingly meager one-third of the respondents said they would be willing to spend an extra $1,000 on an energy-efficient home, even though it would save them $1,000 a year on utility bills. What is clearly more important in these decisions is the home's amenities. According to an NHBA economist: 'They want their friends and relatives to say 'Wow! You have a Jacuzzi, two fireplaces and a huge kitchen'' (Salant, 1997, p. E8). These kinds of survey findings certainly speak volumes about the difficulty of the task ahead. Perhaps because of the dominant view of the home as a primary financial investment, increasing importance is placed on large rooms in large homes. Really, nothing less than a change in how Americans view homeownership is required, and such a major shift will be admittedly slow in coming. Nevertheless many of the European-style initiatives described here will help to push along these attitudinal changes.

Nurturing a different, broader notion of home ownership is one necessary direction: several American examples can be cited of efforts to educate and instill in new homeowners a deeper sense of place and connection to natural environment. Two modest examples of these ideas can be seen in Dewees Island and Spring Island (both in South Carolina), two new communities that have received much attention lately for the importance they place on sustainability and especially the great emphasis placed on educating new residents about the ecology and biodiversity of these places. In both cases, new homeowners receive a large property owner's report—a kind of owner's manual—with extensive discussions of the plant and animal life on the islands, as well as the geology, hydrology, and the management programs and restrictions that apply there. There are also extensive educational programs offered to residents throughout the year. These are minimum responsibilities that should be taken on perhaps by local governments but also by neighborhood-based ecological groups.

In addition to giving builders and housing consumers additional information about alternative building techniques and strategies for energy- and environment-conserving construction, greater efforts might also be made to promote more ecologically conscious choices about location. One innovative strategy has been the publishing and distribution by the Hill Country Foundation, in the Austin area, of an "Eco-Location Map." The map displays the location of the main ecological features of the region, including aquifer recharge zones, sensitive wildlife habitat areas, and the 100-year floodplain. A preferred growth area is also delineated (mostly the eastern portions of the region), and builders, business owners, and housing consumers are encouraged to avoid these ecologically sensitive areas and to locate projects (or purchase their homes) within the desired growth corridors (Greenbeat, 1996). Maps were sold for a modest $3.50 and were distributed at a number of local sites, including grocery stores, travel offices, and bookstores. The Hill Country Foundation also held a series of workshops with real estate offices, business groups, and others about how to effectively use the eco-location maps. This combination of education and asking housing and development consumers to more directly assume responsibility for the ecological impacts of their respective choices is another promising strategy, perhaps more suited to our American individualism.

The dramatic rise in house sizes in the United States also represents a uniquely American sustainable building issue. The European housing projects profiled here generally involve mixtures of different housing types, with considerably less emphasis on detached single-family units and with most dwelling units considerably smaller in size. Robert Frank, in his book *Luxury Fever* describes this amazing trend of rising home sizes, which is occurring despite the decline in household size. Indeed, while the average home built in the 1950s—a time many Americans look back upon with nostalgia—was about 1,100 square feet, by 1996 this average size had nearly doubled. The largest homes have become much larger (6,000-square-foot homes are now not uncommon, not to mention Bill Gates's 45,000-square-foot home in Seattle), and their share of the market is growing. (Frank's data shows the number of homes 2,400 square feet or larger growing to 30 percent by 1996, compared with 18 percent in 1986) (Frank, 1999, p. 21).

This growth in size and amenities in new American homes also has serious implications for our ability to provide affordable housing. In California, for example, house prices have tracked this remarkable rise in housing size. The average new home in California is even larger than the national average—a record 2,095 square feet (compared to 1,610 square feet in 1982). According to a study by the Construction Industry Research Board, almost half of the new homes built in California have four bedrooms or more. Average new single-family homes sold in California bring a whopping $263,200. Amazingly, in California the number of new homes selling for less than $150,000 is an alarmingly small 24 percent (Inman, 1999). In the United States, opulence and consumption in housing have real and serious affordability implications for average Americans.

Creative design for smaller homes is essential and will also facilitate taking advantage of compact, infill development opportunities. In Minneapolis, for example, a number of architects recently participated in a design contest for homes that would fit on the vacant ultra-narrow lots (34 to 38 feet wide) that exist in the city's Powderhorn Park neighborhood, close to downtown. The winning entry (and some 165 architects from all around the country submitted plans) will be built, and the hope is to publish the best plans in a book. As the organizer of the contest observes, "What we're really hoping to do is to restore the density of the city, rather than have these lots cut in half and given away as side lots. . . . There are hundreds of small city lots in the Twin Cities and if other neighborhoods want to use these plans, we'd be excited by that" (Hawley, 1999, p. 2). Many other American cities have similar opportunities for creative infill, and clearly some of the green building impulse in this country should be directed to designing and building space-efficient, highly daylighted, smaller homes that fit well into existing urban neighborhoods.

NOTES

1. The Ecolonia evaluation studies also helped identify problems with certain materials and technology. Edwards (1996) notes the following problem areas: a risk of moisture and rotting in compressed cellulose insulation; extra attention needed to ensure proper ventilation in structures; the expensive and unreliable nature of PVs; and unreliable compost toilets; see the many more detailed evaluation studies prepared by NOVEM. Other problems noted in the evaluation studies: plants that did not grow on the grass roofs and water flowing over the rim of the roof; many residents did not wash their cars in the designated car-washing area, resulting in damaging runoff entering the lake (in part due to insufficient information about the objectives of this design); recycling closets were rarely used, mostly due to their inconvenient location near the entrance hall of homes; natural paints were found to peel, discolor, and provide inadequate pro-

tection; and complaints were made about the noise generated by central vacuum cleaner systems.

2. Literature on the project claims even higher efficiency—specifically, that this unit requires 250 to 300 cubic meters of gas annually, compared to an average Dutch home in this area, which uses between 1,200 and 1,800 cubic meters (VROM, undated).

3. Things about the project that have not worked as well include the passive solar design (the solar rooms are frequently too hot in the summer and too cool in the winter to be very usable), the lack of social interaction between the different parts of the development (they tend to be isolated islands), and an inability to effectively restrict or control automobiles (almost all units have automobiles and many have garages; residents drive cars frequently, despite the project being very pedestrian- and bicycle-friendly). Problems in enforcing restrictions on building materials have also been cited.

4. The financial limits of building rental homes meant that some features were not included. For instance, built-in "waste collection cupboards," included in the private homes, were not included in the rental units.

5. It was estimated that the additional energy features cost about US $700,000, but that the annual energy savings were on the order of US $2.4 million.

6. The expected electrical output of the photovoltaics is 106,000 kWh/year, while the expected total electrical demand for the building is 175,000 kWh/year.

7. The first action plan covered the period 1996–97, and the second covered the period 1998–99; VROM is required to submit an evaluation report on the action program to Parliament twice yearly.

8. Such as cash back at closing, high qualifying ratios, assured appraised values, free interest lock-ins, and discounted interest rates (USEPA, undated).

9. More specifically, the following greenpoints are required for approval of building permits for new residential construction, or additions to existing residential greater than 500 square feet in size (City of Boulder, undated, p. 3):

   - New dwelling units that have a floor area of 2,500 square feet or less must earn at least 25 points.
   - One additional point must be earned for every 200 square feet or fraction thereof of floor area over 2500 square feet, up to a maximum of 10 additional points.
   - All additional over 500 square feet but less than 1,001 square feet must earn 10 points.
   - All additional of 1,001 square feet of floor area or larger must earn at least 15 points.
   - Applicants for new dwelling units must earn a minimum of 2 points from "sustainable buildings materials and methods" (measures marked with *) and 2 points from "indoor air quality" (measures marked with **).

Part V

Governance and Economy

Chapter 11

Ecological Governance in Green-Urban Cities

Among the leading green-urban cities, there is a strong recognition of the need to take a hard look at the unsustainable practices of local government and to reform the way government itself works. Clearly, municipalities and other sub-national forms of government (e.g., provincial governments in the Netherlands and cantons in Switzerland) can have a significant direct impact in the direction of sustainability by changing the unsustainable practices of its employees, its investment and purchasing practices, and the ways in which it delivers services to the public. A general conclusion is that these European cities, to varying degrees, are attempting to understand these impacts and to aggressively change them in support of sustainability. A frequent rationale offered by interviewees is that it is difficult and inappropriate to call attention to inappropriate and unsustainable practices in the private sector without first making real strides within the governmental structure itself.

The European cities visited and studied here have taken a number of steps to directly reduce their environmental impacts and footprints, and these are reviewed later. The efforts range from creative approaches to gauging sustainability of projects or practices (e.g., sustainability indicators) to techniques for structuring decisions in the future (e.g., ecological budgeting) to a variety of more specific actions, programs, and policies designed to reduce environmental impacts (e.g., the management of public buildings, ecological procurement, and environmental public vehicles). Taken together, these cities have shown convincingly that local and municipal governments have a tremendous range and variety of ways in which they can make a difference and can "practice what they preach."

Audits, Indicators, and Targets

Many European cities have been involved in an ongoing assessment, in one way or another, of the environmental trends and circumstances in their communities. In some places this takes the form of a state-of-the-local-environment study or report. As already mentioned, a number of cities and local government units have developed or are in the process of developing, sustainability indicators. Most of the cities studied have prepared such indicators in one form or another, and the general conclusion is that these techniques have been applied much earlier and are much more widespread among European communities than among American communities. Many local indicators and targets have come directly out of the local Agenda 21 process. Local Agenda 21 (LA21) is an effort arising from the 1992 Rio Conference that is intended to encourage and facilitate the preparation of local or community sustainability plans. Many European municipalities have undertaken such efforts, resulting in a host of specific institutions and actions, including community indicators. (LA21 is discussed in greater detail later.)

Several sustainability indicators have also been prepared at the European Union (EU) level (see Stanners and Bourdeau, 1995). Twelve cities participated in the European Sustainability Index Project. With EU funding, and coordinated by the International Institute for the Urban Environment, these twelve cities (including the cities of Amsterdam, Den Haag, Freiburg, and Leicester) collected data and information on twenty-six different sustainability indicators. Through workshop discussions, these indicators were refined and insights were gained about the ease or difficulty of collecting data and the benefits and uses of such measures. These experiences offer some creative guidance about how to prepare such indicators, as well as how they can be effectively used to guide local policy and shape public discourse about the future.

Leicester was the first city in Britain to develop a set of sustainability indicators. The first set was released in January 1995 and presented trends from fourteen measures. Much of the news was not good, as a majority of the indicators (ten of fourteen) were in fact moving in the wrong direction. There was a conscious decision not to tout the findings (nor to hide them). The feeling was that this would only lead to negative skepticism about the city's efforts (e.g., "We're supposed to be the 'environmental city,' but the trends say otherwise"). Leicester plans to extend the number of indicators over time and to present them in more positive ways. For example, negative trends will be tied to specific and tangible actions that can be taken to address them. These indicators have, nevertheless, been useful in important ways. They have given the city a gauge of how well (or badly) it is doing on a number of measures. And, the indicators have been useful in lobbying, for example, in showing that the city has certain problems (e.g., air quality) that require action.

Den Haag, as another example, has for a number of years, prepared something it calls its Environmental Thermometer (or "Haagse Milieu Thermometer") (see Figure 11.1). This device takes an interesting approach to measuring the distance to targets, and it provides a quick assessment of where progress has been made, as well as where backsliding has occurred. The presentation of the thermometer is innovative. The basic idea is to provide a quick snapshot of how well the city is doing in moving toward important environmental targets. Indicator results are presented in terms of progress (backward or forward) at meeting city targets, as well as the distance to the targets. This method is believed to be a more understandable way to present these annual results (and easier for the public to read). One of the key lessons of the Den Haag experience (and others) suggests the need to include at least some measures unique to the particular community that relate or tie into its unique history or circumstances.

One such unique indicator in Den Haag is the number of nesting storks. The stork is the official symbol for the city and is an example of an indi-

Compensation for lost greenspace

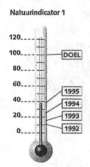

Natuurindicator 1

More than a fifth of Den Haag's land area is composed of various forms of public greenspace. Since 1986, as a result of land use redistribution and replanning, there has been a decline in greenspace, mostly due to the need for building homes. Compensation for this loss of greenspace has been undertaken at other locations, but less than the amount of greenspace lost. The city has gradually made up this loss, but is still 10 hectares behind compared with 1986. This data comes from the city's annual Green Report of 1995/96. This report is published yearly since 1990.

Figure 11.1. Den Haag environmental thermometer

The city of Den Haag in the Netherlands has for a number of years issued an annual "environmental thermometer," which tracks and gauges environmental trends and accomplishments there. The specific indicator shows progress made toward compensating for loss of nature areas in the city. Like all of the indicators, it presents both a goal and the actual achievement level by year, as well as a photograph or picture intended to represent the indicator being measured.

Source: Gemeente Den Haag.

cator with special significance to Den Haag residents. Another creative design aspect of the thermometer is the placement of a photographic image beside each thermometer theme (see Figure 11.1). This has made it easier for the public and decision makers to quickly read and understand these annual results.

Albertslund, Denmark, has collected extensive data on energy and resource consumption and publishes this information each year as a series of *green accounts*. Specifically, the accounts are prepared for the following: carbon dioxide emissions, resulting from consumption of electricity, heat, and traffic; water consumption; sorting of wastes; and use of pesticides (e.g., Albertslund Kommune, 1995). The accounts are published for the city as a whole but also for each district or neighborhood in the city. The latter has permitted city officials, and the residents themselves, to identify districts of high consumption. A citywide user group has been formed with a representative from each district, and comparisons between districts have had the effect of creating positive peer pressure among them, encouraging those neighborhoods showing high consumption to establish plans to curtail the excess.

Albertslund is also impressive in its efforts not only to track resource consumption through these green accounts, but also to work toward reducing its consumption to its fair share. It does this by calculating the environmental space—or its fair share of resource use (with its first calculations done for carbon dioxide and water consumption; see Chapter 1 for a discussion of the meaning of *environmental space*). As Hjalte Aaberg, chairman of the city's Environmental Committee, states: "The general objective is that the consumption of resources and energy must be within the limits of the environmental space by the year 2010" (Aaberg, 1997). To reach this goal, a series of intermediate targets have been set by the city: for example, by 2000, the city hopes to have reduced its carbon dioxide emissions by 30 percent (compared to 1986) (Danish Ministry of Foreign Affairs, 1996). The green accounting system in the city then becomes the means of evaluating progress toward these targets.

Often as a result of local Agenda 21 activities, many municipalities are assessing the environmental functioning of their own offices, agencies, and utilities. Variously called green audits, environmental audits, or eco-audits, they represent attempts to comprehensively study and gauge the ways in which a local government's actions and policies affect the environment. They frequently lead to the preparation of a local state-of-the-environment report and an environmental action plan (see ICLEI, 1992).

Within the EU, municipal governments now have the ability to participate in the EMAS program (Eco-Management and Audit Scheme), a form of environmental auditing and environmental management system formerly available only to private companies. A number of localities are currently in the early stages of EMAS, but only a handful have completed the certification process. One of the first localities to complete the process, the London borough of Sutton is one of the case communities visited and an important leader in this area.

Münster is also a city that has already begun to apply the eco-audit idea to a number of its governmental functions. The city is starting in a gradual and experimental way, and through partnerships. Specifically, a first effort is being undertaken in schools and kindergartens in the city. The goal of the eco-auditing program is to identify and reduce consumption of energy, water, wastewater, transportation impacts, and other materials used in the schools. These programs started voluntarily, and the city's environmental office is providing much of the money and financial incentives for doing the eco-audits, including the hiring of external eco-auditors to help the schools in preparing their eco-audits. An agreement has been made with the schools that half of the savings in reduced energy consumption can be kept for their own use, in whatever way they want to use it; the rest of the savings accrues to the city. In addition to the cost of the eco-auditor, the city also provides the schools with some materials (e.g., new thermostats). Technical advice is also given. The city continues to campaign for partners willing to participate in this eco-auditing program. During the first phases of this experiment, the city's environmental office has itself become a major participant.

Sustainability Matrices and Appraisals

Leicester has prepared a creative Sustainability Appraisal (SA) and applied it to evaluating its local plan. The twenty factors selected are together intended to judge "whether policies and proposals [in the plan] will enable a move towards or away from a more sustainable future" (Leicester City Council, undated, p. 1). These evaluative factors are organized into a matrix and are used to assess each major plan policy, using a system of "checks" and "minuses," accompanied by text commentary (see Table 11.1). The twenty factors used are grouped within three categories: (1) quality of life and local environment (e.g., open space, healthy housing, local economy, and vitality of local centers), (2) natural resources (e.g., landscape, waste, water, and land and soil), and (3) global sustainability (e.g., biodiversity and movement—such as the number of trips made and the level of carbon dioxide emissions generated). The appraised methodology is also applied to specific proposed development sites in the city. (See Table 11.1 for an example of this.)

Table 11.1. Impact Commentary, Proposed Housing Development at Hamilton (H1[a]), Leicester

Sustainability Impact Criteria	Impact	Commentary
QUALITY OF LIFE AND LOCAL ENVIRONMENT		
1 Open Space	+	Opportunities to provide new public open space within development.
2 Health	-	Emissions from new traffic.
3 Safety and Security		Covered by other CLLP policies.
4 Housing	++	Meeting identified housing needs of City.
5 Equity	+	Range/mix of housing together with ancillary community facilities.
6 Accessibility	+	Urban fringe location currently not well served by public transport. Still transport choice location.
7 Local Economy		
8 Vitality of Centers	+	Additional housing will support Hamilton District Center facilities.
9 Built Environment	+	High-quality design could contribute to appearance of development.
10 Cultural heritage		
NATURAL RESOURCES		
11 Landscape	-	Loss of open countryside, but structural planting often an important predevelopment feature.
12 Minerals		
13 Waste		
14 Water	-	Possible disruption to existing ground water/drainage, etc.
15 Land and Soil	-	Loss of agricultural land.
GLOBAL SUSTAINABILITY		
16 Biodiversity	-	Loss of natural habitats (greenfield site), but new development will create parkland and water settings.
17 Movement	-	Increased use of private car due to peripheral location.
18 Transport Mode	-	As above.
19 Energy	?	Depends on detailed layout.
20 Air Quality	-	

SUMMARY:

The proposals that revealed the most negative effects in the appraisal were unsurprisingly the major greenfield sites.

- H1(a) Hamilton Extension
- H1(b) Land east of Thurcaston Road
- H2(a) Glenfrith Hospital

All of these proposals will result in the agricultural land and their development having varying degrees of impact on the natural environment. This has to be balanced against the scale of the city's housing needs and the amount of infrastructure provided already and committed to these development areas. Other policies in the plan can help to counterbalance any adverse effects, e.g., the provision of better public transport services, cycle/footpath networks and local facilities to serve new residential areas can help to reduce the length of car trips and the need to travel generally.

The government already recognizes that urban infill development will not be sufficient or indeed desirable in trying to meet the growth in new households, and it acknowledges that there will still be a need for greenfield sites. A balanced planning strategy is likely to be the best approach toward meeting sustainable development objectives. The CLLP attempts to deliver such a strategy, which has already been endorsed by the inspector who held the inquiry into the local plan in 1993.

Environmental Budgets and Charters

An especially promising idea being promoted by ICLEI is the notion of local environmental budgeting. Here, the notion is that each city should prepare, as it prepares its yearly or semi-yearly financial budget, an ecological budget as well, as an explicit accounting of environmental spending (pollution, resource use) during the period, which must stay within certain limits or targets. Theoretically, a community's global or extra-local environmental impacts could also be taken into account. "Local Environmental Budgeting provides local administration and decisionmakers with a framework for managing natural resources as economically as the artificial resource 'money.' The use of resources, a kind of environmental spending, must remain within the budget limit. This limit is defined by environmental quality targets. When the budget limit is exceeded, overspending begins" (Erdmenger et al., 1997, p. 8).

A pilot project of three German cities (including Heidelberg) and a county is currently under way (to be expanded to ten cities). Funded by the German Federal Environmental Foundation (Deutsche Bundesstiftung Umwelt), these communities are going through the process of preparing, adopting, and implementing an environmental budget (ICLEI, undated).

Environmental budgeting has the advantages of making the various kinds of ecological spending explicit and of holding officials accountable for failing to meet adopted "budgets." In addition to ecological spending, ecological income could also be incorporated into the budget (e.g., desealing surfaces or tree planting) (see Figure 11.2). Ecological assets in the community, such as biodiversity, forests, and groundwater, would also be incorporated.

The process and tool of ecological budgeting would work in ways analogous to conventional financial budgeting. Just as local authorities prepare and enact a budget of projected monetary expenditures for the coming year, so also can (and should) environmental expenditures be budgeted. This budgeting involves communities setting short-range and long-term targets and indicating how expenditures (and revenues) will fall within the budget. As an example, the expansion of impervious or paved surfaces (sealing) in a community could be viewed as an environmental *spending*, while desealing or actions to return paved areas to green and trees could be viewed as environmental *revenue*. The extent to which the ecological budget is balanced at the end of the year would involve calculating net ecological spending and then determining whether it is within the amount budgeted for at the beginning of the budget cycle.

Also analogous to a financial budget, asset summaries can be prepared. Just as it is relevant in the budgeting process to tally the extent and value of assets such as public vehicles, buildings, and office furniture, so also is it relevant to consider how ecological assets—forests, biodiversity, ground-water quality, and other ecological stocks of assets—change over time.

According to ICLEI (undated), the main objectives of ecological budgeting consist of the following:

- to balance the amount of pollution and the consumption of resources in the local community;
- to plan and control the consumption of environmental goods throughout the budgeting period;
- to enable decision makers and the administration to set priorities in environmental policies and to express their needs to other political fields;
- to present the state of the environment in a way that it is understandable for the public; and
- to compare the current state of the environment with targets.

ICLEI identifies several steps to follow in preparing a budget on an annual or semi-annual basis: preparing the environmental budget, enacting or passing the budget, implementing the budget (projects, programs, and actions), and finally preparing of balance sheets at the end of the budget cycle to determine whether and the extent to which the budget has been met.

Ecological budgeting, or ecobudgeting, has a number of potential advantages. It applies a comprehensive, systematic framework for understanding and planning environmental change in a community. It makes visible the cumulative outcomes of many environmental actions and decisions. But perhaps most importantly, the adoption of a budget implies a commitment by local politicians to stay within the budget and to be judged politically by their ability or failure (as we do with conventional fiscal budgets) to do so (see also, Otto-Zimmermann, 1998).

Local governments can express environmental commitments in other ways as well. Several London boroughs have adopted environmental charters, which express intentions to pursue sustainability at every possible policy level and in turn serve as an impetus for reforming government purchasing and other policy. In Westminster borough, the charter (once adopted) was distributed to all city departments, and it led to a series of follow-up seminars for city staff (both general awareness seminars and more specific technical seminars on energy, waste, water, and purchasing were offered). The city has also prepared an online technical handbook that provides more detailed technical information to managers. Many of the localities visited have put into place some form of internal recycling program for employees and government offices (e.g., the London boroughs of Sutton and Ealing).

Odense has found great benefit in preparing a city environmental plan, the first of which was prepared in 1993. Updated yearly, with a new plan prepared every four years, this mechanism has been useful for providing attention and visibility for environmental issues in other departments and for coordinating environmental initiatives among different actors and agencies in the city. The plan identifies city environmental goals and targets in a number of areas, identifies the agency responsible for implementing them, and determines where the necessary funding will be obtained (Odense Kommune, 1997). To Poul Lorenzen, head of the City's Environmental Department, the process behind the plan is extremely important—building a network of contacts and supporters in other departments and generating creative ideas for how different city departments and other organizations can help in achieving environmental goals.

A number of environmental issues in Zürich have been confronted by the city in its fairly comprehensive "Environmental Policy" adopted by the council in October 1995 (City of Zürich, 1995). The policy identifies and discusses a number of environmental topics and presents guidelines for future action for each. More specifically, the policy addresses the following areas: energy; urban planning; traffic; air pollution control; noise abatement; refuse and wastewater; nature; publicly owned buildings; public purchasing; traffic created by the city administration; information, advice, and education; economic measures; management, cooperation, and mediation; and external policy. The policy illustrates that the city is beginning to understand how it can reform a variety of practices and decisions over which it has direct control (e.g., how it manages its buildings and what it purchases. The policy calls for an intensifying of efforts to make public buildings more energy efficient and environmentally benign (city-owned buildings comprise some 1.8 million square meters of floor space). Greater attention is to be given to using ecological criteria in public purchasing decisions. The policy acknowledges that the city, with 22,000 employees, is the single largest employer, and it proposes to undertake a host of actions to discourage car commuting by its employees (e.g., by reducing the availability of and raising the cost of parking) and to encourage other means of transportation (e.g., providing more bicycle stands and restoring a subsidy to cover the cost of public transit). Concerning economic measures, the policy states that the city will explore "green investments" (e.g., through the city's insurance fund). Many of these increasingly common elements of a city environmental policy are further described later.

Freiburg has done many things to incorporate environmental sustainability into the way it manages the city and city property. It was one of the first cities in Germany to create an Environmental Protection Office (in 1986), and later one of the first to reorganize many of its local functions into an Environmental Department (in 1990; combining environmental protection, gardening and forestry, and the motor vehicle fleet) (see Deutsche Umwelthilfe, 1992).

Bologna is unique among Italian cities in requiring the preparation of environmental impact assessments for almost all development projects and proposals in the city. Actually, this preparation is not a law or a requirement, but the result of an agreement between builders and developers and the city. The former have agreed to prepare environmental impact statements, in exchange for which the city has agreed to expedite the processing of development approval. The head of the city's environmental assessment division believes the program has had a positive influence, helping to change the design of projects and the overall attitude of builders and developers. These are but a few techniques European cities are using to make environmental impacts and implications more transparent.

Procurement and Investment Policies

There are a variety of specific strategies local governments have adopted in order to operate more sustainably. One important strategy involves purchasing and procurement. In Freiburg, for example, an environmental impact assessment has been required since 1992 for all municipal purchases. The city of Albertslund requires all suppliers to fill out a questionnaire and to indicate whether they have adopted an environmental management system (EMS) and, if so, which standards have been adopted. The London borough of Sutton has been a leader in promoting sustainable practices throughout the local government and has become the first local government to become certified under the EU's Eco Management and Audit System (EMAS) program, which has typically been utilized by private companies. Its procurement policies are already very strong from a sustainability point of view, and they are gradually becoming more stringent. The borough has for some time had a green purchasing policy (e.g., preventing the purchase of tropical hardwoods and the use of certain pesticides). Sutton's purchasing department has requested that if companies on its list of approved contractors wish to remain on the list, they must develop and adopt an environmental policy and must have put in place a recognized environmental management system (e.g., EMAS) by 1999. The borough has held educational workshops for these local companies, and about one-third (350 companies) have already put environmental policies into place.

Similarly, Münster has developed an extensive set of procurement policies that discourage the purchasing of environmentally destructive products. Among other things, the city forbids the purchase of tropical woods and products that contain CFCs. As Shuman (1994) reports, the Tropical

Timber Campaign in the Netherlands has resulted in a policy adopted by two-thirds of the country's municipalities stating their intention to avoid the use of tropical woods in building projects.

Municipalities can exert considerable influence in shaping consumption patterns that are more ethical and less environmentally damaging. Shuman (1994) reports that some 300 Dutch municipal governments are buying so-called "solidarity coffee"—coffee purchased from small producers, who receive a fair share of the return and who also meet certain environmental production criteria (see Chapter 12). "As a result of the Dutch campaign, low-income coffee farmers are receiving an extra 8 million guilders (US $4 million) of income per year. Moreover, in each of the 300 Dutch munici-palities where civil servants and city officials now drink solidarity coffee, public debate over the purchasing policy has helped to raise awareness about the inequities facing producers of raw commodities in the South" (p. 31). Local authorities also support *wereldwinkels,* or third-world stores, stores that stock products and crafts that guarantee producers a fair return (the support occurs in several ways, including through the provision of building space, or subsidies, and otherwise encouraging constituents to shop there).

Zürich has developed a comprehensive ecological purchasing program, adopted in 1987. Among the results so far: the enforcement of an office quota of using at least 60 percent recycled paper, an emphasis that new office equipment should use minimal energy and an emphasis on its recy-cling potential, the use of less harmful substances in cleaning and mainte-nance (City of Zürich, 1995).

How and where cities invest their resources is another area of reform. The London borough of Sutton has a policy restricting the types of invest-ments that can be made with its pension funds. Specific instructions have been given to Sutton's financial officer to place funds only in environmen-tally and socially acceptable investments (e.g., companies are asked to pro-vide explanations of their environmental policies and practices, and certain companies and investments have been blacklisted).[1] Other municipal coun-cils in the United Kingdom have taken similar actions, and socially respon-sible investment practices appear on the rise at the local level there (UNED-UK, 1997).

Employee Mobility Strategies

Another strategy involves managing a municipality's workforce to reduce reliance on the automobile and to encourage the use of more sustainable forms of mobility. A number of examples of innovative local programs in this area can be cited as well.

Leicester, for example, provides incentives for its employees to ride bicycles, including providing the same car mileage rate for those employees who use their bicycles for job-related trips. They also provide loans to employees who wish to purchase bicycles. Moreover, the city has also just opened a new showering facility and bike-locking facility, directly below city hall. A number of companies have purchased bikes for use by employees when they need them. Environ, in Leicester, provides its employees with a £50-per-year bicycle maintenance grant (about US $80).

In Bristol, in the United Kingdom, the city has adopted a program to provide each government office with at least one bicycle. Bicycle training will also be provided to staff, bicycle parking and showering facilities are to be installed, and a 10p-per-mile (about US $.16) travel allowance will be afforded councillors who travel to meetings by bicycle (Bristol United Press, 1997). The stated intention of this new scheme is for the local authority to "lead by example."

A number of the study cities have developed sustainable mobility plans for their employees. Den Haag, through its plan, is attempting to encourage the use of bicycles and public transit. Specifically, it has eliminated its car-commuter allowance, and instead employees are offered either a bicycle (2,000 bicycles have been made available by the city) or a season ticket on public transit.

To some degree, more sustainable practices by government employees or offices are tied to the example set by those at the top. A recent survey of the Danish Ministry of the Environment found that a relatively high percentage of its employees commute to work by bicycle (40 percent) (Bjornskov, 1995). Partly, this is due to the positive example set by the minister himself, who is reported to ride his bike to work. In Münster, a similar positive example has been set by the Lord Mayor and the Chief of Justice, both of whom ride their bicycles to work.

Management of Municipal Buildings and Properties

Localities also exercise substantial control over how their city-owned properties are managed, including buildings, parks, and open lands. There are many examples of how these areas are being creatively managed to reduce long-term environmental impacts and to achieve other sustainability goals. Several of the cities now prohibit the use of pesticides on publicly owned lands, for example. Albertslund has such a citywide pesticides policy, as do Freiburg and Odense.

The city of Stockholm has adopted a new, more ecological approach to the management of "open grassed areas" within the city. As detailed in the European Sustainable Cities report:

Under the new system, which aims to encourage the growth of taller grass and greater diversity of plant species and insects, the grass is cut only once per summer season and the cuttings removed. Removal of cuttings reduces the quantity of nutrients to the soil, preventing certain plants from dominating and encouraging the growth of wild-flowers. Residents are encouraged to take an active role in the maintenance of open space through activities such as weeding, mowing and the care of ponds. In partnership with users the City's Real Estate, Streets and Traffic Department prepares a maintenance plan for each area to be cared for, drawing up a user contract. The Department also routinely composts organic waste from city-owned green acres and provides composting facilities in some parks for use by residents. (European Commission, 1996, p. 164)

The conclusion about this new approach: it is "not only ecologically beneficial, but cheaper and more energy efficient than previous methods of care" (p. 164).

The city of Freiburg has made special efforts to manage its greenspaces in a more ecologically sustainable way. It is now the city's policy to leave a large percentage of its parks in "long grass." Mowing of these areas has been reduced to two times per year, in contrast to the sometimes fifteen times they would normally be mowed. A rotational system of cleaning streams and drainage ways has also been put in place. The city is now composting most of the brush and cut material it generates. No longer does the city use pesticides in any of its green areas (about 6,000 hectares), and pesticide use is also forbidden in its allotment gardens (described below). The city's landscape office also has prepared a set of ecological management guidelines, which have been distributed to all city departments and personnel involved in management activities. A series of informational workshops for city employees also has been held.

The city of Freiburg operates an impressive system of community gardens (very much like the Copenhagen allotment gardens). Used following World War II as an important source of food for city residents, these are small gardens (called *Kleingärten*), usually only about 200 square meters in size. The city currently has about 4,000 of these but is expanding the number each year (about 3,000 of them are given to garden clubs to distribute). They have become very desirable (increasingly, as much for quiet contemplation as for food production), and the city maintains a waiting list for people who want them. The city maintains ownership of the land and charges a small monthly rent (DM 15 per month). Each renter is required to build a garden house, which can be sold at the end of the lease. It is the goal of the city to provide a garden plot to each resident who wants one. It is estimated that each year the city adds another 300 to 400 gardens to the pool. Another goal is to make these areas as close as possible to where people live. And, the city actively teaches and promotes ecological gardening there. As noted earlier, pesticide use is prohibited in these gardens.

A number of localities are similarly attempting to educate about (and encourage) gardening without chemicals, and some offer courses in green gardening (e.g., Goteburg, Sweden, and Stortrøms County, Denmark; see Juffermans, 1995). The Globorama nature and science education center in Herning provides a series of outside displays showing more organic, natural methods of gardening and yard care.

A number of European cities, including Vienna and Zürich have acquired and manage municipal forests and large systems of open space. These large systems of greenspace serve many local functions and are often managed in ecologically sustainable ways.[2] Berlin owns extensive woodlands as part of its greenbelt and has the goal of managing them in a sustainable fashion (City of Berlin, 1996). It is also common in Europe for municipalities to own one or more city farms, which typically are working farms that serve important educational and recreational functions. Some 80,000 residents are reported to visit Leicester's city farm each year.

How cities choose to operate schools and public facilities provides opportunities as well for promoting sustainability. Albertslund requires the serving of only ecologically grown foodstuffs in its eight schools and forty child-care facilities. Two environmental counselors also work in the schools. Greening schools is another option—for example, the breaking up of pavement around school buildings and the restoration of natural habitats (discussed in earlier chapters).

How city buildings are designed and operated offers yet another opportunity to reduce resource consumption and set positive community examples. Many cities have made special efforts to significantly reduce energy consumption, for example, in city buildings and facilities. Leicester, which owns some 30,000 buildings (much of it council housing), has undertaken major efficiency improvements, including installing building insulation and windows with double-glazed and low-emissivity glass. Many cities are using low-energy light bulbs and lighting systems. City buildings also offer opportunities to demonstrate various sustainable technologies. Leicester, for example, is in the process of installing solar hot water panels on the roof of one of its main city council buildings (which is viewed as a prototype for a district solar hot water heating system). The city of Graz recently installed a greenroof over its tram garage.

Designing and building new government and civic buildings according to sustainability principals is a key way to set positive examples. The municipality of Delft, in the Netherlands, is a good example. There, the new building for Beheer and Milieu (the Department of Public Works and Environmental Control) has been built to minimize environmental impacts, incorporating an energy-saving heat recovery system, a lighting system that adjusts internal lighting according to the amount of natural outside light available, and solar panels for hot water heating. Other public buildings in Delft are being similarly designed, including a new ecologically designed school (Hugo de Groot School). The city has been actively promoting sustainable design and construction for all buildings within the city. It has entered into a covenant with the local social building companies, in which the companies agree to incorporate sustainable design features. A point system is used by which the companies also agree to include a minimum number of such features. Leverage over private projects is less extensive, but the city attempts to encourage commercial developers to incorporate these features as well. Delft officials feel that designing their own buildings to high environmental standards is essential to the strategy of convincing commercial builders to do the same. The city of Delft has also looked for ways to reduce environmental impacts of roads and other infrastructure projects, for example by using recycled concrete in road foundations and reducing the tar content of asphalt. The Delft Environmental Department has also contracted for an environmentally friendly catering service for its canteens and employee food services, designed to minimize waste and packaging materials.

Kolding is another city pursuing a comprehensive strategy of making all the municipal structures and offices as sustainable as possible. The city now insists that social housing companies, and other organizations over which they have some control, design and build according to a new green manual. A recent case in point for Kolding is the new office building of the Technical Division. The exterior of the building is made from recycled aluminum, and a number of energy conservation and other environmental features have been included in the building. Another example is a new city school, which has been designed (and will be managed) so that it is more fully used throughout the day. This is being called the "multifunctional house." To Michael Damm, head of Kolding's Environment Department, the agenda of sustainability implies a new way of presenting these kinds of public investments to politicians in the future. If traditional short-term budgeting techniques are used, many of the features would not look economically defensible to elected officials. But, when long-term budgets are calculated, as they will be in Kolding, these sustainable building investments will look sensible, and indeed even necessary.

Another way in which the city is directly promoting energy conservation is through the rate structure it imposes on utility consumers. Because the utility company in Freiburg is partly owned by the city, it has a degree of control in this regard. The city adopted in January 1992 an innovative system of *linear time-variable electricity charges:* the energy company has modified utility meters so that usage can be gauged according to three different time zones, and consumers are charged accordingly. (The Öko-Institut came up with this idea, which was first tried in a year-long pilot project.) Energy savings of 6 percent were already measured in 1993 (Heller, undated). The price charged to consumers ranges from 12 pfennings per kilowatt hour in the low-peak times to 45 pfennings in the high-peak times. "The experience gained so far has shown that the linear time-variable tariff leads to a significant shift of the consumption into the low demand times. Moreover, it also leads to marked savings on electricity consumption as a whole since the more comprehensible tariff structure, coupled with the financial incentive to save electricity, triggers a more conscious approach to using current" (Heller, forthcoming, p. 11). Other cities, such as Saarbrücken, have also reformed their energy rate structures in this way (see Results Center, undated).

Green Energy

Another way for municipalities to promote green-urban outcomes is in the choice of green power. A number of local governments in the Netherlands have opted to purchase green power—power generated from renewable sources—from regional electric companies. Green energy (what the Dutch call "ecostroom") has been available to consumers in that country since 1996. Leiden has recently adopted a policy of purchasing a certain percentage of green power, currently 10 percent of its municipal needs (or 1.3 million kWh of the city's approximately 13-million kWh annual municipal-energy consumption, including schools). Its policy sets an official goal of 20 percent green power use by the year 2000. While this decision by Leiden currently costs the city an additional 40,000 guilders per year (about US $20,000), it is made more attractive as a consequence of the Dutch national energy tax, which exempts green energy. As a result, the price differential between green energy and conventional energy is not as substantial.

Many other municipal and provincial governments are purchasing green power in the Netherlands, with some entering into long-term contracts. In a number of places, the decision has been made to ensure that 100 percent of the power of the *gemeentehuis,* or city hall (or provincial hall in the case of provincial governments), comes from renewable sources. The Dutch municipality of Wymbritseradiel, in addition to entering into a ten-year contract to purchase green power, has installed PV panels on the rooftop of its *gemeente huis,* and uses the building as a springboard for the teaching and promotion of green energy use among its citizens (Brouwers et al. 1998).

Environmental Vehicles

Another important area involves the operation of a city's motor fleet (e.g., buses, cars, and garbage collection trucks). Many municipalities in this study have taken actions to make their motor fleets more sustainable by purchasing vehicles that are more energy efficient and low polluting and then operating them on renewable fuels. In this way, local governments are able both to reduce their direct environmental impacts and to positively support the development and economic profitability of alternative vehicle technologies.

Few cities have done as much to promote the use of environmentally friendly vehicles as Stockholm. Stockholm operates an environmental vehicles program with the goal of converting a large portion of its current fleet of 1,500 cars and other vehicles (including fire trucks) to environmental vehicles—vehicles that run on biogas, ethanol, or electricity. A number of biogas vehicles are already in use, and a number of projects have been started to help facilitate and promote environmentally friendly vehicles in the city (e.g., the installation of a fast electric charging station, the conversion of waste disposal trucks to biogas, the replacement of 300 conventional city cars with biogas vehicles, among a number of others; see THERMIE, 1996). Also, only buses that run on ethanol are permitted to operate in the central city. In part a result of an EU-funded program (ZEUS, or "Zero and low Emission vehicles in Urban Society"), the city already utilizes 170 biogas vehicles and 70 electric vehicles. (Stockholm Energi, 1997). One of the components of this program is a hybrid bus project (operated by Stockholm Transportation [SL]) that will result in the conversion of gasoline buses to ethanol. Clearly part of the city's goal here has been to positively influence the strength and marketshare of these kinds of environmental vehicles. As the project manager describes it, the city is attempting not only to be more responsible for the impacts of its own fleet, but to influence the development of, and market for, environmental vehicles. They believe that their actions and initiatives will help to show vehicle manufacturers that there exists the potential for a very profitable market in this area. As a small additional example, Stockholm Energi (the city's energy company) has been collaborating with the rental car agency Hertz to make available electric rental cars in the city. The city has also reduced the cost of parking permits for electric vehicles and provided free electric charging at municipal garages.

Other European cities participating in ZEUS and that are developing their own environmental vehicle programs are Athens, Berlin, Copenhagen, Helsinki, London, Luxembourg, and Palermo. The city of Stockholm coordinates this program, and it indicates the extent of interest in greening city transport fleets. A number of European cities have already been shifting to natural gas or other more environmentally friendly buses. As of 1996, Stockholm Transportation (SL) operated 130 ethanol buses and 6 hybrid buses (Stockholm Environment and Health Protection Administration, 1996). Leiden, for example, has recently introduced hybrid gas-electric buses.

Ecological Twinnings and Looking beyond the City's Borders

One is also impressed with the number and variety of programs in these cities designed to assist or facilitate sustainability initiatives in other cities, often in developing countries. There is a pattern in the most progressive, ecominded cities studied here of recognizing an obligation to look beyond the narrow boundaries of one's own city and a duty to share technical advice and moral support to other communities around the globe.

These programs can take many forms and are often quite creative in their content and structure. Shuman (1994) describes a number of interesting twinnings and linkages between European local authorities and their counterparts in the south. Especially high numbers of such programs are found in Germany, France, the Netherlands, and the United Kingdom. The projects undertaken and the kinds of relationships developed vary. They include educational exchanges and mutual visits, the provision of technical assistance for environmental and other community projects, and the sponsoring of a north–south dialogue and educational programs. A high priority is typically given to promoting education in the schools and in communities about environment and development in communities in the south. Many of these educational programs are specifically environmental. Belgian cities have undertaken tree-planting programs in Haiti, for instance (as well as in Belgium). The city of Breda (the Netherlands) has included such linkages in developing its own program for addressing global climate change: "Breda planted a forest near a local highway to compensate for carbon dioxide emissions, while helping its Polish sister city plant another forest and co-financing a forestry association in Botswana" (Shuman, 1994, p. 75) (see Juffermans, 1995, for a good review of European twinning projects).

A number of the green-urban cities studied here have been involved in some form of twinning activity (what in the United States tends to be called "sister cities"), with strong ecological or sustainability dimensions.[3] Freiburg, for instance, has a long history in this area. One of its recent twinnings is with the city of L'viv in the Ukrainian Republic. Here, the city is providing technical assistance in the area of energy-efficient housing and in development of district heating. One recent initiative undertaken in Leicester is the Interfaith Gardening Work Camp. Spearheaded by the nonprofit environmental charity Environ and the Elchanan Elks Association for Intercommunity Understanding, the program brought students to Leicester from all over the world to learn about and work in church gardens in the city. The students, in addition to painting, potting, and weeding, helped build a wetland at the city's eco-house (its environmental education center). The goals of the program were twofold: "passing on eco skills and giving people the chance to learn more about different religions" (Haynes, 1998, p. 21). Participants from Morocco, Slovenia, Poland, and elsewhere also learned about the "environment city," and, will, it is hoped, "spread the message . . . around the globe" (Leicester Mercury. 1998, p. 12).

Educating and Engaging the Public: Local Agenda 21 and Community-Based Initiatives

The case cities examined in this book provide a wealth of examples of ways of involving, educating, and engaging the public in the mission of local sustainability. This can happen at several different levels and by several means. One of the most significant ways in which participation has occurred in the last several years, specifically around the issue of local sustainability, is through the emergence of local Agenda 21 (LA21) efforts. Many local Agenda 21 programs have followed a similar process and structure. Typically, there is a citywide steering committee, with representatives of major community interests (e.g., government, industry, and NGOs). (In the United Kingdom, these tend to be referred to as "environmental forums.") Frequently, there is a series of more specific task groups or work groups, organized around more specific issues or policy sectors. In Leicester, which has adapted a strong partnership ethos, much of the work of LA21 happens through its "Specialists Working Groups." In Den Haag, similar task groups were established to address the following eight issues: international efforts, energy, waste, traffic and transport, nature and landscape, building and living, communication, and neighborhood initiatives. Lahti's process is similar with seven "cross-sectoral working groups" created. The LA21 process typically involves one or more public meetings or conferences, and some cities have gone through a community visioning process as part of Agenda 21. Common projects and activities undertaken in the local Agenda 21 process include the development of a set of community sustainability indicators, a vision statement, and the preparation of a local sustainability action plan.

In another of the U.K. environment cities, Middlesborough, the LA21 process has also included the convening of a series of specialist working groups, focused on analyzing specific sector or policy areas and developing visions and action programs in each area. As in Leicester, an explicitly partnership approach was pursued. Creatively, the vision statement prepared by each working group was published in the local paper. Community involvement was also solicited through the city's network of twenty-six community councils (neighborhood groups). Eventually, these various initiatives led to the convening of a community vision conference and the publishing of an LA21 Action Plan for the Community (Forum for the Future, 1998). The creation of an ongoing Community Environment Forum is also planned. As an example, the following succinct vision statement produced by the Environmental Quality special working group was published in the local newspaper:

> Industry is organized on a more local basis than it used to be, with companies producing whole products (rather than components) for local distribution. Companies have also taken advantage of clean technology and are removing and reusing chemicals that were previously discharged into the River and atmosphere. (Forum for the Future, 1998)

In addition to the community process, there is frequently also a process more specifically directed at local government employees and agencies, encouraging them to find ways to modify their behaviors and policies to reduce environmental impacts and consumption (and addressing many of the subjects discussed under the ecological governance heading). As part of its internal LA21 process, the city of Helsinki engaged in an extensive process of involving and consulting with a large portion of its 40,000 employees. Some nineteen departments (out of thirty) in the municipal government participated. A contact person was designated in each department, and through extensive department meetings employees were asked to consider how sustainability could be incorporated into the work of their respective departments. The process generated some 1,000 suggested changes, with 300 *immediately implemented* (Association of Finnish Local Authorities, 1996). These suggestions addressed such things as waste recycling, energy savings, using more environmentally-friendly ways of getting to work and the need for environmental purchasing policies, among others. This internal initiative is generally seen as a success:

"The network of contact persons has proved to be an active force in other projects as well" (Association of Finnish Local Authorities, 1996, p. 24). Interestingly, in Middlesborough, the Environmental Sustainability Strategy prepared within the local government itself was coordinated through an interdepartmental group called the "Environmental Sustainability Officer Group."

The local Agenda 21 initiatives have placed a great importance on community participation, and local governments have utilized a wide variety of process, participation, and visioning tools along the way. Gloucestershire's (United Kingdom) LA21 has used a creative visioning process called the Time Machine. Described as a "guided meditation," a trained facilitator takes groups of eight to ten people through this process of imaging the future of their community. "The intrepid time travelers are asked to close their eyes and imagine themselves in the utopian Gloucestershire of 2030. The groups then look at the aspects of future life (health, political systems, landscapes, etc.) that they (would like to) see. After being returned to the present, participants reflect on their experiences individually and then discuss what would be contained in their group vision" (Forum for the Future, 1998).

There are many ways in which a public sense of ethical commitment to the future and to an expanded moral community flows from these many local initiatives. We should not underestimate the power of such expressions of commitment, and the long-term force they may have in shaping perception and behavior. One small but potentially powerful example involves the public planting of trees. In the United Kingdom, as part of millennium activities there, a program called Trees of Time and Place has been initiated. Under this public campaign, citizens are asked to select a tree that has had some importance in their lives, collect seeds from the tree, grow them to seedlings, and then plant them as an important gesture of leaving a legacy to the future. "When the new millennium comes, they will rise up, and plant their trees on dedicated sites in public parks, on urban wasteland, around schools and hospitals, behind pubs, beside community centers and in private gardens" (Baines, 1998, p. 2). In Lahti, participants in the LA21 process are encouraged to make declarations of the things that they plan to do to live more sustainably and to hang the written declarations on a tree in the city hall—a cumulative (and visual) declaration of commitments to a more sustainable future there.

Among certain countries, there has been a high participation rate in LA21. In Sweden, nearly all local governments are in one stage or another in the LA21 process. In the United Kingdom, some 73 percent of the local authorities are involved in LA21 activities, with many having hired staff specifically for this program (Selman, 1998). In Finland, about one-third of the country's 453 localities are developing local plans.

The results of the LA21 process are mixed, but on the whole it has represented a considerable effort to engage citizens in thinking about sustainability and what it might mean for their neighborhoods and communities (see Morris, 1998). On the positive side, thousands of citizens have been involved and have had a chance to have their views and ideas heard. Also, the work and products generated from these local processes are considerable. In each city, the LA21 process has involved a large number of people and has often had very productive spinoffs. In the Den Haag LA21, for example, the process of study groups has spurred a group of citizens interested in transportation issues to develop a relatively sophisticated sustainable transport vision for the city. This "manifesto" has been distributed widely to politicians, the local transit company, and the community as a whole, and it has at least the potential of advancing new ideas and dialogue about solving the city's mobility problems.

While the accomplishments have been considerable, some problems or limitations can also be noted. Most of the local programs have been operating with extremely limited funds, which has constrained what they have been able to accomplish. Secondly, in some cities, citizens have been extensively involved without a clear sense of direction or an end goal. This has resulted in extensive meetings that have accomplished little, and which has caused frustration to some participants. The process might also be criticized as accomplishing few tangible outcomes or changes at the local level. Yet, in most cities (and countries) visited, the LA21 process was still in a relatively early stage. It remains to be seen how the ideas and creative input of the public will change local policy.

These programs do show convincingly that municipalities, through modest investments of money and staff time, can help to grow grassroots sustainability. Often, cities provide neighborhoods or community groups with funds to help them undertake various initiatives. While the level of funding in the aggregate is not terribly large, often it does provide important seed money for groups and does appear to have had positive effects in many places. The city of Stockholm, for instance, maintains a green fund, from which it provides small grants to community groups. During the first year of its operation, some sixty different projects were funded. One recent example is an effort to create "butterfly restaurants"—inner-city areas where parks or open areas are set aside and restored with plants providing necessary butterfly food sources.

Supporting local community groups and grassroots environmental initiatives can take other forms as well. Leicester has used an interesting program of green accounts, where local groups can, by collecting and bringing in recyclable materials, earn monetary credits, which are paid out on a quarterly basis. Recyclables accepted and for which payment is given include aluminum foil and cans, paper, and textiles. There are now some 450 green accounts in the city and the amounts of money paid out have risen to significant levels (£11,000, for example, paid out in 1995–96; Environ, 1996). The program has served both to encourage recycling in the city and to provide a badly needed income for local organizations and charities.

Public Awareness Campaigns

Awareness campaigns are an important strategy used in many cities to encourage more sustainable behaviors and practices on the part of businesses and citizens. Leicester's Turning the Tide initiative is one example. Spearheaded by the group Environ, the initiative consists of a series of specific campaigns (e.g., energy, recycling, transport) aimed at educating and inspiring personal action. The campaigns get the word out through several means, including displays at strategic community points, radio spots, and articles in the local newspaper. The campaigns are guided by a steering committee, closely involving representatives of newspaper and radio. These media alliances are a key lesson. Indeed, one of the most important part nerships in Leicester has been with the local media, which have been influential in helping to educate the public and to help to bring about more sustainable lifestyle patterns in the city. Of particular importance has been the positive role played by Leicester's main newspaper, the *Mercury*, which frequently runs environmental stories and has been particularly effective in the Turning the Tide campaigns. During the campaign, there are articles almost daily, and several times a year the paper runs major environmental pull-out sections on particular topics. Each day, the paper also presents news on these issues, and on every Wednesday it has the "Greenlife" page, which discusses current environmental topics and offers readers tangible information about things they can do and actions they can take.

Environ also runs an eco-house: a converted residential structure demonstrating environmental and conservation ideas and technology that can be applied to a conventional home. There have been some 15,000 visitors to the house. The house focuses on the theme of energy conservation and illustrates a variety of relatively inexpensive things that can be done in the average home. This is also an example of a creative partnership. The building was a derelict house owned by the city. The city paid for refurbishment of the house (along with some private funds and funding from the Electricity Board), and Environ now runs the facility.

The Ecohouse in Leicester, England, is used to demonstrate and educate residents about the relatively inexpensive things homeowners can do to reduce energy consumption and to protect the environment. About 15,000 residents visit the house each year.

Partnerships, then, are also clearly an important aspect of Leicester's success. Some of the partners have been particularly influential in carrying out the program. These partners include, again, the media, De Montfort University, and the environmental charity Environ, among others. The Leicester approach is also characterized as a community-based or grassroots program in the sense that many of the elements of the effort involve the daily promotion of sustainability to residents in a variety of ways. The public information campaigns of Environ, for instance, takes full advantage of a network of community friends and partners. (There are a number of places in the community where literature is displayed, including pubs, libraries, and schools.)

Community outreach and education are important governmental roles as well, and there are a number of creative ideas among the case study cities for how this might be done. Several cities have sponsored environmental community centers for this purpose. Leicester operates a community center known as the Ark, complete with an environmental shop, a bulletin board,

Leicester, England, has also created an environmental community center called the Ark through a partnership with the nonprofit group Environ. The Ark is located in the city-center and contains an environment shop, bulletin board, and ecological cafe, as well as internet connections.

a cafe serving organic and vegetarian foods, and computer terminals providing public access to the Internet. The building itself demonstrates ecological principles; for example, it utilizes extensive natural lighting and recycled materials and is located in an underutilized building in the heart of the city-center. The Ark also represents an interesting local collaboration. The educational center is run by Environ, the environmental charity, the cafe is operated by a whole-foods caterer, and the city owns the building but provides it at a highly subsidized lease rate (Environ, 1996).

Other study cities have undertaken similar education and awareness campaigns. The strategy of the city of Heidelberg in promoting awareness of energy and climate change issues ("Klimaschutz Heidelberg") is instructive, communicating tangible actions that can be taken. The city has adopted a decidedly decentralized approach, and city officials believe it is much more effective in the long run to solicit community-level actors and individuals to get out the message. The city's campaign has involved, for instance, the distribution of energy-conserving lightbulbs (at a subsidized price) through a merchant distribution system, in which local hardware store owners become knowledgeable advocates. The city has held workshops to educate the merchants about the bulbs. The city believes the most effective approach is to develop community- or neighborhood-based forms of communication. In its energy-passport program—a program to encourage homeowners to improve the energy efficiency of their homes—a similar approach is taken. The city has worked through the local craft and trade organization, and the program essentially is implemented through builders and contractors.

There are many examples of European cities that have also initiated some form of general environmental education. Kolding has had good luck with its program to involve schoolchildren in stream restoration and cleanup. As a result of a new Danish law, schools must incorporate more hands-on education. Each school in Kolding now adopts a segment of a stream in the city, studies the stream's ecology and ecological condition, and takes actions to restore and improve it (e.g., tree planting and placement of more rocks). Technical assistance, when needed, is provided by the city, and already some 2.5 kilometers of streams have been restored. Michael Damm, Kolding's environmental director, believes the program has had a substantial effect on the way children and their parents view the environment (Damm, 1998). He describes the case of a notable area farmer, who was known for his damaging farming practices. When his son participated in adopting a segment of a stream affected by these practices, the father's farming behavior changed for the better.

Environmental education is also being promoted by the city of Zürich: there are three forest schools and a nature house (in Allmend Brunau). "The aim of these centers is to offer young people an experience related education in near-natural surroundings" (City of Zürich, 1995, p. 19). The city of Helsinki operates a nature school on Hairaken Island, where students learn about the ecology of the region. Local schools have also adopted protected areas, in which the students monitor and act as stewards for some twelve different ecological areas in the city.

Another approach to community awareness and environmental education is to highlight the many environmental demonstrations—buildings, gardens, ecological shops, and so forth—that exist within the community. The city of Copenhagen (more specifically the Danish Town Planning Institute), for example, has produced an impressive and highly usable *Urban Ecology Guide*. This guidebook provides descriptions of some forty-five different urban ecology projects and sites in the Copenhagen region and provides detailed maps and directions for visiting them (including detailed information about which public transit lines to take; see Danish Town Planning Institute, 1996). Similarly, guides to ecological housing and energy demonstration projects have been produced for the city of Berlin by the European Academy of the Urban Environment. These booklets present ecological walking tours in Berlin, which highlight urban ecology and energy innovations in the city (European Academy of the Urban Environment [EAUE], 1995). One product of the LA21 process in Den Haag has been the publication of a comprehensive green guide to services, products, and organizations in the community (called the Haagse Groene Gids; Gemeente Den Haag, 1996). The American-based "green maps" notion has also been applied to a number of European cities, and green maps have been prepared, for example, for Copenhagen, Gouda (in the Netherlands), and others.

The Role of the Nongovernmental Sector

Nongovernmental organizations have played an important role in educating and working with the public, and a number of promising examples of successful groups can be cited. Interviewees in Leicester, for instance, believe that the organization Environ there has a credibility and ability to get things done that would otherwise not be possible, or as easy, for a local government agency. Because of its status as a charity, it may have a greater ability to enlist the local media and business groups in sustainability initiatives.

Building a community information network is another potentially effective strategy. Leicester's Environ has developed a network of about thirty community stands or sites, where its program information is displayed. These sites are in diverse places, including libraries, pubs, restaurants, and the Ark community center. The sites represent a network of community friends, supportive of the group and its goals.

Another interesting example of a creative community-based organization is EcoStad Den Haag, an outgrowth of the Netherlands Global Action Plan initiative. Located in a community center in the middle of the city, with a very small staff, this organization's main function appears to be to operate as a creative, independent catalyst in the community, helping to broker and facilitate creative community enterprises that support sustainability. It operates on every level, from the individual to the neighborhood to the city (it conducts training, for example, for eco-teams in Den Haag).[4]

The community projects EcoStad Den Haag is involved in are numerous, although many are still in an early stage of development. It has, for example, been helping to secure parking spaces in the community for the car-sharing company Greenwheels and helping to identify potential members. It has joined forces with the local energy company to help market solar hot water heating systems, and it serves as an intermediary between the company and local shopkeepers interested in additional energy conservation measures. The organization has also been working with car-sharing companies, public transit agencies, and a bicycle security facility company, to develop a single mobility card, which could be used for a number of different transport modes: to take a tram, to hire a taxi, to rent a car, or to pay for renting a bike, depending upon what one's particular transport needs are that week.

Although many of these ideas are still in the early stages of development, the director of EcoStad Den Haag believes his organization can function in ways that the government is not able to. The advantages are greater flexibility (administratively and politically), being able to move more quickly on potential projects, and the perception of neutrality in the community. It may also have the advantage of avoiding the turf conflicts that can often arise between different public departments and agencies. As the EcoStad director says, "We're too small to be a threat to anyone." EcoStad, then, serves as a nonprofit intermediary between a neighborhood and its residents, and outside companies and municipal and national governments.

The keystone of the EcoStad approach appears to be networking and bringing together interested people and organizations. The EcoStad network begins with a base of neighborhood eco-teams (discussed below), but has expanded to include churches, neighborhood groups, businesses, and others. It has started producing a newsletter and has also been sponsoring a series of ecological lunches (with ecologically produced food). The emphasis given in EcoStad's message is how individuals and neighborhoods can take concrete actions to promote sustainability; the focus is on identifying relatively easy things that can be done to promote more sustainable lifestyles and community.

Bringing sustainability down to the neighborhood level is critical. In Utrecht, the city is attempting to place environmental staff in each of the city's neighborhoods. Currently there are only two of these "neighborhood environmental points," but the number will be expanded soon. So far, these staff have been involved in a variety of neighborhood activities, including the teaching of a class on environmentally friendly gardening, advising on sustainable building practices, and helping to organize a community discussion about the common concerns of residents along a river in the city.

Confronting the Consumer: Eco-Teams and Green Codes

One of the most impressive and creative approaches to promoting consumer lifestyle changes is the idea of "eco-teams," an idea advanced by the Global Action Plan (GAP), which has had a strong presence in the Netherlands and other European countries. In many of the case study cities, there are large and active eco-team programs under way. The idea is basically a simple one, involving the formation of teams of households who together strive to understand and modify their environmental consumption patterns. (One interviewee described them humorously as "environmental tupperware parties.")

The process and logistics are similar from team to team. Teams usually consist of around seven households, often from the same neighborhood or block. They agree to meet together eight times over the course of the program (or about once a month). Each household measures and tabulates their waste and consumption every month (water, electricity, household waste, car travel), and the group as a whole sets targets for reduction in waste and consumption. GAP staff organize and facilitate the meetings, provide technical advice, and tabulate the measurements for homeowners each month, providing a summary report showing trends and progress toward goals.

Eco-teams have been quite active in the Netherlands, with about 10,000 households participating nationally. Studies show that although the households that participate in the program already tend to show lower rates than the average Dutch household of waste and consumption at the start, significant reductions still result. A study of the Dutch participants shows a substantial aggregate reduction in the ecological demands for those participants (Staats and Harland, 1995). In the Netherlands, eco-team participants experienced an average reduction of 26 percent in garbage, 16 percent in electricity, 12 percent in water, and 14 percent in transport (kilometers traveled). Estimates are that some 1,670 tonnes less carbon dioxide were emitted in the Netherlands as a result of the eco-team program as of January 1, 1997 (GAP Netherlands, materials, March 14, 1997). While the average Netherlands citizen has an ecological footprint of 3.50 hectares, the footprint for an eco-team member is only 2.45 hectares.

A series of studies has also attempted to understand whether these behavioral changes last over time (after the program ends) and whether they result in other types of environmental behavioral changes. Both questions have been answered in the positive with findings showing that six to nine months after the end of the formal eco-team programs, environmental behaviors had for the most part been maintained and had been extended to other pro-environment behaviors and activities outside of the household (e.g., energy saving and recycling at work and joining an environmental organization; Staats and Harland, 1995).

The director of the Netherlands GAP emphasizes the positive, hopeful philosophical orientation of the eco-team idea. He believes it is a needed contrast to the moralistic, finger-pointing approach often taken to environmental problems today. Rather, what seems to be emphasized through the process is the fun involved in making these lifestyle changes, as well as the economic savings that accrue to each household. Nevertheless, involving larger numbers of householders remains a challenge and it is not at all clear that the program will be able to reach the majority of consumers (GAP Netherlands would be happy with a 15 percent participation rate). One answer, they believe, is to create more of a community presence, and they have opened seven community eco-team centers around the country (including EcoStad Den Haag, described earlier).

Arguably, for major changes in personal consumption or behavior to be realized, some considerable amount of awareness building and public campaigning is necessary. While in the United States this has been left to non-governmental groups, there is a greater tendency in European countries for these functions to be taken on by the public sector. In the United Kingdom, a major national public awareness campaign—called Going for Green—was initiated in February 1996, spearheaded by the Department of the Environment but also including private sector support. While still rather new, the campaign has already involved an extensive array of specific educational and other actions designed to confront citizens and consumers and to suggest changes that they can make in their lives. Central to the campaign is a Green Code: a five-point guide to green living that "encourages people to take small individual actions which, if adopted by everyone, could make a huge difference to the environment." The five elements of the Green Code are "cutting down on waste, saving energy and natural resources, travelling sensibly, preventing pollution, and looking after the local environment" (Going for Green, 1998, website). The campaign's accomplishments and progress report through 1998 list a truly impressive array of activities: publication of special environmental editions in local papers, posters at bus stations, distribution of information leaflets and environmental action packs, a Going for Green information hotline, the sponsoring of a variety of community events (including a conference on organic farming for local farmers), a pilot TV advertising campaign, and a number of sustainable community pilot initiatives, among many others. The campaign is casting a wide net, reaching out to municipalities, businesses, and even churches (it is currently working on an "Eco-Congregation" campaign, for example).

Admirably, one of the goals of Going for Green is to reshape or redirect social norms about individual and household consumption:

> People will be much more inclined to adopt environmentally responsible behavior once they perceive this to be the "norm" and see that Green Code activities are being carried out by the majority of others. A proactive public rela-

tions campaign involving all the relevant media is very important, there is also a key role to be played by the Government and other image makers.

Going for Green recommends that as part of the work of the Panel on Sustainable Development Education, an initiative is researched and commissioned to "re-brand" environmental action, so that in the public mind, the word "green" is no longer associated with activities which are the privilege of the wealthy or the pursuit of the weird. Language and images need to be found which establish sustainable development as something commonly desirable and a goal with which everyone wishes to be identified and to play their part in achieving. (Going for Green, 1998, website).

A major element of the campaign is developing green programs within schools. The eco-schools program now has 900 schools participating in the United Kingdom. Each participating school involves students in evaluating such things as water consumption and carbon dioxide emissions and in developing programs for reducing these impacts. Schools also participate in local environmental projects and experiential learning about the environment.

Perhaps the most innovative initiative so far has been the development of computer software that allows individuals to assess the extent of the impact of their individual lifestyle choices. Specifically, this user-friendly system asks individuals to answer a series of questions about one's lifestyle and consumption patterns. At the end, the program calculates a person's *ecological calories* or *EcoCal* score. The higher the EcoCal score, the greater the ecological impact of one's lifestyle. The program also allows users to compare their scores with an average household. The user's score is displayed on a dial that indicates whether the individual has done better (green), worse (red), or about the same as others (amber). This easy-to-use computer program is viewed as essential to overcoming one of the main obstacles to personal responsibility taking: the lack of a perceived connection between actions, behavior, consumption, and environmental outcomes and results.

Since the EcoCal system was unveiled in the fall of 1997, there has been considerable interest in and use of the program. Thousands of copies of the program have been distributed, and local authorities have been plugging it into their ongoing local Agenda 21 efforts (Going for Green, 1998). Eco-Cal "clubs" have been formed within companies such as Electrolux to encourage and help employees to understand and reduce their ecological impacts. Going for Green envisions that in the future, the EcoCal program can be used in ways similar to the eco-team concept, and it has proposed starting an EcoCal monitoring project involving groups of households. "Scores would be taken from the households on a quarterly basis, together with feedback on the environmental action taken and any barriers to action encountered. Change in EcoCal scores (either regionally or nationally) could thus be reported as a headline indicator, showing change in household environmental impact as well as measuring the degree of public participation" (Going for Green, 1998, website).

The consensus Natural Step booklet prepared by Karl-Henrik Robert in Sweden represents a similar effort at education and public awareness about sustainability issues on a broad scale. The booklet was mailed to all 4 million Swedish households and all schools. Bradbury (1996) describes the format of this thirty-seven-page booklet:

> It begins with an overview of evolution and explains the development of the cells of plants, animals and humans. It explains the cyclic characteristic of the natural environment and the environmental dangers of non-cyclic energy sources such as nuclear power. It is an alarm document in its call to action. It notes the extinction of species, the ozone layer and rainforest degradation. It makes suggestions for daily life concerning saving energy, recycling and demanding chlorine free paper and mercury free batteries. It ends with a one-page more densely written conclusion which spells out the ramifications of the foregoing. The document appears user friendly, aimed at a general public. It seems almost understandable even to a non-Swedish speaking person as most of the story is told using illustrations. On the back cover the names of contributing scientists and an address for the "Naturaliga Steget/Natural Step" is included. (p. 19)

A willingness to confront households and consumers about sustainability characterizes many of these European cities (and countries). This is an important dimension of ecological governance.

Supporting and Encouraging Ecological Communities

While difficult to precisely understand or explain, many of these cities have developed a sense of obligation to address problems (or their share of problems) of a global nature. The high number of carbon dioxide reduction strategies developed, and the seriousness with which global climate change is taken, reflects this. Moreover, there is in these best cities a longer time-frame at work, one acknowledging that actions and policies today will indeed influence the future and future generations. An analysis of Saar-brücken's energy initiatives, as one example, makes this point well: "Supported by a progressive government and heightened environmental awareness, Saarbrücken's planning horizon is in the hundreds of years and its investments in solar energy resources underscore this commitment to the future. Saarbrücken provides a remarkable example of a community thinking globally and acting locally" (Results Center, undated, p. 18).

There are undoubtedly many influences and factors that help explain the emergence of these exemplary cities. Development of green-urban programs and ecologically sustainable local initiatives is in part encouraged in Europe through a number of organizations. The German environmental organization Deutsche Umwelthilfe (DU) has, since the mid-1980s, sought to promote friendly competition between German localities through ranking and publicizing good practice. Since 1990, DU has generated a quantitative ranking of German cities according to the extent and stringency of their environmental and conservation efforts. The winner is declared the "Federal Capital in Nature and Environmental Protection" for that particular year (Deutsche Umwelthilfe, undated). Past winners have included Erlangen, Freiburg, and Heidelberg. Local officials do indeed take notice of the yearly rankings and are clearly conscious of how well they are doing environmentally compared with other cities. The program seems to encourage and support positive and innovative environmental programs, and it offers positive public relations for winners. DU, among other things, produces a pamphlet/brochure describing and documenting the initiatives and innovations of the winning city, and this publication gets wide distribution. In similar fashion, the Danish environmental organization Danmarks Naturfredningsforening provides an annual ranking of the greenest Danish cities, with similar positive results (see Danmarks Naturfredningsforening, 1997).

At the European level, there are a number of important peer-support networks, including Eurocities, ICLEI, Car Free Cities, and others. These networks are ways of sharing information and technical knowledge and providing political and moral support. The Sustainable Cities and Towns Campaign, supported by the EU (Directorate General XI) is worthy of special note. An outgrowth of the work of the EU Export Committee on the Urban Environment, the first meeting of these cities was held in Aalborg, Denmark, in 1994. A sustainability charter bears the name of the site of this first meeting. Participating cities and towns are asked to sign this charter and become part of what is now a network of nearly 400 cities throughout Europe. Each year, the campaign awards a city or group of cities the Sustainable European City of the Year award, as well as certificates of merit. These awards have become very coveted, and a healthy competition has developed at a Europe-wide level. (See Chapter 2 for a more extensive discussion of the campaign and other peer-support networks.)

Lessons for American Cities

Perhaps the main lesson from these European cities is the tremendous potential that exists to redefine the mission and function of local governments and, by doing so, to have a clear and immediate effect in reducing environmental impacts and enhancing environmental quality. Municipal and local governments can exert tremendous influence by shifting their resources, service decisions, investments, and purchasing power to encourage more ecologically sustainable outcomes. There is an important ecological obligation to how we govern that is now commonly acknowledged by many European municipalities but is rarely considered by American communities.

There are, however, positive trends in certain areas of the United States that might be built upon, as well as examples of some American communities doing exemplary work in this area. One area where there has been considerable activity is in the development and use of sustainability indicators, benchmarks, and targets. In lieu of a real local Agenda 21 process, groups such as Sustainable Seattle (a nonprofit community group) have prepared and disseminated comprehensive sustainability indicators (Beatley and Manning, 1997). Other prominent local examples include Santa Monica (California), Jacksonville (Florida), and Portland (Oregon), among many others.

Few American cities, though, have developed comprehensive local sustainability programs or initiatives. One community leading the way is Austin, Texas. Austin has begun an ambitious Community Sustainability Initiative, which includes a number of activities and projects aimed at making the city more sustainable.[5] Key components of this initiative, some under way and others planned for the future, include the development of a sustainability matrix for evaluating proposed capital improvement projects (already used to evaluate projects proposed for the city's November 1998 bond measure); a regional sustainability indicators project and annual Sustainability Report (planned); a traditional neighborhood district ordinance and innovative local smart growth guidance strategy (mostly adopted); a new sustainable masterplan for redevelopment of the Robert Mueller airport (being replaced with a new airport, and the existing site to be "transformed into a model sustainable development" (under way); a process of undertaking "sustainability assessments and sustainable operation training" for all departments within the city government (within five years; pilot project with Departments of Public Works and Transportation); and adoption of sustainable purchasing guidelines for the city (planned), among others (City of Austin, undated-b; see also City of Austin, 1998a). The city has also appointed a "sustainable community officer" to shepherd the initiative and make sustainability matters more visible in the city.

Austin's CIP (Capital Improvements Program) Sustainability Matrix, in particular, is one potentially effective way to inject consideration of sustainability issues into departmental priorities. Specifically, city departments were asked to use the matrix to evaluate "projects to be brought forth to a bond election" (City of Austin, undated-a). Under the system, city departments are asked to quantitatively evaluate their proposed projects against nine major groupings of criteria: public health/safety, maintenance, socioeconomic impact, neighborhood impact, social justice, alternative funding, coordination with other projects, land use, and environmental. Within the environmental group, scores are assigned on five measures (air, water, energy, biota, and other environmental). Such methods hold much promise for making sustainability tangible and for applying these concepts in a systematic manner.

With major restructuring of the electricity markets under way in many American states, sustainability-minded local governments will have special opportunities to promote and encourage renewable energy. Thus while municipally-owned power companies are less common in the United States, deregulation may allow localities an impressive degree of control over sources of power. The city of Santa Monica, as part of its Sustainable City Program, became in 1999 the first city in the world (it proclaims) to mandate that 100 percent of its energy—energy to power all of its municipal buildings and facilities, from its airport to street lamps—must come from renewable sources. After issuing a request for proposals and reviewing submittals from fourteen different supply companies, the city entered into a contract with Commonwealth Energy Corporation to supply its needed 5 megawatts (the equivalent of the electricity needs of between 5,000 and 6,000 homes). The power will be supplied from geothermal sources and will require the city to pay a 5 percent premium above conventional electric rates (an estimated cost of about $140,000) (Green Power Network, 1999). The city council voted unanimously to make this transition to green power, exhibiting exemplary leadership that may well be followed (and should be) by other American communities. In the words of Santa Monica councilman Michael Feinstein, "The city is taking a leadership role to help show people that buying green power is the environmentally right thing to do" (Green Power Network, 1998, p.1). The city also plans a local education campaign to encourage its citizens to make more informed choices about power selection and to also encourage a shifting to renewables.

In the United States, few cities have aspired to become an "environment city" to the degree that Chattanooga has. Chattanooga, rebounding from being one of the nation's most heavily polluted cities, has redefined its image as a sustainable city and an environmental leader and has adopted a host of initiatives and programs to give meaning to this vision. These have included an electric bus initiative, a series of downtown and riverfront redevelopment initiatives, a metropolitan greenways initiative, a proposed ecoindustrial park, and a proposed environmental trade center. Compared to many of the green-urban cities profiled here, though, even Chattanooga might be viewed as light green (given its considerable, though far from radical, redefinition of itself). The electric vehicle initiative is one of the clearest successes. The regional transit authority now operates a downtown shuttle system using fifteen electric vehicles (with some 400,000 yearly riders), and a local electric bus manufacturer is now exporting electric buses to cities around the world (Chattanooga News Bureau, 1997). An Electric Transit Vehicle Institute also exists in the city, with considerable public sector sponsorship. To be sure, there is a spirit of partnership and collaboration in Chattanooga and a sense that environmental issues and quality can serve as an important organizing theme for this city.

Arcata (California) is another positive American example of a community, albeit a relatively small one (about 17,000 residents), that has sought to comprehensively reconsider a host of its policies and actions. The unique actions taken there, in contrast to typical American communities, include the adoption of a policy on socially responsible investments, efforts to ban McDonald's-style franchise fast-food restaurants (what its policy calls "formula restaurants"), a 50 percent recycling goal (by 2000), a municipal baseball field dubbed "the only one in the USA to be maintained entirely without chemical fertilizers or pesticides," a program to reintroduce endangered fish species in local streams, the sustainable management and harvesting of its own Community Forest, and a police force propelled by bicycles, among others (Jordan, 1998; Painter, 1998).[6]

Many of these initiatives are the direct result of what has been described as the first Green Party–majority city council in the United States. Perhaps Arcata foreshadows the increasingly potent local political agenda of the Green Party. While some in the town view the policies of the Greens to be a bit too radical, the experience there suggests the potential political alliances that might be formed around a green-urbanism agenda. Downtown merchants, for instance, have positive feelings about the tendency of the Green council to stop big box retail. In the words of one downtown retailer: "Our sales are up 30 percent to 40 percent over last year. . . . There are never any vacancies on this plaza. There's no boarded-up store-fronts. The council is not opening us up to the big box stores, and they are keeping this a viable economy. They are not letting anybody just build any-thing they want" (Curtius, 1998b, p. A3).

The possibilities and potential power of green politics at the local level should not be underestimated. There is no question that a stronger politi-cal presence of the Green Party, and local coalitions with Social Democrats, help explain the environmental accomplishments of many European cities such as Freiburg and Münster, as well as a relatively high background level of popular support for environmental issues in Germany and other north-ern European countries.[7] Green members of the city council in Vienna, as a further example, have been the ones to push car-free housing estates and ecological housing there (see European Foundation for the Improvement of Living and Working Conditions, 1996). Green party support and leader-ship help explain the sustainability initiatives in many of the cities profiled.

As an initial start, we should expect of all American communities cer-tain actions and investments in long-term sustainability, typically above and beyond what is currently the norm. The elements of such a program might consist of at least the following:

- Each community should prepare a comprehensive set of local sustain-ability indicators, adapted to the unique issues and circumstances of their place in the world;
- Each community should prepare a community metabolism analysis, which (in various levels of detail and complexity) can chart the external impacts and interconnections between the community and other com-munities and the region, and the broader public impacted by these meta-bolic interconnections;
- Each community should prepare an annual or semi-annual ecological budget; each local government should be required to run a surplus in this budget;
- Each community should appoint a sustainability officer, whose responsi-bility it is to inject considerations of long-term sustainability into all departmental policy making and community decision making;
- Each community should prepare a community sustainability matrix to guide major decisions in the community; and
- Each community should be expected to fundamentally assess the extent to which its investment, procurement, and other decisions affect long-term sustainability, and to identify and consider ways in which these decisions can be adjusted to minimize or reduce their ecological foot-

print. The four system conditions of the Natural Step represent a good starting point and a potential powerful set of criteria for assessing the locality's range of activities and functions and looking for ways to reform them.

Efforts can be made to assist and facilitate the development of comprehensive local sustainability and strategies, and there are a number of promising initiatives around the country to consider. In the American system of governance, states are especially well placed to encourage and facilitate the development of comprehensive local sustainability programs. Florida, in many respects, is leading the way through its creative Sustainable Communities Demonstration Project. An outgrowth of the work of the Governors Commission for a Sustainable South Florida, established in 1996, this is a unique state-local partnership program for encouraging sustainable communities. Under the program the state—spearheaded by the Department of Community of Affairs (DCA)—called for applications from Florida communities interested in participating in the program. Twenty-eight communities applied (showing considerable interest), from which five were selected. Under the program, demonstration communities must enter into a written agreement with the state, indicating the particular programs or initiatives they plan to pursue. Once an approved agreement has been reached, communities benefit from additional regulatory flexibility (certain comprehensive plan amendments and developments of regional impact will not have to go through typical regional and state review). Six sustainability principles are to be advanced by these agreements (Department of Community Affairs [Florida], 1997):

- Restore key ecosystems;
- Create quality communities and jobs;
- Achieve a cleaner, healthier environment;
- Limit urban sprawl;
- Protect wildlife and natural areas; and
- Advance the efficient use of land and other resources.

The five communities chosen were Boca Raton, Martin County, Ocala, Orlando, and Tampa/Hillsborough County. Each community is pursuing a locally unique set of issues, including a variety of sustainability dimensions, such as urban design, growth containment, economic development, protection of environmental lands, and provision of affordable housing.

In response to the initial high number of applicants and a desire to support this interest, a Florida Sustainable Communities Network (FSCN) has been established. The stated purpose of the network is "to bring training, information, technical assistance and peer-to-peer information sharing to communities around the state so as to help them achieve their own sustainable development objectives" (Department of Community Affairs [Florida], 1997). To these ends, DCA has established an Internet site for sharing information and resources. Participating communities are required only to adopt a resolution stating their intention to become more sustainable. (The content of a suggested resolution is included on the website.) The first year's evaluation of the program is generally positive. The report notes some concerns, however, about the permit flexibility given to demonstration communities and about the fact that no small-population cities or counties are represented in the five initial communities chosen (DCA has stated its intention to expand the number of pilot communities by three to incorporate such smaller communities).

There are a number of other things that could be done, taking the lead from Europe, to encourage and support green-urban initiatives. Sponsoring at a national level the equivalent of a United States Sustainable Cities and Towns Campaign, along with a yearly awards program, would be helpful. Environmental organizations in the United States could assume a role similar to groups such as Danmarks Naturfredningsforening in Denmark and Deutsche Umwelthilfe in Germany, evaluating and recognizing the best cities, counties, and regions in terms of their sustainability programs and accomplishments (Deutsche Umwelthilfe, 1996). There is some evidence that mainstream environmental groups are becoming more interested in recognizing the importance of cities and urban development. The Sierra Club's anti-sprawl campaign is one example of this. It would be a natural extension for such groups to move more stridently into the green-urban or sustainable cities agenda, as their counterparts in Europe have.

At the federal government level, there are indeed initiatives upon which to build, including the work of the President's Council on Sustainable Development (PCSD), and the U.S. EPA Sustainable Development Challenge Grants program. The grants program, now in its third year, has certainly helped to push along and support a variety of local initiatives. There have been positive outcomes, but a critical assessment of the grant recipients would suggest that the funded programs, while certainly useful, are (generally) not pushing the envelope and probably are not likely to result in comprehensive sustainable strategies of the kind found in many of the European cities profiled here (e.g., Freiburg, Leicester, Graz, and Albertslund). And, of course, these project-specific grants are rather modest in amount. An alternative federal funding model might be grounded more in the experience of Project Impact—a program implemented by the Federal Emergency Management Agency (FEMA) in an effort to encourage the development of disaster-resistant communities. Under this program, communities are given more sizeable grants ($1 million) and asked to develop a comprehensive package of initiatives to move them in the direction of becoming fundamentally less vulnerable to natural disasters over time. Encouraging the development of comprehensive programs and a commitment to long-term program-building are essential, and a similar approach could be used in the development of green-urban communities in the United States. Perhaps a more limited number of model sustainable communities should be selected, with longer term (and larger) financial commitments made to help them develop and implement comprehensive green-urban programs.

Redirecting the consumer growth machine in U.S. communities may be one of our most significant environmental and social challenges, and these European examples offer some guidance for beginning steps. As Frank (1999) so persuasively demonstrates, the costs of our historically high consumption patterns are considerable: expanding personal debt (and an alarming rise in rates of bankruptcy), low rates of saving, less time for family, and a decline in the resources available for expenditures on public goods (e.g., repairing roads, building libraries, and ensuring clean air and water). These high-consumption lifestyles also have severe global environmental implications, as already noted. There is little indication, moreover, that people are leading happier lives as a result of our excessive consumer culture—perhaps, just the opposite may be true. Many of the European cities profiled here have attempted to educate, demonstrate, and engage the public in a debate about ways and strategies for reducing damaging consumption. And, many of these communities have placed a clear premium on facilitating less consumptive lifestyles—whether through alternatives to dependence on the private auto, more compact resource-efficient housing and living arrangements, or the ability to substitute home-garden produce for store-purchased foods, among others.

As in countries such as the United Kingdom, and in a number of the cities profiled here, it is time in the United States for a national forum or public campaign directly and specifically aimed at consumption. Many believe the economic signals must be adjusted to reduce excessive consumption impulses; important here is the European reliance on value-added taxes, carbon dioxide and other green taxes, and high gasoline and energy prices, which set in motion a more sustainable set of economics signals.[8]

What is effectively illustrated by the extensive efforts to promote greening of household decisions through mechanisms such as eco-teams in the Netherlands (and other countries) and the EcoCal program in the United Kingdom, is that it is possible to significantly (and often voluntarily) reduce environmental impacts at this level. Here, in the most consumptive nation and culture in the world, we desperately need more of these kinds of initiatives in an effort to at least partially reduce and redirect consumption patterns. The obstacles and impediments, especially in such a high consumption culture, are serious and many, of course. What efforts such as the United Kingdom's Going for Green campaign indicate is the need for a real and concerted public awareness campaign, at both national and local levels. Such a serious campaign targeted on national consumption patterns in the United States is appropriate and necessary. In part, this is a recognition that, especially in the United States, the vast majority of popular images lead us in the other direction: consumption without limits and the perception of there being few (if any) societal or environmental costs associated with this. Within the next five years, then, the United States should develop and embark upon a national campaign and dialogue aimed at consumption reduction and environmentally supportive lifestyle changes. Perhaps we should call this "Americans for a Green Tomorrow" (or some version that perhaps yields an appropriately catchy acronym). At the least, such a campaign would be the recognition that representative government—at all levels—has an important role in shaping norms about what is acceptable personal and household behavior.

Notes

1. The borough of Sutton adopted in 1982 a policy (now rescinded) banning investments in South Africa. In 1990, it issued a statement to its fund managers to choose investments in companies "dedicated to good employment practices and demonstrating sensitivity to environment issues," and to avoid companies that do not meet these practice criteria. Furthermore, it requests the managers to send a copy of the borough's environmental policy to all companies invested in and "to raise with them specific issues of environmental or ethical concern" (UNED-UK, 1997, p. 26). Information and commentary about these investments are also contained in the borough's annual report.

2. See Hough's discussion of Zürich's Forest Preserves (Hough, 1995e). Erlangen (Germany), another community frequently praised for its ecological policies, has a 400-hectare municipal forest (Deutsche Umwelthilfe, 1991)

3. It is an interesting question why communities in some European countries have developed especially active initiatives for linking with communities in the south. Shuman (1994) speculates about some of the special reasons that explain involvement by the Netherlands: "The motives for Dutch communities to involve themselves in international affairs mirror those found elsewhere: the global nature of many problems and the need for global action to remedy them, the special skills held by localities, and the proximity of local authorities to the people. But there are some motivations for CDI's [community based development initiatives] that are uniquely Dutch. As a small nation long surrounded by powerful nations,

the Netherlands has historically been an accommodater and peace-maker. Dependent on shipping and trade, the Dutch have maintained an internationalist, 'mercantilist' outlook. A typical Dutch teenager graduating from his school knows three or four languages. And the deep roots of Calvinism nurture a widespread sense of responsibility for fellow human beings" (p. 114).

4. Funding for EcoStad Den Haag has come from a combination of sources, including the central government, the local energy company (providing the majority of funding in the latest year), and the municipality.

5. Much of the following is a result of a series of interviews in Austin in November 1998. Individuals interviewed included Lawrence Doxley, the city's sustainability officer, and other staff from the city's green builder program.

6. Other interesting aspects of the town: the Earthflag flies along with the American flag in the downtown plaza and the annual parade is an all-species parade "featuring townspeople dressed as salmon, spotted owls and other animals" (Curtius, 1998b, p. A3).

7. Pucher (1997) attributes many of the impressive bicycle initiatives in these cities to these green-leaning municipal politics: "In Münster, Freiburg and Bremen, the Green Party has been part of the governing coalition with the Social Democrats. Likewise the Green Party has become increasingly important at the state and national levels. Environmental consciousness in Germany is high among all political parties and most segments of the population, but is highest among university students" (p. 35).

8. Frank (1999) argues persuasively for a "progressive consumption tax," and points out the difficulties and limitations of value-added taxes (see pp. 211–226 especially).

Chapter 12

Building a Sustainable Economy: Innovations in Restorative Commerce

Building a Sustainable Local Economy

The type and composition of a local economy can influence in tremendous ways a city's ecological footprint and impact. In too many cities, however, the environment is a secondary consideration (if considered at all) in crafting economic development policy. There are, however, profoundly important ways in which local or municipal economic development policy and strategy can be reconceived to better support the green-urban and urban sustainability goals described in this book.

In a number of European cities, there is evidence of a different, more ecological approach to commerce and economic development. In this approach, impact on the environment is not secondary but primary, and municipal (and national) governments view their economic development roles as legitimately concerned with encouraging and promoting more ecologically sound commerce. There is a spirit of collaboration, especially between local government and industry in a number of the case study cities, and impressive examples of efforts by these cities to facilitate and encourage movement toward some sustainable, restorative local economies can be found.

The chapter to follow describes a number of the more impressive local initiatives and programs around Europe. It should be emphasized that this is by no means a comprehensive investigation of sustainable local economic development policy. However, the stories that follow identify some of the most important and powerful elements of a new vision of sustainable economy.

Figure 12.1. ECOPROFIT logo (Graz, Austria)

Under Graz's ECOPROFIT program, the logo to the left can only be used by companies that have achieved certain minimum levels of pollution and waste reduction and are making continuous progress at promoting closed-loop production. These companies are considered environmental market leaders and are generally proud to display the logo.

Source: City of Graz.

Supporting Sustainable Local Businesses

There are a number of impressive local efforts in Europe to promote pollution prevention and resource efficiency within private companies. One of the European cities that has done the most in this regard is Graz, Austria. Since 1991, it has operated an innovative program called ECOPROFIT Graz that is intended to educate local businesses and to help them to identify changes in production processes that could reduce waste and resource consumption, and in turn increase profitability. This is a voluntary program, cooperatively run by the city's department of environmental protection and Graz University of Technology. As an incentive for participation, companies that complete the program are awarded the ECOPROFIT logo, which can be used for marketing purposes to promote themselves as "ecological market leaders" (see Figure 12.1).

Graz has historically been an industrial center, which suffers from chronic levels of pollution (especially winter inversions). The ECOPROFIT program was viewed as an important strategy to begin to address these pollution problems, and to promote pollution reduction beyond what is required by environmental regulations alone. Graz was one of the first-year winners of the European Sustainable City award, in large part because of the innovative ECOPROFIT program. The key idea behind the program is to create a partnership between industry and business, the local university, and the local government, in an effort to help businesses find ways to prevent pollution. The program explicitly promotes the philosophy of closed-loop production.

Participation in the program follows several stages. Initially, workshops are held to educate company personnel in closed-loop production, and data and information collection for each company is undertaken (including the preparation of an input-output analysis, documenting flows of energy and materials). A multidisciplinary project team must be appointed within each company, and ideas are generated about how to increase efficiency and minimize waste. The awarding of the ECOPROFIT logo is made contingent on the achieving of a significant reduction in waste and pollution, and continuous progress after the first year is necessary if a company wishes to retain use of the logo.

The program establishes certain criteria for awarding the ECOPROFIT logo. Several quantifiable standards have been established (based essentially on the EU's EMAS program, adjusted for small- and medium-sized companies), including a 30 percent solid waste reduction and a 50 percent hazardous waste and air emissions reduction. The logo is awarded only for one year. To maintain certification, companies must continue to actively participate in the program and achieve additional reductions in pollution. Interestingly, the companies that have gone through the early phases of the program then become the peer group involved in training and bringing along the newer companies participating.

The program has had considerable success with a variety of businesses participating (e.g., the first group included several printing companies, a repair garage, a wholesale coffee roaster, and a large chain-store; see ICLEI, 1994). Many of these companies have made significant environmental improvements. Overall, for example, the companies have experienced a 50 percent reduction in toxic and solid wastes. Examples of tangible changes include the repair garage adopting a paint spray technology that reduces overspray, the switching to water-based paints in the printing companies, and the reduction of container wastes as a result of in-bulk ink purchasing. The author toured a Ford minivan assembly plant in Graz that has been participating for several years and has instituted a number of production changes (including, for example, changes in its painting processes that allow recapture and reuse of paint).

Significant individual examples of dramatic improvements can be cited (ICLEI, 1994, p. 5):

> Specific improvements were achieved through better environmental management including improved housekeeping, changes in material selections, and the implementation of new technologies and process modifications. For example, in the vehicle repair garages, a high volume/low pressure spraying technique reduces the overspray by 25 percent. In printing enterprises, mixing inks in gravure printing cut down on hazardous wastes. Chemical inputs in reproduction processes were reduced by as much as 70 percent. Changing material selection was also effective. Toxic halogenated degreasing agents were replaced with water based cold dip degreasers in garages to reduce solvent emissions. Water based paints were selected wherever

possible for printing enterprises and resulted in a reduction of 80 percent to 90 percent in solvent emissions. Oil-
based offset cleaners were replaced with less volatile vegetable oil cleaners and in bulk purchasing of inks reduced
the generation of empty containers by 50 percent.

At the same time that these types of pollution-reduction techniques and
technologies have been put into place, the companies have experienced significant cost savings, thus effectively showing that environmentally sustainable production processes can also make good economic sense.

One important lesson here is that municipalities can exercise a significant catalytic role. By creating positive incentives for change (e.g., the use
of the ECOPROFIT logo), together with the expertise of the university in
creating an educational and awareness-building process and providing
technical and other support, the city of Graz has taken the lead in gently
pushing industry in the direction of more environmentally friendly production. The city staff responsible for the program make it clear that each individual company or business must identify and implement its own specific
measures and must itself be committed to achieving pollution reduction.

Companies participate in the program voluntarily, and thus the incentives are important. The emphasis of the program is to find low-cost
improvements that will not only reduce pollution but also increase efficiency and profits; thus, there is an obvious financial incentive. There are,
as well, significant public relations benefits. Those companies that participate in the program, meet the ongoing program criteria, and are allowed
to utilize the ECOPROFIT logo clearly view this as a valuable marketing
and public relations tool.

The ECOPROFIT Graz programs illustrate that local governments in
coordination with the technical expertise of universities can play an important role in collaborating with and helping along companies in their communities. It is a distinctly different role than the typical regulatory and
largely adversarial role government often plays, especially in the United
States. The companies involved in the program have themselves seen great
advantages. They represent ". . . financial savings, higher productivity,
improved relations with the municipal administration, and an improved
public image" (p. 5). The program also has the result of demonstrating
locally the technical and financial merits of many pollution-prevention techniques and technologies—at the end of some seven or eight years of operation, there are an abundant number of tangible, practical examples of pollution prevention and closed-loop production. The ECOPROFIT program
publishes an annual report documenting and presenting many of these projects, which allows for a much wider potential impact and replicability and
demonstrates to the larger business community their feasibility and benefits.

The training programs and ongoing involvement of company staff also seem to overcome a major obstacle of trust. In thinking about the transferability of the ECOPROFIT idea to American communities, it would be necessary to overcome a much larger degree of antagonism between government and industry. Creating collaborative mechanisms in which business personnel are actively involved in training and idea generation seems essential, and it is one of the important lessons of the Graz initiative.

Other European cities are pursuing a similar ecoprofit program designed to stimulate environmental efficiency and performance of local firms. Kolding, together with several other cities, for example, has developed a strategy (similar to Graz's) for encouraging environmental and resource efficiency in businesses. Called the Green Network, it is an association of businesses willing to take stock of their environmental impacts and to set and agree to work toward achieving more ambitious environmental goals. In exchange, the cities recognize these efforts by awarding a Green Network diploma and flag. The program has been popular. More than 160 businesses in the Kolding area are participating, and most large companies are involved. The head of the environmental department in Kolding believes that business pride is now at work and that many businesses are embarrassed not to be involved in the network.

A number of other European cities have established formal mechanisms or processes for engaging businesses about the environment. Albertslund has established, for example, an environmental forum for trade and business, designed specifically to assist these enterprises in thinking about preventive approaches to environmental impacts and to promote clean technologies and environmental management and audits in local companies.

Some communities, such as the London borough of Ealing, have prepared green business guides. A pilot project called Greening the High Street has also been under way in Ealing, involving an innovative collaboration between local businesses and the city. Each business looks carefully at its environmental impacts and, specifically in the first stage of the effort, its waste stream. Businesses are then assisted in identifying ways to reduce these impacts (places where waste can be reduced).

Leicester has undertaken a range of programs and initiatives to reach out to local businesses. These have included creating a Business Sector Network, convening business seminars, setting up an environmental helpline, and offering a service to businesses of preparing an environmental review. Conducted by the local nonprofit group Environ, these business reviews involve "a comprehensive analysis of a company's environmental footprint" (Environ, 1996). Usually, the analysis takes place over a one- or two-week period and results in tangible recommendations for improving environmental performance, many of which also aim to enhance economic profitability as well.

Supporting and encouraging small businesses with a green emphasis has been a focus of some programs. EcoStad Den Haag has been working on the development of an eco-pass (based on a concept similar to air-miles/or frequent-flyer programs), where the purchasing of environmentally friendly goods (e.g., public transit, organic foods, and bicycles) would generate points for the purchaser, which could in turn be redeemed for other goods or services (e.g., environmentally friendly recreation). The EcoStad newsletter is also providing an early outlet for green neighborhood businesses to advertise and offer discount coupons. This is seen as a way to "make the market warm" for the eco-pass concept.

Cities can also support the development of new ecological businesses and technologies through strategic funding and technical assistance. Berlin has taken an especially active role in encouraging the development of sustainable industries and technologies. It has for a number of years provided subsidies for these purposes. Specifically, the city will provide, under its Environmental Improvement Program (EIP), up to 50 percent of the cost of business investments in new environmental technologies and equipment. (These technologies have to be new or different, and above and beyond what is required under the law.)

Industrial Symbiosis and Ecoindustrial Parks

There are a number of emerging and promising examples in European cities of *industrial symbiosis*—arrangements in which the wastes of one manufacturer or industry serve as productive inputs to one or more other companies. There exist many partial examples of symbioses in the world, but few full-fledged models. Kalundborg (Denmark), discussed at length in Chapter 9, is the most widely studied and widely cited example of an industrial symbiosis in the world, and it represents a powerful (and inspirational) model for American cities.

In the Kalundborg complex, the Asnæs power plant forms the center of the symbiosis and has itself done much of the work to organize and expand the interrelationships over the years. Specifically, this coal- and oil-fired power plant sells its excess heat to the city of Kalundborg in the form of hot water for the city's district heating system. In addition, it sells excess steam to a nearby (Statoil) refinery for heating and also heats a nearby fish farm. The power company also sells other byproducts and waste, including gypsum from its sulfur dioxide scrubbers to a local plasterboard maker and fly ash (another byproduct) to local building construction firms. The refinery, while taking excess steam from the power plant, sells back flaregas (this would normally be burned off) to the Asnæs plant to be used as fuel to further generate electricity and heat. It also sends fly ash to the plasterboard maker, cooling water to the power plant, and sulfur (from its desulfurization process) to a local sulfuric acid maker. A local pharmaceuticals company, Novo Nordisk, is also part of the symbiosis: it receives district heating from the city and steam from the power station, and it sends its organic sludge to local farms as fertilizer. Surplus yeast, from insulin production, becomes animal feed (Kalundborg Center for Industrial Symbiosis, 1996).

The results of these symbiotic relationships are impressive and include less pollution, more efficient use of resources, least-cost achievement of environmental restrictions, and generally improved cooperation between the different companies involved (including, for example, joint worker training). Among the environmental benefits have been sharp reductions in the need for certain virgin materials and a nearly 60 percent reduction in carbon dioxide and sulfur dioxide emissions (Gertler and Ehrenfeld, 1994).

A new symbiosis under development in Kalundborg involves a contaminated soil remediation company. The heavy metals extracted from the soil are sold to other companies in the area for reuse, and some of the clean soil is then used for construction and building projects. Another recent example involves a Danish oil recycling company, which is planning to extract and reuse waste oil from ships using the Kalundborg harbor. Once refined, the oil results in a base oil, which then can be reused; the power company may use some of this in its oil-fired burners.

Not all recent symbiotic ideas have worked, though. Recently there were plans for the power company to provide cooling water first to a new brewery, then to the Novo Nordisk Pharmaceutical company, then to the refinery, and finally back to the plant, with each user requiring water that is slightly less cool. Ultimately, the idea fell apart through a combination of small problems (e.g., Novo needed to know quickly about feasibility and price), and the brewery ultimately decided it was not the appropriate time to expand its operation. This specific case illustrates the pitfalls and difficulties of pulling together such arrangements and the timing problems that often arise.

Is the Kalundborg industrial complex really a truly sustainable endeavor? There are some paradoxes and some important reservations about the Kalundborg model. First, and perhaps most obviously, the centerpiece of the complex is a power plant, fueled with a combination of coal and oil; large quantities of both are shipped from all over the world. (Indeed, it is Denmark's largest power plant.) Second, the symbiotic interconnections have been mostly restricted to the industries themselves, and there have been few attempts to extend them to include residential and other sectors and the broader set of activities and functions that occur in the city and region. On the last point, the committee established to coordinate environmental activities between companies (the "environmental" club) is beginning to expand its notions of symbiosis to address the larger region. Valdemar Christenson, its chair, has already brought to the group some preliminary ideas about how to do this.

While there has been considerable recent activity here in the United States aimed at creating ecoindustrial parks and zero-emission zones, Europe (still) provides essentially the only working models of these. There has been, understandably, tremendous interest in the Kalundborg program, and for many involved it is clear that one important mission is to attempt to export this model to other parts of the world. A Symbiosis Institute has been formed (with two staff members) partly for this purpose. Groups from other parts of Europe and the world have visited Kalundborg, including a recent delegation from Mississippi.

A number of other creative symbioses can be identified, although few that involve as many interconnections as Kalundborg. One example is the RoCa3 power plant near Rotterdam, which provides 250 hectares of green-houses with heating water (from combined heat and power [CHP] produc-

Ecological commerce and industry can be defined partly by how the power is pro-duced to support these activities. Shown here is an innovative industrial park in Saarbrücken powered through a combination of photovoltaic (PV) panels and a combined heat and power plant. During the winter, the CHP plants provide district heat and electricity along with the PV panels. During the summer, when heat is not needed, all the electricity for the complex is generated through the PV panels.

tion) and carbon dioxide (a waste product). Normally, these greenhouses would generate their own carbon dioxide, but through this symbiosis a portion of waste emissions from the power plant becomes a valuable input to greenhouse production (see Chapter 8; Electriciteitsbedrijf Zuid-Holland [EZH], undated).

A number of similar examples can be cited of large CHP plants providing residual heat (in the form of hot water or steam) to surrounding industries or communities. While the present study is not a comprehensive reporting on industrial symbiosis, others have identified a number of other European examples, including projects in Sweden, Austria, Ireland, and France (see Cote, 1997). These many examples illustrate the potential power of the concept of symbiosis in reducing operating costs and increasing competitiveness of industry, while at the same time significantly reducing the environmental impacts of production. These industrial symbioses illustrate the potential for zero-emission and closed-loop economies, and while European cities have certainly not yet reached the zenith of their potential, they are in many ways much farther down the path than their American counterparts.

Other European cities have focused on developing ecoindustrial parks, seeking to attract and encourage ecologically friendly industries and industries where principles of industrial ecology and symbiosis can occur. Danish cities have been especially active here, with the ecoindustrial park in Kalundborg, again, serving as the best, and perhaps only fully functioning, symbiotic ecoindustrial complex. Another example of this strategy can be seen in the city of Herning (Denmark), which is developing a business park where new businesses must agree to comply with an extensive environmental charter (the 16-point Environmental Charter of the International Chamber of Commerce), which calls for recycling and reuse of materials and the use of environmental technology. Other study cities are developing similar ecological industrial or business parks.

Part of what makes such industrial complexes or ecoindustrial parks more sustainable is the manner in which energy and heat are provided to them, even where other extensive symbioses may not exist. The Innovation and Technology Centre SITZ in Saarbrücken is an example. Here, a very interesting strategy for heating and cooling has been developed. A centralized CHP plant operates during the winter months, providing both electricity and (centralized) district heating to companies in the park, supplemented by photovoltaic panels. However, during the summer months (when heating needs are low), the array of 1,000 photovoltaic modules (50 kilowatt peak) provides all the companies' power needs (European Academy of the Urban Environment [EAUE], 1996).

European governments provide sizable subsidies for the development of these kinds of sustainable technologies. In the Netherlands, under its VAMIL program, industries can depreciate (in an accelerated fashion) investments made in sustainable technology. The Ministry of Housing, Spatial Planning, and Environment (VROM) maintains, and updates yearly, an "environmental list" of acceptable equipment and technological investments, which was begun in 1991. Technologies are only included on the list if they are not currently in common use in the market (defined as a market penetration of no greater than 30 percent). More specifically, qualifying equipment is defined as: ". . . solely equipment which is not in common use in the Netherlands and which can contribute to a substantial degree to preventing, restricting or remedying the detrimental repercussions on the environment of human activity, which includes the use of energy and raw materials, in the form of pollution, degradation or depletion" (VROM, 1994, p. 5). A point system is used by VROM in evaluating the relative priority of proposed additions to the list. Among the criteria for which points are assigned are the nature of the pollutants that would be reduced (the more harmful, the more points); the nature of the technology (e.g., does it combine energy savings with emissions reductions?); and the number of years before investment will be recouped (the shorter the period, the greater the points). Updating the list is based on a process of consultation with a network of contacts at ministries, as well as surveys of specific industry areas (the latter based on the target groups contained in the National Environmental Policy Plan). Individual businesses or organizations can and do submit their own proposed additions to the list. Industry surveys suggest strong support for the program and provide evidence that the financial incentives do affect investment decisions (see VROM, 1994). Industries especially choose technologies and equipment on the list when (as would be expected) price and quality are otherwise about the same.

Envisioning a Sustainable Factory

Another notable European example of sustainable business is the company Ecover, located in Oostmalle near Antwerpen, Belgium. The company produces a range of washing and cleaning products designed to minimize environmental impacts. Indeed, the company's philosophy is explicitly based on principles of sustainability. The company dates back to 1987 and has been steadily growing in size and market coverage. It is currently the market leader in the United States for ecological washing products, and its sales are growing at a fairly dramatic rate each year.

Interestingly, the company's environmental philosophy has extended to its factory as well, which it describes as an *ecological factory*. A picture of the factory, with its distinctive greenroof, even adorns the packages of many of its products. There are a number of features about the factory that make it unusual. It consists of two parts—an older, conventional, rectangular flat-roofed building, and a large addition, designed to emphasize the principles of organic architecture and completed in 1992. The new building is oriented to capture the sun, is wonderfully daylighted, and contains a 6,000-square meter greenroof, perhaps the building's most distinctive environmental feature (and what the company boasts as "the biggest roof garden ever laid on an industrial building") (Ecover, 1992, p. 6). Much of the factory (60 to 70 percent) is constructed of materials that can be recycled. The main trusses are made of northern European spruce, and very little steel is used compared to most standard factory buildings (a steel roof structure is typically used in industrial buildings). Throughout the building, the use of steel is consciously minimized.

Saving the existing building was also a conscious environmental decision, with clear conservation benefits. Beyond that, virtually all aspects of the needed addition were designed with environment in mind. Building materials used in the factory were evaluated and rated according to a system—called the Bouw Initiatief Milieunorm (or BIM)—developed by researchers at the TU-Eindhoven. Building materials were ranked on a scale of 1 to 10 (with 10 representing the highest environmental quality), and whenever possible the least-damaging materials were chosen. Synthetics were avoided, and natural linoleum, earthen tiles, paper insulation, and natural paints were used.

The walls of the factory's addition are built from a unique brick, which possesses several environmental benefits—it is a mixture of sawdust, clay, and coal dust. The presence of the sawdust means that the bricks are essentially fired from the inside out, requiring less energy (fewer baking days, baked at lower temperatures). The bricks are also more environmental in that they use recycled coal dust. The bricks' fine porous quality also enhances their insulation value.

The experience with the Ecover greenroof, its most dramatic feature, has generally been positive. When the author visited in June 1998, it was a lush green, with extensive clover, moss, and grasses growing throughout. The roof has been quite successful in cooling the building in the summer months and containing heat during the winter months. The reported differences between the inside and outside temperatures are quite dramatic (+12° C inside during winter, +4° C outside; +26° C inside in summer, +33° C outside). Clear glass cupolas run down the ridges of the roof and let in a tremendous amount of light, almost eliminating the need for artificial lighting. The calculated energy savings from the daylighting is substantial—usage is estimated at 5,000 kWh per year, compared with the 30,000 kWh needed in a conventional factory of this size (Ecover, 1992, p. 70).[1]

Peter Malaise, concept manager for the Ecover company, explains that there was much experimentation in building the roof, and some problems have been encountered along the way. If they were to do it over again, Malaise says that they would work early on with a plant biologist and plan more carefully the types of biotopes to be created on the roof. One problem has been that during the summer months, high plant mortality is experienced, and Malaise believes this is because inappropriate species were selected. Some water leakages have also been experienced, although not significant. The roof is mowed just once a year.

The factory also employs a wastewater treatment system intended to completely recycle wastewater. Extensive recycling of water in production processes (e.g., rinsing water reused as thinner) means that the factory discharges much less to begin with. Resulting wastewater goes through several steps, including a series of shallow treatment ponds and eventually a reedbed filtration system. The original plan was to recirculate this clean wastewater back for reuse in the factory, for watering the greenroof, for toilet flushing, and for other production uses, but local health regulations have prevented this from happening. Also, use of the reedbed filtration portion of the system has been temporarily halted (the expansion of a local road is taking much of original reedbed), but there are plans to redesign and improve the system in the future.

For Ecover, the factory represents a natural reflection of its sustainability values. It cost about 40 percent more than a conventional factory building would cost, although Malaise says that these extra costs would likely be only 5 to 10 percent if built today.

Employees of the plant are also encouraged to live more sustainably. The

The Ecover ecological factory in Oostmalle, Belgium, incorporates many sustainable features, including extensive use of daylighting, as seen here.

company provides a per-kilometer travel allowance, for example, that is three times higher for bike travel than for car travel. And, employees receive higher travel reimbursements if they use cars that get better fuel mileage (Ecover, 1992). The factory also aims to create extremely positive working conditions. This includes modifying working tasks daily and using a "gentle shift system."[2] The factory is an environmental work in progress, it seems, and there are proposals for making it even more sustainable. Utilizing some form of cogeneration for power/heat production is under consideration. And, again, there has also been the idea that the resulting wastewater from the plant's reedbed system might be applied to the greenroof and used for other purposes in the factory. (At the moment, the clean water—although much reduced in volume—is still required by regulation to be discharged into a municipal sewer.) And perhaps more photovoltaic panels could be placed on the factory's roof—currently, there is only a small experimental array above the main entrance to the building (perhaps the photovoltaics can provide power for the pump to transport wastewater to the grassroof).

The Ecover plant provides the glimmer of a possibility that factories might indeed be seen as more than polluting engines of industry. Rather, they may begin to be viewed and conceived from the beginning as elegant, living organisms. While Ecover admits that all washing and cleaning products are to some degree environmentally damaging, it has taken great strides to design products that do as little harm as possible. All its products must adhere to the "Ecover code." The Ecover products are generally distinguished by their lack of most petrol-chemical substances; instead, they contain natural materials that degrade easily and quickly. Instead of petrol-chemical surfactants, the company uses surfactants made from soap and sugar. These same impressive qualities of responsible, sustainable product design have been creatively applied to the building and site at which they are made—a positive example that other industries could and should emulate.

Sustainable Industrial Estates

Dunkerque, a city on the north coast of France, has developed some creative ways of reconciling heavy industry with the need to protect the natural environment there and the living environments of its population. It has developed what it calls its "Industrial Environment Scheme" (IES). Adopted in 1993, it was largely the basis for the city's selection as one of the first winners of the European Sustainable City award. The development of Dunkerque's strategy really began with the steel crisis in the 1980s, in which the area lost some 6,000 jobs, followed soon after by the closing of the city's shipyard and the loss of another 3,000 jobs. There were real questions then about whether Dunkerque had a future as an industrial city. Most in Dunkerque believed it did, and that the area would continue to be well suited for many kinds of industrial growth. The large port is a major asset, and a large stock of industrial land, some 3,000 hectares, is available. At the same time, though, many in Dunkerque believed industry could not and must not be managed in the same way as in the past and that any future industry in the area would need to be much more environmentally sensitive and respectful of the health of its population.

With these environmental goals in mind, a process was put in motion to design a new kind of industrial development strategy. A series of studies was conducted, and visits were made to other European cities to see how similar industrial endeavors were managed elsewhere. A steering committee was formed, consisting of representatives of the chamber of commerce, the port authority, the urban community (a regional government including 18 different communities), and the local association for the protection of the environment, among others.

What resulted from this process was not a law or a new set of regulations, but rather a visionary and advisory document to guide the actions and decisions of the many parties, including industry itself, involved in planning the location and design of new industrial estates. There are several main components to the scheme. First, it lays down an environmental charter, which is in effect an agreement that environmental protection and conservation will be given major importance in all future decisions. Among the specific requirements imposed by the charter on new industries are the following: they must respect all environmental laws and treaties; they must use clean technologies and the best pollution control technologies available at the time; and they must acknowledge and respect local environmental objectives.

Second, the scheme puts forth a new process for making decisions about new industry. Decisions about industrial siting and management in France have historically been heavily top-down and administrative, with relatively little input from citizens, local communities, and environmental groups. Industry in the past has often even been allowed to construct its building and facilities before receiving operating permits from the central government. The new process provided for under the scheme calls for community consultation and public review at a much earlier stage.

Another key component of the scheme has been the comprehensive delineation of *zones of vigilance*. These are areas that are in close proximity to existing towns and population centers, in which future heavy industrial activities will no longer be permitted. Specifically, within these zones, industries that would present clear and significant risks to adjoining populations and communities will not be permitted. Implementation of this provision is based on a risk classification of different industries, maintained by the French Ministry of Industry. In addition, all major public facilities and uses, such as hospitals, schools, and supermarkets, have been mapped, and potentially hazardous industrial activities are prohibited within 800 meters of them.

Under the IES, certain sensitive natural areas are to be protected and set aside. Specifically, these areas include a dune protection zone and a former industrial site (the *reserve de salines*), which has regenerated into an important natural area. Some 700 hectares of natural dunes and 12 kilometers of sandy beaches are protected. Industry must protect and steer away from the natural areas that form the so-called "green crescent," important areas for recreation and nature. The urban community has developed a masterplan for greenways, which envisions a regionwide, connected system of natural and recreational areas. It will provide pedestrian and bicycle linkages between different parts of the region, as well.

The IES also incorporates a set of detailed landscaping principles for new industry. Safe transport of hazardous materials throughout the region is another factor considered in the scheme. The scheme has delineated a system of roads and interchanges where industrial truck movement will be permitted, generally away from existing towns and developed areas.

No explicit attention in the IES is given to promoting symbiotic interconnections between the different industries in the area, but a number of relationships and interconnections have developed informally. One symbiosis that does exist is the use of the excess energy produced by a major steel factory (a factory responsible for 30 percent of French steel production). This factory's blast furnaces are providing hot water to the local district heating network in amounts sufficient to supply heat to 16,000 homes. There are plans to expand this system as well, and the factory has quite a bit more residual heat that it could provide.

The approach of the IES is clearly not a radical scheme for remaking industry; rather, it is essentially one of reducing industry's environmental impacts and reducing problems of incompatibility. Indeed, it might be argued that although emission standards are higher and levels of pollution control are greater in Dunkerque, the city nevertheless accepts as inevitable the generation of pollutants and the production of many kinds of products and materials (e.g., chemicals and pesticides) that are fundamentally antithetical to an agenda of sustainability. Nevertheless, Dunkerque's strategy holds promise as a model for greening industrial estates in other places, and it would certainly represent a major environmental improvement over how most industrial estates in the world are planned and managed.

Interestingly, many of the ideas of the Dunkerque IES would not be possible if not for the prevailing land use strategy of promoting compact development in the region. The Dunkerque urban community explicitly pursues a compact growth approach, with most future development assumed to occur in areas immediately adjacent to existing villages, towns, and the city itself. Residential development outside of these designated growth areas is essentially prohibited. This makes it much easier to minimize incompatibilities between heavy industry and populations, for example by devising and protecting a road route for transport of hazardous materials and prohibiting high-risk industries within zones of vigilance.

Although much of the scheme is voluntary as far as industry goes, observers believe it has worked quite well, and most industries in Dunkerque are adhering to the environmental charter. Local officials believe this is partly about doing things that are more economical, but largely about concern over their environmental image. Industry has also seen the value of the scheme in reducing uncertainty about future conflicts between industry and nonindustrial activities.

Economic and Ecological Renewal: Economic Development through Landscape Recycling

Reuse and redevelopment of former industrial sites, and the establishment of new economic activities and functions in such areas, represents another important strategy for ecological economic development. If industrial buildings and factories can be adaptively reused, this saves on energy, building materials, and land, and is an important element of an ecological economy. Many exemplary examples of this form of ecological brownfield redevelopment in European cities can be cited. One of the largest examples of ecological restructuring of former industrial sites is the Emscher Park International Building Exhibition (or simply Emscher Park IBA). Not a building exhibition in the typical sense, it is really a series of innovative redevelopment projects and initiatives focused on the heavily industrial Ruhr Valley in northwestern Germany. This is a region with a history of steel mills, coal mines, and chemical plants, all experiencing a long pattern of decline, which has resulted in a largely derelict industrial landscape. The region has been highly polluted as well.

In May 1989, the initiative was begun by the German Länd (state) government of North Rhine Westphalia. The idea is to promote creative projects for redevelopment and reuse of an 800-square-kilometer, 70-kilometer-long corridor from Duisberg to Dortmund. The exhibition area includes some 17 different cities and some 2 million residents. Through a combination of public and private funding (including monies from the lander and national governments, the EU, and private investors), more than 100 projects have been funded. A special company (IBA GmbH) was formed to coordinate and market the projects, and a steering committee and board of trustees also oversees the project[3] (European Commission DGXI, 1996a).

Project ideas have been generated through a variety of processes, including design competitions, symposia, workshops, and expert panels. Each of the seventeen municipalities in the corridor initially joined in the creation of the IBA, and the exhibition reflects an approach of creating collaborative partnerships between local government, industries, environmental groups, and others.

A number of impressive projects have already been completed. A major theme of Emscher Park is the creative reuse of former industrial buildings and sites. These include, for example, a former coal mine in Essen, which has now been converted into a facility housing a graphic design center, a museum, and artist studios. The gasometer, in Oberhausen, has been converted into a theater and exhibition hall (USEPA, undated). Considerable housing has been built and restored as well. Some twenty-six different housing projects have been constructed (including the renovation of large numbers of homes), many reusing industrial lands.

A major ecological feature of the initiative is Emscher Landscape Park, the broader environmental or landscape framework in which the many specific building and rebuilding projects are situated. This park is envisioned as a series of projects that will provide a system of open space and bicycle and pedestrian paths that connect the cities in the region, largely utilizing abandoned industrial roads and rail lines. At the core of this "network of regional open space recreational areas" is a 200-hectare park, created from the former Duisburg-Nord Ironworks (USEPA, undated, p. 6). The Landscape Park concept actually builds upon a 1920s plan (never implemented) for seven "regional green corridors." "Taking up this earlier idea, the individual north-south corridors are being expanded and linked to a new east-west corridor to form a complete park system" (IBA Emscher Park, undated, p. 13). "By connecting isolated open spaces, restoring the landscape, and upgrading the ecological and aesthetic quality of the desolated landscape, the idea is to achieve a lasting improvement of the living and working environment" (MacDonald, undated, p. 4).

Another ecological centerpiece has been the rejuvenation and restoration of the Emscher River System. This river has been heavily polluted, with much of the industrial waste directly transported to the river through open sewers. Elements of this restoration effort have included improvements to the sewage treatment system (such as replacing open sewers), daylighting some streams, desealing portions of the watershed, and taking a number of actions to restore the river system to more natural conditions. An "ecological restructuring" of the river system is ultimately envisioned (IBA Emscher Park, undated).

An emphasis in this reuse and redevelopment has been placed on economic activities and endeavors that emphasize new technologies and ecological industries and companies. A series of technology centers with an ecological emphasis, has been built in the region (including, for example, a company called Eco-Textil, producing low-chemical textiles).

Ecological building and design is another significant theme, and many of the new buildings constructed on Emscher Park sites incorporate significant ecological design measures. The Rheinelbe Science Park (in Gelsenkirchen), built on the site of a former steel mill, incorporates extensive photovoltaic panels on its rooftop (MacDonald, undated). A housing project in the city of Bottrop (constructed on a brownfield site) incorporates a rainwater collection system and centralized district heating (USEPA, undated). This green design emphasis has extended to the cities and towns throughout the region. A new thirty-floor office building in Essen, for instance (the corporate headquarters for RWE AG), has been designed to provide each floor with natural ventilation (through a system of double-skinned insulated glass).

Another major (and unique) theme in Emscher Park is the preservation and reuse of many of the industrial buildings and structures as artifacts of history to be appreciated and remembered. These "industrial monuments" include everything from natural gas storage tanks to reclaimed coal mine tailings to the engine room of a coal mine elevator. All have been reconfigured and reused for other functions. These leftover industrial buildings and landscapes have been viewed as cultural and historical resources preserved and integrated into the productive fabric of this landscape of renewal. Concerts and plays now take place in old steelworks. Former gas storage tanks now house historical exhibits:

> IBA devised an ingenious reuse strategy that preserves these enormous relics as museum pieces of its industrial past and promotes them as centers of cultural activities. The term *industrial monument* captures the essence of the Emscher Landscape Park where concerts are staged against a backdrop of a former steel plant's framework and people hike among the hills of reclaimed coal pilings. The twelve story gas-o-meter in Oberhausen no longer stores natural gas, but is the home for many unique cultural events: concerts, parties, plays, conventions, and meetings. What was once the engine room for a coal mine's elevator at the *Erfahrungsfed Zollverein* in Essen, is now an interactive exploratium for children and adults. Instead of delivering coal miners hundreds of feet below the surface, the turbines, along with other machines and tools, have been creatively incorporated into exhibits for patrons to explore. (USEPA, undated)

By most accounts, and as it approaches the end of its original ten-year mission, Emscher Park has accomplished much. It represents one of the few examples of a regional brownfields redevelopment strategy, has brought about numerous reuse and renovation projects (showing effectively that many buildings and structures can be adaptively reused, preventing the energy and other impacts associated with building new commercial and industrial structures), and has taken the creative approach of saving and heralding its industrial past. Much of the Emscher Landscape Park is already in place, including a 270-kilometer bike path extending from Duisburg to Berkamen. This project has already done much to enhance and restore the quality of the living environment in this part of Germany (IBA Emscher Park, undated).

In addition, the economics appear to strongly favor a strategy of industrial reuse. One state government official estimates that tearing down and disposing of structures at the former Duisburg Plant would cost more than twice the amount of redeveloping and reusing them (Le Pierres, undated). Economic development through industrial reuse, then, may be the most economic option as well as the most sustainable.

While Emscher Park may be the project on the most impressive scale, there are a number of other exemplary examples of industrial site renovation and reuse in Europe. These include the Westergasfabriek in Amsterdam (see USEPA, undated) and the Glasvej district in Odense, among many others (see descriptions of other industrial redevelopment projects in Europe in Pacte Project, 1997).

Green Offices: More Ecological Ways of Working?

How offices and commercial spaces are organized, the ways in which people work and function within them, and their ecological design features constitute equally important ways in which commerce can be more restorative. European cities offer examples of a number of creative design and work arrangements, and several of the more innovative ones are profiled here.

The central government building at Haarlem, the Netherlands, for example, has incorporated a number of interesting environmental features. Among them are an energy-efficient lighting system; an exterior wall design that incorporates so-called "eyebrows," which shield the summer sun, and fully operable windows (and no air conditioning); a great deal of daylighting (the building is designed around a series of staggered atria); solar hot water panels for kitchen use; a rainwater collection system, which provides all the water necessary to flush toilets in the building (water is also collected from the roof of the adjoining train station); and a series of small greenroofs. Conference rooms have been placed on the north side of building and office workspaces on the south side to optimize sun and warmth.

Also, a major environmental feature can be seen in the building's location adjacent to the main train station in Haarlem. There are no auto parking spaces incorporated into the building design (though there is a public parking deck not far away), and most employees use public transit or bicycle to work. (Employees are given the chance to purchase a bicycle at government expense, up to a value of 1,500 guilders, or about US $750).

The most intriguing new innovation being tested in this building, however, is the concept of shared working spaces. It is estimated that in any given day, about 50 percent of the space in a conventional office space goes unused (e.g., because of travel, illness, vacations, or pregnancy). The design of the Haarlem building begins from this premise and aims to reduce the space needed by 25 percent, through a shared workspace arrangement. About half of the employees of the government building agency housed in these offices operate under this shared workspace arrangement. Instead of having a permanent office assigned to them, employees arrive each morning and collect a rollable cart (which contains their personal belongings, files, and their laptop computer) and then simply select an open office, which they can use for the day. At the end of the day, they collect their belongings, roll their (locked) cart back to its stall for the evening, and leave. When employees begin in the morning, they also collect their own portable phone, which they clip to their belt and take with them wherever they go. The laptops plug into a port at each desk, and the desk and workspace furniture is fully adjustable.

The national government building agency in Haarlem is experimenting with shared office space. Workers have movable carts (shown here) instead of permanent office space, which they can roll to wherever they are working on that particular day.

Employees were given the choice in the beginning of whether they wanted to participant in the shared workspace concept. If they wanted their own permanent desk, they were given it, but about half chose this new way of working. They were also told that after a year, an evaluation would be conducted and they could choose to opt out of the shared workspace arrangement at that time if they wished. Peter van Exel, head of the government building agency's regional office, believes that the employees who chose the shared workspace arrangement are generally happy with it. He believes that this notion that people must have their own dedicated space (which they personalize by displaying pictures of family, etc.) is not particularly true. (Interestingly, these employees were given training in the beginning in how to maintain a clean desk.) The evaluation promised to the employees has not yet occurred, mostly because work needs to be done to address several problems with the building itself. A significant problem has been excessive noise, and it has been found that the ceramic separating walls (designed to do a number of things, including keeping the building cool) are not doing an adequate job of absorption.

One key lesson for van Exel is that employees must be given nice facilities in which to work and relax. The government building agency office includes, for example, a large room known as the Pavilion, containing magazines, lounge chairs, and other amenities. It is generally a nice place to relax, as well as to hold more informal meetings.

Offices can fundamentally reduce their ecological footprints in many other ways, and European cities provide abundant examples. One recent example of this in the Netherlands is the *Eco-kantoor* (or "ecological office") in Bunnik. With a floor area of 1,609 square meters, and a total building cost of about 4 million guilders (about US $2 million), it was designed from the beginning with a number of ecological features focused on reducing the level of resource use by occupants of the building. It is designed for natural ventilation in the summer (no air conditioning), with a night ventilation system, operable/openable windows throughout, extensive use of daylighting, heat recovery systems, and extensive insulation. The building is 45 percent more energy efficient than what is required by law. There are 10 square meters of photovoltaic cells on the roof, and it is solar-oriented. The building also incorporates water-conserving toilets and faucets, and a rainwater collection system (with a basement cistern) provides a portion of the water for flushing toilets. Pantries are fitted for separation of wastes, and a general emphasis has been placed on the use of natural, nontoxic materials. Other interesting ecological features include an emphasis on the use of reusable materials throughout, an underground lava material used in the parking area (which absorbs leaking auto oil), and the use of cellulose and natural insulation materials.

Table 12.1. Comparison of the Ecokantoor with Conventional Office Space

	Standard Dutch Office Building	Ecokantoor
Basic rental cost, per square meter (guilders)	225	246
Energy and water usage	39	18
Total rental cost and service cost (per square meter) in guilders	264	264

Source: Comfort, 1996.

One of the more interesting ideas is the design of the building's atrium, where water is released (from the rainwater collection cistern) and flows from the ceiling, when sensors detect that humidity levels are too low. Vegetation and an inside pond create a pleasant working environment as well.

The design of the interior workspace also has important lessons. To maximize the use of daylighting, all workspaces are kept near the exterior of the building, while bathrooms and storage and other installations are placed in the center. Each workspace has its own adjustable lighting and ventilation. The interior spaces are flexible in their dimensions—they can be adjusted to accommodate from one to six different companies.

These energy and ecological features have been estimated to add about 10 percent to the cost of the building. But, the building illustrates that these costs can be fairly quickly recouped through reduced energy and water costs. Table 12.1 shows that when projected environmental savings are taken into account, the per-square-meter cost of the Eco-kantoor is equal to that of a standard Dutch office building.

The overall results of the Eco-kantoor are impressive. The design has resulted in significant reductions in resource use: electricity consumption reduced by 55 percent, gas use reduced by 45 percent, and water use reduced by 50 percent (Comfort, 1996). And, an extremely pleasant working environment has been created.

Ecobusinesses and Green Consumerism

Europe provides many examples of progressive companies and businesses that have sought to reshape themselves in more environmentally sustainable ways. Although it is not always clear what motivates such companies (whether public relations or genuine concern about the environment, or a mixture of both), they do represent positive examples of how companies can significantly reduce their ecological footprints. Many of the world's most environmentally friendly businesses have emerged in western and northern Europe, especially in Sweden, Denmark, Germany, and the Netherlands. Important European exemplars include Electrolux, Scandic Hotels, IKEA, McDonald's, Novotex, and BMW, among others.

Many of these companies have adopted explicit environmental policies, prepared annual environmental reports, and have adopted one or more environmental management systems, including the EU's own "EMAS," or Eco-Management and Audit Scheme. A number of these companies also have endorsed the system principles of the Natural Step, a set of ambitious sustainability goals established by Swedish cancer researcher Karl-Henrik Robèrt. Many companies have gone through the Natural Step training and have modified their product designs and company operations to satisfy the "system conditions" outlined in the Natural Step.

Robèrt, frustrated with the confusion and disagreement over the meaning of sustainability, sought consensus from Sweden's leading scientists. Through an iterative process of consultation (some twenty-two different versions of his report were circulated), consensus emerged. At the heart of this consensus are four critical system conditions: (1) that substances from the earth's crust must not be allowed to systematically increase in the ecosphere; (2) that substances produced by society must not systematically increase in the ecosphere; (3) that the physical basis for productivity and diversity of nature must not be systematically diminished; and (4) that fair and efficient use of resources with respect to meeting human needs must occur (The Natural Step, 1996). (See Box 12.1, which provides additional insights into what these principles mean in practice.) Robèrt's final consensus report, endorsed by the King of Sweden, was mailed to every household

---

Box 12.1. The Four System Conditions of the Natural Step

1. Substances from the earth's crust must not systematically increase in the ecosphere.

This means:
Fossil fuels, metals, and other minerals must not be extracted at a faster pace than their slow redeposit and reintegration into the earth's crust.

Reason:
Otherwise, the concentration of substances in the ecosphere will increase and eventually reach limits—often unknown—beyond which irreversible changes occur.

Question to ask:
Does your organization systematically decrease its economic dependence on underground metals, fuels, and other minerals?

2. Substances produced by society must not systematically increase in the ecosphere.

This means:
Substances must not be produced at a faster pace than they can be broken down and integrated into the cycles of nature or deposited into the Earth's crust.

Reason:
Otherwise, the concentration of substances in the ecosphere will increase and eventually reach limits—often unknown—beyond which irreversible changes occur.

Question to ask:
Does your organization systematically decrease its economic dependence on persistent unnatural substances?

3. The physical basis for productivity and diversity of nature must not be systematically diminished.

This means:
We cannot harvest or manipulate ecosystems in such a way that productive capacity and diversity systematically diminish.

Reason:
Our health and prosperity depend on the capacity of nature to reconcentrate and restructure wastes into new resources.

Question to ask:
Does your organization systematically decrease its economic dependence on activities that encroach on productive parts of nature, such as overfishing?

4. Fair and efficient use of resources with respect to meeting human needs must occur.

This means:
Basic human needs must be met with the most resource-efficient methods possible, and their satisfaction must take precedence over the provision of luxuries.

Reason:
Humanity must prosper with a resource metabolism meeting System Conditions 1 through 3. This is necessary in order to gain the social stability and cooperation for achieving the changes in time.

Question to ask:
Does your organization systematically decrease its economic dependence on using an unnecessarily large amount of resources in relation to added human value?

Source: The Natural Step News, No. 1, Winter 1996.

in the country (4 million households) as well as to every school. An estimated sixty corporations have endorsed the Natural Step, and some fifty cities in Sweden are also using it (Malcolm, 1998; Bradbury, 1996).

Swedish-based Scandic Hotels has adopted the Natural Step and has undertaken some impressive steps to reduce the impact of this industry. The task of incorporating the Natural Step principles was given to each of Scandic's hotels, with employees in charge of developing the plans. The company has also put its 6,500 employees through the Natural Step training. Specifically, it has introduced the notion of the Recyclable Hotel Room—in particular through choosing natural materials and avoiding plastics. It has replaced carpeting and plastic flooring with wood parquet floors derived from sustainably harvested Scandinavian forests. It is minimizing the use of chrome and other metals, and it has installed water-conserving fixtures and a number of features to reduce energy consumption. The hotel decided to no longer wash linens each day and has shifted from bar soap to soap dispensers. All new rooms are declared to be 97 percent recyclable, and the hotel is retrofitting 2,000 rooms each year.

The new Sjölyst hotel in Oslo illustrates these design principles, including an innovative approach to reducing energy consumption in rooms: "Through the hotel's televisions, which also has an alarm clock and message system, the room temperature is transmitted via a sensor to the hotel's central computer system and graphically presented every four minutes—allowing the temperature to be tracked and adjusted" (*Financial Times*, 1997).

The results for Scandic, which had been running in the red, are reported to be considerable and beyond simply doing the right thing for the environment. Redefining itself in this way has led to "enthusiasm and high morale among employees" and "press attention and an ad campaign enhanced the hotel's image." "Occupancy rates jumped from 65 percent to 85 percent. The company returned to profitability" (Malcolm, 1998). The estimated environmental impacts are considerable. In 1997 alone, the retrofitted rooms are estimated to have reduced plastics use by 90 tonnes and metal use by 15 tonnes (Scandic website).

McDonald's in Sweden has taken a number of actions to reduce environmental impacts, again guided by the Natural Step. They have shifted from plastic and polystyrene to the use of paper and are emphasizing the use of renewable energy sources (some restaurants are reported to have installed windmills on their roofs) (Slavin, 1998).

Novotex, based in Denmark, has pioneered the production of "green cotton," which employs "special weaving techniques to avoid the need for formaldehyde or other chemicals for finishing the fabrics" ("Environmental Aspects of Natural Fibres," undated). IKEA markets a number of low-polluting and recyclable home furnishings (including, for example, a ceiling fan that utilizes recycled sheet metal) and takes advantage of natural materials, such as water-soluble glue and organic cotton, where possible.

Electrolux-Sweden has developed a range of products that use less energy and otherwise reduce environmental impacts, including "The world's first portable vacuum cleaner with cadmium-free batteries"; water-saving front-loading washing machines; a no-PVC refrigerator; and a photovoltaic-powered lawnmower (the so-called "solar mower") (Electrolux, 1997). The company has also developed a system of "environmental declarations"—statements of the natural environmental impacts of a product during its full life, which are accessible through the Internet (Electrolux, 1997, p. 9).

A number of these companies have developed product lines that allow product take-back and recycling, and there is a clear European trend in this direction (with some believing there will likely be EU-wide requirements at some point in the near future). The German car manufacturer BMW has made particular strides in designing and manufacturing vehicles to allow disassembly and material reuse. It created the first pilot disassembly plant (in 1990), has established a network of authorized dismantlers, has worked to develop a plastics identification system to make recycling easier and quicker, and now publishes a disassembly handbook for use by recycling companies. The company has established a target of recycling 85 percent of the materials in its cars, now designs for disassembly from the beginning, and has also issued (in 1997) a guarantee to take back all of its automobiles at the end of their lives (BMW, undated).

While there remains skepticism about the Natural Step, and some believe many of these exemplary companies have a long way to go in reaching the four system conditions, the positive movement in the direction of a more sustainable economy seems undeniable (see Vidal and McIvor, 1995; *Financial Times*, 1998). These companies, moreover, appear to demonstrate that ecological impacts can be dramatically reduced at the same time that production costs are cut and profits are enhanced.

To promote and facilitate ecobusinesses and ecological consumerism, a number of national eco-label programs have been established in Europe. Germany's Blue Angel was the first, established in 1977, and another example is the Nordic Swan. The EU instituted its own Eco-label Programme in 1983. This voluntary program works through the establishment of ecological criteria in each different product group and is intended to screen for "those products with the lowest environmental impact" to carry the eco-label or logo (European Union, undated).[4]

Ecological criteria have been established for twelve product groups, including washing machines, dishwashers, laundry detergents, copying paper, and refrigerators, among others. A total of 216 products have now been awarded the EU Eco-logo, a blue-and-green flower. While clearly still in its infancy, this system holds tremendous potential for facilitating more ecologically informed consumer choices and encouraging companies to develop and market more responsible products.[5]

The emergence in European countries of these ecological industries and companies seems the result of a combination of much stronger consumer demand for such products and rational government laws and pricing policies that mandate or strongly encourage more ecological production (e.g., Germany's take-back law for autos, Dutch taxes on new cars to support eventual disassembly and recycling, and Germany's greenpoint program for product packaging). In countries such as Sweden and the Netherlands, moreover, there exists a strong tradition of consensus-based decisions and less acrimony between business and government. Although the market and cultural conditions of northern Europe are more favorable to the emergence of ecoindustries, green businesses have emerged in the United States—and more could be done to promote and facilitate the application of powerful ideas such as the Natural Step. Indeed, American companies (such as the carpet manufacturer Interface) have adopted the system conditions and demonstrate effectively that American companies can fundamentally operate more sustainably while also making a profit.

There also appears to be some direct spillover from the progressive Swedish and European green companies. An American McDonald's is reported, for example, to have installed solar hot water heaters in an effort (albeit a small one) to shift partially to renewable energy (Slavin, 1998). Local officials involved in local economic development can promote (perhaps mandate or strongly suggest) Natural Step principles wherever and whenever the opportunity arises by sponsoring ecological business seminars and training programs and including ecological information materials with all information distributed to prospective businesses.

Encouraging local production of goods and services that might otherwise be imported is another important strategy, and here as well many European examples exist. The London borough of Sutton, for example, has undertaken a number of initiatives to promote local production of goods, including (through the Bioregional Development Group) locally produced charcoal and local paper production (Sustainable London Trust, undated). Efforts to support local agriculture fall under this heading, and the historically prominent (cultural) role of farmers markets in most European cities helps in this regard (e.g., in Dutch cities such as Leiden, the markets are large affairs occurring twice a week; although not all of the goods are locally produced, there is greater likelihood they will be). And, it might be noted that many local efforts at using biomass to fuel CHP plants (and really many of the renewable energy strategies discussed in Chapter 9) represent examples of sustainable local economic development in the sense that local power production is replacing energy produced elsewhere and imported into the community (see Juffermans, 1995, for more examples of this). Community-supported agriculture, moreover, saw its beginnings in Germany and Switzerland and remains a powerful idea for supporting the local economy. Douthwaite (1996) describes in detail a number of such local-based economic development ideas in Europe and elsewhere, from the expansion of microbreweries in Britain to initiatives for growing energy crops. His book is a recommended resource.

Municipalities can also make it easier for citizens to shop in more ecological ways. Kolding and Herning have started, for example, *Green Shops* programs. Although in the early stages, the idea is that shops and businesses agree to stock the latest and best green products in exchange for being awarded a green shops designation (see Figure 12.2), and the ability to display a placard indicating this designation in the front of their stores. So the theory goes, if your store sells shoes, you would agree to stock the most environmentally sound and green shoe products. Early interest has been good, and in Kolding two stores—a grocery store and building supply center—have already been given the green shops designation. Admittedly, the program has to rely on a good faith effort by shopkeepers because city staff have no real way of effectively policing whether the best, most green products are being stocked in the stores.

Figure 12.2. The *grøn butik,* or "green shops" logo, an initiative of Green City Denmark, indicates businesses that have agreed to stock and sell the leading environmental products for their particular business sector.

Source: Green City Denmark.

The impetus for green consumerism has come from many directions. Municipal governments themselves can stimulate product markets through their purchasing power (as discussed in Chapter 11). Environmental organizations have also played a role. The Swedish Nature Conservation Society, for example, initiated a successful "Environment Friendly Shopping" campaign, resulting in substantial reductions in the purchase of environmentally harmful products and leading some companies to modify the content of their products. Swedish municipalities have taken the lead and developed their own environment-friendly shopping campaigns, as have other cities reported on in this book (e.g., Leicester).

European countries also have a long history of promoting more positive economic relationships with third world countries, and this represents another important element of green consumerism. The concept of third world shops—stores (generally run by volunteers) that sell goods produced in third world countries and handled through relationships that guarantee a fair price to third world producers—has found extensive support among European shoppers. The first such shops began appearing in the late 1960s, with the first opening in Sweden. In the beginning years, the mission was seen more in terms of providing information to the public, participating in political rallies and events, and generally being more activist in nature. Over the years, the shops themselves—and the selling of products based on providing a fair return to third world producers—has become the main emphasis. In the Netherlands, there are now almost 400 such shops—called *wereldwinkels* or "world shops"—supported by a national association of *wereldwinkels*, based in Utrecht. About half of these operate in dedicated shop space and are open daily. The other half typically operate on a more limited scale, such as a booth at the weekly market or at special events. In the Netherlands, these stores have been growing in size and business. In 1997, they accounted for 35 million guilders in sales (about US $17 million), obviously still a very small percentage of the quite large Dutch consumer market.

The products offered in these stores range from pottery and wood carvings to coffee and teas to toys made from recycled soda cans. Goods are purchased by each individual store, but *wereldwinkel* shops must buy only from suppliers and importers who meet certain criteria and who are certified by the national organization. In the Netherlands, there are currently about twenty-five suppliers (the largest being the organization Fair Share). To gain certification, the national organization does considerable research on suppliers and importers before certification is awarded. The main requirement is that the producers in third world countries be guaranteed a fair price for their work and their products. In each store, up to 15 percent of the goods can be what is referred to as a "border assortment"—goods from other suppliers or organizations that are consistent with the *wereldwinkel* philosophy (e.g., Greenpeace).

The *wereldwinkels* are supported in a number of ways by the cities and towns in which they are located. In a recent survey of forty-five *wereldwinkels,* about half were found to have been given recent subsidies or support by local governments. In some cases, the municipality even owns the building. In most stores, the employees are unpaid volunteers, although stores in some cities provide jobs under a central government employment program. Because the stores are not out to make a profit and are usually manned by volunteers, more of the price of the product goes back to the third world producers. Where some stores accumulate profits, these monies typically are used to improve the shops or to fund projects in third world countries. In Leiden, the *wereldwinkel* is also combined with a secondhand shop.

Are these stores successful, and do they make a real difference? Erika Spil, of the Dutch national organization of *wereldwinkels,* definitely believes they do. There are now shops in virtually every city and town, and the name recognition among the Dutch population is very high (80 percent in a recent survey). There is no question that *wereldwinkels* have had the positive function of raising consciousness about the third world, and about the necessity of equitable trading between the north and the south. While the criteria suppliers and importers must satisfy do include the environment, it is not always clear that the goods purchased are the most environmentally supportive. There is talk within *wereldwinkel* circles about the need to address

Wereldwinkels, or world shops, such as this one in Leiden, sell products that guarantee a fair return to artisans and craftspeople in developing countries. There are some 400 *wereldwinkels* in the Netherlands.

environmental issues more fully and directly than currently is the case. Nevertheless, *wereldwinkel* supporters believe that their shops match the times well, as consumers (at least European) move away from wanting quantity to wanting quality products. And, the stores are becoming more established and more professional in their operation, and sales are indeed growing. There is now a network of European *wereldwinkels,* and all signs suggest that these more responsible forms of consumerism are gaining ground.

One of the main products found in the *wereldwinkels* is Max Havelaar coffee, a fair trade certified coffee established in the late 1980s. The Max Havelaar label indicates that the coffee beans have been grown by small coffee bean growers who are guaranteed a fair price and who meet certain production criteria. A set of fair trade conditions (see Box 12.2) must be satisfied before the certification is given, including the payment to producers of a "surcharge" (in addition to the world market price), thus guaranteeing small producers a higher price (an additional surcharge is required for an organically grown label). The original certification for coffee has now been extended to other products, including honey, cocoa (chocolate bars), and bananas. The Max Havelaar certification program has been highly successful and has resulted in providing an estimated 40 million guilders (about US $20 million) in surcharges (above the world market price) paid directly to small producers (Max Havelaar Foundation, undated). Market penetration of these products has been extensive in the

---

BOX 12.2. Max Havelaar Fair Trade Conditions

1. *Direct purchase.* The products are purchased directly from small farmer organizations or from plantations. The organizations are registered in the Register of Producers of the Fairtrade Labeling Organizations (FLO) International.
2. *Surcharge.* The price being paid is derived directly from the world market price and is in principle a little bit higher because farmers still have to catch up before arriving at a favorable trading position.
3. *Guaranteed minimum price.* To guarantee the arms a minimum of social security, a minimum price has been established.
4. *Credit allowances.* Part of the harvest can be financed in advance if producers of the cooperatives ask for it.
5. *Long-term relationships.* Producers and importers will have to provide mutual security in supply and purchase. That is the reason to aim for long-term trading relationships.
6. *Production criteria for plantations.* In addition to these trading terms, production criteria concerning working conditions and environmental care have been developed especially for bananas and tea.

Source: Max Havelaar Foundation, undated

Netherlands and now extends into other European nations. Some 90 percent of the grocery stores in the Netherlands carry the certified coffee. These forms of fair trade and product certification programs have tremendous potential for bringing about responsible (and ecological) forms of consumption.

Marketing Sustainable Business and Technologies

There are also good examples of efforts to effectively market green-urban technologies and innovations as an economic development strategy. Green City Denmark A/S, established in 1993 and headquartered in Herning, is one such marketing organization, which is focused on selling the ecological community-building ideas and technology with which Denmark leads much of the rest of the world. The limited liability company was initially formed by the Danish Ministry of Business and Industries, the Ministry of Energy and Environment, and four Danish cities (Herning, Videback, Ikast, and Silkeborg), but it is now open to membership by other cities, companies, or organizations that can purchase shares in the company. There are currently 220 shareholders. The stated purposes of Green City Denmark are to "establish a showcase for Danish expertise within energy and environment . . ." and to market ". . . Danish expertise within environmentally sound production and sustainable solutions for waste treatment, water supply, waste water, energy supply/renewable energy sources/energy savings, urban ecology, etc." (Green City Denmark A/S, undated, p. 4). Green City Denmark achieves these objectives through a variety of marketing activities, including participating and arranging exhibitions and trade fairs, arranging visiting delegations (some 160 delegations from 30 countries so far), and participating in local environmental training and education programs (Green City Denmark, 1997).

This marketing network has been very successful at showcasing and marketing Denmark's environmental businesses and technology. As a national government report concludes: "Local cooperation networks between the municipal environmental authorities and the local enterprises can often combine stricter environmental standards for enterprises with improved opportunities for profit. The combination of expertise that enterprises and municipal authorities can offer is a solid basis for the export of systems and the concomitant operative experience and training opportunities for customers" (The Ecological City, Denmark, 1995, p. 33). A similar network has been formed in Finland, modeled after Green City Denmark (and including the study city of Lahti). Called Green Triangle Finland, its aims are also to market ecological products, services, and innovations of Finnish companies and communities.

Lessons for American Cities

One of the key lessons of these European cities is the proactive role that local authorities can play in helping promote more environmentally restorative forms of commerce and business. As this chapter illustrates, there are a variety of opportunities for playing such a role, and American communities can and should consider a similar charge. While few American cities have been as engaged collaboratively with local companies as cities such as Graz, there are in fact American examples that illustrate that this is possible. Perhaps the most impressive American example is Portland's BEST program (Businesses for a Sustainable Tomorrow). In a strategy similar to Graz's, the city's Energy Office has been encouraging and assisting local businesses in becoming more energy- and resource-efficient, and less environmentally polluting. Each year the program announces its BEST Business Awards, which are similar to ECOPROFIT in that they recognize environmental leaders in the community (see Portland BEST, undated). A program in Boulder called PACE (Partners for a Clean Environment) provides a similar function. Here, the city offers two programs to the business community: access to a clearinghouse and research service (the "connection"), and a voluntary environmental certification program (the PACE "certificate" program) (see Partners for a Clean Environment [PACE], undated). These programs demonstrate that even in the American context of a more regulatory "arms-length" relationship between business and government, localities can indeed play an important, more proactive environmental role.

Many of the other innovative ideas for greening economic development explored here are equally relevant. For example, industrial symbiosis represents a tremendous opportunity in American cities. As already mentioned in Chapter 8, the lessons of Kalundborg are immediately relevant and transferable to many American industrial complexes. Indeed, the surge of activity in the planning and development of ecoindustrial parks around the country is extremely promising, and USEPA and state and local governments should continue to support these initiatives. Although progress to date has been limited, Kalundborg remains a powerful working model—the source of both practical advice and inspiration. Local economic development offices and programs will need to rethink their missions and modes of operation to facilitate such symbioses. An initial step is to more formally and comprehensively study the current inputs and outputs to the local (and regional) economy (e.g., waste generated and materials and energy needs for production). Such a study may help to identify current and future linkages or symbioses.

There will, moreover, often be creative opportunities to utilize former industrial sites as the basis for new industries and economic activity. An inspirational recent example can be seen in Maya Lin's design for the Bronx Community Paper Company. This recycling center, which will recycle some 300,000 tons of used paper per year and provide 400 new jobs, is sited on a former industrial site—the former Harlem River Rail Yards (Muschamp, 1998). American communities do indeed have many opportunities for creative reuse and redevelopment, with the obvious land use benefits of facilitating more compact urban form.

Also, as the Ecover factory in Belgium effectively demonstrates, there will be many opportunities to integrate sustainable industry and economy with sustainable design and architecture. One leading (recent) American example of this is provided by the Green Institute in Minneapolis. Here, an innovative eco-enterprise center in the Phillips neighborhood has recently opened. Built on an urban redevelopment site (a cleared area that was to be used for a garbage transfer station), the 64,000-square-foot facility incorporates a number of impressive ecological design features, including the reuse of steel beams from older buildings, 100 percent daylighting, the use of wind and solar energy, and a rooftop garden, among other features. Energy savings for this building have been estimated at 70 percent, and the building is expected to be able to produce more energy than it consumes (Green Institute, undated; Roundtable Minutes, 1998.) The facility also brings jobs and income to an economically struggling neighborhood. There is no reason why the production of more environmentally sensitive products and services cannot also occur in these kinds of ecologically restorative and nourishing structures.

Rethinking conventional office and working environments to be more environment conserving and less ecologically damaging also holds much promise for U.S. cities. A number of American companies have already been successfully experimenting with these types of new shared-space buildings, suggesting that we will likely see more of these kinds of arrangements. One recent prominent example is AT&T's new shared office in Morristown, New Jersey. There, 225 employees share significantly less space than in a more traditional office arrangement. It was assumed that at any given time, some 60 percent of the sales and technical staff would be out of the office. The building operates in a manner similar to the Haarlem building, where employees reserve space through their laptop, retrieve a mobile file cabinet, and have their phone calls routed to their reserved space. Special features installed by AT&T include a cafe, phone rooms, "personal harbors," and team meeting spaces (Apgar, 1998). The financial and space savings are impressive. Annual savings of $460,000 (or about $2,000 per employee) have been realized, and the required building space has been reduced from 45,000 square feet to 27,000 square feet. Like the Haarlem building, the environmental implications are thus considerable.

More intangible benefits include "closer teamwork, better customer service, and greater employee satisfaction" (Apgar, 1998).

These kinds of shared-office arrangements are but one form of the "alternative workplace." Others that are becoming increasingly popular in the United States include the use of satellite offices (which have also been shown to reduce real estate needs dramatically), telecommuting, and home offices. There are certainly a number of barriers, and one lesson is the importance of programs to support these alternative work concepts (e.g., everything from providing financial allowances for office furnishings to providing training and technical assistance to creating mechanisms by which to connect employees back to the managers and workers on site). Current estimates puts the number of telecommuters or home-based workers at between 30 and 40 million (Apgar, 1998). These kinds of alternative workplaces will likely be increasingly important, with significant implications for sustainability.

The European experience shows that green consumerism can make a significant difference in the marketplace. American consumers have far to go, however, in reaching the same level of concern and commitment when compared to their European counterparts, and they will need assistance and encouragement in making choices about green products. The green-consumer and eco-labeling programs in Europe are clearly helpful in guiding consumers and in strengthening market support for green products. While several nongovernmental eco-label systems are in operation in the United States (e.g., Green Seal), perhaps it is time to establish (or at least to financially support) such a governmental system in the United States. Frankel (1998), in reviewing eco-label programs elsewhere, concludes: "These programs are federally funded in every country but the U.S. . . . for all practical purposes eco-labeling in the U.S. has not gotten off the ground" (Frankel, 1998, p. 161). (See Frankel for a discussion of the problems and complexities of implementing an eco-labeling system.) A national eco-labeling commitment would do much to facilitate responsible consumer choices.

American cities and communities could indeed become much more actively involved in supporting green businesses and green consumer opportunities within their jurisdictions (and regions). Activities could range from distributing guidebooks and information about how and where to purchase green products to some form of certification system for green shops, similar to those used in Denmark and elsewhere. Local governments could recycle buildings and spaces that might be used to support ecologically friendly stores (e.g., *wereldwinkels*)—for example, by providing free or subsidized rents. And again, American communities must learn, as many European cities have, that their own direct buying decisions can help tremendously in supporting fledgling ecobusinesses and services.

Notes

1. Artificial lighting is only needed during winter months, between 8 and 10 A.M., and 5 and 6 P.M.
2. The "gentle shift system" is described in this way: "i.e. between six and two or between two and ten; without the night shift system which disturbs the bio-rhythms; employees work flexible working hours and enjoy the possibility of working at home thanks to their portable computers" (Ecover, 1992, p. 13).
3. The [Steering] Committee decides on the admission of projects to the exhibition, and the Trustees "bring together representatives from public life who promote the Building Exhibition and support its initiatives" (European Commission DGXI, 1996a, p. 2).
4. According to the EU, "Ecological criteria are not based on a single parameter, but rather rest on a study which analyzes the impact of the product on the environment throughout its entire life-cycle, possibly starting from raw material extraction in the pre-production stage, through production, distribution and use of the product, to the disposal of the product" (EU, undated [http://europa.eu.int/comm/dg11/ecolabel/program.html].
5. The EU says the following about success to date: "It is certainly too early to assess the consumers' response and the users' perceptions and reactions. However, the very encouraging reactions from manufacturers in recent months show that the dynamics of supply and demand in a free market are working to the advantage of firms applying for the EU Eco-label. The steady increase in the number of applications from manufacturers will continue as both they and consumers realize the importance of this little flower and the benefits it brings . . . Commissioner Ritt Bjerregaard has said that the proposed revised Eco-label scheme '. . . will be an important market-oriented instrument in the EU's environment policy' and that it' . . . will make it easier for the 373 million European consumers to make their choice for 'green' products by clearly indicating the positive environmental impact of the product. Consumers also have the choice to disregard products which do not carry the Eco-label, thereby putting pressure on producers to apply for the label and change production patterns in order to live up to the criteria of a reduced impact on the environment." (EU, undated [http://europa.eu.int/comm/dg11/erolabel/program.html].

Part VI

Learning from Europe

Chapter 13

The Promise of Green Urbanism: Lessons from European Cities

The Challenges of Green Urbanism

At times, the descriptions of these selected European cities may seem excessively optimistic—these are clearly cities making impressive strides and moving significantly in the direction of more sustainable futures. Even for the most holistic and forward-thinking of the lot, however, implementing the ideas of green urbanism raises serious challenges and dilemmas. These cities, despite their tremendous accomplishments, are not perfect examples of sustainable places, but struggle with difficult conflicts and trade-offs. A number of these dilemmas have emerged from the case studies and are instructive for other cities pursuing urban sustainability.

Several dilemmas arise from the objective of promoting dense, compact development patterns. Although most of the case cities examined have managed to protect extensive parks and open spaces, compact development policies do often result in the gradual loss of vacant green areas within the cities.

Compact growth policies in cities like Amsterdam have indeed resulted in the loss of some neighborhood greenspaces. A report by the Amsterdam Physical Planning Department talks about these negative impacts on greenspace (City of Amsterdam, 1994, p. 156):

> In the past few years Amsterdam's compact-city policies have led to a more intensive use of land, the expansion and compaction of the city have largely been carried out on open space in the city districts. Sports fields have been

rezoned for housing purposes, for example in Geuzenveld, and parks and gardens have also been used, often small plots left over from the days of the General Extension Plan. The urban designers and physical planners at the Physical Planning Department proved unable to redirect the powerful thrust of these policies. The value of this green space for the city as a whole was ignored.

And, in cities such as Amsterdam, although the per-capita greenspace available is considerable (estimated in Amsterdam at 14 square meters per person on average), this space is unevenly distributed across the city. In many of the older areas of cities, greenspace and nature are not prominent features; many of these urban spaces, delightful for other reasons, are admittedly quite gray.

Numerous specific examples of this conflict between compactness and urban greenspace arise from the cases. One example, the IJburg project in Amsterdam, represents to many in the Dutch environmental community an unfortunate loss of aquatic habitat (although its ecological value appears debatable, and Amsterdam officials argue the project is necessary to accommodate new housing in close proximity to the urban center). Other cities in the study have faced similar trade-offs.

Another challenge also arising from the desire to develop in a denser, more land-efficient pattern emerges with respect to the aesthetic and livability qualities of the resulting housing. A number of the larger projects visited (e.g., Rieselfeld in Freiburg and GWL-terrein in Amsterdam) involve large, high-bulk housing blocks, with less than inspirational architectural qualities. Although admittedly subjective (and admittedly premature in the sense that a number of these projects have yet to be finished), the architectural and building qualities of these places are somewhat cold and harsh. This creates a strong challenge to design new dense housing and living environments that are human-scale, enjoyable places to live—as aesthetically uplifting as they are energy- and environment-conserving.

The same might be said for many of the public spaces designed as part of new developments. They almost always fail to live up to the plazas, pleins, and civic spaces of the older city. A related question is whether it is truly possible to create new settlement quarters (e.g., Almere and Houten in the Netherlands) that have all of the human qualities of place that older European cities have. One of the most impressive qualities of many European cities is the organic nature of their development: they have grown, developed, and changed incrementally over many years, and the current environment is the cumulative result of this organic growth. Much of the current approach to building represents large-scale new neighborhoods and communities, and although this undoubtedly has many economic and sustainability advantages (e.g., the ability to extend public transit), the result is often less than ideal visually and socially. The policy ramifications of this issue are not clear, but the issue does lend further support for efforts to infill, to redevelop sensitivity, and to encourage adaptive reuse—all strategies undertaken to various degrees by the study cities. And, it further strengthens the importance of incorporating green features into any future development projects.

Despite these dilemmas and challenges presented by compactness, many of these cities demonstrate creative balancing of public goals. An important observation is that many of the European cities studied and visited are (and have managed to remain) amazingly green. The Scandinavian cities especially have a high green quotient, and at the same time they are highly dense. Other impressive green and dense cities include Berlin and Freiburg, among others. This "greenness" is a function of the presence of trees and vegetation, green vacant land, and the close proximity of cities to a large (protected) natural landscape and surrounding natural topographic features (e.g., lakes and seas). Many of these cities have worked hard to protect this ecological capital, while also growing compactly.

One important response to the gradual loss of greenspaces within cities (in addition to protecting a certain green structure that should at some point be considered untouchable) is to actively "green" existing areas of the built environment, as we have seen in many creative examples in the European cities. This includes tree planting, greenroofs, green walls, taking up impervious surfaces, and many of the other greening strategies that have already been in use in a number of the cities studied. These are essential design and planning ingredients, and a necessary companion to compact land development policies.

Certain other environmental goals may come into conflict with developing in a more compact way. Compactness may suggest the need, for example, for building in close proximity to highways (which raises noise problems) or near airports (or other land use uses, which raises public safety issues), or near former industrial sites (which raises questions of exposure of the public to environmental risks, such as contaminated soil). Cities are presented with trade-offs between growing outwardly and growing in ways that support a more sustainable urban form but that raise other concerns about environmental and social risks.

Some creative ways for resolving these dilemmas can be seen in the cities studied. The Netherlands is experimenting with a flexible environmental standards system, under its *stad en milieu* (city and the environment) initiative. Under this program, selected cities around the country are allowed the flexibility at particular sites to supersede certain environmental regulations (such as noise) in order to allow development projects with strong mitigative features to move forward where a strict interpretation of national standards would otherwise prevent them. For example, the CiBoGa project in

Groningen, a former industrial site, is being allowed to move forward with a less-costly soil remediation plan (one-third of the soil will be removed and the rest will remain on site with high containment). Most of the planners and public officials interviewed felt this new flexibility was badly needed, and at the same time would not put the public at any substantial risk.

There are also clearly opportunities to increase density while at the same time enhancing the environmental qualities and overall livability of an area. Amsterdam is attempting to do this in several places. In one area, the city is simultaneously adding housing density while also converting a straight (unnatural) canal into a bending, greener ecological waterway. In the Bijlmermeer area of the city, plans have been developed to provide substantial infill housing and to at the same time "green" the area (e.g., through the creation of green corridors, tree planting). Berlin has been pursuing a similar strategy to green its large housing blocks as a way of enhancing the natural environment and the quality of living environments.

Amsterdam has also made creative use of, for example, an environmental matrix, which helps to sort out these site-specific tradeoffs (see Groot, 1997; Groot and Vermeulen, 1997). Having a strong set of mitigation standards seems to be another important response to this issue. Berlin has such a system under its landscape protection program. Loss of green areas requires extensive compensating actions, including requirements for extensive tree planting (and a system for allocating these trees across the different districts of the city; see City of Berlin, 1996).

It is also important to recognize that there are indeed significant challenges to urban sustainability even in the most progressive, eco-minded cities profiled here. Deconcentration of growth—albeit in a fundamentally more concentrated form than in the United States—remains a serious force and trend, and the accompanying rise in auto usage and dependence are troubling. Car ownership has grown a whopping 40 percent in the United Kingdom since 1980, for example, and car usage in the Netherlands, as noted earlier, is predicted to grow by 70 percent (from 1986 to 2010). These hardly sound like sustainable trends.

Indeed, even in cities that have managed to create, maintain, and strengthen a compact, walkable urban form, there are powerful political forces working in opposite directions. A recent controversy in Groningen, for example, has thrown into question the city's commitment to keeping the automobile out of the city-center. Specifically, there is a proposal in the works in which Vroom and Dreesmann (V&D), a large Dutch department store, is willing to move to the north end of the Grote Markt, substantially renovating a deteriorating building and thus perhaps serving as a catalyst for other private investments in the area. However, V&D wants, as a condition of doing this, to have the city build a parking garage under the Grote Markt. There is considerable opposition to this move, but it is believed that the city will eventually agree to some version of it, accepting more cars in the city-center than desired. Car-ownership growth in Edinburgh, the fastest growth rate in the United Kingdom, was an amazing 57 percent in the decade of 1981 to 1991 (Johnstone, 1998). While this city is doing many positive things, including building a car-free housing estate, there are many forces working against sustainable mobility.

Although many European cities have pursued and are pursuing compact growth policies, and countries such as the Netherlands have adopted a national compact cities policy, there is still an active European debate about the merits and virtues of compact development. Breheny (1997), in reviewing the United Kingdom's plans to divert a significant amount of future growth to brownfield or vacant urban sites, raises several questions about its feasibility and social acceptability. Concerning feasibility, he cites the current demographic and market forces that are pushing in the opposite direction.[1] He also sites survey data suggesting that housing consumers are—like Americans—mostly looking for single-family homes with gardens and space. "Generally, marketing surveys carried out by housebuilders reveal a strong preference for houses with gardens and as much space in both as possible" (p. 213)

Breheny also cites data that suggest higher rates of "satisfaction" among rural residents compared to "urban" residents and an inverse relationship between density and satisfaction (although, it might be added, the satisfaction rates for urban/city-center locations are not especially low). "The compaction logic implies a need to switch from low-density houses to higher-density houses and particularly flats, but the attitude survey suggests that people overwhelmingly prefer houses" (Breheny, 1997, p. 214). Breheny concludes that the proponents of compact cities, at least in the United Kingdom, may face serious obstacles, not unlike many confronted in the United States: "There is it seems a direct conflict between the dedicated compactionists, who promote the virtues of high-density urban living, and humble consumers, who have consistently voted for the opposite, still expressing a preference for decentralized, spacious living" (Breheny, 1997, p. 215; see also Janks, Williams, and Burton, 1996).

Even in countries such as the Netherlands, there is the growing recognition that the city either must adjust its future development decisions to better respond to the wishes and demands of residents or continue to witness the exodus of residents who can find such housing elsewhere. This adjustment in thinking can certainly be seen in some recent development projects, where the type and density of housing is adapted to reflect market conditions.[2] While Europeans are generally more willing to live in denser, compact neighborhoods, many of these cities still face the challenge of balancing compactness with the desire of housing consumers for more space.

Another significant dilemma involves the overall consumption patterns

Table 13.1. Overview of Environmental Space, Actual Consumption and Targets for 2010 for the European Union

Resource	Present use	Environmental	Change	Target 2010	Target 2010
CO$_2$ emissions[1]	7.3t	1.7t	77	5.4t	26
Primary energy use	123GJ	60GJ	50	98GJ	21
Fossil fuels	100GJ	25GJ	75	78GJ	22
Nuclear	16GJ	0GJ	100	0EJ	100
Renewables	7GI	35GI	+400	20GJ	+74
NONRENEWABLE RAW MATERIALS[2]					
Cement	536kg	80kg	85	423kg	21
Pig iron	273kg	36kg	87	213kg	22
Aluminum	12kg	1.2kg	90	9.2kg	23
Chlorine	23kg	0kg	100	17.2kg	25
Land use (EU12)	0.726ha			0.64 ha	12
Arable	0.237ha	0.10ha	58	0.15ha	37
Pasture	0.167ha	0.09ha	47	0.113ha	32
New import of agricultural land	0.037ha	0.00ha	100	0.0185ha	50
"Unused" agricultural area	0.ha			0.047ha	
Unprotected woodland	0.164ha	0.138ha	16	0.138ha	16
Protected area	0.003ha	0.061ha	+1933	0.064ha	+2000
Urban area	0.053ha	0.0513	3.2	0.0513	3.2
Wood[3]	0.66m3	0.56m3	15	0.56m3	15
Water[4]	768m3	n/a	n/a	n/a	n/a

[1] Present use for Europe-NIS, environmental space and target for Europe.
[2] Present use for EU12, environmental space and target for Europe.
[3] EU+ETA+CEE.
[4] The environmental space of water cannot be calculated on a European level.

of the residents of European cities, and the fact that trends at this level may cancel out many of the impressive strides of municipal governments. As Table 13.1 notes, European countries use much more than their fair share of the world's resources (although substantially less than the United States does). And although great strides are being made to promote sustainable architecture and design, and more aggressive energy and waste reduction policies have been adopted, for example, European consumers are simply consuming and using more. Even in these countries (and cities), where concern and awareness about the environment are relatively high, consumption is excessive. More, then, is required, and consumers and producers within cities must be challenged and motivated to do more to curtail consumption and waste.

In cities such as London, there is a special dilemma about whether and how to mitigate its tremendous ecological impacts nationally and internationally. In London, a city that represents a tremendous economic engine, what responsibility the city must assume for the ecological footprint of these activities is a serious issue. The Sustainable London Trust recognizes the immensity of the challenge. Two specific examples are London's role as an international banking center and the resource needs generated by the growing air traffic at Heathrow Airport. In the words of the Trust:

> Then, what about the city's trading and financial activities: How do these affect the living conditions of other people or the health of ecosystems world-wide? For instance, when a banker makes a loan to a foreign business, his decisions have far-reaching repercussions. If London is to become a sustainable city, we have to examine these effects: how can we ensure that landowners and their institutions play a life-enhancing, not life-destroying, role in the world? (Sustainable London Trust, 1997, p. 5)

The London Energy Study found that some 15 percent of London's energy consumption is accounted for by the fuel consumption of air traffic going in and out of the city. Fuel consumption from air traffic has been rising in recent years, from 950,000 tonnes to more than 3 million tonnes (between 1965 and 1991). It is not clear who should be assigned the moral responsibility for this consumption (e.g., airlines or air travelers), but the responsibility arguably is London's in the sense that it is a key element of the local economy strongly influenced by local decisions and policy (e.g., the issue of whether to build a new terminal at Heathrow, which is currently under debate).

The impressive methodological work done in calculating the ecological footprint of city residents, or the environmental space consumed by them, further complicates the dilemma of high consumption and resource use. As these methods effectively show, there are many "hidden" costs associated with high consumption, in that the environmental impacts and depletion implications are felt many miles away. As Folke et al. (1997, p. 171) correctly observe: "One cannot talk about sustainable cities if the ecological resource base on which they depend is excluded from analysis and policy." Reductions in resource demands and waste generation are one needed response, but also raised is the possibility of making "unhidden" these cross-boundary connections and impacts. European cities could begin to exercise greater control over, and interest in, the methods and practices used to provide their resource needs (for example, London imports some 1.2 million tonnes of timber; arrangements could be brokered to encourage or require the provision of these inputs from sustainably harvested forests; Sustainable London Trust, 1997).

Despite these serious challenges and dilemmas, the accomplishments of the very best of these green-urban, or sustainable, European cities are undeniable and impressive. It is hard to find (or imagine) examples that come closer to the ideals expounded in contemporary planning and environmental circles. The fact that even these most exemplary cities may not be truly or fully sustainable—or meet the green-urban conditions outlined in the beginning of this book—should not diminish the value of their experiences. The lessons are considerable. These cities have substantially and seriously reduced their ecological footprints and have shown without a doubt that cities are as much a necessary part of the solution to our environmental predicament as a cause of it. And, despite the obstacles faced along the way, these cities offer tremendous insights and inspiration. Cities such as Leicester, Albertslund, and Freiburg demonstrate that through comprehensive, forward-looking policies and investments, it is possible to create highly livable places, places where community is strengthened, places where land and resources are used sparingly, and places where long-term benefits more than outweigh the short-term costs of programs, policies, and actions. Perhaps most importantly, these cities illustrate the power and potential of reconceptualizing cities as places of nature, connected to nature (in both direct and indirect ways), where the natural environment becomes more than an afterthought. It becomes, rather, a central organizing theme.

Creating Green and Sustainable Cities in the United States: Lessons from Europe

It might be wondered whether what has been accomplished in these most exemplary European cities can also occur in their American counterparts. There is no question that economic, political, geographic, and other circumstances make many of the programs and initiatives described here more feasible in European countries than in the United States. The background context is clearly different in many significant ways. For example, the density of population and the scarcity of land in countries such as the Netherlands make compact city policies much more of a necessity. The much higher price of gasoline, mostly a result of historically higher government taxes, helps to make automobile use more expensive and public transit more attractive. And, the structure and more extensive role of government, and its stronger land use planning function, is also helpful in achieving many of the outcomes described here. Nevertheless, there are many lessons and broad themes that emerge from these European cities, which American planners and public officials should consider. These lessons include the following:

- *A more sustainable urban development model is possible: the promise of ecological living environments*
  Perhaps the clearest lesson from European urban practice is that alternative patterns of growth and development do exist, and it is possible to

organize space and public investments in ways that create compact, walkable, green communities—places that exhibit many highly attractive qualities. Public transit, walking, and bicycle use, under the right circumstances and with the appropriate long-term public policies, can serve as viable alternatives to reliance on the automobile. Substantially less energy and fewer resources can be consumed by citizens, and at the same time personal choice and mobility can be expanded. In short, these European cities, while clearly not perfect and clearly confronting a host of their own problems, show that different, more sustainable future paths do exist. Moreover, collectively the cases have provided substantial guidance about the tools, techniques, methods, and strategies that can be employed in the pursuit of more sustainable paths.

These cities also strongly demonstrate that compact urban form and other sustainable design measures need not conflict with a high quality of life. Indeed, just the opposite is the case. Compact, denser, walkable communities offer tremendous amenities, social and environmental, and are life-enhancing as well as ecologically restorative. A major lesson can be seen in the multiple objectives achieved and in reinforcing agendas possible in these green-urban cities.

This study provides many tangible examples of the benefits and promise of creating ecological neighborhoods and living environments that are both environmentally sustainable and exhibit high qualities of life and a high degree of attractiveness to residents. These environments that are relatively dense, walkable, have access to public transit, incorporate significant elements of green, and include ecological features that significantly reduce their overall ecological footprints. The design and building of these areas have, in many parts of Europe, moved from the realm of experiment to mainstream practice. The environmental, economic, and human benefits of these development practices are considerable, and it should be possible to successfully adapt these models—or at least important elements of them—to American community planning and building.

Many of the cities studied here have taken amazing steps to experiment with and promote ecological housing and development. From the scale of a single home or building to entire new neighborhoods and urban districts, these experiences demonstrate that new urban development can fundamentally reduce its ecological footprint. Moreover, and very importantly, these new ecological neighborhoods and developments can occur in urban settings and can indeed contribute to a broader, more sustainable urban form. This is a lesson that must be learned in the United States. There is a tendency in the American setting to plant our ecological experiments (e.g., witness the ecoburbs and ecovillage movement) in rural or exurban locations, often exacerbating problems of urban sprawl. The European examples discussed here show that *green* and *urban,* on the contrary, can be effectively fused.

- *Sustainable mobility*

  Many of the European cities are grappling with American trends of decentralization and increasing auto use and thus provide special insights and examples. In the face of these trends, cities such as Freiburg, Zürich, and Amsterdam have made major commitments and investments in other, more sustainable modes of mobility and transportation. These European cities provide important models for how American cities can address their transportation problems. The solution is not a simple one, not a silver bullet, but a package of initiatives, which includes commitment to and investment in comprehensive, integrated public transit systems, coordination of land use and transport investment decisions, increasing opportunities for bicyclists and pedestrians, and looking for creative ways to minimize or reduce auto-mobility and reliance. Although some of the models are still experimental, these European cities offer some important ideas about handling mobility in the future, including the use of car-sharing, comprehensive mobility packages, car-free development and housing areas, and financial incentives to reduce car use (e.g., road pricing), among others.

- *Integrated strategies and solutions*

  The hallmark of many of these successful city efforts is the attempt to take an integrated, holistic approach. This is especially clear in the transportation area, where the most impressive cities have adopted and implemented a variety of reinforcing policies and measures. These measures include simultaneously investing in and expanding public transit, expanding bicycle networks and facilities, pedestrianization and traffic calming, aggressive parking restrictions, and locating major new developments near public transit and where walking and bicycling can take place.

  The integration, however, ideally extends beyond individual sectors. Clearly, for example, the ability to achieve more sustainable mobility means enhancing the attractiveness of urban environments by improving the green structure of the city and by enhancing the attractiveness of public spaces, among many other methods. New ideas about car-free or car-minimal developments are creative and promising, but they will ultimately fall short unless human behavior is addressed and modified (e.g., we know from experience that many people will simply find other places to park their cars and will continue to maintain auto-dependent lifestyles). Integrated approaches to green urbanism are essential.

- *Urban metabolism: the city as an organic whole*

  These European cases illustrate the importance of looking at cities as organic wholes—whether through the lens of urban metabolism, ecological footprints, or ecocycle balancing. Cities require substantial environmental inputs (e.g., water, energy, and food) and generate substantial outputs (e.g., waste). Conventional thinking sees this process as essentially linear—inputs are drawn in, outputs flow out. Many of the cities profiled, however, are attempting (many admittedly in the early stages) to connect these inputs and outputs with the promise of reducing long-term ecological impacts, using resources more efficiently, and reducing economic costs. Stockholm's efforts to promote a balanced ecocycles approach is one such promising example.

An equally powerful metaphor is to see the city as a living environment—fundamentally like a forest, or a wetland, or a prairie. These themes have been increasingly important in Europe. The EU's *Green Paper on the Urban Environment* and later the important report of European Sustainable Cities both strongly emphasize an ecosystem's view of cities. The cities profiled here provide a variety of powerful ideas and tangible examples of how to acknowledge and put into practice this view of cities. They range from the impressive urban-ecological structures of Scandinavian cities (such as Helsinki), which bring wild nature almost to the very city-center, to the very important use of greenroofs (eco-roofs) in Germany and the Netherlands, which create new habitats and nature in the most urban and developed of city spaces. American cities, perhaps because the option of horizontal expansion (ever in pursuit of the elusive nature beyond the boundaries of cities) has always existed, have yet to face squarely the challenge of naturalizing or ecologizing urbanity. The Europeans have not always done it completely or perfectly but they are, nevertheless, on the better course.

- *The shift toward renewable energy cities*

Although there is certainly much still to be done, there are now many positive examples of cities (and national governments) actively promoting a shift toward renewable forms of energy. The support for solar energy is particularly instructive, with governments such as Germany's and the Netherlands' providing significant financial support (as is the European Commission). Development projects such as Nieuwland in Amersfoort, in which a very high percentage of the homes will incorporate some combination of active and passive solar, are impressive and should be emulated here in the United States. Through a mixture of energy conservation and support of renewables, cities and settlements can significantly reduce their overall ecological footprint and make a significant contribution to addressing global climate change.

The integration of and support for solar energy, and a sense of the need to fundamentally move away from dependence on local fuels, are especially impressive in many of these European cities. Organizing entire new residential districts around solar energy, such as in the case of the new solar city in Linz, as well as Nieuwland in Amersfoort, represents extremely forward-looking thinking. Increasingly, it seems, in these most progressive European cities, every new civic building or school represents an opportunity to incorporate new solar and low-energy design strategies. There is a great missed opportunity in American cities to seriously embrace the renewables agenda. Cities in the American Southwest, for example, whose economies and infrastructure could be essentially driven by solar power, seem to have little interest in this (ubiquitous) renewable energy source.

- *The importance of reinforcing actions at each scale; the importance of connections and linkages*
The cases illustrate the importance of reinforcing actions and policies at different jurisdictional levels and geographical scales. Ecological design features at the building or project scale can significantly reduce overall energy or resource demands (e.g., through insulation and passive solar). At a regional or extra-regional level, however, efforts are needed to develop renewable energy resources (e.g., wind energy in Bologna). More sustainable forms of transportation and mobility depend on actions at both a project or neighborhood level (e.g., designing for pedestrians and bicycles and de-emphasizing automobiles) and metropolitan and regional levels (e.g., public transit investments and improvements). Creative attention at each scale is critical to the outcome of creating sustainable places.

Almost all of the cities are working to enhance mobility through a strategy of linkages and connections, which take several forms. One form is the spatial connections between different neighborhoods and districts in the city. In most of the bicycle-friendly cities studied, the urban bike network links up with recreational routes, making it relatively easy to get to more open expanses of land and nature. An emphasis placed on connectedness pays tremendous dividends in these cities.

Attention to detail is another part of the story. For example, while there are many larger locational decisions and land use and infrastructural policies that explain more sustainable transportation systems, one is struck by the attention to detail at every planning level and the important cumulative effect this has. As the tram systems in cities such as Freiburg effectively show, enticing people to use public transit is often a result of the cumulative effect of lots of actions that make it easy and enjoyable to use this mode. Positive design details include comfortable seat configurations, easy ticket purchase and use, real-time reporting of when the next tram will arrive, low-carriage cars for easy loading and unloading, and so forth.

Facilitating the use of bicycles is similarly a matter of detailing, including the many individual design considerations that make bicyclists feel safe, such as the physical separation of cars and bikes, separate traffic lighting for bicycles, special painted surfaces (e.g., the red bike lanes in

Heidelberg and elsewhere), and actions to slow and calm auto traffic. Signage can also be very important and is another example of importance of attention to details. Improving signage includes effective efforts to educate riders about the best and most direct routes to key destinations. If they know how to get to the city-center or to the library or to their place of employment without engaging in a complicated exercise in map-reading, this is a further enticement. Enhancing the speed of mobility is also a matter of details. Cities such as Münster have been able to make cycle commuting attractive because it is fast. Münster has worked aggressively at providing shortcuts for bikes that auto traffic does not enjoy, for example. In a host of these cities, and in a variety of ways, attention to these kinds of design details pays off.

- *Advances in sustainability through partnerships*
Many of the city case studies, and perhaps the European approach more generally, reflect a spirit of collaboration between the industrial and business communities, and government. There appears to be less antagonism and divisiveness between these groups and a sense of the mutuality of their objectives and agendas. This certainly is partly cultural (consider the experiences of the Dutch and the consensus-based nature of their society), but local governments can clearly make the choice to include and collaborate with business in pursuit of sustainability.

Cities such as Leicester have successfully built partnerships among the city, community groups, and the media. Leicester's Turning the Tide Campaign is actually guided by a so-called "Partnership Board." The close involvement of the media has been especially important in helping to get the word out about more sustainable lifestyles and practices. Leicester's Quality Bus Partnership, a collaborative effort with bus operators to improve service, is yet another example. Universities can also be important partners (e.g., consider the positive role played by De Montfort University's Institute for Energy and Sustainable Development, in Leicester). Many of the case cities provide similar positive examples. Successful partnering is clearly a touchstone in these sustainable cities.

In the Netherlands, the National Environmental Policy Plan (NEPP) is fundamentally based on the assumption of collaboration, cooperation, and partnership between government, industry, and other elements of society. The NEPP is directed at specific target groups who generally enter into dialogue and negotiation, resulting in tangible targets that the groups agree to work to achieve. The national government and the construction industry, for example, have worked closely together in developing a set of quantitative targets and measures that will be voluntarily undertaken by the industry. These targets are ambitious and call for sizeable reductions in the use of nonrenewable raw materials, reuse of construction and demolition waste, use of tropical hardwoods only from sustainably harvested sources, reduction in use of solvent paints, and reduction in energy use in new buildings, among others (see VROM, 1994). Similar agreements have been made with other sectors in the Netherlands.

- *Engaging target groups; collaborative, interdisciplinary approaches*
The case studies here illustrate that movement toward a more sustainable society requires efforts and actions by a variety of groups in society, including industry, government, and consumers, among others. Different initiatives and creative approaches are needed to involve and engage these different target groups. Programs such as Graz's ECOPROFIT, for instance, recognize the importance of engaging the industrial and business sectors. The use of eco-teams, a concept pioneered and promoted in a number of cities by Global Action Plan, addresses the changes needed in personal and household consumption. Each of these different groups in society will need to be involved in crafting a more sustainable future.

Many of the most successful urban sustainability initiatives documented in this study, moreover, are the direct result of collaboration among and between different actors and groups in the community, and of the collaborative involvement of different professions and disciplines. The sustainable housing projects being built in the Netherlands, Denmark, and other countries are possible in large part because they explicitly involve environmental planners and local environmental departments early in their design, as well as engineers, developers, and housing associations. There is a creativity and attention to multiple factors that results from these interdisciplinary processes.

Indeed, the extensive local Agenda 21 initiatives under way in many European cities exemplify a collaborative philosophy. Process is very important, and efforts are made to reach out to local businesses, neighborhoods, and public and private sector organizations of all sorts. Much of the policy development work has typically occurred through sector working groups, which are collaborative by design.

Working to promote ecocycle balancing in most cities requires efforts to break down the administrative and disciplinary boundaries of different city agencies and departments. The water company must be willing to talk and work with the city energy company, which must be willing to work with the waste management agency or company, and so on. Although certainly a challenge, effectively developing more sustainable material and energy flows in a city requires overcoming these obstacles.

In Hammarby Sjöstad in Stockholm, involvement of the Stockholm energy company is essential in designing an efficient, sustainable energy strategy for this new district. Involvement of the waste company, from which biofuels will be extracted and used for energy, is also essential. In this way, these companies and utilities are encouraged to think beyond their traditional narrow roles as providers of energy, water, and so forth. Their role is redefined as one of providing a desired service rather than a specific good or product.

- *A shift from products to services in the urban environment*
A significant lesson illustrated by many of these innovative city programs is the importance of a shift in thinking from the provision of *products* or material goods to the provision of the actual *services* or benefits resulting from them. This is a commonly heralded shift among environmentalists in the United States, but rarely do we see evidence of this at an urban level as we do in Europe. The result can clearly be less environmental damage and greater cost-efficiency when focusing on the desired service or benefit, rather than on a specific product. Examples include the promising approach of focusing on the provision of "mobility" rather than on accommodating auto traffic, as well as any specific form of transportation service. Projects such as Amsterdam's IJburg development have the potential of satisfying through mobility packages the movement needs of residents, while minimizing the use of automobiles. The car-sharing services that have developed in many cities in Europe are a similar example. It can be argued that it is not specifically an automobile that people desire or need, but the mobility services provided by them. Car-sharing companies provide the service without product ownership per se. Yet another example can be seen in the innovative public bike programs in Copenhagen, Amsterdam, and other cities.

Europe leads the way, as well, in building economies where goods and materials are recycled and reused, and where companies are increasingly expected to take back their products at the end of their useful life. Whether in the form of a recyclable subway car (as in Stockholm), a recyclable hotel room (e.g., in Scandic hotels), or recyclable industrial landscapes (e.g., Emscher Park), an emphasis on reuse and recycling can be seen in many places and in many ways. This is major lesson for a sustainable society.

- *Making sustainability profitable*
Related to the importance of emphasizing the multiple benefits of sustainable city initiatives is the idea that cities can structure these initiatives in ways that are perhaps not always economically profitable but that at least pay for themselves in the long or even the short term. Examples of such programs include Heidelberg's creative approach to contracting for energy reduction in its city buildings. The idea of hiring a mobility manager (as in several London boroughs) whose salary is paid for out of savings in transportation costs is another example.

Another method is to create positive incentives for users to reduce resource consumption. Several cities, including Heidelberg and Münster, have school energy conservation programs that create incentives for school administrators to find ways to reduce consumption and waste by allowing them to keep a portion of the savings. In Münster, for example, schools can keep half of the energy savings that result, using these funds for books, computers, or other school-related needs. These experiences provide important insights about how to structure similar green-urban initiatives in the United States.

In still other ways, many of these cities have recognized that sustainability is a profitable economic development path. Denmark (at both national and local levels) has recognized the significant economic niche it holds (and can further develop) in the areas of ecological technologies and services. A major shift to wind energy in that country makes sense for environmental and energy security reasons, but it also strengthens and develops a technology sector in which the Danes are leading globally. Green City Denmark is a marvelous example of an effort to economically capitalize on this country's leadership and innovation in sustainable development. In a host of green-urban economic sectors, the Europeans recognize that sustainability can enhance economic growth, competitiveness, and profitability.

- *Ecological governance*
The cities described in this book effectively illustrate that municipal governments can reform *themselves*—their purchasing, building, employee management, and other policies—to significantly reduce use of resources and promote sustainability. A number of creative and far-reaching internal reforms have been undertaken by case communities (and discussed extensively in this book). A common first step is to conduct an extensive audit of the environmental effects of local government policies and decisions and to prepare a local state-of-the-environment study.

The case cities examined in this study have developed and are using extensive systems of local sustainability indicators and targets. From Den Haag to London to Albertslund, these techniques have been shown to have considerable importance in making urban sustainability tangible; linking environmental, economic, and social issues; and clarifying goals for the future.

A lesson repeatedly stated by many interviewees was the importance of local governments setting positive examples at the local level, along with the need for local authorities to take their own serious actions to promote sustainability before proselytizing about what its citizens, businesses, and private organizations should or must do. Such actions are seen as an essential step in ensuring the credibility of the municipality, as well as a matter of fairness.

What is also especially impressive is the more proactive stance assumed by the best of these three green-urban cities. Saarbrücken has taken major proactive initiatives to grow and support a solar energy industry, for example. Stockholm's environmental vehicle initiatives is in large part about stimulating and strengthening a local market for such vehicles. Graz has made exemplary strides in proactively working with local industries to help them become more energy efficient and less polluting. In a host of ways, these cities show the virtues of creative, proactive policies. Government in these cities is not seen as laissez-faire or caretaking in nature, but as an entity exercising important proactive leadership; it is a pacesetter, not a follower or a spectator.

- *The importance of economic signals and incentives for green-urban living*
The green-urban cities profiled here also highlight the important role played by economic signals and incentives, and the direction and type of public investments made. Higher gasoline prices, higher costs associated with auto ownership and use, and the increasing use of green taxes in Europe all help to reinforce more sustainable patterns of land and resource use in these cities. The willingness by these cities (and countries) to invest substantially in public transit is a further example. Such investment also fundamentally shape individual, family, and corporate decisions.

The lessons for the United States are perhaps difficult to embrace politically, but they do suggest that, to a large degree, what is necessary is the shifting of economic incentives and signals (e.g., at least a modest increase in gas taxes, perhaps to more fully fund transit and high-speed rail). These actions represent the conscious decisions of a society to ensure that prices more accurately reflect the true costs of personal choices and behavior and create positive inducements for more sustainable lifestyles.

- *The role of demonstration and experimentation*
The cities examined here have in common a history of creative experimentation with new ideas, new tools, and new strategies. Together, these green-urban cities show how powerful a spirit of experimentation can be, as well as how important this experimentation can be in setting new directions. This study has uncovered numerous demonstration projects sponsored by national and local governments. These demonstration projects, taken as a whole, appear to have played an extremely important role in shaping perception about what actions and policies are possible and feasible. Examples of valuable demonstration projects include Ecolonia (an innovative residential housing project in the Netherlands, sponsored in part by a national group committed to promoting housing innovation), Stockholm's environmental vehicles program and Heidelburg's minimum energy social housing project, among many others. Not only do such efforts effectively illustrate the technical feasibility of par-

ticular sustainability ideas, but they also help to constructively push private companies and markets along in the direction of such new ideas. They can serve as both examples and market catalysts.

Experimentation is often used as an alternative to wholesale (and sometimes premature) adoption of a measure or technology. It permits the waters to be tested and for concerns to be watched, as well as provides a chance for support for a new idea to emerge. Some of the most innovative programs and practices documented here began as test trials, through limited experimentation. Many of these cities have demonstrated the critical importance of research and evaluation studies. Often these studies have helped to deflect unfair skepticism about sustainability practices, as well as to provide tangible guidance about how and in what ways existing programs should be modified.

- *Technology and people*
The experiences of European cities in grappling with sustainability and the green-urban agenda suggest that the challenge is both about technology and people. Attention to both will be needed and, indeed, as these many European initiatives show, one form of solution will not be successful without the other. European cities, as we have seen, are investing in, utilizing, and experimenting with a host of sustainability technologies, including photovoltaics, wind energy, sustainable building techniques, and public bicycle—depot systems, among many others. These innovative techniques, products, and technologies are potentially powerful in their ability to fundamentally reduce environmental impacts while at the same time making life easier and more enjoyable. The Europeans demonstrate convincingly the importance of underwriting and supporting the development and application of these technological innovations.

At the same time, there is a clear recognition that moving people's hearts and changing their behavior are also necessary ingredients. The creative environmental education and consumption-reduction initiatives described in these pages—such as the GAP eco-teams and the United Kingdom's Going for Green initiatives—reflect the central importance given to the social and human element. And, indeed, the extensive local Agenda 21 programs under way in many communities further demonstrate a commitment to community participation, grassroots involvement, and an emphasis on people and community. These are important themes in European green-urban cities, for which emphasis on both technology and people is critical.

Many of the European cities' experiences further demonstrate that technology requires attention to the human users for it to be effective. Numerous examples have emerged, such as in the area of innovative sustainable building technology. Creating special areas for car-washing in Ecolonia (thus separating out this harmful waste stream from water that would normally drain into the community lake) is an idea that sounds good on paper, but if residents do not understand the purpose or need for this device, they are not likely to use it (which was indeed the case). As a further example, research suggests that residents of the Dutch ecological housing project Morra Park did not understand the purpose of the *serres* (sunrooms) attached to their homes. As a consequence, many residents attempted to heat these spaces and to treat them as year-round living areas. Perhaps partly faulty design, this passive design strategy clearly failed at the level of human use. Indeed, the emphasis on educating residents in new ecological housing projects reflects this understanding that human use and behavior are essential elements if the environmental goals behind technology and design innovation are to be realized.

- *City networks and peer recognition*

European cities benefit greatly from the existence of a number of supportive networks or associations of communities and cities that deal with local sustainability issues. Among these are the International Council for Local Environmental Initiatives (ICLEI, with its European Secretariat in Freiburg), Eurocities, and Car Free Cities, among others. These organizations serve a number of useful functions, including lobbying, technical assistance, and publication and dissemination of information about what different communities are doing. And there are also a number of EU-funded programs that further support information dissemination and collaboration between cities and the development of demonstration programs.

Ultimately, the adoption and successful implementation of sustainable practices is a matter of political (and popular) support, and the European context is no different. In this regard, recognition of the accomplishment by a city, or the prospect of this recognition in the future, has proven to be an important influence on the European cities studied. This recognition has occurred in recent years through several mechanisms. In some countries, notably Germany, Denmark, and the United Kingdom, programs have existed for recognizing and issuing awards for special achievement in environmental management. In Germany, a city is chosen each year and designated as the "ecological city" by the well-respected environmental group Deutsche Umwelthilfe. In fact, not only is the top city chosen, but a detailed environmental ranking of cities is also published (see Deutsche Umwelthilfe, undated). A similar ranking is published in Denmark (by the environmental group Danmarks Naturfredningsforening). In the United Kingdom, five cities have been designated "Environment Cities," beginning with Leicester in 1990. Although not an annual designation, the recognition given is quite similar. The program is cosponsored by the Royal Society for Nature Conservation (RSNC), the Wildlife Trust Partnership, and the Leicester Ecology Trust.

More recently, and on an European scale, is the creation of the annual sustainable city award, presented by the European Sustainable Cities and Towns Campaign. The value of these awards is certainly debatable, but interviewees frequently mentioned the awards and there is considerable evidence of their political and other value. They do seem to enhance the position of those promoting sustainability locally and to make the adoption and implementation of sustainability measures that much easier. Cities are clearly using these awards and are proud of receiving them. The attractiveness of the Sustainable Cities and Town Campaign award is further enhanced by the ability to use the award logo on official city stationery and other promotional purposes.

- *The role of national programs, leadership, and coordination*
A major factor helping to explain the creative and bold initiatives in the cities examined has been the pull and the push of governmental units at higher levels, and especially the existence of strong national initiatives. The examples are numerous and can be seen in virtually every sector (such as transportation, energy, and waste management). The financial and other forms of support and encouragement are substantial and should not be underestimated. European national governments, especially those of northern European nations, are not timid in taking the initiative in solving problems of unsustainable development, and they frequently have developed ambitious national goals, plans, and programs, from which this assistance flows.

Examples of national sustainability initiatives that have stimulated or facilitated local programs are numerous. Most countries have prepared national sustainable development plans under Agenda 21, laying a foundation for local actions. The Netherlands government, for example, has national-level strategies and action plans that are backed by substantial funding and that promote a host of sustainable practices and technologies. As mentioned, there is an ambitious strategy for promoting sustainable building nationwide. Similarly, programs exist for promoting bicycle use (see Welleman, undated). In Denmark, tremendous national leadership can be seen in promoting and investing in wind power and other renewable energy technologies of the future. Numerous examples of critical national leadership can be cited.

Important financial incentives are often provided at the national level. The Netherlands has creatively harnessed the power of the tax code by, for example, providing investors in green projects with tax-free status, as well as generating substantial new capital to support sustainable building and other practices. European national governments have adopted carbon and other eco-taxes that encourage more sustainable use of land and water and eco-cycle balancing in cities and households.

The adoption of strong national codes and standards also explains some of the good progress that has been made. Countries such as Denmark, Germany, and the Netherlands have adopted strong energy codes for new housing, for example.

In the area of spatial planning, local initiatives are helped greatly by the existence in many countries of a national development strategy or plan. In the Netherlands, a national compact cities strategy has been effectively advanced, providing a broad structure in which provincial and local planning occurs. Numerous and significant locational decisions have further reinforced this policy and its A-B-C transportation/land use strategy has been a similarly important aid. And symbolically important has been the decision to consolidate the headquarters of the Dutch Ministry of Housing, Spatial Planning and Environment (VROM) in a new building directly adjacent to the main train terminal in Den Haag an "A" location.)

In turn, national spatial plans serve as the basis for more logical, coordinated investment decisions at the national level, as in the form of new, high-speed rail lines or a new justice complex.[3] In numerous ways, the examples in this book show the power and impact of strong national leadership in setting out basic conditions and a supportive climate in which many green-urban cities and green-urban initiatives can occur.

A Final Note: From Aalborg to Austin

While there are few perfect or complete examples of sustainable or green-urban cities among the European examples discussed here, there are many important ideas and initiatives to educate and inspire American planners, elected officials, and citizens. What is perhaps most obvious from this book is the utility of the continued exchange of experience and ideas. It has been especially surprising to me that few of these European urban experiences are discussed or incorporated into U.S. schools of planning and architecture, and that American professionals in these areas are not more familiar (if at all) with these initiatives. And, although the emphasis of this book has been on learning from Europe, there are clearly important lessons and experiences to flow in the other direction.

Also obvious is the need to further nurture and develop closer European–American urban sustainability ties. These ties could take many forms, including course offerings in American (and European) planning schools, exchanges of faculty and students (which already occur to some extent), and green-urban study tours. From the point of view of this author, the education of every aspiring American planner should involve at least a modicum of direct exposure to the experiences of these European cities.

In conclusion, it is important to recognize the common lessons of both American and European experiences, namely that in this period of global environmental crisis, cities represent perhaps the best hope and the most compelling opportunities we have for moving society in the direction of sustainability. While viewed by many as more the problem than the solution, the many positive examples of this book show definitively that cities can be the source of tremendous innovation and inspiration and can provide the essential foundations for a truly sustainable life and culture. Any future vision of a sustainable planet must be necessarily and undeniably a *green-urban vision*—one in which at the core are cities that are truly ecological, restorative, and uplifting.

NOTES

1. As Breheny (1997) observes: "The decentralized focus of economic activity over the last 20 years or so is regarded by many commentators as a profound shift in economic geography, and one to be observed in many western countries. If this is true, then it may be very difficult, if not impossible, to impose a new contrasting logic that requires industry to return to the very places that it has abandoned on ignored" (p. 211).

2. For example, the Piccardthofplas in Groningen mostly consists of single-family detached units, and a portion of the units are in villa housing. As well, it is envisioned that in the future the areas north of the center of this city, which have been problem areas with a high number of flats and a concentration of minorities and lower-income residents, will be targeted for some degree of demolition; some flats are to be replaced with single-family attached units, with gardens and other amenities (still relatively high density, but closer to what residents appear to want in the way of new housing).

3. National policy and legislation can also work against local sustainability, of course, and there are also examples of this. In cities in countries that have undergone extensive privatization, notably the United Kingdom, interviewees held strong opinions that the privatization had undermined sustainability. Interviewees were critical, for example, of the service levels provided by the private bus companies. Here, the privatization ethos is believed to have reduced the public control and leverage over many sectors that influence sustainability. Most car parks, for instance, are privately owned, and cities (such as Leicester) have no control over setting prices in these facilities (they would like to increase the parking rates). Also, municipalities in the United Kingdom do not own their own energy companies, unlike in Germany and other countries in this study. National energy policy may have similar results, it is believed. In the United Kingdom, many believe that the national effort to encourage construction of natural gas–fired power plants (the so-called "dash for the gas") works against more sustainable long-term solutions to the energy problem (including conservation and promoting development of renewable energy sources).

References

Aaberg, Hjalte. 1997. "Agenda for Environmental Sustainability—The Case of Albertslund." Paper presented to Sustainable Cities Conference, Stockholm, June.

Albertslund Kommune. 1995. *Grout Reguskab 1995*. Albertslund: Albertslund Kommune.

Alterman, Rachelle. 1997. "The Challenge of Farmland Preservation: Lessons from a Six-Nation Comparison." *Journal of the American Planning Association*, Spring, Vol. 63, No. 2, pp. 220–243.

Amesberger, Gunter. 1998. "Austria's new solar city takes shape." *Renewable Energy*, July, pp. 54–56.

Apgar, Mahlon IV. 1998. "The Alternative Workplace: Changing Where and How People Work." *Harvard Business Review*, May–June, Vol. 76, p. 121.

Arhus Kommune. 1997. "Cykelbus'ters I Arhus." September.

Arhus Kommune. 1998. "Ta'cyclen i Arhus." January.

Arlidge, John. 1997. "Green Homes for People without Cars." *The Guardian Weekly*, April 27, p. 30.

Associated Press. 1999. "Norway: New Malls Banned," *The Gazette* (Montreal), January 9, p. A16.

Association of Finnish Local Authorities. 1996. *Learning New Skills: Finnish Municipalities Towards Sustainability*. Helsinki: Association of Finnish Local Authorities.

Association of Finnish Local Authorities. 1996. *Making Future Now: Good Practices in Finland*. Helsinki: Association of Finnish Local Authorities.

Aubrey, Chrispen. 1994. "Letting the Grass Grow Over Their Heads." *The Daily Telegraph*, June 18, p. 3

Baines, Chris. 1998. "Trees of Time and Place." *Urban Wildlife News*, Vol. 15, No. 1, February, pp. 2–3.

Bakker, Marien. 1996. "The State of Car-Sharing 'Call-a-Car' in the Netherlands." Paper presented to ACT '96 Conference, Denver.

Baltimore Urban Resources Initiative. 1997. "Baltimore City Government and the Management of Vacant Lots and Open Space." Draft report, September.

Beatley, Timothy, David J. Brower, and William Lucy. 1994. "Representation in Comprehensive Planning: An Analysis of the Austinplan Process." *Journal of the American Planning Association,* Spring, Vol. 60, pp. 185–196.

Beatley, Timothy, and Kristy Manning. 1997. *The Ecology of Place: Planning for Environment, Economy and Community.* Washington, DC: Island Press.

Beckman, Stephanie, Sev Jones, Kevin Liburdy, and Connie Peters. 1997. "Greening Our Cities: An Analysis of the Benefits and Barriers Associated with Green Roofs." Portland, OR: Portland State University, Planning Workshop.

Benjamin, Mark. 1997. "Natuurlijk." *De Dordtenaar,* December 5.

Ben-Joseph, Evan. 1995. "Changing the Residential Street Scene: Adapting the Shared Street (Woonerf) Concept to the Suburban Environment." *Journal of the American Planning Association,* Vol. 61, No. 4, Autumn, pp. 504–515.

Bentley, I., A. Alcock, P. Murrain, S. McGlynn, and G. Smith. 1995. *Responsive Environments.* London: Architectural Press.

Berents, Roy. 1998. "Duurzaam Bouwen." *Plan Amsterdam,* No.4, dienst Ruimtelijke Ordening, Gemeente Amsterdam.

Berger, John J. 1997. *Charging Ahead: The Business of Renewable Energy and What It Means for America.* New York: Henry Holt.

Berger, Paul, and Alex Borer. 1994. "The 'Nature Around the Schoolhouse' Project." *Anthos,* February, pp. 72–75.

Berggrund, Lars. 1996. "Göteburg, Sweden: Ecocycles in the Urban System." In *LA 21 Planning Guide.* Freiburg, Germany: ICLEI.

Berlin Senate. 1996. "Berlin Hellersdorf District: A Sustainable Strategy for Industrially Pre-fabricated Housing Developments." March.

Bernick, Michael, and Robert Cervero. 1997. *Transit Villages in the 21st Century.* New York: McGraw-Hill.

Bigness, Jon. 1998. "CTA Making Fare Cards Smarter." *Chicago Tribune,* March 5, Business section, p. 1.

BINE. 1994. "The Freiburg Self Sufficient Solar House," Freiburg: BINE.

Bjornskov, Leo. 1995. "The Challenge of the Urban Environment." In *The European City—Sustaining Urban Quality.* Copenhagen: Conference proceedings. Danish Ministry of the Environment and Energy.

Blake, Laurie. 1998. "Lessons from a Toll-lane Flop: Official Looks Back on Missteps in Plan to Ease I-394 Congestion," *Star Tribune* (Minneapolis), May 28, p. 2B.

BMW. Undated. *Environmental Report.*

Boplats. 1996. *Urban Development in an Ecocycles Adapted Industrial Society.* Stockholm: Swedish Council for Building Research.

Boverket. 1995. *The Ecological City.* The Swedish Report to OECD, National Board of Housing, Building, and Planning Karlskrona, Sweden.

Bowlin, Mike R. 1999. "Clean Energy: Preparing Today for Tomorrow's Challenges." Remarks presented at Cambridge Energy Research Associates (CER) 18th Annual Executive Conference: Globality & Energy: Strategies for the New Millennium, February 9, Houston.

Boyes, Roger. 1997. "Green Cities Drive Out Plague of Cars," *The Times* (London), June 25.

Brabants Dagblad. 1996. "Natuurmonumenten wil wildviaduct Loon op Zand," *Brabants Dagblad,* March 2, pp. 1 and 17.

Bradbury, Hilary. 1996. "The Swedish Natural Step: A Model for Sustainable Transformation." Website: learning.mit.edu

Bradshaw, Martin. 1996. "Vitality and Variety." In D. Chapman ed., *Creating Neighborhoods and Places in the Built Environment,* New York: Routledge.

Breheny, Michael. 1997. "Urban Compaction: Feasible and Acceptable?" *Cities,* Vol. 14, No. 4, pp. 209–217.

Bristol United Press. 1997. "Pedal Power for Council Workers." *British Evening Post,* November 24, p. 14.

Brooke, James. 1998. "Denver Stands Out in Trend Toward Living Downtown." *The New York Times,* December 29.

Brouwers, Joost, Eric Harms, Jan Juffermans, Willem Koetsenruijter, and Harrie Perebooms. 1998. *De Duurzame Stad.* Best, Netherlands: Aeneas.

Brown, Patricia Leigh. 1998. "It Takes a Pioneer to Save a Prairie." *New York Times,* September 10, p. D1.

Brussaard, Wim. 1991. "Protecting Agricultural Resources in Europe: A Report from the Netherlands." *Indiana Law Review,* Vol. 24, pp. 1525–1542.

Building and Social Housing Foundation. 1996. *World Habitat Awards 1990–1994,* Leicestershire, U.K.: Building and Social Housing Foundation.

Building Design. 1998. "Green Roofs Come of Age." *Building Design,* February 27, p. 24.

BUND. 1995. "Freiburg, Germany: Measures in All Areas of Transport Policy Form Effective, Ecologically-Oriented City-Wide Concept." Technical report, Freiburg, Germany.

Bunde, Jorgen. 1997. "The BikeBus'ters from Arhus, Denmark: We'll Park Our Cars for 200 years . . ." In Rodney Tolley, ed., *The Greening of Urban Transport: Planning for Walking and Cycling in Western Cities.* New York: John Wiley and Sons.

Burke, Maria. 1997. "Environmental Taxes Gaining Grand in Europe." *Environmental Science and Technology News,* Vol. 31, No. 2, pp. 84–88.

Bynes, Susan. 1997. "A Choice in How Seattle Grows." *The Seattle Times.* November 2.

CADDET. 1997. "Solar Panels Supplement District Heating in Denmark." Oxfordshire, UK: CADDET Centre for Renewable Energy.

Callenbach, Ernest. 1996. *Bring Back the Buffalo! A Sustainable Future for America's Great Plains.* Washington, D.C.: Island Press.

Canada Mortgage and Housing Corporation. Undated. "CMHC's Healthy House in Toronto." Ottawa, ON.

Car Free Cities Coordination Office. Undated. "About Car Free Cities." Website: http://www.edc.eu.int/cfc/cfcset.html

Car Sharing Portland, Inc. Undated. "Car Sharing Is the New Way to Drive in Portland." Website: http://www.carsharing-pdx.com

Cervero, Robert. 1994. "Transit Villages: From Idea to Implementation." *Access,* No. 5, Fall, pp. 8–14.

Cervero, Robert. 1995. "Sustainable New Towns: Stockholm's Rail-Served Satellites." *Cities,* Vol. 12, No. 1, pp. 41–51.

Chattanooga Institute. Undated. "SMART Park Eco-Industrial Initiative." Website: http://www.csc2.org

Chattanooga News Bureau. 1997. "Chattanooga's Electric Bus Initiative." Website: http://www.csc2.org

Chattanooga News Bureau. 1997. "Vice President Gore Praises Chattanooga 'Smart Growth' Initiatives." Website: http://www.csc2.org.

City of Amsterdam. 1994. *A City in Progress: Physical Planning in Amsterdam.* Amsterdam, The Netherlands: dienst Ruimtelijke Ordening.

City of Austin. Undated-a. "CIP Sustainability Matrix." *Information and Guidelines.*

City of Austin. Undated-b. "Short and Long Range Activities of the Sustainable Communities Initiative."

City of Austin. 1998a. "Current Sustainable City News." *Sustainable Communities,* Vol. 1, No. 2, Spring.

City of Austin. 1998b. "Current Sustainable City News." *Sustainable Communities,* Vol. 1, No. 3, Fall.

City of Berlin. 1996. "Environmental Strategies for Berlin." Berlin: Ministry of Urban Development, Environmental Protection and Technology.

City of Boulder. Undated. *Greenpoints Program: Guidelines for Resource Conservation Ordinance.* Boulder, CO: Office of Environmental Affairs.

City of Copenhagen. 1996. "Copenhagen Traffic: Plans and Visions." City Engineering Directorate.

City of Davis. Undated. "Parking lot shading guidelines and master parking lot tree list guidelines."

City of Göteburg. Undated. "The Farms and Farmlands in and around the City."

City of Groningen. 1997. "CiBoGa Site Groningen: A Breakthrough in Environmental Quality in the Densely-Populated City." Groningen Local Authority and Buro Nieuwe Gracht, March.

City of Helsinki. 1995. "Biodiversity, Strategy for Urban Nature in Helsinki." Helsinki Environment Department.

City of Helsinki. 1996. "Sustainable Development Principles for City Planning in Helsinki." Helsinki City Planning Department.

City of Helsinki. Undated. "Viikki Ecological Neighborhood." Helsinki City Planning Department.

City of Palm Springs. 1998. "News Release." Department of Transportation, May 6.

City of Portland. 1999. "Peer Review Analysis of the Traffic Circle Program." Office of Transportation.

City of Stockholm. Undated-a. "Hammarby Sjöstad: Leading the World in Ecological, Environmentally-Adapted Construction and Housing."

City of Stockholm. Undated-b. "An Environmental Program for Hammarby Sjöstad."

City of Stockholm. 1996. *Stodens Utveckling*, Stadsbyggnads Kontoret.

City of Stockholm. 1997. "Summary of the Impact Assessments from Best Practices—The City of Stockholm." Agenda 21 Program.

City of the Hague. 1996. "The Hague New Centre: From the Planning to the Project Stage." July.

City of Vienna. 1992. "The Environment in Vienna." Vienna Press and Information Agency.

City of Vienna. 1993. "Vienna: Launching into a New Era." June.

City of West Palm Beach, Florida, 1996. "City Transportation Language Policy." Memo to department directors and division heads, from Michael Wright, city manager, November 14.

City of Zürich. 1995. "Environmental Policy of the City of Zürich: Local Agenda 21." City of Zürich Department of Health and Environment, October.

Collier, Ute, and Ragner E. Löfstedt. 1997. "Think Globally, Act Locally? Local Climate Change and Energy Policies in Sweden and the U.K." *Global Environmental Changes*, Vol. 7, No. 1, pp. 25–40.

Comfort. 1996. "Hoe kom je zonder gas de winter door?" *Comfort*, magazine of Cooperative energie Cominatie U.A., February, pp. 12–13.

Commission of the European Communities. 1990. *Green Paper on the Urban Environment.* Brussels.

Conservation Engineering Limited, in collaboration with Dublin Corporation, Temple Bar Properties Limited. Undated. "Combined Heat and Power: Clean, Economic Energy for Dublin Corporation Civic Offices and Neighboring Buildings."

Cote, Ray. 1997. "Industrial Ecosystems: Evolving and Maturing." *Journal of Industrial Ecology*, Summer, pp. 9–12.

Curtius, Mary. 1998a. "Town Goes with the Low-tech Flow." *L.A. Times*, November 30, p. A3.

Curtius, Mary. 1998b. "How the Greens Got the Blues." *L.A. Times*, October 9, p. A3.

Daimler-Benz, A. G. 1998. "Stockholm's Green Metro." *Environmental Magazine*.

Damm, Michael. 1998. "Tools for Implementing Local Agenda 21—How Does One Involve the Public?" Municipality of Kolding.

Danish Energy Agency. 1998. "Combined Heat and Power in Denmark." Copenhagen, May.

Danish Ministry of Environment and Energy. 1995. *The European City—Sustaining Urban Quality.* Working conference, Copenhagen, April, Spatial Planning Department.

Danish Ministry of Foreign Affairs. 1996. *The Danish National Report to Habitat II.* Also co-issued by Danish Ministry of Housing and Building, and Environment and Energy, March.

Danish Town Planning Institute. 1996. *Urban Ecology Guide—Greater Copenhagen.* Danish Town Planning Institute, Copenhagen.

Danmarks Naturfredningsforening. 1997. *Grone Realiteter: 1 kommunerne 1996-1998.* Kobenhavn: Danmarks Naturfredningsforening.

Davies, H. W. E. 1989. "Development Control in the Netherlands." *The Planner,* April, p. 23.

De Dordtenaar. 1997. "Raadsmeerderheid trekt met tegenzin geld uit voor City Fruitful." *De Dordtenaar,* October 3.

Delft, Department of Public Works and Environmental Control, 1996. "Ecodus, Environmentally-aware Building within a Fixed Scheme or Framework: Evaluation." January.

De Montfort University. 1993. "Queens Building, School of Engineering and Manufacture," opened by Her Majesty the Queen, 9 December 1993.

Den Haag Nieuw Centrum. 1995. "Het Haagsche Hof aan de Parkstraat."

Department of Community Affairs (Florida). 1997. "Sustainable Communities Demonstration Project: 1997 Report to the Legislature."

Deutsche Umwelthilfe. 1991. "Erlangen: Federal Capital for Conservation and the Environment 1990." Radolfzell, Germany.

Deutsche Umwelthilfe. 1992. "Freiburg: Federal Capital for Nature Conservation and Environment 1992." Radolfzell, Germany.

Deutsche Umwelthilfe. 1996. "Kommunal-Wettbewerb." Radolfzell, Germany.

Deutsche Umwelthilfe. Undated. "Projects and Campaigns." Radolfzell, Germany.

Dienst Ruimtelijke Ordening. 1998. *Nieuw Sloten: Van Tuin tot Stad,* Amsterdam: dRO.

Douthwaite, Richard. 1996. *Short Circuit: Strengthening Local Economies in an Unstable World.* White River Junction, VT: Chelsea Green.

Dublin Corporation. 1997. "A Strategic Cycle Network Plan." Environmental Traffic Planning Division, March.

Durning, Allan Thein, and Yoram Bauman, 1998. *Tax Shift: How to Help the Economy, Improve the Environment, and Get the Tax Man Off Your Back.* Seattle; Northwest Environment Watch, Report No. 7, April.

Economist, The. 1991. "When Virtue Pays a Premium." *The Economist,* April 18, pp. 57–58.

Economist, The. 1997. "Living with the Car: No Room, No Room." *The Economist,* December 6, pp. 21–23.

Economist, The. 1998. "California Dreamin." *The Economist,* September 5, survey section, p. 516.

Ecover. 1992. *The Ecological Factory-Manual.* 2nd ed. Oostmalle, Belgium: Ecover International.

Edwards, Brian. 1996. *Towards Sustainable Architecture: European Directives and Building Design.* London: Butterworth Architecture.

Electriciteitsbedrijf Zuid-Holland (EZH). Undated. "RoCa 3: Innovation for the B Triangle." Rotterdam.

Electrolux. 1997. *Environmental Report 1998*. AB Electrolux, Group Environmental Affairs, Stockholm.

Elsennar, Peter M. W., and Jerven A. Fanoy. 1993. "Urban Transport and Sustainable Development in the Netherlands." *ITE Journal*, August.

Elson, Martin J. 1993. *The Effectiveness of Green Belts*. London: Her Majesty's Stationary Office.

Elson, Martin J. 1986. *Greenbelts: Conflict Mediation in the Urban Fringe*. London: William Heinemann Ltd.

Engelund, Claus. 1997. "Marine Windmills to Replace Coal-fired Power Stations." *Danish Environment*, Edition 8, November, pp. 16–17.

Environ. 1996. *Local Sustainability: Turning Sustainable Development into Practical Action in Our Communities*. Leicester, U.K.: Environ.

"Environmental Aspects of Natural Fibres." Undated. Website: http://www.redesign.org/reports/textiles/nattext.hml

Environmental Building News. 1999. "Fort Worth Post Office Tests Green Design." *Environmental Building News*, April.

Erdmenger, Christoph, Birgit Dette, and Konrad Otto-Zimmermann. 1997. "Local Environmental Budgeting: The Controlling Instrument for the Sustainable Development of Local Authorities." ICLEI, Freiburg, Germany, January.

Euronet. 1996. "Toll Ring, Oslo, Norway: Road Pricing in an Urban Area." European Good Practice Information Service, October.

European Academy of the Urban Environment. 1995 (EAUE). "Urban Ecology Excursions in Berlin." Berlin.

European Academy of the Urban Environment (EAUE). 1996. "Saarbrücken: Solar and Wind Energy in the Saarbrücken Energy Concept." Good practice database.

European Academy of the Urban Environment (EAUE). 1997. "Berlin: Model Project of Ecological Urban Renewal in Berlin-Kreuzberg." Good practice case description.

European Commission. 1994. *European Sustainable Cities*. Part One, Brussels: Expert Group on the Urban Environment.

European Commission DGXI. 1996a. "Emscher Park, Germany: Ecological and Urban Renewal of Urban Areas." European Good Practice Information Service, October.

European Commission DGXI. 1996b. "Helsinki Metropolitan Area, Finland: Separate Collection of Biowaste: Closing the Nutrient Circle," European Good Practice Information Service.

European Commission. 1996. *European Sustainable Cities*. Directorate General XI, Brussels, March.

European Commission. 1997. *Agenda 21, The First Five Years*, European Community Progress on the Implementation of Agenda 21, 1992–97. Brussels: European Commission.

European Environment Agency. 1996. *Environmental Taxes: Implementation and Environmental Effectiveness.* Copenhagen: European Environment Agency.

European Environment Agency. 1997. "Towards Sustainable Development for Local Authorities." Copenhagen, February, prepared by Malina Mehra, IMSA Amsterdam.

European Environment Agency. 1997. *Europe's Environment: The Second Assessment.* Copenhagen: European Environment Agency.

European Federation of City Farms. Undated. "A Network of City Farms." Website: http://digitaalbrussel.vgc.be

European Foundation for the Improvement of Living and Working Conditions. 1993. *Innovations for the Improvement of the Urban Environment.* Dublin: European Foundation for the Improvement of Living and Working Conditions.

European Union. Undated. "An Overview of the EU Eco-Label Programme." Website: http://europa.eu.int/comm/dg11/ecolabel/program.ht

Farmers Weekly. 1998. "Inner City Enterprise Can Only Help Farming Cause." *Farmers Weekly,* March 13, p. 1.

Federal Highway Administration. 1998. "Congestion Pricing Notes." No. 4, Spring.

Feldstein, Dan. 1997. "Pedaling Past the Rest." *The Houston Chronicle,* October 12.

Financial Times. 1997. "Rooms with a view to recycling." *Financial Times* (USA Edition) Business and the Environment section, p. 23.

Financial Times. 1998. "Natural Step to Sustainability: Scientists Disagree on the Feasibility of Ecological Cost-benefit Analysis." *Financial Times* (London), January 7, Business and the Environment section, p. 20.

Folke, Carl, Asa Jansson, Jonas Larsson, and Robert Costanza. 1997. "Ecosystem Appropriation by Cities." *Ambio,* Vol. 26, No. 3, May, pp. 167–172.

Forum for the Future. 1997a. "Case Studies: Living over the Shop, in York." Prepared by Oliver Savage, Environ, Leicester.

Forum for the Future. 1997b. "Case Studies: Ecological Urban Improvements in Unionplatz and Teirgarden, Berlin." Prepared by Oliver Savage, Environ, Leicester.

Forum for the Future. 1997c. "Case Studies: Vision 21: Gloucestershire's Local Agenda 21." Prepared by Les Newby, Environ, Leicester.

Forum for the Future. 1998. "Case Studies: Action 2020—Middleborough's Local Agenda 21." Prepared by Duncan Bell, Environ, Leicester.

Frank, Robert H. 1999. *Luxury Fever: Why Money Fails to Satisfy in an Era of Excess.* New York: Free Press.

Frankel, Carl. 1998. *In Earth's Company: Business, Environment and the Challenge of Sustainability.* Gabriola Island, BC: New Society Publishers.

Friends of the Earth. 1998. "Poll Finds U.S. Voters Favor Green Taxes." News release, June 17, Washington, DC.

Friends of the Earth. 1999. "Southern California Voters Curb Sprawl." Website: http://www.foe.org

Friends of the Earth Europe. 1995. *Towards Sustainable Europe.* Summary FDE Europe. Brussels, January.

Gehl, Jan. 1995. "Livable Cities for All—The Danish Experience." In *The European City-Sustaining Urban Quality,* Danish Ministry of Environment and Energy, conference proceedings, Copenhagen.

Gehl, Jan, and Lars Gemzøe. 1996. *Public Spaces—Public Life.* Copenhagen: The Danish Architectural Press.

Gemeente Den Haag. 1996. "Haagse Groene Gids." Lokale Agenda 21.

Gemeente Heerhugowaard. 1999. "Stad Van De Zon." Heerhugowaard information bureau.

Gemeente Leiden. 1998a. "Duurzame Stedebouw in Roomburg." Afdeling Stedebouw, Junio.

Gemeente Leiden, 1998b. *Ideeën: Stad and Milieu Leiden.* September.

Gemeente Utrecht. 1992. Leidsche Rijn Masterplan, Utrecht, Netherlands.

Gemeente Utrecht. Undated. "Leidsche Rijn."

Geografie. 1996. "Spatial Planning in the Netherlands." *Geografie,* Vol. 1996, pp. 1–26.

Gertler, Nicolas and John Ehrenfeld. 1994. "Industrial Symbiosis in Kalundborg: Development and Implications." Program on Technology, Business, and Environment, Massachusetts Institute of Technology, working paper, August.

Ghent, Randy. 1998. "Car-free France." *Earth First!,* February–March, p. 13.

Gill, Allan. 1998. "It Takes a Tenner to Force Cars off the Road," *The Evening Standard,* July 20, p. 8.

Girardet, Herbert. 1994. "Keeping Up with Capital Growth." *Geographical Magazine,* June, Vol. 66, No. 6, pp. 12–16.

Girardet, Herbert. Undated. "Getting London in Shape for 2000: How London Can Compete in the Race for Resource Efficiency." Draft, prepared for London First.

Girling, Cynthia L., and Kenneth I. Helphand. 1994. *Yard, Street, Park: The Design of Suburban Open Space.* New York: John Wiley and Sons.

Glendening, Gov. Parris N. 1999. "'3 Great Challenges': Education, Environment, Equality." Inaugural address published in *The Washington Post,* January 21, p. A12.

Going for Green, 1998. Website: http://www.gfg.iclnet.co.uk

Goodchild, Barry. 1998. "Learning the Lessons of Housing over Shops Initiatives." *Journal of Urban Design,* Vol. 3, No. 1, pp. 73–92.

Goode, David A. 1989. "Urban Nature Conservation in Britain." *Journal of Applied Ecology,* Vol. 26, pp. 859–873.

Government Buildings Agency (The Netherlands). 1997. "Government Housing and the Environment: Sustainable Decisions." Den Haag, The Netherlands, 2nd ed., February.

Grant, Malcolm M. 1992. "Planning Law and the British Land Use Planning System." *Town Planning Review,* Vol. 63, No. 1, pp. 3–11.

Gray, Tom. 1998. "Wind Gets Competitive in the U.S." *Solar Today,* March/April, pp. 18–21.

Green City Denmark A/S. Undated. "Waste Water." Herning.

Green City Denmark A/S. 1997. "Project Reference." Herning.

Green City Denmark A/S. 1997. "European Green Cities Inspiration Guide: A View Into Low Energy Home Building in Europe."

Green Institute. Undated. Website: http://www.greeninstitute.org

Green Power Network. 1998. "Santa Monica Unanimously Approves RFP Process to Switch all City Facilities to Green Power." Press release, October 14. Website: http://www.eren.doe.gov

Green Power Network. 1999. "Santa Monica First City in the World to be Powered by 100% Green Power." Press release, June 1. Website: http://www.eren.doe.gov

Green, Victoria Jane. 1995. "Sustainable Energy Policies—Problems with Implementation: An Examination of the Implementation of Sustainable Energy Policies in Leicester, Middlesborough, Petersborough and Leeds." M.A. thesis in environmental planning, The University of Nottingham.

Greenbeat. 1996. "Eco-location: Charting Sustainability." January, Texas Environmental Center. Website: http://www.tec.org

Gregory, Ted. 1996. "City Gets a Handle on Helping Bicycles." *Chicago Tribune.* September 11.

Groningen Gemeente. 1993. "Hand on Heart: A New City Centre for Groningen." Groningen, The Netherlands.

Groningen Gemeente. 1996. "City for a New Century: Groningen in 2005." Structure Plan, Dienst Ruimtelijke Ordening en Economische Zaken.

Groot, M. M. 1997. "The Environmental Matrix Enhances Planning Processes." Amsterdam Planning Department.

Groot, M. M., and J. W. Vermeulen, 1997. "The Environmental Matrix Enhances Planning Processes: An Indicator Based Approach to Urban Planning and Development in Amsterdam." Advisory team, Environment and Urban Ecology, City of Amsterdam, Planning Department, January.

Haberman, Douglas. 1997. "Experimental Riders Go for in Electric Bike Program." *The Desert Sun,* September 3, p. B3.

Hahn, Ekhart, and Michael LaFond. 1997. "Local Agenda 21 and Ecological Urban Restructuring: A European Model Project in Leipzig." Science Center, Berlin.

Hall, Peter. 1995a. "The European City: Past and Future." In Danish Ministry of the Environment and Energy, *The European City—Sustaining Urban Quality.* Conference proceedings, Copenhagen.

Hall, Peter. 1995b. "A European Perspective on the Spatial Links between Land Use, Development and Transport." In David Banister, ed., *Transport and Urban Development.* London: ESFN Span.

Hall, Peter, Brian Sands, and Walter Streeter. 1993. "Managing the Suburban Commute: A Cross National Comparison of Three Metropolitan Areas." University of California, Berkeley: Institute for Urban and Regional Development, Working Paper #595, August.

Hallett, Graham, ed. 1989. *Land and Housing Policies in Europe and the U.S.* London: Routledge.

Hammon, M. Jeff. 1999. "Tax Reform: State by State." *E/Environmental Magazine,* March–April.

Harper, Keith. 1998. "Norway and Singapore Point the Way with Electronic Charging That Raises Millions and Cuts Traffic Levels." *The Guardian* (London), December 9, p. 130.

Hawley, David. 1999. "Downsizing Domiciles." *Pioneer Planet.* Website: http://www.pioneerplanet.com

Hayes, Mathew. 1997. "Central European Approach to On-Farm Composting." *Bio-Cycle,* June, pp. 34–35.

Haynes, Owen. 1998. "Eco City's a Global Village for Visitors." *Leicester Mercury,* July 18, p. 21.

Heller, Dr. Peter W. 1997. "Urban Development and a Local Environmental Action Plan Exemplified by A Medium-sized City: Freiburg in Breisgau, Germany."

Heller, Dr. Peter W. Undated. "Freiburg—Germany's Green City."

Helsinki Energy. Undated. "Helsinki—The Energy Efficient City: Combined Heat and Electricity Production and District Heating System of Helsinki Energy, Finland."

Helsinki Metropolitan Area Council (YTV). 1993. "Eat What You Can—Recycle the Rest: Separate Collection of Biowaste." Waste Management Departments.

Helsinki Metropolitan Area Council (YTV). Undated. "The Climate Change, Helsinki Regional CO_2 Reduction Strategy."

Herning Kommunale Vaerker. Undated. "Biogas from Source-separated Household Waste." Herning, Denmark.

Hildebrandt, Andreas. 1995. Notes on the Freiburg transit program.

Hough, Michael. 1995. *Cities and Natural Process.* London: Routledge.

Howe, Deborah. 1998. "Metropolitan Portland's Greenspaces Program." In "Creating Sustainable Places" symposium proceedings, January 30–31, Arizona State University, Tempe, AZ.

HSB Stockholm. Undated. "The Story of Understenshojden." Stockholm: HSB Stockholm.

Hufbauer, Rudiger. Undated. "Notes on the Freiburg Transport System." Freiburg, Traffic Planning Division.

Husberger, Lars. 1996. "Development Patterns in the Swedish Spatial Vision, Sweden 2009." In Boplats, *Urban Development in an Ecocycles Adapted Industrial Society.* Stockholm: Swedish Council for Building Research.

IBA Emscher Park. Undated. "The Emscher Park International Building Exhibition: An Institution of the State of North-Rhine Westphalia."

ICLEI. 1992. "Environmental Auditing: Lancashire County, UK." Case Study #6, Toronto.

ICLEI. 1996. "Bologna, Italy: Restriction of Automobile Traffic in the Historic Center City." European Good Practice Information Service, Toronto.

ICLEI. 1997. "STATTAUTO—Germany's largest car-sharing company." Toronto.

ICLEI. Undated. "Local Environmental Budgeting." Website: http://www.iclei. org/ecobudget/envbudpe.htm

ING Bank. Undated. "Building with a Difference: ING Bank Head Office." Amsterdam.

Inman, Bradley. 1999. "Houses Are Getting Bigger, and Pricier." *San Francisco Examiner,* February 21, p. E11.

Interiors Magazine. 1999a. "Miller/SQA Facility." *Interiors,* January, pp. 102–103.

Interiors Magazine. 1999b. "901 Cherry: San Bruno, California." *Interiors,* January, pp. 104–107.

Interiors Magazine. 1999c. "Adam Joseph Lewis Center for Environmental Studies, Oberlin College," *Interiors,* January, pp. 110–111.

International Council of Local Environmental Initiatives (ICLEI). 1994. "Profiting From Pollution: Graz, Austria." Case Study #24, Freiburg: ICLEI.

International Council of Local Environmental Initiatives (ICLEI). 1996. *The Local Agenda 21 Planning Guide: An Introduction to Sustainable Development Planning.* Toronto: ICLEI.

International Institute for the Urban Environment. 1994. "The European Sustainability Index Project." Delft.

Jacobs, Alan. 1994. *Great Streets.* Cambridge, MA: MIT Press.

Jenks, Mike, Katie Williams, and Elizabeth Burton. 1996. "A Sustainable Future through the Compact City? Urban Intensification in the United Kingdom." *Environments by Design,* Vol. 1, No. 1, January, pp. 5–20.

Jenks, Mike, Elizabeth Burton, and Katie Williams, eds. 1996. *The Compact City: A Sustainable Urban Form?* London: E&FN Span.

Jensen, Mari N. 1998. "Ecologists Go to Town: Investigations in Baltimore and Phoenix Forge a New Ecology of Cities." *Science News,* Vol. 153, April 4, pp. 219–221.

Johnston, Jacklyn, and John Newton. 1997. *Building Green: A Guide to Using Plants on Roofs, Walls and Pavements,* London: London Ecology Unit.

Johnstone, Anne. 1998. "The New Economy Drive." *The Herald* (Glasgow), December 9, p. 15.

Jongman, Rob H. G. 1995. "Nature Conservation Planning in Europe: Developing Ecological Networks." *Landscape and Urban Planning,* Vol. 32, pp. 169–183.

Joos, Ernst. 1992. "Three Messages from Zürich Concerning the New Transport Policy." Zürich Transity Authority.

Jordan, Thea. 1998. "Big Mac Hits Trouble in a Town That Turned Green." *The Scotsman.* July 2, p. 11.

Juffermans, Jan. 1995. *Sustainable Lifestyles: Guide to Good Practice.* Den Haag: Towns and Development.

Kalundborg Center for Industrial Symbiosis. 1996. "Individual Symbiosis: Exchange of Resources," September.

Kennedy, Margrit, and Declan Kennedy, eds. 1997. *Designing Ecological Settlements: Ecological Planning and Building: Experiences in New Housing and in the Renewal of Existing Housing Quarters in European Countries.* Berlin: European Academy of the Urban Environment.

Kenworthy, Jeff, Felix Lanbe, Peter Newman, and Paul Barter. 1996. "Indicators of Transport Efficiency in 37 Global Cities." Report prepared for the World Bank, October.

Kolding Kommune. 1995. "Ecological Urban Renewal in Kolding." With Danish Ministry of Housing, August.

Kraay, Joop H. 1996. "Dutch Approaches to Surviving with Traffic and Transport." *Transport Reviews,* Vol. 16, No. 4, pp. 323–343.

Kreiger, Alex. 1998. "Whose Urbanism?" *Architecture Magazine,* November, pp. 73–76.

Kretschmer, Dr. Rolf-Michael. 1995. "Report of Dr. Rolf-Michael Kretschmer—Technical Director of Freiburger Verkehrs AG, Germany—at Light Rail 95 Conference." Fairfield Halls, Croyden.

Kuiper Compagnons. Undated. "City Fruitful: Stedenbouwkundig Ontwerp." Bureau voor Ruimtelijke Ordening en Architectuur BV. Website: http://www.kuiper.nl/p3.htm

Kunz, Pamela Murphy. 1999. "Solar Energy in Europe." *Solar Today,* January/February, pp. 28–31.

Lafferty, William M., and Katarina Eckerberg, eds. 1998. *From Earth Summit to Local Agenda 21: Working Towards Sustainable Development.* London, Earthscan.

Landeshauptstadt Saarbrücken. 1997. "Regenwasser ist zu kostbar für den Kanal!" Saarbrücken, Dezernat für Recht, Umwelt und Gesundheit, Amt für Energie und Umwelt.

Leicester City Council. 1989. "Leicester Ecology Strategy." Part one.

Leicester City Council. 1994. "Land Use Plan."

Leicester City Council. Undated-a. "Cycling."

Leicester City Council. Undated-b. "Pedestrians" and "Traffic Calming."

Leicester City Council. Undated-c. "Sustainability Appraisal." City of Leicester Local Plan.

Leicester Mercury. 1998. "Students Sign Up for Green Crusade." *Leicester Mercury,* July 25, p. 12.

Leinsberger, Christopher. 1996. "Metropolitan Development Trends of the Latter 1990s: Social and Environmental Implications." In *Land Use in America,* Henry L. Diamond and Patrick F. Noonan, eds. Washington, DC: Island Press.

Lennard, Suzanne H.C., and Henry L. Lennard, *Livable Cities Observed: A Source of Images and Ideas for City Officials, Community Leaders, Architects, Planners and All Others Committed to Making Cities Livable.* Carmel, CA: Gondolier Press.

Le Pierres, Laurent. Undated. "Industrial Belt Manufacturing Green Solutions." Website: http://www.herald.ns.ca/archives/laurent/story4.htmp

Letts, Lois. 1998. "Gardening in the Sky." *The Times* (London), February, Features sections, February 18.

Liebman, George W. 1996. "Three Good Community-building Ideas from Abroad." *American Enterprise,* November/December, pp. 72–73, 98.

Lightfoot, Graham. 1996. "Car-sharing Studies: An Investigation." Bremen: European Car-Sharing.

Lisbon Action Plan. 1996. "The Lisbon Action Plan: From Charter to Action." Website: http://www.iclei.org/la21/eurola21.html

Loa, Jeff, and Robert Wolcott. 1994. "Innovation in Community Design: The Davis Experience." Paper prepared for the Making Cities Livable Conference, February 22–26, San Francisco, CA.

London First. 1997. "Capital Punishment: The Effect of Under-Investment on London's Underground." London, March 17.

Louisse, Anneke F. 1998. "Rural Towns and Villages of the Netherlands' Green Heart: Is a Healthy Survival Possible?" *Journal of Architectural and Planning Research,* Vol. 15, No. 1, Spring, pp. 73–84.

Lucas, John. 1994. "Outdoors: Nature Makes a Comeback in London's Docklands." *The Daily Telegraph,* October 15, pg. 3.

MacDonald, Rob. Undated. "IBA Emscher Park." Website: http://rudi.herts.ac.uk/ns-search/ej/udq/56/inter.html

Malcolm, Teresa. 1998. "Program Seeks to Nurture the Planet, Profits." *National Catholic Reporter,* No. 29, Vol. 34, May 22, p. 5.

Mann, Gunter. 1996. "Faunistische Untersuchung von drei Dachbegriinungen in Linz" OKO-L Vol. 18, No. 2, pp. 3–14.

Masser, Ian. 1992. "Learning from Europe." *Journal of the American Planning Association,* Vol. 58, No. 1, Winter, pp. 3–8.

Massie, Allan. 1998. "Driving Taxes That Take a Huge Toll on the Economy." *Daily Mail* (London), July 20, p. 8.

Max Havelaar Foundation. Undated. "Max Havelaar: A Fair Trade Label." Website: http://www.maxhavelaar.nl

McCamant, Kathryn, and Charles Durrett. 1998. *CoHousing: A Contemporary Approach to Housing Ourselves.* Berkeley, CA: Habitat Press/Ten Speed Press.

McKibben, Bill. 1998. "A Special Moment in History." *The Atlantic Monthly.* May, pp. 55–78.

Mega, Voula. 1996. *Utopias and Realities of Urban Sustainable Development.* Dublin: European Foundation for the Improvement of Living and Working Conditions.

Mega, Voula. 1997. *Perceiving, Conceiving, Achieving: The Sustainable City: A Synthesis Report.* Dublin: European Foundation for the Improvement of Living and Working Conditions.

Middleton, D. Scott. 1997. "The Woodlands." *Urban Land,* June, pp. 26–30.

Ministry of Housing, Spatial Planning and the Environment (VROM). 1994. "Accelerated Depreciation on Environmental Investment in the Netherlands." Evaluation report, Den Haag, November.

Ministry of Housing, Spatial Planning and the Environment (VROM). 1995. Stad and Milieu: Rapportage Deelprojecct, Den Haag: VROM.

Ministry of Housing, Spatial Planning and the Environment (VROM). 1996a. "Best Practices: Sustainable Living in the Netherlands." Den Haag.

Ministry of Housing, Spatial Planning and the Environment. 1996b. "Spatial Planning in the Netherlands: Bodies and Instruments." Den Haag: Spatial Planning Directorate.

Ministry of Transport, Public Works and Water Management. 1995. *Cities Make Room for Cyclists: Examples from Towns in the Netherlands, Denmark, Germany, and Switzerland.* Den Haag.

Ministry of Transport, Public Works and Water Management. Undated. "The New HSL Plan in Broad Lines: Dutch Section of the High Speed Rail Connection, Amsterdam-Brussels-Paris/London." Traffic and Transport Structure Plan, Den Haag.

Morris, Jane. 1998. "Coming In from the Cold." *Town and Country Planning,* January/February, p. 18.

Mudd, Lyssa. 1998. "Commons on Wheels." *Whole Earth,* Fall, p. 52.

Municipality of Bologna. 1996. *Energy in Bologna: Innovative Projects for Reducing Energy Consumption and Pollution.* February.

Municipality of Delft. 1984. "Fietsen in Delft: Planning for the Urban Cyclist." Traffic Department, September.

Municipality of Dordrecht. 1994. "Ecological Strategies for Cities." Proceedings of a conference and workshop held in October and November, 1993.

Municipality of Kolding. 1996. "Urban Renewal of Solgarden/Kolding A." Technical Administration, December.

Murphy, Dean E. 1996. "In Copenhagen One-third of All Commuters Reach Their Jobs by Bicycle." *L.A. Times,* July 15, p. A20.

Muschamp, Herbert. 1998. "Greening a South Bronx Brownfield." *The New York Times,* January 23.

National Bicycling and Walking Study. 1994. "Traffic Calming, Auto-restricted Zones and Other Traffic Management Techniques—Their Effects on Bicycling and Pedestrians." FWWA case study #19, January.

Natural Step, The. 1996. "The Four System Conditions from the Natural Step." *The Natural Step News,* No. 1, Winter.

Neild, Nigel. 1998. "Introducing the Concept of Sustainable Development into the Treaties of the European Union." In O'Riordan and Voisey, eds., *The Transition to Sustainability: The Politics of Agenda 21 in Europe.* London: Earthscan.

Netzer, Dick. 1998. "The Relevance and Feasibility of Land Value Taxation in the Rich Countries." In Netzer *Land Value Taxation: Can It and Will It Work Today?* Cambridge, MA: Lincoln Institute of Land Policy.

Newman, Peter, and Jeff Kenworthy. 1991. "Transport and Urban Form in Thirty-two of the World Principal Cities." *Transport Reviews,* Vol. 11, No. 3, pp. 249–272.

Newman, Peter, and Jeff R. Kenworthy. 1989. *Cities and Automobile Dependence: A Sourcebook.* Hants. England: Gower Technical.

Newman, Peter, and Jeff Kenworthy, with Les Robinson. 1992. *Winning Back the Cities*. Leichhardt, Australia: Pluto Press.

Newman, Peter, and Andy Thornley. 1996. *Urban Planning in Europe: International Competition, National Systems and Planning Projects*. London: Routledge.

Nield, Chloe. 1998. "Environment at the Heart of Europe." *Landscape Design*, Vol. 276, December, pp. 52–55.

Nijkamp, Peter, and Adriaan Perrels. 1994. *Sustainable Cities in Europe: A Comparative Analysis of Urban Energy—Environment Policies*. London: Earthscan.

Nivola, Pietro. 1999. "Fit for Fat City: A 'Lite' Menu of European Policies to Improve Our Urban Form." Policy Brief #44, Brookings Institution, January.

Norwood, Ken, and Kathleen Smith. 1995. *Rebuilding Community in America: Housing for Ecological Living, Personal Empowerment, and the New Extended Family*. Berkeley, CA: Shared Living Resource Center.

NOVEM. Undated. *Op weg naar Ecolonia: Evaluatie en bewonersonderzoek*. Sittard, Netherlands: NOVEM.

NOVEM. 1996. "Nul-energiewoning met PV in Zandvoort." Number 5, February.

NOVEM. 1999. "Vergisting van GFT-afval en Opwerking van Biogas." Sittard: NOVEM.

Odense Kommune. 1997. Mijoplan 1997–2000, Odense, Denmark.

O'Meara, Molly. 1998. "How Medium-Sized Cities Can Avoid Strangulation." *Worldwatch Magazine*, September/October, pp. 9–15.

O'Riordan, Tim, and Heather Voisey, eds. 1998. *The Transition to Sustainability: The Politics of Agenda 21 in Europe*. London: Earthscan.

Orr, David. 1994. *Earth in Mind*. Washington, DC: Island Press.

Oskam, A. W. 1995. "A Tale of Two Cities—Amsterdam." In Danish Ministry of Environment and Energy. In *The European City-Sustaining Urban Quality*, conference proceedings, Copenhagen.

Ott, Ruedi. 1996. "Conurbation Transport Policy in Zürich: A Swiss Contribution to the Best Practices Initiative." Genchen, Switzerland: Federal Office of Housing.

Otto-Zimmerman, Konrad. 1998. "New Public Management of Natural Resources: Environmental Budgeting by Municipalities. Website: http://www.iclei.org/ecobudget/konrad.htm

Overholser, Geneva. 1999. "Charleton Heston, Meet Joe Camel." *The Washington Post*, May 4, pg. A23.

PACTE Project. 1997. "Environmental Effects of Structural Changes in Old Industrial Cities." Action Program for Local and Regional Authorities in Europe, Tampere, Finland.

Painter, Sue. 1998. "Greetings from Green City USA." *The Gloucester Citizen*, June 29, p. 6.

Partners for a Clean Environment (PACE). Undated. "Partners for a Clean Environment." Boulder, CO.

Pearce, B. J. 1992. "The Effectiveness of the British Land Use Planning System." *Town Planning Review,* Vol. 63, No. 1, pp. 13–28.

Petherick, Ann. 1998. "Room for Reuse." *Town and Country Planning,* January/February, pp. 35–36.

Pfeifer, Sharon, and Faith Balch. 1999. "Planning for Nature in the Face of Urban Growth: The Metro Greenways Program, Twin Cities Region." Paper presented to Challenge to Urban Sustainability conference, Stanford University, February.

Phillips, Adrian. 1996. "The Challenge of Restoring Europe's Nature and Landscapes." *International Planning Studies,* Vol. 1, No. 1, pp. 73–93.

Pierce, Neal R. 1998. "Atlanta's Bullet Train." *The Washington Post,* June 21.

Pivo, Gary. 1996. "Toward Sustainable Urbanization on Mainstreet Cascadia." *Cities,* Vol. 13, No. 5, pp. 339–354.

Porter, Douglas R. 1996. *Profiles in Growth Management: An Assessment of Current Programs and Guidelines for Effective Management.* Washington, DC: Urban Land Institute.

Portland BEST. Undated. "Businesses for an Environmentally Sustainable Tomorrow." Portland Energy Office. Website: http://www.ci.portland.or.us/energy/bestmain.html

Post, Michel. Undated. "The Green Roof." Photocopied paper obtained from the author.

Public Technology, Inc. Undated. "West Palm Beach, FL: Change on the Ground." Traffic calming case studies. Website: http://pti.nw.dc.us

Pucher, John. 1997. "Bicycling Boom in Germany: A Revival Engineered by Public Policy." *Transportation Quarterly,* Vol. 51, No. 4, Fall, pp. 31–46.

Pucher, John, and Christian Lefevre. 1996. *The Urban Transport Crisis in Europe and North America.* London: MacMillan Press Ltd.

Purves, Libby. 1998. "Move Over Motorists: Home Zones Would Reclaim Our Streets for the Old, the Young and the Poor." *The Times* (London), January 27.

Quinn, Feargal. 1998. "Radical thinking required to case traffic." *The Irish Times,* November 19, News features section, p. 18.

Quinn, Sue. 1999. "Home Zones Reclaim the Streets." *The Guardian,* August 5, p. 10.

Rabobank. 1995. "Een sociale ontmoetingsplaats zonder auto's." *Rabo Vastgoed Magazine,* No. 2, Jaargong 4, July, pp. 6–8.

Rackstraw, Kevein. 1998. "Wind Around the World." *Solar Today,* March/April, pp. 22–25.

Rand, Harry. 1993. *Hundertwasser.* Koln: Benedikt Taschen.

RECITE. Undated. "The Temple Bar Development Program." RECITE Bulletin #11, Urban Pilot projects, European Commission, Brussels.

Reich, K., G. Kleiss, A. Goetzberger, and T. Nordman. 1998. "Photovoltaic Noise Barriers: An Innovation on its way to Market." *The Sustainable Energy Industry Journal,* Vol. 3, No. 2, pp. 66–67.

Reid, Alice. 1998. "Fare-ATM Cards Set for Test by Metro." *The Washington Post,* September 18, p. B1.

Results Center. Undated. "Saarbrücken, Germany: Comprehensive Municipal Energy Efficiency." Profile #78, Denver, CO.

Rigter, Gerard. 1997. "Ook met wildviaducten lijkt Veluwse natuur reddeloos." *Algemeen Dagblad,* July 19, p. 5.

Rimer, Sara. 1997. "An Aging Nation Ill-equipped for Hanging Up the Car Keys." *The New York Times,* December 15, pp. A1, A20.

Ringli, Hellmut. 1989. "Spatial Planning in Switzerland." In International Society of City and Regional Planners, *Planning in the Host Country,* Basel, Bulletin 1989/2.

Ringli, Hellmut. 1995. "Strategies for Sustainable Urban Development in the Zürich Area." In Lars Orrskog, ed., *Adjusting Cities to the Demands of Sustainability—How and by Whom?* Stockholm: Swedish Royal Institute of Technology.

Ringli, Hellmut. 1996. "The Swiss Urban Development Strategy—A Polycentric Urban Network." In International Society of City and Regional Planners, *Migration and the Global Economy: Planning Responses to Disintegrating Patterns and Frontiers,* working paper book, Jerusalem, October 13–16.

Rogers, Sir Richard. 1997. *Cities for a Small Plane.* London: Faber and Faber.

Roundtable Minutes. 1998. "Eco-Industrial Development Program Meeting Minutes." October 27–28, Cape Charles, VA.

Royal Dutch Touring Club. 1978. "Woonerf: Residential Princinct." *Ekistics,* Vol. 273, November/December, pp. 417–423.

Safdie, Moshe. 1997. *The City After the Automobile: An Architect's Vision.* Toronto: Stoddart Publishing.

Salant, Katherine. 1997. "Earning a Star for Improved Energy Efficiency." *The Washington Post,* September 13, pp. E1, E10.

Scandic Hotels. Undated. "The Environmental Room." Website: http://www.scandic-hotels.com/br/30/30rummet.html

Scotsman Publications Ltd. 1998. "Tories Call for City to Reject Road Pricing." *Evening News,* October 5, p. 9.

Selman, Paul. 1998. "A Real Local Agenda for the 21st Century." *Town and Country Planning,* January/February, pp. 15–17.

Sep, Rund. 1998. "Roomburg Wordt Leidse Milieuwijk." Gemeente Leiden.

Shuman, Michael. 1994. *Towards a Global Village: International Community Development Initiatives.* London: Pluto Press.

Shuman, Michael H. 1998. *Going Local: Creating Self-Reliant Communities in a Global Age.* New York: The Free Press.

Slavin, Terry. 1998. "Sustainable Argument Takes a Step Forward." *The Observer,* March 22, Business section, p. 7.

Sofia Statement. 1998. "Towards Local Sustainability in Central and Eastern Europe: The Sofia Statement." Website: http://www.iclei.org/europe/sofiafin.html

South Carolina Sea Grant Consortium. 1998. "113 Calhoun Street Community Sustainability Center." Website: http://www.csc.noaa.gov/scSeaGrant/text/113calhoun.html

Southworth, Michael, and Evan Ben-Joseph. 1997. *Streets and the Shaping of Towns and Cities*. New York: McGraw-Hill.

Southworth, Michael, and Balaji Parthasarathy. 1997. "The Suburban Realm II: Eurourbanism, New Urbanism and the Implications for Urban Design in the American Metropolis." *Journal of Urban Design*, Vol. 2, No. 1, pp. 9–33.

Staats, H. J., and P. Harland. 1995. "The Ecoteam Program in the Netherlands." Leiden: Center for Energy and Environmental Research, Leiden University.

Stanners, David, and Phillippe Bourdeau, eds. 1995. *Europe's Environment: The Dobris Assessment*. Copenhagen: European Environment Agency.

Steele, James. 1997. *Sustainable Architecture: Principles, Paradigms, and Case Studies*. New York: McGraw-Hill.

Stichting Natuur en Milieu. 1994. *Milieusparend Huishouden*. Amsterdam: Stichting Natuur en Milieu.

Stockholm Energi. 1997. *Environmental Report 96*. Stockholm: Stockholm Energi.

Stockholm Environment and Health Protection Administration. 1996. "Environmental Vehicles in Stockholm."

Stuchlik, Gerda, and Klaus Heidler. 1998. "The Freiburg Solar Region—A Model of Sustainable Planning for the Millenium." *The Sustainable Energy Industry Journal*, Vol. 3, No. 2, pp. 30–31.

Sukopp, H. 1980. "Urban Ecology and Its Application in Europe." In Sukopp and Hejny, eds., *Urban Ecology*. SPB Academic Publishing.

Sustainable London Trust. 1997. *Creating a Sustainable London*. London: Sustainable London Trust.

Sustainable London Trust. Undated. "Creating a Sustainable London—Implementation." Website: http://www.greenchannel.com

Sustainable Minnesota. 1998. "Tax Polluters, Not Families and Businesses," February. Website: http://www.me3.org

Swedish Environmental Protection Agency. 1997. "Evaluation of Green Taxes in Sweden: Large Environmental Impact at Small Cost." March 13 press release.

Temple Bar Properties. Undated. "The Green Building, Temple Bar." Dublin.

Templin, Neal. 1998. "Windows That Open Are the Latest Office Amenity," *Wall Street Journal Europe*. August 28–29, p. 8.

Ten Grotenhuis, Dirk H. 1979. "The Woonerf in City and Traffic Planning." Municipality of Delf, March.

THERMIE. 1996. "ZEUS: Zero and Low Emission Vehicles in Urban Society." March.

Thomas, David, John Minett, Steve Hopkins, Steve Hammertt, Andreas Faludi, and David Banell. 1983. *Flexibility and Commitment in Planning: A Com-*

parative Study of Local Planning and Development in the Netherlands and England. The Hague: Martinus Nijhoff.

Thompson, J. William. 1998. "Grass-roofs Movement." *Landscape Architecture*, May, pp. 47–51.

Titheridge, Helena, G. Boyle, and Paul Fleming. 1996. "Development and Validation of a Computer Model for Assessing Energy Demand and Supply Patterns in the Urban Environment." *Energy and Environment*, Vol. 7, No. 1, pp. 29–40.

Torrie, Ralph. 1993. "Findings and Policy Implications from the Urban CO_2 Reduction Project." International Council for Local Environmental Initiatives, January.

Tri-State Transportation Campaign, 1998. "Guiliani Announces Major Traffic Calming Step." *Mobilizing the Region*, Issue 169, April 10.

TROS. 1998. "Meer Tuinplezier." Videotape, August 8. Hilversum: TROS.

U.K. Department of the Environment. 1996. "Leading the Way-CHP for Whitehall." Website: http://www.energy.rochester.edu/uk

U.K. Department of the Environment. Undated. "A UK Strategy for Combined Heat and Power." Website: http://www.energy.rochester.edu/uk/chpstrategy

UNED-UK, 1997. "Green and Ethical Pensions: A Report for Local Authorities." London: United National Environment and Development U.K. Committee, January.

United Nations. 1992. *Agenda 21: The United Nations Programme of Action From Rio*. New York: United Nations.

United Nations Development Program. 1996. *Urban Agriculture: Food, Jobs and Sustainable Cities*. New York: United Nations Department Program.

U.S. Department of Transportation. 1994. *The National Bicycling and Walking Study*. Executive Summary, Washington, D.C.

USEPA. 1998. "The Energy Star Homes Program." Website: http://www.yosemite.epa.gov

USEPA. Undated-a. "The International Building Exhibition (IBA): Preserving Open Space and Our Industrial Heritage through Regional Brownfields Redevelopment." An international brownfields case study. Website: http://www.epa.gov/swerosps/bf/html-doc/emscher.htm

USEPA. Undated-b. "Westergasfabriek: Collaboration of Local Government and Community." An international brownfields case study, USEPA and ICMA, Washington, D.C.

U.S. Postal Service. Undated. "The First Green Post Office." Website: http://www.usps.gov

Van den Brink, Adri. 1994. "Rural Planning in the Netherlands: The Interrelations between Policy Levels and the Role of Land Development." Paper presented to seminar on Provincial Planning, Milan, November 17.

Van den Brink, Adri. 1997. "Urbanization and Land Use Planning: Dutch Policy Perspectives and Experiences." Unpublished paper.

Van der Valk, Arnold. 1997. "Randstad-Green Heart Metropolis: Invention,

Reception and Impact of a National Principle of Spatial Organization." *Built Environment,* Vol. 17, No. 1, pp. 23–33.

Van der Vegt, Henri, Henkter Heide, Sybrand Tjallingii, and Dick van Alphen, eds. 1994. *Sustainable Urban Development: Research and Experiments.* Delft: Delft University Press.

Van Zadelhoff, Erik, and Wim Lammers. 1995. "The Dutch Ecological Network," *Landschap,* Vol. 95–3, pp. 77–88.

Vermeend, Willem, and Jacob van der Vaart. 1998. *Greening Taxes: The Dutch Model.* Deventer, Netherlands: Kluwer.

Vermont Fair Tax Coalition. 1999. "Vermont Tax Coalition Releases Report on Advantages of Tax Shifting." News release, March 31.

VIBA, "Guide to the Permanent Exhibition." S-Hertogenbosch, The Netherlands.

Vidal, John, and Greg McIvor. 1995. "Environment: Is This Man a Natural?" *The Guardian* (London), October 18. Features section, p. 4.

Villiger, Jorg. 1989. "The City of Zürich's Streams Concept." *Authos,* Vol. 2, pp. 6–10.

Von Ungern-Sternberg, Dr. Sven. 1996a. "Reiselfeld—Establishing a New Urban District Applying User-Friendly Principles." February.

Von Ungern-Sternberg, Dr. Sven. 1996b. "The City of Freiburg Integral Traffic Plan." Erster Burgermeister, Bau- und Ordnun-gsdezernent, Stadt Freiburg im Breigau, February.

Vossestein, Jacob. 1998. *Dealing with the Dutch.* Amsterdam: Royal Tropical Institute.

VROM. 1994. "Working with the Construction Sector." *Environmental Policy in Action,* No. 2.

VROM. 1995. *Sustainable Building: Investing in the Future.* Den Haag: Ministry of Housing, Spatial Planning and the Environment.

VROM. 1998. "Cycling for the Climate." *Environmental News from the Netherlands,* June, #3.

VROM. Undated. "Milieu als ambitie: Milieubewust bouwen, wonen en werken in het Morra Park in Drachten." Vierde Nota.

Wagner, Conrad, and Richard Katzev. 1996. "Car Sharing Takes Off in Europe." *Urban Ecologist,* No. 3, p. 13.

Wahrman, Tirza S. 1998. "Breaking the Logjam: The Peak Pricing of Congested Urban Roadways Under the Clean Air Act to Improve Air Quality and Reduce Vehicle Miles Travelled." *Duke Environmental Law and Policy Forum,* Vol. 8, Spring, p. 181.

Warren, Roxanne. 1998. *The Urban Oasis: Guideways and Greenways in the Human Environment.* New York: McGraw-Hill.

Welleman, Ton. 1996. "Bikes Behind the Dikes." *Geographie,* Vol. 1996, pp. 12–15.

Welleman, Ton. Undated. "The Autumn of the Bicycle Master Plan." Den Haag, Dutch Ministry of Transport, Public Works and Water Management

White, Ben. 1999. "Amtrack Announces Partnership Plans." *The Washington Post,* January 21, p. A23.

WHO Regional Office for Europe. 1998. "WHO Healthy Cities Network." Website: http://www.who.dk/healthy-cities/hcu.htm

Wickham, Daniel. 1999. "Sewage Forests: Cleaning Water and Cooling the Planet." *Earth Island Journal,* Winter/Spring, pp. 32–33.

Williams, David. 1998. "Low-tech Start for the Brave New World of Road-pricing." *The Evening Standard* (London), November 25, p. 20.

Williams, R. H. 1996. *European Union Spatial Policy and Planning.* London: Paul Chapman Publishing.

"World's Largest Solar-powered Sports Stadium." 1998. *The Sustainable Energy Industry Journal,* Vol. 3, No. 2, p. 67.

World Media Foundation. 1999. "Living on Earth." Transcript of interview with Jasper Simonsen, Deputy Minister for the Environment, Norway, January 15.

Yardham, Ian, Michael Waite, Andrew Simpson, and Niall Machin. 1994. *Nature Conservation in Lambeth.* London: London Ecology Unit.

Individuals Interviewed

Alberslund (Denmark)
Finn Aaberg, mayor
Maps Hermansen, planning director
Agenda 21 Centre, director and staff
(and others)

Almere (the Netherlands)
Ton van Wijlen, Stadsecoloog
ir. Gerard Jan Hellinga, senior stedenbouwkundige

Amersfoort (the Netherlands)
Heino Abrahams, Gemeente Amersfoort
ing. H. A. Eijpe, REMU
ing. J. J. E. van Aalst, REMU
Elly de Bruin, info-centrum

Amsterdam (the Netherlands)
ir. A. W. Oskam, Managing Director, Physical Planning Department
ir. Hugo Poelstra, Transportation team leader, City of Amsterdam
Jan Brouwer, Nieuw Sloten, city planning department
Herman Bartman, IJburg mobility coordinator
Frans de Rooy, Projectgroep IJburg
Yvonne Ravenstein, Platform Binnenstad Auto Vrij

F. G. Karemaker, projectleider, Stadsdeel Westerpark
Mare Nijboer, Milieucentrum Amsterdam
ir. H.T.M. Hofstede, Stadsdeel Zuidoost
ir. C. M. T. van der Pol, IJburg Projectleider
ir. E. P. T. Smits, Omegam
ir. Joep H. M. Mooren, Ingenieurs Bureau Amsterdam
Luud Schimmelpennink, Depot (Y-Tech)

Bielefeld (Germany) (Waldquelle)
Hans-Friedrich Bültmann, Bültmann, Schröter & Partner

Berlin (Germany)
Cornelia Poczka, Berlin Senate
Monica Schümer-Strucksberg, Berlin Senate, Dept. of Housing and City
    Planning
Dr. Manfred Breitenkamp, head, division environmental policy, energy
    and technology, Berlin Senate
Thorsten Tonndorf, city planning, Berlin Senate
(and others)

Bologna (Italy)
Luca Zingale, Agenzia per il Risparmio Energetico
Luca Bellinato, traffic and transportation
Leonardo Mannini, city planning
Bruno Alampi, Progetto Pegaso
Susanna Crescenzi
Simonetta Tunesi, planificatore ambientale
Gabriele Bollini, planificatore ambientale
dott. urb. Andrea Rumor
Basilio Limuti, Bologna energy agency

Copenhagen (Denmark)
Øle Michael Jensen, Danish Building Research Institute
Annette Blegvad, UIA, Sustainable Development of the Built Environment
Niels Boje Groth, Danish Forest and Landscape Research Institute
Karen Attwell, Danish Building Research Institute

Jørn Ørum-Nielsen, DIS
Eric Skoven, DIS
Torben Dahl, Royal Danish Academy of Fine Arts
Lena Larsen, Royal Danish Academy of Fine Arts
Bo Gronlund, Royal Danish Academy of Fine Arts
Prof. Lise Drewes Nielsen, Copenhagen Business School
Royal Danish Academy of Fine Arts
Peter Newman, visiting professor, Royal Danish Academy
Søren B. Jensen, Copenhagen commune
Vipke Grupe Larson (and family), Bakken CoHousing Project
(and others)

Delft (the Netherlands)
Joop Koetsenruijter, chief, transport section
Robert Blom, planning department
ir. A. Verzijl, Dienst Beheer and Milieu
ir. G. J. Kuipers, Dienst Stadsontwikkeling

Den Haag (the Netherlands)
J.A.M. Kroese-Duijsters, city manager
Theo Kuypers, head LA21 program
ir. Ruud P. Voskuil, project leader, new map of Den Haag
Th. l. Bermoloff, environment department
ir. Johan G. M. Apeldoorn, Transport Theme group, LA21
Simon de Boer, Den Haag Ecostadt
(and others)

Drachten (the Netherlands)
ir. G. L. (Arno) Muis (Morra Park)

Dublin (Ireland)
Voula Mega, European Foundation for the Improvement of Living and
   Working Conditions
Steve Margolis, senior executive planner, Dublin Corporation
Dick Gleeson, deputy Dublin Planning Officer, Dublin Corporation
Michael Smith, An Taisce, The National Trust for Ireland

John McCarthy, Department of the Environment (Ireland)
Con Coll, Dublic Corporation, planning
Dublin Transit Initiative Staff
Temple Bar Properties Staff
(and others)

Dunkerque (France)
Francis Nave, Agence D'urbanisme et de Developement
Christine Masson, LA21 coordinator

Enschede (the Netherlands)
ir. A. J. A. M. Bos (Oikos)
ir. Gerard Jan Hellinga (Oikos)

Freiburg (Germany)
Dr. Peter Heller, chairman, International Council for Local Environmental
    Initiatives
Wülf Daseking, planning director
Rudiger Hufbauer, traffic department
Wolfgang Berger, ISES
Götz Eberhard Kemnitz, city planning
Harald Rehbein, city gardening and landscape division
Andreas Hildebrandt, Freiburger Verkehrs AG
David Hauck, International Solar Energy Society
(and others)

Göteburg (Sweden)
Hans Anders, Senior Comprehensive Planner

Graz (Austria)
Dr. Karl Niederl, director, environment department
Josef Rogl, city planning
Prof. Dagmar Grage
Manfred Hönig, Traffic Department
Karl Heimz Lesch, environment department
Dr. Barbara Moshammer, environment department

Erich Eisner, Eurostar
(and others)

Groningen (the Netherlands)
Ing. W. J. Veldstra, Stadsecoloog, Gemeente Groningen
Marjan Drent, Gemeente Groningen
Luuk Oost, Gemeente Groningen
(and others)

Heerhugowaard (the Netherlands)
R.M. Mellema, Informatiecentrum, Gemeente Heerhugowaard

Heidelberg (Germany)
Thomas Schaller, bürgermeister for environment and energy
Dr. Eckart Würzner, head environmental protection department
Klaus Ziemssen, city planning department
Ralf Bermich, environment
Rüdiger Becker, ecologist
(and others)

Helsinki (Finland)
Camilla v. Bonsdorff, chief, environmental protection
Kari Silfverberg, environmental protection, LA21 coordinator
Maija Hakanen, Association of Finnish Local Authorities
Matti Nieminen, environment center
Reijo Teerioja, head of transport office, YTV, Helsinki Metropolitan Area
     Council
Juha Sipilä, exec. director, YTV, Helsinki Metropolitan Area Council
Olli-Pekka Poutanen, bureau chief, Traffic Planning Division
Jussi Vuorinen, chief master planner, city planning department
Riitta Jalkanen, project chief, town planning division
Heikki Rinne, project manager, Helsinki city office, Economy and Plan-
     ning Division
Tapio Öhman, Helsinki Energy
Lauri Taipale, head, environmental section, Helsinki Energy
Kari Hämekoski, YTV, Helsinki Metropolitan Area Council

Teemu Virtanen, YTV, Helsinki Metropolitan Area Council

Herning (Denmark)
Annette Vestergaard, Environment Department
Helle Andersen, Globorama
Per Jorgensen, Globorama
Erik Lund, director, Herning Boligselskab

Houten (the Netherlands)
Robert J. A. Derks, Derks Stedenbouw b.v.

Kalundborg (Denmark)
Valdemar Christensen, SK Power company

Kolding (Denmark)
Michael Damm, head, environment department
Georg Vnna, planning department
Soren Bjerregaard, planning department

Lahti (Finland)
Timo Permanto, City of Lahti
Sakari Autio, project coordinator, Environmental Management scheme,
    City of Lahti
Paul Carroll, Green Triangle Finland
(and others)

Leicester (United Kingdom)
Anna Dodd, Environmental and Development, Leicester City Council
Ian Roberts, director, Environ
Paul Leonard-Williams, Environment and Development, Leicester City
    Council
Diane Chapman, Environment and Development, Leiscester City Council
Les Newby, Environ
Edward Tyrer, Transport Advisor, Leicester City Council
Dr. Paul Fleming, De Montfort University Institute for Energy and Sus-
    tainable Development

Peter Weber, De Montfort University Institute for Energy and Sustainable Development

Herbert Eppel, De Montfort University Institute for Energy and Sustainable Development

(and others)

Leiden (the Netherlands)

Kees de Wit, energy coordinator, Gemeente Leiden

Inge Schrader, Sustainable Building Coordinator, Gemeente Leiden

drs. Willem Brandhorst, Stadsdistributie Centrum

R.J.F. van Gulick, Juridisch Beleidsmedewerker, Gemeente Leiden

Linda van Mourik, project leider, Stad & Milieu, Gemeente Leiden

Linz (Austria)

Dr. Gerhard Utri, environment department, City of Linz

Ina Jung, Solar city pichling

Dr. Günther Knötig, Land Oberosterreich

Monika Murauer, city planning, City of Linz

Andreas Pühringer, planning, City of Linz

Dipl.-Ing. dr. Leonard Höfler

(and others)

London (United Kingdom)

Prof. David Goode, director, London Ecology Unit

Robin Clements, deputy chief planner, LPAC

Shirley Rodrigues, Assoc. of London Government, LA21 coordinator

John Jopling, Sustainable London Trust

Graham Dean, LA21 Coordinator, London Burrough of Sutton

Michael Calderbank, borough of Ealing

Sue Tarton, London borough of Merton

Kate Kinson, London First

John Heyderman, London Cycling Campaign

Karl Claydon, Camden Community Transport

Iam Hughes, London study

Jane Morris, Local Government Management Board

Münster (Germany)

Wolfgang DuBois, director, environment director
Gunnar Pick, city planning
Rainer Karliczek, city planning director
(and others)

Odense (Denmark)

Poul Lorenzen, department head, Environment
Søren Christensen, Environment
Søren Faereh, city architect/urban design

Oostmalle (Belgium) (Ecover Factory)

Peter Malaise, concept manager, ECOVER

Rotterdam (the Netherlands)

Hette K. Hylkema, project manager Electriciteitsbedrijf Zuid-Holland
Jan Trapman, Electriciteitsbedrijf Zuid-Holland

Saarbrücken (Germany)

Dr. rer. nat. Jürgen Lottermoser, Landeshauptstadt Saarbrücken
Dr. Thomas Rohrback, Stadwerke Saarbrücken
Bernd Dunnzlaff, Saarland Ministry for Environment, Energy and Transport
Elisabeth Streit, Landeshauptstadt Saarbrücken
Dr. Alexander Dörr, ARGE Solar
Thomas Bouillon, Climate Zones Study
(and others)

Stockholm (Sweden)

Krister Skånberg, Borgarråd
Britt Sahleström, Stockholm Energi
Borje Lindvall, Secretary General, SL
Micael Hagman, LA21, Project Leader
Kerstin Blix, Environment and health protection
Jonas Norrman, Svenska Kommunförbundet
Gustaf Landahl, Mijoforvaltningen
Lars Lindblom, manager, water conservation, Stockholm Vatten

Göran Johnson, regional planner, Office of Regional Planning and Urban
Transportation
Mattias Lundberg, Swedish Transport and Communications Research
Board
Jim Nilsson, Eco-cycle division
Peter Wenster, Svenska Kommunforbundet
Mats Pemer, director, Strategic Planning Department
Bengt Bilén (eco-village)
Eva Sandberg, Stockholms Naturskyddsforening
Karl-Henrik Robert, Det Naturliga Steget
(and others)

Tilburg (the Netherlands)
Jan Dictus, environmental project manager

Vienna (Austria)
Helmut Löffler, head, environmental protection
Gordana Janak, environmental protection

Zürich (Switzerland)
Hans Rudolf Rüegg, Stadtbaumeister, City of Zürich
Prof. Dr. Hellmut Ringli, ETH
Prof. Markus Eggenberger, ETH, urban and regional planning
Ernst Joos, director, transportation dept., City of Zürich
Francis Rossé, Landscape planning office, City of Zürich
Prof. Dr. Willy Schmid, ETH, Institut fur Orts-Regional-und Landespla-
nung und Institut fur Kulturtechnik
Dr. Christian Gabathuler, director, provincial planning department
Dr. Michael Koch, ETH
Prof. R. W. Scholz, ETH
Margrot Leuthold, Alliance for Global Sustainability, ETH
Prof. Dr. Marcel Herbst, ETH
(and others)

Utrecht (the Netherlands)
ir. Kees Visser, projectleider Stedelijke projecten, Gemeente Utrecht
drs. Gerard Slag, environment department, Gemeente Utrecht

Michael Post, Het Groene Dak
ir. W. A. J. M. van Loosbroek, Verkeer, Gemeente Utrecht
drs. J. van der Snoek, Milieu, Gemeente Utrecht
Els Stasse, secretaris, Projectbureau Duurzaam Utrecht, Gemeente Utrecht
drs. Margot Stolk, projectleider, Duurzaam Utrecht, Gemeente Utrecht
R. Rijnders, Dienst Water en Milieu, Gemeente Utrecht
Leen DeWit, Leidse Rijn, Gemeente Utrecht
drs. Lutske Lindeman, Leidsche Rijn, Gemeente Utrecht

Zandvoort (the Netherlands)
ir. P. C. Kamp (Zero-energy house)

Zwijndrecht (the Netherlands)
ir. C. Merkus, wethouder van Stedelijke, Gemeente Zwijndrecht
ing. W. T. Los, director, sector Wonen and Bouwen, Gemeente Zwijndrecht

Zwolle (the Netherlands)
Margriet Meindertsma, Gemeente Zwolle
dr. Co Verdaas, strategic planner, Gemeente Zwolle
Joep v. d. Heyden, Stadshager project coordinator, Gemeente Zwolle
(and others)

Dutch National Government
Gerard H. J. Keijzers, director, Directorate for Strategic Planning, VROM
drs. Peter van Exel, chief, Sustainable building program, VROM
ir. L. M. De Wever, Rijksgebouwendienst
Prof. Adri van den Brink, Dienst Landeljk Gebied
drs. Ron Spreekmeester, VROM, international housing affairs
drs. J. J. H. Leerssen, VROM
drs. B. Roes, VNG, Vereniging van Nederlandse Gemeenten
ing. G. J. den Boon, DuBo Centrum, Utrecht
Piet Kruithoff, Directorate-General for Environmental Protection
drs. Th. van Bellegem, Directorate-General for Environmental Protection
J. A. M. Kroese-Duijsters, Director General for Spatial Planning
ir. J. C. Heemrood, project director, Sustainable Building

Hans A. Ruijter, project manager, road pricing

A. A. M. Zimmerman, Ministerie van Verkeer en Waterstaat

Marion G. Bakker, mobility management, Ministry of Transport, Public Works and Water Management

Henry B. J. Meutink, Stichting voor Gedeeld Autogebruik

H. van Hilten, Rijksgebouwendienst

(and others)

National Environmental Organizations

Peter van Lentenfeld, director, Global Action Plan Netherlands

drs. B. Roes, VNG (Den Haag)

Research Institutes

Hugo Priemus, OTB Managing Director, TU-Delft

Maria Buitenkamp, campaign leader, sustainable development, Friends of the Earth Netherlands

Tjeerd Deelstra, director, The International Institute for the Urban Environment

Voula Mega, European Foundation for the Improvement of Living and Working Conditions

Anthony Payne, European Sustainable Cities and Towns Campaign (Brussels)

(and others)

University

Ing. G. W. Nijenhuis, Landbouwuniversiteit Wageningen

Prof. Dr. Hubert van Lier, Wageningen

Prof. Dr. Adri van den Brink, Wageningen

(and others)

Misc.

Mr. Campagne, Greenwheels

Joachim Schwartz, director, European Car Sharing Organization, Bremen

Jan Holstein, VIBA Expo, 's-Hertogenbosch

ing. J. lepsma, Novem (Amersfoort)

Erika Spil, National Association of Wereldwinkels, Utrecht

(and others)

Appendix B

Charter of European Cities
and Towns: Towards Sustainability
(The Aalborg Charter)

(as approved by the participants at the European Conference on Sustainable Cities and Towns in Aalborg, Denmark on 27 May 1994.)

Part I. Consensus Declaration: European Cities and Towns Towards Sustainability

Part II. The European Sustainable Cities and Towns Campaign

Part III. Engaging in Local Agenda 21 Processes: Local Action Plans Towards Sustainability

Explanatory Note

The Aalborg Charter was approved by the participants at the European Conference on Sustainable Cities and Towns held in Aalborg, Denmark, from 24–27 May 1994 under joint sponsorship by the European Commission and the City of Aalborg and organized by the International Council for Local Environmental Initiatives (ICLEI). The responsibility for preparing the Draft Charter was taken by ICLEI and shared with the Ministry of Urban Development and Transport of the Federal State of Northrhine-Westphalia, Germany. The charter reflects ideas and wording from many contributors.

The Aalborg Charter was initially signed by 80 European local authorities and 253 representatives of international organizations, national governments, scientific institutes, consultants, and individuals. By signing the charter, European cities, towns, and counties committed themselves to enter into Local Agenda 21 processes and develop long-term action plans towards sustainability and initiated the European Sustainable Cities and Towns Campaign.

The draft charter was discussed by more than 600 participants in the 36 workshops of the Aalborg conference. Many of their comments and suggestions were incorporated into the final text. However, the Charter Editorial Group felt that numerous basic and substantial proposals for amendments deserved a more intensive consideration and discussion and could not simply be included as a matter of editing. Therefore, it was proposed that the review of the suggested amendments would be a task of the Campaign Coordination, which the charter further developed and submitted to the participants at the Second European Conference on Sustainable Cities and Towns held in Lisbon, Portugal, in September 1996.

Part I. Consensus Declaration: European Cities and Towns Towards Sustainability

I.1. The Role of European Cities and Towns

We, European cities and towns, signatories of this Charter, state that in the course of history, our towns have existed within and outlasted empires, nation states, and regimes and have survived as centres of social life, carriers of our economies, and guardians of culture, heritage, and tradition. Along with families and neighbourhoods, towns have been the basic elements of our societies and states. Towns have been the centres of industry, craft, trade, education, and government.

We understand that our present urban lifestyle, in particular our patterns of division of labour and functions, land use, transport, industrial production, agriculture, consumption, and leisure activities, and hence our standard of living, make us essentially responsible for many environmental problems humankind is facing. This is particularly relevant as 80 percent of Europe's population live in urban areas.

We have learnt that present levels of resource consumption in the industrialised countries cannot be achieved by all people currently living, much less by future generations, without destroying the natural capital.

We are convinced that sustainable human life on this globe cannot be achieved without sustainable local communities. Local government is close to where environmental problems are perceived and closest to the citizens and shares responsibility with governments at all levels for the well-being of humankind and nature. Therefore, cities and towns are key players in the process of changing lifestyles, production, consumption, and spatial patterns.

I.2. The Notion and Principles of Sustainability

We, cities and towns, understand that the idea of sustainable development helps us to base our standard of living on the carrying capacity of nature. We seek to achieve social justice, sustainable economies, and environmental sustainability. Social justice will necessarily have to be based on economic sustainability and equity, which require environmental sustainability.

Environmental sustainability means maintaining the natural capital. It demands from us that the rate at which we consume renewable material, water, and energy resources does not exceed the rate at which the natural systems can replenish them, and that the rate at which we consume non-renewable resources does not exceed the rate at which sustainable renewable resources are replaced. Environmental sustainability also means that the rate of emitted pollutants does not exceed the capacity of the air, water, and soil to absorb and process them.

Furthermore, environmental sustainability entails the maintenance of biodiversity; human health; as well, as air, water, and soil qualities at standards sufficient to sustain human life and well-being, as well as animal and plant life, for all time.

I.3. Local Strategies Towards Sustainability

We are convinced that the city or town is both the largest unit capable of initially addressing the many urban architectural, social, economic, political, natural resource, and environmental imbalances damaging our modern world and the smallest scale at which problems can be meaningfully resolved in an integrated, holistic, and sustainable fashion. As each city is different, we have to find our individual ways towards sustainability. We shall integrate the principles of sustainability in all our policies and make the respective strengths of our cities and towns the basis of locally appropriate strategies.

1.4. Sustainability as a Creative, Local, Balance-Seeking Process

We, cities and towns, recognise that sustainability is neither a vision nor an unchanging state, but a creative, local, balance-seeking process extending into all areas of local decision-making. It provides ongoing feedback in the management of the town or city on which activities are driving the urban ecosystem towards balance and which are driving it away. But building the management of a city around the information collected through such a process, the city is understood to work as an organic whole and the effects of all significant activities are made manifest. Through such a process the city and its citizens may make informed choices. Through a management process rooted in sustainability, decisions may be made which not only represent the interests of current stakeholders, but also of future generations.

I.5. Resolving Problems by Negotiating Outwards

We, cities and towns, recognise that a town or city cannot permit itself to export problems into the larger environment or to the future. Therefore, any problems or imbalances within the city are either brought towards balance at their own level or absorbed by some larger entity at the regional or national level. This is the principle of resolving problems by negotiating outwards. The implementation of this principle will give each city or town great freedom to define the nature of its activities.

I.6. Urban Economy Towards Sustainability

We, cities and towns, understand that the limiting factor for economic development of our cities and towns has become natural capital, such as atmosphere, soil, water, and forests. We must therefore invest in this capital. In order of priority this requires

1. investments in conserving the remaining natural capital, such as groundwater stocks, soil, habitats for rare species;
2. encouraging the growth of natural capital by reducing our level of current exploitation, such as of non-renewable energy;
3. investments to relieve pressure on natural capital stocks by expanding cultivated natural capital (such as parks for inner-city recreation to relieve pressure on natural forests); and
4. increasing the end-use efficiency of products, such as energy-efficient buildings, environmentally friendly urban transport.

I.7. Social Equity for Urban Sustainability

We, cities and towns, are aware that the poor are worst affected by environmental problems (such as noise and air pollution from traffic, lack of amenities, unhealthy housing, lack of open space) and are least able to solve them. Inequitable distribution of wealth both causes unsustainable behaviour and makes it harder to change. We intend to integrate people's basic social needs as well as healthcare, employment, and housing programmes with environmental protection. We wish to learn from initial experiences of sustainable lifestyles, so that we can work towards improving the quality of citizen's lifestyles rather than simply maximising consumption.

We will try to create jobs which contribute to the sustainability of the community and thereby reduce unemployment. When seeking to attract or create jobs we will assess the effects of any business opportunity in terms of sustainability in order to encourage the creation of long-term jobs and long-life products in accordance with the principles of sustainability.

I.8. Sustainable Land-Use Patterns

We, cities and towns, recognise the importance of effective land-use and development planning policies by our local authorities which embrace the strategic environmental assessment of all plans. We should take advantage of the scope for providing efficient public transport and energy which higher densities offer, while maintaining the human scale of development. In both undertaking urban renewal programmes in inner urban areas and in planning new suburbs we seek a mix of functions so as to reduce the need for mobility. Notions of equitable regional interdependency should enable us to balance the flows between city and countryside and prevent cities from merely exploiting the resources of surrounding areas.

I.9. Sustainable Urban Mobility Patterns

We, cities and towns, shall strive to improve accessibility and sustain social welfare and urban lifestyles with less transport. We know that it is imperative for a sustainable city to reduce en-forced mobility and stop promoting and supporting the unnecessary use of motorised vehicles. We shall give priority to ecologically sound means of transport (in particular walking, cycling, public transport) and make a combination of these means the centre of our planning efforts. Motorised individual means of urban transport ought to have the subsidiary function of facilitating access to local services and maintaining the economic activity of the city.

I.10. Responsibility for the Global Climate

We, cities and towns, understand that the significant risks posed by global warming to the natural and built environments and to future human generations require a response sufficient to stabilise and then to reduce emissions of greenhouse gases into the atmosphere as soon as possible. It is equally important to protect global biomass resources, such as forests and phytoplankton, which play an essential role in the earth's carbon cycle. The abatement of fossil fuel emissions will require policies and initiatives based on a thorough understanding of the alternatives and of the urban environment as an energy system. The only sustainable alternatives are renewable energy sources.

I.11. Prevention of Ecosystem Toxification

We, cities and towns, are aware that more and more toxic and harmful substances are released into the air, water, soil, food, and are thereby becoming a growing threat to human health and the ecosystems. We will undertake every effort to see that further pollution is stopped and prevented at source.

I.12. Local Self-Governance as a Pre-Condition

We, cities and towns, are confident that we have the strength, the knowledge, and the creative potential to develop sustainable ways of living and to design and manage our cities towards sustainability. As democratically elected representatives of our local communities we are ready to take responsibility for the task of reorganising our cities and towns for sustainability. The extent to which cities and towns are able to rise to this challenge depends upon their being given rights to local self-governance, according to the principle of subsidiarity. It is essential that sufficient powers are left at the local level and that local authorities are given a solid financial base.

I.13. Citizens as Key Actors and the Involvement of the Community

We, cities and towns, pledge to meet the mandate given by Agenda 21, the key document approved at the Earth Summit in Rio de Janeiro, to work with all sectors of our communities—citizens, businesses, interest groups—when developing our Local Agenda 21 plans. We recognize the call in the European Union's Fifth Environmental Action Programme "Towards Sustainability" for the responsibility for the implementation of the programme to be shared among all sectors of the community. Therefore, we will base our work on cooperation between all actors involved. We shall ensure that all citizens and interested groups have access to information and are able to participate in local decision-making processes. We will seek opportunities for education and training for sustainability, not only for the general population, but for both elected representatives and officials in local government.

I.14. Instruments and Tools for Urban Management Towards Sustainability

We, cities and towns, pledge to use the political and technical instruments and tools available for an ecosystem approach to urban management. We shall take advantage of a wide range of instruments, including those for collecting and processing environmental data; environmental planning; regulatory, economic, and communication instruments such as directives, taxes and fees; and mechanisms for awareness raising, including public participation. We seek to establish new environmental budgeting systems which allow for the management of our natural resources as economically as our artificial resource, "money."

We know that we must base our policy-making and controlling efforts, in particular our environmental monitoring, auditing, impact assessment, accounting, balancing and reporting systems, on different types of indicators, including those of urban environmental quality, urban flows, urban patterns, and most importantly, indicators of an urban systems sustainability.

We, cities and towns, recognize that a whole range of policies and activities yielding positive ecological consequences have already been successfully applied in many cities through Europe. However, while these instruments are valuable tools for reducing the pace and pressure of unsustainability, they do not in and of themselves reverse society's unsustainable direction. Still, with this strong existing ecological base, the cities are in an excellent position to take the threshold step of integrating these policies and activities into the governance process for managing local urban economies through a comprehensive sustainability process. In this process we are called on to develop our own strategies, try them out in practice and share our experiences.

Part II. The European Sustainable Cities and Towns Campaign

We, European cities and towns, signatories of this charter, shall move forward together towards sustainability in a process of learning from experience and successful local examples. We shall encourage each other to establish long-term local action plans (Local Agendas 21), thereby strengthening inter-authority cooperation, and relating this process to the European Union's actions in the field of the urban environment.

We hereby initiate *The European Sustainable Cities and Towns Campaign* to encourage and support cities and towns in working towards sustainability. The initial phase of this Campaign shall be for a two-year period, after which progress shall be assessed at a Second European Conference on Sustainable Cities and Towns to be held in 1996.

We invite every local authority, whether city, town, or county and any European network of local authorities to join the Campaign by adopting and signing this Charter.

We request all the major local authority networks in Europe to undertake the coordination of the Campaign. A Coordinating Committee shall be established of representatives of these networks. Arrangements will be made for those local authorities which are not members of any network.

We foresee the principal activities of the Campaign to be to:

- facilitate mutual support between European cities and towns in the design, development, and implementation of policies towards sustainability;

- collect and disseminate information on good examples at the local level;
- promote the principle of sustainability in other local authorities;
- recruit further signatories to the Charter;
- organise an annual "Sustainable City Award";
- formulate policy recommendations to the European Commission;
- provide input to the Sustainable Cities Reports of the Urban Environment Expert Group;
- support local policy-makers in implementing appropriate recommendations and legislation from the European Union;
- edit a Campaign newsletter.

These activities will require the establishment of a Campaign Coordination.

We shall invite other organisations to actively support the Campaign.

Part III. Engaging in the Local Agenda 21 Processes: Local Action Plans Towards Sustainability

We, European cities and towns, signatories of this Charter, pledge by signing this Charter and joining the European Sustainable Cities and Towns Campaign that we will seek to achieve a consensus within our communities on a Local Agenda 21 by the end of 1996. This will meet the mandate established by Chapter 28 of Agenda 21 as agreed at the Earth Summit in Rio in June 1992. By means of our individual local action plans we shall contribute to the implementation of the European Union's Fifth Environmental Action Programme "Towards Sustainability." The Local Agenda 21 processes shall be developed on the basis of Part I of this Charter.

We propose that the process of preparing a local action plan should include the following stages:

- recognition of the existing planning and financial frameworks as well as other plans and programmes;
- the systematic identification, by means of extensive public consultation, of problems and their causes;
- the prioritisation of tasks to address identified problems;
- the creation of a vision for a sustainable community through a participatory process involving all sectors of the community;
- the consideration and assessment of alternative strategic options;
- the establishment of a long-term local action plan towards sustainability which includes measurable targets;
- the programming of the implementation of the plan, including the preparation of a timetable and statement of allocation of responsibilities among the partners;

- the establishment of systems and procedures for monitoring and reporting on the implementation of the plan.

We will need to review whether the internal arrangements of our local authorities are appropriate and efficient to allow the development of the Local Agenda 21 processes, including long-term action plans towards sustainability. Efforts may be needed to improve the capacity of the organisation which will include reviewing the political arrangements, administrative procedures, corporate and inter-disciplinary working, human resources available and inter-authority cooperation, including associations and networks.

Index

Aalborg Charter. *See* European
    Sustainable Cities and Towns
    Campaign
A-B-C public transit policy, 112–113,
    140–141, 143–144, 427
Accessory units, 80–81
Acquisition. *See* Procurement and
    investment policies
Action Plan Sustainable Netherlands, 23
Adam Joseph Lewis Center, 317
Agenda 21, national development plans,
    426. *See also* Local Agenda 21
    processes
Agricultural practices
    city farms, 214–215, 340
    connections to the city, 238–242, 413
    farmers markets, 395
    farmland preservation, 13, 58–59,
        214–215, 412
    fertilizer from food waste, 236
    government subsidies, 58
    subscription farming, 13
Air quality. *See* Carbon dioxide
    emissions; Carbon monoxide
    emissions; Nitrogen oxide emissions;
    Sulfur dioxide
Air traffic, impacts of, 413
Albertslund, 10
    green accounts, 330
    pesticide policy, 338
    procurement policy, 336
    sustainable business promotion, 373
Algemene Nederlandse Wielrijders Bond
    (ANWB), 154–155, 156, 299
Almere, 10

bus system, 48, 124–125
compact urban planning, 48–49
ecological networks, 200
Almshouses. *See* Housing, buildings
    around a courtyard
Alphen a/d Rijn, Ecolonia building
    project, 291–293, 323 n.1, 423
Altstad. *See* Freiburg, Altstad district
American Forests, 228
American Wind Energy Association, 284
Amersfoort, 10
    bicycle system, 170–171
    greenschools, 216
    Nieuwland, energy balanced housing,
        79–80, 279–280
    schoolhouses, 299
    solar energy, 274–275, 276
Amsterdam, 10
    bicycle system, 171, 180–183
    car-sharing, 151, 152, 156
    city-center, 44, 46
    compact urban planning and
        greenspace, 35, 407–409
    decentralized energy production,
        261–262
    dock area development, Java-eiland,
        46–47
    ecological building projects, 298–299,
        302–303
    GWL-terrein, 230, 312
        car-free approach, 145–148
        greenroofs, 205, 208–209
        rainwater conservation, 217
    industrial site renovations, 387
    infill development, 45, 410

Amsterdam (*continued*)
  land use and transportation data, 30
  Nieuw Sloten, high-density areas with
    livability, 78–79, 112
  parking strategies, 143–144
  public transit, 112
  traffic control in, 140–141
  urban renewal, 306
  "white bikes" program, 178. *See also*
    Bicycles, public-use shared
Antwerpen, Ecover factory, 378–381,
  401
Arcata. *See* California, Arcata
ARGE Solar, 273
Århus, bicycle system, 169–170,
  183–184
Arizona
  Civano ecovillage, 314
  Phoenix land use and transportation
    data, 30
Ark, The, 350–351
Arnhem, 252, 312
Art, civic, 91–92, 98, 99, 113, 121
Asnæs power plant, 374
AT&T, 402
Audits. *See* Sustainability, assessment of
Austria. *See* Graz; Linz; Vienna
Automobiles. *See also* Parking; Traffic
    control
  alternatives to. *See* Bicycles; Public
    transit; Transportation
  car-free housing developments,
    145–151, 297–298
  car-on-demand, 154–156
  car-sharing, 151–154, 421
    Ecostad activities, 354
    Family, Friends & Neighbors, 155
    GWL-terrein activities, 145
    potential for, 165, 165 n.2
    psychological aspects of, 165
  car use statistics, 30, 137, 410
  design for reuse, 394
  disincentives for, 60–61, 134, 335, 423
  gasoline taxes, 60–61, 74 n.5, 134, 176
  incentives for alternatives to, 43,
    51–52, 335, 337–338, 381
  limited access by, 49. *See also*
    Pedestrian-oriented spaces;
    Traffic control
  ownership trends, 61
  roads for. *See* Road-pricing; Roads
  sales tax on, 74 n.6
Awards
  BEST Business Award, 400
  Environmental Cities, 425–426

European Sustainable City Award, 10,
  17, 360
National Environmental Award, 259

Bakken cohousing site, 85
Ballerup, 301
Barcelona, 93
Bebauungsplan, 57
Beijum, 34
Belgium, 344. *See also* Antwerpen;
    Oostmalle
Bergin, 157
Berlin, 10
  bike lanes, 166
  car-sharing, 152, 153
  city-center, 44
  deconcentrated concentration, 48, 52
  desealing of roads, 216
  ecological institutional buildings, 302
  greenspace and ecological networks,
    199, 200
  infill development, 92
  parking strategies, 143
  planning for local climate, 218–219
  public transit statistics, 109
  public transit system, 111, 135
  spatial planning, 53
  sustainable business promotion, 374
  urban renewal, 304–305, 306–307
BEST Business Awards, 400
Bestemmingsplan, 53, 57
Bicycles, 166–167
  bike lanes, kilometers of, 166
  cultural aspects, 183–184, 185, 188,
    189
  models and guidance, 185–193,
    418–419
  mopeds *vs.,* 98, 142
  parking. *See* Parking, for bicycles
  promotion of
    by businesses, 253
    by cities, 167–177
    models for, 418–419
  public-use shared, 135, 146, 151,
    177–183, 190–193
  restricted lanes for, 42, 43, 97
  trip statistics
    Freiburg, 123
    Netherlands, 41
    U.S., 105, 106 n.3, 189–190
Bielefeld, car-free development, 150–151
Binnenstad beter. See Groningen,
    compact urban planning
Biocide Directive, 15
Biodiversity, 4, 222–223, 239

Biogas. *See* Fuel, alternatives
Bioworks pyramid of Kolding, 248–252,
    257 n.3, 305
Birds directive, 201
Block 103 project, 304–305
BMW, 390, 394
Bofœllesskaber. See Cohousing
Bologna, 10
    carbon dioxide emissions, 74 n.1,
        282–283
    city-center, 44
    environmental impact assessments,
        336
    greenspace, 199
    historic building preservation, 90
    infill development, 45
    parking strategies, 143, 144–145
    pedestrian-oriented spaces, 92, 93
    public transit system, 111, 115
    wildlife habitat conservation, 223
    wind energy, 268
Bouw Initiatief Milieunorm (BIM), 379
Boxmeer, 299
Breda, 344
Bridges, ecological, 213–214
Bristol, 215, 338
Britain. *See* United Kingdom
Bronx Community Paper Company, 401
"Brownfields," 56, 74 n.3, 314,
    384–387, 401, 411
Budgets, environmental. *See* Economic
    aspects, budgets and charters
Buildings. *See also* Construction
    materials; Greenroofs; Greenwalls
    aesthetics of, 408
    designed for dismantling and reuse,
        299–300, 421
    ecologically designed, 203–204,
        314–316, 350–351
    governmental, 340–342
    institutional, 302–304, 309,
        316–317, 318–319, 387–390,
        401–402
    mortgages for, 310
    projects, 291–304
    promotion of, 307–310, 316, 318,
        319–320
    pyramids, Kolding wastewater
        treatment site, 248–252, 257 n.3
    retrofitting, 226, 304, 305–307,
        349–350
    windflow and transparent
        construction, 219
    historic preservation of, 90, 97,
        386–387

management of, 338–342
    urban renewal, 304–307
Bunnik, ecological office, 389. 390
Buses. *See* Transportation, bus systems
Business
    environmentally friendly, 390–399
    green manufacturing companies,
        393–394
    industrial estates, 381–384
    industrial symbiosis and ecoindustrial
        parks, 374–378
    local sustainable, 370–374
    marketing, 399–400
    offices. *See* Office buildings
    partnerships with government,
        419–420
    privatization *vs.* sustainability, 428 n.3
    shopping malls, 56
    shops, in mixed-use housing, 75 n.8,
        78, 79–81
    sustainable factory, 378–381, 401
Business Sector Network, 373
Buurt Auto Service, 145–146

California
    Arcata
        sustainability policies, 362
        wastewater treatment wetland, 254
    Davis
        bicycle system, 188
        cohousing, 85–86, 101, 102
        cul-de-sac connections, 67
        Village Homes development,
            228–229
        wastewater treatment wetland,
            255–256
    home size preference, 322–323
    housing-commuting balance, 64
    light rail lines, 130
    Los Angeles
        land use and transportation data,
            30
        public transit statistics, 110
    New Urbanism, 65
    Palm Spring bicycle-sharing program,
        192–193
    Sacramento solar energy promotion,
        286–287
    San Diego road-pricing, 164
    Santa Monica renewable energy policy,
        361–362
    traffic-calming strategies, 67, 161, 164
Canada
    Toronto Healthy House, 314–316
    Victoria car-sharing, 165

Canals
    ecological bridges, 213–214
    as ecological corridors, 200
    for stormwater runoff. See Water,
        green drainage swales
Canton. See Zürich
Capital Improvements Program
    Sustainability Matrix, 361
Carbon dioxide emissions, 130
    European statistics and targets, 6, 74
        n.1, 412
    greenroofs and, 206
    per capita, 4, 74 n.1
    reduction strategies, 22, 264, 282–288
    tree-planting and, 254
    use in greenhouses, 244–246
Carbon monoxide emissions, 61
Carbon tax, 268
Car Busters, 139
Car-Free Cities network, 137–138, 359,
    425
CEMR. See Council of European
    Municipalities and Regions
Childcare, 81, 340
Chip cards. See Public transit, single card
    for integrated use
CiBoGa project, 301, 409
Cities. See also Growth issues
    bicycle-friendly, 167–177
    car-free, 137–139
    city-centers, 43–47, 103
    connections to the hinterland,
        238–242, 418
    cultural perception of, 224
    as ecosystems, 16, 17, 197–198,
        416–417
    hierarchy of centers in, 51
    included in the book
        criteria for, 9
        list of, 10
        structure of field visits, 12
    integration of functions within, 41,
        247
    nature as a paradigm for, 6–7
    organic growth of, 408
    as organisms, 3, 6–7
    ranking systems, 20–21
    re-use of land. See Infill development
    sister, 344–345
    street aesthetics and design, 92–93,
        173
    urban restructuring, 220–221
Cities for a Small Planet, 232
Cities for Climate Protection, 22, 282
City After the Automobile, The, 151

City Bikes, 178, 179, 190
City farms, 214–215, 340
City of the Sun (Heerhugowaard),
    276–277
Climate
    global, 4, 22, 466
    local, 218–219
Climate Alliance of European Cities, 22,
    282
Climate Alliance Treaty, 283
Closed-loop relationships, 7, 11,
    242–246, 276, 370. See also
    Ecocycle balancing
Coevolution of sustainability policy, 14
Cohousing
    Denmark, 85
    United States, 13, 85–86, 101–102
Colorado
    Boulder
        bicycle system, 187, 190, 191
        green building promotion, 320, 321,
            324 n.9
        mini-bus system, 132
        pedestrian-oriented spaces, 104
    Denver
        carbon dioxide emissions, 74 n.1
        city-center housing, 103
    Nyland cohousing, 102
    solar energy promotion, 287
        Combined heat and energy
            production (CHP). See District
            heating systems
        Commission de Villes, 18
        Commonwealth Energy
            Corporation, 361
        Community involvement. See Public
            participation
        Commuting. See also Automobiles,
            disincentives for; Automobiles,
            incentives for alternatives to;
            Public transit
    by bicycle, 166, 167, 170, 183,
        186
    job-housing balance, 64
    suburb-to-suburb, 125
Compact urban form, 13. See also
    Ecocycle balancing; Ecovillages;
    Housing, "mixed use"
    cultural factors, 59–60, 411, 414
    decentralizing trends, 411
    economic signals that influence,
        60–61, 423
    growth districts, 41–43
    loss of greenspace from, 407–409
    models and guidance, 414–415

proximity to noisy or hazardous sites, 409
spatial planning, 29–32, 52–58, 62, 418
strategies for, 32–41, 70
value of rural, agricultural, and undeveloped lands, 58–59
Composting, 238, 240, 255, 339
Computer software, for sustainability assessment, 357
Conflicts of green urbanism, 407–414, 465
Congestion pricing. See Road-pricing
Construction Industry Research Board, 323
Construction materials
avoidance of nonsustainable products, 294, 295, 296–297, 318, 379
insulation, 270–271, 278, 281, 295, 379
procurement policies, 336–337
sawdust-mixture bricks, 379
use of local products, 318
use of recycled products, 204, 270, 295, 318, 379, 421
windows, 271, 278, 295
Consumer trends and perceptions
carbon dioxide emissions, 4
green consumerism, 390–399, 404 n.5
high-consumption lifestyle, 366
housing, 322–323, 411
promotion of lifestyle changes, 354–358
use of world's resources, 411–412
Contaminants
in Aalborg Charter policy, 466–467
in food, 7
pesticide policies, 333
pollution prevention/reduction, 371–372, 466–467
soil remediation, 375
urban development and hazardous sites, 409
Cooperation and partnerships, 17, 419–420
Copenhagen, 10
bicycle-sharing program, 178–179
bicycle system, 166, 171
carbon dioxide emissions, 74 n.1
city-center, 44
cohousing, 85
compact urban planning, 52, 53
district heating, 261
ecological building projects, 300, 301
environmental education, 352–353
land use and transportation data, 30
pedestrian-oriented spaces, 40, 94–96
public transit statistics, 110
Copenhagen Declaration, 137
Council of European Municipalities and Regions (CEMR), 18
Courtyards, 83–85, 212–213, 299
Creating a Sustainable London, 238
Crime, 60
Cul-de-sac connections, 67
Cultural aspects
bicycle riding, 183–184, 185, 188, 189
in compact urban form planning, 59–60
extended family and accessory units, 81
home ownership, 321, 322–323
Netherlands international initiatives, 367–368 n.3
perception of cities, 224
shift from products to services, 421
sustainable industry, 395
trams, 123
transferability of European experience, 13–15, 366, 373
transit ethos, U.S. lack of, 129–130
U.S. television watching, 103
use of terms, 12
Curitibia, 14
Cycles, creation of. See Closed-loop relationships; Ecocycle balancing
Cycle to Work campaign, 184
Cykelbus'ters, 183–184

Danmarks Naturfredningsforening, 21, 359, 365, 425
Davis. See California, Davis
Day care, 81, 340
Deconcentrated concentration, 48, 52, 410
De Helden, 34
Delft
bicycle usage, 168
ecological buildings, 295–296, 341
living street concept, 142–143
De Meern, 41
Den Haag, 10
bicycle promotion, 338
buildings around a courtyard, 84–85
carbon dioxin emissions, 282
city-center, New Centrum, 45
Ecostad, 23, 353–354, 368 n.4, 374
high-density areas with livability, 77
local Agenda 21 processes, 348
sustainability assessment, 329–330
tree planting, 205

Denmark. *See also* Albertslund;
    Copenhagen; Herning; Kalundborg;
    Kolding; Odense; Slagelse; Viborg
    bicycle commuting statistics, 338
    cohousing, 85
    district heating, 260–261, 374–375
    Green Municipalities Project, 20
    green taxes, 257 n.4
    organic waste recycling, 241
    promotion of sustainability, 359
    renewable energy, 268–270, 422
Depot bicycle-sharing system, 180–183
Desealing of roads, 216–218
Deutsche Umwelthilfe, 20, 359, 365
Developing countries, goods from,
    397–399
Developments. *See* Housing
    developments
Die Grüne Hausnummer, 311–312
Dilemmas of green urbanism, 407–414,
    465
Directives of the European Union, 15,
    201
Disabilities, adaptations for, 122–123,
    214
District heating systems, 43, 217,
    259–264
    Denmark, 260–261, 301, 374–375, 377
    GWL-terrein in Amsterdam, 217
    lessons from Europe, 285–286
    symbiosis with industry, 377
    technological background, 288 n.3
    Utrecht Centrum, 43
Dobris Assessment, 19
Dordrecht, ecocycle balancing, 247–248
Drachten, 8, 80, 251–252, 293–295
Drainage swales. *See* Water, green
    drainage swales
Drempels, 139, 161, 162
Dublin, 10
    bicycle system, 177
    city-center, 45, 46, 89–90
    district heating, 263
    ecological buildings, 89–90, 302, 314
DuboCentrum, 309
DuBo-kaart, 313
Dunkerque, 10
    greenwalls, 212
    sustainable industrial estate, 381–384
    tram system development, 113–114
Dynamic Regional Energy Analysis
    Model, 265

Earth Summit, 4, 469
Eco-bridges, 213–214
Ecoburbs. *See* Ecovillages

EcoCal program, 357–358, 366
Ecocycle balancing, 11, 232–242,
    246–257. *See also* Energy balancing
    models and guidance, 416–417, 420
    in neighborhoods, 246–252
    pilot programs, 236, 276, 277, 305,
    374–375
Ecodus, 295–296, 341
Eco-kantoor, 389, 390
Ecological budgeting. *See* Economic
    aspects, budgets, and charters
"Ecological footprint," 4. *See also*
    Compact urban form; Ecovillages;
    Environmental space
    analysis of, 19–20, 233, 235, 239,
    253–254
    of an office, 389–390
    monitoring of reductions in, 329–331
    reduction of, 6, 88–89, 197–231, 290
Ecological networks, 199–203, 224
Ecological regeneration. *See* Restoration,
    ecological
Ecological tax, 70, 252–253, 256–257,
    423, 426
Ecology parks, 199, 214–215
Ecolonia. *See* Alphen a/d Rijn
Economic aspects. *See also* Taxes
    bicycle use/promotion, 175–176, 177,
    183, 189
    budgets and charters, 333–336,
    467–468
    costs associated with automobile use,
    137
    eco-bridges, 214
    electricity pricing by time variables,
    342
    green accounts, 242, 330, 348
    greenroofs, 206, 211
    impact of pedestrian-oriented spaces,
    101
    influence on compact land use
    patterns, 60–61, 75 n.8
    liability of bicycle-sharing programs,
    191
    of Living Over the Shops campaign, 82
    mortgages for green buildings, 310,
    316, 318
    procurement and investment policies,
    335, 336–337
    public transit systems, 118–119, 122
    road-pricing billing, 160–161
    sustainable economy
        in the Aalborg Charter, 465
        local businesses, 370–374
        pilot programs, 18
        profits from, 421–422

Economic Efficiency and Pollution
    Reduction Act, 256
Ecooperation, 184
ECOPROFIT program, 370–373, 400,
    420
Eco-roofs. *See* Greenroofs
Ecostad, 23, 353–354, 368 n.4, 374
Ecosystem approach. *See* Cities, as
    ecosystems; Ecovillages
Eco-team program, 355–356, 366, 424
Eco-Textil, 386
Eco-tickets, 121
Ecover factory, 317, 378–381, 401
Ecovillages, 86, 147, 230, 314, 358–60
Edinburgh, car-free development, 148
Education. *See also* Schools
    bicycle mentors, 189
    community information networks, 353
    in energy efficiency, 266
    exchanges and transfers, 344
    green remodeling techniques, 320
    local ecology, 322
    need for sustainability curriculum, 427
    neighborhood eco-teams program,
        355–356, 366, 424
    organic gardening, 340
    of the public, 313, 322, 345–353
    of residents in ecological
        developments, 146–147, 298,
        312, 321
    role in technology development,
        424–425
    sustainable building, 309
Ekogras, 209
Elderly, public transit and the, 123,
    129–130
Electric Bicycle Demonstration Program,
    192
Electriciteitsbedrijf Zuid-Holland,
    245–246
Electric Transit Vehicle Institute, 362
Electric vehicles. *See* Transportation,
    electric vehicles
Electrolux-Sweden, 390, 394
Emscher Park IBA, 384–387
Energy. *See also* District heating systems
    buildings as percent of world's
        consumption, 290
    decentralized production of, 261–264,
        284–285
    in ecocycle balancing, 234, 242–246,
        247–252
    municipal energy planning and
        conservation, 258–260
    in new housing developments,
        267

nuclear, 412
from organic wastes, 241–242
pilot programs, 18, 258
pricing with time variables, 342
privatization *vs.* sustainability, 428 n.3
renewable
    European statistics and targets,
        412
    hydroelectric, 268
    models and guidance, 417–418
    policies for, 268–270, 342–343,
        361–362
    solar. *See* Solar energy
    wind, 268–269, 284, 289 n.9, 393,
        422
Energy balancing, 277–282, 288 n.5
Energy efficiency, promotion of, 88,
    264–267
Energy Star Homes Program, 316, 318
Enschede, ecological building project,
    217–218, 229, 296–298, 309
Ensheim, 273
Enterprise Zone, 13
Environ, 23, 101, 177, 338, 349, 350,
    373
Environmental criteria, 336, 409–410
Environmental groups. *See*
    Nongovernmental organizations
Environmental Improvement Program
    (EIP), 374
Environmental space, 23, 330
Environmental taxes. *See* Taxes,
    ecological
Environmental Thermometer, 329–330
Eslov, ecocycle balancing, 238
Essen, 386, 387
Ethanol. *See* Fuel, alternatives
Eurocities, 18, 359, 425
Europe
    Car-Free Cities network, 137–138,
        359, 425
    car-sharing, 151–154
    coordination between governments,
        344–345, 367–368 n.3
    eastern, 18
    ecological networks, 200–201,
        359–360
    green taxes, 252–253
    promotion of sustainability, 359–360
    as source of models and guidance,
        336, 414–427
    Sustainablity Index Project, 19, 328
    use of world's resources, 411–412
European Academy of Urban
    Environment, 20
European Carsharing, 151, 152

European City of the Year award, 360
European Ecological Network
    (EECONET), 200–201
European Foundation for the
    Improvement of Living and Working
    Conditions, 20
European Green Cities, 18
European Sustainable Cities and Towns
    Campaign, 359–360
    awards, 10, 17, 381, 426
    on cities as ecosystems, 417
    on city farms, 214–215
    on open grass areas, 338–339
    principals of urban sustainability,
        16–17
    text of charter, 462–470
European Sustainable Communities, 16
European Union directives, 15, 201
Expert Committee on the Urban
    Environment, 16, 22, 135 n.2
Extrapolation. See United States,
    transferability of the European
    experience

Factories, sustainable, 378–381, 401
Fair Share suppliers, 397
Family, Friends, and Neighbors car-
    sharing, 155
Family aspects
    day care, 81, 340
    extended family housing, 81
Farmers markets, 395
Farmland preservation, 13, 58–59,
    214–215, 412
Fast-office, 299–300
Feet First campaign, 141
Fifth Environmental Action Program, 15
Finland. See also Helsinki; Lahti
    energy from organic wastes, 241–242
    legislation, 20
    local Agenda 21 processes, 348
    Local Government Act, 20
Flächennutzungsplan, 57
Florida
    carbon dioxide emissions, 74 n.1
    Sustainable Communities
        Demonstration Project, 364–365
    West Palm Beach traffic-calming
        strategies, 163
Food production and consumption, 6, 7.
    See also Gardens; Greenroofs
Forests, near cities, 31, 49, 91, 198, 255,
    340, 367 n.2
Fourth Memorandum Town Planning
    Extra. See VINEX sites

France. See Dunkerque; Paris
Fraunhofer Institute for Solar Energy
    Systems, 278
Fredengade bioworks project, 248–252,
    257 n.3, 305
Freiburg, 10
    Altstad district, 90–91, 96–97
    bicycle system, 166, 167, 172,
        174–175
    city property management, 335–336
    compact urban planning, 38, 58
    electricity pricing, 342
    energy-balanced housing, 278–279
    energy standards, 267, 288 n.8
    greenspace management, 339–340
    historic building preservation, 90–91
    pedestrian-oriented spaces, 19, 96–97,
        138
    pesticide policy, 338
    planning for local climate, 219
    procurement policy, 336
    public transit, 119–124
    solar energy promotion, 270–271,
        272, 288 n.8
    twinning with L'viv, 345
Freiburg Solar Initiative, 272, 288 n.8
Friends of the Earth, 23
Fuel
    airplane, 413
    alternatives to gasoline, 125, 318,
        343–344
    in ecocycle balancing, 247, 254
    fossil fuel trends, 6, 130, 412
    gasoline taxes, 60–61, 74 n.5

Gap headquarters building, 317
Gardens. See also Tree planting
    communal
        Drachten, 294
        Freiburg, 339–340
        GWL-terrein, 147, 230
        Het Groene Dak, 87–88, 150
    in courtyards, 83–85, 212–213, 299
    eco-tuinen, in ecological building
        projects, 296
    greenhouses, 244–246, 248
    hydroplanting, 210, 231 n.2
    in industrial buildings, 303
    in living street concept, 142
    organic gardening education, 340
    rooftop. See Greenroofs
Gasoline tax, 60–61, 74 n.5, 134, 176
General Electric, 226
German Federal Environmental
    Foundation, 333

Germany. *See also* Berlin; Freiburg;
    Heidelberg; Leipzig; Münster;
    Saarbrücken
  Avoidance of Waste Ordinance, 253
  Berlin Forest Act, 199
  bicycle promotion, 172–176
  car-free developments, 148, 150–151
  car-sharing, 152, 153
  compact urban planning, 35, 38
  composting plants, 240
  Emscher Park, 384–387
  environmental budgeting, 333
  green house number project, 311–312
  green taxes, 253
  high-speed rail system, 128
  infill development, 39
  initiatives, 22
  public transit, 113–114, 116
  renewable energy promotion,
    269–270, 272
  spatial planning, 57, 59
  sustainability promotion, 359
  train system, 114
Global Action Plan (GAP), 353,
    354–355, 420, 424
Global aspects
  climate change, 4, 22, 466
  role of cities in sustainability, 3–5
  use of world's resources, 411–412
  world's energy consumption, 290
Gloucester, 346
Going for Green campaign, 356–357,
    367, 424
Göteburg, 214, 237
Gouda, 263, 271
Governance in green urban cities. *See
    also* Education
  in the Aalborg Charter, 467
  budgets and charters, 333–336,
    467–468
  employee mobility. *See* Automobiles;
    Public transit; Transportation
  evaluation of sustainability. *See*
    Sustainability, assessment of
  management of municipal buildings
    and properties, 338–342
  models and guidance, 422–423
  motor fleet, 343–344
  partnerships, 17, 419–420
  procurement and investment policies,
    335, 336–337
  role of nongovernmental
    organizations, 353–358
Governors Commission for a Sustainable
    South Florida, 364

Grassroofs. *See* Greenroofs
Graz, 10
  composting program, 240–241
  EcoProfit program, 370–373, 400, 420
  greenroofs, 340
  greenspace, 199
  planning for local climate, 218
Great Britain. *See* United Kingdom
Green accounts, 242, 330, 348
Greenbelt Corridor and Home Countries
    Act, 38
Green Builder program, 319
Green buildings. *See* Buildings,
    ecologically designed
Green City Denmark A/S, 399–400, 422
Green Code, 356–357
Green Courtyards program, 213
Green energy. *See* Energy, renewable
Green Heart. *See* Greenspace, Green
    Heart areas in the Netherlands
Green infrastructure, 225
Greening the High Street project, 373
Green mortgages, 310, 316, 318
Green Municipalities project, 20
Green Network, 373
Green Paper on the Urban Environment,
    15–16, 30, 417
Green Party, 234, 362–363, 368 n.7
Greenpeace, 397
Greenpoints program, 320, 321
Green Radial, 11, 220–221
Greenroofs, 7, 206–211
  on an ecofactory, 379
  costs associated with, 216–217
  criteria for, 231 n.3
  as ecological compensation, 203
  GWL-terrein, 147, 209
  in Het Groene Dak, 88, 150
  promotion of, 225–226
Green Shops program, 396
Greenspace, 7, 11, 197–231
  in compact urban planning
    adjacent fingers or wedges, 35, 38,
      56, 63
    forests, near cities, 31, 49, 91, 198,
      255, 340, 367 n.2
    Green Radial hub design, 11,
      220–221
    lessons from Europe, 407–408, 410
    public transit to, 63
  as ecological corridors, 35, 199, 200
  Green Heart area in the Netherlands,
    33, 35, 43
  loss from housing, 329, 407–409
  management of, 339–340

Greenspace (*coninued*)
    planning for local climate, 218–219
    rooftop. *See* Greenroofs
    in tram systems, 120
Greenspaces program, 224
Green taxes. *See* Taxes, ecological
Green Triangle Finland, 400
Green urbanism
    the challenges of, 407–414, 465
    ecological networks in, 199–203
    governance in, 327–367
    promotion of, 358–360
    qualities that exemplify, 6–8
Greenwalls, 211–212
Greenwheels, 152, 153–154, 353
Groningen, 10
    architecture, 92
    bicycle usage, 167
    CiBoGa project, 301, 409
    city-center, 44, 45, 156, 410, 428
    compact urban planning, 34–35,
        409–410
    ecological networks, 200
    pedestrian-oriented spaces, 101
    sustainable building projects, 301, 428
        n.2
Groundwater protection, 71, 199, 302
Growth issues
    containment policies, 66–74
    development of targets, 73, 412
    growth centers, 47–52
    growth districts, 41–43
    legislation against urban sprawl, 63
    models and guidance, 414–415
    public transit planning and, 112
    spatial planning, 52–58, 269
GWL-terrein. *See* Amsterdam, GWL-
    terrein

Haagse Milieu Thermometer, 329–330
Haarlem, 209–210, 309, 387–388
Habitat conservation, 222–223, 383, 412
Habitats Directive, 15, 201
Hammarby Sjöstad site. *See* Stockholm,
    Hammarby Sjöstad site
Healthy Cities program, 22
Healthy House, 314–316
Heathrow Airport, 413
Heating. *See* District heating systems
Heerhugowaard, solar energy, 276–277
Heidelberg, 10, 78
    energy efficiency projects, 268,
        351–352, 421
    greenspace, 199

improved energy efficiency, 265–266,
    267
solar energy promotion, 271
traffic control in, 140, 141
wildlife habitat conservation, 223
Helsinki, 10
    carbon dioxide emissions, 74 n.1, 282
    combined heat and power production,
        259
    compact urban planning, 35, 36–37
    composting and recycling program,
        241
    ecological building projects, 299–300
    environmental education, 352
    greenspace, 198
    high-density areas with livability, 77
    Keskuspuisto Park, 36–37
    local Agenda 21 processes, 346
    public transit statistics, 109
    spatial planning, 54
    Viikki urban gardens, 222, 229, 300
Herman Miller factory, 317
Herning, 10, 377, 396
's-Hertogenbosch, 313
Het Groene Dak project. *See* Utrecht,
    green courtyards
Hill Country Foundation, 322
Historic building preservation, 90, 97,
    386–387
Hofjes. See Housing, buildings around a
    courtyard
Holistic nature of sustainable cities, 9
Home Zones traffic control, 143
Hotels, green, 309, 393, 421
Housing. *See also* Housing developments
    accessory units, 80–81
    buildings around a courtyard, 83–85,
        212–213
    in city-centers, 45–46, 103
    commuting issues in, 64
    cooperative. *See* Cohousing
    creative, 76–105
    energy-balanced, 277–282
    green building/remodeling
        certifications, 316, 318, 319–320,
        321
    green house numbers program,
        311–312
    green mortgages, 310, 316, 318
    high-density areas with livability,
        76–80
    home size preference, 322–323, 411
    by infill development, 39
    low-energy ecological, 18

"mixed use," 45–46, 75 n.8, 78, 79–81
Netherlands, compact urban planning, 32–33
planning, 76–77
promotion of diversity in, 43
on restored brownfields, 385
solar, 270, 274
subsidized, 77
trends in, 64–65
Housing developments, 57, 72, 75 n.8, 132–133
bicycle promotion in, 173
car-free, 145–151
energy standards for, 267, 238 n.8, 427
siting issues, 407–410
with solar energy. 274–277
Houten, 49–50, 51
Hundertwasser Haus, 203–204
Hydroelectric energy, 268
Hydroplanting, 210, 231 n.2

IBA GmbH, 384–385
ICLEI. See International Council for Local Environment Initiatives
IJburg. See Amsterdam, ecological building projects
IKEA, 390, 394
Illinois
Chicago Transit Authority, 124
Chicago bicycle system, 187
Prairie Crossing ecovillage, 230, 314
Indicators. See Sustainability. assessment of
Industrial Environmental Scheme, 381–384
Industrial estates, 381–384
Industrial fields, redevelopment of. See "Brownfields"
Industrial parks, ecocycle balancing in, 254, 374–378
Infill development, 90–92. See also "Brownfields"; Living Over the Shops campaign
Germany, 38–39, 386
lessons from Europe, 410
Netherlands, 39
Sweden, 40
United States, 68–69, 72, 323, 401
Infrastructure, green, 225
ING headquarters building, 302–303
Innovation and Technology Centre SITZ, 377

Integration
of energy sources, 417–418
of functions within a city, 41, 247
of policies, 17, 416
of strategies and solutions, 416
sustainability through partnerships, 17, 419–420
Intermodal Surface Transportation Efficiency Act (ISTEA), 162, 163, 186
International Council for Local Environment Initiatives (ICLEI), 18, 359
Cities for Climate Protection campaign, 22, 282
on environmental budgeting, 333
functions of, 425
guidelines, 20
International Solar Energy Society (ISES), 270–271
Interviewees for the book, 451–461
Investment. See Procurement and investment policies
Ireland. See Dublin
Italy, spatial planning, 54. See also Bologna

Java-eiland, dock area development, 46–47
"Jenni house," 278

Kalundborg, ecocycle balancing, 10, 242–244, 374–376, 401
Keskuspuisto Park, 36–37
Kista, 77
Kleingarten. See Gardens, communal
KLM airline, 155
Kolding, 10, 314
bioworks pyramid, 248–252, 257 n.3, 305
ecocycle balancing and courtyards, 212, 248–251
environmental education, 352
green municipal buildings, 341–342
Green Shops program, 396
urban renewal, 305–306

LA21. See Local Agenda 21
Labeling, eco-friendly, 316, 370, 394–395, 396, 403, 404 n.5
Lahti, 10, 347
Land use, 30, 61–62. See also Compact urban form; Growth issues
in the Aalborg Charter, 466

Land use (*continued*)
  European statistics and targets, 412
  public transit coordination with,
    112–113
  recycling. *See* "Brownfields"
Lees, 21
Legislation and initiatives. *See also*
    Governance in green urban cities
  budgets and charters, 333–336,
    467–468
  Denmark, wind energy, 269
  environmental criteria for development
    siting, 409–410
  European ecological networks,
    201–203
  Finland, 20
  Germany
    Avoidance of Waste Ordinance, 253
    Berlin Forest Act, 199
    Global Action Plan, 353, 354–355,
      420, 424
    green building certifications, 314, 316,
      319–320, 321
    for greening, 20–21, 38
    national differences in, 25 n.1
  Netherlands
    green building promotion, 307–309
    National Action Plan, 307
    National Environmental Policy Plan,
      292, 378, 419
    Nature Policy Plan, 201–202
  solar energy, 287, 423
  sustainability, 15, 360
  United Kingdom, Greenbelt Corridor
    and Home Countries Act, 38
  United States
    Austin, 70–72, 360
    green taxes, 256–257
    Intermodal Surface Transportation
      Efficiency Act, 162, 163, 186
    Minnesota Economic Efficiency and
      Pollution Reduction Act, 256
    Seattle Growth Management Act, 68
    "takings clause" and private land
      ownership, 58
    against urban sprawl, 63
Leicester, 10, 21
  bicycle promotion, 177, 337–338
  community information networks, 353
  ecological institutional buildings,
    303–304
  environmental education, 345,
    349–351
  greenspace, 199
  improved energy efficiency, 265

  partnerships in governance, 419
  pedestrian-oriented spaces, 98–99, 101
  public awareness campaign, 349–350
  recycling program, 242
  road-pricing, 158
  sustainability appraisal, 331–332
  sustainability assessment, 328–329
  sustainable business promotion, 373
  traffic control in, 141, 142
  wildlife habitat conservation, 222, 223
Leicester Ecology Trust, 21
Leiden, 10, 34
  bicycle system, 167–168
  creative housing in, 89
  electric truck system for freight,
    126–128
  greenspace, 205
  high-density areas with livability, 80
  hofjes (buildings around a courtyard),
    84
  infill development, 38–39
  pedestrian-oriented spaces, 97–98
  renewable energy policy, 342
  solar energy promotion, 271
Leidsche Rijn. *See* Utrecht, growth
    districts
Leipzig, 11, 220–221
Lelystad, 48
Leusden, 309
Liability issues, 191
LIFE program, 220
Lifestyle changes, 4, 354–358
Linz, 10
  carbon dioxide emissions, 283–284
  greenroofs, 210–211
  public transit, 110
  solar energy, 275–276
  sustainable building projects, 301
Lisbon Action Plan, 18
Living Over the Shops campaign (LOTS),
    45–46, 82–83
Living street concept *(woonerf)*
  definition, 142
  design and planning, 142–143, 165
    n.3, 205
  for traffic-calming, 139, 142, 143
  United States, 161
Local Agenda 21 processes, 21–22,
    345–349
  in the Aalborg Charter, 467, 469–470
  number of European cities involved in,
    22
  partnerships in, 420
  public participation, 346–347, 420,
    424

sustainable indices and targets from, 328
Local aspects
  of Agenda 21. *See* Local Agenda 21 processes
  ecosystem education, 322
  governance of green urban cities, 327–367, 467
  municipal buildings and properties, 338–342
  municipal procurement policies, 336–337
  planning for climate, 218–219
  renewable energy promotion, 342–343
  self-sufficiency, 7
  sustainable businesses, 370–374, 395–396
Logos. *See* Labeling, eco-friendly
London, 10
  air traffic impacts, 413
  bicycle system, 176–177, 184
  carbon dioxide emissions per day, 6
  car-free developments, 148
  ecocycle balancing, 234
  ecological footprint, 232–233, 238, 412–413
  environmental charters, 334
  environmental groups, 22–23
  food and fuel consumption, 6
  land use and transportation data, 30
  socially responsible investment, 337
  spatial planning, 55
  sustainable business promotion, 373, 395
  wildlife habitat conservation, 222–223
London Cycle Network, 176–177, 184
London Cycling Campaign, 176–177, 184
London Energy Study, 413
Long-Term Ecological Research network (LTER), 231
LOTS. *See* Living Over the Shops campaign
Luxury Fever, 322

Management
  of buildings, 338–342
  of greenspace, 339–340
  of municipal properties, 335–336
  urban, 17, 467–468
Mariahilfstrasse. *See* Vienna, pedestrian-oriented spaces
Marine Windmill Action Plan, 269
Marketing, 14, 399–400

Maryland
  Baltimore infill development, 68
  New Urbanism, 65
Massachusetts, Boston land use and transportation data, 30
Max Havelaar Foundation, 399
MAX light rail system, 131
McDonald's, 390, 393, 395
Media
  role of the, 349–350, 353, 393
  U.S. television watching, 103
Middlesborough, 21, 347
Minnesota
  carbon dioxide emissions, 74 n.1
  ecological taxes, 70
  Economic Efficiency and Pollution Reduction Act, 256
  greenspace, 224–225
  Minneapolis infill development, 323
  road-pricing initiative, 164
Monitoring. *See also* Sustainability, assessment of
  EcoCal software, 357–358
  Environmental Thermometer, 329
  green accounts, 330, 348
Mopeds, 98, 142
Morra Park. *See* Drachten
Mortgages, green, 310, 316, 318
Muir commons, 85–86, 101, 102
Münster, 10, 44
  bicycle system, 172–174, 175, 193, 419
  carbon dioxide emissions, 283
  connections to the farmlands, 240
  historic building preservation, 90
  procurement policy, 336–337
  sustainability assessment, 331

National Action Plan, 307
National Bicycling and Walking Study, 162, 189–190
National Federation of City Farms, 215
National Science Foundation, Long-Term Ecological Research network, 231
Natural areas. *See* Ecological networks; Greenspace; Habitat conservation
Natural Step, 233–236, 358, 391–393, 395
Nature Around the Schoolhouse project, 215–216
Nature Policy Plan, 201–202
Negotiation, 465
Neighborhoods, 8. *See also* Compact urban form; Ecovillages
  coordination and linkages between, 354–355, 418–419

Neighborhoods (*continued*)
   creation of safe. *See* Living street
      concept
   ecocycle balancing, 246–252
   as hierarchy of centers, 51
   Traditional Neighborhood Districts,
      72
   traffic control in, 140
   urban renewal, 304–307
Netherlands, 154–155. *See also* Almere;
      Amersfoort; Amsterdam; Bunnick;
      Den Haag; Drachten; Gouda;
      Groningen; Heerhugowaard;
      Houten; Leiden; Rotterdam;
      Utrecht; Zwolle
   bicycle system, 168, 180, 184
   buildings around a courtyard, 83–85,
      212–213
   call-a-car program, 155–156
   canals as ecological corridors, 200
   car-free developments, 148–150
   car ownership, 61, 410
   car-sharing, 152, 153, 155
   car use statistics, 137
   compact urban development, 32–33
   composting program, 241
   eco-bridges, 213–214
   ecological building projects,
      291–300
   ecological networks, 201–203
   eco-teams in neighborhoods, 355–356,
      366, 424
   energy agency. *See* Novem
   energy balanced housing, 280–282
   Global Action Plan, 353, 354–355,
      420, 424
   green building promotion, 307–309
   greenroofs, 207
   green taxes, 252–253
   growth center development, 48
   high-speed rail system, 128–129
   housing projects, 76–77
   incentives for alternatives to
      automobiles, 43
   infill development, 39
   land use data, 29, 30
   living street concept. *See* Living street
      concept
   National Action Plan, 307
   National Environmental Policy Plan,
      292, 378, 419
   Nature Policy Plan, 201–202
   partnerships in governance, 419–420
   pedestrian-oriented spaces, 95
   population dispersion, 61

   public transit A-B-C policy, 112–113,
      140–141, 143–144, 427
   renewable energy policy, 342–343
   road-pricing, 158–160
   solar energy, 276–277
   spatial planning, 53, 55, 57–58
   urban population density, 31, 32
   World Shops program, 397–399
New Centrum, 45
New Urbanism, 5, 65–66
New York, land use and transportation
      data, 30
Nieuwland, energy balanced housing,
      79–80, 279–280
Nieuw Sloten district, 78–79, 112
Nitrogen oxide emissions, 61, 259
Nongovernmental organizations, 20, 23
   conferences, 139
   role of, 345, 353–358, 365
Norway. *See also* Oslo
   road-pricing, 156–157
   spatial planning, 56
NOVEM, 274, 277, 280–281, 291, 310
Novo Nodisk Pharmaceutical, 375
Novotex, 393–394
Nuclear energy, 412
Nul-energiewoning, 280

"Oberlin building," 317
Odense, 10
   bicycle system, 169
   city-center, 44
   compact urban planning, 33–34
   environmental charters, 334–335
   industrial site renovations, 387
   pedestrian-oriented spaces, 99
   pesticide policy, 338
   traffic control in, 140
OECD. *See* Organization for Economic
      Cooperation and Development
Office buildings, 299–300, 302–304,
      387–390, 402
Ohio, Oberlin College green building,
      317
Oikos. *See* Enschede
Oostmalle, 380
Open spaces. *See* Pedestrian-oriented
      spaces
ORBITALE system, 125
Orebro, 300
Oregon, Portland
   bicycle system, 186, 190
   greenroof study, 226, 227
   greenspace, 224
   growth policy, 67

light rail system, 131
sustainable business program, 400
traffic-calming strategies, 162, 165
Organization for Economic Cooperation
and Development (OECD), 18
Oslo, 157, 393
Overpasses. See Bridges, ecological

Paris, ORBITALE system, 125
Park-and-ride lots, 122, 125
Parking
alternate-side, 123
for bicycles, 169, 170, 171–172,
173–174, 188
in car-free housing developments, 145,
146, 150
with car-sharing, 154
permeable bricks in lots, 294, 296
planting trees among, 204, 205, 218,
229
restrictions, 117, 122, 143–145,
150
siting issues, 410
solar lighting, 263
taxes on spaces, 158
Partners for a Clean Environment
(PACE), 400–401
Pedestrian-oriented spaces
in Car-Free Cities network, 138
in car-free developments, 149
Copenhagen, 40, 94–96
courtyards, 83–85, 212–213, 299
European plazas and squares, 92–93,
96, 103, 106 n.2, 408
Freiburg, 19, 91, 96
incremental approach in development
of, 96
Leicester, 98
Leiden, 97
lessons from Europe, 102–105
Odense, 99
United States, 14, 103–104
Vienna, 99–101
Peterborough, 21
Piccardthofplas, 301, 428 n.2
Planet Works, 242
Planning. See Compact urban form;
Housing, planning; Living street
concept, design and planning;
Public transit, planning; Spatial
planning
Plazas. See Pedestrian-oriented spaces
Poland, sister-city tree planting, 344
Policies
bicycle usage and, 185–185

compact urban form and, 60–61
deconcentrated concentration, 48, 52
environmental charters, 334–335,
467–468
growth containment, 66–74
integration of, 17, 416
open space, 67
procurement and investment, 335,
336–337
public transit, 112–113
renewable energy, 264, 268–270,
342–343
Political aspects
Green Party, 234, 362–363, 368 n.7
transferability of the European
experience, 13–15, 366, 373
Pollution. See Contaminants
Polycentric urban network, 55
Population density in major cities, 30, 31
Portland. See Oregon, Portland
Portugal, Lisbon Action Plan, 18
Potsdamer Platz project, 302
Preservation activities
farmland, 13, 58–59, 214–215, 412
historic buildings, 90, 97, 386–387
President's Council on Sustainable
Development, 365
Privatization, 428 n.3
Procurement and investment policies,
335, 336–337, 361
Property tax, 70
Public participation, 4. See also
Nongovernmental organizations
in the Aalborg Charter, 467
campaigns, 349–353
citywide user groups, 330
in local Agenda 21 processes,
346–347, 420, 424
Public spaces. See Pedestrian-oriented
spaces
Public transit
coordination with land use, 112–113
in ecological building projects,
125–126, 296, 297–298, 299
investment in, 110–111
planning, 111–116
prioritization of, 116–118, 131, 132
single card for integrated use, 121,
124, 135, 135 n.1, 159, 354
usage statistics, 109–111
use of data on, 30
PV (photovoltaics). See Solar energy

Quality of life, 8, 465–466
Queens Building, 303–304

Rail systems. *See* Transportation, rail
    systems
Rainwater. *See* Water, rainwater
    conservation
Recreation
    bicycle-sharing program to, 180, 181
    publit transit to, 134–135
    solar-powered sports stadiums, 270,
        271, 274
Recycling. *See also* Closed-loop
    relationships; Ecocycle balancing
    centers, 401
    design for reuse
        automobiles, 394
        hotel rooms, 421
        industrial landscapes, 421
        offices, 299–300
        subway cars, 421
    green accounts for materials, 242,
        348–349
    of oil, 375
    of organic waste, 234, 236, 238,
        240–241
Redeveloped sites. *See* "Brownfields";
    Infill development
Regeneration. *See* Restoration, ecological
Regiokarte ticket, 121
Regional aspects
    ecological networks, 201, 224–225,
        254
    self-sufficiency, 7
    spacial planning, 52–58, 418
REMU power company, 274, 275, 279
Renewable energy. *See* Energy, renewable
Renewable Portfolio Standard (RPS), 289
    n.10
Research, 20
    Long-Term Ecological Research
        network, 231
    methods, 9–12
    role of demonstration and
        experimentation, 423–424
    technology development, 4, 424–425
Responsibility. *See* Policies, integration of
Restoration, ecological, 7, 219–220, 304,
    352, 385
Retail shops. *See* Housing, "mixed use"
Retrofitting, 226, 266, 304, 305–307,
    349–350
Reuse
    of buildings, 299–300, 421. *See also*
        Infill development
    of products. *See* Recycling, design for
        reuse
Rijkswaterstaat, 213–214

Rio Conference on Environment and
    Development, 4, 469
Rivers. *See* Stream/river restoration
Road-pricing, 14, 156–161, 163–164
Roads
    desealing of, 216–218
    solar energy in design of, 272
    taxes on, 134
RoCa3 power plant, 244–246, 376–377
Romolenpolder. *See* Haarlem
Rooftop for Schools program, 287
Rotterdam, ecocycle balancing (RoCa3),
    244–246, 376–377
Royal Ecopark, 199–200
Royal Society for Nature Conservation,
    21, 426
Runoff. *See* Wastewater treatment;
    Water, green drainage swales
Rural lands. *See* Agricultural practices;
    Farmland preservation; Undeveloped
    land
RWE AG headquarters building, 386

Saarbrücken, 10. *See also* Stadtwerke
    carbon dioxide emissions, 283
    decentralized energy production, 262
    ecoindustrial park, 377
    greenroofs, 206, 207
    improved energy efficiency, 264, 266
    planning activities, 219, 359
    rainwater conservation, 216–217
    solar energy, 272–273
    tram system, 113–114
    wind energy, 264, 266, 268
SAS headquarters building, 302
Scandic Hotels, 390, 393, 421
Schools
    energy efficiency in, 266, 275, 287,
        418, 422
    green, 215–216, 340, 341, 357
    promotion of sustainability, 331
    school houses, 299
Scotland
    car-free developments, 148
    car-sharing, 152
    car use statistics, 137, 410–411
Seattle. *See* Washington, Seattle
Second Structure Scheme for Traffic and
    Transport, 61
Self-sufficiency, 7
Sewage forest, 255
Sewage sludge, 234. *See also* Wastewater
    treatment
Shared streets. *See* Living street concept
Shopping malls, 56

Shops. *See* Business; Housing, "mixed use"
Sierra Club, 365
Singapore, 14
Sister city programs, 344–345
Sjolyst hotel, 393
Skotteparken. *See* Copenhagen, ecological building projects
Skövde, 214
Slagelse, urban renewal, 306
"Smart cards." *See* Public transit, single card for integrated use
SMART Park, 254
Social equity, 465–466
Social housing. *See* Housing, subsidized
Socially responsible investment, 337, 367 n.1
Software, for sustainability assessment, 357
Solar energy, 88, 89. *See also* Buildings, ecologically designed
  cities with, 270–273
  in developments, 274–277, 293, 296, 298
  in district heating, 263–264
  for electric bicycles, 192–193, 193 n.4
  for neighborhoods, 248, 251, 296
  in parking lots, 263
  photovoltaic energy output, 324 n.6
  pilot programs, 270
  rooftop requirements, 289 n.11, 296
  United States, 286–287
Solarhaus Freiburg, 270, 278–279
Solarhaus Heleotrope, 270
Solgarden urban renewal project, 305–306, 314
South Carolina, ecovillages, 314, 321–322
Spain, 93, 128
Spatial planning, 52–58, 62
  butterfly plan, 49, 50
  connections and linkages, 418–419
  finger plan, 52, 53
  renewable energy and, 269
  United States, 66–67
Spokes for Folks program, 191
Spoorwegen, 154
Squares. *See* Pedestrian-oriented spaces
Stad en Milieu infill development, 39, 409
Stadsdistributie Centrum (SdC), 126–128, 136 n.5
Stadtbahn, 116
Stadtwerke, 264–265, 268, 283
STATTAUTO, 153, 154

Stattoil, 374
Stockholm, 10
  compact urban planning, 33, 50–51
  district heating, 259, 260, 268
  ecocycle balancing, 234–238, 246–247
  greenspace, 199–200, 338–339, 348
  Hammarby Sjöstad site, 40, 247–252, 420–421
  high-density areas with livability, 77
  infill development, 39–40
  land use and transportation data, 30
  municipal motor fleet, 343–344
  pedestrian-oriented spaces, 101
  public transit, 109, 113, 119, 125–126
  Royal Ecopark, 199–200
Stockholm Transportation SL, 343
Stormwater runoff. *See* Wastewater treatment; Water, green drainage swales
Stream/river restoration, 7, 219–220, 352, 385
Streekplan, 53
Street design, 92–93
Strøget. *See* Copenhagen, pedestrian-oriented spaces
Subscription farming, 13
Suburbanization. *See* Urban sprawl
Sulfur dioxide, 252, 259
Sustainability
  assessment of, 19
  computer software for, 357
  indicators and targets, 21, 23, 73, 236, 328–331, 412, 422–423
  matrices and appraisals, 331–332, 360, 361
  economic, 369–403
  factory model, 378–381, 401
  global aspects, 3–5
  models and guidance, 414–415
  policy, coevolution of, 14
  principals of, 16, 17, 363–364, 391–392, 464
  privatization and, 428 n.3
  profits from, 421–422
  relevance and role of, in Europe, 15–24
  trade-off issues, 407–414
Sustainable Cities. *See* European Sustainable Cities and Towns Campaign
Sustainable Communities Demonstration Project, 364–365
Sustainable Index project, 19, 328
Sustainable London Trust, 412–413
Sustainable Seattle program, 69, 360

Sutton, 367 n.1, 395
Swales. *See* Water, green drainage swales
Sweden. *See also* Kista; Stockholm;
    Vällingby
  city farms, 214–215
  compact urban planning, 74 n.4
  ecocycle balancing, 234–238
  ecovillages, 86
  energy from organic wastes, 242
  green taxes, 252
  high-speed rail system, 128
  local Agenda 21 processes, 347
  public transit, 31
  summer homes and population
      dispersion, 61, 75 n.7
Swedish Nature Conservation Society,
    397
Switzerland. *See also* Zürich
  infrastructure policy, 118–119
  protection of agricultural land, 58
  spatial planning, 53–54, 55–56
Symbiotic relationships, 7, 374–378. *See
    also* Ecocycle balancing

Taxes
  accessory units, 81
  carbon, 268
  ecological, 70, 252–253, 256–257,
      423, 426
  gasoline, 60–61, 74 n.5, 134, 176
  as incentives/disincentives, 60–61, 70,
      73, 75 n.8, 81, 287
  open space sales, 225
  parking spaces, 158
  property, 70
  road, 134
  solar energy, 287
Taxis, shared, 126
Technology development
  opportunities for, 4
  people and, 424–425
Temple Bar. *See* Dublin
Tennessee, Chattanooga
  ecocycle balancing, 254
  high-speed rail initiative, 133
  infill development, 69
  sustainability policies, 362
Texas
  Austin
    growth planning, 70–72
    promotion of green building, 319
    sustainability initiative, 360–361
  ecosystem education, 322
  Houston
    bicycle system, 186–187

  land use and transportation data, 30
  natural drainage systems, 229
  Woodlands ecovillage, 229, 314
THERMIE program, 18, 274, 300
Third-world shops, 397–399
Tilburg, 301
Time Machine visioning process, 346
Toward a Sustainable Seattle, 69, 360
Towards a Sustainable Europe, 23
Towards Car-Free Cities, 139
Towards Sustainability (Fifth
    Environmental Action Program), 15
Traffic control, 137
  barriers, 123
  for bicycle-priority streets, 170,
      172–173
  express lanes, 163
  Freiburg, 120, 123, 135–136 n.3
  Home Zones program, 143
  living street concept. *See* Living street
      concept
  signal lights, 116, 120
  speed bumps, 139, 161, 162
  speed zones, 140, 143, 172, 174
  traffic circles, 139–140, 161
  tree placement, 139
  use of sheep, 140
  Zürich, 116, 120
Train systems. *See* Transportation, rail
    systems
Tram systems. *See* Transportation, tram
    systems
Transferiums. *See* Transportation, park-
    and-ride lots
Transportation. *See also* Automobiles;
    Bicycles; Fuel; Public transit; Traffic
    control
  in the Aalborg Charter, 466
  air traffic impacts, 413
  bus systems
    Almere, 48
    cultural aspects of, 124–125
    in ecological building projects, 296,
        297–298
    Freiburg, 120
    mini-buses, 126, 132
    mixed with bike traffic, 173
    "night bus," 121
    Zürich, 116, 120
  in compact urban planning, 35, 38,
      50–53, 55–56, 74 n.4
  electric vehicles
    bicycles, 191–192
    buses, 254, 343, 362
    in Hammersby Sjöstad, 247

municipal motor fleet, 343–344, 362
subsidies for, 136 n.4
trucks, 126–128
United States, 362
usage statistics, 136 n.4
innovations and priorities, 109–135
models and guidance, 415, 421
multi-modal and integrated systems, 113–116, 119–120, 132
park-and-ride lots, 122, 125
pilot programs, 18
rail systems, 56, 121–122
Adtranz C2O, 125–126
high-speed, 128–129, 133
light, 129, 130, 131
ORBITALE, 125
to recreational destinations, 134–135
TGV, 128
U-bahn and S-bahn lines, 111
Second Structure Scheme for Traffic and Transport, 61
shared. See Automobiles, car-sharing; Bicycles, public-use shared
single card for. See Public transit, single card for integrated use
taxis, community, 126
tram systems, 111, 113–116
innovations in, Frieburg, 119–122, 418
prioritization of, in Zürich, 116–118
the special feel of, 124
Tunnelbana, 50, 51
Transport of goods, 6, 126–128
Treaty of Maastricht, 15
Tree planting, 204–205, 228, 229, 255, 344, 346–347
Tree tenants, 204
Troncheim, 157
Trucks, electric, 126–128
Turning the Tide campaign, 349–350, 419
Twinning activities, 344–345

Understensbójden ecovillage, 86–87
Undeveloped land, 58–59. See also "Brownfields"; Infill development
Unechten Einbahnstrassen, 173
United Kingdom. See also Leicester; London
car ownership statistics, 410
city farms, 215
compact urban planning, 38

decentralized energy production, 262–263
Greenbelt Corridor and Home Countries Act, 38
greenroofs, 210
Home Zones traffic control, 143
legislation and initiatives, 21, 38
Living Over the Shops campaign, 45–46, 82–83
local Agenda 21 processes, 346–347, 348
public awareness campaign, 356–357
road-pricing, 157–158
solar energy promotion, 271
spatial planning, 55, 56
United Nations Environmental Award, 259
United States. See also specific states
bicycle-sharing programs, 190–191
bicycle systems, 186–187
business and sustainability, 400–402
carbon dioxide emission, 284
coevolution of sustainability policy with Europe, 14
cohousing, 13, 85–86, 101–102
compact urban planning, 62–74
ecovillages in, 314
greenroofs, 225–226
green taxes, 256–257
infill development, 68–69, 72
lessons for the
bicycle promotion, 185–193
ecocycle balancing, 253–257
ecological building design, 313–323
governance, 360–367
green cities, 223–231, 414–427
public transit, 129–135
renewable energy, 284–288
sustainable businesses, 400–403
traffic-calming, 161–165
pedestrian-oriented spaces, 103–105
rail systems, 133, 135
road-pricing, 163–164
sustainability activities, federal, 365–366
transferability of the European experience, 13–15, 366, 373
United Towns Organization (UTO), 18
Urban Containment Movement, 73
Urban Development in an Eco-Cycles Adapted Industrial Society, 238–239
Urban Ecology Guide, 352–353
Urbanism. See Cities; Green urbanism; New Urbanism

Urban management, 17, 467–468
Urban network, 55, 425–426
Urban oases, 104
Urban renewal, 304–307
Urban restructuring, 220–221
Urban runoff. *See* Wastewater treatment;
    Water, green drainage swales
Urban sprawl, 61–62. *See also* Compact
    urban form
Urban villages, 43–47, 68, 69, 77–80
U.S. Department of Energy, Energy Star
    Homes Program, 316, 318
U.S. Environmental Protection Agency,
    Energy Star Homes Program, 316,
    318
U.S. Federal Emergency Management
    Agency (FEMA), 365–366
U.S. Postal Service, 318–319
Utility car, 151
UTO. *See* United Towns Organization
Utrecht, 10
    bicycle system, 169, 170
    car-free developments, 150
    car-sharing, 152, 153
    creative housing in, 87–89
    eco-bridges, 214
    environmental education, 354
    green courtyards, 212–213, 312
    greenspace, 205
    growth districts, 41–43
    public transit statistics, 109

Vällingby, 51, 52
VAMIL program, 38
Ventilation of institutional buildings,
    303–304
VIBA (Vereniging Integrale Bio-logische
    Architectuur), 312–313
Viborg, district heating, 261
Vienna, 10
    bike lanes, 166
    district heating, 259, 261, 262
    energy standards, 267
    forests, 31, 198
    green buildings, 204
    green courtyards, 213
    greenspace, 199
    historic building preservation, 90
    land use and transportation data, 30
    pedestrian-oriented spaces, 99–100
Vierde Nota over de Ruimtelijke
    Ordening Extra. *See* VINEX sites
Viikki urban gardens, 222, 229, 300
Village Homes development, 228–229
VINEX sites, 32, 307

bicycle system, 170
Netherlands, 77, 170, 282, 296, 307
social/public housing criteria, 77
spatial planning in, 170
Violence. *See* Crime
Virginia
    Haymount ecovillage, 314
    pedestrian-oriented spaces, 105
Vleuten, 41
Vroom and Dreesmann (V&D), 410

Wadies. See Wastewater treatment;
    Water, green drainage swales
Walking, 41, 105, 106 n.3
Washington, Seattle
    Growth Management Act, 68
    Sustainable Seattle program, 69, 360
    traffic-calming strategies, 161, 165
    urban housing, 64, 68, 69
Washington Area Bicyclists Association,
    189
Washington, D.C.
    bicycle system, 187, 189
    land use and transportation data, 30
Waste
    in ecocycle balancing, 234, 236, 238,
        240–241, 247, 254
    green taxes on, 253
    reduction, in business, 371
Wastewater treatment
    bacteria in green swales, 218
    constructed wetlands, 251, 254–256,
        294, 317
    industrial, 380
    reedbed filtration
        Arnhem, 252
        in a factory, 280
        Het Groene Dak, 213
        Kolding, 248–252, 257 n.3, 305
        Leiden, 89
    sewage forest, 255
Water
    conservation methods, 147
    European usage, statistics and targets,
        412
    green drainage swales, 43
        Drachten, 294
        Enschede, 217–218
        Leiden, 89
        United States, 228–229
    on greenroofs, 209
    groundwater protection, 71, 199,
        302
    rainwater conservation, 88, 147,
        216–217, 226, 248, 251, 305

separation of "grey," 43, 147, 213, 252
stream restoration, 219–220, 352, 385
Wereldwinkels. See World shops
Westerpark. *See* Amsterdam, GWL-terrein
Wetlands, constructed, 251, 254–256, 294, 317
Wetlands Project, 255–256
"White bikes" program, 178
Wildlife habitat conservation, 35, 199, 200, 213–214, 222–223, 254, 383
Wildlife Trust Partnership, 21, 426
William McDonough and Partners, 317
Wind energy, 268–269, 284, 289 n.10, 393, 422
Window right, 204
Witfiets, 178, 180, 182. *See also* Bicycles, public-use shared
Witkar car-sharing system. *See* Amsterdam, car-sharing
Woonerf. See Living street concept
Workspace, shared, 388–389, 402
World Health Organization, Healthy Cities program, 22

World shops, 397–399, 403

Ystad, ecocycle balancing, 237

Zandfoort, energy balanced housing, 280–282
Zero and Low Emission Vehicles in Urban Society (ZEUS), 343, 344
Zero-energy housing, 277–282
Zevenaar, 208
Zürich, 10
    city-center development, 47
    environmental education, 352
    environmental policy, 335
    greenschools, 215–216
    greenspace, 199
    land use and transportation data, 30
    procurement policy, 337
    public transit statistics, 110
    public transit system, 111, 116–118, 135–136 n.3
    spatial planning, 54, 55–56
    stream restoration, 219–220
Zwijndrecht, 149
Zwolle, 10, 31